Business Communication

Process & Product
Volume Two

7th Edition

Mary Ellen Guffy | Dana Loewy

CENGAGE Learning

Australia • Brazil • Japan • Korea • Mexico • Singapore • Spain • United Kingdom • United States

Business Communication
Process & Product
Volume Two
7th Edition

Senior Project Development Manager:
Linda deStefano

Market Development Manager:
Heather Kramer

Senior Production/Manufacturing Manager:
Donna M. Brown

Production Editorial Manager:
Kim Fry

Sr. Rights Acquisition Account Manager:
Todd Osborne

Printed in the United States of America

Business Communication: Process & Product, Seventh Edition
Mary Ellen Guffy | Dana Loewy

Library of Congress Control Number: 2010930837

ISBN-13: 978-1-285-91813-6

ISBN-10: 1-285-91813-4

Cengage Learning
5191 Natorp Boulevard
Mason, Ohio 45040
USA
Cengage Learning is a leading provider of customized learning solutions with office locations around the globe, including Singapore, the United Kingdom, Australia, Mexico, Brazil, and Japan. Locate your local office at:
international.cengage.com/region.

Cengage Learning products are represented in Canada by Nelson Education, Ltd.
For your lifelong learning solutions, visit **www.cengage.com/custom.**
Visit our corporate website at **www.cengage.com.**

Brief Contents

CHAPTER 4

Planning Business Messages

Want to do well on tests and excel in your course? Go to **www.meguffey.com** for helpful interactive resources.

- **Review the Chapter 4 PowerPoint slides to prepare for the first quiz.**

OBJECTIVES

After studying this chapter, you should be able to

1. Identify four basic principles of business writing, summarize the 3-x-3 writing process, and explain how a writing process helps a writer.
2. Recognize the components of the first phase of the writing process (prewriting), including analyzing your purpose, anticipating the audience, selecting the best channel, and considering how to adapt your message to the audience.
3. Effectively apply audience benefits, the "you" view, and conversational but professional language.
4. Effectively employ positive and courteous tone, bias-free language, simple expression, and vigorous words.
5. Understand how teams approach collaborative writing projects and what collaboration tools support team writing.
6. Summarize the legal and ethical responsibilities of business communicators in the areas of investments, safety, marketing, human resources, and copyright law.

Zooming In — PART 1

Suze Orman Preaches Financial Freedom in Simple Language

Personal finance guru Suze Orman has a mission. She wants to change the way people think, act, and talk about money. One of the most widely read financial authorities of our time, she has written seven best-selling financial guidance books. But she is probably best known for her television programs including specials for PBS, the syndicated *Financial Freedom Hour* on QVC network, and an advice show on CNBC. She is also a columnist for *O*, Oprah Winfrey's magazine, and for Yahoo's personal finance site.

Orman's advice is largely for people who are drowning in debt. "Sweetheart," she says to a caller, "burn those credit cards!" She delivers her gospel of financial freedom with an animated conviction and high-energy style that have become her hallmark.[1] In her books and magazine articles, she speaks with the same assurance. "Having talked to literally tens of thousands of people, I can say that what is good for America ... is not having credit card debt, not leasing a car, and not having mortgage debt. This is not good for a human being. It's just not!"[2]

Orman knows what it is like to be in debt. After graduating with a degree in sociology, she worked for seven years as a waitress at the Buttercup Bakery in Berkeley, California. With a $50,000 loan from her customers, she intended to finance her own restaurant. Because of bad advice from an investment firm, she lost her $50,000 within four months. However, "she made it all up and then some after the firm hired her as its only female broker."[3]

As a broker, she developed her financial planning skills and built a reputation for honesty and ethical advice. Her books and articles combine emotional and spiritual observations about money and how to avoid the financial problems that caused pain for her family as she was growing up. *The Money Book for the Young, Fabulous, & Broke* directs financial advice at young people early in their working lives.

She admits that her message is not new. "It's not the material that I know, but how I communicate the material I know that sets me apart."[4] Orman's advice is practical and cuts through much confusing, contradictory financial information. One of her greatest strengths is breaking complex ideas into easy-to-understand segments. Like many great communicators, she knows her audience, shapes her message accordingly, and uses simple language.

© Newscom

Critical Thinking

- Whether one is writing a book, making a speech, or composing a business letter, why is it important to anticipate the audience for the message?
- What does writing an effective financial help book have in common with writing an effective business message?
- Why is it important to follow a writing process?

http://www.suzeorman.com

Understanding the Writing Process for Business Messages

LEARNING OBJECTIVE 1

Identify four basic principles of business writing, summarize the 3-x-3 writing process, and explain how a writing process helps a writer.

The task of preparing a written business message or a presentation is easier and more efficient if you have a systematic process to follow. When financial expert Suze Orman starts a writing assignment, she focuses totally on the task at hand. She takes no phone calls, answers no e-mails, and allows no interruptions. In delivering a convincing message, she employs many of the writing techniques you are about to learn. This chapter presents a systematic writing process that you can use to approach all business communication problems, whether you are planning an e-mail message, a report, an oral presentation, or even an instant message. The 3-x-3 writing process guides you through three phases, making it easy for you to plan, organize, and complete any message. Following the 3-x-3 writing process takes the guesswork out of writing. It tells you what goes on in each phase and guides you to effective results.

Starting With the Basics

What distinguishes business writing from other kinds of writing?

The first thing you should recognize about business writing is that it differs from other writing you may have done. In preparing high school or college compositions and term papers, you probably focused on discussing your feelings or displaying your knowledge. Your instructors wanted to see your thought processes, and they wanted assurance that you had internalized the subject matter. You may have had to meet a minimum word count. Business writers, however, have different goals. For business messages and oral presentations, your writing should be:

- **Purposeful.** You will be writing to solve problems and convey information. You will have a definite purpose to fulfill in each message.
- **Persuasive.** You want your audience to believe and accept your message.
- **Economical.** You will try to present ideas clearly but concisely. Length is not rewarded.
- **Audience oriented.** You will concentrate on looking at a problem from the perspective of the audience instead of seeing it from your own.

These distinctions actually ease the writer's task. You will not be searching your imagination for creative topic ideas. You won't be stretching your ideas to make them appear longer. Writing consultants and businesspeople complain that many college graduates entering industry have at least an unconscious perception that quantity enhances quality. Wrong! Get over the notion that longer is better. Conciseness and clarity are prized in business.

The ability to prepare concise, audience-centered, persuasive, and purposeful messages does not come naturally. Very few people, especially beginners, can sit down and compose a terrific letter or report without training. However, following a systematic process, studying model messages, and practicing the craft can make nearly anyone a successful business writer or speaker.

Following the 3-x-3 Writing Process

What are the three phases of the writing process?

Whether you are preparing an e-mail message, memo, letter, or oral presentation, the process will be easier if you follow a systematic plan. The 3-x-3 writing process breaks the entire task into three phases: *prewriting, writing,* and *revising*, as shown in Figure 4.1.

To illustrate the writing process, let's say that you own a popular local McDonald's franchise. At rush times, you face a problem. Customers complain about the chaotic multiple waiting lines to approach the service counter. You once saw two customers nearly get into a fistfight over cutting into a line. What's more, customers often are so intent on looking for ways to improve their positions in line that they fail to examine the menu. Then they are

FIGURE 4.1 The 3-x-3 Writing Process

1 Prewriting

Analyze: Decide on your purpose. What do you want the receiver to do or believe? What channel or form is best? Should you deliver your message in writing, orally, electronically, or graphically?

Anticipate: Profile the audience. What does the receiver already know? Will the receiver's response be neutral, positive, or negative? Use the direct method for positive messages; consider using the indirect method for negative or persuasive messages.

Adapt: What techniques can you use to adapt your message to its audience and the audience's anticipated reaction? Include audience benefits and the "you" view, as well as positive, conversational, and courteous language.

2 Writing

Research: Gather data to provide facts. Search company files, previous correspondence, and the Internet. What do you need to know to write this message? How much does the audience already know?

Organize: Group similar facts together. Organize direct messages with the big idea first, followed by an explanation and an action request in the closing. For persuasive or negative messages, use an indirect, problem-solving plan. For short messages, make quick notes. For longer messages, outline your plan and make notes.

Compose: Prepare a first draft, usually writing quickly. Focus on short, clear sentences using the active voice. Link ideas to build paragraph coherence.

3 Revising

Revise: Edit your message to be sure it is clear, conversational, concise, and readable. Revise to eliminate wordy fillers, long lead-ins, redundancies, compound prepositions, wordy noun phrases, and trite business phrases. Develop parallelism and consider using headings and numbered and bulleted lists for quick comprehension.

Proofread: Take the time to read over every message carefully. Look for errors in spelling, grammar, punctuation, names, numbers, and format.

Evaluate: Decide whether this message will achieve your purpose. Have you thought enough about the audience to be sure this message is appropriate and appealing?

undecided when their turn arrives. You want to convince other franchise owners that a single-line (serpentine) system would work better. You could telephone the other owners. But you want to present a serious argument with good points that they will remember and be willing to act on when they gather for their next district meeting. You decide to write a letter that you hope will win their support.

What tasks are involved in the first phase of the writing process?

Prewriting. The first phase of the writing process prepares you to write. It involves *analyzing* the audience and your purpose for writing. The audience for your letter will be other franchise owners, some highly educated and others not. Your purpose in writing is to convince them that a change in policy would improve customer service. You are convinced that a single-line system, such as that used in banks, would reduce chaos and make customers happier because they would not have to worry about where they are in line.

Prewriting also involves *anticipating* how your audience will react to your message. You are sure that some of the other owners will agree with you, but others might fear that customers seeing a long single line might go elsewhere. In *adapting* your message to the audience, you try to think of the right words and the right tone that will win approval.

What tasks are involved in the second phase of the writing process?

Writing. The second phase involves researching, organizing, and then composing the message. In *researching* information for this letter, you would probably investigate other kinds of businesses that use single lines for customers. You might check out your competitors. What are Wendy's and Burger King doing? You might do some calling to see whether other franchise owners are concerned about chaotic lines. Before writing to the entire group, you might brainstorm with a few owners to see what ideas they have for solving the problem.

Once you have collected enough information, you would focus on *organizing* your letter. Should you start out by offering your solution? Or should you work up to it slowly, describing the problem, presenting your evidence, and then ending with the solution? The final step in the second phase of the writing process is actually *composing* the letter. Naturally, you will do it at your computer so that you can revise easily.

Revising. The third phase of the process involves revising, proofreading, and evaluating your letter. After writing the first draft, you will spend a lot of time *revising* the message for clarity, conciseness, tone, and readability. Could parts of it be rearranged to make your point more effectively? This is the time when you look for ways to improve the organization and tone of your message. Next, you will spend time *proofreading* carefully to ensure correct spelling, grammar, punctuation, and format. The final phase involves *evaluating* your message to decide whether it accomplishes your goal.

Scheduling the Writing Process

What percentage of your time should you spend on each phase of the writing process?

Although Figure 4.1 shows the three phases of the writing process equally, the time you spend on each varies depending on the complexity of the problem, the purpose, the audience, and your schedule. One expert gives these rough estimates for scheduling a project:

- Prewriting—25 percent (thinking and planning)
- Writing—25 percent (organizing and composing)
- Revising—50 percent (45 percent revising and 5 percent proofreading)

These are rough guides, yet you can see that good writers spend most of their time on the final phase of revising and proofreading. Much depends, of course, on your project, its importance, and your familiarity with it. What is critical to remember, though, is that revising is a major component of the writing process.

It may appear that you perform one step and progress to the next, always following the same order. Most business writing, however, is not that rigid. Although writers perform the tasks described, the steps may be rearranged, abbreviated, or repeated. Some writers revise every sentence and paragraph as they go. Many find that new ideas occur after they have begun to write, causing them to back up, alter the organization, and rethink their plan. Beginning business writers often follow the writing process closely. With experience, though, you will become like other good writers and presenters who alter, compress, and rearrange the steps as needed.

Ethics Check

Essays for Sale

Web sites with playful names such as Cramster, Course Hero, Koofers, and Spark Notes provide ready-made solutions and essays for students. Do such sites encourage cheating and undermine the mental sweat equity of day-to-day learning?

Analyzing Your Purpose and Selecting Your Channel

We devote the remainder of this chapter to the first phase of the writing process. You will learn to analyze the purpose for writing, anticipate how your audience will react, and adapt your message to the audience. It's surprising how many people begin writing and discover only as they approach the end of a message what they are trying to accomplish. If you analyze your purpose before you begin, you can avoid backtracking and starting over.

LEARNING OBJECTIVE 2
Recognize the components of the first phase of the writing process (prewriting), including analyzing your purpose, profiling the audience, and selecting the best channel.

Identifying Your Purpose

As you begin to compose a message, ask yourself two important questions: (a) Why am I sending this message? and (b) What do I hope to achieve? Your responses will determine how you organize and present your information.

What are the primary and secondary purposes of most business messages?

Your message may have primary and secondary purposes. For college work your primary purpose may be merely to complete the assignment; secondary purposes might be to make yourself look good and to earn an excellent grade. The primary purposes for sending business messages are typically to inform and to persuade. A secondary purpose is to promote goodwill. You and your organization want to look good in the eyes of your audience.

Most business messages do nothing more than *inform*. They explain procedures, announce meetings, answer questions, and transmit findings. Some business messages, however, are meant to *persuade*. These messages sell products, convince managers, motivate employees, and win over customers. Informative messages are developed differently from persuasive messages.

Selecting the Best Channel

After identifying the purpose of your message, you need to select the most appropriate communication channel. Some information is most efficiently and effectively delivered orally. Other messages should be written, and still others are best delivered electronically. Whether to set up a meeting, send a message by e-mail, or write a report depends on some of the following factors:

What factors influence your selection of the best delivery channel?

- Importance of the message
- Amount and speed of feedback and interactivity required
- Necessity of a permanent record
- Cost of the channel
- Degree of formality desired
- Confidentiality and sensitivity of the message

An interesting theory, called the media richness theory, describes the extent to which a channel or medium recreates or represents all the information available in the original message. A richer medium, such as face-to-face conversation, permits more interactivity and feedback. A leaner medium, such as a report or proposal, presents a flat, one-dimensional message. Richer media enable the sender to provide more verbal and visual cues, as well as allow the sender to tailor the message to the audience.

Many factors help you decide which of the channels shown in Figure 4.2 on page 116 is most appropriate for delivering a workplace message.

Switching to Faster Channels

Technology and competition continue to accelerate the pace of business today. As a result, communicators are switching to ever-faster means of exchanging information. In the past business messages within organizations were delivered largely by hard-copy memos. Responses would typically take a couple of days. However, that's too slow for today's communicators. They want answers and action now! Mobile phones, instant messaging, faxes, Web sites, and especially e-mail can deliver that information much faster than can traditional channels of communication.

FIGURE 4.2 Choosing Communication Channels

Channel	Best Use
Blog	When one person needs to present digital information easily so that it is available to others.
E-mail	When you need feedback but not immediately. Lack of security makes it problematic for personal, emotional, or private messages.
Face-to-face conversation	When you need a rich, interactive medium. Useful for persuasive, bad-news, and personal messages.
Face-to-face group meeting	When group decisions and consensus are important. Inefficient for merely distributing information.
Fax	When your message must cross time zones or international boundaries, when a written record is significant, or when speed is important.
Instant message	When you are online and need a quick response. Useful for learning whether someone is available for a phone conversation.
Letter	When a written record or formality is required, especially with customers, the government, suppliers, or others outside an organization.
Memo	When you want a written record to clearly explain policies, discuss procedures, or collect information within an organization.
Phone call	When you need to deliver or gather information quickly, when nonverbal cues are unimportant, and when you cannot meet in person.
Report or proposal	When you are delivering considerable data internally or externally.
Voice mail message	When you wish to leave important or routine information that the receiver can respond to when convenient.
Video- or audioconference	When group consensus and interaction are important, but members are geographically dispersed.
Wiki	When digital information must be made available to others. Useful for collaboration because participants can easily add, remove, and edit content.

Why is e-mail so popular for business messages?

Within many organizations, hard-copy memos are still written, especially for messages that require persuasion, permanence, or formality. They are also prepared as attachments to e-mail messages. Clearly, however, the channel of choice for corporate communicators today is e-mail. It's fast, inexpensive, and easy. Businesspeople are sending fewer hard-copy interoffice memos and fewer customer letters. Customer service functions can now be served through Web sites or by e-mail.

Many businesses now help customers with live chat, shown in Figure 4.3. Customers visit the company Web site and chat with representatives by keying their questions and answers back and forth. Customer representatives must have not only good keying skills but also an ability to write conversational and correct responses. One company found that it could not easily convert its telephone customer service people to chat representatives because many lacked the language skills necessary to write clear and correct messages. They were good at talking but not at writing, again making the point that the Internet has increased the need for good writing skills.

Whether your channel choice is live chat, e-mail, a hard-copy memo, or a report, you will be showcasing your communication skills and applying the writing process. The best writers spend sufficient time in the prewriting phase.

Anticipating the Audience

A good writer anticipates the audience for a message: What is the reader or listener like? How will that person react to the message? Although you can't always know exactly who the receiver is, you can imagine some of that person's characteristics. Even writers of direct-mail sales letters have a general idea of the audience they wish to target. Picturing a typical receiver is important in guiding what you write. One copywriter at Lands' End, the catalog company, pictures his sister-in-law whenever he writes product descriptions for the catalog. By profiling your audience and shaping a message to respond to that profile, you are more likely to achieve your communication goals.

FIGURE 4.3 Live Chat Connects Service Reps and Customers

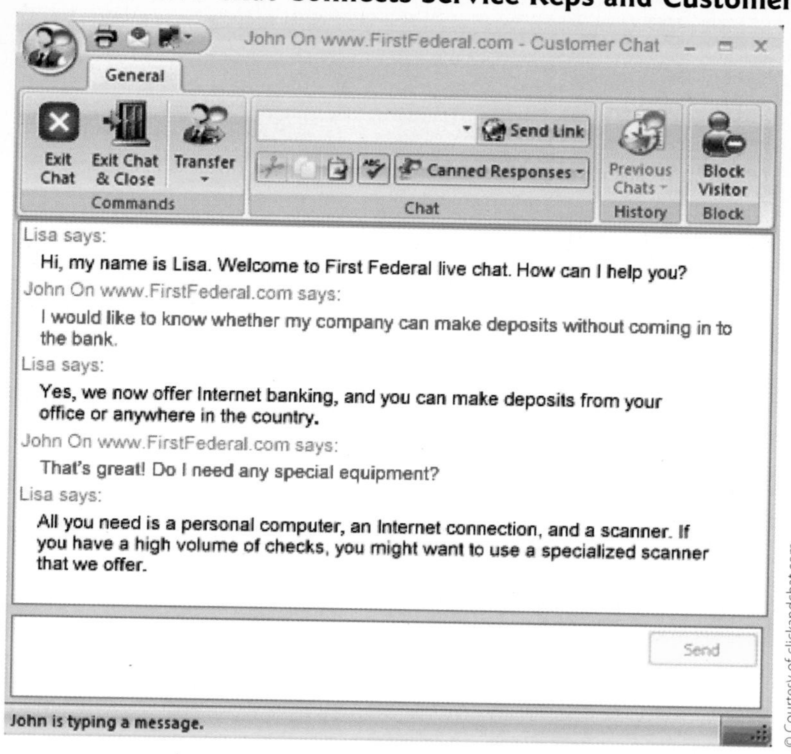

Customer service reps in chat sessions require good writing skills to answer questions concisely, clearly, and conversationally. It takes special talent to be able to think and key immediate responses that are spelled correctly and are error-free.

Profiling the Audience

Why is it important to profile the audience for a business message?

Visualizing your audience is a pivotal step in the writing process. The questions in Figure 4.4 will help you profile your audience. How much time you devote to answering these questions depends on your message and its context. An analytical report that you compose for management or an oral presentation before a big group would, of course, demand considerable audience anticipation. On the other hand, an e-mail message to a coworker or a letter to a familiar supplier might require only a few moments of planning. No matter how short your message, though, spend some time thinking about the audience so that you can tailor your words to your readers or listeners. Remember that most receivers will be thinking, *What's in it for me?* or, *What am I supposed to do with this information*?

Responding to the Audience Profile

Profiling your audience helps you make decisions about shaping the message. You will discover what kind of language is appropriate, whether you are free to use specialized technical terms, whether you should explain everything, and so on. You will decide whether your tone should be formal or informal, and you will select the most desirable channel. Imagining whether the receiver is likely to be neutral, positive, or negative will help you determine how to organize your message.

Another advantage of profiling your audience is considering the possibility of a secondary audience. For example, let's say you start to write an e-mail message to your supervisor, Sheila, describing a problem you are having. Halfway through the message you realize that Sheila will probably forward this message to her boss, the vice president. Sheila will not want to summarize what you said; instead she will take the easy route and merely forward your e-mail. When you realize that the vice president will probably see this message, you decide to back up and use a more formal tone. You remove your inquiry about Sheila's family, you reduce your complaints, and you tone down your language about why things went wrong. Instead, you provide more background information, and you are more specific in identifying items the vice

Spotlight on Communicators

Warren Buffett, the second richest man in the United States and one of the most successful investors of all time, offers advice on how to improve your messages by profiling your audience and responding to that profile. When writing annual reports, he pretends that he's talking to his sisters. "I have no trouble picturing them. Though highly intelligent, they are not experts in accounting or finance. They will understand plain English but jargon may puzzle them. . . . No sisters to write to? Borrow mine. Just begin with 'Dear Doris and Bertie,'" he suggested.

FIGURE 4.4 Asking the Right Questions to Profile Your Audience

Primary Audience	Secondary Audience
Who is my primary reader or listener?	Who might see or hear this message in addition to the primary audience?
What are my personal and professional relationships with this person?	How do these people differ from the primary audience?
What position does this person hold in the organization?	Do I need to include more background information?
How much does this person know about the subject?	How must I reshape my message to make it understandable and acceptable to others to whom it might be forwarded?
What do I know about this person's education, beliefs, culture, and attitudes?	
Should I expect a neutral, positive, or negative response to my message?	

president might not recognize. Analyzing the task and anticipating the audience help you adapt your message so that you can create an efficient and effective message.

Adapting to the Task and Audience

LEARNING OBJECTIVE 3

Effectively apply audience benefits, the "you" view, and conversational but professional language.

After analyzing your purpose and anticipating your audience, you will begin to think about how to adapt your message to the task and the audience. Adaptation is the process of creating a message that suits your audience. One important aspect of adaptation is *tone*. Conveyed largely by the words in a message, tone affects how a receiver feels upon reading or hearing a message. Tone is how you say something. It reveals the writer's attitude toward the receiver. For example, how you would react to these statements?

You must return the form by 5 p.m.

Would you please return the form by 5 p.m.

The wording of the first message establishes an aggressive or negative tone—no one likes being told what to do. The second message is reworded in a friendlier, more positive manner. Poorly chosen words may sound demeaning, condescending, discourteous, pretentious, or demanding. Notice in the Lands' End letter in Figure 4.5 that the writer achieves a courteous and warm tone. The letter responds to a customer's concern about the changing merchandise mix available in Lands' End catalogs. The customer also wants to receive fewer catalogs. The writer explains the company's expanded merchandise line and reassures the customer that Lands' End has not abandoned its emphasis on classic styles.

What techniques help a writer achieve a positive tone?

Skilled communicators create a positive tone in their messages by using a number of adaptive techniques, some of which are unconscious. These include spotlighting audience benefits, cultivating a "you" view, sounding conversational but professional, and using positive, courteous expression. Additional adaptive techniques include using bias-free language and preferring plain language with familiar but vigorous words.

Developing Audience Benefits

Focusing on the audience sounds like a modern idea, but actually one of America's early statesmen and authors recognized this fundamental writing principle over 200 years ago. In describing effective writing, Ben Franklin observed, "To be good, it ought to have a tendency to benefit the reader."[5] These wise words have become a fundamental guideline for today's business communicators. Expanding on Franklin's counsel, a contemporary communication consultant gives this solid advice to his business clients: "Always stress the benefit to the audience of whatever it is you are trying to get them to do. If you can show them how you are going to save them frustration or help them meet their goals, you have the makings of a powerful message."[6]

What is *empathy*?

Adapting your message to the receiver's needs means putting yourself in that person's shoes. It's called *empathy*. Empathic senders think about how a receiver will decode a message. They try to give something to the receiver, solve the receiver's problems, save the receiver's

FIGURE 4.5 Customer Response Letter

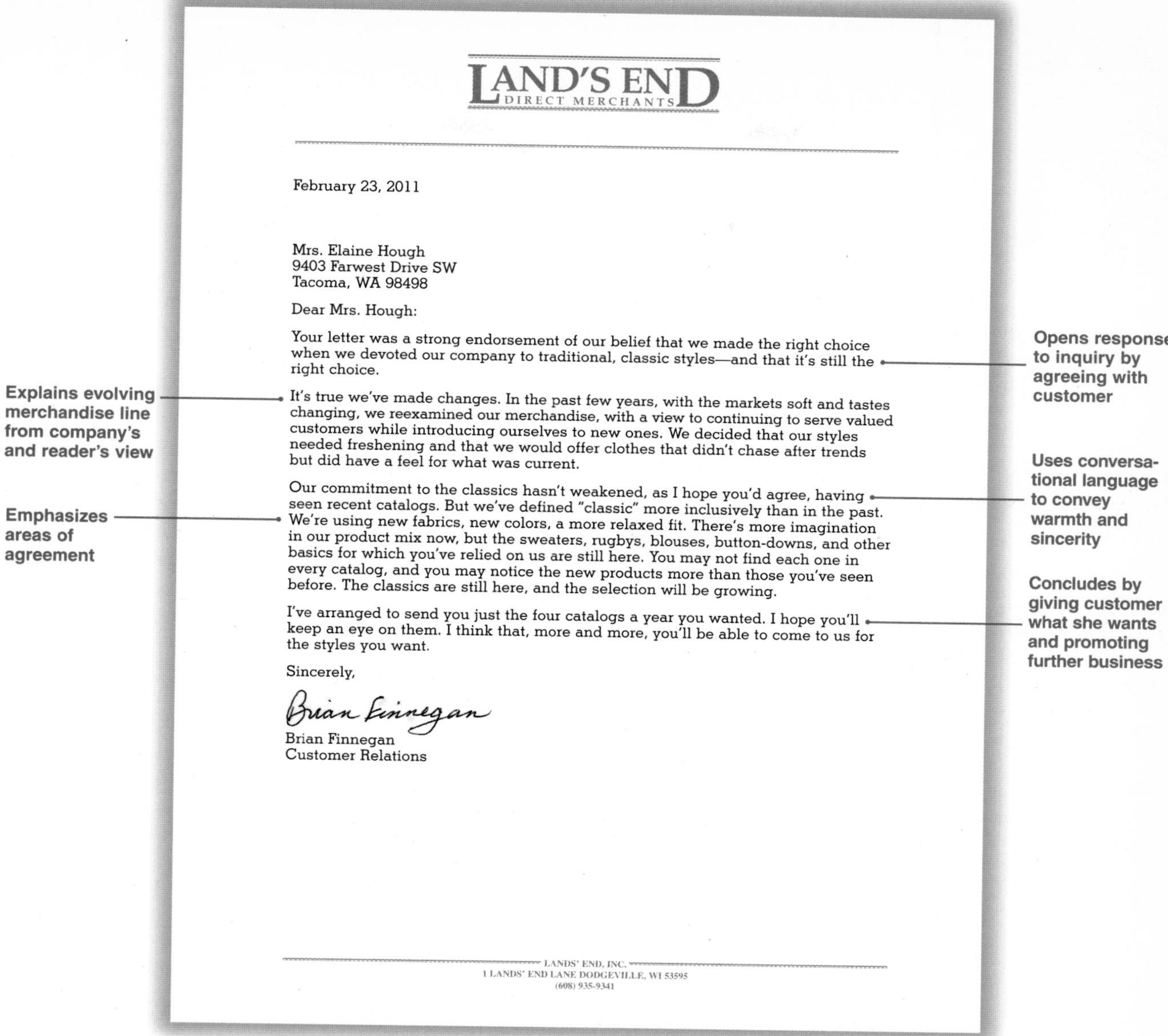

LAND'S END
DIRECT MERCHANTS

February 23, 2011

Mrs. Elaine Hough
9403 Farwest Drive SW
Tacoma, WA 98498

Dear Mrs. Hough:

Your letter was a strong endorsement of our belief that we made the right choice when we devoted our company to traditional, classic styles—and that it's still the right choice.

It's true we've made changes. In the past few years, with the markets soft and tastes changing, we reexamined our merchandise, with a view to continuing to serve valued customers while introducing ourselves to new ones. We decided that our styles needed freshening and that we would offer clothes that didn't chase after trends but did have a feel for what was current.

Our commitment to the classics hasn't weakened, as I hope you'd agree, having seen recent catalogs. But we've defined "classic" more inclusively than in the past. We're using new fabrics, new colors, a more relaxed fit. There's more imagination in our product mix now, but the sweaters, rugbys, blouses, button-downs, and other basics for which you've relied on us are still here. You may not find each one in every catalog, and you may notice the new products more than those you've seen before. The classics are still here, and the selection will be growing.

I've arranged to send you just the four catalogs a year you wanted. I hope you'll keep an eye on them. I think that, more and more, you'll be able to come to us for the styles you want.

Sincerely,

Brian Finnegan
Brian Finnegan
Customer Relations

LANDS' END, INC.
1 LANDS' END LANE DODGEVILLE, WI 53595
(608) 935-9341

Explains evolving merchandise line from company's and reader's view
Emphasizes areas of agreement
Opens response to inquiry by agreeing with customer
Uses conversational language to convey warmth and sincerity
Concludes by giving customer what she wants and promoting further business

money, or just understand the feelings and position of that person. Which version of the following messages is more appealing to the audience?

Sender Focus	**Audience Focus**
The Human Resources Department requires that the enclosed questionnaire be completed immediately so that we can allocate our training resource funds to employees.	By filling out the enclosed questionnaire, you can be one of the first employees to sign up for our training resource funds.
Our warranty becomes effective only when we receive an owner's registration.	Your warranty begins working for you as soon as you return your owner's registration.
We are proud to announce our new software virus checker that we think is the best on the market!	Now you can be sure that all your computers will be protected with our real-time virus scanning.

Cultivating the "You" View

Notice that many of the previous audience-focused messages included the word *you*. In concentrating on receiver benefits, skilled communicators naturally develop the "you" view. They

Spotlight on Communicators

Voted the greatest minority entrepreneur in American history, John H. Johnson was a master at profiling potential customers and cultivating the "you" view. He always focused on what they wanted rather than on what he wanted. His emphasis on the "you" view helped him build *Ebony* and *Jet* magazines, along with *Fashion Fair Cosmetics*, into multimillion-dollar businesses. In explaining his customer approach, he said, "I want to know where they came from, what are their interests, [and] what can I talk to them about." He worked to establish rapport with people by learning their interests.

emphasize second-person pronouns (*you, your*) instead of first-person pronouns (*I/we, us, our*). Whether your goal is to inform, persuade, or promote goodwill, the catchiest words you can use are *you* and *your*. Compare the following examples.

"I/We" View	"You" View
We are requiring all employees to respond to the attached survey about health benefits.	Because your ideas count, please complete the attached survey about health benefits.
I need your account number before I can do anything.	Would you mind giving me your account number so that I can locate your records and help you solve this problem?
We have shipped your order by UPS, and we are sure it will arrive in time for your sales promotion December 1.	Your order will be delivered by UPS in time for your sales promotion December 1.

How can you use the word *you* skillfully?

Although you want to focus on the reader or listener, don't overuse or misuse the second-person pronoun *you*. Readers and listeners appreciate genuine interest; on the other hand, they resent obvious attempts at manipulation. The authors of some sales messages, for example, are guilty of overkill when they include *you* dozens of times in a direct-mail promotion. Furthermore, the word can sometimes create the wrong impression. Consider this statement: *You cannot return merchandise until you receive written approval.* The word *you* appears twice, but the reader feels singled out for criticism. In the following version the message is less personal and more positive: *Customers may return merchandise with written approval.*

Another difficulty in emphasizing the "you" view and de-emphasizing *we/I* is that it may result in overuse of the passive voice. For example, to avoid *We will give you* (active voice), you might write *You will be given* (passive voice). The active voice in writing is generally preferred because it identifies who is doing the acting. You will learn more about active and passive voice in Chapter 5.

Should you remove all incidents of *I* and *we* in your messages?

In recognizing the value of the "you" attitude, writers do not have to sterilize their writing and totally avoid any first-person pronouns or words that show their feelings. Skilled communicators are able to convey sincerity, warmth, and enthusiasm by the words they choose. Don't be afraid to use phrases such as *I'm happy* or *We're delighted*, if you truly are.

When speaking face-to-face, communicators show sincerity and warmth with nonverbal cues such as a smile and a pleasant voice tone. In letters, memos, and e-mail messages, however, only expressive words and phrases can show these feelings. These phrases suggest hidden messages that say *You are important, I hear you,* and *I'm honestly trying to please you.* Mary Kay Ash, one of the most successful cosmetics entrepreneurs of all time, gave her salespeople wise advice. She had them imagine that any person they were addressing wore a sign saying, *Make me feel important.*

Being Conversational but Professional

How can a message be conversational and also professional?

Most instant messages, e-mail messages, business letters, memos, and reports replace conversation. Thus, they are most effective when they convey an informal, conversational tone instead of a formal, pretentious tone. Workplace messages should not, however, become so casual that they sound low level and unprofessional.

Instant messaging (IM) enables coworkers to have informal, spontaneous conversations. Some companies have accepted IM as a serious workplace tool. With the increasing use of instant messaging and e-mail, however, a major problem has developed. Sloppy, unprofessional expression appears in many workplace messages. You will learn more about the dangers of e-mail in Chapter 7. At this point, though, we focus on the tone of the language.

To project a professional image, you must sound educated and mature. Overuse of expressions such as *totally awesome, you know,* and *like,* as well as reliance on needless abbreviations (*BTW* for *by the way*), make a businessperson sound like a teenager. Professional messages do not include IM abbreviations, slang, sentence fragments, and chitchat. We urge you to strive for a warm, conversational tone that avoids low-level diction. Levels of diction, as shown in Figure 4.6, range from unprofessional to formal.

FIGURE 4.6 Levels of Diction

Unprofessional (Low-level diction)	Conversational (Middle-level diction)	Formal (High-level diction)
badmouth	criticize	denigrate
guts	nerve	courage
pecking order	line of command	dominance hierarchy
ticked off	upset	provoked
rat on	inform	betray
rip off	steal	expropriate
Sentence example: If we just hang in there, we can snag the contract.	**Sentence example:** If we don't get discouraged, we can win the contract.	**Sentence example:** If the principals persevere, they can secure the contract.

Your goal is a warm, friendly tone that sounds professional. Although some writers are too casual, others are overly formal. To impress readers and listeners, they use big words, long sentences, legal terminology, and third-person constructions. Stay away from expressions such as *the undersigned, the writer*, and *the affected party*. You will sound friendlier with familiar pronouns such as *I, we*, and *you*. Study the following examples to see how to achieve a professional, yet conversational tone:

Unprofessional	Professional
Hey, boss, Gr8 news! Firewall now installed!! BTW, check with me b4 announcing it.	Mr. Smith, our new firewall software is now installed. Please check with me before announcing it.
Look, dude, this report is totally bogus. And the figures don't look kosher. Show me some real stats. Got sources?	Because the figures in this report seem inaccurate, please submit the source statistics.

Zooming In — PART 2

Suze Orman

America's most listened-to personal finance expert, Suze Orman, appears on TV, makes personal appearances, prepares magazine columns, and has written seven best-selling books. One might expect her to be a master multitasker, taking on many jobs at once and juggling all of them perfectly. Wrong, way wrong! When Orman starts a writing task, she focuses on that task only and allows no interruptions. "I came to this conclusion after watching the way racehorses win," she explained. "They come out of the gate with blinders on and go for the finish line." That's how she writes. "All I care about is what I do, and I do absolutely nothing else while I am doing it."[7] Trying to complete more than one task at the same time ends in the "absolute ruination" of any project, she contended. "When I'm writing, I don't answer phones. I don't care what else is going on."[8]

Her total focus enables her to target her advice to specific audiences. She seems to really care about people and is nonjudgmental toward those who have dug themselves into terrible financial trouble. Although much financial information is contradictory and confusing, she offers practical advice in simple, positive language. She explains the reasoning behind her advice and encourages others to learn to make their own financial decisions wisely.

Critical Thinking

- When writing, what are the advantages and disadvantages of multitasking?
- Suze Orman is known for using simple, familiar language to express complex ideas. Does a business writer lose credibility when using this kind of language?
- Why does it make sense for a business writer to express ideas positively instead of negatively?

© Newscom

Overly Formal	Conversational
All employees are herewith instructed to return the appropriately designated contracts to the undersigned.	Please return your contracts to me.
Pertaining to your order, we must verify the sizes that your organization requires prior to consignment of your order to our shipper.	We will send your order as soon as we confirm the sizes you need.

Expressing Yourself Positively

LEARNING OBJECTIVE 4
Effectively employ positive and courteous tone, bias-free language, simple expression, and vigorous words.

What are examples of loaded words that convey a negative tone?

You can improve the clarity, tone, and effectiveness of a message if you use positive rather than negative language. Positive language generally conveys more information than negative language does. Moreover, positive messages are uplifting and pleasant to read. Positive wording tells what *is* and what *can be done* rather than what *isn't* and what *can't be done*. For example, *Your order cannot be shipped by January 10* is not nearly as informative as *Your order will be shipped January 20*. An office supply store adjacent to an ice cream parlor in Portland, Maine, posted a sign on its door that reads: *Please enjoy your ice cream before you enjoy our store*. That sounds much more positive and inviting than *No food allowed!*[9]

Using positive language also involves avoiding negative words that create ill will. Some words appear to blame or accuse your audience. For example, opening a letter to a customer with *You claim that* suggests that you don't believe the customer. Other loaded words that can get you in trouble are *complaint, criticism, defective, failed, mistake,* and *neglected*. Often the writer is unconscious of the effect of these words. Notice in the following examples how you can revise the negative tone to create a more positive impression.

Negative	Positive
This plan definitely cannot succeed if we don't obtain management approval.	This plan definitely can succeed if we obtain management approval.
You failed to include your credit card number, so we can't mail your order.	We look forward to completing your order as soon as we receive your credit card number.
Your letter of May 2 claims that you returned a defective headset.	Your May 2 letter describes a headset you returned.
Employees cannot park in Lot H until April 1.	Employees may park in Lot H starting April 1.
You won't be sorry that....	You will be happy that....

Being Courteous

Why is it smart for a business communicator to remain cool and courteous even when angry?

Maintaining a courteous tone involves not just guarding against rudeness but also avoiding words that sound demanding or preachy. Expressions such as *you should, you must,* and *you have to* cause people to instinctively react with *Oh, yeah?* One remedy is to turn these demands into rhetorical questions that begin with *Will you please....* Giving reasons for a request also softens the tone.

Even when you feel justified in displaying anger, remember that losing your temper or being sarcastic will seldom accomplish your goals as a business communicator: to inform, to persuade, and to create goodwill. When you are irritated, frustrated, or infuriated, keep cool and try to defuse the situation. In dealing with customers in telephone conversations, use polite phrases such as *I would be happy to assist you with that, Thank you for being so patient,* and *It was a pleasure speaking with you.*

Less Courteous	More Courteous and Helpful
Can't you people get anything right? This is the second time I've written!	Please credit my account for $340. My latest statement shows that the error noted in my letter of May 15 has not yet been corrected.
Stewart, you must complete all performance reviews by Friday.	Stewart, will you please complete all performance reviews by Friday.

Less Courteous	More Courteous and Helpful
You should organize a car pool in this department.	Organizing a car pool will reduce your transportation costs and help preserve the environment.
Am I the only one who can read the operating manual?	Let's review the operating manual together so that you can get your documents to print correctly next time.

Choosing Bias-Free Language

In adapting a message to its audience, be sure your language is sensitive and bias-free. Few writers set out to be offensive. Sometimes, though, we all say things that we never thought might be hurtful. The real problem is that we don't think about the words that stereotype groups of people, such as *the boys in the mail room* or *the girls in the front office.* Be cautious about expressions that might be biased in terms of gender, race, ethnicity, age, and disability. Generally, you can avoid gender-biased language by leaving out the words *man* or *woman*, by using plural nouns and pronouns, or by changing to a gender-free word (*person* or *representative*). Avoid the *his or her* option whenever possible. It's wordy and conspicuous. With a little effort, you can usually find a construction that is graceful, grammatical, and unselfconscious.

Specify age only if it is relevant, and avoid expressions that are demeaning or subjective (such as *spry old codger*). To avoid disability bias, do not refer to an individual's disability unless it is relevant. When necessary, use terms that do not stigmatize disabled individuals. The following examples give you a quick look at a few problem expressions and possible replacements. The real key to bias-free communication, though, lies in your awareness and commitment. Be on the lookout to be sure that your messages do not exclude, stereotype, or offend people.

What is biased language, and why should business communicators avoid it?

Gender Biased	Improved
female doctor, woman attorney, cleaning woman	doctor, attorney, cleaner
waiter/waitress, authoress, stewardess	server, author, flight attendant
mankind, man-hour, man-made	humanity, working hours, artificial
office girls	office workers
the doctor … he	doctors … they
the teacher … she	teachers … they
executives and their wives	executives and their spouses
foreman, flagman, workman	lead worker, flagger, worker
businessman, salesman	businessperson, sales representative
Each employee had his picture taken.	Each employee had a picture taken. All employees had their pictures taken. Each employee had his or her picture taken.

Racially or Ethnically Biased	Improved
An Indian accountant was hired.	An accountant was hired.
James Lee, an African American, applied.	James Lee applied.

Age Biased	Improved
The law applied to old people.	The law applied to people over 65.
Sally Kay, 55, was transferred.	Sally Kay was transferred.
a spry old gentleman	a man
a little old lady	a woman

Disability Biased	Improved
afflicted with arthritis, suffering from …, crippled by …	has arthritis
confined to a wheelchair	uses a wheelchair

Why should business communicators strive to use familiar language?

Using Plain Language and Familiar Words

In adapting your message to your audience, use plain language and familiar words that you think audience members will recognize. Don't, however, avoid a big word that conveys your idea efficiently and is appropriate for the audience. Your goal is to shun pompous and pretentious language. Instead, use "GO" words. If you mean *begin,* don't say *commence* or *initiate.* If you mean *pay*, don't write *compensate*. By substituting everyday, familiar words for unfamiliar ones, as shown here, you help your audience comprehend your ideas quickly.

Unfamiliar	Familiar
commensurate	equal
interrogate	question
materialize	appear
obfuscate	confuse
remuneration	pay, salary
terminate	end

At the same time, be selective in your use of jargon. *Jargon* describes technical or specialized terms within a field. These terms enable insiders to communicate complex ideas briefly, but to outsiders they mean nothing. Human resources professionals, for example, know precisely what's meant by *cafeteria plan* (a benefits option program), but most of us would be thinking about lunch. Geologists refer to *plate tectonics,* and physicians discuss *metastatic carcinomas*. These terms mean little to most of us. Use specialized language only when the audience will understand it. In addition, don't forget to consider secondary audiences: Will those potential receivers understand any technical terms used?

How can you improve your vocabulary so that you can use precise, vigorous words?

Employing Precise, Vigorous Words

Strong verbs and concrete nouns give receivers more information and keep them interested. Don't overlook the thesaurus (or the thesaurus program on your computer) for expanding your word choices and vocabulary. Whenever possible, use specific words as shown here.

Imprecise, Dull	More Precise
a change in profits	a 25 percent hike in profits a 10 percent plunge in profits
to say	to promise, confess, understand to allege, assert, assume, judge
to think about	to identify, diagnose, analyze to probe, examine, inspect

The accompanying checklist feature on page 126 reviews important elements in the first phase of the 3-x-3 writing process. As you review these tips, remember the three basics of prewriting: analyzing, anticipating, and adapting. Figure 4.7 on page 125 illustrates a number of poor techniques that create a negative tone in an e-mail message. Notice what a difference revision makes. Many negative ideas could have been expressed positively. After revision, the message is shorter, is more conversational, and emphasizes audience benefits.

Writing in Teams

LEARNING OBJECTIVE 5

Understand how teams approach collaborative writing projects and what collaboration tools support team writing.

As you learned in Chapter 2, many of today's workers will work with teams to deliver services, develop products, and complete projects. It is almost assumed that today's progressive organizations will employ teams in some capacity to achieve their objectives. Because much of a team's work involves writing, you can expect to be putting your writing skills to work as part of a team.

FIGURE 4.7 Improving the Tone in an E-Mail Message

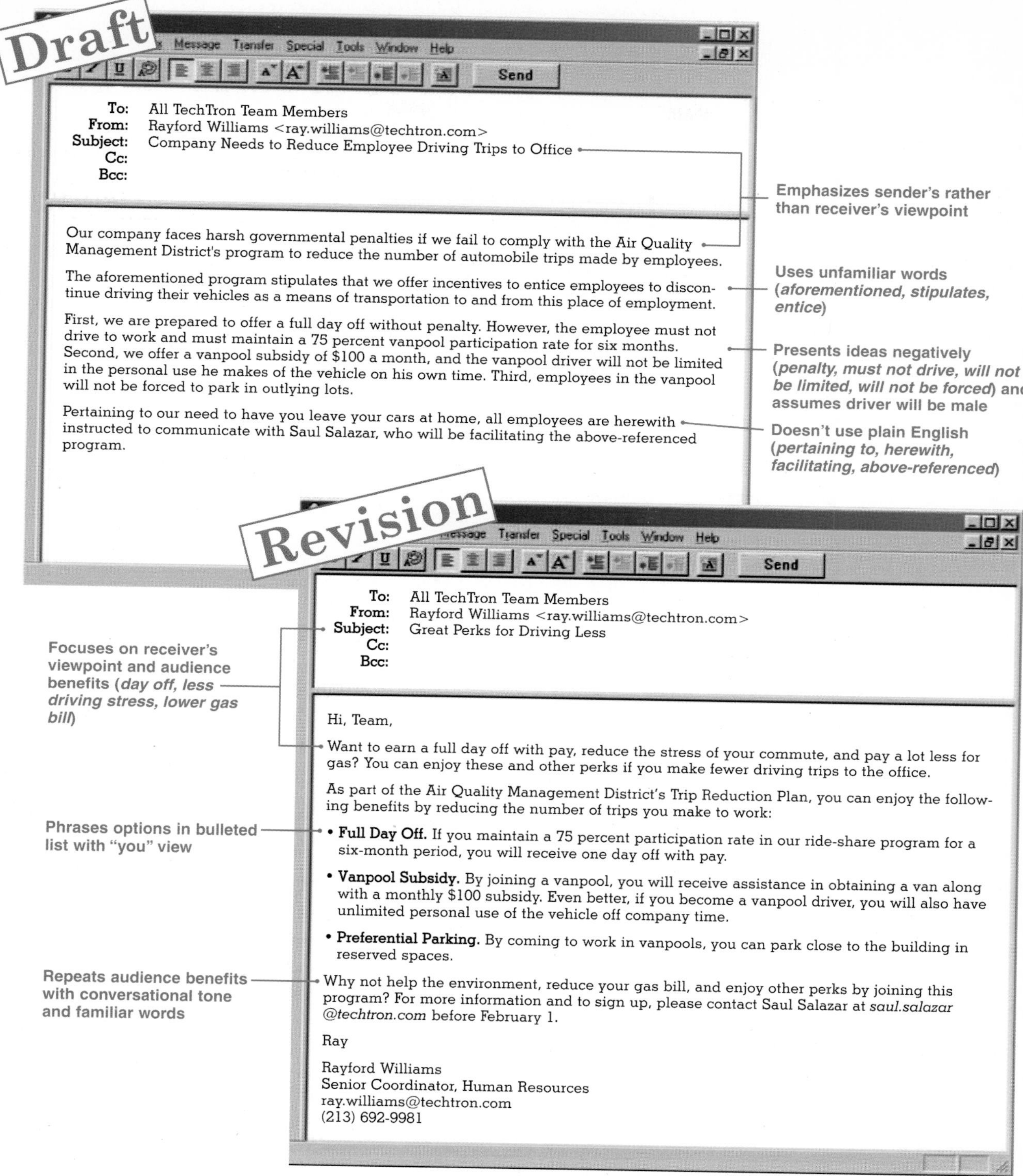
Draft
Message Transfer Special Tools Window Help
Send
To: All TechTron Team Members
From: Rayford Williams <ray.williams@techtron.com>
Subject: Company Needs to Reduce Employee Driving Trips to Office
Cc:
Bcc:
Our company faces harsh governmental penalties if we fail to comply with the Air Quality Management District's program to reduce the number of automobile trips made by employees.
The aforementioned program stipulates that we offer incentives to entice employees to discontinue driving their vehicles as a means of transportation to and from this place of employment.
First, we are prepared to offer a full day off without penalty. However, the employee must not drive to work and must maintain a 75 percent vanpool participation rate for six months. Second, we offer a vanpool subsidy of $100 a month, and the vanpool driver will not be limited in the personal use he makes of the vehicle on his own time. Third, employees in the vanpool will not be forced to park in outlying lots.
Pertaining to our need to have you leave your cars at home, all employees are herewith instructed to communicate with Saul Salazar, who will be facilitating the above-referenced program.
Emphasizes sender's rather than receiver's viewpoint
Uses unfamiliar words (aforementioned, stipulates, entice)
Presents ideas negatively (penalty, must not drive, will not be limited, will not be forced) and assumes driver will be male
Doesn't use plain English (pertaining to, herewith, facilitating, above-referenced)
Revision
Message Transfer Special Tools Window Help
Send
To: All TechTron Team Members
From: Rayford Williams <ray.williams@techtron.com>
Subject: Great Perks for Driving Less
Cc:
Bcc:
Hi, Team,
Want to earn a full day off with pay, reduce the stress of your commute, and pay a lot less for gas? You can enjoy these and other perks if you make fewer driving trips to the office.
As part of the Air Quality Management District's Trip Reduction Plan, you can enjoy the following benefits by reducing the number of trips you make to work:
• Full Day Off. If you maintain a 75 percent participation rate in our ride-share program for a six-month period, you will receive one day off with pay.
• Vanpool Subsidy. By joining a vanpool, you will receive assistance in obtaining a van along with a monthly $100 subsidy. Even better, if you become a vanpool driver, you will also have unlimited personal use of the vehicle off company time.
• Preferential Parking. By coming to work in vanpools, you can park close to the building in reserved spaces.
Why not help the environment, reduce your gas bill, and enjoy other perks by joining this program? For more information and to sign up, please contact Saul Salazar at saul.salazar@techtron.com before February 1.
Ray
Rayford Williams
Senior Coordinator, Human Resources
ray.williams@techtron.com
(213) 692-9981
Focuses on receiver's viewpoint and audience benefits (day off, less driving stress, lower gas bill)
Phrases options in bulleted list with "you" view
Repeats audience benefits with conversational tone and familiar words

When Are Team-Written Documents Necessary?

Collaboration on team-written documents is necessary for projects that (a) are big, (b) have short deadlines, and (c) require the expertise or consensus of many people. Businesspeople sometimes collaborate on short documents, such as memos, letters, information briefs, procedures, and policies. But more often, teams work together on big documents and presentations.

In what situations can you expect to share writing duties with a team?

Checklist

Adapting a Message to Its Audience

- **Identify the message purpose.** Ask yourself why you are communicating and what you hope to achieve. Look for primary and secondary purposes.
- **Select the most appropriate form.** Determine whether you need a permanent record or whether the message is too sensitive to put in writing.
- **Profile the audience.** Identify your relationship with the reader and your knowledge about that individual or group. Assess how much the receiver knows about the subject.
- **Focus on audience benefits.** Phrase your statements from the readers' viewpoint, not the writer's. Concentrate on the "you" view (*Your order will arrive, You can enjoy, Your ideas count*).
- **Avoid gender and racial bias.** Use bias-free words (*businessperson* instead of *businessman; working hours* instead of *man-hours*). Omit ethnic identification unless the context demands it.
- **Avoid age and disability bias.** Include age only if relevant. Avoid potentially demeaning expressions (*spry old gentleman*), and use terms that do not stigmatize disabled people (*he is disabled* instead of *he is a cripple* or *he has a handicap*).
- **Be conversational but professional.** Strive for a warm, friendly tone that is not overly formal or familiar. Avoid slang and low-level diction.
- **Express ideas positively rather than negatively.** Instead of *Your order can't be shipped before June 1*, say *Your order can be shipped June 1*.
- **Use short, familiar words.** Use technical terms and big words only if they are appropriate for the audience (*end* not *terminate, required* not *mandatory*).
- **Search for precise, vigorous words.** Use a thesaurus if necessary to find strong verbs and concrete nouns (*announces* instead of *says, brokerage* instead of *business*).

Why Are Team-Written Documents Better?

Team-written documents and presentations are standard in most organizations because collaboration has many advantages. Most important, collaboration usually produces a better product because many heads are better than one. In addition, team members and organizations benefit from team processes. Working together helps socialize members. They learn more about the organization's values and procedures. They are able to break down functional barriers, and they improve both formal and informal chains of communication. Additionally, they buy in to a project when they are part of its development. Members of effective teams are eager to implement their recommendations.

How Are Team-Written Documents Divided?

In what phases of the writing process do team members work together and separately?

With big writing projects, teams may not actually function together for each phase of the writing process. Typically, team members gather at the beginning to brainstorm. They iron out answers to questions about the purpose, audience, content, organization, and design of their document or presentation. They develop procedures for team functioning, as you learned in Chapter 2. Then, they often assign segments of the project to individual members.

Teams work together closely in Phase 1 (prewriting) of the writing process. However, members generally work separately in Phase 2 (writing), when they conduct research, organize their findings, and compose a first draft. During Phase 3 (revising) teams may work together to synthesize their drafts and offer suggestions for revision. They might assign one person the task of preparing the final document, and another, the job of proofreading. The revision and evaluation phase might be repeated several times before the final product is ready for presentation.

What Online Collaboration Tools Support Team Writing?

One of the most frustrating tasks for teams is writing shared documents. Keeping the various versions straight and recognizing who made what comment can be difficult. Fortunately, online collaboration tools are constantly being developed and improved. They range from simple to complex, inexpensive to expensive, locally installed to remotely hosted, commercial to open source, and large to small. Online collaboration tools are especially necessary when team members are not physically in the same location. However, even when members are nearby, they may find it necessary to use online collaboration tools, such as the following:[10]

- **E-mail.** Despite its many drawbacks, e-mail remains a popular tool for online asynchronous (intermittent data transmission) collaboration. However, as projects grow more complex and involve more people who are not working nearby, e-mail becomes a clumsy, ineffective tool, especially for collaborative writing tasks.
- **Mailing lists.** With the right software, mailing lists can be archived online, providing a threaded listing of posts and full-text searching.
- **Discussion boards.** Participants can upload documents to the board instead of sending large files to everyone.
- **Instant messaging.** Because it ensures immediate availability, instant messaging is gaining acceptance. It allows members to clear up minor matters immediately, and it is helpful in initiating a quick group discussion.
- **Blogs and wikis.** A *blog* is a Web site with journal entries usually written by one person with comments added by others. A *wiki* is a Web site that allows multiple users to collaboratively create and edit pages. Wikis are good tools for building a knowledge repository that can be edited by participants. You will learn more about blogs and wikis in Chapter 7.
- **Groupware and portals.** Groupware and portals in the past involved expensive software featuring online discussion areas, document- and file-sharing areas, integrated calendaring, and collaborative authoring tools. More recently, less expensive tools including Basecamp, Box, Huddle, and Socialtext are available.

A team of investors and organic farmers in Bloomington, Indiana, began using Basecamp, an inexpensive Web-based collaboration program, to help the people in the field keep in touch with those in town. The 81-acre farm grows organic produce and sells it to Whole Foods Market, food co-ops, and farmers' markets. The farm's founders brought on four partners, but their jobs elsewhere prevented them from visiting the farm very often. One partner decided to install Basecamp on the farm house computer. For $24 a month this program offers to-do lists, a wiki, a chat room, 3 gigabytes of file storage, and a function that tracks due dates. Now the city folks can stay in the loop with the farmers and can share in decision making and farm progress.[11]

Collaboration software isn't just for multinational corporations. Stranger's Hill Organics, the oldest certified organics farm in Indiana, has joined the ranks of Adidas, Patagonia, Kellogg's and others in using Basecamp, a popular project-management tool that allows professionals to work together from different locations. The local grower, which serves markets and co-ops in Bloomington and Indianapolis, uses Basecamp to coordinate tasks, from crop maintenance and harvesting to tax planning. The results show in the farm's healthy squash, beans, cucumbers, and herbs. *How might farmers use online collaboration tools?*

PLUGGED IN

Using Technology to Edit and Revise Collaborative Documents

Collaborative writing and editing projects are challenging. Fortunately, Microsoft Word offers useful tools to help team members edit and share documents electronically. Two simple but useful editing tools are **Text Highlight Color** and **Font Color**. These tools, which are found on the **Home** tab in MS Office 2007, enable reviewers to point out errors and explain problematic passages through the use of contrast. However, some projects require more advanced editing tools such as **Track Changes** and **Comment**.

Track Changes. To suggest specific editing changes to other team members, **Track Changes** is handy. The revised wording is visible on screen, and deletions show up in callout balloons that appear in the right-hand margin (see Figure 4.2). Suggested revisions offered by various team members are identified and dated. The original writer may accept or reject these changes. In Office 2007 you will find **Track Changes** on the **Review** tab.

Comment. Probably the most useful editing tool is the **Comment** function, also shown in Figure 4.8. This tool allows users to point out problematic passages or errors, ask or answer questions, and share ideas without changing or adding text. When more than one person adds comments, the comments appear in different colors and are identified by the writer's name and a date/time stamp. To use this tool in Word 2007, click **New Comment** from the drop-down **Review** tab. Then type your comment, which can be seen in the Web or print layout view (click **View** and **Print Layout** or **Web Layout**).

Completing a Document. When a document is finished, be sure to accept or reject all changes on the **Review** tab, a step that removes the tracking information.

Career Application

Organize into groups of three. Using the latest version of Word, copy and respond to the Document for Analysis in 4.11. Set up a round-robin e-mail file exchange so that each member responds to the other group members' documents by using the **Comment** feature of Word to offer advice or suggestions for improvement. Submit a printout of the document with group comments, as well as a final edited document.

What Tools Work Well for Student Collaboration?

Student groups collaborating on assignments may find several helpful software tools. Google Docs is a free Web-based word processor, spreadsheet, presentation, and form application program that keeps documents current and lets team members update files from their own computers. A favorite feature of Google Docs is offline editing via Google Gears or the Chrome browser. In addition, Google Docs enables you to compose offline using your own word processor and upload into Docs to share and edit with teammates. Another free collaborative writing tool is Whiteboard. Check out either of these free tools by searching Google.

A number of tools accompanying Microsoft Word enable team writers to track changes and insert comments while editing one team document. The above Plugged In box discusses these tools, and Figure 4.8 illustrates how they work.

Adapting to Legal and Ethical Responsibilities

LEARNING OBJECTIVE 6

Summarize the legal and ethical responsibilities of business communicators in the areas of investments, safety, marketing, human resources, and copyright law.

One of your primary responsibilities in writing for an organization or for yourself is to avoid language that may land you in court. Another responsibility is to be ethical. Both of these concerns revolve around the use and abuse of language. You can protect yourself and avoid litigation by knowing what is legal and by adapting your language accordingly. Be especially careful when your messages address or include mentions of investments, safety, marketing, human resources, and copyright law.

Investment Information

Writers describing the sale of stocks or financial services must follow specific laws written to protect investors. Any messages—including e-mails, letters, newsletters, and pamphlets—must be free of misleading information, exaggerations, and half-truths. One company in Massachusetts inadvertently violated the law by declaring that it was "recession-proof." After going bankrupt, the company was sued by angry stockholders claiming that they had been

FIGURE 4.8 **Track Changes and Comment Features in Team Document**

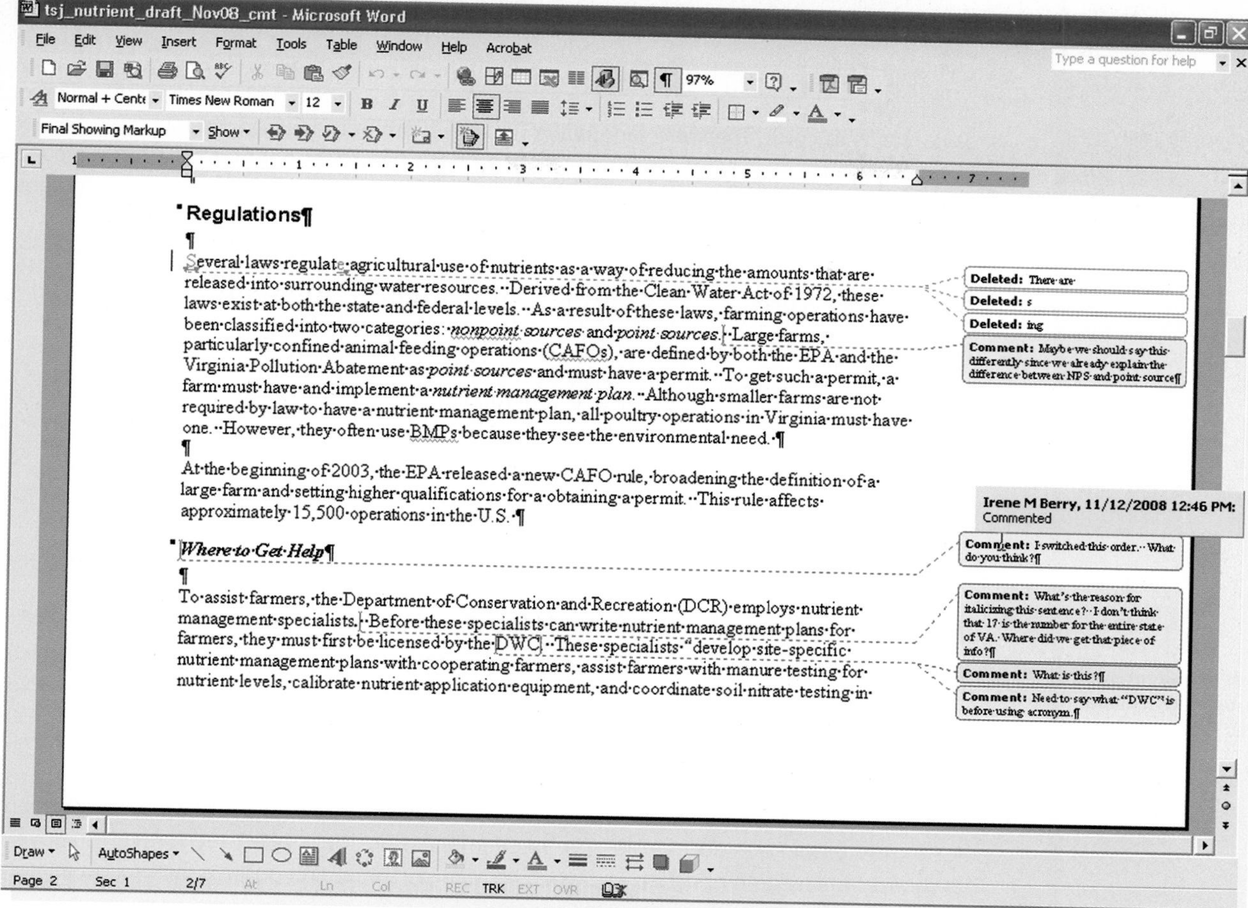

deceived. A software company caused a flurry of lawsuits by withholding information that revealed problems in a new version of one of its most popular programs. Stockholders sued, charging that managers had deliberately concealed the bad news, thus keeping stock prices artificially high. Experienced financial writers know that careless language and even poor timing may provoke litigation.

Safety Information

Writers describing potentially dangerous products worry not only about protecting people from physical harm but also about being sued. During the past three decades, litigation arising from product liability has been one of the most active areas of tort law (*tort law* involves wrongful civil acts other than breach of contract). Manufacturers are obligated to warn consumers of any risks in their products. These warnings must do more than suggest danger; they must also clearly tell people how to use the product safely. In writing warnings, concentrate on major points. Omit anything that is not critical. In the work area describe a potential problem and tell how to solve it. For example, *Lead dust is harmful and gets on your clothes. Change your clothes before leaving work.*

Why should warnings on dangerous products be written especially clearly?

Clearly written safety messages use easy-to-understand words, such as *doctor* instead of *physician*, *clean* instead of *sanitary*, and *burn* instead of *incinerate*. Technical terms are defined; for example, *Asbestos is a carcinogen (something that causes cancer)*. Effective safety messages also include highlighting techniques such as headings and bullets. In coming chapters you will learn more about these techniques for improving readability.

Marketing Information

Sales and marketing messages are illegal if they falsely advertise prices, performance capability, quality, or other product characteristics. Marketing messages must not deceive the buyer in any

What kinds of sales and marketing messages are illegal?

way. The marketers of CortiSlim and CortiStress paid huge fines and were forbidden to claim that their products caused rapid weight loss and reduced the risk of cancer, heart disease, and other ailments.[12]

Sellers of services must also be cautious about the language they use to describe what they will do. Letters, reports, and proposals that describe services to be performed are interpreted as contracts in court. Therefore, language must not promise more than intended. In Chapter 10 on page 315, you will learn more about what's legal and what's not in sales letters. Here are some dangerous words (and recommended alternatives) that have created misunderstandings leading to lawsuits.[13]

Dangerous Word	Court Interpretation	Recommended Alternative
inspect	to examine critically, to investigate and test officially, to scrutinize	to review, to study, to tour the facility
determine	to come to a decision, to decide, to resolve	to evaluate, to assess, to analyze
assure	to render safe, to make secure, to give confidence, to cause to feel certain	to facilitate, to provide further confidence, to enhance the reliability of

Human Resources Information

What kinds of statements should you avoid in evaluating employees in the workplace?

The vast number of lawsuits relating to human resources and employment makes this a treacherous area for business communicators. In evaluating employees in the workplace, avoid making unsubstantiated negative comments. It is also unwise to assess traits (*she is unreliable*) because doing so requires subjective judgment. Concentrate instead on specific incidents (*in the last month she missed four work days and was late three times*). Defamation lawsuits have become so common that some companies no longer provide letters of recommendation for former employees. To be safe, give recommendations only when the former employee authorizes the recommendation and when you can say something positive. Stick to job-related information.

Statements in employee handbooks also require careful wording, because a court might rule that such statements are "implied contracts." Consider the following handbook remark: "We at Hotstuff, Inc., show our appreciation for hard work and team spirit by rewarding everyone who performs well." This seemingly harmless statement could make it difficult to fire an employee because of the implied employment promise.[14] Companies are warned to avoid promissory phrases in writing job advertisements, application forms, and offer letters. Phrases that suggest permanent employment and guaranteed job security can be interpreted as contracts.[15]

ETHICS CHECK

Barack Rip-Off

Poster artist Shepard Fairey created a popular "Hope" poster of Barack Obama from a striking photo he saw on the Internet. Freelance photographer Mannie Garcia cried foul and demanded licensing fees, which Fairey refused. Are items on the Internet free for the taking if they have been changed a little?

In statements to existing and prospective employees, companies must recognize that oral comments may trigger lawsuits. A Minnesota television news anchor won damages when she gave up her job search because her station manager promised to extensively market her in a leading role. But he failed to follow through. A Vermont engineer won his case of negligent misrepresentation when he was not told that the defense project for which he was hired faced a potential cutback. Companies are warned to require employees to sign employment agreements indicating that all terms of employment orally agreed upon must be made in writing to be valid.[16]

In adapting messages to meet today's litigious business environment, be sensitive to the rights of others and to your own rights. The key elements in this adaptation process are awareness of laws, sensitivity to interpretations, and careful use of language.

Copyright Information

What is *fair use* in relation to copyright law?

The Copyright Act of 1976 protects authors—literary, dramatic, and artistic—of published and unpublished works. The word *copyright* refers to "the right to copy," and a key provision is *fair use*. Under fair use, individuals have limited use of copyrighted material without requiring permission. These uses are for criticism, comment, news reporting, teaching, scholarship, and research. Unfortunately, the distinctions between fair use and infringement are not clearly defined.

Four-Factor Test to Assess Fair Use. What is fair use? Actually, it is a shadowy territory with vague and often disputed boundaries—now even more so with the addition of cyberspace. Courts use four factors as a test in deciding disputes over fair use:

- **Purpose and character of the use, particularly whether for profit.** Courts are more likely to allow fair use for nonprofit educational purposes than for commercial ventures.
- **Nature of the copyrighted work.** When information is necessary for public good—such as medical news—courts are more likely to support fair use.
- **Amount and substantiality of portion used.** Copying a 200-word passage from a 200,000-word book might be allowed but not 200 words from a 1,000-word article or a substantial part of a shorter work. A total of 300 words is mistakenly thought by many to be an acceptable limit for fair use, but courts have not upheld this figure. Don't rely on it.
- **Effect of the use on the potential market.** If use of the work may interfere with the author's potential profit from the original, fair use copying would not be allowed.

How to Avoid Copyright Infringement. Whenever you borrow words, charts, graphs, photos, music, or anything created privately, be sure you know what is legal and acceptable. The following guidelines will help:

Why should writers assume that everything is copyrighted?

- **Assume that everything is copyrighted.** Nearly everything created privately and originally after 1989 is copyrighted and protected whether or not it has a copyright notice.
- **Realize that Internet items are NOT in the public domain.** Nothing modern is in the public domain (free to be used by anyone) unless the owner explicitly says so.
- **Observe fair-use restrictions.** Be aware of the four-factor test. Avoid appropriating large amounts of outside material.
- **Ask for permission.** You are always safe if you obtain permission. Write to the source, identify the material you wish to include, and explain where it will be used. Expect to pay for permission.
- **Don't assume that a footnote is all that is needed.** Including a footnote to a source prevents plagiarism but not copyright infringement. Anything copied beyond the boundaries of fair use requires permission. You will learn more about citation methods and ways to avoid plagiarism in Chapter 12.

For more information about *copyright law, fair use, public domain,* and *work for hire,* you can search the Web with these keywords.

Want to do well on tests and excel in your course? Go to **www.meguffey.com** for helpful interactive resources.

- **Review the Chapter 4 PowerPoint slides to prepare for the first quiz.**

Zooming In — YOUR TURN

Applying Your Skills With Suze Orman

As an applicant for a research assistant at the Suze Orman Financial Group, you have been asked to submit a writing sample. Your assignment is to compose a one-page memo discussing why so many college students are in debt. All applicants are to provide tips to students who want to avoid getting into college-related debt. As a writing sample, your memo will be judged on its clear expression, simple language, and precise words.

Your Task

Address your memo to Melissa M., who is a recruiter hired by Suze Orman to screen applicants. See Chapter 8 for information about preparing memos.

Summary of Learning Objectives

1 Identify four basic principles of business writing, summarize the 3-x-3 writing process, and explain how a writing process helps a writer. Business writing differs from academic writing in that it strives to solve business problems. It is also economical, persuasive, and audience oriented. Phase 1 of the 3-x-3 writing process (prewriting) involves analyzing the message, anticipating the audience, and considering ways to adapt the message to the audience. Phase 2 (writing) involves researching the topic, organizing the material, and composing the message. Phase 3 (revising) includes proofreading and evaluating the message. A writing process helps a writer by providing a systematic plan describing what to do in creating messages.

2 Recognize the components of the first phase of the writing process (prewriting) including analyzing your purpose, profiling the audience, and selecting the best channel. Communicators must decide why they are delivering a message and what they hope to achieve. Although many messages only inform, some must also persuade. After identifying the purpose of a message, communicators must choose the most appropriate channel. That choice depends on the importance of the message, the amount and speed of feedback required, the need for a permanent record, the cost of the channel, and the degree of formality desired. Communicators should also anticipate the primary and secondary audiences in order to adapt the message appropriately.

3 Effectively apply audience benefits, the "you" view, and a conversational but professional tone. Skilled communicators strive to emphasize audience benefits in business messages. This involves looking for ways to give something to the receiver, solve the receiver's problems, save the receiver's money, or just understand the feelings and position of that person. Skilled communicators look at a message from the receiver's perspective applying the "you" view without attempting to manipulate. Effective business messages convey a warm, friendly tone but avoid expressions that may make the writer sound immature or unprofessional.

4 Effectively employ positive and courteous tone, bias-free language, simple expression, and vigorous words. Skilled communicators improve the clarity, tone, and effectiveness of messages by using positive language that tells what can be done rather than what can't be done (*The project will be successful with your support* rather than *The project won't be successful without your support*). A courteous tone means guarding against rudeness and avoiding sounding preachy or demanding. Messages should also avoid language that excludes, stereotypes, or offends people, such as *lady lawyer, spry old gentlemen,* and *confined to a wheelchair*). Messages are improved by strong verbs and concrete nouns rather than imprecise, dull expressions.

5 Understand how teams approach collaborative writing projects and what collaboration tools support team writing. Team writing, which is necessary for large projects or when wide expertise is necessary, alters the writing process. Teams often work together in brainstorming and working out their procedures and assignments. Then individual members write their portions of the report or presentation during Phase 2. During Phase 3 (revising) teams may work together to combine their drafts. Teams use online collaboration tools such as e-mail, mailing lists, discussion boards, instant messaging, blogs, wikis, groupware, and portals.

6 Summarize the legal and ethical responsibilities of business communicators in the areas of investments, safety, marketing, human resources, and copyright law. In writing about investments, communicators must avoid misleading information, exaggerations, and half-truths. Safety information, including warnings, must tell consumers clearly how to use a product safely and motivate them to do so. In addition to being honest, marketing information must not promise more than intended. Communicators in human resources must use careful wording (particularly in employment recommendations and employee handbooks) to avoid lawsuits. They must also avoid oral promises that can result in lawsuits. In publication, one must be mindful of copyright laws. Writers should assume that everything is copyrighted, even items borrowed from the Internet, and know the implications and limitations of *fair use*.

Chapter Review

1. Why do you think business writing differs from school essay writing? (Obj. 1)
2. List the three phases of the writing process and summarize what happens in each phase. Which phase requires the most time? (Obj. 1)
3. What six factors are important in selecting an appropriate channel to deliver a message? What makes one channel richer than another? (Obj. 2)
4. How does profiling the audience help a business communicator prepare a message? (Obj. 2)
5. What is meant by "audience benefits"? (Obj. 3)
6. When is the "you" view appropriate, and when is it inappropriate? (Obj. 3)
7. Why is it OK to use instant messaging abbreviations (such as *BTW*) and happy faces in messages to friends but not OK in business messages? (Obj. 3)
8. What is wrong with using expressions such as *you claim, complaint, criticism, defective, failed, mistake,* and *neglected?* (Obj. 4)
9. What is wrong with the following statement? *Pertaining to the above-referenced infraction, all employees are herewith warned by the undersigned not to install private software on company computers.* (Obj. 4)
10. What is bias-free language? List original examples. (Obj. 4)
11. Why should business writers strive to use short, familiar, simple words? Does this "dumb down" business messages? (Obj. 4)
12. What is *jargon*, and when is it appropriate for business writing? (Obj. 4)
13. What are the advantages and disadvantages of team-written documents? (Obj. 5)
14. Under copyright law, what does *fair use* mean? (Obj. 6)
15. What kinds of works are protected by copyright laws? (Obj. 6)

Critical Thinking

1. Why do you think employers prefer messages that are not written like high school and college essays? (Obj. 1)
2. A wise observer once said that bad writing makes smart people look dumb. Do you agree or disagree, and why? (Objs. 1–4)
3. Discuss the following statement: "The English language is a land mine—it is filled with terms that are easily misinterpreted as derogatory and others that are blatantly insulting . . . . Being fair and objective is not enough; employers must also appear to be so."[17] (Obj. 4)
4. Why do you think that writing in a natural, conversational tone is difficult for many people? (Obj. 3)
5. **Ethical Issue:** Peter Whitney, an employee at Wells Fargo, launched an Internet blog to chat about his life, his friends, and his job. After criticizing some of his coworkers in his blog, he was fired from his job handling mail and the front desk. Whitney said, "There needs to be clearer guidelines. Some people go to a bar and complain about workers. I decided to do it online. Some people say I deserve what happened, but it was really harsh. It was unfair."[18] Do you agree or disagree, and why?

Writing Improvement Exercises

4.1 Audience Benefits and the "You" View (Obj. 3)

Your Task. Revise the following sentences to emphasize the perspective of the audience and the "you" view.

a. To avoid suffering the kinds of monetary losses we have experienced in the past, our credit union prohibits the cashing of third-party checks presented by our members.
b. To help us process your order with our new database software, we need you to go to this Web site and fill out the required customer information.
c. We regret to announce that our electronics center is able to honor iPhone discounts only for a limited initial offering during the next 30 days.
d. Under a new policy, reimbursement of travel expenses will be restricted to those related to work only.
e. We are pleased to announce that you have been approved to enroll in our management trainee program.
f. To allow us to continue our policy of selling name brands at discount prices, we can give store credit but we cannot give cash refunds on returned merchandise.

4.2 Conversational but Professional (Obj. 3)

Your Task. Revise the following to make the tone conversational yet professional.

a. Under separate cover the above-referenced items (printer toner and supplies) are being sent to your Oakdale office, as per your telephone conversation of April 1.
b. Kindly inform the undersigned whether or not your representative will be making a visitation in the near future.
c. It is recommended that you conceptualize and submit your departmental budget ASAP.
d. BTW, we've had some slippage in the schedule but don't have to scrap everything and start from ground zero.
e. To facilitate ratification of this agreement, your negotiators urge that the membership respond in the affirmative.
f. She didn't have the guts to badmouth him 2 hz face.

4.3 Positive and Courteous Expression (Obj. 4)

Your Task. Revise the following sentences to reflect positive and courteous expression.

a. Customers are ineligible for the 10 percent discount unless they show their membership cards.
b. Titan Insurance Company will not process any claim not accompanied by documented proof from a physician showing that the injuries were treated.
c. If you fail to follow each requirement, you will not receive your $50 rebate.
d. You have definitely not completed the job satisfactorily, and we will exercise our legal right to withhold payment until you do.
e. In the message you left at our Web site, you claim that you returned a defective headset.
f. We regret to announce that the special purchase netbook computers will be available only to the first 25 customers.

4.4 Bias-Free Language (Obj. 4)

Your Task. Revise the following sentences to reduce gender, racial, ethnic, age, and disability bias.

a. Any applicant for the position of fireman must submit a medical report signed by his physician.
b. Every employee is entitled to see his personnel file.
c. All waiters and waitresses are covered under our new benefits package.
d. A salesman would have to use all his skills to sell those condos.
e. Serving on the panel are a lady veterinarian, a female doctor, two businessmen, and an Indian CPA.
f. All conference participants and their wives are invited to the banquet.
g. How many man-hours are required to complete the project?

4.5 Plain Language and Familiar Words (Obj. 4)

Your Task. Revise the following sentences to use plain language and familiar words.

a. Please ascertain whether we must perpetuate our current contract despite perplexing profits.
b. He hypothesized that the vehicle was not operational because of a malfunctioning gasket.
c. Because we cannot monitor all cash payments, we must terminate the contract.
d. The contract stipulates that management must perpetuate the retirement plan.
e. I'll interface with Mark to access his people.
f. Unilateral nullification of the terms and conditions of the expiring agreement absent bona fide impasse is prohibited. (Legal talk!)

4.6 Precise, Vigorous Words (Obj. 4)

Your Task. From the choices in parentheses, select the most precise, vigorous words.

a. We plan to (*acknowledge, publicize, applaud*) the work of exemplary employees.
b. When replying to e-mail, (*bring in, include, put*) enough of the old message for (*someone, the person, the recipient*) to recognize the original note.
c. For a (*hard, long, complicated*) e-mail message, (*make, create, do*) the message in your word processing program.
d. If an e-mail (*thing, catch, glitch*) interferes while writing, you can easily (*get, have, retrieve*) your message.

For the following sentences provide more precise alternatives for the italicized words.

e. After (a) *going over* the proposal, I decided it was (b) *bad*.
f. In her e-mail message, she said that she would (a) *change* overtime hours in order to (b) *fix* the budget.
g. Our new manager (a) *said* that only (b) *the right kind of* applicants should apply.

4.7 Legal Language (Obj. 6)

Your Task. To avoid possible litigation, revise the italicized words in the following sentences taken from proposals.

a. We have *inspected* the environmental project and will send a complete report.
b. Our goal is to *assure* completion of the ecological program on schedule.
c. We will *determine* the amount of stress for each supporting column.

Activities

4.8 Document for Analysis: Improving the Tone of an E-Mail Message (Objs. 3–5)

Team

Your Task. Analyze the following demanding e-mail to be sent by the vice president to all employees. In teams or individually, discuss the tone and writing faults in this message. Your instructor may ask you to revise the message so that it reflects some of the writing techniques you learned in this chapter. How can you make this message more courteous, positive, and precise? Focus on conciseness, familiar words, and developing the "you" view. Consider revising this e-mail as a collaboration project using Word's **Comment** feature.

To: All Employees
From: B. A. Cartwright <bacartwright@integrity.com>
Subject: Your Excessive Use of E-Mail!
Cc:
Attached: E-Mail and Internet Policy

Once again I have the decidedly unpleasant task of reminding all employees that you may NOT utilize company computers or the Internet other than for work-related business and essential personal messages. Effective immediately a new policy will be implemented.

Our guys in IT tell me that our bandwidth is now seriously compromised by some of you boys and girls who are using company computers for gaming, blogging, shopping, chatting, and downloading streaming video. Yes, we have given you the right to use e-mail responsibly for essential personal messages. But that does not include checking your Facebook or MySpace accounts during work hours or downloading your favorite shows or sharing music.

We distributed an e-mail policy a little while ago. We have now found it necessary to amplify and extrapolate that policy to include use of the Internet. If our company does not control its e-mail and Internet use, you will continue to suffer slow downloads. You may also lose the right to use e-mail at all. In the past every employee has had the right to send a personal e-mail occasionally, but he must use that right carefully. We may have to prohibit the personal use of e-mail entirely. Don't make me do this!

You will be expected to study the attached E-Mail and Internet policy and return the signed form with your agreement to adhere to this policy. You must return this form by March 1. No exceptions!

4.9 Channel Selection: Burger King and the $1 Double Cheeseburger (Obj. 2)

To offer a budget sandwich during tough times, Burger King Holdings Inc. proposed a four-month promotion offering its double cheeseburger for $1 in the United States. But franchisees rejected the proposal because they thought it made no sense to sell the sandwich at a lower price than the cost of its ingredients. Burger King has 11,100 restaurants in more than 65 countries, and almost 90 percent of them are owned and operated by independent franchisees. Burger King management tried again by asking its U.S. franchisees to consider a six-week period for the $1 special, but operators voted against the modified plan as well. Results of the vote were delivered to franchisees in an audio recording.[19]

Your Task. Discuss the factors Burger King management may have considered before choosing a communication channel to deliver this important news. Was an audio recording (probably a recorded phone message) the best channel to deliver this news to thousands of franchisees in the United States?

4.10 Channel Selection: Various Business Scenarios (Obj. 2)

Your Task. Using Figure 4.2 on page 116, suggest the best communication channels for the following messages. Assume that all channels shown are available. Be prepared to explain your choices.

a. You need to know whether Crystal in Reprographics can produce a rush job for you in two days.
b. As part of a task force to investigate cell phone marketing, you need to establish a central location where each team member can see general information about the task as well as add comments for others to see. Task force members are located throughout the country.
c. You want to know what team members are available immediately for a quick teleconference meeting. They are all workaholics and glued to their computers.
d. As human resources manager during a company reorganization, you must tell six employees that they will lose their jobs.
e. A prospective client in Japan wants price quotes for a number of your products as soon as possible.
f. You must respond to a notice from the Internal Revenue Service insisting that you did not pay the correct amount for last quarter's employer's taxes.
g. As a member of the Information Technology Department, you must collect information about virus protection software for your office computers and make a recommendation to the hands-on company president.

4.11 Analyzing Audiences (Obj. 3)

Your Task. Using the questions in Figure 4.4 on page 118, write a brief analysis of the audience for each of the following communication tasks.

a. You are about to send an e-mail to your regional sales manager describing your visit to a new customer who is demanding special discounts.
b. You are preparing a cover letter for a job that you saw advertised in a local newspaper. You are confident that your qualifications match the job description.
c. As an administrator at the municipal water department, you must write a letter to water users explaining that the tap water may taste and smell bad; however, it poses no threats to health.
d. You are planning to write an e-mail to your boss to try to persuade her to allow you to attend a computer class that will require you to leave work early two days a week for ten weeks.
e. You are preparing an unsolicited sales letter to a targeted group of executives promoting part-time ownership in a corporate jet plane.

4.12 Copyright Confusion: Myths and Facts (Obj. 6)

Ethics

Your Task. You overheard the following statements as a group of college students discussed copyright issues.[20] Which of these statements do you think are true, and which are false?

a. If it doesn't have a copyright notice, it's not copyrighted.
b. If I don't charge for it, it's not a violation.
c. If it's posted to the Internet, it's in the public domain.
d. I can always argue that my posting was just fair use.
e. If you don't defend your copyright, you lose it.
f. If I make up my own stories, but base them on another work, my new work belongs to me.
g. They can't get me; defendants in court have powerful rights!
h. Copyright violation isn't a crime or anything, is it?
i. It doesn't hurt anybody. In fact, it's free advertising.
j. They e-mailed me a copy, so I can post it.

Video Resource

Video Library 1, Guffey's 3-x-3 Writing Process Develops Fluent Workplace Skills

This video combines narrative and role-playing to illustrate each phase of Guffey's 3-x-3 writing process. It shows three phases of the writing process including prewriting, writing, and revising. You will see how the writing process guides the development of a complete message. This video illustrates concepts in Chapters 4, 5, and 6. After viewing the film, be prepared to answer these questions:

- How can a writing process help a writer?
- Does the writing process always follow the same order?
- Why does revising take more time than any other part of the process?

Chat About It

In each chapter you will find five discussion questions related to the chapter material. Your instructor may assign these topics for you to discuss in class, in an online chat room, or on an online discussion board. Some of the discussion topics may require outside research. You may also be asked to read and respond to postings made by your classmates.

Topic 1: List and analyze the steps that you followed to write a document before you started this course. Based on what you are learning in this course, which steps were effective? Which were ineffective? How will you change your approach to writing?

Topic 2: After searching an alumni database, you decide to e-mail a professional who is working in the career you hope to enter. Your goal in writing this professional is to obtain firsthand information about this person's career and to receive career advice. However, you know nothing about this person. Why might this person help you? Why might this person refuse? Should you organize your message directly or indirectly?

Topic 3: Why should you avoid words such as *really, totally, very*, and *quite* in your business writing? Provide an example of a sentence with and without such words. How did the meaning of the sentence change?

Topic 4: Think back to the last time you were involved in a team project. What did the team do that resulted in an efficient working process and a successful product? What did the team do that resulted in an inefficient working process and an unsuccessful product?

Topic 5: Find a news article online that describes a company that used careless language in its communication with its customers, stockholders, or employees. Briefly explain what the company did and what it should have done instead.

Grammar and Mechanics C.L.U.E. Review 4

Adjectives and Adverbs

Review Guides 19–20 about adjectives and adverbs in Appendix A, Grammar and Mechanics Guide, beginning on page A-9. On a separate sheet, revise the following sentences to correct errors in adjectives and adverbs. For each error that you locate, write the guide number that reflects this usage. Some sentences may have two errors. If a sentence is correct, write *C*. When you finish, check your answers on page Key-1.

1. Business writers strive to use easy to understand language and familiar words.
2. Luis said he did good in his employment interview.
3. Having prepared for months, we won the contract easy.
4. Collaboration on team written documents is necessary for big projects.
5. Jenna felt badly when her team project was completed.
6. The 3-x-3 writing plan provides step by step instructions for writing messages.
7. Our recently-revised office handbook outlined all recommended document formats.
8. The project ran smooth after Maria organized the team.
9. Locally-installed online collaboration tools are easy-to-use and work well.
10. Well written safety messages include short, familiar words.

CHAPTER 5

Organizing and Writing Business Messages

Want to do well on tests and excel in your course? Go to **www.meguffey.com** for helpful interactive resources.

- **Review the Chapter 5 PowerPoint slides to prepare for the first quiz.**

OBJECTIVES

After studying this chapter, you should be able to

1. Apply Phase 2 of the 3-x-3 writing process, which begins with formal and informal methods for researching data and generating ideas.
2. Explain how to organize data into lists and alphanumeric or decimal outlines.
3. Compare direct and indirect patterns for organizing ideas.
4. Compose the first draft of a message, avoiding sentence fragments, run-on sentences, and comma splices as well as emphasizing important ideas, avoiding misplaced modifiers, and using active and passive voice effectively.
5. Compose effective paragraphs using three classic paragraph plans as well as applying techniques for achieving paragraph coherence.

Zooming In PART 1

Once the Height of Hip, Gap Struggles to Stop Sagging Sales

From humble beginnings in San Francisco, Gap Inc. grew to become the largest clothing chain in the United States. However, after spectacular growth, it fell from favor. Critics accused it of making every bad move a retailer could. Besides major misses in fashion, the company failed to differentiate among its three major brands—Banana Republic, Gap, and Old Navy—and it opened too many stores.

The company that had pioneered the casual cool look with fitted jeans, khakis, and simple T-shirts lost its fashion compass. "The Gap doesn't seem hip any longer," said one shopper. "They're too preppy and sterile." [1] Another young shopper said, "Gap seems to be stuck in the '90s. I always think of it as the clothes my parents wear."[2] Once the king of casual but classic clothing, Gap has been stung by retailing upstarts that woo young people with trendy fashions at affordable prices. Retailers such as Zara, Mango, Hot Topic, and Hollister are snagging customers with hip styles and competitive pricing.

At its zenith in 1994, Gap launched Old Navy as a fun fashion label with good prices and street-chic attitude. Emphasizing humor and mass appeal, Old Navy gave shoppers music and bright colors while promoting a quirky image. But like Gap, Old Navy lost its cult status and its aura of campy fashion. In attempting to right the sinking ship, Old Navy overcorrected and went overboard with inexpensive fashions.

Further compounding their woes, both Gap and Old Navy have saturated the market. Gap has 2,688 U.S. stores, and Old Navy has 1,066.[3] They are almost as ubiquitous as Starbucks. In the fashion business, bigness is not necessarily a plus. With stores in nearly every shopping center, Gap has overexposed the brand. Customers are staying away because its styles no longer seem unique or special.

Under new management, Gap Inc. is working to improve its merchandise mix, reduce inventories, halt capital spending, and enhance its online and global presence. Ultimately, though, Gap and Old Navy must find a way to lure their customers back.

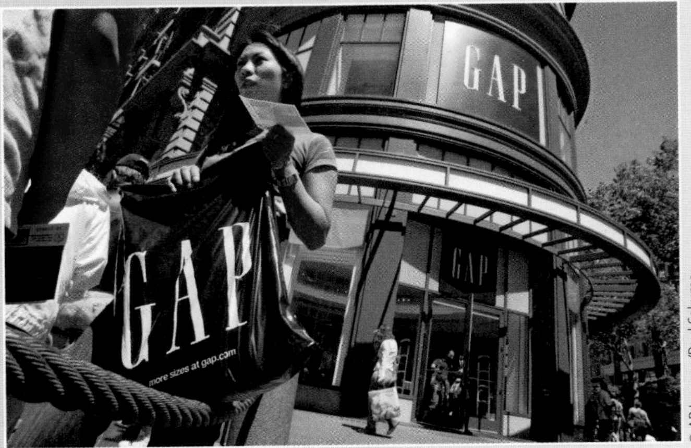

© AP Images/Paul Sakuma

Critical Thinking

- In what ways would research (gathering information) be important to Gap and Old Navy in getting their customers back?
- Why is it important for Gap managers, as well as other business communicators, to gather all necessary information before making management decisions?
- What techniques can business communicators at Gap Inc. and other companies use to generate ideas for new products as well as to improve business processes?

http://www.gap.com

Gathering Information Through Research

LEARNING OBJECTIVE 1

Apply Phase 2 of the 3-x-3 writing process, which begins with formal and informal methods for researching data and generating ideas.

Why is it necessary to gather information before beginning to write rather than gathering it as you write?

Business communicators at Gap and Old Navy face daily challenges that require data collection, idea generation, and concept organization. Before they can make decisions and convey those decisions in written messages or presentations, they must gather information and organize that information. These activities are part of the second phase of the 3-x-3 writing process. You will recall that the 3-x-3 writing process, as reviewed in Figure 5.1, involves three phases. This chapter focuses on the second phase of the process: researching, organizing, and writing.

No smart businessperson would begin writing a message before collecting all the needed information. We call this collection process *research*, a rather formal-sounding term. For simple documents, though, the process can be quite informal. Research is necessary before beginning to write because the information you collect helps shape the message. Discovering significant data after a message is half completed often means starting over and reorganizing. To avoid frustration and inaccurate messages, collect information that answers a primary question:

- What does the receiver need to know about this topic?

When the message involves action, search for answers to secondary questions:

- What is the receiver to do?
- How is the receiver to do it?

FIGURE 5.1 **Guffey's 3-x-3 Writing Process**

1 Prewriting	2 Writing	3 Revising
Analyze: Decide on the purpose of your message. What do you want the receiver to do or believe? What communication channel is best? **Anticipate:** Profile the audience. What does the receiver already know? Will the receiver's response be neutral, positive, or negative? **Adapt:** What writing techniques and strategies can you use to adapt your message to its audience? How can you shape the message to achieve your purpose?	**Research:** Gather background data to provide facts. Search company files, previous correspondence, and the Internet. What do you need to know to write this message? **Organize:** Group similar information together. Decide whether to organize your information directly or indirectly. Outline your plan and make notes. **Compose:** Prepare a first draft, usually writing quickly. Remember that you will be revising it to improve its readability and impact.	**Revise:** Edit your message to be sure it is clear, conversational, concise, and readable. Look for ways to highlight important information. Consider bullets, lists, and headings to help the reader understand related points. **Proofread:** Read carefully to find and correct errors in spelling, grammar, punctuation, names, numbers, and format. **Evaluate:** Will this message achieve your purpose? Have you thought enough about the audience to be sure this message is appropriate and appealing?

- When must the receiver do it?
- What will happen if the receiver doesn't do it?

Whenever your communication problem requires more information than you have in your head or at your fingertips, you must conduct research. This research may be formal or informal.

Formal Research Methods

How can you gather information formally?

Long reports and complex business problems generally require some use of formal research methods. Let's say you are part of the management team at Gap Inc. and you want to evaluate several locations for the placement of a new Old Navy store. Or, let's assume you must write a term paper for a college class. Both tasks require more data than you have in your head or at your fingertips. To conduct formal research, you could do the following:

- **Access electronically.** Much information is now available on the Internet, on CDs or DVDs, and in databases that can be accessed by computer. College and public libraries subscribe to retrieval services that permit you to access most periodic literature. You can

As consumers increasingly turn to the Internet to shop, recommend products, and rate businesses on their customer service, management teams are turning to a new kind of research to inform business decisions—online "buzz-tracking." Research firms such as Nielsen BuzzMetrics and Brandimensions traverse millions of fan sites, blogs, and chat rooms to analyze user feedback and spot consumer trends. *How can buzz-tracking research help communication professionals develop more effective written messages and presentations?*

FIGURE 5.2 Creating Cluster Diagram to Generate Ideas for an Old Navy/Gap Recruiting Brochure

Tips for Activating Ideas

- In the center of a clean sheet of paper, write your topic name and circle it.
- Around that circle record any topic ideas that pop into your mind.
- Circle each idea.
- Avoid censoring ideas; record everything.
- If ideas seem related, join them with lines, but don't spend time on organization just yet.

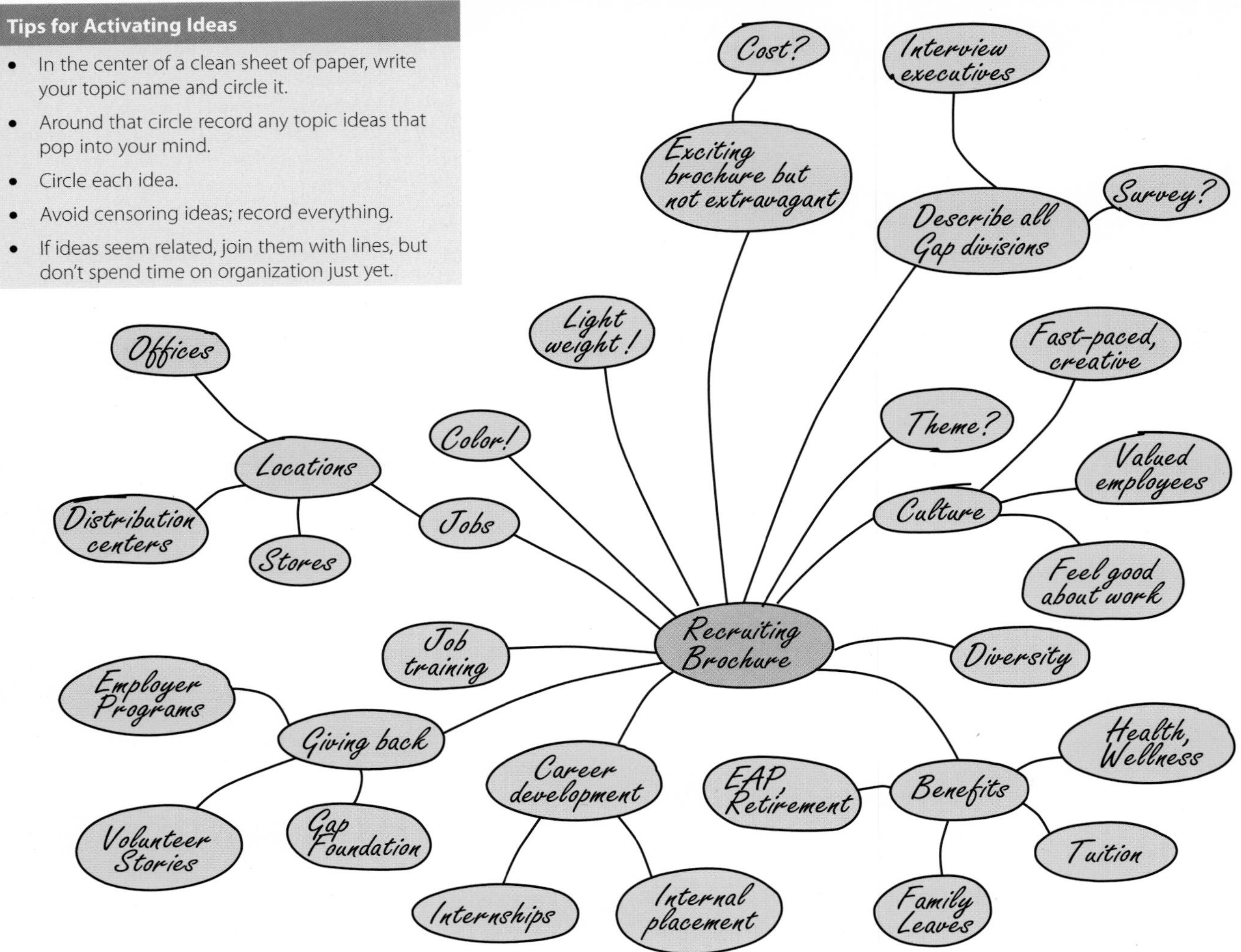

also find extraordinary amounts of information by searching the Web. You will learn more about using electronic sources in Chapter 11.

- **Search manually.** Helpful background and supplementary information is available through manual searching of resources in public and college libraries. These traditional sources include books and newspaper, magazine, and journal articles. Other sources are encyclopedias, reference books, handbooks, dictionaries, directories, and almanacs.
- **Go to the source.** For firsthand information, go directly to the source. If you were comparing the taste of Coca-Cola and Pepsi, for example, you could find out what consumers really think by conducting interviews or surveys, by putting together questionnaires, or by organizing focus groups. Formal research includes structured sampling and controls that enable investigators to make accurate judgments and valid predictions.
- **Investigate primary sources.** To develop firsthand, primary information for a project, go directly to the source. In searching for locations for Old Navy stores, you might travel to possible sites and check them out. If you need information about how many shoppers pass by a location or visit a shopping center, you might conduct a traffic count. To learn more about specific shoppers who might become Old Navy customers, you could use questionnaires, interviews, or focus groups. Formal research includes scientific sampling methods that enable investigators to make accurate judgments and valid predictions.
- **Conduct scientific experiments.** Another source of primary data is experimentation. Instead of merely asking for the target audience's opinion, scientific researchers present

FIGURE 5.3 Organizing Ideas From a Cluster Diagram Into Subclusters

Tips for Organizing Ideas

- Analyze the ideas generated in the original cluster diagram.
- Cross out ideas that are obviously irrelevant; simplify and clarify.
- Add new ideas that seem appropriate.
- Study the ideas for similarities.
- Group similar ideas into classifications (such as Content, Development, and Form).
- If the organization seems clear at this point, prepare an outline.
- For further visualization, make subcluster circles around each classification.

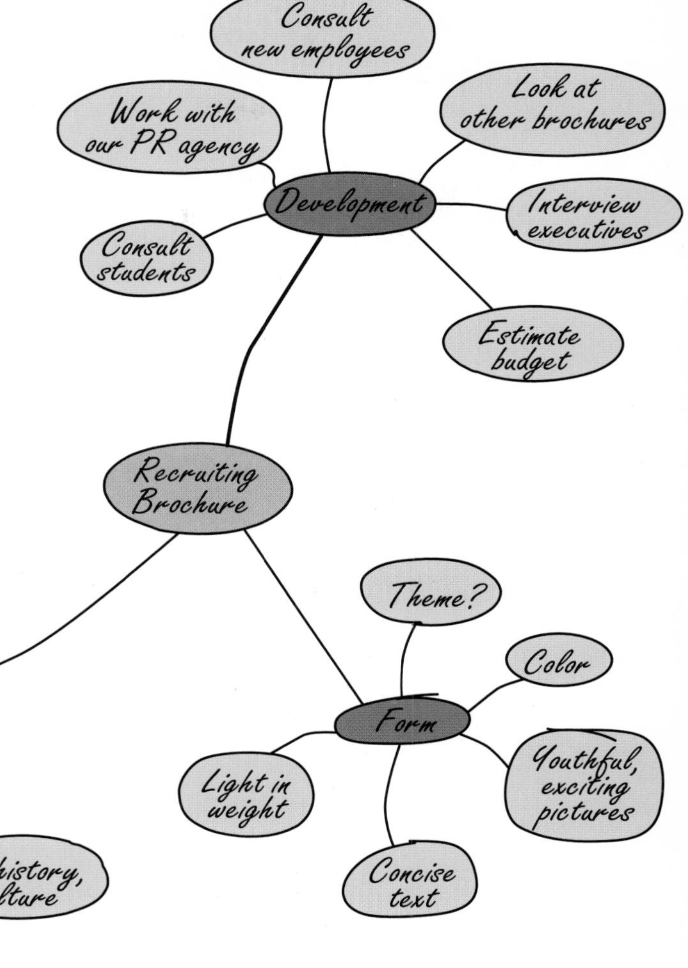

choices with controlled variables. Assume, for example, that the management team at Gap wants to know at what price and under what circumstances consumers would purchase jeans from the Gap instead of from Abercrombie & Fitch. Instead of jeans, let's say that management wants to study the time of year and type of weather conditions that motivate consumers to begin purchasing sweaters, jackets, and cold-weather gear. The results of such experimentation would provide valuable data for managerial decision making. Because formal research techniques are particularly necessary for reports, you will study resources and techniques more extensively in Unit 4.

Informal Research Methods

Most routine tasks—such as composing e-mails, memos, letters, informational reports, and oral presentations—require data that you can collect informally. For some projects, though, you rely more on your own ideas instead of—or in addition to—researching existing facts. Here are some techniques for collecting informal data and for generating ideas:

- **Look in the files.** If you are responding to an inquiry, you often can find the answer to the inquiry by investigating the company files or by consulting colleagues.

Spotlight on Communicators

© Ravi S Sahani/The India Today Group/Getty Images

Chris Heatherly and Len Mazzocco use systematic brainstorming to overhaul the Disney toy lineup every six months. A diverse group of designers, engineers, artists, animators, video game designers, marketers, and theme park employees gather 20 to 30 times a year for two- or three-day brainstorming sessions at hotels around the world. Three elements are crucial to their success: (a) icebreaker activities from 10 minutes to a half hour, (b) 45- to 60-minute brainstorming sessions in which teams list as many ideas as they can and then vote for their favorites, and (c) a product pitch including a storyboard record of the best toy ideas. When people have tried to ignore the icebreaker segment and cut to the chase, Chris says, "it just doesn't work. . . . You have to have some decompression time to be creative."

How can you gather information informally?

- **Talk with your boss.** Get information from the individual making the assignment. What does that person know about the topic? What slant should you take? What other sources would he or she suggest?
- **Interview the target audience.** Consider talking with individuals at whom the message is aimed. They can provide clarifying information that tells you what they want to know and how you should shape your remarks. Suggestions for conducting more formal interviews are presented in Chapter 11.
- **Conduct an informal survey.** Gather unscientific but helpful information through questionnaires, telephone surveys, or online surveys. In preparing a memo report predicting the success of a proposed company fitness center, for example, circulate a questionnaire asking for employee reactions.

What is brainstorming, and how should it be conducted for best results?

Generating Ideas by Brainstorming

One popular method for generating ideas is brainstorming. We should point out, however, that some critics argue that brainstorming groups "produce fewer and poorer quality ideas than the same number of individuals working alone." Even brainstorming proponents agree that, when done poorly, it can be a waste of time. But done properly, brainstorming is quite effective in unleashing ideas and creative energy.[4] One recent writer claims that groups can generate more and better ideas when "brainwriting"; that is, silently sharing written ideas in a structured group format.[5] Another group suggests using Twitter to exchange brainstorming ideas quickly.[6] Most business communicators, however, meet face to face to brainstorm, and they follow these suggestions to produce the best ideas:

- Define the problem and create an agenda that outlines the topics to be covered.
- Establish time limits, remembering that short sessions are best.
- Set a quota, such as a minimum of 100 ideas. The goal is quantity, not quality.
- Require every participant to contribute ideas, accept the ideas of others, or improve on ideas.
- Encourage wild, out-of-the-box thinking. Allow no one to criticize or evaluate ideas.
- Write ideas on flipcharts or on sheets of paper hung around the room.
- Organize and classify the ideas, retaining the best. Consider using cluster diagrams, discussed shortly.

Thousands of hospital patients die every year after receiving the wrong medicine. To prevent this tragic loss and to improve overall hospital efficiency, one large managed care facility holds brainstorming sessions bringing together doctors, nurses, patients, and vendors. Their ground rules include focusing on quantity of ideas rather than quality, withholding criticism, welcoming unusual ideas, and combining and improving ideas. The facilitator begins with a clear problem statement. Participants write ideas on Post-It notes using Sharpie pens to prevent wordiness. *Why is it necessary for successful brainstorming to begin with a clear problem statement, and what is the benefit of conciseness?*

Collecting Information and Generating Ideas on the Job

Let's assume that you work in the corporate offices of Gap Inc. and that you have been given the task of developing a college recruiting brochure for all Gap stores. You think this is a great idea because Gap Inc. has thousands of stores, and many college students don't know about the exciting career opportunities and benefits it offers. You know right away that you want the brochure to be colorful, exciting, concise, youth oriented, lightweight (because it has to be carried to college campuses), and easily updated. Beyond that, you realize that you need ideas from others on how to develop this recruiting brochure.

To collect data for this project, you decide to use both formal and informal research methods. You study recruiting brochures from other companies. You talk with college students about information they would like to see in a brochure. You conduct more formal research among recently hired employees and among Gap division presidents and executives to learn what they think a recruiting brochure should include. Working with an outside consultant, you prepare a questionnaire to use in personal interviews with employees and executives. The interviews include some open-ended questions such as, *How did you start with the company?* The questionnaire also asks specific questions about career paths, degree requirements, personality traits desired, and so forth.

Next you ask five or six fellow employees and team members to help brainstorm ideas for the brochure. In a spirited session, your team comes up the cluster diagram shown in Figure 5.2. The ideas range from the cost of the brochure to career development programs and your company's appealing location in the San Francisco Bay area.

From the jumble of ideas in the initial cluster diagram, you see that you can organize most of the information into three main categories relating to the brochure—Development, Form, and Content. You eliminate, simplify, and consolidate some ideas and add other new ideas. Then you organize the ideas into subclusters, shown in Figure 5.3. This set of subclusters could form the basis for an outline, which we will talk about shortly. Or you could make another set of subclusters, further outlining the categories.

Organizing Ideas

LEARNING OBJECTIVE 2
Explain how to organize data into lists and alphanumeric or decimal outlines.

One of the most important tasks in preparing well-organized messages is grouping similar ideas together. These groups of ideas are then sequenced in a way that helps the reader understand relationships and accept the writer's views. Unorganized messages proceed free-form, jumping from one thought to another. They look like the jumbled ideas in our Figure 5.2 cluster diagram. Such messages fail to emphasize important points. Puzzled readers can't see how the pieces fit together, and they become frustrated and irritated. Many communication experts regard poor organization as the greatest failing of business writers. Two simple techniques can help you organize data: the scratch list and the outline.

Using Lists and Outlines

What are two techniques for organizing data?

In developing simple messages, some writers make a quick scratch list of the topics they wish to cover. Writers often jot this scratch list in the margin of the letter or memo to which they are responding (the majority of business messages are written in response to other documents). These writers then compose a message at their computers directly from the scratch list.

Most writers, though, need to organize their ideas—especially if the project is complex—into a hierarchy, such as an outline. The beauty of preparing an outline is that it gives you a chance to organize your thinking before you get bogged down in word choice and sentence structure. Figure 5.4 shows two outline formats: alphanumeric and decimal. The familiar alphanumeric format uses Roman numerals, letters, and numbers to show major and minor ideas. The decimal format, which takes a little getting used to, has the advantage of showing how every item at every level relates to the whole. Both outlining formats force you to focus on the topic, identify major ideas, and support those ideas with details, illustrations, or evidence.

Probably the hardest part of outlining is grouping ideas into components or categories—ideally three to five. These categories are very important because they will become the major headings in your report. If you have more than five components, look for ways to combine smaller segments into broader topics. The following example shows how a portion of the Gap recruiting brochure subclusters (Figure 5.3) can be organized into an alphanumeric outline.[7]

FIGURE 5.4 Two Outlining Formats

Format for Alphanumeric Outline	Format for Decimal Outline
Title: Major Idea, Purpose	Title: Major Idea, Purpose
I. First major component	1.0. First major component
A. First subpoint	1.1. First subpoint
1. Detail, illustration, evidence	1.1.1. Detail, illustration, evidence
2. Detail, illustration, evidence	1.1.2. Detail, illustration, evidence
B. Second subpoint	1.2. Second subpoint
1.	1.2.1.
2.	1.2.2.
II. Second major component	2.0. Second major component
A. First subpoint	2.1. First subpoint
1.	2.1.1.
2.	2.1.2.
B. Second subpoint	2.2. Second subpoint
1.	2.2.1.
2.	2.2.2.
III. Third major component	3.0. Third major component
A.	3.1.
1.	3.1.1.
2.	3.1.2.
B.	3.2.
1.	3.2.1.
2.	3.2.2.
(This method is simple and familiar.)	*(This method relates every item to the overall outline.)*

Tips for Making Outlines

- Define the main topic (purpose of message) in the title.
- Divide the main topic into major components or classifications (preferably three to five). If necessary, combine small components into one larger category.
- Break the components into subpoints.
- Don't put a single item under a major component; if you have only one subpoint, integrate it with the main item above it or reorganize.
- Strive to make each component exclusive (no overlapping).
- Use details, illustrations, and evidence to support subpoints.

How are alphanumeric and decimal outlines different, and how are they similar?

I. Introduction
  A. Brief history of Gap Inc.
    1. Founding
    2. Milestones
  B. Corporate culture
    1. Emphasize upbeat attitude
    2. Value diversity, employees
    3. Value social responsibility

II. Careers
  A. Opportunities
    1. Internships
    2. Management trainee programs
    3. MBA programs
  B. Development
    1. Internal promotion
    2. Job training

Notice that each major category is divided into at least two subcategories. These categories are then fleshed out with examples, details, statistics, case histories, and other data. In moving

FIGURE 5.5 **Typical Major Components in Business Outlines**

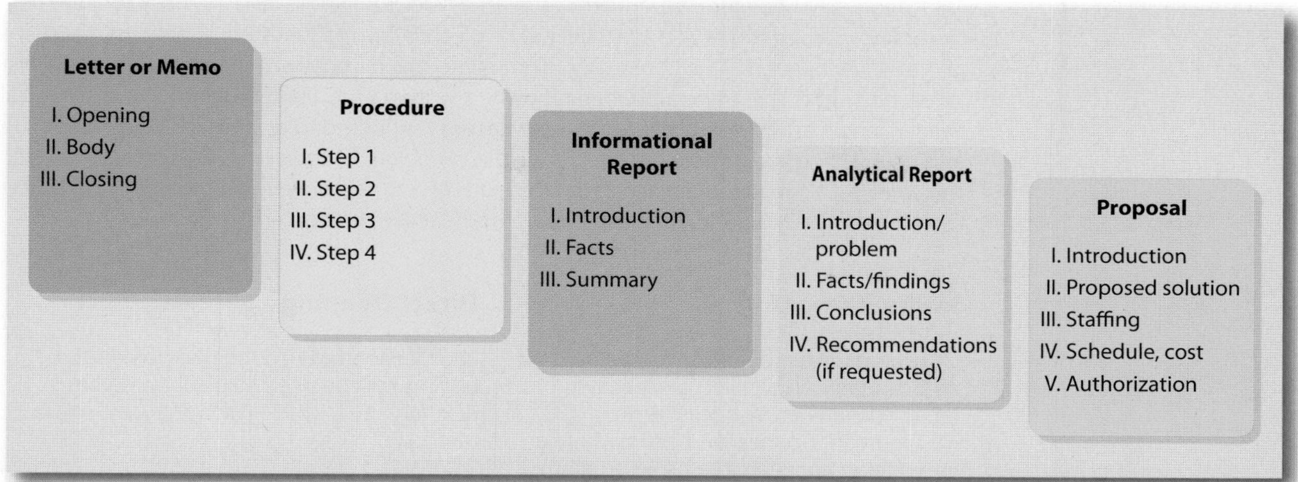

from major point to subpoint, you are progressing from large, abstract concepts to small, concrete ideas. Each subpoint could be further subdivided with more specific illustrations if you desired. You can determine the appropriate amount of detail by considering what your audience (primary and secondary) already knows about the topic and how much persuading you must do.

How you group ideas into components depends on your topic and your channel of communication. Business documents usually contain typical components arranged in traditional patterns, as shown in Figure 5.5.

Thus far, you've seen how to collect information, generate ideas, and prepare an outline. How you order the information in your outline, though, depends on the pattern or strategy you choose.

Organizing Ideas into Patterns

LEARNING OBJECTIVE 3
Compare direct and indirect patterns for organizing ideas.

Two organizational patterns provide plans of action for typical business messages: the direct pattern and the indirect pattern. The primary difference between the two patterns is where the main idea is placed. In the direct pattern, the main idea comes first, followed by details, explanation, or evidence. In the indirect pattern, the main idea follows the details, explanation, and evidence. The pattern you select is determined by how you expect the audience to react to the message, as shown in Figure 5.6.

FIGURE 5.6 **Audience Response Determines Pattern of Organization**

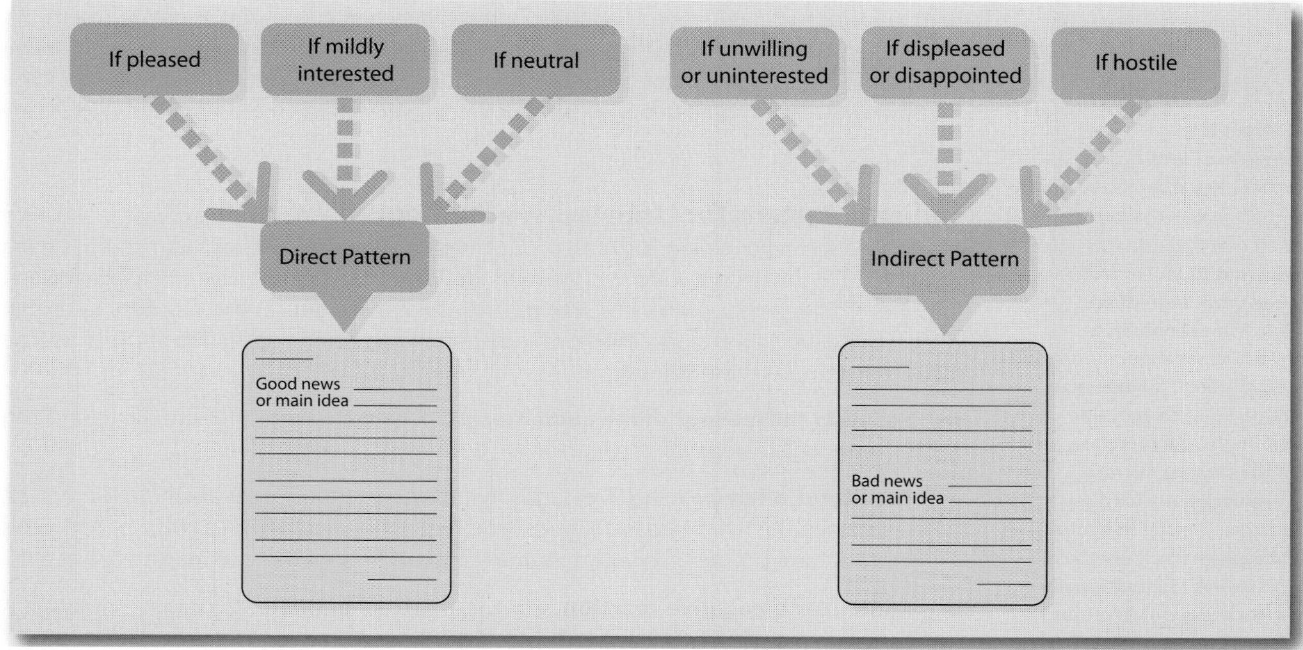

What pattern do business messages usually follow? Why?

Direct Pattern for Receptive Audiences. In preparing to write any message, you need to anticipate the audience's reaction to your ideas and frame your message accordingly. When you expect the reader to be pleased, mildly interested, or, at worst, neutral—use the direct pattern. That is, put your main point—the purpose of your message—in the first or second sentence. Dianna Booher, renowned writing consultant, pointed out that typical readers begin any message by saying, "So what am I supposed to do with this information?" In business writing you have to say, "Reader, here is my point!"[8] As quickly as possible, tell why you are writing. Compare the direct and indirect patterns in the following memo openings. Notice how long it takes to get to the main idea in the indirect opening.

Indirect Opening	Direct Opening
Our company has been concerned with attracting better-qualified prospective job candidates. For this reason, the Management Council has been gathering information about an internship program for college students. After considerable investigation, we have voted to begin a pilot program starting next fall.	The Management Council has voted to begin a college internship pilot program next fall.

What is frontloading, and how does it benefit receivers?

Explanations and details follow the direct opening. What's important is getting to the main idea quickly. This direct method, also called *frontloading*, has at least three advantages:

- **Saves the reader's time.** Many of today's businesspeople can devote only a few moments to each message. Messages that take too long to get to the point may lose their readers along the way.
- **Sets a proper frame of mind.** Learning the purpose up front helps the reader put the subsequent details and explanations in perspective. Without a clear opening, the reader may be thinking, "Why am I being told this?"
- **Reduces frustration.** Readers forced to struggle through excessive verbiage before reaching the main idea become frustrated. They resent the writer. Poorly organized messages create a negative impression of the writer.

This frontloading technique works best with audiences that are likely to be receptive to or at least not disagree with what you have to say. Typical business messages that follow the direct pattern include routine requests and responses, orders and acknowledgments, nonsensitive memos, e-mails, informational reports, and informational oral presentations. All these tasks have one element in common: none has a sensitive subject that will upset the reader. It should be noted, however, that some business communicators prefer to use the direct pattern for nearly all messages.

Ethics Check

How Sweet It Is

The makers of artificial sweetener Equal sued competitor Splenda because the latter claimed that Splenda was "made from sugar." In reality, Splenda's core ingredient is made from sucralose, a nonnutritive synthetic compound manufactured in laboratories. Although Splenda contains a sugar molecule, sucralose is not the same as sucrose, the technical name for pure table sugar, despite its similar-sounding name. Is it unethical for companies to intentionally advertise using wording that would confuse consumers?

Indirect Pattern for Unreceptive Audiences. When you expect the audience to be uninterested, unwilling, displeased, or perhaps even hostile, the indirect pattern is more appropriate. In this pattern you reveal the main idea only after you have offered explanation and evidence. This approach works well with three kinds of messages: (a) bad news, (b) ideas that require persuasion, and (c) sensitive news, especially when being transmitted to superiors. The indirect pattern has these benefits:

- **Respects the feelings of the audience.** Bad news is always painful, but the trauma can be lessened by preparing the receiver for it.
- **Facilitates a fair hearing.** Messages that may upset the reader are more likely to be read when the main idea is delayed. Beginning immediately with a piece of bad news or a persuasive request, for example, may cause the receiver to stop reading or listening.
- **Minimizes a negative reaction.** A reader's overall reaction to a negative message is generally improved if the news is delivered gently.

Zooming In PART 2

Gap Inc.

Rebuilding its customer base and correcting its fashion missteps are major initiatives at Gap and its offspring, Old Navy. At the same time, the stores must be ever watchful that their garments are not made in sweatshops. Stiff competition and consumer demand for low prices have forced many U.S. apparel manufacturers to shift production offshore. Some of that production ends up in sweatshops, such as those found in Cambodia, Bangladesh, and Honduras. The worst sweatshops use child labor and demand 80-hour workweeks without overtime pay. Bosses routinely shout at workers and may send them home for talking on the job. Workers earn as little as 29 cents an hour.

Like other major apparel manufacturers, Gap Inc. strives to control working conditions with factory-monitoring and labor-standards programs. Around the world Gap Inc. has more than 90 employees whose sole focus is working to improve conditions in the factories that make its clothing. In one year these employees conducted 4,438 inspections at 2,118 garment factories around the world.[9] When a problem is found, Gap takes action. It works with contractors and factories to improve practices and conditions. If conditions don't improve, the retailer stops using errant contractors.[10] Enforcing its standards worldwide requires an ongoing effort.

When complaints from human rights activists and other watchdog groups arrive, Gap Inc. must investigate and respond to each inquiry.

© AP Images/Paul Sakuma

Critical Thinking

- When a business communicator responds to an inquiry, such as a letter about human rights violations among contractors, is "research" necessary?
- What are the differences between formal and informal research?
- What are the advantages and disadvantages of brainstorming with groups?

Typical business messages that could be developed indirectly include letters, e-mails, and memos that refuse requests, deny claims, and disapprove credit. Persuasive requests, sales letters, sensitive messages, and some reports and oral presentations may also benefit from the indirect strategy. You will learn more about using the indirect pattern in Chapters 9 and 10.

In summary, business messages may be organized directly, with the main idea first, or indirectly, with the main idea delayed. Although these two patterns cover many communication problems, they should be considered neither universal nor inviolate. Every business transaction is distinct. Some messages are mixed: part good news, part bad; part goodwill, part persuasion. In upcoming chapters you will practice applying the direct and indirect patterns in typical situations. Then, you will have the skills and confidence to evaluate communication problems and vary these patterns depending on the goals you wish to achieve.

Composing the First Draft

LEARNING OBJECTIVE 4

Compose the first draft of a message, avoiding sentence fragments, run-on sentences, and comma splices as well as emphasizing important ideas, avoiding misplaced modifiers, and using active and passive voice effectively.

Once you have researched your topic, organized the data, and selected a pattern of organization, you are ready to begin composing. Most writers expect to use their computers for composition, but many are unaware of all the ways a computer can help create better written messages, oral presentations, and Web pages. See the accompanying Plugged In box to learn how you can take full advantage of your computer.

Even with a computer, some writers have trouble getting started, especially if they haven't completed the preparatory work. Organizing your ideas and working from an outline are very helpful in overcoming writer's block. Composition is also easier if you have a quiet environment in which to concentrate. Businesspeople with messages to compose set aside a given time and allow no calls, visitors, or other interruptions. This is a good technique for students as well.

What is freewriting, and how is it helpful?

As you begin composing, think about what style fits you best. Some experts suggest that you write quickly (*freewriting*). Get your thoughts down now and refine them in later versions. As you take up each idea, imagine that you are talking to the reader. Don't let yourself get bogged down. If you can't think of the right word, insert a substitute or type *find perfect word later.* Freewriting works well for some writers, but others prefer to move more slowly and think through their ideas more deliberately. Whether you are a speedy or a deliberate writer, keep in mind that you are writing the first draft. You will have time later to revise and polish your sentences.

PLUGGED IN

Seven Ways Computers Can Help You Create Better Written Messages, Oral Presentations, and Web Pages

Although computers can't actually do the writing for you, they provide powerful tools that make the composition process easier and the results more professional. Here are seven ways your computer can help you improve your written documents, oral presentations, and even Web pages.

1. **Fighting writer's block.** Because word processors enable ideas to flow almost effortlessly from your brain to a screen, you can expect fewer delays resulting from writer's block. You can compose rapidly, and you can experiment with structure and phrasing, later retaining and polishing your most promising thoughts.
2. **Collecting information electronically.** As a knowledge worker in an information economy, you must find information quickly. Much of the world's information is now accessible in databases or on the Web. You will learn more about these exciting electronic resources in Unit 4.
3. **Outlining and organizing ideas.** Most word processors include some form of "outliner," a feature that enables you to divide a topic into a hierarchical order with main points and subpoints. Your computer keeps track of the levels of ideas automatically so that you can easily add, cut, or rearrange points in the outline.
4. **Improving correctness and precision.** Nearly all word processing programs today provide features that catch and correct spelling and typographical errors. Grammar checkers detect many errors in capitalization, word use (such as *it's, its*), double negatives, verb use, subject–verb agreement, sentence structure, number agreement, number style, and other writing faults. But the errors are merely highlighted—not corrected. You have to do that.
5. **Adding graphics for emphasis.** Your letters, memos, and reports may be improved by the addition of graphs and artwork to clarify and illustrate data. You can import charts, diagrams, and illustrations created in database, spreadsheet, graphics, or draw-and-paint programs. Clip art is available to symbolize or illustrate ideas.
6. **Designing and producing professional-looking documents, presentations, and Web pages.** Most software now includes a large selection of scalable fonts (for a variety of character sizes and styles), italics, boldface, symbols, and styling techniques to help you format consistently and produce professional-looking results. Presentation software enables you to incorporate illustrative slide effects, color, sound, pictures, and video clips into your talks for management or customers. Web document builders also help you design and construct Web pages.
7. **Using collaborative software for team writing.** Special programs with commenting and revision features, described in Chapter 4, allow you to make changes and to identify each team member's editing.

Career Application

Individually or in teams, identify specific software programs that perform the tasks described here. Prepare a table naming each program, its major functions, and its advantages and disadvantages for business writers in your field.

Creating Effective Sentences

In creating your first draft, you will be working at the sentence level of composition. Although you have used sentences all your life, you may be unaware of how they can be shaped and arranged to express your ideas most effectively.

Recognizing Basic Sentence Elements

To avoid writing sentence fragments and making punctuation errors, let's review some basic sentence elements. Complete sentences have subjects and verbs and make sense.

What makes a sentence complete?

SUBJECT (The manager) — VERB (sent)

The manager of Information Technology sent an e-mail to all employees.

Clauses and phrases, the key building blocks of sentences, are related groups of words. Clauses have subjects and verbs; phrases do not.

PHRASE (of Information Technology) — PHRASE (to all employees)

The manager of Information Technology sent an e-mail to all employees.

PHRASE (By reading carefully) — PHRASE (about the latest computer viruses)

By reading carefully, we learned about the latest computer viruses.

CLAUSE | CLAUSE

Because he is experienced, Adam can repair most computer problems.

CLAUSE | CLAUSE

When we have technology problems, we call a technician in our support group.

How are clauses different from phrases?

Clauses may be divided into two groups: independent and dependent. Independent clauses are grammatically complete. Dependent clauses depend for their meaning on independent clauses. In the two preceding examples the clauses beginning with *Because* and *When* are dependent. Dependent clauses are often introduced by words such as *if, when, because,* and *as.*

How are independent clauses different from dependent clauses?

INDEPENDENT CLAUSE

Adam solves our technology problems.

DEPENDENT CLAUSE | INDEPENDENT CLAUSE

When employees need help, Adam solves our technology problems.

By learning to distinguish phrases, independent clauses, and dependent clauses, you will be able to punctuate sentences correctly and avoid three basic sentence faults: the fragment, the run-on sentence, and the comma splice.

Avoiding Three Common Sentence Faults

What are sentence fragments?

As you craft your sentences, beware of three common traps: fragments, run-on (fused) sentences, and comma-splice sentences. If any of these faults appears in a business message, the writer immediately loses credibility.

Fragments. One of the most serious errors a writer can make is punctuating a fragment as if it were a complete sentence. A fragment is usually a broken-off part of a complex sentence.

Fragment	Revision
Because most transactions require a permanent record. Good writing skills are critical.	Because most transactions require a permanent record, good writing skills are critical.
The recruiter requested a writing sample. Even though the candidate seemed to communicate well.	The recruiter requested a writing sample even though the candidate seemed to communicate well.

Fragments often can be identified by the words that introduce them—words such as *although, as, because, even, except, for example, if, instead of, since, such as, that, which,* and *when*. These words introduce dependent clauses. Make sure such clauses always connect to independent clauses.

What is a run-on (fused) sentence?

Run-On (Fused) Sentences. A sentence with two independent clauses must be joined by a coordinating conjunction (*and, or, nor, but*) or by a semicolon (;) or separated into two sentences. Without a conjunction or a semicolon, a run-on sentence results.

Run-On Sentence	Revision
Most job seekers present a printed résumé some are also using Web sites as electronic portfolios	Most job seekers present a printed résumé. Some are also using Web sites as electronic portfolios.
One candidate sent an e-mail résumé another sent a traditional résumé.	One candidate sent an e-mail résumé; another sent a traditional résumé.

What is a comma splice?

Comma-Splice Sentences. A comma splice results when a writer joins (splices together) two independent clauses with a comma. Independent clauses may be joined with a coordinating conjunction (*and, or, nor, but*) or a conjunctive adverb (*however, consequently, therefore,* and others). Notice that clauses joined by coordinating conjunctions require only a comma. Clauses joined by a coordinating adverb require a semicolon. On the following page are three possible revisions that rectify a comma splice.

Comma Splice	Possible Revisions
Some employees responded by e-mail, others picked up the telephone.	Some employees responded by e-mail, and others picked up the telephone. Some employees responded by e-mail; however, others picked up the telephone. Some employees responded by e-mail; others picked up the telephone.

Sentences should average how many words?

Preferring Short Sentences

Because your goal is to communicate clearly, you should strive for sentences that average 20 words. Some sentences will be shorter; some will be longer. The American Press Institute reports that reader comprehension drops off markedly as sentences become longer.[11] Therefore, in crafting your sentences, think about the relationship between sentence length and comprehension.

Sentence Length	Comprehension Rate
8 words	100%
15 words	90%
19 words	80%
28 words	50%

Instead of stringing together clauses with *and, but,* and *however*, break some of those complex sentences into separate segments. Business readers want to grasp ideas immediately. They can do that best when thoughts are separated into short sentences. On the other hand, too many monotonous short sentences will sound "grammar schoolish" and may bore or even annoy the reader. Strive for a balance between longer sentences and shorter ones. Your computer probably can point out long sentences and give you an average sentence length.

What techniques can be used to emphasize important ideas?

Emphasizing Important Ideas

You can stress prominent ideas mechanically by underscoring, italicizing, or boldfacing. You can also emphasize important ideas with five stylistic devices.

- **Use vivid words.** Vivid words are emphatic because the reader can picture ideas clearly.

General	Vivid
One business uses personal selling techniques.	Avon uses face-to-face selling techniques.

- **Label the main idea.** If an idea is significant, tell the reader as shown here.

Unlabeled	Labeled
Explore the possibility of leasing a site, but also hire a consultant.	Explore the possibility of leasing a site; but, *most important*, hire a consultant

- **Place the important idea first or last in the sentence.** Ideas have less competition from surrounding words when they appear first or last in a sentence. Observe how the date of the meeting can be emphasized.

Unemphatic	Emphatic
All production and administrative personnel will meet on May 23, at which time we will announce a new plan of salary incentives.	On May 23 all personnel will meet to learn about salary incentives.

- **Place the important idea in a simple sentence or in an independent clause.** Don't dilute the effect of the idea by making it share the spotlight with other words and clauses.

Unemphatic	Emphatic
Although you are the first trainee that we have hired for this program, we have interviewed many candidates and expect to expand the program in the future. (Main idea lost in introductory dependent clause.)	You are the first trainee that we have hired for this program. (Simple sentence contains main idea.)

- **Make sure the important idea is the sentence subject.** You will learn more about active and passive voice shortly, but at this point just focus on making the important idea the subject.

Unemphatic	Emphatic
The environmental report was written by Courtney. (De-emphasizes *Courtney*; emphasizes the report.)	Courtney wrote the environmental report. (Emphasizes *Courtney*.)

Managing Active and Passive Voice

In sentences with active-voice verbs, the subject is the doer of the action. In passive-voice sentences, the subject is acted upon.

How are active- and passive-voice sentences different?

Passive-Voice Verb	Active-Voice Verb
The tax return *was completed* before the April 15 deadline. (The subject, *tax return*, is acted upon.)	Marcelo *completed* his tax return before the April 15 deadline. (The subject, *Marcelo*, is the doer of the action.)

In the first sentence, the passive-voice verb emphasizes the tax return. In the second sentence, the active-voice verb emphasizes Marcelo. Active-voice sentences are more direct because they reveal the performer immediately. They are easier to understand and shorter. Most

FIGURE 5.7 Using Active and Passive Voice Effectively

Use active voice for directness, vigor, and clarity.

Direct and Clear in Active Voice	Indirect and Less Clear in Passive Voice
The manager completed performance reviews for all employees.	Performance reviews were completed for all employees by the manager.
Evelyn initiated a customer service blog last year.	A customer service blog was initiated last year.
IBM will accept applications after January 1.	Applications will be accepted after January 1 by IBM.
Coca-Cola created a Sprite page in Facebook to advertise its beverage.	A Sprite page was created in Facebook by Coca-Cola to advertise its beverage.

Use passive voice to be tactful or to emphasize the action rather than the doer.

Less Tactful or Effective in Active Voice	More Tactful or Effective in Passive Voice
We cannot grant you credit.	Credit cannot be granted.
The CEO made a huge error in projecting profits.	A huge error was made in projecting profits.
I launched a successful fitness program for our company last year.	A successful fitness program was launched for our company last year.
We are studying the effects of the Sarbanes-Oxley Act on our accounting procedures.	The effects of the Sarbanes-Oxley Act on our accounting procedures are being studied.

Spotlight on Communicators

Courtesy of Bob Knight

"Wordiness and murkiness come from misuse of the passive voice," says writing coach Bob Knight. The passive voice also shields people from responsibility. For example, government officials often say, *Mistakes were made.* Passive voice abounds in corporate writing, he suspects, because writers are afraid to say things clearly or they don't want to stand out. He suggests, however, using passive voice for effect, especially when the subject is overwhelmingly important, as in, *A Rembrandt was stolen by two men in janitors' uniforms.* Passive voice is also helpful when you don't know who or what the subject would be in active voice, as in, *The cargo was damaged during an intercontinental flight.*

business writing should be in the active voice. Nevertheless, passive voice is useful in certain instances such as the following:

- **To emphasize an action or the recipient of the action.** *An investigation was launched.*
- **To de-emphasize negative news.** *Cash refunds cannot be made.*
- **To conceal the doer of an action.** *An error was made in our sales figures.*

How can you tell whether a verb is active or passive? Identify the subject of the sentence and decide whether the subject is doing the acting or is being acted upon. For example, in the sentence *An appointment was made for January 1*, the subject is *appointment*. The subject is being acted upon; therefore, the verb (*was made*) is passive. Another clue in identifying passive-voice verbs is that they generally include a *to be* helping verb, such as *is, are, was, were, be, being,* or *been*. Figure 5.7 summarizes effective uses for active and passive voice.

What happens when modifiers are not close to the words they describe or limit?

Avoiding Dangling and Misplaced Modifiers

For clarity, modifiers must be close to the words they describe or limit. A dangling modifier describes or limits a word or words that are missing from the sentence. A misplaced modifier occurs when the word or phrase it describes is not close enough to be clear. To remedy a dangling modifier, supply the missing modifier. To remedy a misplaced modifier, move the modifier closer to the word(s) it describes or limits. Introductory verbal phrases are particularly dangerous; be sure to follow them immediately with the words they logically describe or modify.

Dangling Modifier	Improved
After working nine hours, the report was finally finished. *(Did the report work nine hours? The introductory verbal phrase must be followed by a logical subject.)*	After working nine hours, we finally finished the report.
Driving through Malibu Canyon, the ocean suddenly came into view. (*Is the ocean driving through Malibu Canyon?*)	As we drove through Malibu Canyon, the ocean suddenly came into view.
Speaking before the large audience, Luke's knees began to knock. (*Are Luke's knees making a speech?*)	Speaking before the large audience, Luke felt his knees begin to knock.

Try this trick for detecting and remedying these dangling modifiers. Ask the question *Who?* or *What?* after any introductory phrase. The words immediately following should tell the reader *who* or *what* is performing the action. Try the *who?* test on the previous danglers and on the following misplaced modifiers.

Misplaced Modifier	Improved
Seeing her error too late, the envelope was immediately resealed by Luna. (*Did the envelope see the error?*)	Seeing her error too late, Luna immediately resealed the envelope.
A wart appeared on my left hand that I want removed. (*Is the left hand to be removed?*)	A wart that I want removed appeared on my left hand.
The busy recruiter interviewed only candidates who had excellent computer skills in the morning. (*Were the candidates skilled only in the morning?*)	In the morning the busy recruiter interviewed only candidates who had excellent computer skills.

Drafting Powerful Paragraphs

LEARNING OBJECTIVE 5
Compose effective paragraphs using three classic paragraph plans as well as applying techniques for achieving paragraph coherence.

A paragraph is a group of sentences about one idea. To avoid muddled paragraphs, writers should be able to recognize basic paragraph elements, conventional sentence patterns, and ways to organize sentences using one of three classic paragraph plans. They must also be able to polish their paragraphs by building coherence and using transitional expressions.

Well-constructed paragraphs discuss only one topic. They reveal the primary idea in a topic sentence that usually, but not always, appears first. Paragraphs may be composed of three kinds of sentences:

How many topics should be covered in one paragraph?

Topic Sentence	Expresses the primary idea of the paragraph.
Supporting Sentences	Illustrates, explains, or strengthens the primary idea.
Limiting sentence	Opposes the primary idea by suggesting a negative or contrasting thought; may precede or follow the topic sentence.

These sentences may be arranged in three classic paragraph plans: direct, pivoting, and indirect.

Using the Direct Paragraph Plan to Define, Classify, Illustrate, or Describe

When should the direct paragraph plan be used?

Paragraphs arranged in the direct plan begin with the topic sentence, followed by supporting sentences. Most business messages use this paragraph plan because it clarifies the subject immediately. This plan is useful whenever you must define (a new product or procedure), classify (parts of a whole), illustrate (an idea), or describe (a process). Start with the topic sentence; then strengthen and amplify that idea with supporting ideas, as shown here:

Topic Sentence	A social audit is a report on the social performance of a company.
Supporting Sentences	Such an audit may be conducted by the company itself or by outsiders who evaluate the company's efforts to produce safe products, engage in socially responsible activities, and protect the environment. Many companies publish the results of their social audits in their annual reports. Ben & Jerry's Homemade, for example, devotes a major portion of its annual report to its social audit. The report discusses Ben & Jerry's efforts to support environmental restoration. Moreover, it describes workplace safety, employment equality, and peace programs.

You can alter the direct plan by adding a limiting sentence if necessary. Be sure, though, that you follow with sentences that return to the main idea and support it, as shown here:

Topic Sentence	Flexible work scheduling could immediately increase productivity and enhance employee satisfaction in our entire organization.
Limiting Sentence	Such scheduling, however, is impossible for all employees.
Supporting Sentences	Managers would be required to maintain their regular hours. For many other employees, though, flexible scheduling permits extra time to manage family responsibilities. Feeling less stress, employees are able to focus their attention better at work; hence they become more relaxed and more productive.

Using the Pivoting Paragraph Plan to Compare and Contrast

When is the pivoting paragraph plan appropriate?

Paragraphs using the pivoting plan start with a limiting sentence that offers a contrasting or negative idea before delivering the topic sentence. Notice in the following example how two limiting sentences about drawbacks to foreign service careers open the paragraph; only then do the topic and supporting sentences describing rewards in foreign service appear. The pivoting plan is especially useful for comparing and contrasting ideas. In using the pivoting plan, be sure you emphasize the turn in direction with an obvious *but* or *however*.

Limiting Sentences	Foreign service careers are certainly not for everyone. Many representatives are stationed in remote countries where harsh climates, health hazards, security risks, and other discomforts exist.
Topic Sentence	However, careers in the foreign service offer special rewards for the special people who qualify.
Supporting Sentences	Foreign service employees enjoy the pride and satisfaction of representing the United States abroad. They enjoy frequent travel, enriching cultural and social experiences in living abroad, and action-oriented work.

Using the Indirect Paragraph Plan to Explain and Persuade

When is the indirect paragraph plan appropriate?

Paragraphs using the indirect plan start with the supporting sentences and conclude with the topic sentence. This useful plan enables you to build a rationale, a foundation of reasons, before hitting the audience with a big idea—possibly one that is bad news. It enables you to explain your reasons and then in the final sentence draw a conclusion from them. In the following example, the vice president of a large accounting firm begins by describing the trend toward casual dress and concludes with a recommendation that his firm change its dress code. The indirect plan works well for describing causes followed by an effect.

Supporting Sentences	According to a recent poll, more than half of all white-collar workers are now dressing casually at work. Many high-tech engineers and professional specialists have given up suits and ties, favoring khakis and sweaters instead. In our own business, our consultants say they stand out like "sore thumbs" because they are attired in traditional buttoned-down styles, while the businesspeople they visit are usually wearing comfortable, casual clothing.
Topic Sentence	Therefore, I recommend that we establish an optional business casual policy allowing consultants to dress casually, if they wish, as they perform their duties both in and out of the office.

You will learn more techniques for implementing direct and indirect writing strategies when you prepare letters, memos, e-mails, reports, and oral presentations in subsequent chapters.

Building Paragraph Coherence

What is coherence, and what four techniques help build it in paragraphs?

Paragraphs are coherent when ideas cohere—that is, when the ideas stick together and when one idea logically leads to the next. Well-written paragraphs take the reader through a number of steps. When the author skips from Step 1 to Step 3 and forgets Step 2, the reader is lost. You can use several techniques to keep the reader in step with your ideas.

- **Sustaining the key idea.** Repeating a key expression or using a similar one throughout a paragraph helps sustain a key idea. In the following example, notice that the repetition of *guest* and *VIP* connects ideas.

  Our philosophy holds that every customer is really a ***guest****. All new employees to our theme parks are trained to treat* ***guests*** *as* ***VIPs****. We take great pride in respecting our guests. As* ***VIPs,*** *they are never told what they can or cannot do.*

- **Dovetailing sentences.** Sentences are "dovetailed" when an idea at the end of one connects with an idea at the beginning of the next. Dovetailing sentences is especially helpful with dense, difficult topics. It is also helpful with ordinary paragraphs, such as the following.

  New hosts and hostesses learn about the theme park and its ***facilities****. These* ***facilities*** *include telephones, food services, bathrooms, and attractions, as well as the location of* ***offices****. Knowledge of* ***offices*** *and the internal workings of the company is required of all staffers.*

- **Using pronouns.** Familiar pronouns, such as *we, they, he, she,* and *it,* help build continuity, as do demonstrative pronouns, such as *this, that, these,* and *those*. These words confirm that something under discussion is still being discussed. However, be careful with such

Ethics Check

Blogging for Pay

One single mother earned nearly $500 a month by putting her writing skills to use on "opps" (opportunities) at PayPerPost .com. This site pays consumers to write favorable comments in blogs about specific products. Is it ethical for bloggers to hide their motivation and affiliation when rating products?

pronouns. They often need a noun with them to make their meaning absolutely clear. In the following example, notice how confusing *this* would be if the word *training* were omitted.

All new park employees receive a two-week orientation. They learn that every staffer has a vital role in preparing for the show. This training includes how to maintain enthusiasm.

- **Including transitional expressions.** Transitional expressions are another excellent device for showing connections and achieving paragraph coherence. These words, some of which are shown in Figure 5.8 on page 156 act as verbal road signs to readers and listeners. Transitional expressions enable the receiver to anticipate what's coming, reduce uncertainty, and speed comprehension. They signal that a train of thought is moving forward, being developed, possibly detouring, or ending. As Figure 5.8 shows, transitions can add or strengthen a thought, show time or order, clarify ideas, show cause and effect, contradict thoughts, and contrast ideas. Look back at the examples of direct, pivoting, and indirect paragraphs to see how transitional expressions and other techniques build paragraph coherence. Remember that coherence in communication rarely happens spontaneously; it requires effort and skill.

Want to do well on tests and excel in your course? Go to **www.meguffey.com** for helpful interactive resources.
▸ **Review the Chapter 5 PowerPoint slides to prepare for the first quiz.**

Composing Short Paragraphs for Readability

Although no rule regulates the length of paragraphs, business writers recognize that short paragraphs are more attractive and readable than longer ones. Paragraphs with eight or fewer lines look inviting. Long, solid chunks of print appear formidable. If a topic can't be covered in eight or fewer printed lines (not sentences), consider breaking it up into smaller segments.

The accompanying Checklist summarizes the key points of composing a first draft.

To be inviting and readable, paragraphs should have no more than how many printed lines?

Checklist

Composing Sentences and Paragraphs

For Effective Sentences

- **Avoid common sentence faults.** To avoid un-on sentences, do not join two clauses without appropriate punctuation. To avoid comma splices, do not join two clauses with a comma. To avoid fragments, be sure to use periods only after complete sentences.
- **Control sentence length.** Use longer sentences occasionally, but rely primarily on short and medium-length sentences.
- **Emphasize important ideas.** Place main ideas at the beginning of short sentences for emphasis.
- **Apply active- and passive-voice verbs carefully.** Use active-voice verbs (*She sent the e-mail* instead of *The e-mail was sent by her*) most frequently; they immediately identify the doer. Use passive verbs to emphasize an action, to be tactful, or to conceal the performer.
- **Eliminate misplaced modifiers.** Be sure that introductory verbal phrases are followed by the words that can logically be modified. To check the placement of modifiers, ask *Who?* or *What?* after such phrases.

For Meaningful Paragraphs

- **Develop one idea.** Use topic, supporting, and limiting sentences to develop a single idea within each paragraph.
- **Use the direct plan.** Start most paragraphs with the topic sentence followed by supporting sentences. This direct plan is useful in defining, classifying, illustrating, and describing.
- **Use the pivoting plan.** To compare and contrast ideas, start with a limiting sentence; then, present the topic sentence followed by supporting sentences.
- **Use the indirect plan.** To explain reasons or causes first, start with supporting sentences. Build to the conclusion with the topic sentence at the end of the paragraph.
- **Build coherence with linking techniques.** Hold ideas together by repeating key words, dovetailing sentences (beginning one sentence with an idea from the end of the previous sentence), and using appropriate pronouns.
- **Provide road signs with transitional expressions.** Use verbal signals to help the audience know where the idea is going. Words and phrases such as *moreover, accordingly, as a result,* and *therefore* function as idea pointers.
- **Limit paragraph length.** Remember that paragraphs with eight or fewer printed lines look inviting. Consider breaking up longer paragraphs if necessary.

FIGURE 5.8 **Transitional Expressions That Build Coherence**

To Add or Strengthen	To Show Time or Order	To Clarify	To Show Cause and Effect	To Contradict	To Contrast
additionally	after	for example	accordingly	actually	as opposed to
accordingly	before	for instance	as a result	but	at the same time
again	earlier	I mean	consequently	however	by contrast
also	finally	in other words	for this reason	in fact	conversely
beside	first	put another way	hence	instead	on the contrary
indeed	meanwhile	that is	so	rather	on the other hand
likewise	next	this means	therefore	still	previously
moreover	now	thus	thus	yet	similarly

Zooming In

YOUR TURN

Applying Your Skills at Gap Inc.

The management team at Gap Inc. is struggling to regain its premier position in retailing. As part of a focus group, you and your team have been asked to brainstorm ideas that will help turn around its fortunes. Your team members are to visit a Gap or Old Navy store and take notes on store appearance, merchandise selection, and customer service. Team members should also look at the Gap Web site to learn about its commitment to social responsibility.

Your Task

Form teams of four or five people. Discuss your task and decide on a goal. Make assignments. Who will investigate Gap's Web site? Who will visit stores? Who will lead the brainstorming session? Hold a 10-minute brainstorming session following the suggestions in this chapter for generating ideas. What could be changed to attract more customers in your age group to Gap and Old Navy? Set a quota of at least 50 suggestions. Take notes on all suggestions. After 10 minutes, organize and classify the ideas, retaining the best. Prepare a cluster diagram. Organize the cluster diagram into an outline, and submit your cluster diagram and outline to your instructor. Your instructor may ask for individual or team submissions.

© AP Images/Paul Sakuma

Summary of Learning Objectives

1 Apply Phase 2 of the 3-x-3 writing process, which begins with formal and informal methods for researching data and generating ideas. The second phase of the writing process includes researching, organizing, and writing. Researching means collecting information using formal or informal techniques. Formal research for long reports and complex problems may involve searching electronically or manually, as well as conducting interviews, surveys, focus groups, and experiments. Informal research for routine tasks may include looking in company files, talking with your boss, interviewing the target audience, conducting informal surveys, brainstorming for ideas, and creating cluster diagrams.

2 Explain how to organize data into lists and alphanumeric or decimal outlines. One method for organizing data in simple messages is to list the main topics to be discussed. Organizing more complex messages usually requires an outline. To prepare an outline, divide the main topic into three to five major components. Break the components into subpoints consisting of details, illustrations, and evidence. For an alphanumeric outline, arrange items using Roman numerals (I, II), capital letters (A, B), and numbers (1, 2). For a decimal outline, show the ordering of ideas with decimals (1., 1.1, 1.1.1).

Are you ready? Get more practice at **www.meguffey.com**

3 Compare direct and indirect patterns for organizing ideas. The direct pattern places the main idea first. This pattern is useful when audiences will be pleased, mildly interested, or neutral. It saves the reader's time, sets the proper frame of mind, and reduces reader frustration. The indirect pattern places the main idea after explanations. This pattern is useful for audiences that will be unwilling, displeased, or hostile. It respects the feelings of the audience, encourages a fair hearing, and minimizes negative reactions.

4 Compose the first draft of a message, avoiding sentence fragments, run-on sentences, and comma splices as well as emphasizing important ideas, avoiding misplaced modifiers, and using active and passive voice effectively. Compose the first draft of a message in a quiet environment where you won't be interrupted. Compose quickly but plan to revise. Avoid fragments (breaking off parts of sentences), comma splices (joining two clauses improperly), and run-on sentences (fusing two clauses improperly). Understand the difference between clauses and phrases so that you can write complete sentences. Remember that sentences are most effective when they are short (20 or fewer words). A main idea may be emphasized by making it the sentence subject, placing it first, and removing competing ideas. Effective sentences use active-voice verbs, although passive-voice verbs may be necessary for tact or de-emphasis. Effective sentences avoid dangling and misplaced modifiers.

5 Compose effective paragraphs using three classic paragraph plans as well as applying techniques for achieving paragraph coherence. Typical paragraphs follow one of three plans. Direct paragraphs (topic sentence followed by supporting sentences) are useful to define, classify, illustrate, and describe. Pivoting paragraphs (limiting sentence followed by topic sentence and supporting sentences) are useful to compare and contrast. Indirect paragraphs (supporting sentences followed by topic sentence) build a rationale and foundation of ideas before presenting the main idea. Paragraphs are more coherent when the writer links ideas by (a) sustaining a key thought, (b) dovetailing sentences, (c) using pronouns effectively and (d) employing transitional expressions.

Chapter Review

1. Compare the first phase of the writing process with the second phase. (Obj. 1)
2. For routine writing tasks, what are some techniques for collecting informal data and generating ideas? (Obj. 1)
3. Name seven specific techniques for a productive group brainstorming session. (Obj. 1)
4. What is the difference between a list and an outline? (Obj. 2)
5. What are the major components in a letter or memo? (Obj. 2)
6. What are the major components in an analytical report? (Obj. 2)
7. Why do many readers prefer the direct method for organizing messages? (Obj. 3)
8. When is the indirect pattern appropriate, and what are the benefits of using it? (Obj. 3)
9. What is the primary difference between the direct and indirect patterns of organization? (Obj. 3)
10. List four techniques for emphasizing important ideas in sentences. (Obj. 4)
11. When should business writers use active-voice sentences? When should they use passive-voice sentences? Give an original example of each. (Obj. 4)
12. What's wrong with this sentence? *After reading it carefully, the proposal doesn't interest us.* (Obj. 4)
13. What is a topic sentence, and where is it usually found? (Obj. 5)
14. Describe three paragraph plans. Identify the uses for each. (Obj. 5)
15. What is coherence, and how is it achieved? (Obj. 5)

Critical Thinking

1. Why is cluster diagramming considered an intuitive process whereas outlining is considered an analytical process? (Obj. 2)
2. Why is audience analysis so important in the selection of the direct or indirect pattern of organization for a business message? (Obj. 3)
3. How are speakers different from writers in the way they emphasize ideas? (Obj. 4)
4. Why are short sentences and short paragraphs appropriate for business communication? (Objs. 4, 5)
5. **Ethical Issue:** Discuss the ethics of the indirect pattern of organization. Is it manipulative to delay the presentation of the main idea in a message?

Writing Improvement Exercises

5.1 Sentence Elements (Obj. 4)

Your Task. Identify the following groups of words using these abbreviations: independent clause (IC), dependent clause (DC), or phrase(s) (P). For clauses, circle the subject. Be prepared to explain your choices.

a. although you want to make a good impression during your interview
b. the interviewer will size you up in about seven seconds
c. during a study conducted by neuro-scientists from New York
d. when they examined brain activity
e. MRI results showed significant activity in two brain areas
f. as a matter of fact
g. because people make 11 decisions about you in the first seven seconds
h. in the areas of education, believability, trustworthiness, and economic level

5.2 Sentence Faults (Obj. 4)

In the following, identify the sentence fault (fragment, run-on, comma splice). Then revise to remedy the fault.

a. Because 90 percent of all business transactions involve written messages. Good writing skills are critical.
b. The recruiter requested a writing sample. Even though the candidate seemed to communicate well orally.
c. Major soft-drink companies considered a new pricing strategy, they tested vending machines that raise prices in hot weather.
d. Thirsty consumers may think that variable pricing is unfair they may also refuse to use the machine.
e. About half of Pizza Hut's 7,600 outlets make deliveries, the others concentrate on walk-in customers.
f. McDonald's sold its chain of Chipotle Mexican Grill restaurants the chain's share price doubled on the next day of trading.
g. Private equity players are betting they can breathe new life into old brands. Which explains why Golden Gate Partners paid millions for defunct retailer Eddie Bauer.

5.3 Emphasis (Obj. 4)

For each of the following sentences, circle (1) or (2). Be prepared to justify your choice.

a. Which is more emphatic?
   1. Our dress code is good.
   2. Our dress code reflects common sense and good taste.
b. Which is more emphatic?
   1. A budget increase would certainly improve hiring.
   2. A budget increase of $70,000 would enable us to hire two new people.
c. Which is more emphatic?
   1. The committee was powerless to act.
   2. The committee was unable to take action.
d. Which de-emphasizes the refusal?
   1. Although our resources are committed to other projects this year, we hope to be able to contribute to your worthy cause next year.
   2. We can't contribute to your charity this year.
e. Which sentence places more emphasis on the date?
   1. The deadline is November 30 for health benefit changes.
   2. November 30 is the deadline for health benefit changes.
f. Which sentence is *less* emphatic?
   1. One division's profits decreased last quarter.
   2. Profits in beauty care products dropped 15 percent last quarter.
g. Which sentence gives more emphasis to video game sales?
   1. Sales of video game consoles and software rose 40 percent in June.
   2. During the period ending June 30, sales of video game consoles and software rose significantly.
h. Which sentence gives more emphasis to leadership?
   1. Jason has many admirable qualities, but most important is his leadership skill.
   2. Jason has many admirable qualities, including leadership skill, good judgment, and patience.
i. Which sentence format is more emphatic?
   1. We notified three departments: (a) Marketing, (b) Accounting, and (c) Distribution.
   2. We notified three departments:
      (a) Marketing
      (b) Accounting
      (c) Distribution

5.4 Active Voice (Obj. 4)

Business writing is more forceful if it uses active-voice verbs.

Passive: Antivirus software was installed by Craig on his computer.
Active: Craig installed antivirus software on his computer.

Your Task. Revise the following sentences so that verbs are in the active voice. Put the emphasis on the doer of the action.

a. Employees were given their checks at 4 p.m. every Friday by the manager.
b. New spices and cooking techniques were tried by McDonald's to improve its hamburgers.
c. Our new company logo was designed by my boss.
d. The managers with the most productive departments were commended by the CEO.
e. All team members were asked by the leader to brainstorm for 10 minutes.

5.5 Passive Voice (Obj. 4)

Your Task. Revise the following sentences so that they are in the passive voice.

a. The auditor discovered a computational error in the company's tax figures.
b. We cannot ship your order for ten monitors until June 15.
c. Stacy did not submit the accounting statement on time.
d. The Federal Trade Commission targeted deceptive diet advertisements by weight-loss marketers.
e. Thieves are stealing corporate and financial information by using data-stealing malware on the Web.

5.6 Dangling and Misplaced Modifiers (Obj. 4)

Your Task. On a separate sheet, revise the following sentences to remedy dangling and misplaced modifiers. Add subjects as needed, but retain the introductory phrases. Mark *C* if correct.

a. By advertising extensively, all the open jobs were filled quickly.
b. To apply for early admission, submit your application by November 1. (Tricky!)
c. After leaving the midtown meeting, Angela's car would not start.
d. Walking up the driveway, the Hummer parked in the garage was immediately spotted by the detectives.
e. The manager's rules were to be observed by all staff members, no matter how silly they seemed.
f. To complete the project on time, a new deadline was established by the team.

g. Acting as manager, several new employees were hired by Mr. Lopez.
h. Michelle Mitchell presented a talk about workplace drug problems in our boardroom.

5.7 Paragraph Organization (Obj. 5)

In a memo to the college president, the athletic director is arguing for a new stadium scoreboard. One paragraph will describe the old scoreboard and why it needs to be replaced. Study the following list of ideas for that paragraph.

1. The old scoreboard is a tired warhorse that was originally constructed in the 1960s.
2. It's now hard to find replacement parts for it when something breaks.
3. The old scoreboard is not energy efficient.
4. Coca-Cola has offered to buy a new sports scoreboard in return for exclusive rights to sell soda on campus.
5. The old scoreboard should be replaced for many reasons.
6. It shows only scores for football games.
7. When we have soccer games or track meets, we are without a functioning scoreboard.

   a. Which sentence should be the topic sentence? ______
   b. Which sentence(s) should be developed in a different paragraph? ______
   c. Which supporting sentences should follow the topic sentence? ______
   d. Now write a well-organized paragraph using the preceding information. Strive to incorporate coherence techniques described in this chapter.

5.8 Paragraph Organization and Revision (Obj. 5)

Your Task. The following paragraphs are poorly organized and poorly expressed. Decide what the main idea is in each paragraph. Then revise each paragraph so that it has a topic sentence and is organized directly. Improve the sentence flow, structure, coherence, and correctness by using the techniques described in this chapter and the previous chapter.

a. We feel that the "extreme" strategy has not been developed fully in the fast-food market. Pizza Hut is considering launching a new product called The Extreme. We plan to price this new pizza at $19.99. It will be the largest pizza on the market. It will have double the cheese. It will also have double the toppings. The plan is to target the X and Y Generations. The same target audience that would respond to an extreme product also reacts to low prices. The X and Y Generations are the fastest-growing segments in the fast-food market. These population segments have responded well to other marketing plans using the extreme strategy.
b. You should always have your sound and video files ready for your PowerPoint presentation. When you move the presentation to a network folder or send it to someone else, the presentation has no sound. A common problem in PowerPoint involves lost sound and video files. Create a new folder for your presentation, and copy the sound and video files to that folder before you put them in your presentation. Then you will always have your sound files ready for use with your presentation.
c. Current employees may be interested in applying for new positions within the company. The Human Resources Department has a number of jobs available immediately. The positions are at a high level. Current employees may apply immediately for open positions in production, for some in marketing, and jobs in administrative support are also available. Interested people should come to the Human Resources Department. We have a list showing the open positions, what the qualifications are, and job descriptions are shown. Many of the jobs are now open, but application must be made immediately. That's why we are sending this now. To be hired, an interview must be scheduled within the next two weeks.

Activities

Note: All Documents for Analysis may be downloaded from **www.meguffey.com** so that you do not have to rekey the entire message.

5.9 Document for Analysis: Weak E-Mail Message (Objs. 3–5)

Team

Your Task. The following e-mail suffers from numerous writing faults such as dangling modifiers, overuse of passive voice, and fragments. Notice that small superscript numbers identify each sentence. Individually or in a group, analyze this message. For each sentence or group of words, identify the following faults: dangling modifier (DM), passive voice (PV), and fragment (FR). Your group should agree on its analysis. Your instructor may ask you to revise the message to remedy its faults.

To: Jeremy.Gibbons12@aol.com
From: Andrea Kelly <akelly@bodyfitness.com>
Subject: Improving Your Experience at Body Fitness Center
Cc:
Bcc:

Dear Mr. Gibbons,

[1]Body Fitness Center here in Scottsdale was probably chosen by you because it is one of the top-rated gyms in the Southwest. [2]Our principal goal has always been making your workouts enjoyable. [3]To continue to provide you with the best equipment and programs, your feedback is needed.

[4]An outstanding program with quality equipment and excellent training programs has been provided by Body Fitness. [5]However, more individual attention could be given by us to our customers if our peak usage time could be extended. [6]You have probably noticed that attendance at the gym increases from 4 p.m. to 8 p.m. [7]We wish it were possible to accommodate all our customers on their favorite equipment during those hours. [8]Although we can't stretch an hour. [9]We would like to make better use of the time between 8 p.m. and 11 p.m. [10]With more members coming later, we would have less crush from 4 p.m. to 8 p.m.

[11]To encourage you to stay later, security cameras for our parking area are being considered by my partner and me. [12]Cameras for some inside facilities may also be added. [13]This matter has been given a lot of thought. [14]Although Body Fitness has never previously had an incident that endangered a member.

[15]Please fill in the attached interactive questionnaire. [16]Which will give us instant feedback about scheduling your workouts. [17]By completing this questionnaire, your workouts and training sessions can be better planned so that you can enjoy exactly the equipment and trainers you prefer.

Cordially,

5.10 Collaborative Brainstorming (Obj. 1)

Team

Brainstorming can be a productive method for generating problem-solving ideas. You can improve your brainstorming skills through practice.

Your Task. In teams of four or five, analyze a problem on your campus such as the following: unavailable classes, unrealistic degree requirements, a lack of student intern programs, poor parking facilities, an inadequate registration process, a lack of diversity among students on campus, and so forth. Use brainstorming techniques to generate ideas that clarify the problem and explore its solutions. Each team member should prepare a cluster diagram to record the ideas generated. Either individually or as a team, organize the ideas into an outline with three to five main points and numerous subpoints. Assume that your ideas will become part of a letter to be sent to an appropriate campus official or to your campus newspaper discussing the problem and your solution. Remember, however, your role as a student. Be polite, positive, and constructive—not negative, hostile, or aggressive.

5.11 Individual Brainstorming (Objs. 1, 2)

E-mail

Brainstorming techniques can work for individuals as well as groups. Assume that your boss or department chair wants you to submit a short report analyzing a problem.

Your Task. Analyze a problem that exists where you work or go to school, such as long lines at the copy or fax machines, overuse of express mail services, understaffing during peak customer service hours, poor scheduling of employees, inappropriate cell phone use, an inferior or inflexible benefits package, outdated equipment, or one of the campus problems listed in **Activity 5.10.** Select a problem about which you have some knowledge. Prepare a cluster diagram to develop ideas. Then, organize the ideas into an outline with three to five main points and numerous subpoints. Be polite, positive, and constructive. E-mail the outline to your boss (your instructor). Include an introduction (such as, *Here is the outline you requested in regard to . . .*). Include a closing that offers to share your cluster diagram if your boss would like to see it.

5.12 Brainstorming Tips for Productive Sessions (Obj. 1)

Web

Casandra M., your supervisor at Gap Inc., has been asked to lead a brainstorming group in an effort to generate new ideas for the company's product line. Although Casandra knows a great deal about the company and its products, she doesn't know much about brainstorming. She asks you to research the topic quickly and give her a concise guide on how to brainstorm. One other thing—Casandra doesn't want to read a lot of articles. She wants you to outline tips for productive brainstorming.

Your Task. Conduct an Internet or database keyword search for brainstorming tips. Locate a number of articles with helpful tips. Prepare an outline that tells how to (a) prepare for a brainstorming session, (b) conduct the session, and (c) follow up after the meeting. Submit your outline in a memo or an e-mail to your supervisor (your instructor).

5.13 Collecting Primary Information: Research Interviewing (Obj. 1)

Team

In your follow-up meeting with Casandra M. from **Activity 5.12**, she asks you to complete one more task in preparation for the brainstorming session. She needs further insight in defining the problem and creating an agenda for the outline of topics to be covered in the brainstorming session. She asks you to conduct informal interviews of Gap and Old Navy shoppers.

Your Task. Form five-member class groups. Two members of each group, if possible, should be familiar with Gap and Old Navy. Decide who will role-play the interviewer and the two interviewees (those most familiar with Gap and Old Navy), and who will act as recorder and group spokesperson. If your group has fewer than five members, some will have to fill more than one role. The interviewer asks both interviewees the same three questions outlined below. The recorder takes notes, and the group spokesperson summarizes the group's research results during the class discussion. Use the following interview questions:

a. During your last two visits to Gap or Old Navy, were there any products you expected the two stores to carry but couldn't find?
b. Can you think of any seasonal products you would like Gap or Old Navy to carry? Specifically, identify products for winter, spring, summer, and fall.
c. If you were in charge of Gap or Old Navy's product lines, what three changes would you make to the existing product lines? What three totally new product lines would you want to create?

As a team or individually, prepare an outline that summarizes the information gathered from the in-class interviews.

5.14 Brainstorming: Are Ethics Programs Helpful? (Obj. 1)

Ethics | Team | Web

In the wake of the banking collapse and previous corporate scandals, more companies are hiring ethics officers—sometimes called "ethics cops." Companies are also investing in expensive interactive Web-based ethics training. You have been named to a team to discuss ethics compliance in your company, a large firm with thousands of employees. It has no current program. Other companies have ethics codes, conflicts-of-interest policies, ethics officers, training programs, and hotlines. Some authorities, however, say that ethics failures are usually not the result of ignorance of laws or regulations.[12] A variety of pressures may cause ethics lapses.

Your Task. Your boss, the Human Resources vice president, wants to learn more about employee feelings in regard to ethics programs. In teams, brainstorm to find reactions to these questions. What kinds of ethical dilemmas do typical entry-level and midlevel managerial employees face? Do you think ethics codes help employees be more ethical? What conditions might force employees to steal, lie, or break the rules? Can ethics be taught? What kind of workplace ethics program would you personally find helpful? Before your brainstorming session, you might want to investigate the topic of ethics programs on the Web. Record your ideas during the session. Then organize the best ones into an outline to be presented to Rita Romano, Human Resources Vice President.

5.15 Researching, Brainstorming, and Organizing: Student Loans (Objs. 1–3)

Team | Web

Sarah was all smiles when she graduated and got that degree in her hand. Soon, however, she began to worry about her student loans. Student debt has risen 58 percent in the last decade, according to the College Board, a New York–based college testing and information firm. One study showed that about one third of all recent graduates are unprepared to make their first student loan payment.[13] Another report stated that the average borrower leaves college owing more than $22,000.[14]

Your Task. In teams collect information about student debt. Who has it? How much debt does an average student carry? How do most students repay their loans? What strategies are proposed for helping students avoid, reduce, and repay educational loans? As a group, discuss your findings. Brainstorm for additional strategies. Then organize your findings into an outline with a title, an introduction, and recommendations for helping current students avoid, reduce, and repay their student loans. Submit your outline to your instructor.

Video Resource

Video Library 1, Guffey's 3-x-3 Writing Process Develops Fluent Workplace Skills

If you didn't see *Guffey's 3-x-3 Writing Process Develops Fluent Workplace Skills* when you studied a previous chapter, your instructor may show it with this chapter. It shows all three phases of the writing process so that you can see how it guides the development of a complete message. This video illustrates concepts in Chapters 4, 5, and 6.

Chat About It

In each chapter you will find five discussion questions related to the chapter material. Your instructor may assign these topics for you to discuss in class, in an online chat room, or on an online discussion board. Some of the discussion topics may require outside research. You may also be asked to read and respond to postings made by your classmates.

Topic 1: This chapter describes various techniques for generating ideas. Explore other methods by using Google to search for *generating writing ideas.* Select a method that appeals to you and explain why it would be effective.

Topic 2: In which phase of the 3-x-3 writing process do you suppose most beginners at business writing spend their time? In which phase have you been spending most of your time?

Topic 3: Some writers have trouble writing the opening sentence of a message. Occasionally, a quotation makes for an appropriate opening. Assume that you need to motivate an employee to achieve more at work. Find a famous quotation online about motivation that might be an appropriate opening for such a message. In addition, write a sentence that would effectively transition from this opening.

Topic 4: In your opinion, how many business managers know what a comma splice is? If some managers don't know what a comma splice is, then is it critical that you avoid comma splices in your writing?

Topic 5: Learn how to display the average sentence length in a document using Microsoft Office Word 2007. Not everyone using Word 2007 knows how to do that. Explain the process briefly.

Grammar and Mechanics C.L.U.E. Review 5

Commas

Review Guides 21–26 about commas in Appendix A, Grammar and Mechanics Guide, beginning on page A-10. On a separate sheet, revise the following sentences to correct errors in comma usage. For each error that you locate, write the guide number and abbreviation that reflects this usage. The more you recognize the reasons, the better you will learn these punctuation guidelines. If a sentence is correct, write *C.* When you finish, check your answers on page Key-1.

Guide 21, CmSer (Comma series)	Guide 24, CmDate (Comma, dates, addresses, geographical names, etc.)
Guide 22, CmIntr (Comma introductory)	Guide 25, CmIn (Comma, internal sentence interrupters)
Guide 23, CmConj (Comma conjunction)	

Example: Before beginning a message always collect the necessary information.
Revision: Before beginning a message, always collect the necessary information. [Guide 22, Cm Intr]

1. The 3-x-3 writing process includes prewriting, writing and revising.
2. Before asking others for information see what you can find yourself.
3. Formal research methods include accessing electronically, searching manually and investigating primary sources.
4. If a project is complex consider organizing it by outlining the major points.
5. Careful writers define the main topic and they divide it into three to five components.
6. We decided that Jill Hawkins who is the best writer on the team should prepare the final draft.
7. The company's executives expected new office construction to be finished by September 1, 2012 in Boulder Colorado.
8. Grammar checkers by the way often highlight passive voice as a grammar fault.
9. When you must be tactful and avoid naming the doer of an action the passive voice can be helpful.
10. The direct paragraph plan is useful when you want to define a process or when you must describe something such as a product.

CHAPTER 6

Revising Business Messages

OBJECTIVES

After studying this chapter, you should be able to

1. Complete business messages by revising for conciseness, which includes eliminating flabby expressions, long lead-ins, *there is/are* and *it is/was* fillers, redundancies, and empty words.
2. Improve clarity in business messages by keeping the ideas simple, dumping trite business phrases, dropping clichés and slang, unburying verbs, and controlling exuberance.
3. Enhance readability by understanding document design including the use of white space, margins, typefaces, fonts, numbered and bulleted lists, and headings.
4. Recognize proofreading problem areas and apply effective techniques to proofread both routine and complex documents.
5. Evaluate a message to judge its success.

Want to do well on tests and excel in your course? Go to **www.meguffey.com** for helpful interactive resources.

- **Review the Chapter 6 PowerPoint slides to prepare for the first quiz.**

© iStockphoto.com/Josh Hodge

Zooming In

PART 1

Taco Bell Tweaks Menu to Rebuild Customer Base

After an outbreak of *E. coli* linked to its restaurants in five states followed by a highly publicized video of rats cavorting in one of its New York restaurants, Taco Bell struggled to regain its reputation. Eventually the restaurant chain overcame the bad publicity, and customers returned to its tacos, burritos, and tostadas. Taco Bell realized, however, that it had to keep rebuilding its customer base by improving its image and its menu.

Yum Brands—owner of Taco Bell, Pizza Hut, and KFC—is the world's largest restaurant company, with more than 36,000 restaurants around the world.[1] Although Taco Bell is the most successful of Yum's fast-food chains, it must compete for customers with McDonald's, Burger King, and Wendy's as well as with trendy upstarts Baja Fresh, Chipotle, and Qdoba. Despite the competition, Taco Bell holds a commanding lead in the Mexican fast-food market.

In overcoming its bad image, Taco Bell plans to remodel or rebuild 375 locations. Major emphasis, however, goes to revamping its menu. One portion of the plan focuses on new breakfast products such as a sausage and bacon Grilled Stuft burrito; a Southwest sausage burrito; an egg, bacon, and cheese burrito; and cinnamon Toastadas.

Looking beyond breakfast fare, Emil Brolick, president of brand building at Yum, suggested that Taco Bell had higher aspirations. "[W]e believe we have a unique opportunity because while all the sandwich players are trying to one-up each other in the same game, we're going to play a different game."[2] His interest lies in unique flavors and better products. However, Taco Bell is also concerned with healthful food. Stinging from criticism that fast food contributes to the worldwide obesity epidemic, Taco Bell is looking for more nutritious menu choices.[3]

In the increasingly crowded fast-food market, customers are slowly but surely shifting away from the traditional burger and chicken fast foods. One food industry executive said, "Burgers are your dad's food, and Mexican is the choice of the new generation."[4] Poised to capitalize on this movement, Taco Bell remains keenly aware that (a) it sells a quasi-Mexican food, and (b) its customers are changing. Although its products cannot veer too far from what appeals to the masses, Taco Bell must also compete with new flavors, low-fat items, and fresh ingredients. A recently hired culinary product manager is charged with the task of coming up with menu suggestions and communicating them to management. You will learn more about this case on page 171.

© AP Images/Phil Coale

Critical Thinking

- When new ideas must be generated and sold to management, what role does communication skill play in the process?
- Do you think the Taco Bell culinary product manager will be making an oral or a written presentation of new menu ideas?
- Why is a writing process helpful in developing a presentation of new ideas?

http://www.tacobell.com

Applying Phase 3 of the Writing Process

LEARNING OBJECTIVE 1
Complete business messages by revising for conciseness, which includes eliminating flabby expressions, long lead-ins, *there is/are* and *it is/was* fillers, redundancies, and empty words.

The final phase of the 3-x-3 writing process focuses on revising, proofreading, and evaluating. Revising means improving the content and sentence structure of your message. Proofreading involves correcting its grammar, spelling, punctuation, format, and mechanics. Evaluating is the process of analyzing whether your message achieves its purpose. One would not expect people in the restaurant business to require these kinds of skills. However, the new culinary product manager at Taco Bell—and many other similar businesspeople—realize that bright ideas are worth little unless they can be communicated effectively to fellow workers and to management. In the communication process, the techniques of revision can often mean the difference between the acceptance or rejection of ideas.

Although the composition process differs depending on the person and the situation, this final phase should occupy a significant share of the total time you spend on a message. As you learned earlier, some experts recommend devoting about half the total composition time to revising and proofreading.[5]

Why is the revision stage of the writing process so important?

Rarely is the first or even second version of a message satisfactory. Only amateurs expect writing perfection on the first try. The revision stage is your chance to make sure your message says what you mean. Many professional writers compose the first draft quickly without worrying about language, precision, or correctness. Then they revise and polish extensively. Other writers, however, prefer to revise as they go—particularly for shorter business documents.

Whether you revise immediately or after a break, you will want to examine your message critically. You should be especially concerned with ways to improve its conciseness, clarity, and readability.

Revising for Conciseness

In business, time is indeed money. Translated into writing, this means that concise messages save reading time and, thus, money. In addition, messages that are written directly and efficiently are easier to read and comprehend. In the revision process, look for shorter ways to say what you mean. Examine every sentence that you write. Could the thought be conveyed in fewer words? Your writing will be more concise if you eliminate flabby expressions, drop unnecessary introductory words, get rid of redundancies, and purge empty words.

Why is conciseness so important in business messages?

Eliminating Flabby Expressions

As you revise, focus on eliminating flabby expressions. This takes conscious effort. As one expert copyeditor observed, "Trim sentences, like trim bodies, usually require far more effort than flabby ones."[6] Turning out slim sentences and lean messages means that you will strive to "trim the fat." For example, notice the flabbiness in this sentence: *Due to the fact that sales are booming, profits are good*. It could be said more concisely: *Because sales are booming, profits are good.* Many flabby expressions can be shortened to one concise word as shown here and illustrated in Figure 6.1. Also notice in this figure that you may use different methods for revising printed documents and digital documents.

Flabby	Concise
as a general rule	generally
at a later date	later
at this point in time	now, presently
despite the fact that	although
due to the fact that, inasmuch as, in view of the fact that	because
feel free to	please
for the period of	for
in addition to the above	also
in all probability	probably
in the event that	if
in the near future	soon
in very few cases	seldom
until such time as	until

Why should you avoid long lead-ins in your messages?

Limiting Long Lead-Ins

Another way to create concise sentences is to delete unnecessary introductory words. Consider this sentence: *I am sending you this e-mail to announce that we have hired a new manager*. A more concise and more direct sentence deletes the long lead-in: *We have hired a*

FIGURE 6.1 Revising Manually and Digitally

Revising Digital Documents Using Strikethrough and Color

When revising digital documents, you can use simple word processing tools such as strikethrough and color. In this example, strikethroughs in red identify passages to be deleted. The strikethrough function is located on the **Font** tab. We used blue to show inserted words, but you may choose any color you prefer. If you need to add comments, use the MS Word **Comment** feature, shown in Chapter 4, Figure 4.8, on page 129.

~~This is a short note to let you know that, as~~ As you requested, I ~~made an investigation of~~ investigated several of our competitors' Web sites. Attached ~~hereto~~ is a summary of my findings. ~~of my investigation.~~ I was ~~really~~ most interested in ~~making a comparison of the employment of strategies for~~ comparing marketing strategies as well as ~~the use of~~ navigational graphics ~~used~~ to guide visitors through the sites. ~~In view of the fact that~~ Because we will be revising our own Web site ~~in the near future~~ soon, I was ~~extremely~~ intrigued by the organization, ~~kind of~~ marketing tactics, and navigation at ~~each and~~ every site I visited.

Revising Printed Documents Using Proofreading Symbols

When revising printed documents, use standard symbols to manually show your revisions.

~~This is a short note to let you know that,~~ as you requested, I ~~made an~~ investigat~~ion of~~ several of our competitors' Web sites. Attached ~~hereto~~ is a summary of my findings ~~of my investigation.~~ I was ~~really~~ most interested in ~~making a comparison of the employment of~~ strategies ~~for marketing~~ as well as ~~the use of~~ navigational graphics ~~used~~ to guide visitors through the sites. ~~In view of the fact that~~ we will be revising our own Web site ~~in the near future,~~ I was ~~extremely~~ intrigued by the organization, ~~kind of~~ marketing tactics, and navigation at ~~each and~~ every site I visited.

Popular Proofreading Symbols

Delete	℘
Capitalize	≡
Insert	∧
Insert comma	∧,
Insert period	⊙
Start paragraph	¶

new manager. The meat of the sentence often follows the words *that* or *because*, as shown in the following:

Wordy	Concise
We are sending this announcement to let everyone know that new parking permits will be available January 1.	New parking permits will be available January 1.
This is to inform you that you may find lower airfares at our Web site.	You may find lower airfares at our Web site.
I am writing this letter because Professor John Donnellan suggested that your organization was hiring trainees.	Professor John Donnellan suggested that your organization was hiring trainees.

Dropping Unnecessary *there is/are* and *it is/was* Fillers

In many sentences the expressions *there is/are* and *it is/was* function as unnecessary fillers. In addition to taking up space, these fillers delay getting to the point of the sentence. Eliminate them by recasting the sentence. Many—but not all—sentences can be revised so that fillers are unnecessary.

Wordy	Concise
There are only two administrative assistants to serve five managers.	Only two administrative assistants serve five managers.
There was an unused computer in the back office.	An unused computer was in the back office.
It was our auditor who discovered the theft.	Our auditor discovered the theft.

Rejecting Redundancies

What are redundancies?

Expressions that repeat meaning or include unnecessary words are redundant. Saying *unexpected surprise* is like saying *surprise surprise* because *unexpected* carries the same meaning as *surprise*. Excessive adjectives, adverbs, and phrases often create redundancies and wordiness. Redundancies do not add emphasis, as some people think. Instead, they identify a writer as inexperienced. As you revise, look for redundant expressions such as the following:

Redundant	Concise
absolutely essential	essential
adequate enough	adequate
basic fundamentals	fundamentals *or* basics
big in size	big
combined together	combined
exactly identical	identical
each and every	each *or* every
necessary prerequisite	prerequisite
new beginning	beginning
refer back	refer
repeat again	repeat
true facts	facts

Purging Empty Words

Familiar phrases roll off the tongue easily, but many contain expendable parts. Be alert to these empty words and phrases: *case, degree, the fact that, factor, instance, nature,* and *quality.* Notice how much better the following sentences sound when we remove all the empty words:

> ~~*In the case of*~~ USA Today, ~~*the newspaper*~~ *improved its readability.*
>
> *Because of* ~~*the degree of*~~ *active participation by our sales reps, profits soared.*
>
> *We are aware* ~~*of the fact*~~ *that many managers need assistance.*
>
> *Except for* ~~*the instance of*~~ *Toyota, Japanese imports sagged.*
>
> *She chose a career in a field that was analytical* ~~*in nature*~~. [OR: *She chose a career in an analytical field.*]
>
> *Student writing in that class is excellent* ~~*in quality*~~.

Also avoid saying the obvious. In the following examples, notice how many unnecessary words we can omit through revision:

> ~~*When it arrived,*~~ *I cashed your check immediately.* (Announcing the check's arrival is unnecessary. That fact is assumed in its cashing.)
>
> ~~*We need printer cartridges; therefore,*~~ *please send me two dozen laser cartridges.* (The first clause is obvious.)

Finally, look carefully at clauses beginning with *that, which,* and *who.* They can often be shortened without loss of clarity. Search for phrases such as *it appears that.* These phrases often can be reduced to a single adjective or adverb, such as *apparently.*

> *successful*
> *Changing the name of a* ∧ *company* ~~*that is successful*~~ *is always risky.*
>
> *All employees* ~~*who are among those*~~ *completing the course will be reimbursed.*
>
> *final*
> *Our* ∧ *proposal,* ~~*which was*~~ *slightly altered* ~~*in its final form*~~, *won approval.*
>
> *weekly*
> *We plan to schedule* ∧ *meetings* ~~*on a weekly basis*~~.

Revising for Clarity

LEARNING OBJECTIVE 2
Improve clarity in business messages by keeping the ideas simple, dumping trite business phrases, dropping clichés and slang, unburying verbs, and controlling exuberance.

A major revision task involves assessing the clarity of your message. A clear message is one that is immediately understood. Employees, customers, and investors increasingly want to be addressed in a clear and genuine way. Fuzzy and bombastic writing alienates these stakeholders.[7] Business writers appreciate clear messages that are immediately understandable. Techniques that improve clarity include applying the KISS formula (Keep It Short and Simple), dumping trite business phrases, and avoiding clichés and slang.

Keep It Short and Simple

What is the KISS formula, and how does it apply to business messages?

To achieve clarity, resist the urge to show off or be fancy. Remember that your goal is not to impress a reader. Instead, the goal of business writing is to *express,* not *impress.* One way to achieve clear writing is to apply the familiar KISS formula. Use active-voice sentences that avoid indirect, pompous language.

Wordy and Unclear	**Improved**
Employees have not been made sufficiently aware of the potentially adverse consequences regarding the use of these perilous chemicals.	Warn your employees about these dangerous chemicals.

Communicating in clear, simple language is an uphill battle for some firms. That's why plain-language advocate Christopher Balmford founded Cleardocs.com, a document management company that helps law firms, accounting firms, and other highly technical businesses communicate clearly and effectively with clients. Cleardocs' online technology turns complex documents into market-focused plain language, transforming elaborate or technical letters and reports into easily understandable written communications. *What types of businesses have difficulty producing simple, conversational messages, and why?*

Wordy and Unclear	Improved
In regard to the matter of obtaining optimal results, it is essential that employees be given the implements that are necessary for jobs to be completed satisfactorily.	To get the best results, give employees the tools they need to do the job.

Dumping Trite Business Phrases

To sound "businesslike," many writers repeat the same stale expressions that other writers have used over the years. Your writing will sound fresher and more vigorous if you eliminate these trite phrases or find more original ways to convey the idea.

Trite Phrase	Improved
as per your request	as you request
pursuant to your request	at your request
enclosed please find	enclosed is
every effort will be made	we'll try
in accordance with your wishes	as you wish
in receipt of	have received
please do not hesitate to	please
thank you in advance	thank you
under separate cover	separately
with reference to	about

Dropping Clichés and Slang

Clichés are expressions that have become exhausted by overuse. Many cannot be explained, especially to those who are new to our culture. Clichés lack not only freshness but also clarity. Instead of repeating clichés such as the following, try to find another way to say what you mean.

below the belt	last but not least
better than new	make a bundle
beyond a shadow of a doubt	pass with flying colors
easier said than done	quick as a flash
exception to the rule	shoot from the hip
fill the bill	stand your ground
first and foremost	think outside the box
good to go	true to form

Spotlight on Communicators

© AP Images/Jack Plunket

Former Secretary of State Colin Powell believes that effective leaders apply the KISS formula in keeping things simple. They articulate vivid, overarching goals and values. Their visions and priorities are lean and compelling, not cluttered and laden with buzzwords. One of Secretary Powell's favorite quotations illustrates his conviction: "Great leaders are almost always great simplifiers, who can cut through argument, debate and doubt, to offer a solution everybody can understand."

What is slang, and when is it appropriate in business messages?

Slang is composed of informal words with arbitrary and extravagantly changed meanings. Slang words quickly go out of fashion because they are no longer appealing when everyone begins to understand them. Consider the following statement of a government official who had been asked why his department was dropping a proposal to lease offshore oil lands: "The Administration has an awful lot of other things in the pipeline, and this has more wiggle room so they just moved it down the totem pole." He added, however, that the proposal might be offered again since "there is no pulling back because of hot-potato factors."

The meaning here, if the speaker really intended to impart any, is considerably obscured by the use of slang. If you want to sound professional, avoid expressions such as *snarky, lousy, blowing the budget, bombed,* and *getting burned.*

Unburying Verbs

What is a buried verb?

Buried verbs are those that are needlessly converted to wordy noun expressions. This happens when verbs such as *acquire, establish,* and *develop* are made into nouns such as *acquisition, establishment,* and *development.* Such nouns often end in *-tion, -ment,* and *-ance.* Using these nouns increases sentence length, drains verb strength, slows the reader, and muddies the thought. Notice how you can make your writing cleaner and more forceful by avoiding wordy verb/noun conversions:

Buried Verbs	Unburied Verbs
conduct a discussion of	discuss
create a reduction in	reduce
engage in the preparation of	prepare
give consideration to	consider
make an assumption of	assume
make a discovery of	discover
perform an analysis of	analyze
reach a conclusion that	conclude
take action on	act

Controlling Exuberance

Occasionally we show our exuberance with words such as *very, definitely, quite, completely, extremely, really, actually,* and *totally*. These intensifiers can emphasize and strengthen your meaning. Overuse, however, sounds unbusinesslike. Control your enthusiasm and guard against excessive use.

Excessive Exuberance	Businesslike
We *totally* agree that we *actually* did not *really* give his proposal a *very* fair trial.	We agree that we did not give his proposal a fair trial.
The manufacturer was *extremely* upset to learn that its printers were *definitely* being counterfeited.	The manufacturer was upset to learn that its printers were being counterfeited.

Designing Documents for Readability

LEARNING OBJECTIVE 3
Enhance readability by understanding document design including the use of white space, margins, typefaces, fonts, numbered and bulleted lists, and headings.

Well-designed documents improve your messages in two important ways. First, they enhance readability and comprehension. Second, they make readers think you are a well-organized and intelligent person. In the revision process, you have a chance to adjust formatting and make other changes so that readers grasp your main points quickly. Significant design techniques to improve readability include the appropriate use of white space, margins, typefaces, numbered and bulleted lists, and headings for visual impact.

Employing White Space

Empty space on a page is called *white space*. A page crammed full of text or graphics appears busy, cluttered, and unreadable. To increase white space, use headings, bulleted or numbered lists, and effective margins. As discussed earlier, short sentences (20 or fewer words) and short paragraphs (eight or fewer printed lines) improve readability and comprehension. As you revise, think about shortening long sentences. Consider breaking up long paragraphs into shorter chunks. Be sure, however, that each part of the divided paragraph has a topic sentence.

What is a ragged-right margin?

Understanding Margins and Text Alignment

Margins determine the white space on the left, right, top, and bottom of a block of type. They define the reading area and provide important visual relief. Business letters and memos usually have side margins of 1 to 1 ½ inches.

Your word processing program probably offers four forms of margin alignment: (a) lines align only at the left, (b) lines align only at the right, (c) lines align at both left and right (*justified*), and (d) lines are centered. Nearly all text in Western cultures is aligned at the left and reads from left to right. The right margin may be *justified* or *ragged right*. The text in books, magazines, and other long works is often justified on the left and right for a formal appearance.

However, justified text may require more attention to word spacing and hyphenation to avoid awkward empty spaces or "rivers" of spaces running through a document. When right margins are "ragged"—that is, without alignment or justification—they provide more white space and improve readability. Therefore, you are best served by using left-justified text and ragged-right margins without justification. Centered text is appropriate for headings but not for complete messages.

What is the difference between serif and sans serif fonts?

Choosing Appropriate Typefaces

Business writers today may choose from a number of typefaces on their word processors. A typeface defines the shape of text characters. As shown in Figure 6.2, a wide range of typefaces is available for various purposes. Some are decorative and useful for special purposes. For most business messages, however, you should choose from *serif* or *sans serif* categories.

Serif typefaces have small features at the ends of strokes. The most common serif typeface is Times New Roman. Other popular serif typefaces are Century, Georgia, and Palatino. Serif typefaces suggest tradition, maturity, and formality. They are frequently used for body text in

FIGURE 6.2 Typefaces With Different Personalities for Different Purposes

All-Purpose Sans Serif	Traditional Serif	Happy, Creative Script/Funny	Assertive, Bold Modern Display	Plain Monospaced
Arial	Century	Brush Script	Britannic Bold	Courier
Calibri	Garamond	Comic Sans	Broadway	Letter Gothic
Helvetica	Georgia	Gigi	Elephant	Monaco
Tahoma	Goudy	Jokerman	Impact	Prestige Elite
Univers	Palatino	Lucinda	Bauhaus 93	
Verdana	Times New Roman	Kristen	SHOWCARD	

business messages and longer documents. Because books, newspapers, and magazines favor serif typefaces, readers are familiar with them.

Sans serif typefaces include Arial, Calibri, Helvetica, Tahoma, Univers, and Verdana. These clean characters are widely used for headings, signs, and material that does not require continuous reading. Web designers often prefer sans serif typefaces for simple, pure pages. For longer documents, however, sans serif typefaces may seem colder and less accessible than familiar serif typefaces.

For less formal messages or special decorative effects, you might choose one of the happy fonts such as Comic Sans or a bold typeface such as Impact. You can simulate handwriting with a script typeface. Despite the wonderful possibilities available on your word processor, don't get carried away with fancy typefaces. All-purpose sans serif and traditional serif typefaces are most appropriate for your business messages. Generally, use no more than two typefaces within one document.

Capitalizing on Type Fonts and Sizes

Font refers to a specific style (such as *italic*) within a typeface family (such as Times New Roman). Most typeface families offer various fonts such as CAPITALIZATION, SMALL CAPS, **boldface**, *italic*, and underline, as well as fancier fonts such as outline and shadow.

How can font styles and typeface families be used to emphasize your words?

Font styles are a mechanical means of adding emphasis to your words. ALL CAPS, SMALL CAPS, and **bold** are useful for headings, subheadings, and single words or short phrases in the text. ALL CAPS, HOWEVER, SHOULD NEVER BE USED FOR LONG STRETCHES OF TEXT BECAUSE ALL THE LETTERS ARE THE SAME HEIGHT, MAKING IT DIFFICULT FOR READERS TO DIFFERENTIATE WORDS. In addition, excessive use of all caps feels like shouting and irritates readers. **Boldface,** *italics*, and underlining are effective for calling attention to important points and terms. Be cautious, however, when using fancy or an excessive number of font styles. Don't use them if they will confuse, annoy, or delay readers.

During the revision process, think about type size. Readers are generally most comfortable with 10- to 12-point type for body text. Smaller type enables you to fit more words into a space. Tiny type, however, makes text look dense and unappealing. Slightly larger type makes material more readable. Overly large type (14 points or more), however, looks amateurish and out of place for body text in business messages. Larger type, however, is appropriate for headings.

Numbering and Bulleting Lists for Quick Comprehension

What is "skim value," and how can it be enhanced in business messages?

One of the best ways to ensure rapid comprehension of ideas is through the use of numbered or bulleted lists. Lists provide high "skim value." This means that readers can browse quickly and grasp main ideas. By breaking up complex information into smaller chunks, lists improve readability, understanding, and retention. They also force the writer to organize ideas and write efficiently.

In the revision process, look for ideas that could be converted to lists and follow these techniques to make your lists look professional:

- **Numbered lists:** Use for items that represent a sequence or reflect a numbering system.
- **Bulleted lists:** Use to highlight items that don't necessarily show a chronology.

Spotlight on Communicators

© AP Images/Jennifer Szymaszek

Arthur Levitt, former chair of the U.S. Securities and Exchange Commission, is said to have been the most activist chair in the SEC's history. As a champion of "plain English," he was instrumental in requiring that disclosure documents written for investors be readable. To improve their readability, he advocated using the active voice, familiar words, and graphic techniques. He recommended emphasizing important ideas with boldface, graphics, headings, lists, and color. All of these techniques can vastly improve the readability of any business document.

- **Capitalization:** Capitalize the initial word of each line.
- **Punctuation:** Add end punctuation only if the listed items are complete sentences.
- **Parallelism:** Make all the lines consistent; for example, start each with a verb.

In the following examples, notice that the list on the left presents a sequence of steps with numbers. The bulleted list does not show a sequence of ideas; therefore, bullets are appropriate. Also notice the parallelism in each example. In the numbered list, each item begins with a verb. In the bulleted list, each item follows an adjective/noun sequence. Business readers appreciate lists because they focus attention. Be careful, however, not to use so many that your messages look like grocery lists.

What helps you decide whether to use a bulleted or a numbered list?

Numbered List

Our recruiters follow these steps when hiring applicants:

1. Examine the application.
2. Interview the applicant.
3. Check the applicant's references.

Bulleted List

To attract upscale customers, we feature the following:

- Quality fashions
- Personalized service
- A generous return policy

Should headings be used in business messages other than reports?

Adding Headings for Visual Impact

Headings are an effective tool for highlighting information and improving readability. They encourage the writer to group similar material together. Headings help the reader separate major ideas from details. They enable a busy reader to skim familiar or less important information. They also provide a quick preview or review. Headings appear most often in reports, which you will study in greater detail in Chapters 9 and 10. However, main headings, subheadings, and

Zooming In PART 2

Taco Bell

The newly hired culinary product manager at Taco Bell has her job cut out for her. Management expects her to anticipate trends in Mexican foods and improve restaurant menus. Part of the challenge is recognizing trends that consumers haven't even picked up yet and then working these trends into restaurant products. In her words, "We want to kick it up a notch, but we still have to deliver to mainstream consumers." She needs to read the market and then create innovative menu ideas. The new chef is eager to incorporate some of the rich, complex flavors of authentic Mexican cuisine. But she must do it in ways that are acceptable to fast-food customers. Although she has excellent culinary references, the new chef has not been trained in communication. She has plenty of ideas to put into a memo or a presentation. Her job now depends on how well she can communicate these ideas to management.

© AP Images/Phil Coale

Critical Thinking

- Based on what you learned in this chapter, what specific advice can you give about keeping a message clear? Should a business message be conversational?
- Why is conciseness important, and what techniques can be used to achieve it?
- Would you advise the culinary chef to be direct with her ideas? What advice can you give for improving the directness and readability of a business message?

category headings can also improve readability in e-mails, memos, and letters. In the following example, they are used with bullets to summarize categories:

Category Headings

Our company focuses on the following areas in the employment process:

- **Attracting applicants.** We advertise for qualified applicants, and we also encourage current employees to recommend good people.
- **Interviewing applicants.** Our specialized interviews include simulated customer encounters as well as scrutiny by supervisors.
- **Checking references.** We investigate every applicant thoroughly. We contact former employers and all listed references.

In Figure 6.3 on page 174, the writer was able to convert a dense, unappealing e-mail message into an easier-to-read version by applying document design. Notice that the all-caps font in the first paragraph makes its meaning difficult to decipher. Justified margins and lack of white space further reduce readability. In the revised version, the writer changed the all-caps font to upper- and lowercase and also used ragged-right margins to enhance visual appeal. One of the best document design techniques in this message is the use of headings and bullets to help the reader see chunks of information in similar groups. All of these improvements are made in the revision process. You can make any message more readable by applying the document design techniques presented here.

Ethics Check

Costly Writing

Bad writing can be expensive: A Philadelphia lawyer was charged with malpractice to the tune of $6.6 million for drafting a poor commercial lease. The judge in Los Angeles said the draft was "inartfully written and done so in a confusing fashion, which lends itself to ambiguities and disagreements." Can you think of other situations in which writing can be deliberately or accidentally misleading and cost money?

Proofreading

LEARNING OBJECTIVE 4

Recognize proofreading problem areas and apply effective techniques to proofread both routine and complex documents.

Once you have the message in its final form, it's time to proofread. Don't proofread earlier because you may waste time checking items that eventually are changed or omitted. Important messages—such as those you send to management or to customers or turn in to instructors for grades—deserve careful revision and proofreading. When you finish a first draft, plan for a cooling-off period. Put the document aside and return to it after a break, preferably after 24 hours or longer. Proofreading is especially difficult because most of us read what we thought we wrote. That's why it's important to look for specific problem areas.

What to Watch for in Proofreading

Careful proofreaders check for problems in the following areas.

- **Spelling.** Now is the time to consult the dictionary. Is *recommend* spelled with one or two *c*'s? Do you mean *affect* or *effect*? Use your computer spell checker, but don't rely on it totally.
- **Grammar.** Locate sentence subjects; do their verbs agree with them? Do pronouns agree with their antecedents? Review the grammar and mechanics principles in Appendix A if necessary. Use your computer's grammar checker, but be suspicious, as explained in the Plugged In box on page 175.
- **Punctuation.** Make sure that introductory clauses are followed by commas. In compound sentences put commas before coordinating conjunctions *(and, or, but, nor)*. Double-check your use of semicolons and colons.
- **Names and numbers.** Compare all names and numbers with their sources because inaccuracies are not always visible. Especially verify the spelling of the names of individuals receiving the message. Most of us immediately dislike someone who misspells our name.
- **Format.** Be sure that your document looks balanced on the page. Compare its parts and format with those of standard documents shown in Appendix B. If you indent paragraphs, be certain that all are indented.

Spotlight on Communicators

Courtesy of The Washington Post Writers Group - www.washpost.com

Pulitzer Prize–winning *Washington Post* columnist William Raspberry frequently promotes the value of language skills in relation to career success: "Misused words, haphazard sentences, failed subject–verb agreement can distract people from our ideas and get them concentrating on our inadequacies. Good English, carefully spoken and written, can open more doors than a college degree. Bad English can slam doors we don't even know about."

FIGURE 6.3 **Using Document Design to Improve E-Mail Readability**

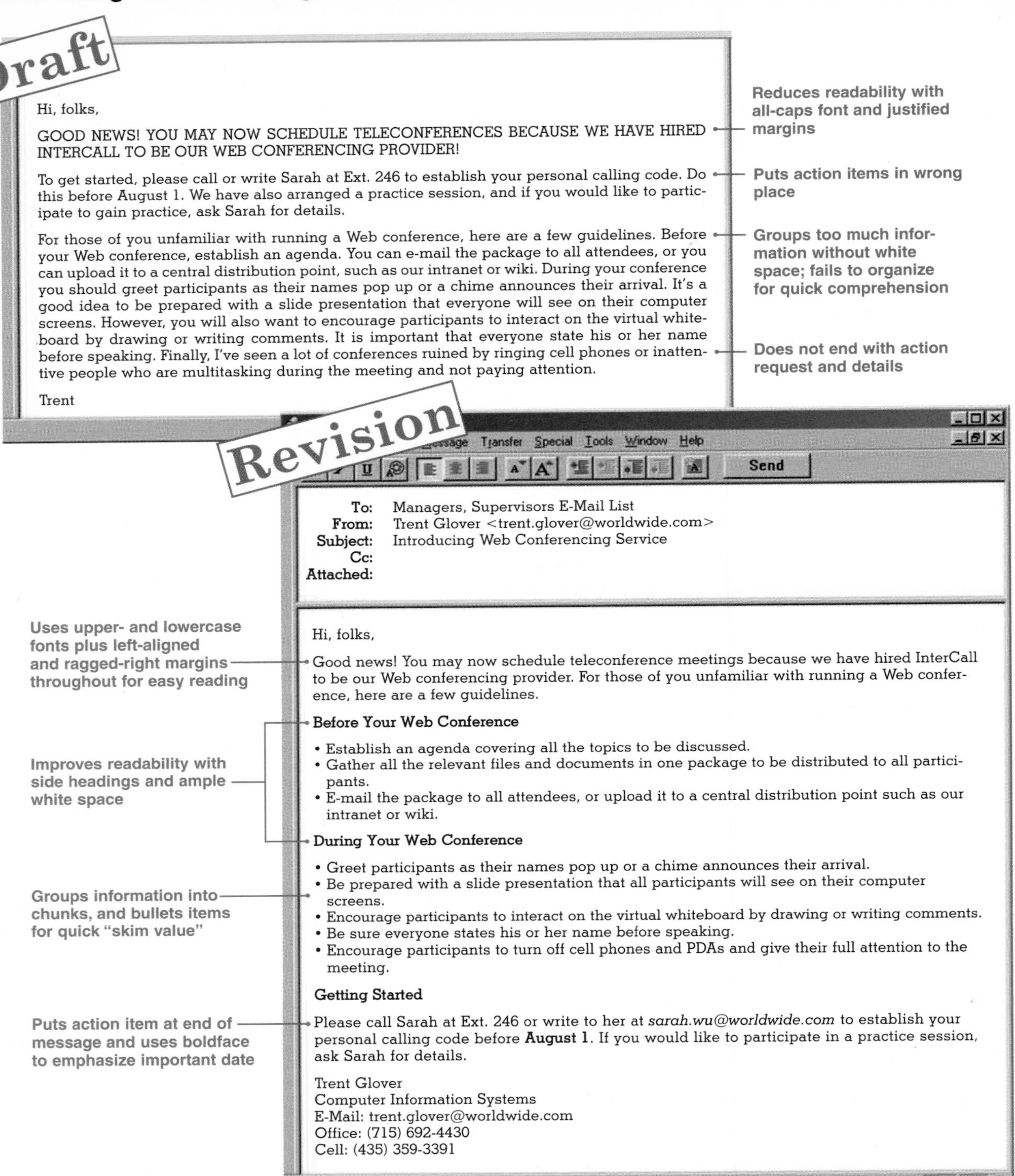

Draft

Hi, folks,

GOOD NEWS! YOU MAY NOW SCHEDULE TELECONFERENCES BECAUSE WE HAVE HIRED INTERCALL TO BE OUR WEB CONFERENCING PROVIDER!

To get started, please call or write Sarah at Ext. 246 to establish your personal calling code. Do this before August 1. We have also arranged a practice session, and if you would like to participate to gain practice, ask Sarah for details.

For those of you unfamiliar with running a Web conference, here are a few guidelines. Before your Web conference, establish an agenda. You can e-mail the package to all attendees, or you can upload it to a central distribution point, such as our intranet or wiki. During your conference you should greet participants as their names pop up or a chime announces their arrival. It's a good idea to be prepared with a slide presentation that everyone will see on their computer screens. However, you will also want to encourage participants to interact on the virtual whiteboard by drawing or writing comments. It is important that everyone state his or her name before speaking. Finally, I've seen a lot of conferences ruined by ringing cell phones or inattentive people who are multitasking during the meeting and not paying attention.

Trent

Revision

To: Managers, Supervisors E-Mail List
From: Trent Glover <trent.glover@worldwide.com>
Subject: Introducing Web Conferencing Service
Cc:
Attached:

Hi, folks,

Good news! You may now schedule teleconference meetings because we have hired InterCall to be our Web conferencing provider. For those of you unfamiliar with running a Web conference, here are a few guidelines.

Before Your Web Conference

- Establish an agenda covering all the topics to be discussed.
- Gather all the relevant files and documents in one package to be distributed to all participants.
- E-mail the package to all attendees, or upload it to a central distribution point such as our intranet or wiki.

During Your Web Conference

- Greet participants as their names pop up or a chime announces their arrival.
- Be prepared with a slide presentation that all participants will see on their computer screens.
- Encourage participants to interact on the virtual whiteboard by drawing or writing comments.
- Be sure everyone states his or her name before speaking.
- Encourage participants to turn off cell phones and PDAs and give their full attention to the meeting.

Getting Started

Please call Sarah at Ext. 246 or write to her at *sarah.wu@worldwide.com* to establish your personal calling code before **August 1**. If you would like to participate in a practice session, ask Sarah for details.

Trent Glover
Computer Information Systems
E-Mail: trent.glover@worldwide.com
Office: (715) 692-4430
Cell: (435) 359-3391

How to Proofread Routine Documents

How does proofreading routine documents differ from proofreading complex documents?

Most routine documents require a light proofreading. If you read on screen, use the down arrow to reveal one line at a time. This focuses your attention at the bottom of the screen. A safer proofreading method, however, is reading from a printed copy. Regardless of which method you use, look for typos and misspellings. Search for easily confused words, such as *to* for *too* and *then* for *than*. Read for missing words and inconsistencies. For handwritten or printed messages, use standard proofreading marks, shown in Figure 6.4, to indicate changes. For digital documents and collaborative projects, use the simple word processing tools shown in Figure 6.1 or use the **Comment** and **Track Changes** functions described in Figure 4.8 on page 129.

How to Proofread Complex Documents

Long, complex, or important documents demand more careful proofreading. Apply the previous suggestions but also add the following techniques:

- Print a copy, preferably double-spaced, and set it aside for at least a day. You will be more alert after a breather.
- Allow adequate time to proofread carefully. A common excuse for sloppy proofreading is lack of time.
- Be prepared to find errors. One student confessed, "I can find other people's errors, but I can't seem to locate my own." Psychologically, we don't expect to find errors, and we don't want to find them. You can overcome this obstacle by anticipating errors and congratulating, not criticizing, yourself each time you find one.
- Read the message at least twice—once for word meanings and once for grammar and mechanics. For very long documents (book chapters and long articles or reports), read a third time to verify consistency in formatting.
- Reduce your reading speed. Concentrate on individual words rather than ideas.
- For documents that must be perfect, enlist a proofreading buddy. Have someone read the message aloud. Spell names and difficult words, note capitalization, and read punctuation.
- Use standard proofreading marks shown in Figure 6.4 to indicate changes.

PLUGGED IN

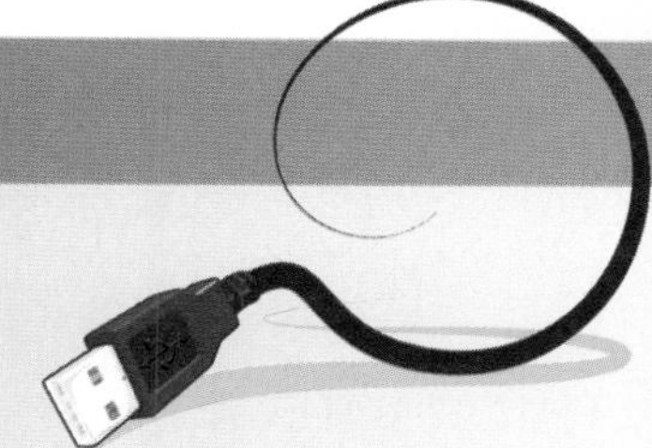

Using Spell Checkers and Grammar/Style Checkers Wisely

Spell-checking and grammar-checking software are two useful tools that can save you from many embarrassing errors. They can also greatly enhance your revision techniques—if you know how to use them wisely.

Spell Checking

Although some writers dismiss spell checkers as an annoyance, most of us are only too happy to have our typos, repeated words, and misspelled words detected. If you are using Microsoft Word 2007, you need to set relevant options. (Click the **MS Office** button, choose **Word Options,** select **Proofing,** and check **Flag repeated words, Check spelling as you type,** and **Use contextual spelling**). When you see a wavy line under a word, you know that the highlighted word may be faulty. Right-click for a list of suggested replacements and other actions. Word 2007 can even detect the misuse of words in context. For example, it usually knows whether *they're, their,* and *there* are being used correctly and may automatically correct errors.

The latest spell checkers are indeed wonderful, but they are far from perfect. When you mistype a word, the spell checker may not be sure what you meant and the suggested replacements may be way off target. What's more, a spell checker cannot know when you type *form* that you meant *from*. Lesson: Don't rely totally on spell checkers to find all typos and spelling errors.

Grammar and Style Checking

Like spell checkers, today's grammar and style checkers are amazingly sophisticated. Microsoft Word marks faults in capitalization, possessives, plurals, punctuation, subject–verb agreement, and gender-specific words as well as misused words, double negatives, fragments, wordiness, and many other problems.

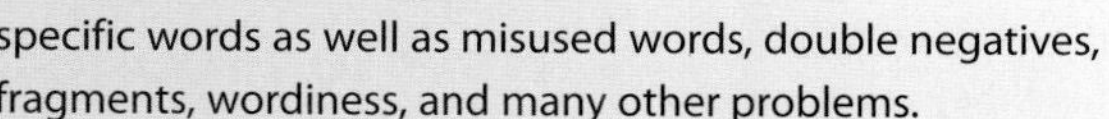

How does a grammar checker work? Say you typed the sentence, *The office and its equipment is for sale*. You would see a wavy line appear under *is*. If you right-click on it, a box identifies the subject–verb agreement error and suggests the verb *are* as a correction. When you click **Change**, the error is corrected. Be sure to set your grammar and style options (**MS Office** button **→ Word Options → Proofing → When correcting spelling and grammar in Word → Settings**). However, before you decide that a grammar checker will solve all your writing problems, think again. Even Word's highly developed software misses plenty of errors, and it also mismarks some correct expressions.

Career Application

Study the spelling and grammar/style settings on your computer. Decide which settings are most useful to you. As you prepare written messages for this class, analyze the suggestions made by your spell checker and grammar checker. For one or two documents, list the spelling, grammar, and style corrections suggested by Word. How many were valid?

FIGURE 6.4 Proofreading Marks

Mark	Meaning	Mark	Meaning
℘	Delete	∧	Insert
≡	Capitalize	# ∧	Insert space
/lc	Lowercase (don't capitalize)	∧ ,	Insert punctuation
∩∪	Transpose	⊙	Insert period
⁀‿	Close up	¶	Start paragraph

Marked Copy

~~This is to inform you that~~ beginning september 1 the doors leading to the Westside of the building will have alarms. Because ~~of the fact that~~ these ~~exits~~ doors also function as fire exits they can not ~~actually~~ be locked consequently we are instaling alrams. Please ~~utilize~~ use the east side exists to avoid setting off the ear piercing alarms.

Many of us struggle with proofreading our own writing because we are seeing the same information over and over. We tend to see what we expect to see as our eyes race over the words without looking at each one carefully. We tend to know what is coming next and glide over it. To change the appearance of what you are reading, you might print it on a different colored paper or change the font. If you are proofing on screen, enlarge the page view or change the background color of the screen.

ETHICS CHECK

Overly Helpful

Students may visit writing centers where they receive useful advice and help. However, some well-meaning tutors take over, revising documents until they don't resemble the original student work. Instructors worry that the resulting documents amount to cheating. Yet in the workplace today, writers must collaborate, and drafts go through multiple revisions. Individual authorship is often not relevant. How much revision is acceptable in a college setting? How much is acceptable in the workplace?

How to Proofread and Revise PDF Files

As documents are increasingly sent as PDF (portable document format) files, business writers are learning to proof without a pen. "Soft proofing" involves using Adobe Acrobat markup tools. The advantages of soft proofing include enabling collaborators in distant locales to proof each other's work electronically and saving days of time in sending hard-copy proofs back and forth. Corrections and edits can be transferred electronically among authors, editors, proofreaders, and typesetters—and then on to the printer without pen ever touching paper. The disadvantages of soft proofing include tired eyes, especially if you are working on long documents, and the fear of losing your work because of a computer crash.

Adobe Acrobat Pro and Standard provide a rich array of tools that can make markup and work flow fairly intuitive. You can insert, replace, highlight, delete, or underline material as well as add notes, all with an insertion point that looks like that used in traditional proofreading, as shown in Figure 6.5. Adobe Acrobat enables you to add comment easily, but the markup tools require practice to use effectively. You can even make your own proofreading marks using the **Create Custom Stamp** feature.

Evaluating

LEARNING OBJECTIVE 5

Evaluate a message to judge its success.

As part of applying finishing touches, take a moment to evaluate your writing. Remember that everything you write, whether for yourself for someone else, takes the place of a personal appearance. If you were meeting in person, you would be certain to dress appropriately and professionally. The same standard applies to your writing. Evaluate what

FIGURE 6.5 Proofreading and Marking PDF Files

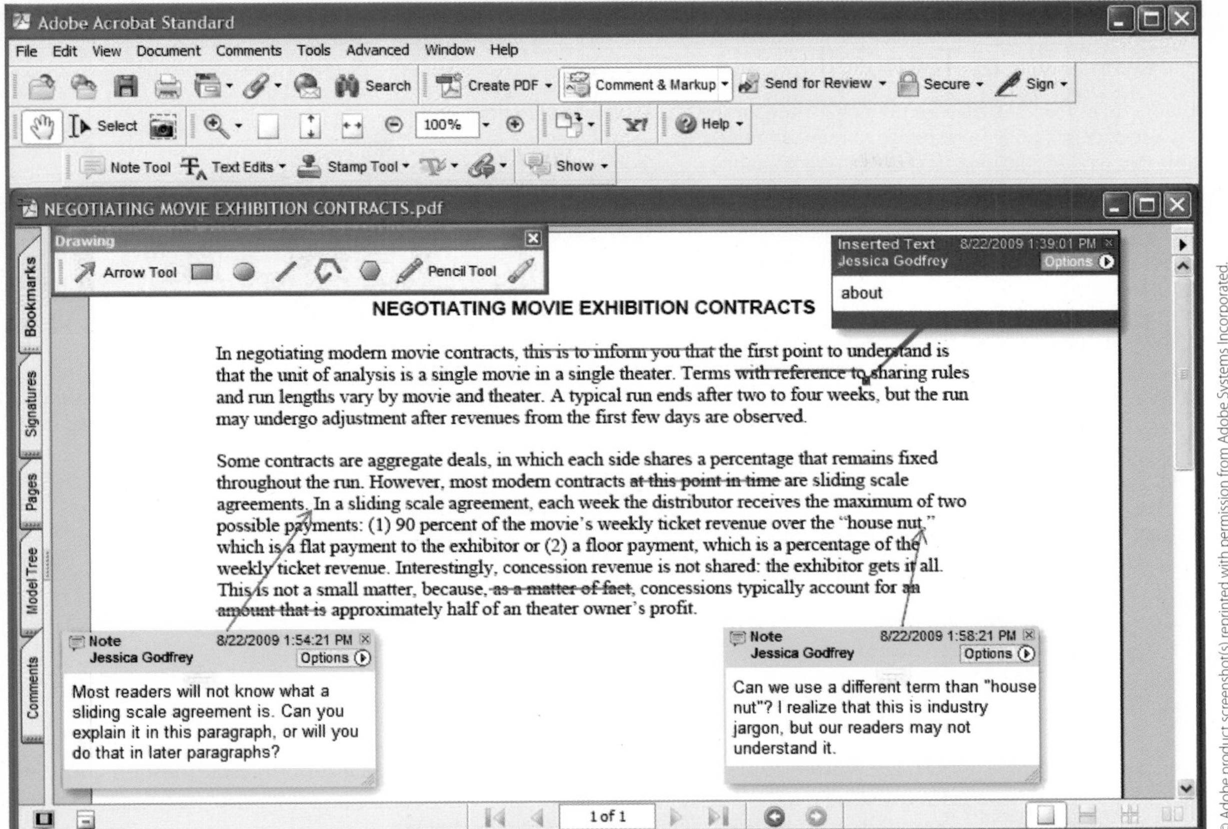

You may proofread and edit PDF files by using Adobe Acrobat software that allows you to insert, replace, highlight, delete, and underline material as well as add notes.

Checklist

Proofreading, Revising, and Evaluating

- **Eliminate flabby expressions.** Strive to reduce wordy phrases to single words (*as a general rule* becomes *generally*; *at this point in time* becomes *now*).
- **Avoid opening fillers and long lead-ins.** Revise sentences so that they don't start with fillers (*there is, there are, it is, it was*) and long lead-ins (*this is to inform you that*).
- **Shun redundancies.** Eliminate words that repeat meanings, such as *refer back.* Watch for repetitious adjectives, adverbs, and phrases.
- **Tighten your writing.** Check phrases that include *case, degree, the fact that, factor*, and other words and phrases that unnecessarily increase wordiness. Avoid saying the obvious.
- **Keep the message simple.** Express ideas directly. Don't show off or use fancy language.
- **Avoid trite business phrases.** Keep your writing fresh, direct, and contemporary by skipping such expressions as *enclosed please find* and *pursuant to your request.*
- **Don't use clichés or slang.** Avoid expressions that are overused and unclear (*below the belt, shoot from the hip*). Don't use slang, which is not only unprofessional but also often unclear to a wide audience.
- **Unbury verbs.** Keep your writing vigorous by not converting verbs to nouns ((*analyze* not *make an analysis of).*
- **Control exuberance.** Avoid overusing intensifiers such as *really, very, definitely, quite, completely, extremely, actually,* and *totally.*
- **Improve readability through document design.** Use bullets, lists, headings, capital letters, underlining, boldface, italics, and blank space to spotlight ideas and organization.
- **Proofread for correctness.** Check spelling, grammar, and punctuation. Compare names and numbers with their sources. Double-check the format to be sure you have been consistent.
- **Evaluate your final product.** Will your message achieve its purpose? Could it be improved? How will you know whether it is successful?

Zooming In — YOUR TURN

Applying Your Skills at Taco Bell

Upgrading the menu at Taco Bell is an exciting challenge for the new culinary product manager. In response to management's request, she comes up with terrific ideas for capitalizing on eating trends and converting them to mainstream tastes. She has been asked to submit a memo summarizing her longer report, which will be presented at a management meeting next week.

Although the new culinary product manager has exceptional talent in cuisine, she realizes that her writing skills are not as well developed as her cooking skills. She comes to the corporate communication department and shows your boss the first draft of her memo. Your boss is a nice guy; and, as a favor, he revises the first two paragraphs, as shown in Figure 6.6.

Your Task

Your boss, the head of corporate communication, has many important tasks to oversee. He hands the product manager's memo to you, his assistant, and tells you to finish cleaning it up. He adds, "Her ideas are right on target, but the main points are totally lost in wordy sentences and solid paragraphs. Revise this and concentrate on conciseness, clarity, and readability. Don't you think some bulleted lists would help this memo a lot?" Revise the remaining four paragraphs of the memo using the techniques you learned in this chapter. Prepare a copy of the complete memo to submit to your boss (your instructor).

you have written to be certain that it attracts the reader's attention. Is it polished and clear enough to convince the reader that you are worth listening to? How successful will this message be? Does it say what you want it to? Will it achieve your purpose? How will you know whether it succeeds?

How is feedback helpful in evaluating the effectiveness of a message?

As you learned in Chapter 1, the best way to judge the success of your communication is through feedback. For this reason you should encourage the receiver to respond to your message. This feedback will tell you how to modify future efforts to improve your communication technique.

Your instructor will also be evaluating some of your writing. Although any criticism is painful, try not to be defensive. Look on these comments as valuable advice tailored to your specific writing weaknesses—and strengths. Many businesses today spend thousands of dollars bringing in communication consultants to improve employee writing skills. You are getting the same training in this course. Take advantage of this chance—one of the few you may have—to improve your skills. The best way to improve your skills, of course, is through instruction, practice, and evaluation.

In this class you have all three elements: instruction in the writing process, practice materials, and someone to guide and evaluate your efforts. Those three elements are the reasons this book and this course may be the most valuable in your entire curriculum. Because it's almost impossible to improve your communication skills alone, take advantage of this opportunity.

The task of revising, proofreading, and evaluating, summarized in the checklist on the preceding page, is hard work. It demands objectivity and a willingness to cut, cut, cut. Though painful, the process is also gratifying. It's a great feeling when you realize your finished message is clear, concise, and effective.

Want to do well on tests and excel in your course? Go to **www.meguffey.com** for helpful interactive resources.

- **Review the Chapter 6 PowerPoint slides to prepare for the first quiz.**

FIGURE 6.6 Partially Revised First Draft

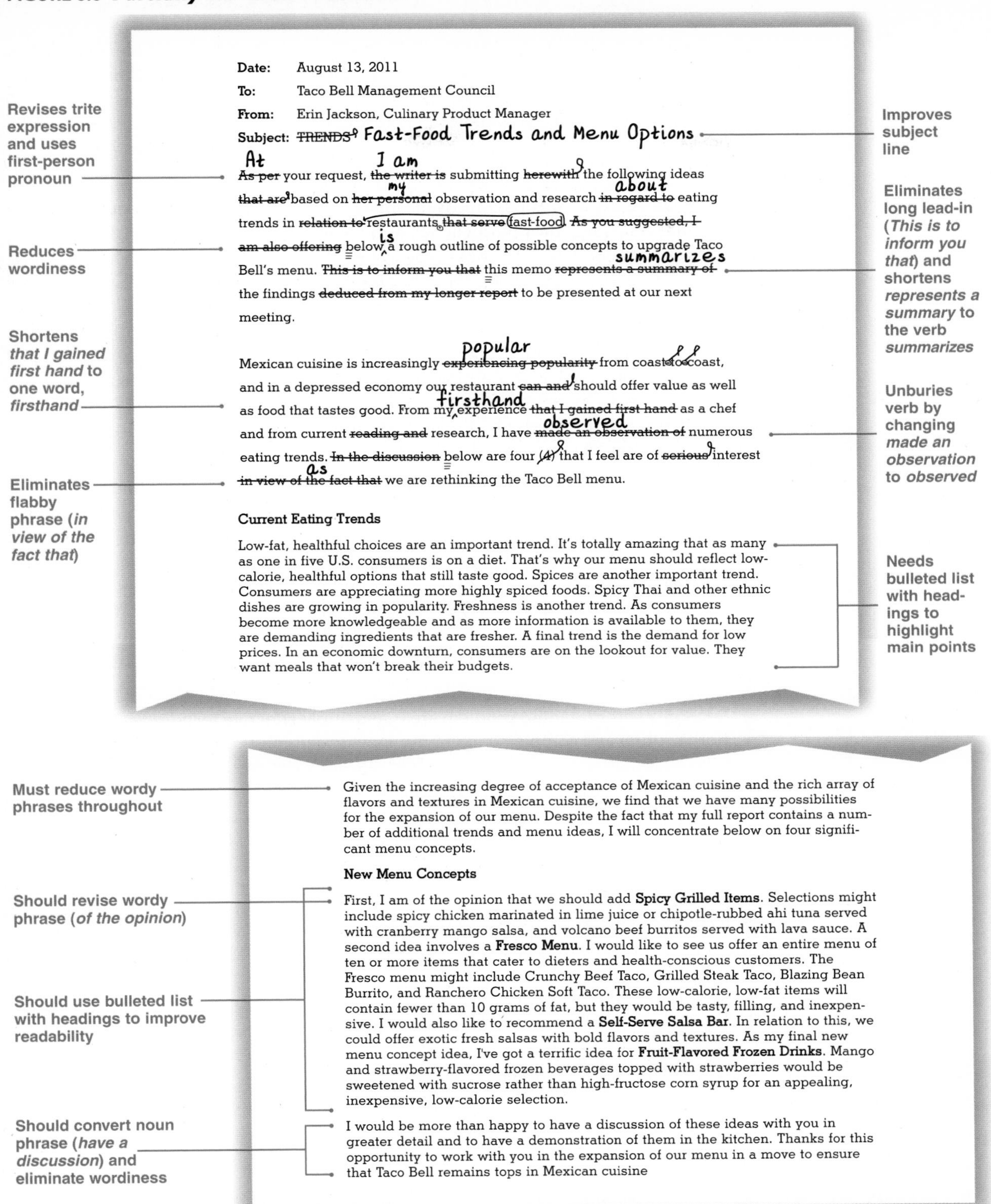

Date: August 13, 2011

To: Taco Bell Management Council

From: Erin Jackson, Culinary Product Manager

Subject: ~~TRENDS~~ Fast-Food Trends and Menu Options

~~As per~~ At your request, ~~the writer is~~ I am submitting ~~herewith~~ the following ideas ~~that are~~ based on ~~her personal~~ my observation and research ~~in regard to~~ about eating trends in ~~relation to~~ restaurants ~~that serve~~ fast-food. ~~As you suggested, I am also offering~~ below is a rough outline of possible concepts to upgrade Taco Bell's menu. ~~This is to inform you that~~ this memo ~~represents a summary of~~ summarizes the findings ~~deduced from my longer report~~ to be presented at our next meeting.

Mexican cuisine is increasingly ~~experiencing popularity~~ popular from coast ~~to~~ coast, and in a depressed economy our restaurant ~~can and~~ should offer value as well as food that tastes good. From my firsthand experience ~~that I gained first hand~~ as a chef and from current ~~reading and~~ research, I have ~~made an observation of~~ observed numerous eating trends. ~~In the discussion~~ below are four ~~(4)~~ that I feel are of ~~serious~~ interest ~~in view of the fact that~~ as we are rethinking the Taco Bell menu.

Current Eating Trends

Low-fat, healthful choices are an important trend. It's totally amazing that as many as one in five U.S. consumers is on a diet. That's why our menu should reflect low-calorie, healthful options that still taste good. Spices are another important trend. Consumers are appreciating more highly spiced foods. Spicy Thai and other ethnic dishes are growing in popularity. Freshness is another trend. As consumers become more knowledgeable and as more information is available to them, they are demanding ingredients that are fresher. A final trend is the demand for low prices. In an economic downturn, consumers are on the lookout for value. They want meals that won't break their budgets.

Given the increasing degree of acceptance of Mexican cuisine and the rich array of flavors and textures in Mexican cuisine, we find that we have many possibilities for the expansion of our menu. Despite the fact that my full report contains a number of additional trends and menu ideas, I will concentrate below on four significant menu concepts.

New Menu Concepts

First, I am of the opinion that we should add **Spicy Grilled Items**. Selections might include spicy chicken marinated in lime juice or chipotle-rubbed ahi tuna served with cranberry mango salsa, and volcano beef burritos served with lava sauce. A second idea involves a **Fresco Menu**. I would like to see us offer an entire menu of ten or more items that cater to dieters and health-conscious customers. The Fresco menu might include Crunchy Beef Taco, Grilled Steak Taco, Blazing Bean Burrito, and Ranchero Chicken Soft Taco. These low-calorie, low-fat items will contain fewer than 10 grams of fat, but they would be tasty, filling, and inexpensive. I would also like to recommend a **Self-Serve Salsa Bar**. In relation to this, we could offer exotic fresh salsas with bold flavors and textures. As my final new menu concept idea, I've got a terrific idea for **Fruit-Flavored Frozen Drinks**. Mango and strawberry-flavored frozen beverages topped with strawberries would be sweetened with sucrose rather than high-fructose corn syrup for an appealing, inexpensive, low-calorie selection.

I would be more than happy to have a discussion of these ideas with you in greater detail and to have a demonstration of them in the kitchen. Thanks for this opportunity to work with you in the expansion of our menu in a move to ensure that Taco Bell remains tops in Mexican cuisine

Revises trite expression and uses first-person pronoun
Reduces wordiness
Shortens *that I gained first hand* to one word, *firsthand*
Eliminates flabby phrase (*in view of the fact that*)
Improves subject line
Eliminates long lead-in (*This is to inform you that*) and shortens *represents a summary* to the verb *summarizes*
Unburies verb by changing *made an observation* to *observed*
Needs bulleted list with headings to highlight main points
Must reduce wordy phrases throughout
Should revise wordy phrase (*of the opinion*)
Should use bulleted list with headings to improve readability
Should convert noun phrase (*have a discussion*) and eliminate wordiness

Summary of Learning Objectives

1 Complete business messages by revising for conciseness, which includes eliminating flabby expressions, long lead-ins, *there is/are* and *it is/was* fillers, redundancies, and empty words. Concise messages make their points using the least number of words. Revising for conciseness involves eliminating flabby expressions (*as a general rule, at a later date, at this point in time*). Concise writing also excludes opening fillers *(there is, there are)*, redundancies *(basic essentials*), and empty words (*in the case of, the fact that).*

2 Improve clarity in business messages by keeping the ideas simple, dumping trite business phrases, dropping clichés and slang, unburying verbs, and controlling exuberance. To be sure your messages are clear, apply the KISS formula: Keep It Short and Simple. Avoid foggy, indirect, and pompous language. Do not include trite business phrases (*as per your request, enclosed please fine, pursuant to your request*), clichés (*better than new, beyond a shadow of a doubt, easier said than done*), and slang (*snarky, lousy, bombed).* Also avoid transforming verbs into nouns (*to conduct an investigation* rather than *to investigate, to perform an analysis* rather than *to analyze*). Noun conversion lengthens sentences, saps the force of the verb, and muddies the message. Finally, do not overuse intensifiers that show exuberance (*totally, actually, very, definitely*). These words can emphasize and strengthen meaning, but overusing them makes your messages sound unbusinesslike.

3 Enhance readability by understanding document design including the use of white space, margins, typefaces, fonts, numbered and bulleted lists, and headings. Well-designed messages enhance readability and comprehension. The most readable messages have ample white space, appropriate side margins, and ragged-right (not justified) margins. Serif typefaces (fonts with small features at the ends of strokes, such as Times New Roman, Century, and Palatino) are most used for body text. Sans serif typefaces (clean fonts without small features, such as Arial, Helvetica, and Tahoma) are often used for headings and signs. Numbered and bulleted lists provide high "skim value" in messages. Headings add visual impact and aid readability in business messages as well as in reports.

4 Recognize proofreading problem areas and apply effective techniques to proofread both routine and complex documents. Proofreaders must be especially alert to spelling, grammar, punctuation, names, numbers, and document format. Routine documents may be proofread immediately after completion. They may be read line by line on the computer screen or, better yet, from a printed draft copy. More complex documents, however, should be proofread after a breather. To do a good job, you must read from a printed copy, allow adequate time, reduce your reading speed, and read the document at least three times—for word meanings, for grammar and mechanics, and for formatting.

5 Evaluate a message to judge its success. Encourage feedback from the receiver so that you can determine whether your communication achieved its goal. Try to welcome any advice from your instructor on how to improve your writing skills. Both techniques help you evaluate the success of a message.

Chapter Review

1. How is proofreading different from revising? (Objs. 1, 4)
2. Why should business writers strive for conciseness? (Obj. 1)
3. What's wrong with expressions such as *due to the fact that* and *in view of the fact that*? (Obj. 1)
4. What is a redundancy? Give an example. Why should writers avoid redundancies? (Obj. 1)
5. Why should a writer avoid the opening *I am sending this e-mail because we have just hired a new manager, and I would like to introduce her*? (Obj. 1)
6. Why should writers avoid opening a sentence with *There is* or *There are*? (Obj. 1)
7. What is a buried verb? Give an original example. Why should they be avoided? (Obj. 2)
8. Why would a good writer avoid this sentence? *When it arrived, I read your message and am now replying.* (Obj. 2)
9. What are five document design techniques that business writers can use to enhance readability? (Obj. 3)

10. How can writers increase white space to improve readability? (Obj. 3)
11. What is the difference between serif and sans serif typefaces? What is the preferred use for each? (Obj. 3)
12. What are five specific items to check in proofreading? Be ready to discuss methods you find useful in spotting these errors. (Obj. 4)
13. In proofreading, why is it difficult to find your own errors? How can you overcome this barrier? (Obj. 4)
14. List four or more effective techniques for proofreading complex documents. (Obj. 4)
15. How can you overcome defensiveness when your writing is criticized constructively? (Obj. 5)

Critical Thinking

1. Is the revision and proofreading process different for short and long documents? Can you skip revising if your message is brief? (Objs. 1, 4)
2. Would you agree or disagree with the following statement by writing expert William Zinsser? "Plain talk will not be easily achieved in corporate America. Too much vanity is on the line." (Objs. 1–5)
3. Because business writing should have high "skim value," why not write everything in bulleted lists? (Obj. 3)
4. Conciseness is valued in business. However, can messages be too short? (Obj. 1)
5. **Ethical Issue:** What advice would you give in this ethical dilemma? Becky is serving as interim editor of the company newsletter. She receives an article written by the company president describing, in abstract and pompous language, the company's goals for the coming year. Becky thinks the article will need considerable revising to make it readable. Attached to the president's article are complimentary comments by two of the company vice presidents. What action should Becky take?

Writing Improvement Exercises

6.1 Flabby Expressions (Obj. 1)

Your Task. Revise the following sentences to eliminate flabby expressions.

a. Despite the fact that we lost the contract, we must at this time move forward.
b. Inasmuch as prices are falling, we will invest in the very near future.
c. We cannot fill the order until such time as payment is received for previous shipments.
d. As a general rule, we would not accept the return; however, we will in all probability make an exception in this case.

6.2 Long Lead-Ins (Obj. 1)

Your Task. Revise the following to eliminate long lead-ins.

a. This message is to let you know that I received your e-mail and its attachments.
b. This memo is to notify everyone that we will observe Monday as a holiday.
c. I am writing this letter to inform you that your homeowner's coverage expires soon.
d. This is to warn everyone that the loss of laptops endangers company security.

6.3 *There is/are* and *It is/was* Fillers (Obj. 1)

Your Task. Revise the following to avoid unnecessary *there is/are* and *it is/was* fillers.

a. There are many businesses that are implementing strict e-mail policies.
b. It is the CEO who must approve the plan.
c. There are several Web pages you must update.
d. The manager says that there are many employees who did not return the health surveys.

6.4 Redundancies (Obj. 1)

Your Task. Revise the following to avoid redundancies.

a. Because the proposals are exactly identical, we need not check each and every item.
b. All requests for iPods and BlackBerrys were combined together in our proposal.
c. The office walls were painted beige in color.
d. Our supervisor requested that team members return back to the office.

6.5 Empty Words (Obj. 1)

Your Task. Revise the following to eliminate empty words and saying the obvious.

a. He scheduled the meeting for 11 a.m. in the morning.
b. Because of the surprising degree of response, the company expanded its free gift program.
c. I have before me your proposal sent by FedEx, and I will distribute it immediately.
d. Are you aware of the fact that our budget has a deficit in the amount of approximately $100,000?

6.6 Trite Business Phrases (Obj. 2)

Your Task. Revise the following sentences to eliminate trite business phrases.

a. As per your request, we will no longer send you e-mail offers.
b. Thank you in advance for considering our plea for community support.
c. Pursuant to your request, we are sending the original copies under separate cover.
d. Enclosed please find a check in the amount of $700.

6.7 Clichés, Slang, and Wordiness (Obj. 2)

Your Task. Revise the following sentences to avoid confusing slang, clichés, and wordiness.

a. Although our last presentation bombed, we think that beyond the shadow of a doubt our new presentation will fly.
b. Our team must be willing to think outside the box in coming up with marketing ideas that pop.
c. True to form, our competitor has made a snarky claim that we think is way below the belt.

d. If you will refer back to the budget, you will see that there are provisions that prevent blowing the budget.

6.8 Buried Verbs (Obj. 2)

Your Task. Revise the following to unbury the verbs.

a. Ms. Nelson gave an appraisal of the home's value.
b. Web-based customer service causes a reduction in overall costs.
c. Management made a recommendation affirming abandonment of the pilot project.
d. The board of directors will give consideration to the contract at its next meeting.

6.9 Lists, Bullets, and Headings (Obj. 3)

a. Use the information in the following dense paragraph to compose a concise, easy-to-read bulleted vertical list with an introductory statement.

   Here at SecurityPlus we specialize in preemployment background reports, which we describe in the following. Among our preemployment background reports are ones that include professional reference interviews, criminal reports, driving records, employment verification, and credit information.

b. Create an introduction and a list from the following wordy paragraph.

   A high-powered MBA program costs hundreds of dollars an hour. Our program covers the same information. That information includes how to start a business. You will also learn information about writing a business plan and understanding taxes. In addition, our MBA program covers how to go about writing a marketing feasibility study. Another topic that students cover in our program is employment benefits plans and licensing requirements.

c. From the following wordy paragraph, create a concise bulleted list with category headings.

   This is to inform you that our on-site GuruGeek computer technicians can provide you with fast, affordable solutions to residential and also to small business clients. Our most popular offerings include antivirus security. This service involves having our GuruGeek protect your computer against viruses, worms, and spyware as well as help you avoid e-mail attacks, identity theft, and malicious hacker programs. Our wireless networking service enables you to share Internet access through a single wireless router so that many computer users use one network at the same time. They are all using the same network. Another popular service is data backup and recovery. Our technicians focus on helping small businesses and home users protect their data without making an investment of a lot of time and energy.

Activities

Note: All Documents for Analysis may be downloaded from **www.meguffey.com** so that you do not have to rekey the entire message.

6.10 Document for Analysis: Ineffective Customer Letter (Objs. 1–5)

Your Task. Study the following message. In teams or in class discussion, list at least five specific weaknesses. If your instructor directs, revise to remedy flabby expressions, long lead-ins, *there is/are* fillers, trite business expressions, clichés, slang, buried verbs, lack of parallelism, and general wordiness. Look for ways to improve readability with bulleted or numbered points.

Current date

Mr. Michael Chatham
329 Sycamore Street
Pikeville, KY 41605

Dear Mr. Chatham:

This is to inform you that we are changing your World Bank Credit Card Agreement. These changes will be effective for all billing periods that will be beginning on or after the date of February 3.

First, we want to tell you about the change in how the calculation of your APR is done. We are increasing your variable APR (annual percentage rate) for purchases. Your APR will be exactly identical to the U.S. prime rate plus 10.99 percent with a minimum APR of 16.99 percent.

Second, we must make an explanation of how the default APR will change. All of your APRs on all balances may automatically increase to the default APR in the event that you default under any card agreement you have with us because for either of the two following reasons: You do not make the minimum payment when due. You make a payment to us that is not honored.

The default APR takes effect as of the first day of the billing period in which you default. However, every effort will be made to lower the APR for new purchases or cash advances if you are able to meet the terms of all card agreements that you have with us for six billing periods.

To Opt Out
To opt out of these changes, call or write us by the date of March 31. It is absolutely essential for you to include your name, address, and account number in the letter that you write. Should you decide to opt out of these changes, you may use your account under the current terms until the ultimate end of your current membership year or the expiration date on your card. We will close your account at that point in time. You must then repay the balance under the current terms.

Please do not hesitate to take advantage of your World Card revolving line of credit and all the benefits and services we offer you.

Sincerely,

6.11 Document for Analysis: Poorly Written E-Mail Message (Objs. 1–5)

Your Task. Study the following message. In teams or in class discussion, list at least five specific weaknesses. If your instructor directs, revise to remedy flabby expressions, long lead-ins, *there is/are* fillers, trite business expressions, clichés, slang, buried verbs, lack of parallelism, and general wordiness. Look for ways to improve readability with bulleted or numbered points.

To: Marcy Love <marcy.love@sokia.com>
From: Shelton Matthews <shelton.matthews@sokia.com>
Subject: Improving Presentation Techniques
Cc:

Marcy,

I am writing this message because, pursuant to your request, I attended a seminar about the use of PowerPoint in business presentations. You suggested that there might be tips that I would learn that we could share with other staff members, many of whom make presentations that almost always include PowerPoint. The speaker, Gary Dixon, made some very good points on the subject of PowerPoint. There were several points of an important nature that are useful in avoiding what he called a "PowerPoint slumber party." Our staff members should give consideration to the following:

Create first the message, not the slide. Only after preparing the entire script should you think about how to make an illustration of it.

You should prepare slides with short lines. Your slides should have only four to six words per line. Short lines act as an encouragement to people to listen to you and not read the slide.

Don't put each and every thing on the slide. If you put too much on the slide, your audience will be reading Item C while you are still talking about Item A. As a last and final point, she suggested that presenters think in terms of headlines. What is the main point? What does it mean to the audience?

Please let me know whether you want me to elaborate and expand on these presentation techniques subsequent to the next staff meeting.

Shelton

6.12 Document for Analysis: Poorly Written Response Letter (Objs. 1–5)

Your Task. Study the following message. In teams or in class discussion, list at least five specific weaknesses. If your instructor directs, revise to remedy flabby expressions, long lead-ins, *there is/are* fillers, trite business expressions, clichés, slang, buried verbs, lack of parallelism, and general wordiness. Look for ways to improve readability with bulleted or numbered points.

Current date

Mr. DeJuan Wilson
Fairfield Associates, Inc.
4290 Park Avenue
Fairfield, CT 06435

Dear Mr. Wilson:

We have received your request for information. As per your request, the undersigned is transmitting to you the attached documents with regard to the improvement of security in your business. To ensure the improvement of your after-hours security, you should initially make a decision with regard to exactly what you contemplate must have protection. You are, in all probability, apprehensive not only about your electronic equipment and paraphernalia but also about your company records, information, and data.

Due to the fact that we feel you will want to obtain protection for both your equipment and data, we will make suggestions for taking a number of judicious steps to inhibit crime. First and foremost, we make a recommendation that you install defensive lighting. A consultant for lighting, currently on our staff, can design both outside and inside lighting, which brings me to my second point. Exhibit security signs, because of the fact that nonprofessional thieves are often as not deterred by posted signs on windows and doors.

As my last and final recommendation, you should install space alarms, which are sensors that look down over the areas that are to receive protection, and activate bells or additional lights, thus scaring off intruders.

After reading the materials that are attached, please call me to initiate a verbal discussion regarding protection of your business.

Sincerely,

6.13 Document for Analysis: Poorly Written Customer Letter (Objs. 1–5)

Your Task. Study the following message. In teams or in class discussion, list at least five specific weaknesses. If your instructor directs, revise to remedy flabby expressions, long lead-ins, *there is/are* fillers, trite business expressions, clichés, slang, buried verbs, lack of parallelism, and general wordiness. Look for ways to improve readability with bulleted or numbered points.

Current date

Ms. Monique Faria
Grey Wolf BioSolutions
4210 Geddes Road
Ann Arbor, MI 48105

Dear Ms. Faria:

This message is an opportunity to thank you for your interest in employee leasing through Enterprise Staffing Services. Small businesses like yours can, at this point in time, enjoy powerful personnel tools previously available only to firms that were larger.

The employee leasing concept allows you to outsource personnel duties so that you can focus on the basic fundamentals of running your business. There are many administrative burdens that you can reduce such as monthly payroll, quarterly taxes, and records related to personnel matters. There is also expert guidance available in the areas of human resources, compliance, and matters of a safety nature. In view of the fact that we have extensive experience, your employer liability can be reduced by a significant degree. You can be assured that the undersigned, as well as our entire staff, will assemble together a plan that will save you time and money as well as protect you from employee hassles and employer liability.

Whether or not you offer no benefits or a full benefits package, Enterprise Staffing Services can make an analysis of your needs and help you return back to the basics of running your business and improvement in profits. Please allow me to call you to arrange a time to meet and talk about your specific needs.

Cordially,

6.14 Learning About Writing Techniques in Your Field (Objs. 1–5)

How much writing is required by people working in your career area? The best way to learn about on-the-job writing is to talk with someone who has a job similar to the one you hope to have one day.

Your Task. Interview someone working in your field of study. Your instructor may ask you to present your findings orally or in a written report. Ask questions such as these: *What kind of writing do you do? What kind of planning do you do before writing? Where do you get information? Do you brainstorm? Make lists? Do you compose with pen and paper, a computer, or a dictating machine? How many e-mail messages do you typically write in a day? How long does it take you to compose a routine one- or two-page memo or letter? Do you revise? How often? Do you have a preferred method for proofreading? When you have questions about grammar and mechanics, what or whom do you consult? Does anyone read your drafts and make suggestions? Can you describe your entire composition process? Do you ever work with others to produce a document? How does this process work? What makes writing easier or harder for you? Have your writing methods and skills changed since you left school?*

6.15 Searching for Deadwood (Objs. 1, 2)

Team | Web

Many writers and speakers are unaware of "deadwood" phrases they use. Some of these are flabby expressions, redundancies, or trite business phrases.

Your Task. Using your favorite Web browser, locate two or three sites devoted to deadwood phrases. Your instructor may ask you to (a) submit a list of ten deadwood phrases (and their preferred substitutes) not mentioned in this textbook, or (b) work in teams to prepare a comprehensive "Dictionary of Deadwood Phrases," including as many as you can find. Be sure to include a preferred substitute.

6.16 Conciseness Is Hard Work (Objs. 1, 2)

Just as most people are unmotivated to read wordy documents, most are unmotivated to listen to wordy speakers. Effective communicators work to eliminate "rambling" in both their written and spoken words.

Abraham Lincoln expressed the relationship between conciseness and hard work with his reply to the question, "How long does it take you to prepare a speech?" "Two weeks for a 20-minute speech," he replied. "One week for a 40-minute speech; and I can give a rambling, two-hour talk right now." Rambling takes little thought and effort; conciseness takes a great deal of both.

Your Task. For a 24-hour period, think about conciseness violations in spoken words. Consider violations in five areas you studied in this chapter: (a) fillers, (b) long lead-ins, (c) redundancies, (d) buried verbs, and (e) empty words. Identify the source of the violation using descriptors such as *friend, family member, coworker, boss, instructor, actor in TV sitcom, interviewer or interviewee on a radio or TV talk show*, and so forth. Include the communication medium for each example (telephone, conversation, radio, television, etc.). Be prepared to share the results of this activity during a class discussion.

6.17 Communicating With a Nonnative English Speaker

Intercultural | Web

In the three chapters devoted to the writing process, most of the advice focuses on communicating clearly and concisely. As the world becomes more globally connected, businesspeople may be increasingly communicating with nonnative speakers and writers. Assume that you have been asked to present a talk to businesspeople in your area. What additional advice would you give to speakers and writers in communicating with nonnative English speakers?

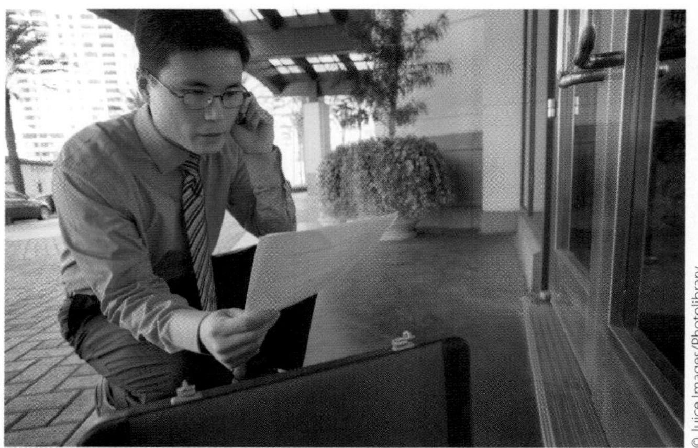

© Juice Images/Photolibrary

Your Task. Search the Web for advice in communicating with nonnative English speakers. Prepare a list of ten significant suggestions.

6.18 How Plain Is the English in Your Apartment Lease? (Objs. 1–3)

E-mail | Ethics | Team

Have you read your apartment lease carefully? Did you understand it? Many students—and their friends and family members—are intimidated, frustrated, or just plain lost when they try to comprehend an apartment lease.

Your Task. Locate an apartment lease—yours, a friend's, or a family member's. In teams, analyze its format and readability. What size is the paper? How large are the margins? Is the type large or small? How much white space appears on the page? Are paragraphs and sentences long or short? Does the lease contain legalese or obscure language? What makes it difficult to understand? In an e-mail message to your instructor, summarize your team's reaction to the lease. Your instructor may ask you to revise sections or the entire lease to make it more readable. In class, discuss how ethical it is for an apartment owner to expect a renter to read and comprehend a lease while sitting in the rental office.

Video Resource

Video Library 2, Writing Skills: The Little Guys

The Little Guys Home Electronics specializes in selling and installing home theater equipment. In just 12 years, it has grown from a start-up company to an established business with annual sales of more than $10 million. The owners—Dave and Evie Wexler and Paul Gerrity—describe their goals, motivations, and experiences in making their business successful. As you watch this video, look for (a) good business practices that helped the owners launch a successful business, (b) characteristics of successful entrepreneurs, and (c) reasons some small businesses remain successful whereas others fail.

Your Task. After watching the video, assume that you have been asked to summarize reasons for the success of The Little Guys. Building on what you have learned in this writing process chapter, compose a bulleted list with ten or more items. Use this opening sentence: *The Little Guys Home Electronics business succeeded because the owners did the following.*

Chat About It

In each chapter you will find five discussion questions related to the chapter material. Your instructor may assign these topics for you to discuss in class, in an online chat room, or on an online discussion board. Some of the discussion topics may require outside research. You may also be asked to read and respond to postings made by your classmates.

Topic 1: When you tackle a serious writing project, do you prefer freewriting, in which you rapidly record your thoughts, or do you prefer to polish and revise as you go? What are the advantages and disadvantages of each method for you? Do you use the same method for both short and long messages?

Topic 2: Think about your own speaking and writing. Do you recognize some favorite redundancies that you use in spoken or written messages? When did you realize that you could be more concise and precise by eliminating these expressions?

Topic 3: The default font in Microsoft Word used to be Times New Roman, a serif typeface. With Word 2007, the new default font is Calibri, a sans serif typeface. Why do you think Microsoft made the switch? In your opinion, is Calibri more readable than Times New Roman in printed documents, documents displayed on a computer screen, both, or neither?

Topic 4: What proofreading tasks can you safely ask a proofreading buddy to perform? What if that person is not a skilled writer?

Topic 5: Are you a good proofreader? Is it easier to find other people's errors than your own? Why? What are you good at finding? What do you frequently miss?

Grammar and Mechanics C.L.U.E. Review 6

Semicolons, Colons

Review Guides 27–30 about semicolons and colons in Appendix A, Grammar and Mechanics Guide, beginning on page A-12. On a separate sheet, revise the following sentences to correct errors in semicolon and colon usage. Do not start new sentences. For each error that you locate, write the guide number that reflects this usage. The more you recognize the reasons, the better you will learn these punctuation guidelines. If a sentence is correct, write C. When you finish, check your answers on page Key-1.

Example: Companies find it difficult to name new products consequently they often hire specialists.
Revision: Companies find it difficult to name new products; consequently, they often hire specialists. [Guide 27]

1. Successful product names may appear to have been named by magic, however the naming process is methodical and deliberate.
2. Choosing the right name and tagline is critical consequently companies are eager to hire specialists.
3. Naming is a costly endeavor, fees may range up to $70,000 for a global name.
4. Expanding markets are in Paris France Beijing China and Dubai City United Arab Emirates.
5. As she was about to name a fashion product, Rachel Hermes said "If I am launching a new fashion label, the task becomes very difficult. I have to find a name that communicates the creative style that the brand is to embody."
6. For a new unisex perfume, Hermes considered the following names Declaration, Serenity, and Earth.
7. Naming is not a problem for small companies however it is a big problem for global brands.
8. Hermes started with a thorough competitive analysis it included quantifying the tone and strength of competing names.
9. Attending the naming sessions were James Harper, marketing director, Reva Cruz, product manager, and Cheryl Chang, vice president.
10. Distribution of goods has become global therefore names have to be registered in many countries.

Are you ready? Get more practice at **www.meguffey.com**

UNIT 3

Workplace Communication

CHAPTER 7

Electronic Messages and Digital Media

Want to do well on tests and excel in your course? Go to **www.meguffey.com** for helpful interactive resources.

- **Review the Chapter 7 PowerPoint slides to prepare for the first quiz.**

OBJECTIVES

After studying this chapter, you should be able to

1. Describe the role digital media play in the changing world of business in contrast to traditional paper-based messages.
2. Meet professional e-mail standards for usage, structure, and format; and follow the rules of netiquette and other best practices.
3. Explain how business professionals communicate by instant messaging and texting.
4. Identify professional uses of podcasts, blogs, and wikis; and describe prudent policies to protect authors of electronic content.
5. Understand business uses of social and professional networking sites as well as RSS feeds and social bookmarking.

Zooming In PART 1

Twitter: From Obscure Tech Fad to Internet Sensation

Basketball giant Shaquille O'Neal has a Twitter account. Governor Arnold Schwarzenegger has one. Actor Ashton Kutcher was an early adopter. Paula Abdul announced her departure from *American Idol* on the popular microblogging service. During labor and childbirth, Sara Williams, wife of Twitter CEO Evan Williams, kept in touch by tweets (short public messages of up to 140 characters) with more than 16,000 followers.[1] Tweets also transmitted the first images of the US Airways jet that safely landed in the Hudson River in early 2009. Twitter allows users to share brief status updates about their lives and their whereabouts online.

What seemed like a novelty for tech heads when the service first emerged a few years ago has become an Internet phenomenon. The ranks of twitterers and users of other social sites have been swelling so explosively—currently to about 7 million on Twitter—that some investors see huge opportunities. They even speak of a new technological revolution, the "real-time Web."[2] High-speed Internet connections, smart mobile devices with Web browsers, and Internet messaging applications have enabled easy around-the-clock, real-time communication. Like other social sites, Twitter has yet to turn a profit. However, nearly 45 million visitors recently accessed its Web site. Roughly the same number used other sites and services to connect to it.[3]

That Twitter had come of age was evident when it became the target of hackers. Similarly, security breaches and other user missteps have highlighted the need for Twitter netiquette: Michigan Rep. Peter Hoekstra broke a national security embargo when he tweeted about his congressional trip to Baghdad, Iraq.[4]

First the tech companies, and now mainstream businesses, are looking for ways to make money using the service. For advice on what not to do on Twitter, see Part 2 of Zooming In later in this chapter. Your Turn on page 212 discusses how businesses are trying to harness the potential of Twitter and other social networks.

Critical Thinking

- In what ways have social media and the "real-time Web" changed how Internet users communicate? Have services such as Twitter improved the way we exchange information?
- What trends have facilitated the emergence of social media, specifically Twitter?
- What could be advantages and drawbacks of using Twitter for business?

http://twitter.com

How Organizations Exchange Messages and Information

LEARNING OBJECTIVE 1

Describe the role digital media play in the changing world of business in contrast to traditional paper-based messages.

Although today's workplaces are still far from paperless, increasingly information is exchanged electronically and on the go, as the preceding discussion of Twitter shows. Social media sites such as Twitter have highlighted the appetite of many people today for instant status updates and the immediate sharing of information. The Web itself has evolved from a mere repository of passively consumed information to Web 2.0—a dynamic, interactive environment. Users are empowered, active participants who create content, review products, and edit and share information.

Ever more data are stored on and accessed from remote networks, not individual computers. This storing and accessing of data along with software applications in remote network clusters, or "clouds," is called *cloud computing*. Mobile communication and cloud computing are the two prevailing technological trends today. In many businesses, desktop computers are fast becoming obsolete with the advent of ever smaller laptops, netbooks, smartphones, personal digital assistants (PDAs), and other compact mobile devices. Furthermore, virtual private networks (VPN) offer secure access to company information from any location in the world that provides an Internet connection.

Today's workforce must stay connected at all times. Knowledge and information workers are expected to remain tethered to their jobs wherever they are, even on the weekends or on vacation. The technological revolution of the last 25 years has resulted in amazing productivity gains. However, technological advances have also made 50-hour workweeks without overtime pay a reality for those "i-workers" lucky enough to snag or keep a promising position in a tough economy. Also, more employees than ever before are telecommuting.

Electronic communication is the lifeblood of a functioning organization today. Fewer layers of management after downsizing and the flattening of corporate hierarchies have meant that more rank-and-file staff members are now empowered to make decisions and tend to work in cross-functional teams. These significant changes would not be possible without a speedy yet accurate exchange of information. In this fast-paced workplace, you will be expected to collect, evaluate, and exchange information in clearly written messages, whether electronic or paper-based.

You may already be sharing digitally with your friends and family, but chances are that you need to understand how businesses transmit information electronically and how they use new technology. This chapter explores professional electronic communication, specifically e-mail, corporate blogs, instant messaging, and text messaging. Moreover, you will learn about business uses of podcasts, wikis, and social networking sites. You will read about best practices in composing e-mails and interacting through other electronic media. Knowing how to prepare an effective message and understanding business technology can save you time, reduce stress, and build your image as a professional.

Communicating With Paper-Based Messages

What role do paper-based messages play in organizations today?

Although the business world is quickly switching to electronic communication channels, paper-based documents still have definite functions.

Business letters. Writers prepare business letters on letterhead stationery. This is the best channel when a permanent record is necessary, when confidentiality is important, when sensitivity and formality are essential, and when you need to make a persuasive, well-considered presentation.

Interoffice memos. Paper-based interoffice memos were once the chief form of internal communication. Today, employees use memos primarily to convey confidential information, emphasize ideas, introduce lengthy documents, or lend importance to a message. Memos are especially appropriate for explaining organizational procedures or policies that become permanent guidelines. In Chapter 8 you will learn more about positive letters, memos, and e-mail messages that follow the direct pattern of organization.

Communicating With Electronic Messages

What role do electronic messages play in organizations today?

A number of electronic communication channels enable businesspeople to exchange information rapidly and efficiently. All of these new electronic channels showcase your writing skills.

Electronic mail. In most businesses today, e-mail is the communication channel of choice. It has been hailed as one of the greatest productivity tools of our time.[5] Users can send messages to single addressees or broadcast them to multiple recipients. When a message arrives in the inbox, the recipient may read, print, forward, store, or delete it. E-mail is most appropriate for short messages. It is inappropriate for sensitive, confidential, or lengthy documents. Increasingly, e-mail is written on laptops, netbooks, and smart devices such as the BlackBerry, Palm, and iPhone. The smaller screen poses its own challenges, yet even short mobile messages need to be correct and professional. You will learn more about safe e-mail practices later in the chapter.

Instant messaging. More interactive and immediate than e-mail, instant messaging (IM) involves the exchange of text messages in real time between two or more people logged into an IM service. IM creates a form of private chat room so that individuals can carry on conversations similar to telephone calls. IM is especially useful for back-and-forth online conversations, such as a customer communicating with a tech support person to solve a problem. Like e-mail, instant messaging creates a permanent text record and must be used carefully.

Text messaging. Sending really short messages (160 or fewer characters) from mobile phones and other wireless devices is called *text messaging* or *texting*. This method uses short message service (SMS) and is available on most mobile phones and personal digital assistants (PDAs). SMS gateways exist to connect mobile phones with instant message services, the Web, desktop computers, and even landline telephones. Busy communicators use text messaging for short person-to-person inquiries and responses that keep them in touch while away from the office.

Podcasts. A podcast is a digital media file that is distributed over the Internet and downloaded on portable media players and personal computers. Podcasts, also called *netcasts* or *webcasts*, are distinguished by their ability to be syndicated, subscribed to, or downloaded automatically when new content is added. In business, podcasts are useful for improving customer relations, marketing, training, product launches, and viral marketing (creating online buzz about new products).

Blogs. A blog is a Web site with journal entries (posts) usually written by one person with comments added by others. It may combine text, images, and links to other blogs or Web pages. Businesses use blogs to keep customers and employees informed and to receive feedback. Company news can be posted, updated, and categorized for easy cross-referencing. Blogs may be a useful tool for marketing and promotion as well as for showing a company's personal side. Twitter is often referred to as a microblogging site, but it also functions as a social networking site.

Wikis. A wiki is a public or private Web site that enables multiple users to collaboratively create, post, edit, and access information. A wiki serves as a central location where shared documents can be viewed and revised by a large or dispersed team. Unlike a standard Web site, a wiki is linked to a database that records all changes thus allowing the viewing of previous versions. The best-known wiki is the online encyclopedia Wikipedia, currently featuring 13 million articles in 262 languages.[6] Because a wiki can be used to manage and organize meeting notes, team agendas, and company calendars, it is a valuable project management tool.

Social networking. Over the past few years, social networking has grown to become one of the most popular uses of the Internet. Also called *social online communities,* social networking sites such as Facebook, MySpace, Classmates.com, and LinkedIn allow participants with various interests to connect and collaborate. Businesses have recognized e-commerce opportunities and use social media to reach out to customers and the public. Most of the sites are now targeting professionals who are welcome to establish business contacts, network, post their career credentials, apply for jobs, and seek advice.

Preparing and Composing Professional E-Mail Messages

LEARNING OBJECTIVE 2

Meet professional e-mail standards for usage, structure, and format; and follow the rules of netiquette and other best practices.

In what way has e-mail matured as a medium?

E-mail has replaced paper memos for many messages inside organizations and for some letters to external audiences. However, as Chapter 8 explains, paper-based documents still have their proper functions. Because they are committed to paper, hard-copy messages tend to carry more weight and are taken more seriously in certain situations. They are considered more formal than electronic communication. Moreover, even if e-mail writers have access to sophisticated HTML mail, the recipient may receive only plaintext messages. Poor layout and little eye appeal may result when elaborate formatting disappears on the receiver's end. The e-mail message may also be difficult to print. This is why business communicators often deliver electronic copies of memos or letters as attachments accompanied by a brief e-mail cover message. PDF documents in particular guarantee that the reader receives a message that looks exactly as the writer intended it.

Early e-mail users were encouraged to ignore stylistic and grammatical considerations. They thought that "words on the fly" required little editing or proofing. Correspondents used emoticons (such as sideways happy faces) to express their emotions. Some e-mail today is still quick and dirty. As this communication channel continues to mature, however, messages are becoming more proper and more professional.

Today it is estimated that more than 210 billion e-mails are sent each day worldwide.[7] E-mail is twice as likely as the telephone to be used to communicate at work.[8] E-mail growth has slowed recently, and rival services are booming. Twitter and Facebook, for example, offer faster, always-on connectedness. However, e-mail in the workplace is here to stay.

Because e-mail is a standard form of communication within organizations, it will likely be your most common business communication channel. E-mails perform critical tasks such as informing employees, giving directions, outlining procedures, requesting data, supplying responses, and confirming decisions.

Analyzing the Components of E-Mail Messages

Much like hard-copy memos, routine e-mails generally contain four parts: (a) an informative subject line that summarizes the message; (b) an opening that reveals the main idea immediately; (c) a body that explains and justifies the main idea; and (d) a closing that presents action information, summarizes the message, or offers a closing thought. Remember that routine messages deliver good news or standard information.

Subject Line. In e-mail messages an informative subject line is essential. It summarizes the central idea, thus providing quick identification for reading and filing. Busy readers glance at a subject line and decide when and whether to read the message. Those without subject lines are often automatically deleted.

What is the purpose of a subject line?

What does it take to get your message read? For one thing, stay away from meaningless or dangerous words. A sure way to get your message deleted or ignored is to use a one-word heading such as *Issue, Problem, Important,* or *Help.* Including a word such as *Free* is dangerous because it may trigger spam filters. Try to make your subject line "talk" by including a verb. Explain the purpose of the message and how it relates to the reader (*Need You to Showcase Two Items at Our Next Trade Show* rather than *Trade Show*). Finally, update your subject line to reflect the current message (*Staff Meeting Rescheduled for May 12* rather than *Re: Re: Staff Meeting*). Remember that a subject line is usually written in an abbreviated style, often without articles *(a, an, the)*. It need not be a complete sentence, and it does not end with a period.

Opening. Most e-mails cover nonsensitive information that can be handled in a straightforward manner. Begin by frontloading; that is, reveal the main idea immediately. Even though the purpose of the e-mail is summarized in the subject line, that purpose should be restated—and amplified—in the first sentence. As you learned in Chapters 5 and 6, busy readers want to know immediately why they are reading a message. Notice how the following indirect opener can be improved by frontloading.

How do most routine e-mails open?

Has Starbucks lost its soul? That's the claim made by Starbucks founder Howard Schultz in an e-mail to top management. According to Schultz, the coffee company's chain-oriented growth has watered down the Starbucks experience, turned the brand into a commodity, and created a "sterile cookie-cutter" atmosphere in the stores. After lamenting numerous changes, including the disappearance of Starbucks' traditional Italian espresso makers, Shultz's memo closes: "Let's get back to the core…and do the things necessary to once again differentiate Starbucks from all others." *What makes this an effective closing?*

Indirect Opening

For the past six months, the Human Resources Development Department has been considering changes to our employees' benefits plan.

Direct Opening

Please review the following proposal regarding employees' benefits, and let me know by May 20 if you approve these changes.

What type of information is covered in the body?

Body. The body provides more information about the reason for writing. It explains and discusses the subject logically. Good e-mails generally discuss only one topic. Limiting the topic helps the receiver act on the subject and file it appropriately. A writer who describes a computer printer problem and also requests permission to attend a conference runs a 50 percent failure risk. The reader may respond to the printer problem but delay or forget about the conference request.

Design your data for easy comprehension by using numbered lists, headings, tables, and other document design techniques introduced in Chapter 6. Compare the following versions of the same message. Notice how the graphic devices of bullets, columns, headings, and white space make the main points easier to comprehend.

Hard-to-Read Paragraph Version

Effective immediately are the following air travel guidelines. Between now and December 31, only account executives may take company-approved trips. These individuals will be allowed to take a maximum of two trips, and they are to travel economy or budget class only.

Improved Version

Effective immediately are the following air travel guidelines:

- Who may travel: Account executives only
- How many trips: A maximum of two trips
- By when: Between now and December 31
- Air class: Economy or budget class only

Which three features typically appear in the closing of a message?

Closing. Generally conclude an e-mail with (a) action information, dates, or deadlines; (b) a summary of the message; or (c) a closing thought. Here again the value of thinking through the message before actually writing it becomes apparent. The closing is where readers look for deadlines and action language. An effective e-mail closing might be, *Please submit your report by June 15 so that we can have your data before our July planning session.*

In more detailed messages, a summary of main points may be an appropriate closing. If no action request is made and a closing summary is unnecessary, you might end with a simple concluding thought *(I'm glad to answer your questions* or *This sounds like a useful project)*. You needn't close messages to coworkers with goodwill statements such as those found in letters to customers or clients. However, some closing thought is often necessary to prevent a feeling of abruptness. Closings can show gratitude or encourage feedback with remarks such as *I sincerely appreciate your help* or *What are your ideas on this proposal?* Other closings look forward to what's next, such as *How would you like to proceed?* Avoid closing with overused expressions such as *Please let me know if I may be of further assistance*. This ending sounds mechanical and insincere.

Which components are generally used to format e-mail messages?

Applying E-Mail Formats

Although e-mail is still a fairly new communication channel, people are beginning to agree on specific formatting and usage conventions. The following suggestions identify current formatting standards. Always check with your organization, however, to observe its practices.

Guide Words. Following the guide word *To*, some writers insert just the recipient's electronic address, such as *william.harding@schilling-voigt.com*. Other writers prefer to

ETHICS CHECK

Hiding Blind Copies

Some workers use *Bcc* (*blind carbon copy*) to copy their friends and colleagues on e-mails when they do not want the recipient to know that a third party will also read the message. Do you believe that hiding copies from the recipient is harmless and acceptable? Or is secretly distributing messages wrong because it means "going behind someone's back"?

include the receiver's full name plus the electronic address, as shown in Figure 7.1. By including full names in the *To* and *From* slots, both receivers and senders are better able to identify the message. By the way, the order of *Date, To, From*, *Subject*, and other guide words varies depending on your e-mail program and whether you are sending or receiving the message.

Most e-mail programs automatically add the current date after *Date*. On the *Cc* line (which stands for *carbon copy* or *courtesy copy*), you can type the address of anyone who is to receive a copy of the message. Remember, though, to send copies only to those people directly involved with the message. Most e-mail programs also include a line for *Bcc (blind carbon copy)*. This sends a copy without the addressee's knowledge. Many savvy writers today use *Bcc* for the names and addresses of a list of receivers, a technique that avoids revealing the addresses to the entire group. On the subject line, identify the subject of the message. Be sure to include enough information to be clear and compelling.

What purpose do greetings serve?

Greeting. Begin your message with a friendly greeting such as the following:

Hi, Rudy,	Thank you, Haley,
Greetings, Amy,	Dear Mr. Cotter:
Mike,	Dear Leslie:

Where do you include the e-mail writer's contact information, and why is it helpful?

In addition to being friendly, a greeting provides a visual cue marking the beginning of the message. Many messages are transmitted or forwarded with such long headers that finding the beginning of the message can be difficult. A greeting helps, as shown in Figure 7.1 on page 194.

In what contexts may e-mail messages be dangerous?

Body. When typing the body of an e-mail message, use standard caps and lowercase characters—never all uppercase or all lowercase characters. Cover just one topic, and try to keep the total message under three screens in length. To assist you, many e-mail programs have basic text-editing features, such as cut, copy, paste, and word-wrap.

Complimentary Closing and Signature Block. In closing your message, you may elect to sign off with a complimentary closing such as *Cheers, All the best*, or *Many thanks*. Such a closing is optional. However, providing your name is mandatory. It is also smart to include full contact information as part of your signature block. Some writers prepare a number of "signatures" in their e-mail programs, depending on what information they want to reveal. They can choose a complete signature with all their contact information, or they can use a brief version. See Figure 7.1 for an example of a complete signature.

Composing Professional E-Mail Messages

Wise business communicators are aware of the importance as well as the dangers of e-mail as a communication channel. They know that their messages can travel, intentionally or unintentionally, long distances. A quickly drafted e-mail may end up in the boss's inbox or be forwarded to an enemy. Making matters worse, computers—like elephants and spurned lovers—never forget. Even erased messages can remain on multiple servers that are backed up by companies or Internet service providers. Increasingly, e-mail has turned into the "smoking gun" uncovered by prosecutors to prove indelicate or even illegal intentions.

E-mail has become the digital equivalent of DNA evidence. A workplace study found that 21 percent of companies have been ordered by courts to surrender employee e-mail, and 13 percent of companies have battled discrimination claims stemming from e-mail or Internet abuse.[9] "E-mail has become the place where everybody loves to look," according

Spotlight on Communicators

Network consultant and author James E. Gaskin recommends writing e-mails backward: "Common e-mail composition problems include forgetting the attachment, too much information in the body of the message, a poor subject, and sending the message to the wrong people. So write your e-mails in that order: attachment, message body, subject, addressees.

When you attach your files first, you won't forget them (if you have a file attachment, of course). When you write your message text, focus on the single bit of information you are providing or the request you are making of the recipient. If you're attaching a file, the message text should address the recipient's responsibility for the attached file or files. Edit and return? Agree or not? Forward to the boss? Explain exactly why you're sending the person a file, and what you want them to do with that file."

Despite its dangers and limitations, e-mail has become a mainstream channel of communication. That's why it's important to take the time to organize your thoughts, compose carefully, and be concerned with correct grammar and punctuation. Understanding netiquette and proper tone is also important if you wish to be perceived as a professional. The pointers in Figure 7.2 will help you get off to a good start in using e-mail smartly and safely.

FIGURE 7.1 Formatting an E-Mail Message

Prewriting

Analyze: The purpose of this e-mail is to solicit feedback regarding a casual-dress policy.

Anticipate: The message is going to a subordinate who is busy but probably eager to be consulted in this policy matter.

Adapt: Use a direct approach beginning with the most important question. Strive for a positive, professional tone rather than an autocratic, authoritative tone.

2 Writing

Research: Collect secondary information about dress-down days in other organizations. Collect primary information by talking with company managers.

Organize: Begin with the main idea followed by a brief explanation and questions. Conclude with an end date and a reason.

Compose: Prepare the first draft remembering that the receiver is busy and appreciates brevity.

3 Revising

Revise: Rewrite questions to ensure that they are parallel and readable.

Proofread: Decide whether to hyphenate *casual-dress policy* and *dress-down days*. Be sure commas follow introductory clauses. Check question marks.

Evaluate: Does this memo encourage participatory management? Will the receiver be able to answer the questions and respond easily?

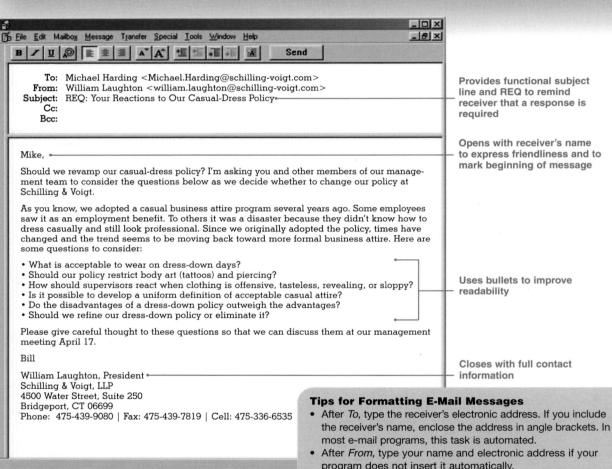

File Edit Mailbox Message Transfer Special Tools Window Help

Send

To: Michael Harding <Michael.Harding@schilling-voigt.com>
From: William Laughton <william.laughton@schilling-voigt.com>
Subject: REQ: Your Reactions to Our Casual-Dress Policy
Cc:
Bcc:

Provides functional subject line and REQ to remind receiver that a response is required

Mike,

Opens with receiver's name to express friendliness and to mark beginning of message

Should we revamp our casual-dress policy? I'm asking you and other members of our management team to consider the questions below as we decide whether to change our policy at Schilling & Voigt.

As you know, we adopted a casual business attire program several years ago. Some employees saw it as an employment benefit. To others it was a disaster because they didn't know how to dress casually and still look professional. Since we originally adopted the policy, times have changed and the trend seems to be moving back toward more formal business attire. Here are some questions to consider:

- What is acceptable to wear on dress-down days?
- Should our policy restrict body art (tattoos) and piercing?
- How should supervisors react when clothing is offensive, tasteless, revealing, or sloppy?
- Is it possible to develop a uniform definition of acceptable casual attire?
- Do the disadvantages of a dress-down policy outweigh the advantages?
- Should we refine our dress-down policy or eliminate it?

Uses bullets to improve readability

Please give careful thought to these questions so that we can discuss them at our management meeting April 17.

Bill

William Laughton, President
Schilling & Voigt, LLP
4500 Water Street, Suite 250
Bridgeport, CT 06699
Phone: 475-439-9080 | Fax: 475-439-7819 | Cell: 475-336-6535

Closes with full contact information

Tips for Formatting E-Mail Messages

- After *To*, type the receiver's electronic address. If you include the receiver's name, enclose the address in angle brackets. In most e-mail programs, this task is automated.
- After *From*, type your name and electronic address if your program does not insert it automatically.
- After *Subject*, present a clear description of the message.
- Insert the addresses of anyone receiving courtesy or blind copies.
- Include a salutation (such as *Mike; Hi, Mike*) or honorific and last name (*Dear Mr. Harding*), especially in messages to outsiders.
- Double-space (skip one line) between paragraphs.
- Do not type in all caps or in all lowercase letters.
- Include full contact information in the signature block.

Checklist

Professional E-Mail

Subject Line

- **Summarize the central idea.** Express concisely what the message is about and how it relates to the reader.
- **Include labels if appropriate.** Labels such as *FYI* (for your information) and *REQ* (required) help receivers recognize how to respond.
- **Avoid empty or dangerous words.** Don't write one-word subject lines such as *Help, Problem*, or *Free*.

Opening

- **State the purpose for writing.** Include the same information that is in the subject line, but expand it.
- **Highlight questions.** If you are requesting information, begin with the most important question, use a polite command *(Please answer the following questions about ...)*, or introduce your request courteously.
- **Supply information directly.** If responding to a request, give the reader the requested information immediately in the opening. Explain later.

Body

- **Explain details.** Arrange information logically. For detailed topics develop separate coherent paragraphs.
- **Enhance readability.** Use short sentences, short paragraphs, and parallel construction for similar ideas.
- **Apply document design.** If appropriate, provide bulleted or numbered lists, columns, tables, or other graphic devices to improve readability and comprehension.
- **Be cautious.** Remember that e-mail messages often travel far beyond their intended audiences.

Closing

- **Request action.** If appropriate, state specifically what you want the reader to do. Include a deadline, with reasons, if possible.
- **Provide a goodwill statement or a closing thought.** When communicating outside of the company or with management, include a positive goodwill statement such as *Our team enjoyed working on the feasibility report, and we look forward to your feedback*. If no action request is necessary, end with a closing thought.
- **Avoid cliché endings.** Use fresh remarks rather than overused expressions such as *If you have additional questions, please do not hesitate to call* or *Thank you for your cooperation.*

to Irwin Schwartz, president of the National Association of Criminal Defense Lawyers.[10] Recently, hundreds of e-mail messages and files were hacked from accounts owned by acclaimed British and American climate scientists, encouraging climate-change skeptics to believe that the scientists conspired to overstate the case for a human contribution to global warming. In one exchange a scientist was discussing a statistical "trick" in illustrating a sharp warming trend. Another scientist referred to climate skeptics as "idiots."[11]

Writers simply forget that their e-mail messages are permanent and searchable and can be forwarded as easily to a thousand people as to just one.[12] Another observer noted that e-mail is like an electronic truth serum.[13] Writers blurt out thoughts without thinking. For these reasons, e-mail and other electronic communication channels pose a number of dangers, to both employees and employers. Best practices for using electronic media in general are discussed at the end of the chapter.

Sometimes taken lightly, e-mail messages, like other business documents, should be written carefully. Once they leave the author's hands, they are essentially published. They can't be retrieved, corrected, or revised. Review the accompanying Checklist and Figure 7.2 for tips for writing typical e-mail messages that will accomplish what you intend.

Using Instant Messaging and Texting Professionally

Making their way from teen bedrooms to office boardrooms, instant messaging (IM) and text messaging have become permanent and powerful communication tools. IM enables you to use the Internet to communicate in real time in a private chat room with one or more individuals. It is like live e-mail or a text telephone call. More and more workers are using it as a speedy communication channel to exchange short messages.

LEARNING OBJECTIVE 3
Explain how business professionals communicate by instant messaging and texting.

FIGURE 7.2 Using E-Mail Safely and Smartly

Tips	E-Mail Best Practices Explained
Try composing offline.	Especially for important messages, use your word processing program to write offline. Then upload your message to your e-mail. This avoids "self-destructing" (losing all your writing through some glitch or pressing the wrong key) when working online.
Get the address right.	If you omit one character or misread the character *l* for the number 1, your message bounces. Solution: Use your electronic address book for people you write to frequently. Double-check every address that you key in manually. Don't accidentally reply to a group of receivers when you intend to answer only one.
Avoid misleading subject lines.	Make sure your subject line is relevant and helpful. Generic tags such as *Hi!* and *Important!* may cause your message to be deleted before it is opened.
Apply the top-of-screen test.	When readers open your message and look at the first screen, will they see what is most significant? Your subject line and first paragraph should convey your purpose. Frontload the message.
Be concise.	Omit unnecessary information. Remember that monitors are small and typefaces are often difficult to read. Organize your ideas tightly.
Don't send anything you wouldn't want published.	E-mail creates a permanent record that does not go away even when deleted. Every message is a corporate communication that can be used against you or your employer. Don't write anything that you wouldn't want your boss, your family, or a judge to read.
Don't use e-mail to avoid contact.	E-mail is inappropriate for breaking bad news or for resolving arguments. For example, it's improper to fire a person by e-mail. It is also a poor channel for clashing with supervisors, subordinates, or others. Before risking hurt feelings, call or pay the person a visit.
Care about correctness.	People are still judged by their writing, whether electronic or paper based. Sloppy e-mail messages (with missing apostrophes, haphazard spelling, and jumbled writing) make readers work too hard. They resent not only the message but also the writer.
Care about tone.	Your words and writing style affect the reader. Avoid sounding curt, negative, or domineering.
Resist humor and sarcasm.	Without the nonverbal cues conveyed by your face and your voice, humor and sarcasm can easily be misunderstood.
Limit any tendency to send blanket copies.	Send copies only to people who really need to see a message. Don't document every business decision and action with an electronic paper trail.
Never send "spam."	Sending unsolicited advertisements ("spam") either by fax or e-mail is illegal in the United States.
Use capital letters only for emphasis.	Avoid writing entire messages in all caps, which is like SHOUTING.
Don't forward without permission, and beware of long threads.	Obtain approval before forwarding a message. Beware of forwarding e-mail consisting of a long thread (string) of messages. Some content at the beginning of the thread may be inappropriate for the third receiver. Leaving sensitive information in the thread can lead to serious trouble.
Use attachments sparingly.	Because attachments may carry viruses, some receivers won't open them. Consider including short attachments within an e-mail message. If you must send a longer attachment, announce it.
Scan all messages in your inbox before replying to each individually.	Because subsequent messages often affect the way you respond, skim all messages first (especially all those from the same individual). Respond immediately to messages that can be answered in two minutes or less.
Print only when necessary.	Read and answer most messages online without saving or printing. Use folders to archive messages on special topics. Print only those messages that are complex, controversial, or involve significant decisions and follow-up.
Acknowledge receipt.	If you can't reply immediately, tell when you can (*Will respond Friday*).
Don't automatically return the sender's message.	When replying, cut and paste the relevant parts. Avoid irritating your recipients by returning the entire thread (sequence of messages) on a topic.
Revise the subject line if the topic changes.	When replying or continuing an e-mail exchange, revise the subject line as the topic changes.
Provide a clear, complete first sentence.	Avoid fuzzy replies such as *That's fine with me* or *Sounds good!* Busy respondents forget what was said in earlier messages, so be sure to fill in the context and your perspective when responding.
Never respond when you are angry.	Calm down before shooting off a response to an upsetting message. You will come up with different and better options after thinking about what was said. If possible, iron out differences in person.

(continued)

FIGURE 7.2 (Continued)

Tips	E-Mail Best Practices Explained
Don't use company computers for personal matters.	Unless your company specifically allows it, never use your employer's computers for personal messages, personal shopping, or entertainment.
Assume that all e-mail is monitored.	Employers legally have the right to monitor e-mail, and about 75 percent of them do.
Design your messages effectively.	When a message requires several screens, help the reader with headings, bulleted lists, side headings, and perhaps an introductory summary that describes what will follow. Although these techniques lengthen a message, they shorten reading time.
Consider cultural differences.	Be clear and precise in your language. Remember that figurative clichés (*pull up stakes, playing second fiddle,*) sports references (*hit a home run, play by the rules*), and slang (*cool, stoked*) may confuse nonnative speakers of English.
Double-check before hitting the Send button.	Avoid the necessity of sending a second message, which makes you look careless. Use spell check and reread for fluency before sending. Verify important facts and the spelling of names.

How do instant messaging and text messaging work?

Text messaging, or texting, is another popular means for exchanging brief messages in real time. Usually delivered by smartphone, texting requires a short message service (SMS) supplied by a cell phone service provider. Increasingly, both IM and text messages are sent by computer or handheld device.

How Instant Messaging and Texting Work

To send an instant message, you might use a public IM service, called a client, such as AOL's Instant Messenger, Yahoo Messenger, Google Talk, Jabber, or Microsoft's Windows Live Messenger. These are public IM services. Once the client is installed, you enter your name and password to log on. The software checks whether any of the users in your contact list are currently logged on. If the server finds any of your contacts, it sends a message to your computer. If the person you wish to contact is online, you can click that person's name and a window opens that you can enter text into. You enter a message such as that shown in Figure 7.3 and click **Send**. Because your client has the Internet address and port number for the computer of the person you addressed, your message is sent directly to the client on that person's computer.

Typically, IM communication is exchanged between two computers that are linked by servers. However, new applications allow people to use IM not only on their computers but also on their handheld devices such as the popular iPhone shown in Figure 7.4. Many smartphones work on a 3G cell phone network where they consume minutes, but they may also allow generally "free" Wi-Fi access where available.

Texting, on the other hand, usually requires a smartphone or PDA, and users are charged for the service, often by choosing a flat rate for a certain number of text or media messages per month. Lately, voice over Internet providers such as Skype offer texting. For a small fee, Skype subscribers can send text messages to SMS-enabled cell phones in the United States and IM messages both domestically and internationally. Again, Skype and other formerly computer-based applications are simultaneously available on mobile devices and are making communication on the go more convenient than ever before.

Pros and Cons of Instant Messaging and Texting

What are the pros and cons of instant messaging and text messaging?

In today's fast-paced world, instant messaging (IM) offers numerous benefits. Its major attraction is real-time communication with colleagues anywhere in the world—so long as a cell phone signal or a Wi-Fi connection is available. IM is a convenient alternative to the telephone and may eventually even replace e-mail. Because IM allows people to share information immediately and make decisions quickly, its impact on business communication has been dramatic. Group online chat capabilities allow coworkers on far-flung project teams to communicate instantly. The popular Skype, the voice over Internet protocol powerhouse, is but one of many providers.

Texting by SMS is rapidly spreading around the world within individual markets and regions, but incompatible wireless standards have prevented the reach of SMS across continents. Like IM, texting can be a low-cost substitute for voice calls, delivering a message

FIGURE 7.3 Instant Message for Brief, Fast Communication

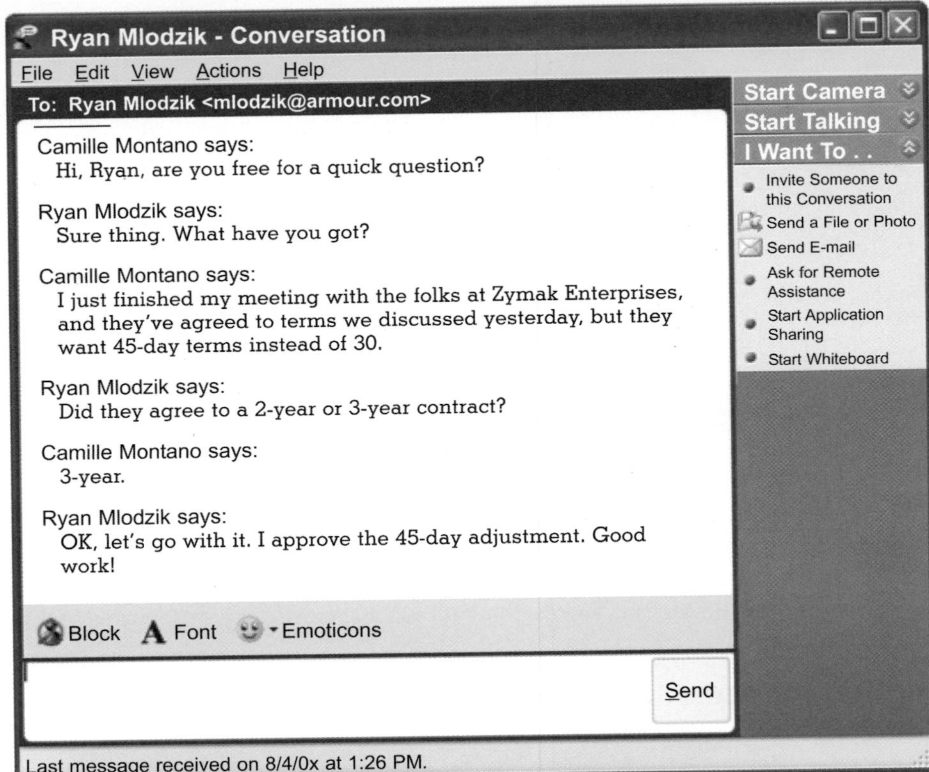

Figure 7.3 shows a brief IM exchange between a supervisor and a subordinate. Both are using a computer-based IM program. Texting is a convenient tool that enables team members to locate quick information and answers in solving immediate problems even when they are apart.

between private mobile phone users quietly and discreetly. SMS is particularly popular in Europe, New Zealand, Australia, and Asia.[14] In bulk text messages, companies around the world provide news alerts, financial information, and advertising to customers. Texts have been used in game shows for TV voting, in the United States most notably to select contestants on *American Idol.*

FIGURE 7.4 Texting and Instant Messaging with the iPhone

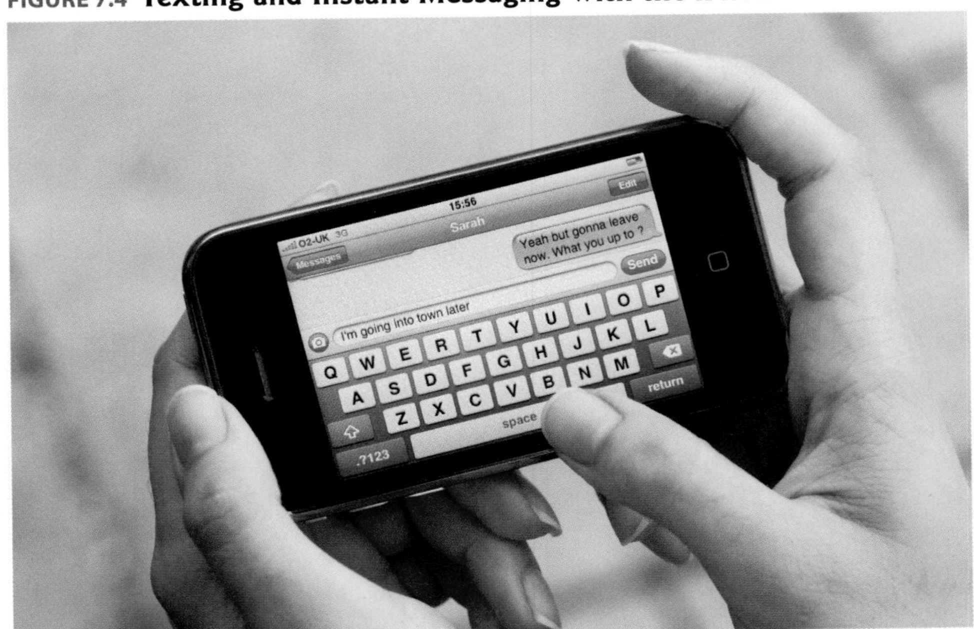

Despite Apple's exclusive distribution agreement with AT&T, the iPhone is one of the most popular handheld devices in the United States. Users like the touch-screen interface and access to countless smart applications ("apps"), many of which are free.

The immediacy of instant and text messaging has created many fans. A user knows right away whether a message was delivered. Messaging avoids phone tag and eliminates the downtime associated with personal telephone conversations. Another benefit includes "presence functionality." Coworkers can locate each other online, thus avoiding wild goose chases hunting someone who is out of the office. Many people consider instant messaging and texting productivity boosters because they enable users to get answers quickly and allow multitasking.

Despite its popularity among workers, some organizations forbid employees to use instant and text messaging for a number of reasons. Employers consider instant messaging yet another distraction in addition to the telephone, e-mail, and the Web. Organizations also fear that privileged information and company records will be revealed through public instant messaging systems, which hackers can easily penetrate. The First National Bank of Bosque County in Valley Mills, Texas, banned IM because of the risk of information leaving the institution without approval.

Companies also worry about *phishing* (fraudulent) schemes, viruses, malware (malicious software programs), and *spim* (IM spam). Like e-mail, instant and text messages are subject to discovery (disclosure); that is, they can become evidence in lawsuits. Moreover, companies fear instant messaging and texting because the services necessitate that businesses track and store messaging conversations to comply with legal requirements. This task may be overwhelming. Finally, IM and texting have been implicated in traffic accidents and inappropriate uses such as the notorious *sexting*.

Best Practices for Instant Messaging and Texting

What are some useful guidelines for writers of instant messages and text messages?

Instant messaging and texting can definitely save time and simplify communication with coworkers and customers. Before using IM or text messaging on the job, however, be sure you have permission. Do not use public systems without checking with your supervisor. If your organization does allow IM or texting, you can use it efficiently and professionally by following these best practice guidelines:

- Learn about your organization's IM policies. Are you allowed to use instant and text messaging? With whom may you exchange messages?
- Don't text or IM while driving a car. Pull over if you must read or send a message.
- Make yourself unavailable when you need to complete a project or meet a deadline.
- Organize your contact lists to separate business contacts from family and friends.
- Keep your messages simple and to the point. Avoid unnecessary chitchat, and know when to say goodbye.
- Don't use IM or text messages to send confidential or sensitive information.
- Be aware that instant or text messages can be saved. As with e-mail, don't say anything that would damage your reputation or that of your organization.
- If personal messaging is allowed, keep it to a minimum. Your organization may prefer that personal chats be done during breaks or the lunch hour.
- Show patience by not blasting multiple messages to coworkers if a response is not immediate.
- Keep your presence status up-to-date so that people trying to reach you don't waste their time.
- Beware of jargon, slang, and abbreviations, which, although they may reduce keystrokes, may be confusing and appear unprofessional.
- Respect your receivers by using good grammar and proper spelling and by proofreading carefully.

Spotlight on Communicators

© Jill & Rose Bennett Photography

Nancy Flynn, founder and executive director of the ePolicy Institute, says it's important that employers create a clear online policy and then explain it. She offers advice to companies that wish to lower their Internet risk and enhance electronic communication. Flynn believes not enough employers have instituted formal training on confidentiality and online liability. She warns any employee: "Don't start blogging. Don't start tweeting. Don't even start e-mailing until you read the company policy."

Zooming In — PART 2

Got Something to Tweet About at Work? Think Again.

The modern workplace is a potential digital minefield. The imprudent use of practically any online tool—whether e-mail, IM, texting, tweeting, blogging, or posting to Facebook—can land workers in hot water and even lead to dismissal. Here are five ways Twitter can get you canned for showing poor judgment:

1. **Sending hate tweets about the boss.** Example: *My retard boss said he put in for raises. I think he lies. He is known for that. His daddy owns the company.*

   The difference between venting around the water cooler or over lunch to a close friend and trumpeting to the world one's dislike for the superior could not be more obvious. Twitter messages can be forwarded (retweeted) and find their way to unintended recipients.

2. **Lying to the boss and bragging about it.** Example: *I so lied to my boss … I was late but I said I forgot my badge and got away with it.*

   Although lying to the boss may be woefully common, broadcasting it to one's followers on Twitter is risky. The Web and Twitter make it easy to track people, and lies have a way of emerging most unexpectedly.

3. **Romancing the boss (kissing and telling).** Example: *I give the boss what he wants, and the fringe benefits are amazing.*

   Again, even if the indiscreet twitterer had a private profile, a contact could easily retweet the message and make it retrievable. Besides, amorous relationships between superiors and subordinates are frowned on in many companies because they could open firms up to sexual harassment lawsuits. Also, the boss could be tracking the tattletale on Twitter and would probably not appreciate the leaking of the affair.

4. **Announcing the desire to quit.** Example: *So close to quitting my job right now. Sometimes I can't [expletive] stand this place [expletive] moron assistant plant manager I'm about to deck him.*

   The wish to quit may come true, but prematurely so and not according to plan. If you hate your job, complain to your pet or vent with your friends over dinner, but don't shout it out on Twitter. Smart workers leave a workplace on good terms knowing that they may need references. They do not burn bridges, much less publicly.

© JOHN MACDOUGALL/AFP/Getty Images

5. **Blocking your boss.** Example: *i kept my promise … my boss thought she was gonna follow me on here … i BLOCKED her* [expletive] *ASAP.*

   Preventing the boss from seeing your profile is no guarantee that he or she won't receive your hateful missives through another source. As Mark, an expert blogger, advises: "The golden rule of not getting yourself fired over 'tweets' is simple—just don't vent your work and boss frustrations publicly."[15]

Critical Thinking

- How do you explain the amazing lapses of judgment apparent in the tweets above?
- How widespread is the use of Twitter among your friends, and how do they benefit from the service?
- What are the most effective ways to warn young people about the dangers to their careers that lurk online?

Using Podcasts or Webcasts, Blogs, and Wikis for Business

LEARNING OBJECTIVE 4

Identify professional uses of podcasts, blogs, and wikis; and describe prudent policies to protect authors of electronic content.

Like Twitter, podcasts, blogs, and wikis are part of the new user-centered virtual environment called Web 2.0. Far from being passive consumers, today's Internet users have the power to create Web content; interact with businesses and each other; review products, self-publish, or blog; contribute to wikis; or tag and share images and other files. Individuals wield enormous power because they can potentially reach huge audiences. Businesses often rightly fear the wrath of disgruntled employees and customers, or they curry favor with influential plugged-in opinion leaders.

What is Web 2.0, and what are its characteristics?

The democratization of the Web means that in the online world, Internet users can bypass gatekeepers who filter content in the traditional print and visual media. Hence, even extreme views often reach audiences of thousands or even millions. The dangers are obvious. Fact checking often falls by the wayside, buzz may become more important than truth, and a single keystroke can make or destroy a reputation. This section addresses prudent business uses of podcasts, blogs, and wikis because you are likely to encounter these and other electronic communication tools on the job.

What purposes do business podcasts serve?

Business Podcasts or Webcasts

Although the terms *podcast* and *podcasting* have caught on, they are somewhat misleading. The words *broadcasting* and *iPod* combined to create the word *podcast*; however, audio and video files can be played on any number of devices, not just Apple's iPod. *Webcasting* for audio and *vcasting* for video content would be more accurate, but most people simply refer to them as podcasting. Podcasts can extend from short clips of a few minutes to 30-minute or longer digital files. Naturally, large video files gobble up a lot of memory, so they tend to be streamed on a Web site rather than downloaded.

Spotlight on Communicators

© Terri Miller/E-Visual Communications, Inc.

Donagh Herlihy, chief information officer of Avon Products, says "The big vision: We're finally getting there. Today, wherever you are, you can connect to all the information you need." Avon's 150,000 sales leaders are now equipped with a cloud-based computer system that they can tap into with smartphones and PCs anywhere in the world. No longer is information stored on individual machines; rather, it is combined into a digital "cloud," or remote computer networks, accessible from various smart devices.

How Organizations Use Podcasts. Like blogging, podcasting has experienced large growth and has spread among various user groups online. Major news organizations and media outlets podcast radio shows (e.g., National Public Radio) and TV shows, from ABC to Fox. Podcasts are also used in education. Students can access instructors' lectures, interviews, sporting events, and other content. Apple's iTunes U is perhaps the best-known example of free educational podcasts from Berkeley, Stanford, and other universities. Unlike streaming video that users can view only with an active Internet connection, podcasts encoded as MP3 files can be downloaded to a computer, a smartphone, or an MP3 player to be enjoyed on the go, often without subsequent Web access.

Delivering and Accessing Podcasts. Businesses have embraced podcasting for sending audio and video messages that do not require a live presence yet offer a friendly human face. Because they can broadcast repetitive information that does not require interaction, podcasts can replace costlier live teleconferences. IBM is training its sales force with podcasts that are available anytime. Real estate agents create podcasts to enable buyers to take virtual walking tours of available properties at their leisure. HR policies can also be presented in the

LUGGED IN

Cloud Computing

© iStockphoto.com/Alex Slobodkin

For businesses, cloud computing might as well mean "cloud nine." Companies are increasingly relying on "cloud-based" computer systems that can be accessed by mobile phones and PCs anytime and anywhere. Google is spearheading efforts to enable future consumers to use inexpensive gadgets to manage their files and media in huge data centers on the Internet. If you use Flickr, Gmail, or Facebook, to name a few, you are already participating in cloud computing. Your photos and other data are stored in a remote location, and you can access them by using your PC, laptop, netbook, smartphone, or PDA.

The Lure and Lucre of the Cloud. Companies are lured to cloud computing by the promise of greater efficiency and higher profits. Avon hopes that its move to manage a sales force of 6 million reps worldwide with cloud computing will lead to greater effectiveness and higher sales. Blue Cross of Pennsylvania has enabled its 300,000 members to access medical histories and claims information with their smartphones. Like other tech companies, Serena Software has fully embraced the cloud, even using Facebook as the primary source of internal communication. Coca-Cola Enterprises has provided 40,000 sales reps, truck drivers, and other workers in the field with portable devices to connect with the home office instantly to respond to changing customer needs and problems on the road.

Vast Opportunities and Risks. The shift from storing information on isolated machines to information sharing in digital and social networks is seen by some as the largest growth opportunity since the Internet boom. The market for cloud products and services will likely soar. However, skeptics warn that caution about the risks of convenience is in order. For one thing, once the information leaves our computing device for the cloud, we don't know who may intercept it. In addition to data security, networks must be reliable, so that users can access them anytime. Google's recent software glitch allowed unauthorized access to a certain percentage of user files and left some Gmail customers unable to use their online applications.

Career Application

Which cloud services or applications are you already using? What are their advantages and disadvantages? Can you identify security risks that our desire for convenience may invite? Is convenience worth the risk? Should sensitive data and potentially revealing information be entrusted to the cloud?

form of podcasts for unlimited viewing on demand or as convenient. Marketing pitches also lend themselves to podcasting.

Podcasts are featured on media Web sites and company portals or shared on social networking sites and blogs. They can usually be streamed or downloaded as media files. As we will see, really simple syndication (RSS) allows the distribution of current information published in podcasts, blogs, video files, and news items. Users can select RSS feeds from various sources and personalize the information they wish to receive. GreenTalk Radio, shown in Figure 7.5, is just one example of a Web site that provides podcasts on many topics, such as green living and environmental stewardship. Frequently, business podcasts include short commercial segments. Nonprofit organizations may play public-service announcements to raise money. Interestingly, this ease of access has not produced multitudes of independent podcasters; the medium is still dominated by professional news organizations such as National Public Radio. Moreover, despite its growth in the last three years, podcasting is far from being a huge Internet phenomenon: fewer than 20 percent of Internet users have listened to a podcast this year.[16]

How is a simple podcast created?

Creating a Podcast. Producing a simple podcast does not require sophisticated equipment. With inexpensive recording, editing, and publishing software such as the popular Propaganda, ePodcast Creator, Audacity, or Gabcast, users can inform customers, mix their own music, or host interviews. In fact, any digital recorder can be used to create a quality primitive podcast, especially if the material is scripted and well rehearsed. If you are considering creating your own podcast, here are a few tips:

- **Decide whether to record one podcast or a series.** You can create a one-time podcast for a specific purpose or a series of podcasts on a related subject. Make sure you have enough material to sustain a steady flow of information.
- **Download software.** The program Audacity is available for free; other popular recording and editing software programs are relatively inexpensive.

FIGURE 7.5 GreenTalk Radio Podcasts

In his audio podcasts, host Sean Daily examines eco-friendly lifestyles and dispenses tips on becoming more "green." Although he maintains a Web site shown here, Daily connects more personally with viewers and listeners through his podcasts.

- **Obtain hardware.** Depending on the sound quality you desire, you may need a sophisticated microphone and other audio equipment. The recording room must be properly shielded against noise, echo, and other interference. Many universities and some libraries provide language labs that feature recording booths.
- **Organize the message.** Make sure your broadcast has a beginning, middle, and end. Build in some redundancy. Tell the listeners what you will tell them, then tell them, and finally, tell them what you've told them. This principle, known to effective PowerPoint users, also applies to podcasting. Previews, summaries, and transitions are important to help your audience follow the message.
- **Choose an extemporaneous or scripted delivery.** Think about how you will deliver the information, whether speaking freely or using a manuscript. Extemporaneous delivery means that you prepare, but you use only brief notes. It usually sounds more spontaneous and natural than reading from a script, but it can also lead to redundancy, repetition, and flubbed lines. Reading from a script, if done skillfully, can sound natural and warm. However, in the wrong hands, reading can come across as mechanical and amateurish.
- **Prepare and practice.** Before recording, do a few practice runs. Editing audio or video is difficult and time-consuming. Try to get your recording right, so that you won't have to edit much.
- **Publish and distribute your message.** If you post the podcast to a blog, you can introduce it and solicit your audience's feedback. Consider distributing your podcast by an RSS feed.

Professional Blogs

How do companies use blogs?

A blog is a Web site with journal entries on any imaginable topic usually written by one person, although some blogs feature multiple commentators. Typically, readers leave feedback. Businesses use blogs to keep customers and employees informed and to interact with them. The biggest advantage of business blogs is that they potentially reach a far-flung, vast audience. Marketing firms and their clients are looking closely at blogs because blogs can produce unbiased consumer feedback faster and more cheaply than such staples of consumer research as focus groups and surveys. Employees and executives at companies such as Google, Sun Microsystems, IBM, and Hewlett-Packard maintain blogs. They use blogs to communicate internally with employees and externally with clients. Currently, 78 (15.6 percent) of Fortune 500 companies are blogging.[17]

As an online diary or journal, a blog allows visitors to leave public comments. At this time, writers have posted 70 million blogs, up nearly 30 percent in one year.[18] However, only about half of these blogs are active, meaning that posts were published within three months. A recent Forrester Research study suggests that 25 percent of the U.S. population read a blog once a month.[19] Although blogs may still be underused, they do represent an amazing new information stream if used wisely.

How Companies Use Blogs

The potential applications of blogs in business are vast. Like other Web 2.0 phenomena, corporate blogs usually invite feedback and help build communities. Specifically, companies use blogs for public relations, customer relations, crisis communication, market research, viral marketing, internal communication, and recruiting.

Public Relations, Customer Relations, and Crisis Communication.

One of the prominent uses of blogs is to provide up-to-date company information to the press and the public. Blogs can be written by executives or by rank-and-file employees. Jonathan Schwartz, president and CEO of Sun Microsystems, is an occasional blogger. General Electric's Global research blog addresses industry insiders and the interested public. Ask a Blueshirt, a site authored by Best Buy employees, offers tips and other types of customer support.

A company blog is a natural forum for late-breaking news, especially when disaster strikes. Business bloggers can address rumors and combat misinformation. Although a blog cannot replace other communication channels in an emergency, it should be part of the overall effort to soothe the public's emotional reaction with a human voice of reason.

Market Research and Viral Marketing. Because most blogs invite feedback, they can be invaluable sources of opinion from customers and industry experts. In addition to monitoring visitor comments on their corporate blogs, many companies now have appointed employees who scrutinize the blogosphere for buzz and positive or negative postings about their organization and products.

The term *viral marketing* refers to the rapid spread of messages online, much like infectious diseases that pass from person to person. Marketers realize the potential of getting the word out about their products and services in the blogosphere, where their messages are often cross-referenced and linked by interested bloggers. Viral messages must be unexpected and elicit an emotional response, much like BMW's hip series of short films by popular directors starring Clive Owen.

Online Communities. Like Twitter, which has a loyal core following, company blogs can attract a devoted community of participants who want to keep informed about company events, product updates, and other news. In turn, those enthusiasts can contribute new ideas. Similar to Dell's Ideastorm, Starbucks' blog Ideas In Action solicits product and service ideas from customers.

Internal Communication and Recruiting. Blogs can be used to keep virtual teams on track and share updates on the road. Members in remote locations can stay in touch by smartphone and other devices, exchanging text, images, sound, and video clips. In many companies, blogs have replaced hard-copy publications in offering late-breaking news or tidbits of interest to employees. They may feature profiles of high-performing workers, information about benefits, and so forth.

Blogs mirror the company culture and present an invaluable opportunity for job candidates to size up a potential employer and the people working there.

What are some tips for crafting effective professional blogs?

Tips for Creating a Professional Blog

Blogging has grown up as a commercial activity and now offers sound business opportunities. Some bloggers make a living, although most remain unknowns in the boundless thickets of information on the Internet. To even have a shot at competing with established blog sites, consider the following guidelines if you would like to start a successful business blog:

- **Identify your audience.** As with any type of communication, you must know your audience to decide what to write to get people to read your blog. Does your blog stand out? What makes you interesting and unique?
- **Find a home for your blog.** You can use software that will let you attach a blog function to your Web site. Alternatively, you can join a blog hosting site that will provide a link on your Web site to attract visitors. You can usually find templates and other options to help build traffic to your site, especially if you use trackers that identify recent posts and popular message threads. Visit **http://www.businessblogconsulting.com** to learn more about blog publishing. Windows Live Spaces at **http://home.spaces.live.com** will help you set up a blog effortlessly and quickly.
- **Craft your message.** Blog about topics that showcase your expertise and insights. Offer a fresh, unique perspective on subjects your audience cares about. Your writing should be intriguing and sincere. Experts suggest that authors get to know the blogosphere in their industry and comment on what other bloggers are writing about. Stick with what you know.
- **Make "blogrolling" work for you.** Your goal is to attract repeat visitors to your blog. One way to achieve this objective is to increase traffic between blogs. "Blogrolling" means that you provide links to other sites or blogs on the Web that you find valuable and that are related to your business or industry. Respond to other bloggers' postings and link to them.
- **Attract search engines by choosing the right keywords.** In headlines and text, emphasize potential search terms that may draw traffic to your site. Focus on one topic and use a variety of synonyms to propel your blog to the top of search engine listings. An import

Ethics Check

Fired for Blogging

Former flight attendant Ellen Simonetti was fired by Delta Air Lines for posting on her blog "Queen of Sky" photos showing her in uniform. Simonetti claims that her dismissal violated her free-speech rights and was an act of sexual discrimination. She has been fighting her firing since 2004, parlaying her fame into a book and even a few talk show appearances. Whose rights take precedence, the employee's or the employer's?

company doing business with China would want to stress the keywords *import* and *China* as well as *trade, Asia,* and so forth, in addition to more industry-specific terms, such as *toys.*

- **Blog often.** Provide fresh content regularly. Stay current. Stale information puts off visitors. Post short, concise messages, but do so often.
- **Monitor the traffic to your site.** If necessary, vary your subjects to attract interest. If traffic slows down, experiment with new themes while staying with your core business and expertise. Also, evaluate the effectiveness of your publishing platform. Some blog publishing sites are more valuable than others in increasing your blog's visibility to search engines.
- **Seek permission.** If you are employed, explore your company's blogging policy. Even if neither a policy nor a prohibition against blogging exists, avoid writing about your employer, coworkers, customers, and events at the office, however veiled your references may be. The Internet is abuzz with stories about bloggers who got fired for online indiscretions.
- **Stay away from inappropriate topics.** Whether you are a rank-and-file employee or a freelance blogger, remember not to write anything you wouldn't want your family, friends, and the public at large to read. Blogs are not private journal entries; therefore, don't entrust to them any risqué, politically extreme, or private information.

Wikis and Collaboration

What is a wiki, and how is it useful to businesses?

At least as important to business as blogs are new communication tools such as wikis and social networking sites. A wiki is a Web site that employs easy-to-use collaborative software to allow users to create documents that can be edited by tapping into the same technology that runs the well-known online encyclopedia Wikipedia. Large companies, such as British Telecom, encourage their employees to team up to author software, launch branding campaigns, and map cell phone stations. Most projects are facilitated with the help of wikis, a tool that's especially valuable across vast geographic distances and multiple time zones.[20]

How Businesses Use Wikis. Far from being just a tool for geeks, wikis are used beyond information technology departments. The five main uses range from providing a shared internal knowledge base to storing templates for business documents:

- **The global wiki.** For companies with a global reach, a wiki is an ideal tool for information sharing between headquarters and satellite offices. Team members can easily edit their work and provide input to the home office and each other.
- **The wiki knowledge base.** Teams or departments use wikis to collect and disseminate information to large audiences creating a database for knowledge management. For example, an IT department may compile frequently asked questions that help users resolve the most common problems themselves. Human resources managers may update employee policies, make announcements, and convey information about benefits.
- **Wikis for meetings.** Wikis can facilitate feedback before and after meetings or serve as repositories of meeting minutes. In fact, wikis may replace some meetings, yet still keep a project on track. An often-cited example of a huge global wiki meeting is IBM's famous massive online discussion and brainstorming session that involved more than 100,000 participants from more than 160 countries.
- **Project management with wikis.** Wikis offer a highly interactive environment ideal for projects by enabling information to be centralized for easy access and user input. All participants have the same information available and can share ideas freely, more freely than in traditional face-to-face meetings. Instead of a top-down information flow, wikis empower employees and foster a team environment in which ideas can thrive.
- **Documentation and wikis.** Wikis can help to document projects large and small as well as technical and nontechnical. Wikis may also provide templates for reports.

FIGURE 7.6 Creating a Wiki With Google Sites and Google Docs

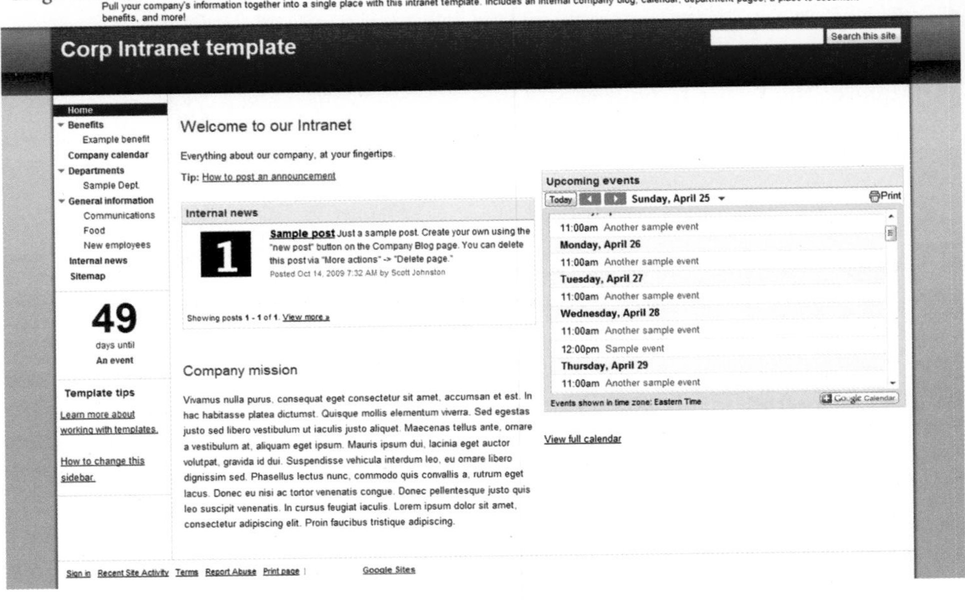

This screen shot of Organic City's intranet shows a template created in Google Sites, a simple, template-driven wiki and document editor. Google Sites and the user-friendly document editing and revision tool Google Docs allow users to create, edit, share, and manage documents online in real time. Unlike in typical wikis, here multiple editors can modify files simultaneously.

What are a few helpful guidelines for wiki contributors?

How to Be a Valuable Wiki Contributor. Whether you wish to contribute to a wiki on the Web or at work, try to be an effective participant. As with most electronic communication, abide by the conventions of polite society, and follow the commonsense rules explained here.

First, show respect and watch out for improper or ambiguous language. Don't attack or otherwise severely criticize another contributor. Don't be a "troll," an annoying individual who posts irrelevant, controversial, or provocative comments online that may anger fellow users and disrupt a discussion. Because expression online allows for little subtlety, give some thought to how your words could be interpreted. Members of online communities can form deep bonds and strongly dislike contributors they consider vicious or mean.

Pay attention to correct grammar and spelling, and verify your facts. Every comment you contribute is essentially published on the Web and available to any reader. If the content appears on the company intranet, it is for the whole company to see. Don't be sloppy; it could cause you to suffer embarrassment or worse. Wikipedia, a wiki that is trying to marry credibility with its desire for openness, recently tightened the rules for its editors after Internet vandals prematurely announced Senator Edward Kennedy's death and pronounced his colleague, Senator Robert Byrd, dead as well. Errors introduced by cyber attacks and innocent errors alike are often perpetuated by people who blindly trust wiki content.

Follow the guidelines for contributors, and give credit where credit is due. Read the rules to make sure your work fits into the group effort in style, content, and format. As a newbie, ask for help if necessary. Leave your ego behind. Contributors to a wiki are part of a team, not individual authors who can reasonably expect recognition or maintain control over their writing. When borrowing, be sure to cite your sources to avoid plagiarism.

Negotiating Social and Professional Networking Sites

LEARNING OBJECTIVE 5

Understand business uses of social and professional networking sites as well as RSS feeds and social bookmarking.

Far from being only entertaining leisure sites, social networking sites such as Facebook, MySpace, and Twitter are used by businesses for similar reasons and in much the same way as podcasts, blogs, and wikis. Social networking sites enable businesses to connect with customers and employees, share company news, and exchange ideas. Social online communities for professional audiences (e.g., LinkedIn) help recruiters find talent and encounter potential employees before hiring them.

Tapping Into Social Networks

How are businesses using social networking sites?

Business interest in social networking sites is not surprising if we consider that 73 percent of millennials, also called Generation Y, regularly socialize and chat online. An average of 55 percent of all consumers between 14 and 75 regularly visit social online communities. All groups spend between 11 and 19 hours a week on the Internet solely for entertainment.[21] Not surprisingly, then, businesses are trying to catch on and tap the vast potential of social networking.

How Businesses Use Social Networks. Some firms use social online communities for brainstorming and teamwork. They provide the collaboration tools and watch what happens. British Telecom (BT) has about 11,000 employees on Facebook in addition to offering its own internal social network. A British Telecom IT executive says that his company can observe online relationships to see how information travels and decision making occurs. The company is able to identify teams that form spontaneously and naturally and then assigns targeted projects to them. Idea generators are easy to spot. The BT executive considers these contributors invaluable, suggesting that "a new class of supercommunicators has emerged."[22] The key to all the new media is that they thrive in a highly mobile and interactive Web 2.0 environment.

Other companies harness the power of online communities to boost their brand image or to provide a forum for collaboration. McDonald's has a strong presence on Facebook boasting nearly 1.5 million "fans." The fast-food chain also maintains a private networking site, StationM, for its 650,000 hourly employees in 15,000 locations across the United States and Canada.[23]

McDonald's and British Telecom are not the only companies running their own social networks. Insurer MetLife has launched connect.MetLife, an online social network collaboration tool. Resembling Facebook, this internal networking tool sits safely behind the corporate firewall.[24] Best Buy has created its own social network, Blue Shirt Nation, with currently more than 20,000 participants, most of them sales associates. IBM's in-house social network, Beehive, has 30,000 employees on it. Managers notice avid networkers who create buzz and promote the brand. The drawback is that quieter employees may be overlooked.[25]

What dangers does social networking pose for businesses?

Potential Risks of Social Networks for Businesses. Online social networks hold great promise for businesses while also presenting some risk. Most managers want plugged-in employees with strong tech skills. They like to imagine their workers as brand

FIGURE 7.7 Big Companies Rule on Facebook: Netflix

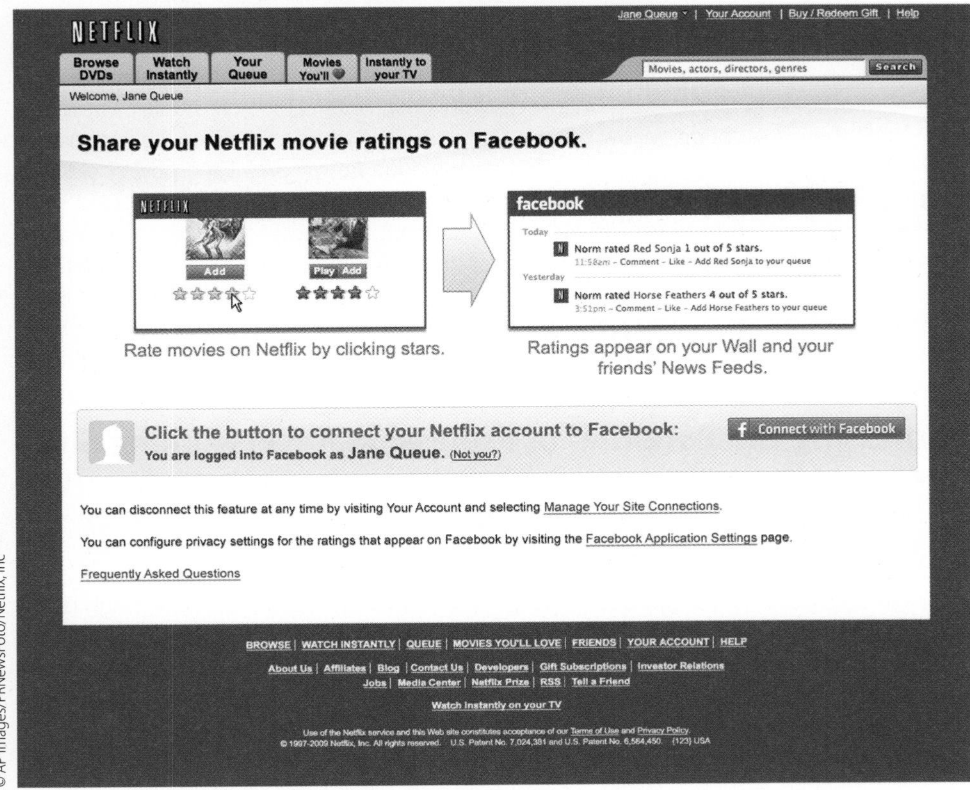

Facebook recently reached 350 million users. The site allows registered users to create individual home pages and to choose from more than 200 groups based on their interests. Large corporations seem to thrive on Facebook. *Slate* magazine ranked Coca-Cola "first among companies with the best Facebook presences." Newer companies such as online film rental service Netflix may draw 100,000 fans, as opposed to Coca-Cola's whopping 5,300,000 fans.

ambassadors. They fantasize about their products becoming overnight sensations thanks to viral marketing. However, they also fret about incurring productivity losses, compromising trade secrets, attracting the wrath of huge Internet audiences, and facing embarrassment over inappropriate and damaging employee posts.[26]

Businesses take different approaches to the "dark side" of social networking. Some, such as Zappos.com, take a hands-off approach to employee online activity. Others, such as IBM, have drafted detailed policies to cover all forms of self-expression online. Some of IBM's guidelines include being honest about one's identity, accepting personal responsibility for published posts, and hitting **Send** only after careful thought. The technology giant asks its workers to avoid any controversies outside their professional role. The company wants workers to "add value" as they are building their social reputations, not dwell on trivia.[27] Finally, Enterprise Rent-A-Car and other organizations block some or all social sites.

Ethics Check

Social Media Help Spread Errors Like Wildfire

Electronics retailer Best Buy recently offered a 52-inch flat-screen TV worth $1,799.99 for $9.99 on its Web site. Within hours bloggers and Twitter users posted jokes about this "steal," and some insisted that Best Buy honor the advertised price. The company quickly corrected the online pricing error and would not accept orders at the incorrect price. Was Best Buy obligated to honor the offer?

Younger workers in particular are often stunned when their employers block access to Facebook, Gmail, and other popular Web destinations. One 27-year-old Chicago resident complained about his former employer: "It was a constant battle between the people that saw technology as an advantage, and those that saw it as a hindrance."[28] The key is to strike a balance between allowing employees access to the Web and protecting security and ensuring productivity. Consultant Gary Rudman sees parallels to old-fashioned chatting around the water cooler or making personal phone calls, grudgingly accepted as they were by managers: "These two worlds will continue to collide until there's a mutual understanding that performance, not Internet usage, is what really matters."[29]

Personal mobile devices make monitoring during work time tougher, and some companies are beginning to open access. Kraft Foods allows "reasonable" personal use as long as it does not interfere with job duties. Because the lines between work time and personal time are increasingly blurry, many companies hesitate to ban the Internet outright on the job. Some allow partial access by limiting what employees can do online. They may disable file sharing to protect sensitive information.

Tips for Using Social Networking Sites and Keeping Your Job. Experts agree that, as with any public online activity, users of social networking sites would do well to exercise caution. Privacy is a myth, and sensitive information should not be shared lightly, least of all risqué photographs. Furthermore, refusing "friend" requests or "unfriending" individuals could jeopardize professional relationships. Consider the following tip by career counselor Julie Powell[30] if you like to visit social networking sites and want to keep your job: Establish boundaries. Don't share information online that you would not be comfortable sharing openly in the office.

The advice to think twice before posting online applies to most communication channels used on the job. Facebook expert and blogger Nick O'Neill cautions account holders never to assume that the content they post on a social networking site is protected unless they have activated the privacy option. Many users leave their pages open and risk trouble with their employers by assuming that online comments are hidden from view.[31] Even privacy settings, however, do not guarantee complete protection from prying eyes.

Among the many risks in the cyber world are inappropriate photographs and making "friends" online. Tags make pictures searchable so that an embarrassing college incident may resurface years later. Another potential minefield, says consultant Rachel Weingarten, is rejecting friend requests from some colleagues while accepting such offers from others.[32] The snubbed coworker may harbor ill feelings as a result. Blocking a user for no apparent reason could also be interpreted as a rude rejection.

Harnessing the Potential of Professional Networking Sites

What are the potential rewards of using professional networking sites such as LinkedIn?

Experts agree that connecting online offers professional opportunities by expanding the traditional Rolodex. They see social networking online as a natural extension of work.[33] Small businesses may view such sites as forums for sharing slideshow presentations and other office documents. Artists may feature their work. Medical doctors can discuss surgical techniques with peers.

As we have seen, the lines between social and professional networking are increasingly blurry. However, among business-oriented Web sites where users can post job openings, résumés, and career profiles, LinkedIn is the most popular networking tool, at least in the United States. Xing is attracting large professional audiences in Europe. A great value of such business networking sites is that they can serve as a source for referrals and recommendations. Job seekers can also browse jobs posted by a company with a LinkedIn presence, such as Adobe Systems shown in Figure 7.8.

FIGURE 7.8 Adobe Systems Jobs on LinkedIn

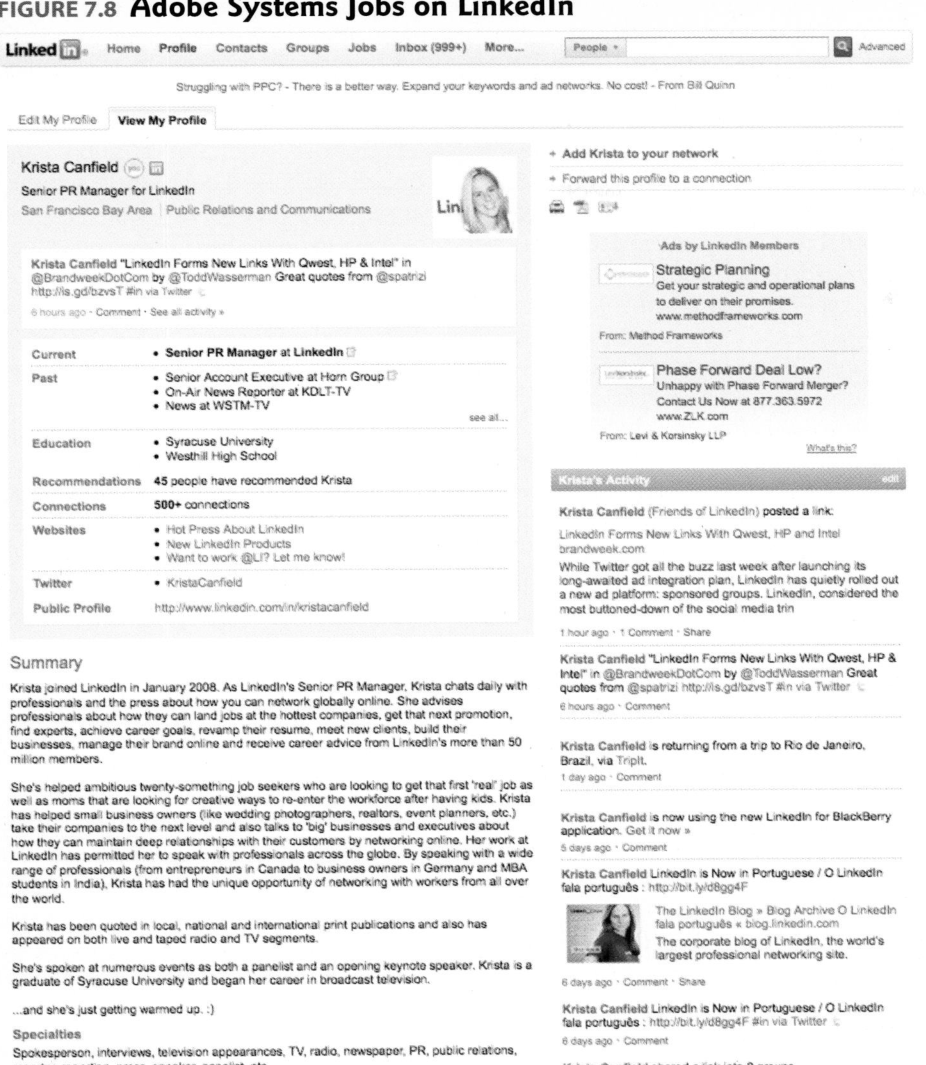

Multimedia and creativity software company Adobe Systems uses the professional networking site LinkedIn to post job openings in its global branch offices.

Hiring experts agree that about three quarters of U.S. companies view social media—mostly LinkedIn—as indispensable outlets for recruiting.[34] They recommend that job seekers keep their profiles "clean"—that is, free of risqué photos, profanity, and negative comments. Instead, job candidates are encouraged to highlight awards, professional goals, and accomplishments. Although professional networking sites cannot replace face-to-face interviews, they allow hiring managers to form first impressions before inviting job hunters, or to vet interviewees being considered for an open position.

The advantages that social and professional networking sites offer recruiters and applicants are plain. In the right hands, the sites are inexpensive, simple, and fast ways to advertise current business opportunities and to connect. However, as innovative as this new type of job search seems to be, the basics remain the same. Candidates need to craft their profiles with the same care they use when putting together their traditional résumés and cover letters. The job hunter's public appearance online must always be professional, and the profile should be up-to-date. You will learn more about job searching online in Chapter 15.

Sharing Information Through RSS Feeds and Social Bookmarking

What is really simple syndication (RSS), and how is it used?

You may wonder how businesspeople navigate the vast resources available on the Internet. Seeking information on the Web that is relevant to you and your business can be time-consuming and sometimes tedious, especially if it means browsing many Web sites for updates. Really simple syndication, RSS for short, is a time-saver, allowing users to monitor many news sources in one convenient spot. Likewise, social bookmarking helps busy professionals stay informed about topics of interest and negotiate the vast information jungle of the Web.

© VectorZilla/Shutterstock.com

Really Simple Syndication. RSS, a fast and easy way to search and manage information, is a data file format capable of transmitting changing Web content. News organizations, bloggers, and other online information providers syndicate (i.e., publish and distribute) their content to subscribers. RSS documents are called feeds or channels, and they can be read most efficiently with a Web-based feed reader (also known as an aggregator), an easy-to-use software application. Feeds help alert subscribers to up-to-the-minute blog entries, news items, videos, and podcasts from various sources.

How does RSS work? Each time a syndicated Web site is updated, a summary of the new information travels by RSS feed to the site's subscribers. Users can read RSS feeds within their Internet browsers and in e-mail programs such as MS Outlook, but local files are likely to become very large. This is why many subscribers prefer stand-alone "cloud" reader programs online that automatically receive updates from the subscribers' favorite Web sites. Some of the popular news aggregators are Google Reader, Bloglines, SharpReader, NetNewsWire, and Straw. Web-based feed readers also work well with mobile devices, helping busy executives keep up with customized news feeds on the go.

Content providers have a vital interest in providing RSS feeds. For one thing, feeds increase traffic to syndicated Web sites because they can be indexed in search engines and tagged to appear in feed lists, making them easier to find. This helps content providers stay ahead of the vast competition in cyberspace. A number of software applications automatically create RSS feeds—Mambo or Drupal are just two among many free, open-source programs available. Forward-looking companies such as retailer Target, online travel sites such as Travelocity, and many airlines have been using RSS feeds to alert customers to weekly sales and special offers.

In what ways is social bookmarking helpful to business users?

Social Bookmarking. In the battle for "eyeballs" on the Internet, social bookmarking is another critical component. Business Web sites, blogs, and other online content gain an edge if readers link to them and, thus, share content with other online users. Digg, Del.icio.us, Reddit, StumbleUpon, and Squidoo are just a few of the many fast-growing social bookmarking and content aggregator (collector) Web sites. Social bookmarking helps users search, organize, manage, and store bookmarks on the Web with the help of metadata—that is, information tags or keywords.

Many Web sites, blogs, and other content providers on the Internet offer various widgets or icons of social bookmarking sites to enable content sharing. Web publishers hope readers will link their information to social bookmarking sites and alert others to the information. Figure 7.9 shows

FIGURE 7.9 Social Bookmarking Sites

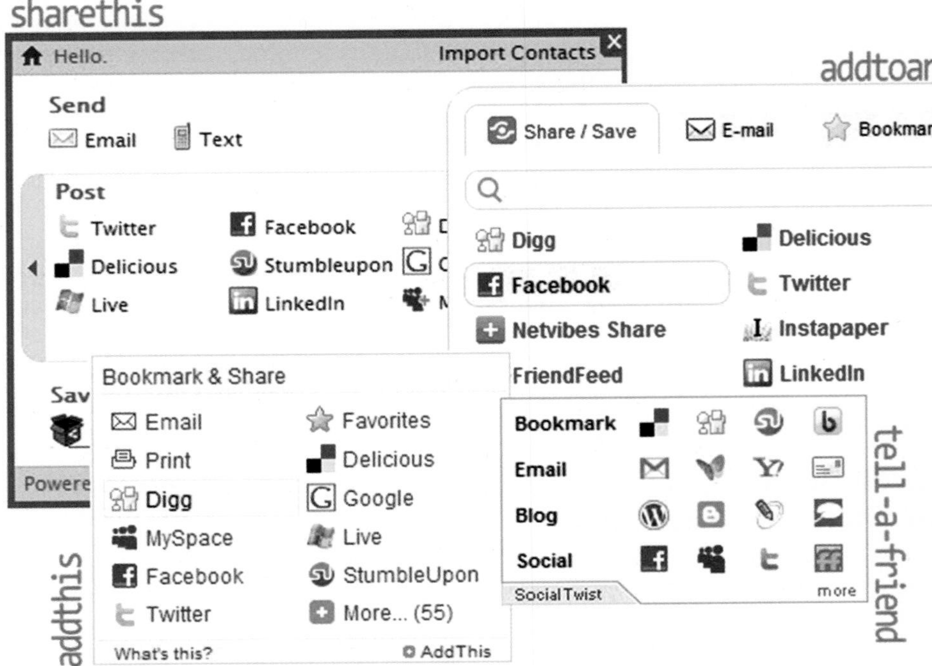

Bloggers and other online content providers don't need to list dozens of buttons so that users can spread content on the Internet. Just one *Share* widget allows visitors to choose which social service they want to use for sharing or bookmarking.

common configurations of bookmarking icons that Web designers insert into Web pages to allow visitors to share content.

Typical search engines favor Web resources generating the most traffic. High-traffic Web sites are those that rack up the most hits and are indexed and bookmarked the most. As a result, they receive a high ranking and pop up topmost in keyword searches. Social bookmarking sites are aggregators, which means that they compile and list current, popular news items that will most likely appeal to their readers.

Perhaps you can see now how RSS feeds and social bookmarking sites could help you stay abreast of breaking news from many sources and save you valuable time. Whether you wish to grab a broadcast from CNN.com or check the most recent sports scores, look for the square orange RSS feed icon on your favorite Web sites or a rectangular button with the letters RSS or XML. On most high-traffic Web sites, you will also see *Share* links, or widgets, that will take you to social bookmarking sites.

Spotlight on Communicators

© Scott Townsend

Scott Townsend, marketing director for United Linen & Uniform Services in Oklahoma, uses Twitter along with a corporate blog to share information with customers and to listen to them: "Businesses need to be careful when using social media outlets such as Twitter because they tend to want to start selling.... But Twitter is more about creating and furthering a relationship with a customer, becoming a resource to them and yourself [to be] available to provide solutions."

Checklist

Using Electronic Media Professionally: Dos and Don'ts

Dos: Know Workplace Policies and Avoid Private Use of Media at Work

- **Learn your company's rules.** One employee knew that her employer restricted personal use of work computers, but she believed it focused on Web surfing, not e-mail. She was stunned when her agency fired her after finding 418 personal e-mail messages on her PC.[37] Companies have been slow to adapt Internet policies to advances such as IM, texting, and tweeting. Being informed is your best protection.
- **Avoid or minimize sending personal e-mail, IM messages, or texts from work.** Even if your company allows personal use during lunch or after hours, keep it to a minimum. Better yet, wait to use your home computer to access your personal e-mail and social networking sites.
- **Separate work and personal data.** Keep information that could embarrass you or expose you to legal liability on your personal storage devices or hard drives, never on your office computer.

Dos: Treat All Online Speech as Public and Protect Your Computer

- **Be careful when blogging, tweeting, or posting on social networking sites.** A Canadian blogger lost his job for an entry that read, "Getting to blog for three hours while being paid: priceless."[38]
- **Keep your virus and malicious software protection current.** Always download the newest definitions and updates to your operating system, browser, antivirus program, and antispyware.
- **Pick strong passwords and vary them.** Use a combination of letters, numbers, and symbols. Select a different password for each Web service, and never use your Web passwords as PIN codes on credit or debit cards. Change your passwords every few months.
- **Keep sensitive information private.** Monitor the privacy settings on social networking sites, but don't trust the "private" areas on Facebook, Flickr, and other services that provide public access to most material they store.

Don'ts: Avoid Questionable Content, Personal Documents, and File Sharing

- **Don't send, download, print, or exhibit pornography, sexually explicit jokes, or inappropriate screen savers.** Anything that might "poison" the work environment is prohibited.
- **Don't open attachments sent by e-mail.** Attachments with executable files or video files may carry viruses, spyware, or other malware (malicious programs).
- **Don't download free software and utilities to company machines.** Employees can unwittingly introduce viruses, phishing schemes, and other cyber "bugs."
- **Don't store your music library and photos on a company machine (or server), and don't watch streaming videos.** Capturing precious company bandwidth for personal use is a sure way to be shown the door.
- **Don't share files and avoid file-sharing services.** At work, clarify whether you may use Google Docs and other services that offer optional file sharing. As with any free cloud-based application, exercise caution. Security breaches are always possible. Stay away from LimeWire, and other distributors of pirated files. File-sharing services and downloads can subject you to breaches by third parties.

Best Practices for Using Electronic Media Smartly, Safely, and Professionally

What are some guidelines for the effective and professional use of electronic media?

As advances in computer technology continue to change the way we work and play, Internet use on and off the job has become a danger zone for employees and employers. Misuse costs employers millions of dollars in lost productivity and litigation, and it can cost employees their jobs. A survey by the American Management Association revealed that 26 percent of employers fired employees for e-mail misuse. In addition, 2 percent terminated employees for using instant messaging, and another 2 percent for posting offensive blog content from a company or even a home computer.[35] Companies struggle with fair Internet use policies knowing that over half of their employees with Web access shop online from the office.[36]

Want to do well on tests and excel in your course? Go to **www.meguffey.com** for helpful interactive resources.

- **Review the Chapter 7 PowerPoint slides to prepare for the first quiz.**

Recreational activities, as well as unintentional but careless miscues, can gobble up precious network resources and waste valuable work time. Even more important is concern over lawsuits and network security. Companies must maintain a workplace free of harassment. If employees download pornography, transmit sexually explicit jokes, or use inappropriate screen savers, the work environment can become "poisoned" and employers may be sued. Furthermore, security problems arise when employees open phishing e-mail or fall for malware when browsing the Web.

The accompanying Checklist feature highlights some employee dos and don'ts that you should abide by to keep out of trouble on the job.

Zooming In — YOUR TURN

Twitter

Most mainstream businesses are waiting on the sidelines to see how Twitter will evolve. However, in some industries companies are already using Twitter and other social media to monitor what is being said about them, to engage with customers, and to market to other businesses. Take the airlines: JetBlue's Cheeps and United's Twares offer special deals on domestic and international flights in 140-character tweets. JetBlue and Southwest appointed "tweet watchers" who troubleshoot air travelers' problems. American, Alaska, Air New Zealand, and the Virgin group also tweet actively.[39]

IT firms were not the only early adopters of Twitter. Many large companies have discovered Twitter as a tool to avert public-relations disasters. Eastman Kodak seeks customers' conversations by searching Twitter and creates marketing campaigns focused on Twitter. Ford teaches employees to represent the company and communicate with customers on Twitter. Coca-Cola and PepsiCo are both quick to apologize to irate customers and to correct problems that they discover on Twitter or other social media network sites. Southwest Airlines employs a six-member "emerging-media team." Coke even appointed its first head of social media, Adam Brown, who says: "We're getting to a point if you're not responding, you're not being seen as an authentic type of brand."[40]

Your Task

You are one of three staffers working for Adam Brown at Coca-Cola. Your job is to comb through tweets to find those that are both positive about and critical of your company and to inform your boss about any that could potentially end up hurting Coke's image. Deciding which post could cause trouble is difficult, given that even with tracking software you may need to scan hundreds of posts every day. You know that if many users "retweet," or redistribute the news, the problem may get out of hand. Create a Twitter account at **http://twitter.com** and search for posts about Coca-Cola or any other company your instructor may assign. Search long enough until you have a good sense of what posters are saying. If you identify a trend, make a note of it and report it either in class or in writing as directed by your instructor.

© JOHN MACDOUGALL/AFP/Getty Images

Summary of Learning Objectives

1 **Describe the role digital media play in the changing world of business in contrast to traditional paper-based messages.** The exchange of information in organizations today is increasingly electronic and mobile, although office workers still send paper-based messages when they need a permanent record; wish to maintain confidentiality; and need to convey formal, long, and important messages. E-mail is still the lifeblood of businesses today, but instant messaging is gaining popularity. Likewise, phone-based SMS services enable cellular customers to send each other short text messages, images, and videos. Businesses have embraced podcasts, blogs, wikis, and social networking to help them communicate with employees, customers, and clients. The use of all digital media requires professionalism and caution because they create permanent records.

2 **Meet professional e-mail standards for usage, structure, and format; and follow the rules of netiquette and other best practices.** Direct (nonsensitive) e-mails begin with a subject line that summarizes the central idea. The opening repeats that idea and amplifies it. The body explains and provides more information. The closing includes (a) action information, dates, and deadlines; (b) a summary; and/or (c) a closing thought. E-mail messages should be formatted with a meaningful subject line, a greeting, a single-spaced body that is typed with a combination of upper- and lowercase letters, and a closing "signature" that includes contact information. Careful e-mail users write concisely and don't send anything they wouldn't want published. They care about correctness, resist humor, never send spam, use identifying labels when appropriate, and use attachments sparingly. They don't access company computers for personal use unless specifically allowed to do so, and they realize that e-mail may be monitored. They strive to improve readability through design and consider cultural differences.

3 **Explain how business professionals communicate by instant messaging and texting.** Both instant messaging (IM) and text messaging have become increasingly relevant for business in communicating with customers, employees, and suppliers. IM participants must share the same software to conduct private chats in real time. Texting generally requires a smartphone-delivered SMS service from a wireless company. Text and IM messages can be delivered by a computer or a handheld device. To keep IM and texts professional, know your company's policies, separate personal from business contacts, stay away from personal messaging at work, make yourself unavailable when you need to concentrate, wait until receiving a reply before shooting off multiple messages, avoid sending confidential information, and use correct grammar and spelling.

4 **Identify professional uses of podcasts, blogs, and wikis; and describe prudent policies to protect authors of electronic content.** Business podcasts are digital audio or video files ranging from short clips to long media files. Any applications that do not require a human presence (e.g., certain training videos) lend themselves to podcast recordings that users can stream or download on demand. Creating simple podcasts requires only inexpensive or free recording software and low-cost equipment. Blogs help businesses to keep customers, employees, and suppliers informed and receive feedback. Online communities can form around a blog. Companies employ blogs for public relations and crisis communication, market research and viral marketing, internal communication, and recruiting. Before blogging, seek permission and know company policies. Avoid sensitive or inappropriate topics. Wikis enable far-flung team members to share information and build a knowledge base, and can be used to replace meetings, manage projects, and document projects large and small. When contributing to a wiki, don't post irrelevant or annoying content, check your facts and your grammar, follow guidelines for contributors, and give credit where appropriate.

5 **Understand business uses of social and professional networking sites as well as RSS feeds and social bookmarking.** Facebook, MySpace, and Twitter allow firms to share company news; exchange ideas; and connect with customers, employees, other stakeholders, and the public at large. Tech companies in particular harness the power of social networking for teamwork and brainstorming. Other companies boost their brand recognition and provide a forum for collaboration by participating in established social networks or by creating their own

in-house communities. The downsides of social media participation are productivity losses, fallout from inappropriate employee posts, leaking of trade secrets, and angry Internet users. Keep safe by sharing only information that you would openly discuss in the office. Be sure to activate your privacy options. Don't post questionable photographs. Professional networking sites such as LinkedIn help companies and job seekers to connect. The virtual network is a logical extension of face-to-face networking, and members need to conduct themselves professionally in both. Really simple syndication and social bookmarking allow users to navigate the huge resources on the Internet. RSS feeds are time-savers because they allow businesspeople to monitor many news sources in one convenient online location. Social bookmarking sites such as Digg, Del.icious, and Reddit can help you search, organize, share, and store bookmarks on the Web.

Chapter Review

1. What is Web 2.0, and how has it changed the way users engage with information? (Obj. 1)
2. Name and describe the two prevailing technological trends today. (Obj. 1)
3. List and concisely describe at least six electronic communication channels used most commonly by businesspeople today. (Obj. 1)
4. List and briefly describe the four parts of typical e-mails. (Obj. 2)
5. Suggest at least ten pointers that you could give to a first-time e-mail user. (Obj. 2)
6. How can you use instant messaging and texting safely on the job? (Obj. 3)
7. Name at least five reasons some organizations forbid employees to use instant and text messaging. (Obj. 3)
8. How can you show professionalism and respect for your receivers in writing business IM messages and texts? (Obj. 3)
9. Describe the process of creating a simple podcast. (Obj. 4)
10. Explain why companies use blogs. (Obj. 4)
11. What is a wiki, and what are its advantages to businesses? (Obj. 4)
12. Name a few of the potential risks that social networking sites may pose to business. (Obj. 5)
13. What do employment and hiring experts recommend to young job seekers who wish to connect with companies on LinkedIn and other professional networking sites? (Obj. 5)
14. What is really simple syndication (RSS), and why is it helpful? (Obj. 5)
15. Explain the role of social bookmarking sites such as Digg, Del.icio.us, Reddit, StumbleUpon, and Squidoo. (Obj. 5)

Critical Thinking

1. How could IM be useful in your career field? Does IM produce a permanent record? Do you think that common abbreviations such as *lol* and *imho* and all-lowercase writing are acceptable in text messages for business? Will the use of shorthand abbreviations as well as creative spelling negatively affect writing skills? (Obj. 3)
2. Tweeting, texting, and quickie e-mailing all may foster sloppy messages. Author Mark Garvey argued, "In business, in education, in the arts, in any writing that takes place outside the linguistic cul-de-sac of our close friends and relatives, writers are expected to reach for certain standards of clarity, concision and care."[41] What did Garvey mean? Do you agree? (Objs. 2, 3)
3. Why are lawyers and technology experts warning companies to store, organize, and manage computer data, including e-mails and instant messages, with sharper diligence? (Obj. 2)
4. Discuss the ramifications of the following statement: *Once an e-mail, instant message, text, or any other document leaves your hands, you have essentially published it.* (Obj. 2)
5. **Ethical Issue:** What Internet behavior could get employees fired? Do employees deserve broad Internet access on the job—if they are responsible? Should employers block access to Web sites? If so, what kind? (Objs. 2, 3, 4, and 5)

Activities

Note: All Documents for Analysis are provided at **www.meguffey.com** for you to revise online.

7.1 Document for Analysis: Jumbled E-Mail Message (Obj. 2)

Your Task. Analyze the following poorly written e-mail. List its weaknesses. Consider redundancies, wordiness, poor organization, weak subject line, and lack of contact information. If your instructor directs, revise it.

To: Greta Targa <greta.targa@gamma.com>
From: Jim Morales <jim.morales@gamma.com>
Subject: HELP!
Cc:
Bcc:

As you already know, we have been working hard to plan the Gamma Fall Training Conference. It will be held in Miami. Here are the speakers I have lined up for training sessions. I'm thinking that on Tuesday, November 12, we will have Nicole Gold. Her scheduled topic is "Using E-Mail and IM Effectively." Anthony Mills said he could speak to our group on November 13 (Wednesday). "Leading Groups and Teams" is the topic for Mills. Here are their e-mail addresses: tony.mills@sunbelt.net. and n.gold@etc.com.

You can help us make this one of the best training sessions ever. I need you to send each of these people an e-mail and confirm the dates and topics. Due to the fact that we must print the program soon (by September 1), I will need this done as soon as possible. Don't hesitate to call if you have any questions.

Jim

7.2 Document for Analysis: Poorly Organized E-Mail (Obj. 2)

Your Task. Analyze the following poorly written and poorly organized e-mail. List its specific weaknesses. Would bulleted headings improve readability? If your instructor directs, revise it.

To: Mitchell Moraga <mitchell.moraga@media.com>
From: Eleanor Hutchinson <ehutchinson@media.com>
Subject: My Report
Cc:
Bcc:

Mitchell,

This is in response to your request that I attend the Workplace Issues and tell you about it. As you know, I attended the Workplace Issues conference on November 3, as you suggested. The topic was how to prevent workplace violence, and I found it very fascinating. Although we have been fortunate to avoid serious incidents at our company, it's better to be safe than sorry. Because I was the representative from our company and you asked for a report, here it is. Kit Adkins was the presenter, and she made suggestions in three categories, which I will summarize here.

Ms. Atkins cautioned organizations to prescreen job applicants. As a matter of fact, wise companies do not offer employment until after a candidate's background has been checked. Just the mention of a background check is enough to make some candidates withdraw. These candidates, of course, are the ones with something to hide.

A second suggestion was that companies should prepare a good employee handbook that outlines what employees should do when they suspect potential workplace violence. This handbook should include a way for informers to be anonymous.

A third recommendation had to do with recognizing red-flag behavior. This involves having companies train managers to recognize signs of potential workplace violence. What are some of the red flags? One sign is an increasing number of arguments (most of them petty) with coworkers. Another sign is extreme changes in behavior or statements indicating depression over family or financial problems. Another sign is bullying or harassing behavior. Bringing a firearm to work or displaying an extreme fascination with firearms is another sign.

I think that the best recommendation is prescreening job candidates. This is because it is most feasible. If you want me to do more research on prescreening techniques, do not hesitate to let me know. Let me know by November 18 if you want me to make a report at our management meeting, which is scheduled for December 3.

Ellie

7.3 Document for Analysis: Instant Messaging at Local Auto Dealer (Obj. 3)

Read the following log of a live IM chat between a customer service representative and a visitor to a Glendora car dealership's Web site. **Your Task.** In class discuss how Alex could have made this interaction with a customer more effective. Is his IM chat with Mr. Rhee professional, polite, and respectful? If your instructor directs, rewrite Alex's responses to Mr. Rhee's queries.

Service rep: Hey, I'm Alex. How's it goin? Welcome to Harkin BMW of Glendora!

Customer: ??

Service rep: Im supposed to provid live assistance. What can I do you for?

Customer: I want buy car.

Service rep: May I have your name fist?

Customer: Jin Bae Rhee

Service rep: Whoa! Is that a dude's name? Okay. What kind? New inventory or preowned?

Customer: BMW. 2011 model. for family, for business.

Service rep: New, then, huh? Where are you from?

Customer: What car you have?

Service rep: We got some that will knock your socks off.

Customer: I want green car, low mileage, less gasoline burn.

Service rep: My man, if you can't afford the gas on these puppies, you shouldn't buy a Beemer, you know what I mean? Or ya want green color?

Customer: ?

Service rep: Okeydoke, we got a full lineup. Which series, 3, 5, 6, or 7? Or an X3 or X5? A Z4 convertible?

Customer: 760 sedan?

Service rep: Nope. We got just two 550i, one for $68,695 and one for 71,020

Customer: Eureopean delivery?

Service rep: Oh, I know zip about that. Let me find someone who does. Can I have your phone number and e-mail?

Customer: i prefer not get a phone call yet ... but 299-484-9807 is phone numer and jrhee@techtrade.com email

Service rep: Awsome. Well give you a jingle back or shoot you an email pronto! Bye.

7.4 Choosing a Holiday Plan (Obj. 2)

E-mail

In the past your company offered all employees 11 holidays, starting with New Year's Day in January and proceeding through Christmas Day the following December. Other companies offer similar holiday schedules. In addition, your company has given all employees one floating holiday. That day was determined by a company-wide vote. As a result, all employees had the same day off. Now, however, management is considering a new plan that involves a floating holiday that each employee may choose. Selections, however, would be subject to staffing needs within individual departments. If two people wanted the same day, the employee with the most seniority would have the day off.

Your Task. As a member of the Human Resources staff, write an e-mail to employees asking them to choose between continuing the current company-wide uniform floating holiday or instituting a new plan for an individual floating holiday. Be sure to establish an end date.

7.5 Reaching Consensus About Business Attire (Obj. 2)

E-mail Team

Casual dress in professional offices has been coming under attack. Your boss, Michael Harding, received the e-mail shown in Figure 7.1. He thinks it would be a good assignment for his group of management trainees to help him respond to that message. He asks your team to research answers to the first five questions in CEO William Laughton's message. He doesn't expect you to answer the final question, but any information you can supply to the first questions would help him shape a response.

Schilling & Voigt is a public CPA firm with a staff of 120 CPAs, bookkeepers, managers, and support personnel. Located in downtown Bridgeport, Connecticut, the plush offices on Water Street overlook Waterfront Park and the Long Island Sound. The firm performs general accounting and audit services as well as tax planning and preparation. Accountants visit clients in the field and also entertain them in the downtown office.

Your Task. Decide whether the entire team will research each question in Figure 7.1 or whether team members will be assigned certain questions. Collect information, discuss it, and reach consensus on what you will report to Mr. Harding. As a team write a concise one-page response. Your goal is to inform, not persuade. Remember that you represent management, not students or employees.

7.6 Twitter: Learning to Write Superefficient Tweets (Objs. 1, 4, and 5)

Twitter forces its users to practice extreme conciseness. Some music reviewers have risen to the challenge and reviewed whole albums in no more than 140 characters. National Public Radio put Stephen Thompson, one of its music editors, to the test. "I approach Twitter as a science," Thompson says.[42] He sees well-designed tweets as online equivalents of haiku, a highly structured type of Japanese poetry. Thompson believes that tweets should be properly punctuated, be written in complete sentences, and of course, not exceed the 140-character limit. His rules also exclude abbreviations.

Here are two samples of Thompson's mini reviews: "Mos Def is a hip-hop renaissance man on smart songs that look to the whole world and its conflicts. Slick Rick's guest spot is a nice touch." The second one reads: "The Phenomenal Handclap Band: Chugging, timeless, jammy throwback from eight shaggy Brooklyn hipsters. Starts slowly, gets hypnotically fun."[43]

Your Task. As an intern in Stephen Thompson's office, review your favorite album in 140 characters or fewer, following your boss's rules. After you have warmed up, your instructor may direct you to other concise writing tasks. Send a tweet to your instructor, if appropriate, or practice writing Twitter posts in MS Word. The best tweets could be shared with the class.

7.7 Instant Messaging: Practicing Your Professional IM Skills (Obj. 3)

Web Team

Your instructor will direct this role-playing group activity. Using instant messaging, you will simulate one of several typical business scenarios—for example, responding to a product inquiry, training a new-hire, troubleshooting with a customer, or making an appointment. For each scenario, two or more students will chat professionally with only a minimal script to practice on-the-spot yet courteous professional interaction by IM. Your instructor will determine which software you will need and provide brief instructions to prepare you for your role in this exercise.

If you don't have instant messaging software on your computer or smart device yet, download the application first—for example, AOL's Instant Messenger, Yahoo Messenger, Microsoft's Windows Live Messenger, or Skype. Yahoo Messenger, for instance, allows you to IM your friends on Yahoo Messenger but also on Windows Live Messenger. You control who sees you online; if you don't wish to be interrupted, you can use stealth settings. All IM software enables users to share photos and large media files (up to 2 gigabytes on Yahoo). You can make voice calls and use webcam video as well. These advanced features turn IM software into a simple conferencing tool and video phone. You can connect with users who have the same software all around the world. Contrary to calling landlines or cell phones, peer-to-peer voice calls are free. Most IM clients also have mobile applications for your smartphone, so that you can IM or call other users while you are away from a computer.

Your Task. Log on to the IM program your instructor chooses. Follow your instructor's directions closely as you role-play the business situation you were assigned with your partner or team. The scenario will involve two or more people who will communicate by instant messaging in real time.

7.8 Podcast, Twitter, Texting: Analyzing a Podcast (Obj. 4)

E-mail

Browsing the podcasts at iTunes, you stumble across the Quick and Dirty Tips series, specifically Money Girl, who dispenses financial advice. You sign up for the free podcasts that cover a variety of business topics. You also visit the Web site at **http://www.quickanddirtytips.com/**.

Your Task. Pick a QDNow.com podcast that interests you. Listen to it or obtain a transcript on the Web site and study it for its structure. Is it direct or indirect? Informative or persuasive? At your instructor's request, write an e-mail that discusses the podcast you analyzed. Alternatively, if your instructor allows, you could also send a very concise summary of the podcast by text message from your cell phone or an ultrashort tweet (140 characters or fewer) to your instructor.

7.9 Podcast: Turning Text to Video in a Jiffy (Obj. 4)

Web

Have you ever wondered how software converts text to video in a matter of minutes? Article Video Robot (AVR) is an application that automates the process of animating your text. You can create something resembling a simple podcast by inputting your text and letting the application do the rest. The AVR Web site provides an entertaining video with step-by-step instructions. To get a taste of creating an animated video from a text you prepare, use the free trial version. When you finish your trial video, you will see that the software makes distribution to about 17 Web sites very easy. Of course, this service may require a fee. Even though the voices sound a bit tinny and robotic, you will have created a rudimentary video in no time.

Your Task. Write a page-long text that delivers information, provides instructions, or conveys a sales pitch. Go to **http://www.articlevideorobot.com/** and view the introduction video. After that, you can register for the free trial. You can use the application only once at no cost, so prepare your text ahead of time. This video tool is suitable for informational, instructional, and persuasive messages.

7.10 Blog: Analyzing the Nuts About Southwest Blog (Obj. 4)

Web

When you browse the Southwest Airlines blog, you will find the following terms of use:

> *We want to build a personal relationship between our Team and you, and we need your participation. Everyone is encouraged to*

join in, and you don't need to register to read, watch, or comment. However, if you would like to share photos or videos or rate a post, among other things, you will need to complete a profile. . . .

This is the point where we insert the "fine print" and discuss the guidelines for posting. Nuts About Southwest is a moderated site because we want to ensure that everyone stays on topic—or at least pretty close to it. We would LUV for you to post your thoughts, comments, suggestions, and questions, but when you post, make sure that they are of general interest to most readers. Of course, profanity, racial and ethnic slurs, and rude behavior like disparaging personal remarks won't be tolerated nor published.

Even though Nuts About Southwest is moderated, we pledge to present opposing viewpoints as we have done since our blog first went "live" several years ago, and we will strive to keep posts interesting, diverse, and multi-sided. Our Team wants to engage in a conversation with you, but not every post will receive a response from us. . . .

Your Task. Visit the Southwest.com blog at **www.blogsouthwest.com/about**. Click About and read the entire User Guide. In class, discuss the tone of the guidelines. How are they presented? Who is authoring the blog, and what is its purpose? What assumptions can you make about the company culture when you read the guidelines and the blog entries? If your instructor directs, write a clear, direct memo or an e-mail message reporting your observations.

7.11 Blog and Wiki: Reviewing Fortune 500 Business Blogging Wiki (Obj. 4)

Web

Here is your opportunity to view and evaluate a corporate blog. The site Socialtext.net is a wiki listing the 78 Fortune 500 companies that have a business blog at this time, defined as "active public blogs by company employees about the company and/or its products." You will find a range of large business organizations such as Amazon.com, Disney, Motorola, Safeway, and Toys"R"Us. Socialtext.net is hosting a wiki of reviews that critique Fortune 500 business blogs. The reviews are posted on a variety of blogs authored by various writers and hyperlinked to the Socialtext.net wiki.

Your Task. Browse the Fortune 500 Business Blogging Wiki at **http://www.socialtext.net/bizblogs/index.cgi**. Follow the links provided there to view some of the corporate blogs on the site. Select a company blog you find interesting, browse the pages, and read some of the contents. Pick a corporate blog that has already been reviewed by an independent blogger. Read the blogger's review. Consider the style and length of the review. If your instructor directs, write a brief informational memo or e-mail describing the business blog as well as its review, the style of the blogger's critique, the review's accuracy, and so forth.

Alternatively, your instructor may ask you to write an original review of a Fortune 500 company blog that has not yet been evaluated. You may be called on to write your own blog entry discussing an unreviewed company blog of your choice. You could compose the blog response in MS Word or e-mail it to your instructor as appropriate.

7.12 Creating a Twitter Group (Obj. 4)

Web

Tweetworks.com is designed to make microblogging useful for private individuals and businesses. The site is based on the premise that people like to talk with other like-minded people. Users come together in communities around specific topics (politics, sports, art, business, and so on). Tweetworks invites members to talk about the big news stories of the day, bounce ideas off other participants online, or just join the conversation—all in fewer than 140 characters. Your instructor may choose to create a public or private group for the class. Within this Tweetworks group for your course, you may be asked to complete short assignments in the form of tweets. Posts in a private group are not shared with other general users, yet they should be relevant to the class content and professional.

Your Task. Use your Twitter username and password to log on at **www.tweetworks.com/groups**. Sign into and follow the group designated by your instructor. Your instructor may ask you to comment on a topic he or she assigns or may encourage you to enter into a freewheeling discussion with other members of your class online. Your instructor may act as a group moderator evaluating the frequency and quality of your contributions.

7.13 Social Networking: Building an Online Community on Facebook (Obj. 5)

Web Team

Chances are you already have a Facebook profile and communicate with friends and family. You may be a fan of a celebrity or a business. Now you can also become a fan of your business communication class if your instructor decides to create a course page on Facebook. The main purpose of such a social networking site for a class is to exchange links and interesting stories relevant to the material being learned. Intriguing tidbits and business news might also be posted on the "wall" to be shared by all signed-up fans. Everybody, even students who are quiet in class, could contribute. However, before you can become a fan of your business communication class, it needs to be created online.

Your Task. If you posted a profile on Facebook, all you need to do is search for the title of the newly created business communication Facebook page and become a fan. If you don't have an account yet, begin by signing up at **www.facebook.com**. On-screen prompts will make it easy for you to build a profile.

7.14 Social Networking: Preparing a Professional LinkedIn Profile (Obj. 5)

Team

Virtual networking on a professional networking site such as LinkedIn is an extension of seeking face-to-face contacts—the most effective way to find a job to date. Consider creating a credible, appealing presence on LinkedIn to make yourself attractive to potential business connections and hiring managers. Your LinkedIn site should serve purely to build your career and professional reputation.

Your Task. Go to **www.linkedin.com** and sign up for a free account. Follow the on-screen directions to create a profile, add a professional-looking photograph, and upload a polished résumé. You will be prompted to invite contacts from your e-mail address books. If your instructor directs, form teams and critique each other's profiles. Link to those profiles of your peers that have been prepared most diligently and strike you as having the best eye appeal.

7.15 E-Mail Simulation: Writeaway Hotels (Obj. 2)

At **www.meguffey.com**, you can build your e-mail skills in our Writeaway Hotels simulation. You will be reading, writing, and responding to messages in an exciting game that helps you make appropriate decisions about whether to respond to e-mail messages and how to write clear, concise messages under pressure. The game can be played in a computer lab, in a classroom, or even on your own computer and on your own time.

Your Task. Check out the Writeaway Hotels simulation at your student site. If your instructor directs, follow the instructions to participate.

Video Resource

Video Library 1, Technology in the Workplace

What is the proper use of technology in today's workplace? This video takes you to H. B. Jones, a small landscape design and supply firm. You will meet Elliott, the owner and founder; Helena, a competent office worker; James, East Coast manager; and Ian, an inept employee. This fast-paced video gives you a glimpse of appropriate and inappropriate uses of workplace technology. It moves so quickly that you may want to watch it twice to be able to answer these questions:

- Do you see significant differences between Helena's and Ian's use of social networking sites? Are their visits to Facespace legitimate?
- What efficiencies and inefficiencies do you detect in how each character uses his or her smartphone?
- Is the featured company a technologically functional workplace, or can it be called dysfunctional? Which remedies would you propose if you identify any shortcomings?
- How would you describe Ian's and Helena's behavior upon entering the office in the morning?

Chat About It

In each chapter you will find five discussion questions related to the chapter material. Your instructor may assign these topics for you to discuss in class, in an online chat room, or on an online discussion board. Some of the discussion topics may require outside research. You may also be asked to read and respond to postings made by your classmates.

Topic 1: How could dashing off quick e-mails, tweets, or instant messages with incorrect style, grammar, or mechanics hurt one's ability to write longer, more formal messages correctly?

Topic 2: Describe a time when you should have had a face-to-face meeting instead of sending an electronic message. Why would the face-to-face meeting have been better?

Topic 3: Find an example of an e-mail that caused a problem for the sender because the message found its way to an unintended recipient. What problem did the situation cause?

Topic 4: What is your strategy to avoid sending an IM, tweet, or text message that you might regret later?

Topic 5: Why do businesses host public blogs with negative postings of their products or services?

Grammar and Mechanics C.L.U.E. Review 7

Apostrophes and Other Punctuation

Review Guides 31–38 about apostrophes and other punctuation in Appendix A, Grammar and Mechanics Guide, beginning on page A-14. On a separate sheet or on your computer, revise the following sentences to correct errors in the use of apostrophes and other punctuation. For each error that you locate, write the guide number that reflects this usage. The more you recognize the reasons, the better you will learn these punctuation guidelines. If a sentence is correct, write *C*. When you finish, check your answers on page Key-1.

Example: We needed the boss signature before we could mail the report.

Revision: We needed the **boss's** signature before we could mail the report. [Guide 32]

1. Facebook users accounts will be suspended if the members don't abide by the sites policies.
2. James performance review was outstanding again.
3. Would you please give me directions to your downtown headquarters
4. The shipping supervisor resented Barbara being late almost every morning.
5. Is it true that the CEO decided to write a weekly blog
6. You must replace the ink cartridge see page 8 in the manual, before printing.
7. Justin wondered whether all sales managers databases needed to be updated.
8. (Direct quotation) Health care costs said the CEO will increase substantially this year.
9. In just two months time, we expect to interview five candidates for the opening.
10. The meeting starts at 10 a.m. sharp, doesn't it

CHAPTER 8

Positive Messages

Want to do well on tests and excel in your course? Go to **www.meguffey.com** for helpful interactive resources.

- **Review the Chapter 8 PowerPoint slides to prepare for the first quiz.**

OBJECTIVES

After studying this chapter, you should be able to

1. Apply the 3-x-3 writing process to creating successful positive messages, including e-mails, interoffice memos, and business letters.
2. Understand the appropriate use of e-mails, interoffice memos, and business letters.
3. Compose direct messages that make requests and respond to inquiries.
4. Write messages that clearly explain step-by-step instructions.
5. Prepare messages that make direct claims.
6. Create adjustment messages that regain the confidence of customers and promote further business.
7. Write special messages that convey kindness and goodwill.
8. Modify international messages to accommodate readers from other cultures.

Zooming In PART 1

Ben & Jerry's Uses Positive Messages to Sweeten Relations With Customers

America's love affair with numbingly rich ice cream may have finally plateaued. Health and weight worries have apparently cut the breakneck growth of superpremium ice creams. However, Ben & Jerry's Homemade, premier purveyor of the superpremiums, remains one of the country's most visible ice cream companies.

In growing from a 12-flavor miniparlor in Burlington, Vermont, into a Fortune 500 company called a "national treasure," Ben & Jerry's has been showered with publicity. The flood of press notices flowed partly from its rapid ascent and its funky flavor hits such as Chubby Hubby, Half Baked Carb Karma, New York Super Fudge Chunk, and Phish Food. During the 2008 presidential campaign, it introduced Yes Pecan (a variation of Barack Obama's campaign mantra, "Yes we can"), made of "amber waves of buttery ice cream with roasted nonpartisan pecans." Of even greater media interest was the New Age business philosophy of founders Ben Cohen and Jerry Greenfield. Unlike most entrepreneurs, their aim was to build a successful business but, at the same time, have fun and be a force for social change.

Some time ago Ben and Jerry resigned their symbolic positions as brand icons after the company was purchased by the Anglo-Dutch megaconglomerate Unilever. Despite the change in ownership, Ben & Jerry's continues its efforts to improve local and global quality of life. The company promotes a progressive, nonpartisan social mission to balance economic, product, and social goals on the way to a sustainable business.

Although no longer locally owned, Ben & Jerry's is a visible company with a popular national product and a strong social image. It naturally generates a good deal of correspondence. Customer messages typically fall into three categories: (a) fan mail, (b) information requests, and (c) claims. Fan mail contains praise and testimonials: "Tried the new Cherry Garcia Frozen Yogurt and . . . I want to go to Vermont and shake your sticky hands." Information requests may involve questions about ingredients or food processing. Some messages inquire about Ben & Jerry's position on milk from cloned cows or eggs from caged chickens. Claim requests generally present a problem and require immediate response. Responding to customer messages in all three categories is a critical element in maintaining customer goodwill and market position for Ben & Jerry's.[1] You will learn more about this case on page 239.

© Andre Jenny/Alamy

Critical Thinking

- Have you ever written a letter or sent an e-mail to a company? What might motivate you to do so? Would you expect a response?
- If a company such as Ben & Jerry's receives a fan letter complimenting products or service, is it necessary to respond?
- Why is it important for companies to answer claim messages immediately?

http://www.benjerry.com

Successful Positive Messages Start With the Writing Process

LEARNING OBJECTIVE 1

Apply the 3-x-3 writing process to creating successful positive messages, including e-mails, interoffice memos, and business letters.

Business and professional organizations thrive on information that is exchanged externally and internally. At Ben & Jerry's external messages go to customers, vendors, other businesses, and the government. Internal messages travel upward to superiors, downward to employees, and horizontally among workers. Most of those messages are positive, straightforward communications that conduct everyday business and convey goodwill.

In this book we divide business messages into three content areas: (a) **positive** messages communicating straightforward requests, replies, and goodwill, covered in this chapter; (b) **negative** messages delivering refusals and bad news, covered in Chapter 9; and (c) **persuasive** messages, including sales pitches, covered in Chapter 10. Most of these business messages are exchanged in the form of e-mails, memos, or letters. As you study how to prepare positive, negative, and persuasive messages, you will also be learning which channel is appropriate for the message and situation you face. Should you send an e-mail or a memo? If the message is going outside the organization, should it be a letter?

This chapter focuses on routine, positive messages. These will make up the bulk of your messages. Although such messages may be short and straightforward, they benefit from attention to the composition process. "At the heart of effective writing is the ability to organize a series of thoughts," says writing expert and executive Max Messmer. Taking the time to think through what you want to achieve and how the audience will react makes writing much easier.[2] Here is a quick review of the 3-x-3 writing process to help you think through its application to positive messages.

Phase 1: Analysis, Anticipation, and Adaptation

What questions should you ask yourself before you begin a message?

In Phase 1, prewriting, you will need to spend some time analyzing your task. It is amazing how many of us are ready to put our pens or computers into gear before engaging our minds. Too often, writers start a message without enough preparation. Alice Blachly, a veteran writer from Ben & Jerry's, realized the problem. She said, "If I'm having trouble with a letter and it's not coming out right, it's almost always because I haven't thought through exactly what I want to say."[3] In the Ben & Jerry's letter shown in Figure 8.1, Blachly responds to a request from a young Ben & Jerry's customer. Before writing the letter, she thought about the receiver and tried to find a way to personalize what could have been a form letter.

As you prepare a message, ask yourself these important questions:

- **Do I really need to write this e-mail, memo, or letter?** A phone call or a quick visit to a nearby coworker might solve the problem—and save the time and expense of a written message. On the other hand, some written messages are needed to provide a permanent record or to show a well-conceived plan.
- **Why am I writing?** Know why you are writing and what you hope to achieve. This will help you recognize what the important points are and where to place them.
- **How will the reader react?** Visualize the reader and the effect your message will have. In preparing written messages, imagine that you are sitting and talking with your reader. Avoid speaking bluntly, failing to explain, or ignoring your reader's needs. Consider ways to shape the message to benefit the reader. Also remember that with e-mails, your message may very well be forwarded to someone else.
- **What channel should I use?** It's tempting to use e-mail for much of your correspondence. However, a phone call or face-to-face visit is a better channel choice if you need to (a) convey enthusiasm, warmth, or another emotion; (b) supply a context; or (c) smooth over disagreements. A business letter is better when the matter requires (a) a permanent record, (b) confidentiality, or (c) formality.
- **How can I save my reader's time?** Think of ways that you can make your message easier to comprehend at a glance. Use bullets, asterisks, lists, headings, and white space to improve readability. Notice in the Ben & Jerry's letter in Figure 8.1 that Alice Blachly used bullets to highlight the enclosures.

Phase 2: Research, Organization, and Composition

What steps should you take in Phase 2 of the writing process?

In Phase 2, writing, you will first want to check the files, gather documentation, and prepare your message. Make an outline of the points you wish to cover. For short messages jot down notes on the document you are answering or make a scratch list at your computer. In Alice Blachly's letter shown in Figure 8.1, she made a scratch outline of the points she wanted to cover before writing.

For longer documents that require formal research, use a cluster diagram or the outlining techniques discussed in Chapter 5. As you compose your message, avoid amassing huge blocks of text. No one wants to read endless lines of type. Instead, group related information into paragraphs, preferably short ones. Paragraphs separated by white space look inviting. Be sure that each paragraph includes a topic sentence backed up by details and evidence. If you bury your main point in the middle of a paragraph, the reader may miss it. Also plan for revision, because excellence is rarely achieved on the first effort.

Phase 3: Revision, Proofreading, and Evaluation

What questions should you ask yourself in Phase 3 of the writing process?

Phase 3, revising, involves putting the final touches on your message. Careful and caring writers ask themselves the following questions:

FIGURE 8.1 Analyzing Ben & Jerry's Customer Response

1 Prewriting

Analyze: The purpose of this letter is to build goodwill and promote Ben & Jerry's products.

Anticipate: The reader is young, enthusiastic, and eager to hear from Ben & Jerry's. She will appreciate personalized comments.

Adapt: Use short sentences, cheerful thoughts, and plenty of references to the reader, her club, her school, and her request.

2 Writing

Research: Reread the customer's letter. Decide on items to enclose and locate them.

Organize: Open directly with a positive response. Explain the enclosed items. Find ways to make the reader feel a special connection with Ben & Jerry's.

Compose: Write the first draft quickly. Realize that revision will improve it.

3 Revising

Revise: Revise the message striving for a warm tone. Use the receiver's name. Edit long paragraphs and add bulleted items.

Proofread: Check the address of the receive Decide whether to hyphenate *cofounder* an how to punctuate quotations.

Evaluate: Consider how you would feel if you received this letter.

January 18, 2012

Ms. Jennifer Ball
1401 Churchville Lane
Bel Air, MD 21014

Dear Jennifer:

We're delighted to hear of your Ben & Jerry's Club at Franklin Middle School and to send the items you requested.

Your club sounds as though it resembles its parent in many ways. We, too, can't seem to control our growth; and we, too, get a little out of control on Friday afternoons. Moreover, the simplicity of your club rules mirrors the philosophy of our cofounder, who says, "If it's not fun, why do it?"

Enclosed are the following items:

- A list of all flavors available in pints. If you can't find these flavors at your grocer's, I'm sending you some "ballots" for your club's use in encouraging your grocer to stock your favorites.
- The latest issue of Ben & Jerry's "Chunk Mail." We're also putting you on our mailing list so that your club will receive our Chunk Mail newsletter regularly.

We hope, Jennifer, that you'll soon tour our plant here in Vermont. Then, you can be on an equal footing with your prez and sport one of our tour buttons. This seems only appropriate for the consensus-building, decision-making model you are pioneering in your Ben & Jerry's Club!

Sincerely,

Alice

Alice Blanchly
Consumer Affairs

Enc: Flavor list, ballots, Chunk Mail

P.O. BOX 240, WATERBURY, VERMONT 05676 (802)244-6957 FAX (802)244-5944
100% Post-Consumer Recycle Paper

Personalizes reply and builds goodwill with reference to writer's letter

Uses receiver's name to make letter sound conversational and personal

Opens directl with respons to customer's request

Itemizes and explains enclosures requested by customer

Ties in cordia closing with more referenc to customer's letter

- **Is the message clear?** Viewed from the receiver's perspective, are the ideas clear? Did you use plain English? If the message is passed on to others, will they need further explanation? Consider having a colleague critique your message if it is an important one.
- **Is the message correct?** Are the sentences complete and punctuated properly? Did you overlook any typos or misspelled words? Remember to use your spell checker and grammar checker to proofread your message before sending it.
- **Did I plan for feedback?** How will you know whether this message is successful? You can improve feedback by asking questions (such as *Are you comfortable with these suggestions?* or *What do you think?*). Remember to make it easy for the receiver to respond.
- **Will this message achieve its purpose?** The last step in the 3-x-3 writing process is evaluating the product. Before any message left her desk at Ben & Jerry's, Alice Blachly always reread it and put herself in the shoes of the reader: "How would I feel if I were receiving it?"

Spotlight on Communicators

Peggy Foran, who has served as executive vice president at Sara Lee Corporation and senior executive with Pfizer Pharmaceutical, was known for "pushing the envelope" in practicing good communication with investors. In correspondence, news releases, and proxy statements, Foran insisted on clear, basic English. Although accustomed to dense legal language, she admitted to confusion. "I do this for a living, and I can't understand a lot of [corporate material] on the first read." She demands clear expression in all messages. "Transparency is part of our culture. We believe in plain English." To be sure their communication is clear, company writers are encouraged to put themselves in the shoes of readers, which is good advice for all business communicators.

Watching the Writing Process in Action

To see how the writing process can improve an internal message, look at Figure 8.2. It shows the first draft and revision of an e-mail that Madeleine Espinoza, senior marketing manager, wrote to her boss, Keith Milton. Although it contained solid information, the first draft was so wordy and dense that the main points were lost.

In the revision stage, Madeleine realized that she needed to reorganize her message into an opening, body, and closing. She desperately needed to improve the readability. In studying what she had written, she recognized that she was talking about two main problems. She discovered that she could present a three-part solution. These ideas didn't occur to her until she had written the first draft. Only in the revision stage was she able to see that she was talking about two separate problems as well as a three-part solution. The revision process can help you think through a problem and clarify a solution.

As she revised, Madeleine was more aware of the subject line, opening, body, and closing. She used an informative subject line and opened directly by explaining why she was writing. Her opening outlined the two main problems so that her reader understood the background of the following recommendations. In the body of the message, Madeleine identified three corrective actions, and she highlighted them for improved readability. Notice that she listed her three recommendations using numbers with boldface headings, and she started each item with an action verb. Madeleine closed her message with a deadline and a reference to the next action to be taken.

Positive Messages: E-Mails, Memos, and Letters

LEARNING OBJECTIVE 2
Understand the appropriate use of e-mails, interoffice memos, and business letters.

In the workplace positive messages may take the form of e-mails, memos, and letters. When you need information from a team member in another office, you might send an e-mail. If you must explain to employees a new procedure for ordering supplies, you would probably write an interoffice memo. When you respond to a customer asking about your products, you would most likely prepare a letter.

Comparing E-Mails and Memos

What kinds of messages are most appropriate for workplace e-mails?

Most internal messages will be exchanged as e-mails or interoffice memos. E-mail is most appropriate for short messages, such as sharing "need to know" facts, setting up appointments, distributing documents, giving updates, requesting information, getting answers to specific questions, and documenting conversations when a paper trail is needed. You probably have already written many e-mails to your friends. However, professional e-mails sent on the job are

FIGURE 8.2 Applying the Writing Process to an E-Mail

1 Prewriting

Analyze: The purpose of this memo is to describe database problems and recommend solutions.

Anticipate: The audience is the writer's boss, who is familiar with the topic and who appreciates brevity.

Adapt: Because the reader requested this message, the direct strategy is most appropriate.

2 Writing

Research: Gather data documenting the customer database and how to use Access software.

Organize: Announce recommendations and summarize problems. In the body, use action verbs to list the three actions for solving the problem. In the closing, describe reader benefits, provide a deadline, and specify the next action.

Compose: Prepare the first draft.

3 Revising

Revise: Highlight the two main problems and the three recommendations. Use bullets, caps, and headings to improve readability. Make the bulleted ideas parallel.

Proofread: Double-check to see whether *database* is one word or two. Use spell checker.

Evaluate: Does this e-mail supply concise information the boss wants in an easy-to-read format?

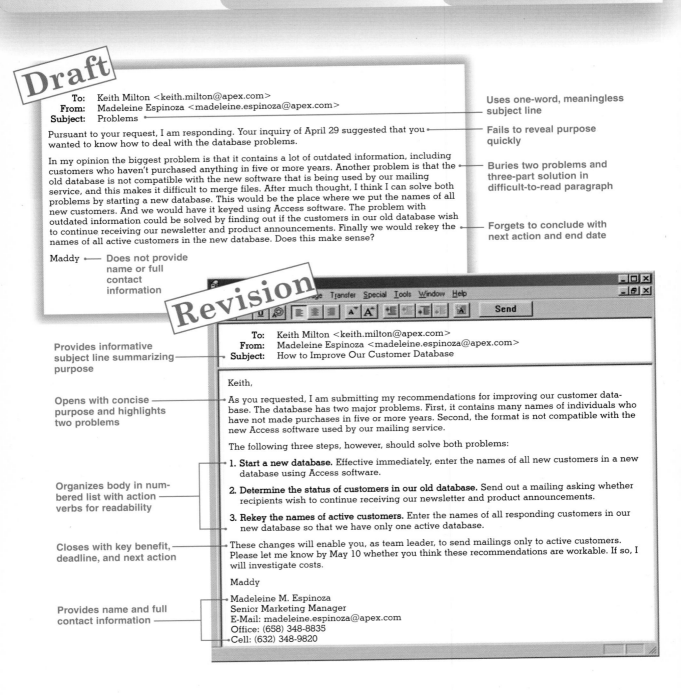

Draft

To: Keith Milton <keith.milton@apex.com>
From: Madeleine Espinoza <madeleine.espinoza@apex.com>
Subject: Problems ← Uses one-word, meaningless subject line

Pursuant to your request, I am responding. Your inquiry of April 29 suggested that you wanted to know how to deal with the database problems. ← Fails to reveal purpose quickly

In my opinion the biggest problem is that it contains a lot of outdated information, including customers who haven't purchased anything in five or more years. Another problem is that the old database is not compatible with the new software that is being used by our mailing service, and this makes it difficult to merge files. After much thought, I think I can solve both problems by starting a new database. This would be the place where we put the names of all new customers. And we would have it keyed using Access software. The problem with outdated information could be solved by finding out if the customers in our old database wish to continue receiving our newsletter and product announcements. Finally we would rekey the names of all active customers in the new database. Does this make sense? ← Buries two problems and three-part solution in difficult-to-read paragraph ← Forgets to conclude with next action and end date

Maddy ← Does not provide name or full contact information

Revision

To: Keith Milton <keith.milton@apex.com>
From: Madeleine Espinoza <madeleine.espinoza@apex.com>
Subject: How to Improve Our Customer Database ← Provides informative subject line summarizing purpose

Keith,

As you requested, I am submitting my recommendations for improving our customer database. The database has two major problems. First, it contains many names of individuals who have not made purchases in five or more years. Second, the format is not compatible with the new Access software used by our mailing service. ← Opens with concise purpose and highlights two problems

The following three steps, however, should solve both problems:

1. **Start a new database.** Effective immediately, enter the names of all new customers in a new database using Access software.
2. **Determine the status of customers in our old database.** Send out a mailing asking whether recipients wish to continue receiving our newsletter and product announcements.
3. **Rekey the names of active customers.** Enter the names of all responding customers in our new database so that we have only one active database.

← Organizes body in numbered list with action verbs for readability

These changes will enable you, as team leader, to send mailings only to active customers. Please let me know by May 10 whether you think these recommendations are workable. If so, I will investigate costs. ← Closes with key benefit, deadline, and next action

Maddy

Madeleine M. Espinoza
Senior Marketing Manager
E-Mail: madeleine.espinoza@apex.com
Office: (658) 348-8835
Cell: (632) 348-9820

← Provides name and full contact information

quite different from notes to friends. The purpose of business e-mails is to get work done rather than interact socially with people.[4] In Chapter 7 you learned about formatting of e-mail, and you studied best practices for using e-mail effectively and safely in the workplace. In this chapter we discuss composing e-mails, interoffice memos, and business letters. You may be thinking, *What are memos? Haven't memos been eclipsed by e-mail?*

The truth is that, although e-mail is very popular, printed hard-copy memos still serve vital functions in the workplace. They remain useful for important internal messages that require a permanent record or formality. For example, organizations use memos to deliver instructions, official policies, short reports, long internal documents, and important announcements. The formatting of memos makes them easy to read and understand, especially when compared with e-mails that have long threads of comments by many receivers. The sender and receiver of memos are always recognizable. The guide words in memos immediately tell you what you want to know—who wrote the message, who was the intended receiver, the date it was sent, and what it is about.

ETHICS CHECK

Surprising the Boss

Kyra M. uses e-mail for nearly all messages. She is ecstatic over a new job offer and quickly sends an e-mail to her manager announcing that she is leaving. He did not know she was looking for a new position. Is this an appropriate use of e-mail?

Preparing Interoffice Memos

How do you format an interoffice memo prepared on plain paper?

The formatting of interoffice memos has much in common with e-mails, which you studied in Chapter 7. Like e-mails, interoffice memos begin with guide words such as *Date, To, From*, and *Subject*. Some organizations have preprinted memo letterhead paper with the name of the organization at the top. In addition to guide words, these forms may include other identifying headings, such as *File Number*, *Floor*, *Extension*, *Location*, and *Distribution*. Because of the difficulty of aligning computer printers with preprinted forms, business writers may use default templates available on their word processors (sometimes called *wizards)*. Writers can customize these templates with their organization's name.

If you are preparing a memo on plain paper, set 1-inch top and bottom margins and left and right margins of 1.25 inches. Provide a heading that includes the name of the company plus the word *Memo* or *Memorandum.* Begin the guide words a triple space (two blank lines) below the last line of the heading. Key in bold the guide words: **Date:, To:, From:,** and **Subject:** at the left margin. The guide words may appear in all caps or with only the initial letter capitalized. Triple-space (two blank lines) after the last line of the heading. Do not justify the right margins. As discussed in the document design section of Chapter 6, ragged-right margins in printed messages make them easier to read. Single-space the message, and double-space between paragraphs, as shown in Figure 8.3.

Preparing Memos as E-Mail Attachments

E-mail has become increasingly important for exchanging internal messages. However, it is inappropriate for long documents or for items that require formality or permanence. For such messages, writers may prepare the information in standard memo format and send it as an attachment to a cover e-mail.

In preparing e-mail attachments, be sure to include identifying information. Because the cover e-mail may become separated from the attachment, the attachment must be fully identified. Preparing the e-mail attachment as a memo provides a handy format that identifies the date, sender, receiver, and subject.

Understanding Business Letters

Thus far we have discussed positive messages that circulate inside an organization. Now let's talk about positive messages that are delivered outside an organization. One important channel for external communication is business letters. Even with the new media available today, a business letter remains one of the most powerful and effective ways to get your message across.

Knowing When to Send a Letter

When should you send a business letter rather than an e-mail?

You will know when to send a business letter by the situation and by the preference of your organization. Although you may be tempted to dash off an e-mail, think twice before descending into digital mode. This section discusses reasons business letters are still indispensable.

Business letters are necessary when the situation calls for a permanent record. For example, when a company enters into an agreement with another company, business letters introduce the agreement and record decisions and points of understanding. Although telephone

FIGURE 8.3 **Interoffice Memo That Responds to a Request**

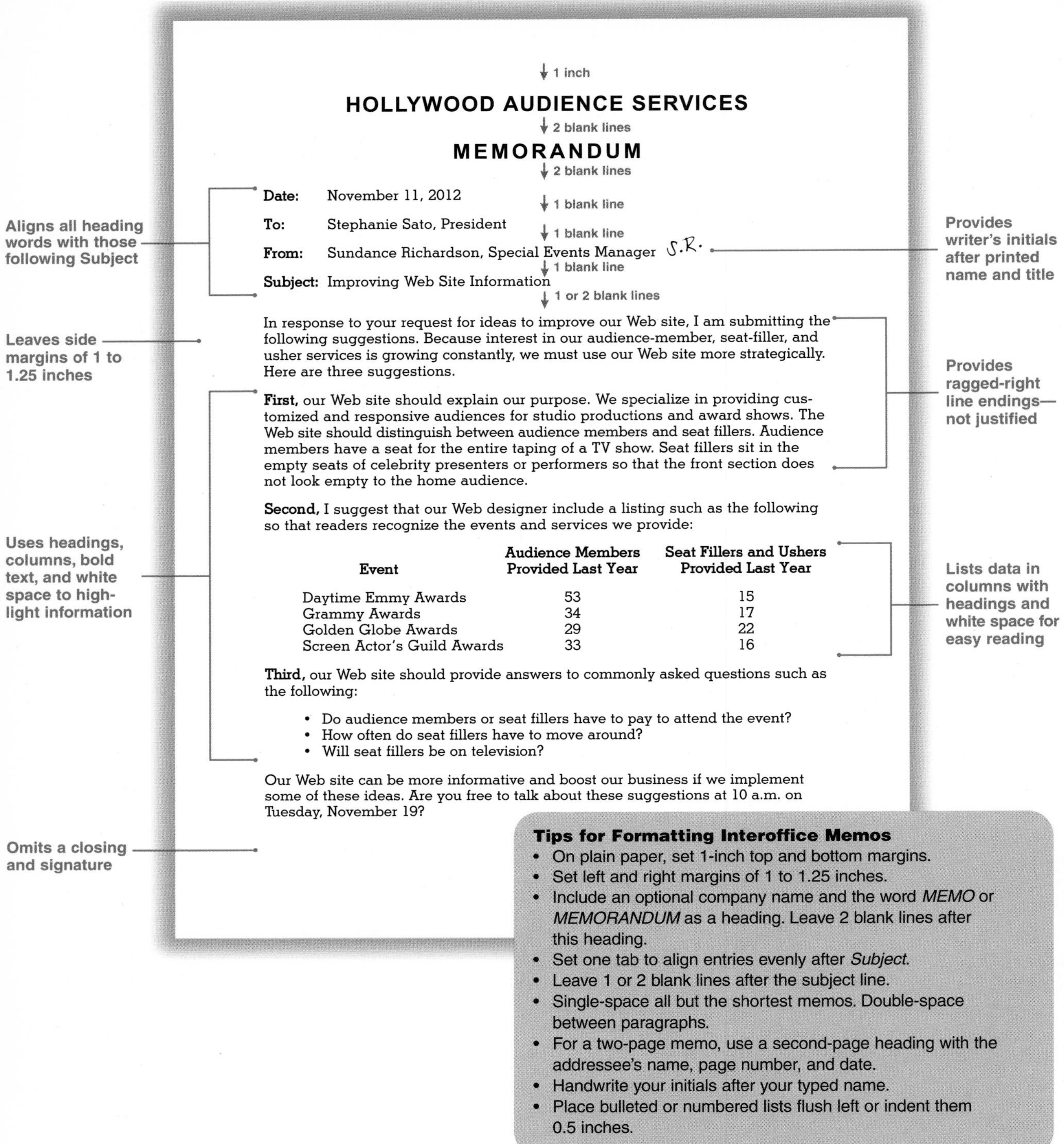

↓ 1 inch

HOLLYWOOD AUDIENCE SERVICES

↓ 2 blank lines

MEMORANDUM

↓ 2 blank lines

Date: November 11, 2012 ↓ 1 blank line

To: Stephanie Sato, President ↓ 1 blank line

From: Sundance Richardson, Special Events Manager S.R.

↓ 1 blank line

Subject: Improving Web Site Information

↓ 1 or 2 blank lines

In response to your request for ideas to improve our Web site, I am submitting the following suggestions. Because interest in our audience-member, seat-filler, and usher services is growing constantly, we must use our Web site more strategically. Here are three suggestions.

First, our Web site should explain our purpose. We specialize in providing customized and responsive audiences for studio productions and award shows. The Web site should distinguish between audience members and seat fillers. Audience members have a seat for the entire taping of a TV show. Seat fillers sit in the empty seats of celebrity presenters or performers so that the front section does not look empty to the home audience.

Second, I suggest that our Web designer include a listing such as the following so that readers recognize the events and services we provide:

Event	Audience Members Provided Last Year	Seat Fillers and Ushers Provided Last Year
Daytime Emmy Awards	53	15
Grammy Awards	34	17
Golden Globe Awards	29	22
Screen Actor's Guild Awards	33	16

Third, our Web site should provide answers to commonly asked questions such as the following:

- Do audience members or seat fillers have to pay to attend the event?
- How often do seat fillers have to move around?
- Will seat fillers be on television?

Our Web site can be more informative and boost our business if we implement some of these ideas. Are you free to talk about these suggestions at 10 a.m. on Tuesday, November 19?

Aligns all heading words with those following Subject
Leaves side margins of 1 to 1.25 inches
Uses headings, columns, bold text, and white space to highlight information
Omits a closing and signature
Provides writer's initials after printed name and title
Provides ragged-right line endings—not justified
Lists data in columns with headings and white space for easy reading

Tips for Formatting Interoffice Memos

- On plain paper, set 1-inch top and bottom margins.
- Set left and right margins of 1 to 1.25 inches.
- Include an optional company name and the word *MEMO* or *MEMORANDUM* as a heading. Leave 2 blank lines after this heading.
- Set one tab to align entries evenly after *Subject*.
- Leave 1 or 2 blank lines after the subject line.
- Single-space all but the shortest memos. Double-space between paragraphs.
- For a two-page memo, use a second-page heading with the addressee's name, page number, and date.
- Handwrite your initials after your typed name.
- Place bulleted or numbered lists flush left or indent them 0.5 inches.

conversations and e-mails may be exchanged, important details are generally recorded in business letters that are kept in company files. Business letters deliver contracts, explain terms, exchange ideas, negotiate agreements, answer vendor questions, and maintain customer relations.

Business letters are confidential. Carefree use of e-mail was once a sign of sophistication. Today, however, communicators know how dangerous it is to entrust confidential and sensitive information to digital channels. A writer in *The New York Times* explained, "Despite the sneering term *snail mail*, plain old letters are the form of long-distance communication least likely to be intercepted, misdirected, forwarded, retrieved, or otherwise inspected by someone you didn't have in mind."[5]

Business letters presented on company stationery carry a sense of formality and importance not possible with e-mail. They look important. They carry a nonverbal message that the writer considered the message so significant and the receiver so prestigious that the writer cared enough to write a real message. Business letters deliver more information than e-mail because they are written on stationery that usually is printed with company information such as logos, addresses, titles, and contact details.

Finally, business letters deliver persuasive, well-considered messages. When a business communicator must be persuasive and can't do it in person, a business letter is more effective than other communication channels. Letters can persuade people to change their actions, adopt new beliefs, make donations, contribute their time, and try new products. Direct-mail letters remain a powerful tool to promote services and products, boost online and retail traffic, and solicit contributions. Business letters represent deliberate communication. They give you a chance to think through what you want to say, organize your thoughts, and write a well-considered argument. You will learn more about writing persuasive and sales messages in Chapter 10.

Using Correct Form in Business Letters

What are justified margins, and should business letters have them?

A business letter conveys silent messages beyond those contained in its printed words. The letter's appearance and format reflect the writer's carefulness and experience. A short letter bunched at the top of a sheet of paper, for example, looks as though it were prepared in a hurry or by an amateur.

For your letters to make a good impression, you need to select an appropriate format. The block style shown in Figure 8.4 is a popular format. In this style the parts of a letter—dateline, inside address, body, and so on—are set flush left on the page. The letter is arranged on the page so that it is centered and framed by white space. Most letters have margins of 1 to 1.5 inches.

In preparing business letters, be sure to use ragged-right margins; that is, don't allow your computer to justify the right margin and make all lines end evenly. Unjustified margins improve readability, say experts, by providing visual stops and by making it easier to tell where the next line begins. Although book publishers use justified right margins, as you see on this page, your letters should use ragged-right margins. Study Figure 8.4 for more tips on making your letters look professional. Appendix B provides more information about letter forms and formats.

Routine Request and Response Messages

LEARNING OBJECTIVE 3
Compose direct messages that make requests and respond to inquiries.

The majority of your business messages will involve routine requests and responses to requests, which are organized directly. Requests and replies may take the form of e-mails, memos, or letters. You might, for example, need to request information from a hotel as you plan a company conference. You might be answering an inquiry from a customer about your services or products. These kinds of routine requests and replies follow a similar pattern.

Creating Request Messages

When you write messages that request information or action and you think your request will be received positively, start with the main idea first. The most emphatic positions in a message are the opening and closing. Readers tend to look at them first. You should capitalize on this tendency by putting the most significant statement first. The first sentence of an information request is usually a question or a polite command. It should not be an explanation or justification, unless resistance to the request is expected. When the information or action requested is likely to be forthcoming, immediately tell the reader what you want.

A letter inquiring about hotel accommodations, shown in Figure 8.4, begins immediately with the most important idea: Can the hotel provide meeting rooms and accommodations for 250 people? Instead of opening with an explanation of who the writer is or why the writer happens to be writing this message, the letter begins directly.

FIGURE 8.4 Formatting a Direct Request Business Letter in Block Style

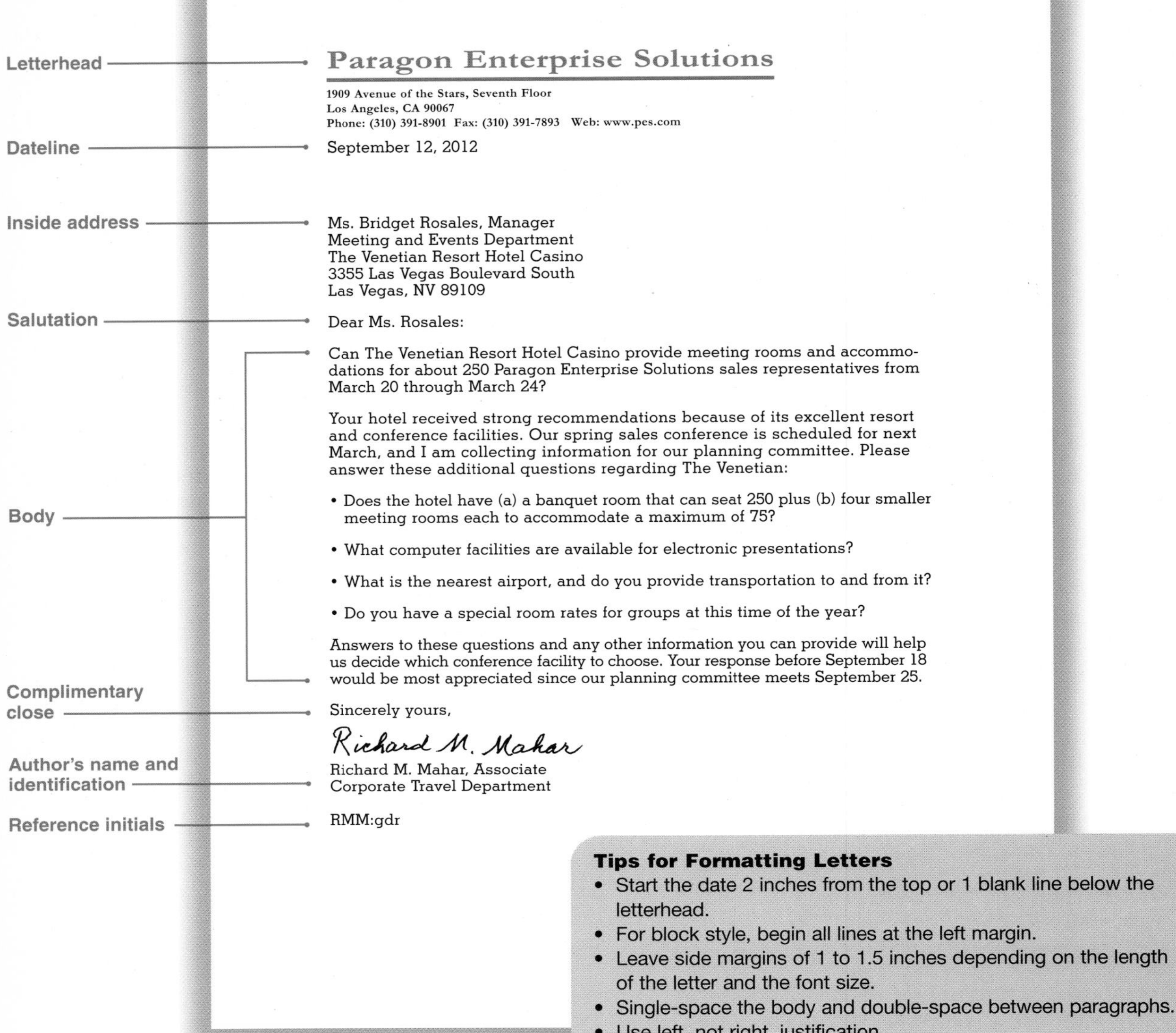

Paragon Enterprise Solutions

1909 Avenue of the Stars, Seventh Floor
Los Angeles, CA 90067
Phone: (310) 391-8901 Fax: (310) 391-7893 Web: www.pes.com

September 12, 2012

Ms. Bridget Rosales, Manager
Meeting and Events Department
The Venetian Resort Hotel Casino
3355 Las Vegas Boulevard South
Las Vegas, NV 89109

Dear Ms. Rosales:

Can The Venetian Resort Hotel Casino provide meeting rooms and accommodations for about 250 Paragon Enterprise Solutions sales representatives from March 20 through March 24?

Your hotel received strong recommendations because of its excellent resort and conference facilities. Our spring sales conference is scheduled for next March, and I am collecting information for our planning committee. Please answer these additional questions regarding The Venetian:

- Does the hotel have (a) a banquet room that can seat 250 plus (b) four smaller meeting rooms each to accommodate a maximum of 75?
- What computer facilities are available for electronic presentations?
- What is the nearest airport, and do you provide transportation to and from it?
- Do you have a special room rates for groups at this time of the year?

Answers to these questions and any other information you can provide will help us decide which conference facility to choose. Your response before September 18 would be most appreciated since our planning committee meets September 25.

Sincerely yours,

Richard M. Mahar

Richard M. Mahar, Associate
Corporate Travel Department

RMM:gdr

Tips for Formatting Letters

- Start the date 2 inches from the top or 1 blank line below the letterhead.
- For block style, begin all lines at the left margin.
- Leave side margins of 1 to 1.5 inches depending on the length of the letter and the font size.
- Single-space the body and double-space between paragraphs.
- Use left, not right, justification.
- Place the title of the receiver wherever it best balances the inside address.
- Place the title of the author wherever it best balances the closing lines.

If several questions must be asked, you have two choices. You can ask the most important question first, as shown in Figure 8.4, or you can begin with a summary statement, such as *Please answer the following questions about providing meeting rooms and accommodations for 250 people from March 20 through March 24.* Avoid beginning with *Will you please. . . .* Although such a statement sounds like a question, it is actually a disguised command. Because you expect an action rather than a reply, you should punctuate this polite command with a period instead of a question mark. To avoid having to choose between a period and a question mark, just omit *Will you* and start with *Please answer.*

How do you make a group of questions parallel in construction?

Providing Details. The body of a message that requests information or action provides necessary details. Remember that the quality of the information obtained from a request depends on the clarity of the inquiry. If you analyze your needs, organize your ideas, and frame your request logically, you are likely to receive a meaningful answer that doesn't require a follow-up message. Whenever possible, focus on benefits to the reader (*To ensure that you receive the exact sweater you want, send us your color choice*). To improve readability, itemize appropriate information in bulleted or numbered lists. Notice that the questions in Figure 8.4 are bulleted, and they are parallel. That is, they use the same balanced construction.

Closing With Appreciation and an Action Request. In the closing tell the reader courteously what is to be done. If a date is important, set an end date to take action and explain why. Some careless writers end request messages simply with *Thank you*, forcing the reader to review the contents to determine what is expected and when. You can save the reader time by spelling out the action to be taken. Avoid other overused endings such as *Thank you for your cooperation* (trite), *Thank you in advance for ...* (trite and presumptuous), and *If you have any questions, do not hesitate to call me* (suggests that you didn't make yourself clear).

Showing appreciation is always appropriate, but try to do so in a fresh and efficient manner. For example, you could hook your thanks to the end date *(Thanks for returning the questionnaire before May 5, when we will begin tabulation)*. You might connect your appreciation to a statement developing reader benefits *(We are grateful for the information you will provide because it will help us serve you better)*. You could briefly describe how the information will help you *(I appreciate this information, which will enable me to ...)*. When possible, make it easy for the reader to comply with your request *(Note your answers on this sheet and return it in the postage-paid envelope* or *Here is my e-mail address so that you can reach me quickly)*.

Ethics Check

Stretching the Truth

A magazine publisher sends you a letter saying that you should renew your subscription immediately to ensure continued delivery. Your subscription is paid for at least a year in advance, but nowhere in the letter or magazine label does your subscription end date appear. How far can a writer go in stretching the truth to achieve a purpose?

Responding to Requests

Often, your messages will respond directly and favorably to requests for information or action. A customer wants information about a product, a supplier asks to arrange a meeting, an employee inquires about a procedure, or a manager requests your input on a marketing campaign. In complying with such requests, you will want to apply the same direct strategy you used in making requests.

Why might a business letter include a subject line?

The opening of a customer response letter might contain an optional subject line, as shown in Figure 8.5. A subject line helps the reader recognize the topic immediately. Usually appearing two lines below the salutation, the subject line refers in abbreviated form to previous correspondence and/or summarizes the message *(Subject: Your July 12 Inquiry About WorkZone Software)*. Knowledgeable business communicators use a subject line to refer to earlier correspondence so that in the first sentence, the most emphatic spot in a letter, they are free to emphasize the main idea.

In the first sentence of a direct response letter, deliver the information the reader wants. Avoid wordy, drawn-out openings such as *I have before me your letter of August 5, in which you request information about....* More forceful and more efficient is an opener that answers the inquiry *(Here is the information you wanted about ...)*. When agreeing to a request for action, announce the good news promptly *(Yes, I will be happy to speak to your business communication class on the topic of ...)*.

In the body of your response, supply explanations and additional information. Because a letter written on company stationery is considered a legally binding contract, be sure to check facts and figures carefully. If a policy or procedure needs authorization, seek approval from a supervisor or executive before writing the letter.

Should a customer response message include more than the information requested?

When customers or prospective customers inquire about products or services, your response should do more than merely supply answers. Try to promote your organization and products. Be sure to present the promotional material with attention to the "you" view and to reader benefits *(You can use our standardized tests to free you from time-consuming employment screening)*.

In concluding a response message, refer to the information provided or to its use. *(The enclosed list summarizes our recommendations. We wish you all the best in redesigning your Web site.)* If further action is required, describe the procedure and help the reader with specifics *(The Small Business Administration publishes a number of helpful booklets. Its Web address is ...)*. Avoid signing off with clichés (*If I may be of further assistance, don't hesitate to ...*).

The checklist on page 231 reviews the direct strategy for information or action requests and replies to such messages.

FIGURE 8.5 Customer Response Letter

Prewriting

Analyze: The purpose of this letter is to provide helpful information and to promote company products.

Anticipate: The reader is the intelligent owner of a small business who needs help with personnel administration.

Adapt: Because the reader requested this data, he will be receptive to the letter. Use the direct strategy.

2 Writing

Research: Gather facts to answer the business owner's questions. Consult brochures and pamphlets.

Organize: Prepare a scratch outline. Plan for a fast, direct opening. Use numbered answers to the business owner's three questions.

Compose: Write the first draft on a computer. Strive for short sentences and paragraphs.

3 Revising

Revise: Eliminate jargon and wordiness. Look for ways to explain how the product the reader's needs. Revise for the "you" vie

Proofread: Double-check the form of numbers *(July 12, page 6, 8 to 5 PST)*.

Evaluate: Does this letter answer the customer's questions and encourage an order?

SONOMA SOFTWARE, INC.
520 Sonoma Parkway
Petaluma, CA 94539
(707) 784-2219
www.sonomasoft.com

July 15, 2012

Mr. Jeffrey M. White
Director, Human Resources
White-Rather Enterprises
1349 Century Boulevard
Wichita Falls, TX 76308

Dear Mr. White:

Subject: Your July 12 Inquiry About WorkZone Software

Yes, we do offer personnel record-keeping software specially designed for small businesses like yours. Here are answers to your three questions about this software:

1. Our WorkZone software provides standard employee forms so that you are always in compliance with current government regulations.
2. You receive an interviewer's guide for structured employee interviews, as well as a scripted format for checking references by telephone.
3. Yes, you can update your employee's records easily without the need for additional software, hardware, or training.

Our WorkZone software was specially designed to provide you with expert forms for interviewing, verifying references, recording attendance, evaluating performance, and tracking the status of your employees. We even provide you with step-by-step instructions and suggested procedures. You can treat your employees as if you had a professional human resources specialist on your staff.

On page 6 of the enclosed pamphlet, you can read about our WorkZone software. To receive a preview copy or to ask questions about its use, just call 1-800-354-5500. Our specialists are eager to help you weekdays from 8 to 5 PST. If you prefer, visit our Web site to receive more information or to place an order.

Sincerely,

Linda DeLorme

Linda DeLorme
Senior Marketing Representative

Enclosure

Identifies previous correspond and subject

Puts most important information first

Lists answers to sender's questions in order asked

Emphasizes "you" view

Links sales promotion to reader benefits

Helps reader find information by citing pages

Makes it ea to respond

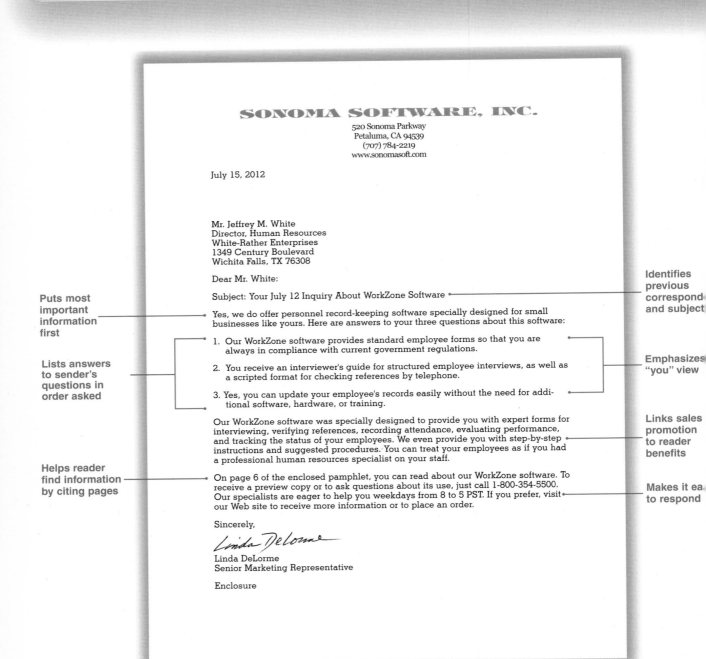

Checklist

Writing Direct Requests and Reponses

Requesting Information or Action

- **Open by stating the main idea.** To elicit information, ask a question or issue a polite command *(Please answer the following questions ...)*.
- **Explain and justify the request.** In the body arrange questions or information logically in parallel, balanced form. Clarify and substantiate your request.
- **Request action in the closing.** Close a request by summarizing exactly what is to be done, including dates or deadlines. Express appreciation. Avoid clichés *(Thank you for your cooperation, Thanking you in advance)*.

Responding to Requests

- **Open directly.** Immediately deliver the information the receiver wants. Avoid wordy, drawn-out openings (*I have before me your request of August 5*). When agreeing to a request, announce the good news immediately.
- **Supply additional information.** In the body provide explanations and expand initial statements. For customer letters, promote products and the organization.
- **Conclude with a cordial statement.** Refer to the information provided or its use. If further action is required, describe the procedures and give specifics. Avoid clichés (*If you have questions, please do not hesitate to let me know)*.

Instruction Messages

LEARNING OBJECTIVE 4
Write messages that clearly explain step-by-step instructions.

Instruction messages describe how to complete a task. You may be asked to write instructions about how to repair a paper jam in the photocopier, order supplies, file a grievance, or hire new employees. Instructions are different from policies and official procedures, which establish rules of conduct to be followed within an organization. We are most concerned with creating messages that clearly explain how to complete a task.

Like requests and responses, instruction messages follow a straightforward, direct approach. Before writing instructions for a process, be sure you understand the process completely. Practice doing it yourself. A message that delivers instructions should open with an explanation of why the procedure or set of instructions is necessary.

Dividing Instructions Into Steps

Why should instructions be written in steps using the imperative mood?

The body of an instruction message should use plain English and familiar words to describe the process. Your messages explaining instructions will be most readable if you follow these guidelines:

- Divide the instructions into steps.
- List the steps in the order in which they are to be carried out.
- Arrange the items vertically with numbers.
- Begin each step with an action verb using the imperative (command) mood rather than the indicative mood.

Indicative Mood	**Imperative (Command) Mood**
The contract should be sent immediately.	Send the contract immediately.
The first step involves loading the software.	Load the software first.
A survey of employees is necessary to learn what options they prefer.	Survey employees to learn the options they prefer.

In the closing of a message issuing instructions, consider connecting following the instructions with benefits to the organization or individual.

If you are asked to prepare a list of instructions that is not part of a message, include a title such as *How to Clear Paper Jams*. Include an opening paragraph explaining why the instructions are needed.

Revising a Message Delivering Instructions

Figure 8.6 shows the first draft of an interoffice memo written by Troy Bell. His memo was meant to announce a new method for employees to follow in advertising open positions. However, the tone was negative, the explanation of the problem rambled, and the new method was

FIGURE 8.6 Interoffice Memo Delivering Instructions

Draft

Date: January 5, 2012
To: Ruth DiSilvestro, Manager
From: Troy Bell, Human Resources
Subject: Job Advertisement Misunderstanding

We had no idea last month when we implemented a new hiring process that major problems would result. Due to the fact that every department is now placing Internet advertisements for new-hires individually, the difficulties occurred. This cannot continue. Perhaps we did not make it clear at the time, but all newly hired employees who are hired for a position should be requested through this office.

Do not submit your advertisements for new employees directly to an Internet job bank or a newspaper. After you write them, they should be brought to Human Resources, where they will be centralized. You should discuss each ad with one of our counselors. Then we will place the ad at an appropriate Internet site or other publication. If you do not follow these guidelines, chaos will result. You may pick up applicant folders from us the day after the closing date in an ad.

- Uses vague, negative subject line
- Fails to pinpoint main idea in opening
- New process is hard to follow
- Uses threats instead of showing benefits to reader

MEMORANDUM

Date: January 5, 2012
To: Ruth DiSilvestro, Manager
From: Troy Bell, Human Resources TB
Subject: Please Follow New Job Advertisement Process

To find the right candidates for your open positions as fast as possible, we are implementing a new routine. Effective today, all advertisements for departmental job openings should be routed through the Human Resources Department.

A major problem resulted from the change in hiring procedures implemented last month. Each department is placing job advertisements for new-hires individually, when all such requests should be centralized in this office. To process applications more efficiently, please follow these steps:

1. Write an advertisement for a position in your department.
2. Bring the ad to Human Resources and discuss it with one of our counselors.
3. Let Human Resources place the ad at an appropriate Internet job bank or submit it to a newspaper.
4. Pick up applicant folders from Human Resources the day following the closing date provided in the ad.

Following these guidelines will save you work and will also enable Human Resources to help you fill your openings more quickly. Call Ann Edmonds at Ext. 2505 if you have questions about this process.

- Employs informative, courteous, upbeat subject line
- Combines "you" view with main idea in opening
- Explains why change in procedures is necessary
- Lists easy-to-follow steps and starts each step with a verb
- Closes by reinforcing benefits to reader

Tips for Writing Instructions

- Arrange each step in the order it should be completed.
- Start each instruction with an action verb in the imperative (command) mood.
- Be careful of tone when writing messages that give orders.
- Show reader benefits if you are encouraging use of the process.

unclear. Notice, too, that Troy's first draft told readers what they *shouldn't* do (*Do not submit advertisements for new employees directly to an Internet job bank or a newspaper*). It is more helpful to tell readers what they *should* do. Finally, Troy's first memo closed with a threat instead of showing readers how this new practice will help them.

In the revision Troy improved the tone considerably. The subject line contains a *please*, which is always pleasant to see even if one is giving an order. The subject line also includes a verb and specifies the purpose of the memo. Instead of expressing his ideas with negative words and threats, Troy revised his message to explain objectively and concisely what went wrong.

Why do numbered steps and action verbs improve the clarity of instructions?

Troy realized that his original explanation of the new procedure was vague and unclear. To clarify the instructions, he itemized and numbered the steps. Each step begins with an action verb in the imperative (command) mood (*Write, Bring, Let,* and *Pick up*). It is sometimes difficult to force all the steps in a list into this kind of command language. Troy struggled, but by trying different wording, he finally found verbs that worked.

Why should you go to so much trouble to make lists and achieve parallelism? Because readers can comprehend what you have said much more quickly. Parallel language also makes you look professional and efficient.

In writing messages that deliver instructions, be careful of tone. Today's managers and team leaders seek employee participation and cooperation. These goals can't be achieved, though, if the writer sounds like a dictator or an autocrat. Avoid making accusations and fixing blame. Rather, explain changes, give reasons, and suggest benefits to the reader. Assume that employees want to contribute to the success of the organization and to their own achievement. Notice in the Figure 8.6 revision that Troy tells readers that they will save time and have their open positions filled more quickly if they follow the new method.

Learning More About Writing Instructions

Where can you go to learn more about how to write instructions?

The writing of instructions is so important that we have developed a special bonus online supplement called *How to Write Instructions.* It provides more examples and information. This online supplement at **www.meguffey.com** extends your textbook with in-depth material including links to real businesses showing you examples of well-written instructions.

Direct Claims

LEARNING OBJECTIVE 5
Prepare messages that make direct claims.

In business, things can and do go wrong—promised shipments are late, warrantied goods fail, or service is disappointing. When you as a customer must write to identify or correct a wrong, the letter is called a *claim*. Straightforward claims are those to which you expect the receiver to agree readily. Even these claims, however, often require a letter. Your first action may be a telephone call or an e-mail to submit your claim, but you may not be satisfied with the result. Claims written as letters are taken more seriously than telephone calls or e-mails, and letters also establish a record of what happened. Straightforward claims use a direct approach. Claims that require a persuasive response are presented in Chapter 10.

Opening a Claim With a Clear Statement

Why is a letter better than a telephone call or e-mail when making a claim?

When you, as a customer, have a legitimate claim, you can expect a positive response from a company. Smart businesses want to hear from their customers. They know that retaining a customer is far less costly than recruiting a new customer.

Open your claim with a compliment, point of agreement, statement of the problem, brief review of action you have taken to resolve the problem, or a clear statement of the action you want. You might expect a replacement, a refund, a new product, credit to your account, correction of a billing error, free repairs, free inspection, or cancellation of an order. When the remedy is obvious, state it immediately *(Please send us 25 Sanyo digital travel alarm clocks to replace the Sanyo analog travel alarm clocks sent in error with our order shipped January 4)*. When the remedy is less obvious, you might ask for a change in policy or procedure or simply for an explanation *(Because three of our employees with confirmed reservations were refused rooms September 16 in your hotel, would you please clarify your policy regarding reservations and late arrivals)*.

Explaining and Justifying a Claim

In the body of a claim letter, explain the problem and justify your request. Provide the necessary details so that the difficulty can be corrected without further correspondence. Avoid becoming angry or trying to fix blame. Although you may be upset, bear in mind that the person reading your letter is seldom responsible for the problem. Instead, state the facts logically, objectively, and unemotionally; let the reader decide on the causes. Include copies of all pertinent documents such as invoices, sales slips, catalog descriptions, and repair records. By the way, be sure to send copies and NOT your originals, which could be lost. When service is involved, cite the names of individuals you spoke to and the dates of the calls. Assume that a company honestly wants to satisfy its customers—because most do. When an alternative remedy exists, spell it out *(If you are unable to send 25 Sanyo digital travel alarm clocks immediately, please credit our account now and notify us when they become available).*

ETHICS CHECK

Renting or Buying?

Lucky U.S. consumers enjoy some of the world's most generous merchandise return policies. It is no wonder, perhaps, that some customers presumably buy video cameras or dresses for special events and return them afterward, no questions asked. Is this so-called renting, or wardrobing, wrong? Do retailers invite such behavior with their liberal policies?

Concluding a Claim With an Action Request

End a claim with a courteous statement that promotes goodwill and summarizes your action request. If appropriate, include an end date *(We realize that mistakes in ordering and shipping sometimes occur. Because we've enjoyed your prompt service in the past, we hope that you will be able to send us the Sanyo digital travel alarm clocks by January 15).* Finally, in making claims, act promptly. Delaying claims makes them appear less important. Delayed claims are also more difficult to verify. By taking the time to put your claim in writing, you indicate your seriousness. A written claim starts a record of the problem, should later action be necessary. Be sure to keep a copy of your message.

Why do you think claims submitted promptly are taken more seriously than delayed ones?

When Keith Krahnke received a statement showing a charge for a three-year service warranty that he did not purchase, he was furious. He called the store but failed to get satisfaction. Then he decided to write. You can see the first draft of his direct claim letter in Figure 8.7. This draft gave him a chance to vent his anger, but it accomplished little else. The tone was belligerent, and it assumed that the company intentionally mischarged him. Furthermore, it failed to tell the reader how to remedy the problem. The revision, also shown in Figure 8.7, tempered the tone, described the problem objectively, and provided facts and figures. Most important, it specified exactly what Keith wanted to be done.

Notice in Figure 8.7 that Keith used the personal business letter style, which is appropriate for you to use in writing personal messages. Your return address, but not your name, appears above the date.

Royal Caribbean International's service reputation ran aground temporarily when a scheduling error sank one couple's plans for a romantic honeymoon cruise. The vacation company's alternate arrangements also went adrift when representatives failed to notify the newlyweds about their rescheduled trip. Although the newlyweds eventually received a $1,700 voucher from Royal Caribbean for a future cruise, the couple was disappointed that Royal Caribbean's initial apology letter wasn't accompanied by a full refund. *What are the key elements of an effective adjustment letter?*

FIGURE 8.7 Direct Claim Letter

Draft

Dear Good Vibes:

You call yourselves Good Vibes, but all I'm getting from your service is bad vibes! I'm furious that you have your salespeople slip in unwanted service warranties to boost your sales.

Sounds angry; jumps to conclusions

When I bought my Panatronic DVR from Good Vibes, Inc., in August, I specifically told the salesperson that I did NOT want a three-year service warranty. But there it is on my Visa statement this month! You people have obviously billed me for a service I did not authorize. I refuse to pay this charge.

Forgets that mistakes happen

How can you hope to stay in business with such fraudulent practices? I was expecting to return this month and look at HDTVs, but you can be sure I'll find an honest dealer this time.

Fails to suggest solution

Angrily,

Revision

Personal business letter style

1201 Lantana Court
Lake Worth, FL 33461
September 3, 2012

Ms. Ernestine Sanborn
Manager, Customer Satisfaction
Good Vibes, Inc.
2003 53rd Street
West Palm Beach, FL 33407

Dear Ms. Sanborn:

States simply and clearly what to do

Please credit my Visa account, No. 0000-0046-2198-9421, to correct an erroneous charge of $299.

Doesn't blame or accuse; uses friendly tone

Explains objectively what went wrong

Documents facts

On August 1, I purchased a Panatronic DVR from Good Vibes, Inc. Although the salesperson discussed a three-year extended warranty with me, I decided against purchasing that service for $299. However, when my credit card statement arrived this month, I noticed an extra $299 charge from Good Vibes, Inc. I suspect that this charge represents the warranty I declined. Enclosed is a copy of my sales invoice along with my Visa statement on which I circled the charge.

Summarizes request and courteously suggests continued business once problem is resolved

Please authorize a credit immediately and send a copy of the transaction to me at the above address. I'm enjoying all the features of my Panatronic DVR and would like to be shopping at Good Vibes for an HDTV shortly.

Sincerely,

Keith Krahnke

Keith Krahnke

Enclosure

Tips for Submitting Claims

- Begin with a compliment, point of agreement, statement of the problem, brief review of action you have taken to resolve the problem, or clear statement of the action you want taken.
- Prove that your claim is valid; explain why the receiver is responsible.
- Enclose document copies supporting your claim.
- Appeal to the reader's fairness, ethics, legal responsibilities, or desire for return business.
- Avoid sounding angry, emotional, or irrational.
- Close by restating what you want done and looking forward to future business.

Adjustments

LEARNING OBJECTIVE 6
Create adjustment messages that regain the confidence of customers and promote further business.

Even the best-run and best-loved businesses occasionally receive claims from consumers. When a company receives a claim and decides to respond favorably, the message is called an *adjustment*. Most businesses make adjustments promptly: they replace merchandise, refund money, extend discounts, send coupons, and repair goods. Businesses make favorable adjustments to legitimate claims for two reasons. First, consumers are protected by contractual and tort law for recovery of damages. If, for example, you find an insect in a package of frozen peas, the food processor of that package is bound by contractual law to replace it. If you suffer injury, the processor may be liable for damages. Second, and more obviously, most organizations genuinely want to satisfy their customers and retain their business.

What is an adjustment message?

In responding to customer claims, you must first decide whether to grant the claim. Unless the claim is obviously fraudulent or excessive, you will probably grant it. When you say yes, your adjustment message will be good news to the reader. Deliver that good news by using the direct strategy. When your response is no, the indirect strategy might be more appropriate. Chapter 9 discusses the indirect strategy for conveying negative news. You have three goals in adjustment letters:

- Rectifying the wrong, if one exists
- Regaining the confidence of the customer
- Promoting further business

Revealing Good News Up Front in an Adjustment Message

Why should adjustment messages begin with the good news?

Instead of beginning with a review of what went wrong, present the good news immediately. When Kimberly Patel responded to the claim of customer Yonkers Digital & Wireless about a missing shipment, her first draft, shown at the top of Figure 8.8, was angry. No wonder. Yonkers Digital had apparently provided the wrong shipping address, and the goods were returned. Once Kimberly and her company decided to send a second shipment and comply with the customer's claim, however, she had to give up the anger. Her goal was to regain the goodwill and the business of this customer. The improved version of her letter announces that a new shipment will arrive shortly.

If you decide to comply with a customer's claim, let the receiver know immediately. Don't begin your letter with a negative statement (*We are very sorry to hear that you are having trouble with your dishwasher*). This approach reminds the reader of the problem and may rekindle the heated emotions or unhappy feelings experienced when the claim was written. Instead, focus on the good news. The following openings for various letters illustrate how to begin a message with good news:

> *You're right! We agree that the warranty on your American Standard Model UC600 dishwasher should be extended for six months.*
>
> *You will be receiving shortly a new slim Nokia cell phone to replace the one that shattered when dropped recently.*
>
> *Please take your portable Admiral microwave oven to A-1 Appliance Service, 200 Orange Street, Pasadena, where it will be repaired at no cost to you.*
>
> *The enclosed check for $325 demonstrates our desire to satisfy our customers and earn their confidence.*

In announcing that you will make an adjustment, be sure to do so without a grudging tone—even if you have reservations about whether the claim is legitimate. Once you decide to comply with the customer's request, do so happily. Avoid halfhearted or reluctant responses (*Although the American Standard dishwasher works well when used properly, we have decided to allow you to take yours to A-1 Appliance Service for repair at our expense).*

Explaining Compliance in the Body of an Adjustment Message

Why do most businesses comply with claims?

In responding to claims, most organizations sincerely want to correct a wrong. They want to do more than just make the customer happy. They want to stand behind their products and services; they want to do what is right.

FIGURE 8.8 Customer Adjustment Letter

Draft

Dear Sir:

I have before me your recent complaint about a missing shipment. First, let me say that it's very difficult to deliver merchandise when we have been given the wrong address.

After receiving your complaint, our investigators looked into your problem shipment and determined that it was sent immediately after we received the order. According to the shipper's records, it was delivered to the warehouse address given on your stationery: 451 Main Street, Yonkers, NY 10708. Unfortunately, no one at that address would accept delivery, so the shipment was returned to us. I see from your current stationery that your company has a new address. With the proper address, we probably could have delivered this shipment.

Although we feel that it is entirely appropriate to charge you shipping and restocking fees, as is our standard practice on returned goods, in this instance we will waive those fees. We hope this second shipment finally catches up with you at your current address.

Sincerely,

Blames customer and fails to reveal good news immediately

Creates ugly tone with negative words and sarcasm

Sounds grudging and reluctant in granting claim

Revision

DD

DIGITAL DEPOT
1405 Chambersburg Road
Trenton, NJ 08619-3590

Phone: (619) 839-2202
Fax: (619) 839-3320
Web: www.ddepot.com

April 24, 2012

Mr. Christopher Durante
Yonkers Digital & Wireless
359 South Broadway Avenue
Yonkers, NY 10705

Dear Mr. Durante:

Subject: Your April 19 Letter About Your Purchase Order

You should receive by April 26 a second shipment of the speakers, VCRs, headphones, and other digital equipment that you ordered April 2.

The first shipment of this order was delivered April 10 to 451 Main Street, Yonkers, NY. When no one at that address would accept the shipment, it was returned to us. Now that I have your letter, I see that the order should have been sent to 359 South Broadway Avenue, Yonkers, NY 10705. When an order is undeliverable, we usually try to verify the shipping address by telephoning the customer. Somehow the return of this shipment was not caught by our normally painstaking shipping clerks. You can be sure that I will investigate shipping and return procedures with our clerks immediately to see if we can improve existing methods.

Your respect is important to us, Mr. Durante. Although our rock-bottom discount prices have enabled us to build a volume business, we don't want to be so large that we lose touch with valued customers like you. Over the years our customers' respect has made us successful, and we hope that the prompt delivery of this shipment will retain yours.

Sincerely,

Kimberly Patel

Kimberly Patel
Distribution Manager

c Emanuel Chavez
Shipping Department

Uses customer's name in salutation

Announces good news immediately

Regains confidence of customer by explaining what happened and by suggesting plans for improvement

Closes confidently with genuine appeal for customer's respect

In the body of the letter, explain how you are complying with the claim. In all but the most routine claims, you should seek to regain the confidence of the customer. You might reasonably expect that a customer who has experienced difficulty with a product, with delivery, with billing, or with service has lost faith in your organization. Rebuilding that faith is important for future business.

How to rebuild lost confidence depends on the situation and the claim. If procedures need to be revised, explain what changes will be made. If a product has defective parts, tell how the product is being improved. If service is faulty, describe genuine efforts to improve it. Notice in Figure 8.8 that the writer promises to investigate shipping procedures to see whether improvements might prevent future mishaps.

Sometimes the problem is not with the product but with the way it is being used. In other instances customers misunderstand warranties or inadvertently cause delivery and billing mix-ups by supplying incorrect information. Remember that rational and sincere explanations will do much to regain the confidence of unhappy customers.

In your explanation avoid emphasizing negative words such as *trouble, regret, misunderstanding, fault, defective, error, inconvenience,* and *unfortunately*. Keep your message positive and upbeat.

Deciding Whether to Apologize

What are the arguments for and against apologies in adjustment messages?

Whether to apologize is a debatable issue. Attorneys generally discourage apologies fearing that they admit responsibility and will trigger lawsuits. However, both judges and juries tend to look on apologies favorably. More than 20 U.S. states have passed some form of an "apology law" that allows an expression of regret without fear that those statements would be used as a basis for liability in court.[6] Some business writing experts advise against apologies, contending that they are counterproductive and merely remind the customer of the unpleasantness related to the claim. If, however, apologizing seems natural, do so.

People like to hear apologies. It raises their self-esteem, shows the humility of the writer, and acts as a form of "psychological compensation."[7] Don't, however, fall back on the familiar phrase, *I'm sorry for any inconvenience we may have caused*. It sounds mechanical and insincere. Instead, try something like this: *We understand the frustration our delay has caused you, We're sorry you didn't receive better service,* or *You're right to be disappointed.* If you feel that an apology is appropriate, do it early and briefly. You will learn more about delivering effective apologies in Chapter 9 when we discuss negative messages.

The primary focus of an adjustment message is on how you are complying with the request, how the problem occurred, and how you are working to prevent its recurrence.

Using Sensitive Language in Adjustment Messages

What are examples of words that create negative reactions?

The language of adjustment messages must be particularly sensitive, because customers are already upset. Here are some don'ts:

- Don't use negative words *(trouble, regret, misunderstanding, fault, error, inconvenience, you claim).*
- Don't blame customers—even when they may be at fault.
- Don't blame individuals or departments within your organization; it's unprofessional.
- Don't make unrealistic promises; you can't guarantee that the situation will never recur.

To regain the confidence of your reader, consider including resale information. Describe a product's features and any special applications that might appeal to the reader. Promote a new product if it seems appropriate.

Showing Confidence in the Closing

How should you close an adjustment message?

End positively by expressing confidence that the problem has been resolved and that continued business relations will result. You might mention the product in a favorable light, suggest a new product, express your appreciation for the customer's business, or anticipate future business. It's often appropriate to refer to the desire to be of service and to satisfy customers. Notice how the following closings illustrate a positive, confident tone:

> *You were most helpful in informing us of this situation and permitting us to correct it. We appreciate your thoughtfulness in writing to us.*

Checklist

Direct Claim and Adjustment Messages

Messages That Make Claims

- **Begin directly with the purpose.** Present a clear statement of the problem or the action requested such as a refund, a replacement, credit, an explanation, or the correction of an error. Consider adding a compliment if you have been pleased in other respects.
- **Explain objectively.** In the body tell the specifics of the claim. Consider reminding the receiver of ethical and legal responsibilities, fairness, and a desire for return business. Provide copies of necessary documents.
- **Conclude by requesting action.** Include an end date, if important. Add a pleasant, forward-looking statement. Keep a copy of the letter.

Messages That Make Adjustments

- **Open with approval.** Comply with the customer's claim immediately. Avoid sounding grudging or reluctant.
- **In the body win back the customer's confidence.** Explain the cause of the problem, or describe your ongoing efforts to avoid such difficulties. Focus on your efforts to satisfy customers. Apologize if you feel that you should, but do so early and quickly. Avoid negative words, accusations, and unrealistic promises. Consider including resale and sales promotion information.
- **Close positively.** Express appreciation to the customer for writing, extend thanks for past business, anticipate continued patronage, refer to your desire to be of service, and/or mention a new product if it seems appropriate.

Thanks for writing. Your satisfaction is important to us. We hope that this refund check convinces you that service to our customers is our No. 1 priority. Our goals are to earn your confidence and continue to justify that confidence with quality products and excellent service.

For your patience and patronage, we are truly grateful.

Zooming In — PART 2

Ben & Jerry's

Customer letters arriving at Ben & Jerry's received special attention from Alice Blachly, a former consumer affairs coordinator. In responding to fan letters, Blachly prepared handwritten cards or printed letters that promoted good feelings and cemented a long-lasting bond between Ben & Jerry's and its satisfied consumers. To letters with questions, Blachly located the information and responded. For example, a consumer worried that cottonseed oil, formerly contained in the one of the nut-butter portions of an exotic ice cream, might be contaminated by pesticides. Blachly checked with company quality assurance experts and also investigated articles about cottonseed oil before responding. Other consumers wondered about Ben & Jerry's position on using milk from cloned cows and eggs from cage-free egg growers.

However, letters with consumer grumbles, such as *My pint didn't have quite enough cookie dough*, always received top priority. "We have trained our consumers to expect the best," said Blachly, "so they are disappointed when something goes wrong. And we are disappointed, too. We refund the purchase price, and we explain what caused the problem, if we know."

© Andre Jenny/Alamy

Critical Thinking

- When customers write to Ben & Jerry's for information and the response must contain both positive and negative news, what strategy should the respondent follow?
- If a customer writes to complain about something for which Ben & Jerry's is not responsible (such as ice in frozen yogurt), should the response letter contain an apology? Why or why not?
- Why is responding to customer inquiries an important function for a company such as Ben & Jerry's?

Your Asus Netbook will come in handy whether you are connecting with friends, surfing the net, listening to music, watching movies, or playing games. What's more, you can add an HDTV tuner and built-in GPS for a little more. Take a look at the enclosed booklet detailing the big savings for essential technology on a budget. We value your business and look forward to your future orders.

Although the direct strategy works for many requests and replies, it obviously won't work for every situation. With more practice and experience, you will be able to alter the pattern and apply the writing process to other communication problems. See the checklist on page 239 for a summary of what to do when you must write claim and adjustment messages.

Goodwill Messages

LEARNING OBJECTIVE 7
Write special messages that convey kindness and goodwill.

Many communicators are intimidated when they must write goodwill messages expressing thanks, recognition, and sympathy. Finding the right words to express feelings is often more difficult than writing ordinary business documents. That is why writers tend to procrastinate when it comes to goodwill messages. Sending a ready-made card or picking up the telephone is easier than writing a message. Remember, though, that the personal sentiments of the sender are always more expressive and more meaningful to readers than are printed cards or oral messages. Taking the time to write gives more importance to our well-wishing. Personal notes also provide a record that can be reread, savored, and treasured.

Why are personal goodwill messages more meaningful than ready-made cards?

In expressing thanks, recognition, or sympathy, you should always do so promptly. These messages are easier to write when the situation is fresh in your mind. They also mean more to the recipient. Don't forget that a prompt thank-you note carries the hidden message that you care and that you consider the event to be important. The best goodwill messages—whether thanks, congratulations, praise, or sympathy—concentrate on the five Ss. Goodwill messages should be

- **Selfless.** Be sure to focus the message solely on the receiver, not the sender. Don't talk about yourself; avoid such comments as *I remember when I. . . .*
- **Specific.** Personalize the message by mentioning specific incidents or characteristics of the receiver. Telling a colleague *Great speech* is much less effective than *Great story about McDonald's marketing in Moscow.* Take care to verify names and other facts.
- **Sincere.** Let your words show genuine feelings. Rehearse in your mind how you would express the message to the receiver orally. Then transform that conversational language to your written message. Avoid pretentious, formal, or flowery language *(It gives me great pleasure to extend felicitations on the occasion of your firm's twentieth anniversary).*
- **Spontaneous.** Keep the message fresh and enthusiastic. Avoid canned phrases *(Congratulations on your promotion, Good luck in the future).* Strive for directness and naturalness, not creative brilliance.
- **Short.** Although goodwill messages can be as long as needed, try to accomplish your purpose in only a few sentences. What is most important is remembering an individual. Such caring does not require documentation or wordiness. Individuals and business organizations often use special note cards or stationery for brief messages.

Spotlight on Communicators

Courtesy of Intel Corporation

Andrew S. Grove, cofounder and former chairman of Intel, the nation's principal computer chip maker, is best known as an Information Age leader and a technology visionary. But he also recognized the value of promoting personal relationships through goodwill messages. A mere thank-you followed by general comments is rather hollow, he said. Instead, when sending thanks or good wishes, Grove suggested making the thanks match the deed. Ask yourself what was special, unusual, extraordinary, or over and above the call of duty—and then describe it. Being specific, warm, and sincere is as important as the difference between a personal note and a computerized form letter.

Expressing Thanks

When someone has done you a favor or when an action merits praise, you need to extend thanks or show appreciation. Letters of appreciation may be written to customers for their orders, to hosts and hostesses for their hospitality, to individuals for kindnesses performed, and especially to customers who complain. After all, complainers are actually providing you with "free consulting reports from the field." Complainers who feel that their complaints were heard often become the greatest promoters of an organization.[8]

Written notes that show appreciation and express thanks are significant to their receivers. In expressing thanks, you generally write a short note on special notepaper or heavy card stock. The following messages provide models for expressing thanks for a gift, for a favor, and for hospitality.

To Express Thanks for a Gift. When expressing thanks, tell what the gift means to you. Use sincere, simple statements.

> *Thanks, Laura, to you and the other members of the department for honoring me with the elegant Waterford crystal vase at the party celebrating my twentieth anniversary with the company. The height and shape of the vase are perfect to hold roses and other bouquets from my garden. Each time I fill it, I'll remember your thoughtfulness in choosing this lovely gift for me.*

To Send Thanks for a Favor. In showing appreciation for a favor, explain the importance of the gesture to you.

> *I sincerely appreciate your filling in for me last week when I was too ill to attend the planning committee meeting for the spring exhibition. Without your participation, much of my preparatory work would have been lost. Knowing that competent and generous individuals like you are part of our team, Mark, is a great comfort. Moreover, counting you as a friend is my very good fortune. I'm grateful to you.*

To Extend Thanks for Hospitality. When you have been a guest, send a note that compliments the fine food, charming surroundings, warm hospitality, excellent host and hostess, and good company.

> *Jeffrey and I want you to know how much we enjoyed the dinner party for our department that you hosted Saturday evening. Your charming home and warm hospitality, along with the lovely dinner and sinfully delicious chocolate dessert, combined to create a truly memorable evening. Most of all, though, we appreciate your kindness in cultivating togetherness in our department. Thanks, Jennifer, for being such a special person.*

Responding to Goodwill Messages

Why should you respond to goodwill messages?

Should you respond when you receive a congratulatory note or a written pat on the back? By all means! These messages are attempts to connect personally; they are efforts to reach out, to form professional and/or personal bonds. Failing to respond to notes of congratulations and most other goodwill messages is like failing to say *You're welcome* when someone says *Thank you.* Responding to such messages is simply the right thing to do. Do avoid, though, minimizing your achievements with comments that suggest you don't really deserve the praise or that the sender is exaggerating your good qualities.

To Answer a Congratulatory Note. In responding to congratulations, keep it short and simple.

> *Thanks for your kind words regarding my award, and thanks, too, for sending me the newspaper clipping. I truly appreciate your thoughtfulness and warm wishes.*

To Respond to a Pat on the Back. When acknowledging a pat-on-the-back note, use simple words in conveying your appreciation.

> *Your note about my work made me feel good. I'm grateful for your thoughtfulness.*

Conveying Sympathy

What should go into a message of sympathy?

Most of us can bear misfortune and grief more easily when we know that others care. Notes expressing sympathy, though, are probably more difficult to write than any other kind of message. Commercial "In sympathy" cards make the task easier—but they are far less meaningful. Grieving friends want to know what you think—not what Hallmark's card writers think. To help you get started, you can always glance through cards expressing sympathy. They will supply ideas about

Checklist

Goodwill Messages

General Guidelines: The Five Ss

- **Be selfless.** Discuss the receiver, not the sender.
- **Be specific.** Instead of generic statements *(You did a good job)*, include special details *(Your marketing strategy to target key customers proved to be outstanding)*.
- **Be sincere.** Show your honest feelings with conversational, unpretentious language *(We are all very proud of your award)*.
- **Be spontaneous.** Strive to make the message natural, fresh, and direct. Avoid canned phrases *(If I may be of service, please do not hesitate . . .)*.
- **Keep the message short.** Remember that, although they may be as long as needed, most goodwill messages are fairly short.

Giving Thanks

- **Cover three points in gift thank-yous.** (a) Identify the gift, (b) tell why you appreciate it, and (c) explain how you will use it.
- **Be sincere in sending thanks for a favor.** Tell what the favor means to you. Avoid superlatives and gushiness. Maintain credibility with sincere, simple statements.
- **Offer praise in expressing thanks for hospitality.** Compliment, as appropriate, the (a) fine food, (b) charming surroundings, (c) warm hospitality, (d) excellent host and hostess, and (e) good company.

Responding to Goodwill Messages

- **Respond to congratulations.** Send a brief note expressing your appreciation. Tell how good the message made you feel.
- **Accept praise gracefully.** Don't make belittling comments *(I'm not really all that good!)* to reduce awkwardness or embarrassment.

Extending Sympathy

- **Refer to the loss or tragedy directly but sensitively.** In the first sentence, mention the loss and your personal reaction.
- **For deaths, praise the deceased.** Describe positive personal characteristics *(Howard was a forceful but caring leader)*.
- **Offer assistance.** Suggest your availability, especially if you can do something specific.
- **End on a reassuring, positive note.** Perhaps refer to the strength the receiver finds in friends, family, colleagues, or religion.

the kinds of thoughts you might wish to convey in your own words. In writing a sympathy note, (a) refer to the death or misfortune sensitively, using words that show you understand what a crushing blow it is; (b) in the case of a death, praise the deceased in a personal way; (c) offer assistance without going into excessive detail; and (d) end on a reassuring, forward-looking note. Sympathy messages may be typed, although handwriting seems more personal. In either case, use notepaper or personal stationery.

Businesses express condolences to bereaved employees in many ways. Flowers, cards, "comfort baskets," and pictures are popular corporate sympathy gifts that allow coworkers to grieve their loss with caring support from the company. Though such gift ideas are appropriate, a note of personal sympathy from a boss or colleague can be a more meaningful way to console an individual who is coping with misfortune and loss. *What important guidelines should be followed when extending sympathy in a personal message?*

To Express Condolences. Mention the loss tactfully, recognize good qualities of the deceased, assure the receiver of your concern, offer assistance, and conclude on a reassuring note.

> *We are deeply saddened, Gayle, to learn of the death of your husband. Warren's kind nature and friendly spirit endeared him to all who knew him. He will be missed.*
>
> *Although words seem empty in expressing our grief, we want you to know that your friends at QuadCom extend their profound sympathy to you. If we may help you or lighten your load in any way, you have but to call.*
>
> *We know that the treasured memories of your many happy years together, along with the support of your family and many friends, will provide strength and comfort in the months ahead.*

International Messages

LEARNING OBJECTIVE 8
Modify international messages to accommodate readers from other cultures.

The writing suggestions you have just studied work well for correspondence in this country. You may need, however, to modify the organization, format, and tone of messages going abroad.

American businesspeople appreciate efficiency, straightforwardness, and conciseness in messages. American business letters, for example, tend to be informal and conversational. Foreign correspondents, however, may look upon such directness and informality as inappropriate, insensitive, and abrasive.[9] Letters in Japan may begin with deference, humility, and references to nature:

> *The season for cherry blossoms is here with us and everybody is beginning to feel refreshed. We sincerely congratulate you on becoming more prosperous in your business.*[10]

How do Chinese sales letters differ from American sales letters?

The writers of Chinese letters strive to build relationships. A sales letter might begin with the salutation *Honored Company*, indicating a high level of respect. Figure 10.8 in Chapter 10 illustrates a Chinese persuasive letter, which contains a low-key sales approach. Although American business writers might use high-pressure tactics and direct requests, Chinese writers are more tentative. For example, a Chinese sales letter might say, *I hope you will take a moment to complete and mail the enclosed application.* The verb *hope* reduces the imposition of a direct request. Avoiding pressure tactics results from the cultural need to show respect and preserve harmony. Demonstrating humility, Chinese writers may refer to their own supposedly meager skills.[11] A typical closing in Chinese letters, *wishing good health*, emphasizes the importance of showing respect and developing reciprocal relationships.

Business letters in Germany tend to be informal. Business correspondents, however, generally address each other with honorifics and last names (Sehr geehrter Herr Woerner = Dr. Mr. Woerner), even if they have known each other for years. Letter introductions may refer to past encounters, meetings, or subjects previously discussed.[12] Italian business letters may refer to the receiver's family and children.

French correspondents would consider it rude to begin a letter with a request before it is explained. French letters typically include an ending with this phrase (or a variation of it): *I wish to assure you* [insert reader's most formal title] *of my most respectful wishes* [followed by the writer's title and signature].[13] Foreign letters are also more likely to include passive-voice constructions *(your letter has been received)*, exaggerated courtesy *(great pleasure, esteemed favor)*, and obvious flattery *(your distinguished firm)*.

Foreign letters may use different formatting techniques than American letters. Whereas American business letters are typewritten and single-spaced, in other countries they may be handwritten and single- or double-spaced. Address arrangements vary as well, as shown in the following:

German	**Japanese**
Herr [title, Mr., on first line]	Ms. Atsuko Takagi [title, name]
Dieter Woerner [name]	5-12 Koyo-cho 4 chome [street, house number]
Fritz-Kalle-Straβe 4 [street, house number]	Higashinada-ku [city]
6200 Wiesbaden [postal district, city]	Tokyo 194 [prefecture, postal district]
Germany [country]	Japan [country]

Zooming In

YOUR TURN

Applying Your Skills at Ben & Jerry's

Alice Blachly, former customer affairs coordinator at Ben & Jerry's, is overloaded with work. She asks you, her assistant, to help as she hands you a stack of letters. The top one is from a customer who complains that she didn't get quite enough cookie and chocolate chunks in her last pint. The customer also wants to know why Ben & Jerry's has strayed from its Vermont roots and rural values by setting up dairy operations in Nevada. However, she agrees with Ben & Jerry's strong stand against using milk from cloned cows.

Blachly tells you to explain that, although we work hard and long at it, the chunking equipment for nuts, chocolate, and cookies is as not always as consistent as B & J would like and that you will report the problem of cookie and chocolate chunks to production. She tells you to refund the estimated purchase price for one pint of ice cream. As she walks away, she says that B & J went to Nevada to supply its product to ice cream eaters on the West Coast. "Saves energy costs," she said. "We don't truck milk across the country."

© Andre Jenny/Alamy

Your Task

Respond to all three of the comments in the letter of Cora Nicol, 246 Falls Overlook Drive, Niagara Falls, NY 14109. Although her complaint was gentle, it is, nevertheless, a complaint that warrants an adjustment. In your response strive to maintain her goodwill and favorable opinion of Ben & Jerry's.

Dates and numbers can be particularly confusing, as shown here:

United States	Some European Countries
June 3, 2012	3rd of June 2012
6/3/12	3.6.12
$5,320.00	US $5.320,00

Want to do well on tests and excel in your course? Go to **www.meguffey.com** for helpful interactive resources.

- **Review the Chapter 8 PowerPoint slides to prepare for the first quiz.**

To be safe, spell out the names of months instead of using figures. Verify sums of money and identify the currency unit.

Because the placement and arrangement of letter addresses and closing lines vary greatly, you should always research local preferences before writing. For important letters going abroad, have someone familiar with local customs read and revise the message. An American graduate student learned this lesson when she wrote a letter, in French, to a Paris museum asking for permission to do research. She received no response. Before writing a second time, she took the letter to her French tutor, who said: "No, no, mademoiselle! It will never do! It must be more respectful. You must be very careful of individuals' titles. Let me show you!" The second letter won the desired permission.

Summary of Learning Objectives

1 **Apply the 3-x-3 writing process to creating successful positive messages, including e-mails, interoffice memos, and business letters.** Positive messages—whether e-mails, interoffice memos, or business letters—can be straightforward and direct because they carry nonsensitive, routine information. In applying Phase 1 of the writing process for positive messages, you should determine your purpose, visualize the audience, and anticipate the reaction of the reader to your message. In Phase 2 you should collect information, make an outline of the points to cover, and write the first draft. In Phase 3 you should revise for clarity,

proofread for correctness, and look for ways to promote "skim value." Finally, you should decide whether the message accomplishes its goal.

2 **Understand the appropriate use of e-mails, interoffice memos, and business letters.** E-mail is appropriate for short, informal messages. Interoffice memos are appropriate for internal messages that are important, lengthy, or formal. Like e-mails, interoffice memos follow a standard form with guide words *Date, To, From,* and *Subject*. Memos that serve as attachments to e-mails must be properly identified. Business letters are necessary when a permanent record is required; when confidentiality is critical; when formality and sensitivity are essential; and when a persuasive, well-considered presentation is important. Business letters written on company stationery often use block style with all lines starting at the left margin.

3 **Compose direct messages that make requests and respond to inquiries.** In direct messages requesting information or action, the opening immediately states the purpose of the message, perhaps asking a question. The body explains and justifies the request. If many questions are asked, they should be expressed in parallel form and balanced grammatically. The closing tells the reader courteously what to do and shows appreciation. In a message that replies directly and complies with a request, a subject line may identify previous correspondence, and the opening immediately delivers the good news. The body explains and provides additional information. The closing is cordial and personalized. If action is necessary, the ending tells the reader how to proceed and gives helpful details.

4 **Write messages that clearly explain step-by-step instructions.** When writing messages that explain instructions, you should (a) divide the instructions into steps, (b) list each step in the order in which it is to be carried out, (c) arrange the items vertically with bullets or numbers, and (d) begin each step with an action verb using the imperative (command) mood rather than the indicative mood (e.g., *Open the paper drawer, load the paper, and push the Start button)*. Messages that give instructions should not sound dictatorial. When changing existing procedures, avoid making accusations and fixing blame. Explain changes, give reasons, and suggest benefits to the reader.

5 **Prepare messages that make direct claims.** When a customer writes to identify a wrong and request a correction, the message is called a *claim*. A direct claim is one to which the receiver is expected to readily agree. A well-written claim begins by describing the problem clearly or telling what action is to be taken. The body of the claim explains and justifies the request without anger or emotion. The closing summarizes the request or action to be taken. It includes an end date, if appropriate, and courteously looks forward to continued business if the problem is resolved. Copies of relevant documents should be enclosed.

6 **Create adjustment messages that regain the confidence of customers and promote further business.** When a company grants a customer's claim, it is called an *adjustment*. An adjustment message has three goals: (a) rectifying the wrong, if one exists; (b) regaining the confidence of the customer; and (c) promoting further business. The opening immediately grants the claim without sounding grudging. To regain the confidence of the customer, the body may explain what went wrong and how the problem will be rectified. However, the writer may strive to avoid accepting responsibility for any problems. The closing expresses appreciation, extends thanks for past business, refers to a desire to be of service, and may mention a new product. If an apology is offered, it should be presented early and briefly.

7 **Write special messages that convey kindness and goodwill.** Messages that deliver thanks, praise, or sympathy should be selfless, specific, sincere, spontaneous, and short. Gift thank-yous should identify the gift, tell why you appreciate it, and explain how you will use it. Favor thank-yous should tell, without gushing, what the favor means to you. Expressions of sympathy should mention the loss tactfully; recognize good qualities in the deceased (in the case of a death); offer assistance; and conclude on a positive, reassuring note.

8 **Modify international messages to accommodate readers from other cultures.** Messages going to individuals in some areas, such as South Asia and Europe, should probably use a less direct organizational strategy and be more formal in tone. Because the placement and arrangement of business letter addresses and closing lines vary greatly, always research local preferences before writing business letters. For important messages going abroad, have someone familiar with local customs read and revise the message.

Are you ready? Get more practice at **www.meguffey.com**

Chapter Review

1. Into what three content categories can most business messages be organized? What group will make up the bulk of your messages? (Obj. 1)
2. How can you save the reader's time and make your business message easy to comprehend at a glance? (Obj. 1)
3. What kinds of messages are sent as are interoffice memos? (Obj. 2)
4. When is it important to send a business letter rather than an e-mail? (Obj. 2)
5. What are the most emphatic positions in a message, and what goes there? (Obj. 3)
6. What should you include in the closing of a request message? (Obj. 3)
7. How should instructions be written? Give a brief original example. (Obj. 4)
8. What is the imperative mood, and why is it important to use it in writing instructions? (Obj. 4)
9. What is a claim? When should it be straightforward? (Obj. 5)
10. Why should a direct claim be made by letter rather than by e-mail or a telephone call? (Obj. 5)
11. What is an adjustment message? (Obj. 6)
12. What are a writer's three goals in composing adjustment messages? (Obj. 6)
13. What are five characteristics of goodwill messages? (Obj. 7)
14. What are four groups of people to whom business communicators might write letters of appreciation? (Obj. 7)
15. What are three elements of business letters going abroad that might be modified to accommodate readers from other cultures? (Obj. 8)

Critical Thinking

1. Are the writing skills that are required for sending business e-mails and text messages different from those required for writing interoffice memos and business letters? Explain. (Objs. 1, 2)
2. In promoting the value of letter writing, a well-known columnist recently wrote, "To trust confidential information to e-mail is to be a rube."[14] What did he mean? Do you agree? (Obj. 2)
3. Why is it important to regain the confidence of a customer in an adjustment message? How can it be done? (Obj. 6)
4. How are American business letters different from those written in other countries? Why do you suppose this is so? (Obj. 8)
5. **Ethical Issue:** Assume that you have drafted a letter to a customer in which you apologize for the way the customer's account was fouled up by the Accounting Department. You show the letter to your boss, and she instructs you to remove the apology. It admits responsibility, she says, and the company cannot allow itself to be held liable. You are not an attorney, but you can't see the harm in a simple apology. What should you do? Refer to the section "Tools for Doing the Right Thing" in Chapter 1 to review the five questions you might ask yourself in trying to do the right thing.

Writing Improvement Exercises

8.1 Direct Openings (Objs. 1–7)

Revise the following openings so that they are more direct. Add information if necessary.

a. Despite the economy, Liberty Bank has been investigating the possibility of initiating an internship program within our Financial Services Department. I have been appointed as the point person to conduct research regarding our proposed program. We are fully aware of the benefits of a strong internship program, and our management team is eager to take advantage of some of these benefits. We would be deeply appreciative if you would be kind enough to help us out with answers to a number of specific questions.

b. My name is Kimberly Sanchez, and I am assistant to the manager of Information Services & Technology at Onyz, Inc. We are interested in your voice recognition software that we understand allows you to dictate and copy text without touching a keyboard. We are interested in answers to a number of questions, such as the cost for a single-user license and perhaps the availability of a free trial version. Will you please answer the following questions.

c. Your letter of March 4 has been referred to me. Pursuant to your inquiry, I have researched your question in regard to whether or not we offer our European-style patio umbrella in colors. This unique umbrella is one of our most popular items. Its 10-foot canopy protects you when the sun is directly overhead, but it also swivels and tilts to virtually any angle for continuous sun protection all day long. It comes in two colors: cream and forest green.

d. I am pleased to receive your inquiry regarding the possibility of my acting as a speaker at the final semester meeting of your business management club on May 2. The topic of online résumés interests me and is one on which I think I could impart helpful information to your members. Therefore, I am responding in the affirmative to your kind invitation.

8.2 Writing Instructions (Obj. 4)

Revise each of the following wordy, dense paragraphs into a set of concise instructions. Include an introductory statement.

a. Orders may be placed at our Web site by following certain steps. Here they are. As a visitor to our site, you should first look over everything and find the items you want from our catalog. Then your shopping cart is important. You will add items to your shopping cart. When you are finished adding things to your shopping cart, the next step is to proceed to checkout. But wait! Have you created a new account? After creating a new account, we next need to know what shipping address to ship your items to. We will also need to have you choose a shipping method. Then you will be expected to provide payment information. Finally, you are nearly done! Payment information must be provided, and then you are ready to review your order and submit it.

b. If you want to make a YouTube video, here are some important tips for those who have not done it before. First, you will need to obtain a video recording device such as a cell phone, webcam, or camcorder. Another thing you will have to do is make a decision on whether or not to make a video blog, comedy skit, how-to video, or a video that is about travel. Remember that your video must be 10 minutes or less for traditional YouTube membership accounts. You will want to create a video with good light quality, and that usually means daytime recording. Finally, be sure to use computer editing software to change or delete anything.

c. A number of employees have asked about how to make two-sided copies. Here's what to do. The copy for Side 1 of the original goes facedown on the document glass. Then the document cover should be closed. Next you should select the quantity that you require. To copy Side 1, you should then press Start. Now you remove the first original and place the second original facedown on the document glass. The document cover should be closed. Now you remove Side 1 copy from the output tray. It should be inserted facedown into the paper bypass tray. Then select the alternate paper tray and press Start.

Activities

Note: All Documents for Analysis are provided at **www.meguffey.com** for you to download and revise.

8.3. Document for Analysis: Direct Request (Obj. 3)

Your Task. Analyze the following poorly written message. List at least five weaknesses. If your instructor directs, revise the message using the suggestions you learned in this and previous chapters.

To: Amsoft Manager List
From: Stella Soto <stella.soto@amsoft.com>
Subject: E-Mail Problems
Cc:
Bcc:

Dear Managers,

As Amsoft vice president, I am troubled by a big problem. I am writing this note to ask for your help and advice to address an urgent problem—the problem of excessive e-mail. If you will do me the favor of answering the questions below, I'm sure your ideas will assist us in the development of a plan that should benefit your staff, yourself, and our organization will be improved. Your replies in writing to these questions (preferably by May 5) will help me prepare for our supervisory committee meeting on May 10.

Although e-mail is a great productivity tool, I'm afraid that its use is becoming extremely excessive. For our organization it is actually cutting into work time. Did you know that one study found that the average office worker is spending 3 hours a day on e-mail? In our organization we may be spending even more than this. It's exceedingly difficult to get any work done because of writing and answering an extraordinary number of e-mails coming in each and every day. Excessive e-mail is sapping the organization's strength and productivity. I would like to have your answers to some questions before the above referenced dates to help us focus on the problem.

Can you give a ballpark figure for how many e-mails you receive and answer on a personal basis each day? Think about how many hours the staff members in your department spend on e-mail each day. Approximately how many hours would you estimate? Do you have any ideas about how we can make a reduction in the volume of e-mails being sent and received within our own organization? Do you think that e-mail is being used by our employees in an excessive manner?

I'm wondering what you think about an e-mail-free day once a week. How about Fridays? I appreciate your suggestions and advice in developing a solution to the problem of controlling e-mail and making an improvement in productivity.

Stella Soto
Vice President, Operations

8.4 Document for Analysis: Direct Response (Obj. 3)

Your Task. Analyze the following poorly written interoffice memo that reports information from a symposium. List at least five weaknesses. If your instructor directs, revise the message.

Date: March 4, 2012
To: Trevor Kurtz, CEO
From: Emily Lopez-Rush
Subject: Instant Messaging

Thanks for asking me to attend the Instant Messaging Symposium. It was sponsored by Pixel Link and took place March 2. Do you think you will want me to expand on what I learned at the next management council meeting? I believe that meeting is March 25.

Anyway, here's my report. Jason Howard, the symposium leader told us that over 80 million workers are already using instant messaging and that it was definitely here to stay. But do the risks outweigh the advantages? He talked about benefits, providers, costs involved, and risks. The top advantages of IM are speed, documentation, and it saves costs. The major problems are spam, security, control, and disruptive. He said that the principal IM providers for consumers were AOL Instant Messenger, Windows Live Messenger, and Yahoo Messenger.

Misuse of IM can result in reductions in productivity. However, positive results can be achieved with appropriate use. Although some employees are using consumer IM services, for maximum security many organizations are investing in enterprise-level IM systems, and they are adopting guidelines for employees. These enterprise-level IM systems range in cost from $30 to $100 per user license. The cost depends on the amount of functionality.

This is just a summary of what I learned. If you want to hear more, please do not hesitate to call.

8.5 Document for Analysis: Direct Claim (Obj. 5)

Your Task. Analyze the following poorly written claim letter. List at least five weaknesses. If your instructor directs, revise it using the suggestions you learned in this chapter.

Current date

Ms. Melanie Cholston, Manager
Nationwide Car Rentals
1325 Commerce Street
Dallas, TX 75202

Dear Melanie Cholston:

I am writing this letter to inform you that you can't have it both ways. Either you provide customers with cars with full gas tanks or you don't. And if you don't, you shouldn't charge them when they return with empty tanks!

In view of the fact that I picked up a car at the Dallas-Ft. Worth International Airport on June 23 with an empty tank, I had to fill it immediately. Then I drove it until June 26. When I returned the car to Houston, as previously planned, I naturally let the tank go nearly empty, since that is the way I received the car in Dallas-Ft. Worth.

But your attendant in Houston charged me to fill the tank—$49.43 (premium gasoline at premium prices)! Although I explained to her that I had received it with an empty tank, she kept telling me that company policy required that she charge for a fill-up. My total bill came to $426.50, which, you must agree, is a lot of money for a rental period of only three days. I have the signed rental agreement and a receipt showing that I paid the full amount and that it included $49.43 for a gas fill-up when I returned the car. Any correspondence should be directed to the undersigned at Criterion Enterprises, 402 North Griffin Street, Dallas, TX 74105.

Inasmuch as my company is a new customer and inasmuch as we had hoped to use your agency for our future car rentals because of your competitive rates, I trust that you will give this matter your prompt attention.

Your unhappy customer,

8.6 Document for Analysis: Instructions (Obj. 4)

Your Task. This e-mail message is addressed to one employee, but it will also be sent to others. List at least five weaknesses. If your instructor directs, revise the message.

To: Sam Oliver <sam.oliver@stcc.edu>
From: Alexandra Tutson <alex.tutson@stcc.edu>
Cc:
Subject: Repairs

This message is to let you know that we have recently instituted a new process for all equipment repairs. Effective immediately, we are no longer using the "Equipment Repair Form" that we formerly used. We want to move everyone to an online database system. This new process will help us repair your equipment faster and keep track of it better. You will find the new procedure at http://www.BigWebDesk.net. That's where you log in. You should indicate the kind of repair you need. It may be for AudioVisual, Mac, PC, or Printer. Then you should begin the process of data entry for your specific problem by selecting **Create New Ticket**. The new ticket should be printed and attached securely to the equipment. Should you have questions or trouble, just call Sylvia at Extension 255. You can also write to her at *sylvia.freeman@stcc.edu.* The warehouse truck driver will pick up and deliver your equipment as we have always done in the past.

Alexandra Tutson, Manager
Operations and Facilities
alex.tutson@stcc.edu
(813) 355-3200, Ext. 230

8.7 Direct Request: Seeking a New Look for the Company Web Site (Obj. 3)

E-mail

You are part of the newly formed Committee on Web Site Redesign. Its function is to look into the possible redesign of your company Web site. Some managers think that the site is looking a bit dated. The committee delegates you to ask Cole Prewarski, Web master and manager, some questions. The committee wonders whether he has done any usability tests on the current site. The committee wants to know how much a total Web redesign might cost.

It also would like to know about the cost of a partial redesign. Someone wanted to know whether animation, sound, or video could be added and wondered if Cole would recommend doing so. Someone else thought that the timing of a redesign might be important. The committee asks you to add other questions to your memo. Invite Cole to a meeting April 6. Assume that he knows about the committee.

Your Task. Write an e-mail to Cole Prewarski (*cprewarski@global.net*) requesting answers to several questions and inviting him to a meeting.

8.8 Direct Request: Heading to Las Vegas (Obj. 3)

Web

Your company, Software.com, wants to hold its next company-wide meeting in a resort location. The CEO has asked you, as marketing manager, to find a conference location for your 85 engineers, product managers, and marketing staff. He wants the company to host a four-day combination sales conference/vacation/retreat at some spectacular spot. He suggests that you start by inquiring at the amazing Caesars Palace Las Vegas. You check its Web site and discover interesting information. However, you decide to write a letter so that you can have a permanent, formal record of all the resorts you investigate.

You estimate that your company will require about 80 rooms. You will also need three conference rooms (to accommodate 25 or more) for one and a half days. You want to know room rates, conference facilities, and entertainment options for families. You have two periods that would be possible: April 20-24 or July 10-14. You know that one of these is at an off-peak time, and you wonder whether you can get a good room rate. You are interested in entertainment at Caesars during these times. One evening the CEO will want to host a banquet for about 125 people.

Your Task. Write a well-organized letter to Ms. Isabella Cervantes, Manager, Convention Services, Caesars Palace, 257 Palace Drive, Las Vegas, NV 87551. Before writing, you might like to look at the Caesars Web site for information.

8.9 Direct Response: Restaurants Join Obesity Fight (Obj. 3)

As consumers become increasingly concerned about obesity and the health risks associated with nutrition, many seek more information about restaurant foods. American families are estimated to spend as much as half of their food dollars at restaurants and to consume about one third of their calories outside the home.

One U.S. senator is pushing a bill to require chain restaurants to list nutritional information for all menu items. Although this law has not been passed, your city would like to encourage restaurants to offer more nutritious menu choices.

Assume that you work for Partners for a Healthier Community (PHC), which is part of the City Health and Human Services Department. PHC has been working on a program called Healthy Dining. Its goal is to offer food establishments the opportunity to be recognized as Healthy Dining restaurants. In order to be listed, owners must meet certain criteria.

A PHC team devoted to the Healthy Dining program discussed a number of requirements. The team thought that restaurants ought to offer at least two choices of fruits or vegetables. They wanted choices other than potato dishes. The team was much opposed to french fries. What could be substituted for them? Perhaps salads? In regard to the menu, the team thought that Healthy Dining restaurants should have some low-fat and low-calorie menu items, and when they are offered, customers should know what they are. However, no minimum on the number of such items would be required. The team also thought that Healthy Dining restaurants should try to provide at least some dishes in smaller portion sizes or perhaps half portions. Milk was discussed, and team members suggested that restaurants move away from offering whole milk. Team members preferred 1 percent or skim milk when milk was offered as a beverage.

The team gave you the task of drafting a letter to restaurant owners who inquired about the Health Dining rating.

Your Task. Prepare a response letter to be sent to owners who want to know how to earn the Healthy Dining rating for their restaurants. Explain the goal of the Healthy Dining program, and show the requirements in a bulleted list. Address the first letter as a response to Mr. Adrian Hammersmith, Adrian's Steak House, 974 South Cobb Drive, Marietta, GA 30060. Explain that an application form and additional information are available at http://www.healthydining.com.

8.10 Direct Response Memo: Luxury Hotels Embrace Signature Scents (Obj. 3)

Web

Hotel chains are constantly seeking new ways to make guests want to return. Comfy beds and smiling clerks are not enough. Many hotels are now developing signature scents to waft through lobbies, restaurants, meeting rooms, and pool areas.

As an assistant to Michelle Long, CEO of a small hotel chain, you received an interesting assignment. Ms. Long recently visited the Park Hyatt in Washington, DC, and was impressed not only with its $24 million makeover and chic guest rooms but also with its custom fragrance. She asks you to conduct research online to discover what hotels are using fragrances and what scents are associated with each property. Her goal is to decide whether this trend is something her small hotel chain might follow.

In your research you discovered that Omni Hotels engage hidden machines to spray a lemongrass and green tea scent into the lobby. Omni also uses a coconut fragrance, for a tropical effect, near the pool. Apparently finding that scents are appealing, Omni plans to extend its fragrances to its meeting spaces. It is considering citrus, which is supposed to enhance energy.

You discovered that Westin Hotels & Resorts favors a white tea aroma. In Paris the fashionable Hotel Costes treats guests to an exclusive custom scent with notes of lavender, bay tree, coriander, white pepper, rose, incense, woods, and musk. Luxury properties are embracing signature fragrances to create an emotional connection to their hotels.

Your research also reveals a Web site complaining that hotels are contributing to the "sick building syndrome" by masking chemical smells with fragrances. Proponents of fragrance-free hotels recommend striving for fresh, not perfumed, air.

Your Task. Conduct additional Web research so that you can report on at least five hotels and their signature scents. Address a concise interoffice memo (or an e-mail if your instructor directs) to CEO Michelle Long. Decide whether to mention the argument for fragrance-free hotels. In addition, think about how you can make your findings most readable.

8.11 Direct Response Memo: Arranging Interviews for Environmental Architect/Designer (Obj. 3)

James F. Becker, founder and CEO of Becker & Associate Architects, is a busy architect. As he expands his business, he is looking for ecologically conscious designers who can develop sustainable architecture that minimizes the negative environmental impact of buildings. His company has an open position for an environmental architect/designer. Three candidates were scheduled to be interviewed on March 14. However, Mr. Becker now finds he must be in Dallas during that week to consult with the builders of a 112-unit planned golf course community. He asks you, his office manager, to call the candidates, reschedule for March 28 or March 29, and prepare a memo with the new times as well as a brief summary of the candidates' backgrounds.

Fortunately, you were able to reschedule all three candidates. Scott Hogarth will come on March 29 at 11 a.m. Mr. Hogarth specializes in passive solar energy and has two years of experience with SolarPlus, Inc. He has a bachelor's degree from the University of Southern California. Amanda Froescher has a master's degree from Boise State University and worked for five years as an architect planner for Boise Builders, with expertise in sustainable building materials. She will come on March 28 at 2 p.m. Without a degree but with ten years of building experience, Raul Ramirez is scheduled for March 28 at 10 a.m. He is the owner of Green Building Consulting and has experience with energy efficiency, sustainable materials, domes, and earth-friendly design. You are wondering whether Mr. Becker forgot to include Stanley Grafsky, his partner, who usually helps make personnel selections.

Your Task. Prepare a memo (or e-mail if your instructor directs) to Mr. Becker with all the information he needs in the most readable format. Consider using a three-column table format for the candidate information.

8.12 Instruction E-Mail or Memo: New Process for Purchase Requests (Obj. 4)

E-mail

Along with your parents, brothers, and sisters, you own a share of a growing family business with 55 employees. As the head of the Purchasing Department, you realize that the business must keep better track of purchases. Some employees use the company purchasing order forms, but others submit sloppy e-mails or handwritten notes that are barely legible. What's worse, you are not sure whether the requested purchase has been authorized by the budget manager. You talk to the family management council, and they urge you to establish a standard procedure for submitting purchase requests.

Because the business has a good Web site, you decide that purchase requests must now be downloaded from the company intranet (http://www.lynch.com/intranet). To provide the fastest service, employees should fill out the new purchase request form. This may be done manually or digitally. Employees must include complete information for each requested purchase: date, quantities, catalog numbers, complete descriptions, complete vendor mailing address and contact information, delivery requirements, and shipping methods (usually f.o.b.). The Purchasing Department should be sent the original, and a copy should be kept by the requesting employee. An important step in the new procedure is approval by the budget manager on the request form. That is, employees should talk to the budget manager and get her approval before submitting the purchase request. You think this new procedure will solve many problems for you and for employees.

Your Task. As Purchasing Department manager, write an e-mail or a hard-copy memo (as your instructor directs) to all employees informing them of the new procedure.

8.13 Instruction E-Mail or Memo: Cell Phone Use and Texting While Driving (Obj. 4)

E-mail | Team | Web

As one of the managers of Capri, a hair care and skin products company, you are alarmed at a newspaper article you just saw. A stockbroker for Morgan Stanley Smith Barney was making cold calls on his personal cell phone while driving. His car hit and killed a motorcyclist. The brokerage firm was sued and accused of contributing to an accident by encouraging employees to use cell phones while driving. To avoid the risk of paying huge damages awarded by an emotional jury, the brokerage firm offered the victim's family a $500,000 settlement.

You begin to worry, knowing that your company has provided its 75 sales representatives with cell phones to help them keep in touch with the home base while they are in the field. You are also worried about texting while driving. At the next management meeting, other members agree that you should draft a message detailing some cell phone safety rules for your sales reps. On the Web you learn several tips: Anyone with a cell phone should get to know its features, including speed dial, automatic memory, and redial. Another suggestion involves using a hands-free device. (Management members decide to purchase these for every sales rep and have the devices available within one month.)You also learn that cell phones in cars should be within easy reach so drivers can grab them without removing their eyes from the road. If they get an incoming call at an inconvenient time, they should allow their voice mail to pick up the call. They should never talk, of course, during hazardous driving conditions, such as rain, sleet, snow, and ice.

Texting while driving is totally out of the question! In addition, taking notes or looking up phone numbers is also dangerous. The more you think about it, the more you think that sales reps should not use their cell phones while the car is moving. They really should pull over. But you know that would be hard to enforce.

Your Task. Individually or in teams, write a memo or e-mail to Capri sales reps outlining company suggestions (or should they be rules?) for the safe use of wireless devices in cars. You may wish to check the Web for additional safety ideas. Try to suggest reader benefits in this message. How is safety beneficial to the sales reps? The message is from you acting as operations manager.

8.14 Instruction E-Mail or Memo: Describing a Workplace Procedure (Obj. 4)

E-mail

At your job or organization, assume that a new employee has joined the staff and the boss has asked you to write out a set of instructions for some task. It could be sending faxes, printing copies, answering the phone, setting up appointments, scheduling conferences, training employees, greeting customers, closing a cash register, opening the office, closing the office, or any other task that has at least five steps.

Your Task. Prepare an e-mail or memo to your manager, Josh Washington, in response to his request for a set of instructions for the task.

8.15 Instruction E-Mail or Memo: How to be Safe at Work (Obj. 4)

E-mail | Web

After a recent frightening experience, your boss, Kathryn Gossoni, realized that she must draft a memo about office security. Here's why she's concerned. A senior associate, Barbara Williams, was working overtime cleaning up overdue reports. At about 9 p.m. she heard the office door open, but the intruder quickly left when it was clear that someone was in the office. Your boss hurriedly put together the following memo to be distributed to office managers in five branch offices. But she was on her way out of town, and she asked you to revise her draft and have it ready for her approval when she returns. One other thing—she wondered whether you would do online research to find other helpful suggestions. Your boss trusts you to totally revise, if necessary.

Your Task. Conduct a database or Web search to look for reasonable office security suggestions. Study the following memo. Then improve its organization, clarity, conciseness, correctness, and readability. Don't be afraid to do a total overhaul. Bulleted points are a must, and check the correctness, too. Your boss is no Ms. Grammar! Be sure to add an appropriate closing. This may be either a memo or an e-mail, as your instructor directs.

Date: Current
To: Branch Managers
From: Kathryn Gossoni, Vice President
Subject: Staying Safe in the Office

Office security is a topic we have not talked enough about. I was terrified recently when a senior associate, who was working late, told me she heard the front door of the branch office open and she thought she heard a person enter. When she called out, the person apparently left. This frightening experience reminded me there are several things that each branch can do to improve it's office security. The following are a few simple things, but we will talk more about this at our next quarterly meeting (June 8?). Please come with additional ideas.

If an office worker is here early or late, then it is your responsibility to talk with them about before and after hours security. When someone comes in early it is not smart to open the doors until most of the rest of the staff arrive. Needless to say, employees working overtime should make sure the door is locked and they should not open there office doors after hours to people they don't know, especially if you are in the office alone. Dark offices are especially attractive to thieves with valuable equipment.

Many branches are turning off lights at points of entry and parking areas to conserve energy. Consider changing this policy or installing lights connected to motion detectors, which is an inexpensive (and easy!) way to discourage burglars and intruders. I also think that "cash-free" decals are a good idea because they make thieves realize that not much is in this office to take. These signs may discourage breaking and entering. On the topic of lighting, we want to be sure that doors and windows that are secluded and not visible to neighbors or passersby is illuminated.

We should also beware of displaying any valuable equipment or other things. When people walk by, they should not be able to look in and see expensive equipment. Notebook computers and small portable equipment is particularly vulnerable at night. It should be locked up. In spite of the fact that most of our branches are guarded by Broadview Security, I'm not sure all branches are displaying the decals prominently—especially on windows and doors. We want people to know that our premises are electronically protected.

8.16 Writing Clear Instructions (Obj. 4)

At **www.meguffey.com**, you will find a supplement devoted to writing instructions. It includes colorful examples and links to Web sites with relevant examples of real sets of instructions from business Web sites.

Your Task. Locate "How to Write Instructions" and study all of its sections. Then choose one of the following application activities:

A-5, "Revising the Instructions for an Imported Fax Machine," or A-6, "Evaluation: Instructions for Dealing With Car Emergencies." Complete the assignment and submit it to your instructor.

8.17 Direct Claim: Protesting Unexpected Charges (Obj. 5)

As vice president of Rochester Preferred Travel, you are upset with Premier Promos. Premier is a catalog company that provides imprinted promotional products for companies. Your travel service was looking for something special to offer in promoting its cruise ship travel packages. Premier offered free samples of its promotional merchandise, under its "No Surprise" policy.

You thought, *What can we lose?* So on January 11, you placed a telephone order for a number of samples. These included an insulated lunch sack, a portable power strip in a zippered case, a square-ended barrel bag with fanny pack, as well as a deluxe canvas attaché case and two colors of garment-dyed sweatshirts. All items were supposed to be free. You did think it odd that you were asked for your company's MasterCard number, but Premier promised to bill you only if you kept the samples.

When the items arrived, you were not pleased, and you returned them all on January 21 (you have a postal receipt showing the return). But your February credit card statement showed a charge of $258.20 for the sample items. You called Premier in February and spoke to Virginia, who assured you that a credit would be made on your next statement. However, your March statement showed no credit. You called again and received a similar promise. It's now April and no credit has been made. You realize that this situation is now too complicated for another telephone call, and you decide to write and demand action.

Your Task. Write a claim letter that documents the problem and states the action that you want taken. Add any information you feel is necessary. Address your letter to Ms. Arletta Sandusky, Customer Services, Premier Promos, 2445 Bermiss Road, Valdosta, GA 31602.

8.18 Direct Claim: Short Door for Tall Player (Obj. 5)

As the owner of Contempo Interiors, you recently worked on the custom Indiana home of an NBA basketball player. He requested an oversized 12-foot mahogany entry door. You ordered by telephone the solid mahogany door ("Provence") from American Custom Wood on May 17. When it arrived on June 28, your carpenter gave you the bad news. Magnificent as it was, the huge door was cut too small. Instead of measuring a total of 12 feet 2 inches, the door measured 11 feet 10 inches. In your carpenter's words, "No way can I stretch that door to fit this opening!" You waited four weeks for this handcrafted custom door, and your client wanted it installed immediately. Your carpenter said, "I can rebuild this opening for you, but I'm going to have to charge you for my time." His extra charge came to $940.50.

You feel that the people at American Custom Wood should reimburse you for this amount since it was their error. In fact, you actually saved them a bundle of money by not returning the door. You decide to write to American Custom Wood and enclose a copy of your carpenter's bill. You wonder whether you should also include a copy of the invoice, even though it does not show the exact door measurements. You are a good customer of American Custom Wood, having used its quality doors and windows on many other jobs. You are confident that it will grant this claim.

Your Task. Write a claim letter to Michael Medina, Operations Manager, American Custom Wood, 140 NE 136 Avenue, Vancouver, WA 98654.

8.19 Direct Claim: The Real Thing (Obj. 5)

Like most consumers, you have probably occasionally been unhappy with service or with products you have used.

Your Task. Select a product or service that has disappointed you. Write a claim letter requesting a refund, replacement, explanation, or whatever seems reasonable. Generally, such letters are addressed to customer service departments. For claims about food products, be sure to include bar-code identification from the package, if possible. Your instructor may ask you to actually mail this letter. Remember that smart companies want to know what their customers think, especially if a product could be improved. Give your ideas for improvement. When you receive a response, share it with your class.

8.20 Direct Claim: Barking Mad With Happpypets.com (Obj. 5)

E-mail

As the owner/operator of Posh Paws, a mobile dog grooming service, you recently purchased several items from Happypets.com. You encountered the Web site when surfing the Internet and were impressed with the variety and prices of its products. Because Happypets.com offered free shipping on orders over $100, you decided to take a chance on a company you had never heard of and place an order.

Using the online shopping cart, you ordered two bottles each of Top Performance UltraCoat Hot Oil Treatment and UltraCoat A-1 Hot Oil Shampoo. To qualify for the free shipping, you added one Very Berry Bow Canister. The holidays are approaching, and customers like bows on their freshly groomed pets. As you entered your credit card and delivery information, you had to check a box and agree to no exchanges because the items were on sale. You had previously used the hot oil products, so you figured you had nothing to lose and completed the $107.93 transaction. To be safe, you printed a copy of your order (number 0095644-1) for your records.

When the package arrived, you were barking mad. Although the packing slip accurately listed the items you requested, Happypets.com must have shipped you someone else's order: six bottles each of Pet Effects Watermelon and Pear Shampoo and Top Performance Soothing Suds Shampoo. Because the holiday season is fast approaching, you must purchase your supplies locally.

Your Task. Write an e-mail that documents the problem and states the action you want taken. Add any information you feel is necessary. Send the e-mail to *Customer Services@Happypets.com.*

8.21 Direct Claim: But It Doesn't Work! (Obj. 5)

E-mail

After you receive an unexpected bonus, you decide to indulge and buy a new HDTV. You conduct research to compare prices and decide on a Panasonic 42-inch Plasma HDTV Model TC-P42X1. You find a great deal at Digital Depot for $599.95 plus tax. Although the closest store is a 45-minute drive, the price is so good you decide it's worth the trip. You sell your old TV to make room for the Panasonic and spend several hours installing the new set. It works perfectly, but the next day when you go to turn it on, nothing happens. You check everything, but no matter what you do, you can't get a picture. You're irritated! You are without a TV and have wasted hours hooking up the Panasonic. Assuming it's just a faulty set, you pack up the TV and drive back to Digital Depot. You have no trouble returning the item and come home with a second Panasonic.

Again you install the TV, and again you enjoy your new purchase. But the next day, you have no picture for a second time. Now you are fuming! Not looking forward to your third trip to Digital Depot, you repack the Panasonic and return it. The customer service representative tries to offer you another Panasonic, but you decline. You point out all the trouble you have been through and say you would prefer a more reliable TV from a different manufacturer that is the same size and in the same price range as the Panasonic. Digital Depot carries a Samsung (Model PN42B450B1D) that fits your criteria, but at $729.00, it is more than you had budgeted. You feel that after all the problems you have endured, Digital Depot should sell you the Samsung at the same price. However, when you called to discuss the matter, you were told to submit a written request.

Your Task. Write a direct claim letter to Dennis Garcia, Manager, Digital Depot, 2300 Austin Street, Houston, TX 77074, asking him to sell you the TV for less than the advertised price.

8.22 Adjustment: Responding to Short Door for Tall Player (Obj. 6)

As Michael Medina, operations manager, American Custom Wood, you have a problem. Your firm manufactures quality precut and custom-built doors and frames. You have received a letter from Erica Adams (described in **Activity 8.18**), an interior designer. Her letter explained that the custom mahogany door ("Provence") she received was cut to the wrong dimensions. She ordered an oversized door measuring 12 feet 2 inches. The door that arrived was 11 feet 10 inches.

Ms. Adams kept the door because her client, an NBA basketball player, insisted that the front of the house be closed up. Therefore, she had her carpenter resize the opening. He charged $940.50 for this corrective work. She claims that you should reimburse her for this amount, since your company was responsible for the error. You check her May 17 order and find that the order was filled correctly. In a telephone order, Ms. Adams requested the Provence double-entry door measuring 11 feet 10 inches, and that is what you sent. Now she says that the doors should have been 12 feet 2 inches.

Your policy forbids refunds or returns on custom orders. Yet, you remember that around May 15 you had two new people working the phones taking orders. It is possible that they did not hear or record the measurements correctly. You don't know whether to grant this claim or refuse it. But you do know that you must look into the training of telephone order takers and be sure that they verify all custom order measurements. It might also be a good idea to have your craftspeople call a second time to confirm custom measurements.

Ms. Adams is a successful interior designer who has provided American Custom Wood with a number of orders. You value her business but aren't sure how to respond. You would like to remind her that American Custom Wood has earned a reputation as a premier manufacturer of wood doors and frames. Your doors feature prime woods, meticulous craftsmanship, and award-winning designs. What's more, the engineering is ingenious. You also have a wide range of classic designs.

Your Task. After much deliberation, you decide to grant this claim. Respond to Erica Adams, Contempo Interiors, 2304 River Ridge Road, Indianapolis, IN 46031. You might mention that you have a new line of greenhouse windows that are available in three sizes. Include a brochure describing these windows.

8.23 Adjustment: We Can Restretch But Not Replace (Obj. 6)

E-mail

Your company, ArtWorkOnline, sells paintings through its Web site and catalogs. It specializes in workplace art intended for offices, executive suites, conference rooms, and common areas. To make shopping for office art easy, your art consultants preselect art, making sure that the finished product is framed and delivered in perfect shape. You are proud that ArtWorkOnline can offer fine works of original art at incredibly low prices.

© dbimages/Alamy

Recently you received an e-mail from Huntzinger Construction claiming that a large canvas of an oil painting that your company sent had arrived in damaged condition. The e-mail said, "This painting sags, and we can't possibly hang it in our executive offices." You were surprised at this message because the customer had signed for delivery and not mentioned any damage. The e-mail went on to demand a replacement.

You find it difficult to believe that the painting is damaged because you are so careful about shipping. You give explicit instructions to shippers that large paintings must be shipped standing up, not lying down. You also make sure that every painting is wrapped in two layers of convoluted foam and one layer of Perf-Pack foam, which should be sufficient to withstand any bumps and scrapes that negligent shipping may cause. On the other hand, you will immediately review your packing requirements with your shippers.

It's against your company policy to give refunds or replace paintings that the receiver found acceptable when delivered. However, you could offer Huntzinger Construction the opportunity to take the painting to a local framing shop for restretching at your expense. The company could send the restretching bill to ArtWorkOnline at 438 West 84th Street, New York, NY 10024.

Your Task. Compose an e-mail adjustment message that regains the customer's confidence. Send it to Charles M. Huntzinger at *cmhuntzinger@huntzconstruction.com*.

8.24 Adjustment: Pigeon Problems (Obj. 6)

You didn't want to do it. But guests were complaining about the pigeons that roost on the Scottsdale Hilton's upper floors and tower. Pigeon droppings splattered sidewalks, furniture, and people. As the hotel manager, you had to take action. You called an exterminator, who recommended Avitrol. This drug, he promised, would disorient the birds, preventing them from finding their way back to the Hilton. The drugging, however, produced a result you didn't expect: pigeons began dying.

After a story hit the local newspapers, you began to receive complaints. The most vocal came from the Avian Affairs Coalition, a local bird-advocacy group. It said that the pigeons are really Mediterranean rock doves, the original "dove of peace" in European history and the same species the Bible said Noah originally released from his ark during the great flood. Activists claimed that Avitrol is a lethal drug causing birds, animals, and even people who ingest as little as 1/600th of a teaspoon to convulse and die lingering deaths of up to two hours.

Repulsed at the pigeon deaths and the bad publicity, you stopped the use of Avitrol immediately. You are now considering installing wires that offer a mild, nonlethal electrical shock. These wires, installed at the Maricopa County Jail in downtown Phoenix for $50,000, keep thousands of pigeons from alighting and could save $1 million in extermination and cleanup costs over the life of the building. You are also considering installing netting that forms a transparent barrier, sealing areas against entry by birds.

Your Task. Respond to Mrs. Tia Walsh, 24 Canyon Lake Shore Drive, Spring Branch, TX 52319, a recent Scottsdale Hilton guest. She sent a letter condemning the pigeon poisoning and threatening to never return to the hotel unless it changed its policy. Try to regain the confidence of Mrs. Walsh and promote further business.[15]

8.25 Adjustment: Backing Up "No Surprise" Offer (Obj. 6)

Premier Promos prides itself on its "No Surprise" offer. This means that anything ordered from its catalog of promotional products may be returned for a full refund within two weeks of purchase. The claim from Rochester Preferred Travel (see **Activity 8.17**) describes an order placed January 11 and returned January 21. As assistant to the Customer Services manager, you check the return files and see that items were received January 25. You speak with service agent Virginia, who agrees with you—the credit of $258.20 should have been granted to Rochester Preferred Travel. She reminds you that a new system for handling returns was implemented in February. Perhaps the Rochester return slipped through the cracks. Regardless of the reason, you decide to tell accounting to issue the credit immediately.

Your Task. In an adjustment letter, try to regain the confidence and the business of Rochester Preferred Travel, 245 East Avenue, Rochester, NY 14604. Include a sample imprinted travel mug in a gift box and a Coleman 8-quart jug cooler. You know that you are the most reliable source for the lowest-priced imprinted promotional products in the field, and this travel agency should be able to find something suitable in your catalog. Address your letter to Leticia Vascellaro, and sign it with your name.

8.26 Thanks for a Favor: Got the Job! (Obj. 7)

Congratulations! You completed your degree and got a terrific job in your field. One of your instructors was especially helpful to you when you were a student. This instructor also wrote an effective letter of recommendation that was instrumental in helping you obtain your job.

Your Task. Write a letter thanking your instructor.

8.27 Thanks for the Hospitality: Holiday Entertaining (Obj. 7)

You and other members of your staff or organization were entertained at an elegant dinner during the winter holiday season.

Your Task. Write a thank-you letter to your boss (supervisor, manager, vice president, president, or chief executive officer) or to the head of an organization to which you belong. Include specific details that will make your letter personal and sincere.

8.28 Sending Good Wishes: Personalizing Group Greeting Cards (Obj. 7)

Team | Web

When a work colleague has a birthday, gets promoted, or retires, someone generally circulates a group greeting card. In the past it wasn't a big deal. Office colleagues just signed their names and passed the store-bought card along to others. But the current trend is toward personalization with witty, oh-so-clever quips. And that presents a problem. What should you say—or not say?

You know that people value special handwritten quips, but you realize that you are not particularly original and you don't have a store of *bon mots* (clever sayings, witticisms). You are tired of the old standbys, such as *This place won't be the same without you* and *You are only as old as you feel.*

Your Task. To be prepared for the next greeting card that lands on your desk at work, you decide to work with some friends to make a list of remarks appropriate for business occasions. Use the Web to research witty sayings appropriate for promotions, birthdays, births, weddings, illnesses, or personal losses. Use a search term such as *birthday sayings, retirement quotes,* or *cool sayings.* You may decide to assign each category (birthday, retirement, promotion, and so forth) to a separate team. Submit the best sayings in a memo to your instructor.

8.29 Responding to Good Wishes: Saying Thank You (Obj. 7)

Your Task. Write a short note thanking a friend who sent you good wishes when you recently completed your degree.

8.30 Extending Sympathy: To a Spouse (Obj. 7)

Your Task. Imagine that the spouse of a coworker recently died of cancer. Write the coworker a letter of sympathy.

8.31 International Message: Negotiating a Cool Deal With a Chinese Supplier (Obj. 8)

E-mail | Intercultural

Your company, Pioneer Cable, seeks a cable assembly supplier in China. A few representatives of Pioneer just had a videoconference with AmRep China, a company specializing in finding Chinese manufacturers for American companies. Terrance Shaw, CEO and son of the owner, has been corresponding with Michael Zhu, who represents AmRep. The videoconference went well, but Mr. Shaw, the owner, wants Terrance to confirm in writing what was discussed. Terrance, better known as Terry around the office, is an upbeat, gadget-loving young executive who would rather be using IM than writing e-mail. He manages to put together a rough draft, but he asks you to help him improve it.

Your Task. Revise the following e-mail to make it more formal, readable, and interculturally acceptable.

To: Michael Zhu <Michael.zhu@AmRep.com>
From: Terrance Shaw <tshaw@pioneercable.com>
Subject: Videoconference Info
Cc:

Hey, Michael, it was great seeing and talking with you and your crew in the September 14 videoconference. Everyone here at Pioneer Cable is totally stoked about having AmRep China hook us up with a Chinese cable assembly supplier. We're sure you'll turn over every stone to find us a terrific supplier!

Because of all the heavy accents, it was a little hard to understand some speakers in our videoconference, so let me go over some things we agreed on. AmRep China is going to look for a cable assembly supplier for Pioneer. Right? You'll make no bones about getting us the best price/quality ratio you can possibly manage. This is obviously easier for you to do than for us because you'll be communicating in Chinese.

Unless I misunderstood, I heard one of your staff say that there would be continuous data feedback on quality control and that your company would provide technical conformance to the specifications that we submit. Is that right? There was also quite a discussion on ISO 9001:2000 standards and procedures, and you said that AmRep would definitely find a supplier that adheres to those standards. This is super important to us. I believe I also heard that AmRep would help us manage production and delivery schedules with our Chinese supplier.

The owner says that we must have confirmation of these points before we can continue our negotiations. Hope to hear from you soon!

Terry
CEO, Pioneer Cable
E-Mail: tshaw@pioneercable.com
Phone: (814) 739-2901
FAX: (814) 739-3445

Video Resource

Video Library 2, Adjustment Letter: Ben & Jerry's

In this video you see Ben & Jerry's managers discussing six factors that determine its continuing success. Toward the end of the video, you hear staffers discuss a new packaging material made with unbleached paper. As a socially responsible company, Ben & Jerry's wanted to move away from ice cream packages made from bleached papers. Bleaching requires chlorine, a substance that contains dioxin, which is known to cause cancer, genetic and reproductive defects, and learning disabilities. In producing paper, pulp mills using chlorine are also adding to dioxin contamination of waterways. After much research, Ben & Jerry's found a chlorine-free, unbleached paperboard for its packages. That was the good news. The bad news is that the inside of the package is now brown.

Assume you have been hired at Ben & Jerry's to help answer incoming letters. Although you are fairly new, your boss gives you a letter from an unhappy customer. This customer opened a pint of Ben & Jerry's World's Best Vanilla and then threw it out. After seeing the brown inner lid, he decided that his pint must have been used for chocolate before it was used for vanilla. Or, he said, "the entire pint has gone bad and somehow turned the sides brown." Whatever the reason, he wasn't taking any chances. He wants his money back.

Your Task. Write a letter that explains the brown carton, justifies the reason for using it, and retains the customer's business. Address the letter to Mr. Daniel Gilstrap, 17263 Blackhawk Avenue, Friendswood, TX 77546.

Chat About It

In each chapter you will find five discussion questions related to the chapter material. Your instructor may assign these topics for you to discuss in class, in an online chat room, or on an online discussion board. Some of the discussion topics may require outside research. You may also be asked to read and respond to postings made by your classmates.

Topic 1: In preparing to write a message, you learned that you should ask yourself (a) whether a written message is necessary, (b) what your goal is in writing, (c) how the reader might react, (d) what the best channel is, and (e) how you can write the message in a way that saves the reader time. Which of these questions do you feel is most important, and why?

Topic 2: Describe a time when you or someone you know wrote a letter that was successful in its purpose, such as gaining a refund, changing a decision, or achieving something that the reader might have opposed. Was another form of communication, such as a phone call, tried first? Why do think the letter was successful?

Topic 3: When responding favorably to a request that you are not thrilled to grant, why is it important in business to nevertheless sound gracious or even agreeable?

Topic 4: Conduct research regarding costly mistakes that resulted from unclear instructions. What is the most costly mistake you discovered?

Topic 5: Describe an occasion when you should have written a goodwill message but failed to do so. Why was it difficult to write that message? What would make it easier for you to do so?

Grammar and Mechanics C.L.U.E. Review 8

Capitalization

Review Guides 39–46 about capitalization in Appendix A, Grammar and Mechanics Guide, beginning on page A-16. On a separate sheet, revise the following sentences to correct capitalization errors. For each error that you locate, write the guide number that reflects this usage. Sentences may have more than one error. If a sentence is correct, write *C*. When you finish, check your answers on page Key-1.

Example: Neither the President nor the Operations Manager would comment on the Company rumor that it would close its midwest factory.

Revision: Neither the **president** nor the **operations manager** would comment on the **company** rumor that it would close its **Midwest** factory. [Guides 41, 43]

1. Once the Management Team and the Union members finally agreed, mayor knox signed the Agreement.
2. All delta airlines passengers must exit the Plane at gate 14 when they reach los angeles international airport.
3. The vice president of the united states urged members of the european union to continue to seek peace in the middle east.
4. My Uncle, who lives in the south, has Skippy Peanut Butter and coca-cola for Breakfast.
5. Our Marketing Manager and Director of Sales thought that the Company should purchase BlackBerry Smartphones for all Sales Reps.
6. Personal Tax Rates for japanese citizens are low by International standards, according to professor yamaguchi at osaka university.
7. Jinhee Kim, who heads our customer communication division, has a Master's Degree in social psychology from the university of new mexico.
8. Please consult figure 4.5 in chapter 4 to obtain U.S. census bureau population figures for the pacific northwest.
9. Last Fall did you see the article titled "The global consequences of using crops for fuel"?
10. Toby plans to take courses in Marketing, Business Law, and English in the Spring.

CHAPTER 9

Negative Messages

OBJECTIVES

After studying this chapter, you should be able to

1. Describe the goals and strategies of business communicators in conveying negative news effectively, including applying the writing process and avoiding legal liability.
2. Decide whether to use the direct or indirect strategy in conveying negative news.
3. Analyze the components of effective negative messages, including opening with a buffer, apologizing, conveying empathy, presenting the reasons, cushioning the bad news, and closing pleasantly.
4. Describe and apply effective techniques for refusing typical requests.
5. Explain and apply effective techniques for handling bad news with customers.
6. Understand and apply effective techniques for delivering bad news within organizations.
7. Compare strategies for revealing bad news in other cultures.

Want to do well on tests and excel in your course? Go to **www.meguffey.com** for helpful interactive resources.

- **Review the Chapter 9 PowerPoint slides to prepare for the first quiz.**

Zooming In

PART 1

Being Proactive Lessens Bad-News Nightmares at Southwest Airlines

Delayed flights, mishandled baggage, and passengers stranded on tarmacs are among the many nightmares of today's flyers. One carrier, however, leads the industry with the fewest consumer complaints. Southwest Airlines takes a proactive approach, giving its customers timely and regular updates—even when the news is bad. An ice storm caused a several-hour delay on a flight leaving St. Louis. Southwest flight attendants and pilots walked through the plane regularly, answering passengers' questions and providing information on connecting flights. Passengers on that flight were pleasantly surprised when vouchers for free round-trip flights arrived a few days later. The vouchers were accompanied by a letter from the airline apologizing for the inconvenience.

Such practices are the norm for Southwest. The Dallas-based discount airline—known for its low fares, lack of frills, and efficient service—has become a powerful brand in a competitive industry since its humble beginnings in 1971. Founders Rollin King and Herb Kelleher had a unique vision for their new company: Get passengers where they want to go, on time, at the lowest price—and make flying fun for both employees and passengers.

Their formula worked. Today, Southwest is the largest carrier in the United States based on domestic departures. It currently operates more than 3,100 flights a day and has nearly 35,000 employees.[1] Whereas other airlines are struggling and adding baggage and fuel fees, Southwest remains profitable and prides itself on its theme of "Fees Don't Fly With Us."[2]

High satisfaction ratings have won Southwest a spot on *BusinessWeek's* ranking of the country's 25 best customer service providers. Like its peers, however, Southwest has its share of problems. Irate customers complain about lost baggage, weather delays, and canceled flights. The difference is its response strategy. Fred Taylor, senior manager of proactive customer communications, tracks operating disruptions across the organization. He meets daily with department representatives to discuss possible problems and develop strategies to minimize difficulties before they happen. Capitalizing on social media, Southwest uses Twitter to send tweets with chatty trivia as well as travel updates and official announcements.[3]

Regardless of his proactive efforts to minimize customer complaints, Taylor still must respond occasionally to disappointed customers.[4] Delivering bad news and responding to customer complaints are major responsibilities of his job. You will learn more about this case on page 277.

© Justin Sullivan/Getty Images

Critical Thinking

- Suppose you applied for a job that you really wanted, but the company hired someone else. To notify you of the bad news, the company sends a letter. Should the letter blurt out the bad news immediately or soften the blow somewhat?
- What are some techniques you could use if you have to deliver bad news in business messages?
- What goals should you try to achieve when you have to give disappointing news to customers, employees, suppliers, or others on behalf of your organization?

http://www.southwest.com

Conveying Negative News Effectively

LEARNING OBJECTIVE 1

Describe the goals and strategies of business communicators in conveying negative news effectively, including applying the writing process and avoiding legal liability.

Bad things happen in all businesses. At Southwest Airlines, storms cancel or delay flights, baggage is misplaced, and air traffic interrupts schedules. In other businesses, goods are not delivered, products fail to perform as expected, service is poor, billing gets fouled up, or customers are misunderstood. You may have to write messages ending business relationships, declining proposals, announcing price increases, refusing requests for donations, terminating employees, turning down invitations, or responding to unhappy customers. You might have to apologize for mistakes in orders, errors in pricing, the rudeness of employees, overlooked appointments, substandard service, pricing errors, faulty accounting, defective products, or jumbled instructions. As a company employee, you may even have to respond to complaints voiced to the world on Twitter, Facebook, or complaint Web sites.

The sad truth is that everyone occasionally must deliver bad news in business. Because bad news disappoints, irritates, and sometimes angers the receiver, such messages must be written carefully. The bad feelings associated with disappointing news can generally be reduced if the receiver (a) knows the reasons for the rejection, (b) feels that the news was revealed sensitively, and (c) believes the matter was treated seriously and fairly.

In this chapter you will learn when to use the direct strategy and when to use the indirect strategy to deliver bad news. You will study the goals of business communicators in working with bad news and learn techniques for achieving those goals.

Establishing Goals in Communicating Negative News

What can the writer of a bad-news message strive to achieve in minimizing bad feelings?

Delivering negative news is not the happiest communication task you may have, but it can be gratifying if you do it effectively. As a business communicator working with bad news, you will have many goals, the most important of which are these:

- **Explaining clearly and completely.** Your message should be so clear that the receiver understands and, we hope, accepts the bad news. The receiver should not have to call or write to clarify the message.
- **Projecting a professional image.** You will strive to project a professional and positive image of you and your organization. Even when irate customers use a threatening tone or overstate their claims, you must use polite language, control your emotions, and respond with clear explanations of why a negative message was necessary.
- **Conveying empathy and sensitivity.** Bad news is better accepted if it is delivered sensitively. Use language that respects the receiver and attempts to reduce bad feelings. Accepting blame, when appropriate, and apologizing goes far in smoothing over negative messages. But avoid creating legal liability or responsibility for you or your organization.
- **Being fair.** Show that the situation or decision was fair, impartial, and rational. Receivers are far more likely to accept negative news if they feel they were treated fairly.
- **Maintaining friendly relations.** Make an effort to include statements that show your desire to continue pleasant relations with the receiver. As you learned in Chapter 8 in writing adjustment messages, one of your goals is to regain the confidence of customers.

These are ambitious goals, and we are not always successful in achieving them all. However, many senders have found the strategies and techniques you are about to learn helpful in conveying disappointing news sensitively and safely. With experience, you will be able to vary these strategies and adapt them to your organization's specific communication tasks.

Applying the 3-x-3 Writing Process

Why is the 3-x-3 writing process especially helpful in crafting bad-news messages?

Thinking through the entire writing process is especially important in bad-news messages because the way bad news is revealed often determines how it is accepted. You have probably heard people say, "I didn't mind the news so much, but I resented the way I was told!" Certain techniques can help you deliver bad news sensitively, beginning with the familiar 3-x-3 writing process.

Analysis, Anticipation, and Adaptation. In Phase 1 (prewriting), you need to analyze the bad news and anticipate its effect on the receiver. When Microsoft launched its first widescale layoff, an administrative glitch caused it to pay more severance than intended to some laid-off employees. After the mistake was discovered, Microsoft sent a bad-news letter bluntly asking the ex-workers to return the money. Employees not only suffered the loss of their jobs, but, adding insult to injury, Microsoft then demanded the return of $4,000 to $5,000 in severance pay. Some employees had already spent the money, and others were planning their futures with it. Obviously, the sender of the bad-news message had not considered the effect it would have on its readers. After the letters seeking repayment began to surface on the Web, Microsoft reversed course and allowed the workers to keep the overpayment.[5] However, the entire situation might have been handled better if Microsoft had given more thought to analyzing the situation and anticipating its effect.

When you have bad news to convey, one of your first considerations is how that message will affect its receiver. If the disappointment will be mild, announce it directly. For example, a small rate increase in a newspaper or Web subscription can be announced directly. If the bad news is serious or personal, consider techniques to reduce the pain. In the Microsoft situation, the bad-news letter should have prepared the reader, given reasons for the payback request, possibly offered alternatives, and sought the goodwill of the receiver.

Choose words that show you respect the reader as a responsible, valuable person. Select the best channel to deliver the bad news. In many negative situations, you will be dealing with a customer. If your goal is retaining the goodwill of a customer, a letter on company stationery will be more impressive than an e-mail.

Research, Organization, and Composition. In Phase 2 (writing), you will gather information and brainstorm for ideas. Jot down all the reasons you have that explain the bad news. If four or five reasons prompted your negative decision, concentrate on the strongest and safest ones. Avoid presenting any weak reasons; readers may seize on them to reject the entire message. Include ample explanation of the negative situation, and avoid fixing blame.

When the U.S. Post Office has to deliver damaged mail, it includes an explanation, such as the following: "Because the Post Office handles millions of pieces of mail daily, we must use mechanical methods to ensure prompt delivery. Damage can occur if mail is insecurely enveloped or bulky contents are enclosed. When this occurs and the machinery jams, it often causes damage to other mail that was properly prepared." Notice that the Post Office message offers the strongest reason for the problem, although other reasons may have been possible. Notice, too, that the explanation tactfully skirts the issue of who caused the problem.

In composing any negative message, conduct research if necessary to help you explain what went wrong and why a decision or action is necessary.

Revision, Proofreading, and Evaluation. In Phase 3 (revising), you will read over your message carefully to ensure that it says what you intend. Check your wording to be sure you are concise without being brusque. If you find that you have overused certain words, click on your word processing thesaurus to find synonyms. Read your sentences to see if they sound like conversation and flow smoothly. This is the time to edit and improve coherence and tone. In bad-news messages, the tone is especially important. Readers are more likely to accept negative messages if the tone is friendly and respectful. Even when the bad news can't be changed, its effect can be reduced somewhat by the way it is presented.

In the last phase of the writing process, proofread to make sure your verbs agree with their subjects, your sentences are properly punctuated, and all words are spelled correctly. Pay attention to common mistakes (*its/it's; than/then; their/there*). If your word processing program checks grammar, be sure to investigate those squiggly underscores. Finally, evaluate your message. Is it too blunt? Too subtle? Have you delivered the bad news clearly but professionally?

Avoiding Legal Liability in Conveying Negative News

Before we examine the components of a negative message, let's look more closely at how you can avoid exposing yourself and your employer to legal liability in writing negative messages. Although we can't always anticipate the consequences of our words, we should be alert to three causes of legal difficulties: (a) abusive language, (b) careless language, and (c) the good-guy syndrome.

Abusive Language. Calling people names (such as *deadbeat, crook*, or *quack*) can get you into trouble. *Defamation* is the legal term for any false statement that harms an individual's reputation. When the abusive language is written, it is called *libel*; when spoken, it is *slander*.

When does language become legally actionable?

To be actionable (likely to result in a lawsuit), abusive language must be (a) false, (b) damaging to one's good name, and (c) "published"—that is, written or spoken within the presence of others. Therefore, if you were alone with Jane Doe and accused her of accepting bribes and selling company secrets to competitors, she couldn't sue because the defamation wasn't published. Her reputation was not damaged. However, if anyone heard the words or if they were written, you might be legally liable.

In a new wrinkle, you may now be prosecuted if you transmit a harassing or libelous message by e-mail or post it on social networking sites such as Facebook and Twitter.[6] Such electronic transmissions are considered to be published. Moreover, a company may incur liability for messages sent through its computer system by employees. That's why many companies

When accelerator defects threatened Toyota's quality reputation and defied easy diagnosis in Lexus and other models, management took to the Internet to communicate directly with customers. President Akio Toyoda led the public relations blitz with an 800-word letter published at online news outlets, and Internet teams posted recall videos and information for more than 100,000 followers at Toyota's Twitter, Facebook, and YouTube accounts. *Is the Internet an appropriate channel for addressing customers negatively affected by product recalls?*

are increasing their monitoring of both outgoing and internal messages. "Off-the-cuff, casual e-mail conversations among employees are exactly the type of messages that tend to trigger lawsuits and arm litigators with damaging evidence," says e-mail guru Nancy Flynn.[7] Instant messaging adds another danger for companies. Whether your message is in print or electronic, avoid making unproven charges or letting your emotions prompt abusive language.

What does careless language include, and why is it dangerous?

Careless Language. As the marketplace becomes increasingly litigious, we must be certain that our words communicate only what we intend. Take the case of a factory worker injured on the job. His attorney subpoenaed company documents and discovered a seemingly harmless letter sent to a group regarding a plant tour. These words appeared in the letter: "Although we are honored at your interest in our company, we cannot give your group a tour of the plant operations as it would be too noisy and dangerous." The court found in favor of the worker, inferring from the letter that working conditions were indeed hazardous.[8] The letter writer did not intend to convey the impression of dangerous working conditions, but the court accepted that interpretation.

What is meant by the good-guy syndrome?

The Good-Guy Syndrome. Most of us hate to have to reveal bad news—that is, to be the bad guy. To make ourselves look better, to make the receiver feel better, and to maintain good relations, we are tempted to make statements that are legally dangerous. Consider the case of a law firm interviewing job candidates. One of the firm's partners was asked to inform a candidate that she was not selected. The partner's letter said, "Although you were by far the most qualified candidate we interviewed, unfortunately, we have decided we do not have a position for a person of your talents at this time." To show that he personally had no reservations about this candidate and to bolster the candidate, the partner offered his own opinion. However, he differed from the majority of the recruiting committee. When the rejected interviewee learned later that the law firm had hired two male attorneys, she sued, charging sexual discrimination. The court found in favor of the rejected candidate. It agreed that a reasonable inference could be made from the partner's letter that she was the "most qualified candidate."[9]

Two important lessons emerge. First, business communicators act as agents of their organizations. Their words, decisions, and opinions are assumed to represent those of the organization. If you want to communicate your personal feelings or opinions, use your home computer or write on plain paper (rather than company letterhead) and sign your name without title or affiliation. Second, volunteering extra information can lead to trouble. Therefore, avoid supplying data that could be misused, and avoid making promises that can't be fulfilled. Don't admit or imply responsibility for conditions that caused damage or injury. Even apologies *(We're sorry that a faulty bottle cap caused damage to your carpet)* may suggest liability.

Examining Negative News Strategies

LEARNING OBJECTIVE 2
Decide whether to use the direct or indirect strategy in conveying negative news.

You have at your disposal two basic strategies for delivering negative news: direct and indirect. Which approach is best suited for your particular message? One of the first steps you will take before delivering negative news is analyzing how your receiver will react to this news. In earlier chapters we discussed applying the direct strategy to positive messages. We suggested using the indirect strategy when the audience might be unwilling, uninterested, displeased, disappointed, or hostile. In this chapter we expand on that advice and suggest additional considerations that help you decide which strategy to use.

When to Use the Direct Strategy

Many actual bad-news messages are organized indirectly, beginning with a buffer and reasons. However, the direct strategy, with the bad news first, may be more effective in situations such as the following:

- **When the bad news is not damaging.** If the bad news is insignificant (such as a small increase in cost) and doesn't personally affect the receiver, then the direct strategy certainly makes sense.
- **When the receiver may overlook the bad news.** Changes in service, new policy requirements, legal announcements—these critical messages may require boldness to ensure attention.
- **When the organization or receiver prefers directness.** Some companies and individuals expect all internal messages and announcements—even bad news—to be straightforward and presented without frills.
- **When firmness is necessary.** Messages that must demonstrate determination and strength should not use delaying techniques. For example, the last in a series of collection letters that seek payment of overdue accounts may require a direct opener.

Notice in Figure 9.1 that a small rate increase for a newspaper subscription is announced directly because it is unlikely to upset or irritate the receiver. However, many companies prefer to announce even small rate increases more indirectly. They usually want to explain why the increase is necessary before announcing it. Let's now explore when and how to use the indirect strategy in delivering negative news.

When to Use the Indirect Strategy

What guides you in deciding whether to announce bad news directly or indirectly?

Many communicators prefer to use the indirect strategy to present negative news. Whereas good news can be revealed quickly, bad news may be easier to accept when broken gradually. Here are instances when the indirect strategy works well:

- **When the bad news is personally upsetting.** If the negative news involves the receiver personally, such as a layoff notice, the indirect strategy makes sense. Telling an employee that he or she no longer has a job is probably best done in person and by starting indirectly and giving reasons first. When a company has made a mistake that inconveniences or disadvantages a customer, the indirect strategy makes sense.
- **When the bad news will provoke a hostile reaction.** When your message will irritate or infuriate the recipient, the indirect method may be best. It begins with a buffer and reasons, thus encouraging the reader to finish reading or hearing the message. A blunt announcement may make the receiver stop reading.

FIGURE 9.1 Announcing Bad News Directly

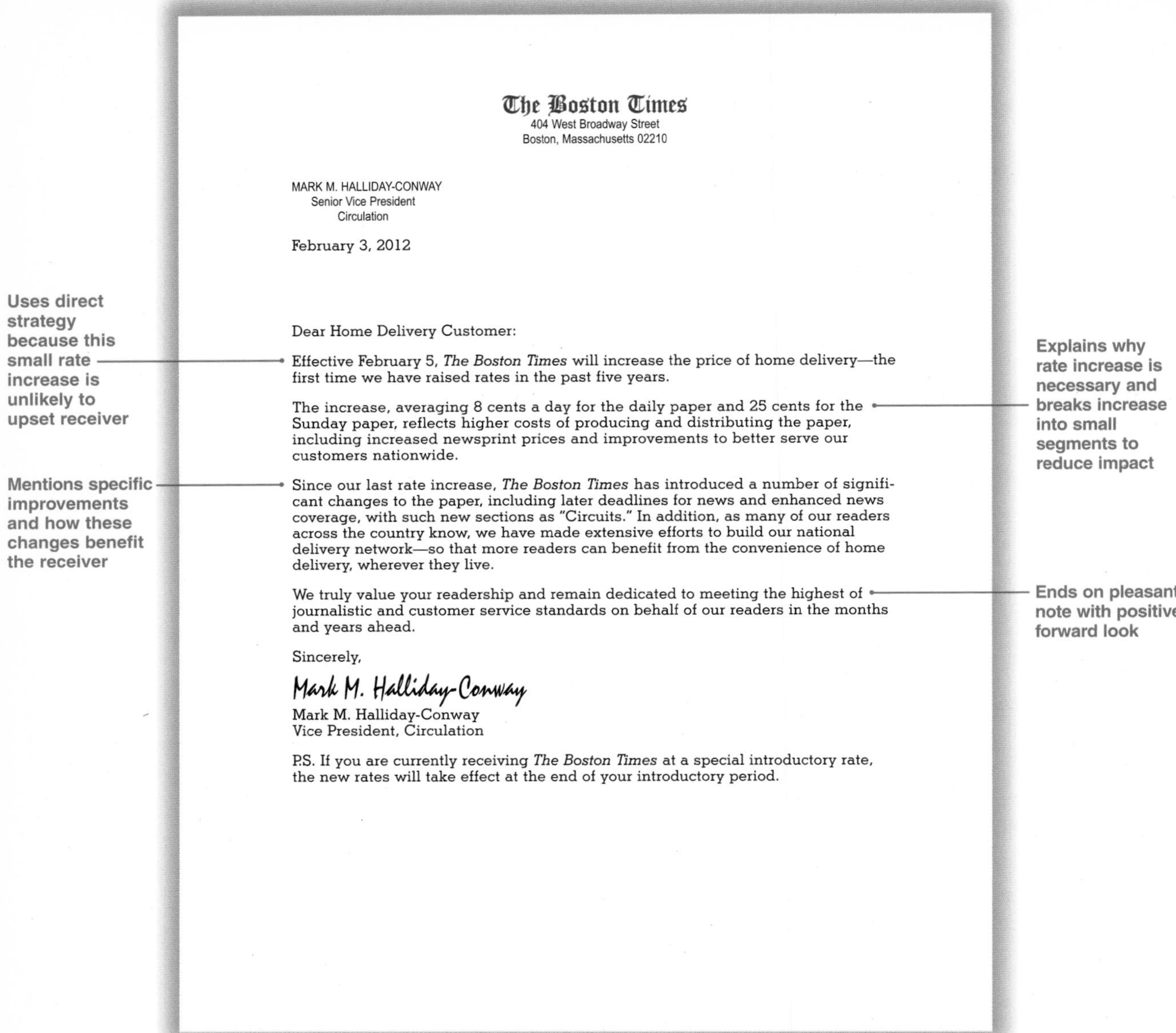

The Boston Times
404 West Broadway Street
Boston, Massachusetts 02210

MARK M. HALLIDAY-CONWAY
Senior Vice President
Circulation

February 3, 2012

Dear Home Delivery Customer:

Effective February 5, *The Boston Times* will increase the price of home delivery—the first time we have raised rates in the past five years.

The increase, averaging 8 cents a day for the daily paper and 25 cents for the Sunday paper, reflects higher costs of producing and distributing the paper, including increased newsprint prices and improvements to better serve our customers nationwide.

Since our last rate increase, *The Boston Times* has introduced a number of significant changes to the paper, including later deadlines for news and enhanced news coverage, with such new sections as "Circuits." In addition, as many of our readers across the country know, we have made extensive efforts to build our national delivery network—so that more readers can benefit from the convenience of home delivery, wherever they live.

We truly value your readership and remain dedicated to meeting the highest of journalistic and customer service standards on behalf of our readers in the months and years ahead.

Sincerely,

Mark M. Halliday-Conway

Mark M. Halliday-Conway
Vice President, Circulation

P.S. If you are currently receiving *The Boston Times* at a special introductory rate, the new rates will take effect at the end of your introductory period.

Uses direct strategy because this small rate increase is unlikely to upset receiver
Mentions specific improvements and how these changes benefit the receiver
Explains why rate increase is necessary and breaks increase into small segments to reduce impact
Ends on pleasant note with positive forward look

- **When the bad news threatens the customer relationship.** If the negative message may damage a customer relationship, the indirect strategy may help salvage the customer bond. Beginning slowly and presenting reasons that explain what happened can be more helpful than directly announcing bad news or failing to adequately explain the reasons.
- **When the bad news is unexpected.** Readers who are totally surprised by bad news tend to have a more negative reaction than those who expected the bad news. If a company suddenly closes an office or a plant and employees had no inkling of the closure, that bad news would be better received if it were revealed cautiously with reasons first.

Whether to use the direct or indirect strategy depends largely on the situation, the reaction you expect from the audience, and your goals. The direct method saves time and is preferred by some who consider it to be more professional and even more ethical than the indirect method. Others think that revealing bad news slowly and indirectly shows sensitivity to the receiver. By preparing the receiver, you tend to soften the impact. As you can see in Figure 9.2, the major

FIGURE 9.2 Comparing the Direct and Indirect Strategies for Negative Messages

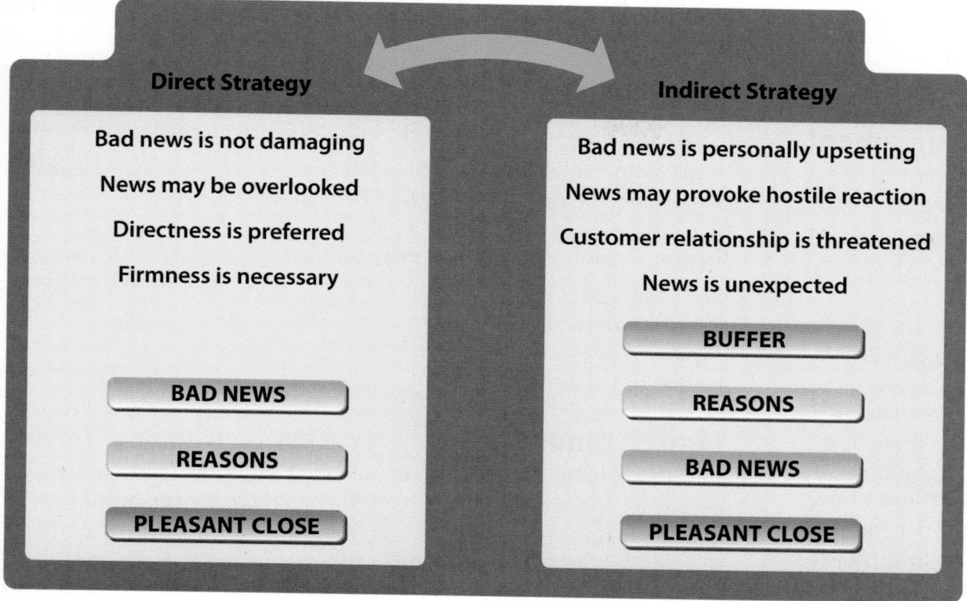

differences between the two strategies depend on whether you start with a buffer and how early you explain the reasons for the negative news.

Analyzing the Components of Effective Negative Messages

LEARNING OBJECTIVE 3
Analyze the components of effective negative messages, including opening with a buffer, apologizing, conveying empathy, presenting the reasons, cushioning the bad news, and closing pleasantly.

Even though it may be impossible to make the receiver happy when delivering negative news, you can reduce bad feelings and resentment by structuring your message sensitively. Most negative messages contain some or all of these parts: buffer, reasons, bad news, and closing. This section also discusses apologies and how to convey empathy in delivering bad news.

Buffer to Open Indirect Messages

If you decide to use the indirect strategy, your message might begin with a buffer. A buffer is a device to reduce shock or pain. To buffer the pain of bad news, begin with a neutral but meaningful statement that makes the reader continue reading. The buffer should be relevant and concise and provide a natural transition to the explanation that follows. The individual situation, of course, will help determine what you should put in the buffer. Avoid trite buffers such as *Thank you for your letter.*

It should be noted that not all business communication authors agree that buffers actually increase the effectiveness of negative messages. However, in many cultures softening bad news is appreciated. Following are various buffer possibilities.

Best News. Start with the part of the message that represents the best news. For example, a message to workers announced new health plan rules limiting prescriptions to a 34-day supply and increasing co-payments. With home delivery, however, employees could save up to $24 on each prescription. To emphasize the good news, you might write, *You can now achieve significant savings and avoid trips to the drugstore by having your prescription drugs delivered to your home.*[10]

Compliment. Praise the receiver's accomplishments, organization, or efforts, but do so with honesty and sincerity. For instance, in a letter declining an invitation to speak, you could write, *The Thalians have my sincere admiration for their fund-raising projects on behalf of hungry children. I am honored that you asked me to speak Friday, November 5.*

How can you buffer the opening of a bad-news message?

Appreciation. Convey thanks for doing business, for sending something, for showing confidence in your organization, for expressing feelings, or simply for providing feedback. Suppose you had to draft a letter that refuses employment. You could say, *I appreciated learning about the hospitality management program at Cornell and about your qualifications in our interview last Friday.* Avoid thanking the reader, however, for something you are about to refuse.

Agreement. Make a relevant statement with which both reader and receiver can agree. A letter that rejects a loan application might read, *We both realize how much the export business has been affected by the relative weakness of the dollar in the past two years.*

Spotlight on Communicators

Courtesy of Marshall Goldsmith

When leaders accept blame or apologize, executive coach Marshall Goldsmith believes, it is "one of the most powerful and resonant gestures in the human arsenal—almost as powerful as a declaration of love. If love means, 'I care about you, and I'm happy about it,' then an apology means, 'I hurt you, and I'm sorry about it.'" Named one of the 50 greatest thinkers and business management leaders, Goldsmith explains that the best thing about apologizing is that it forces everyone to let go of the past. In effect, an apology says, *I screwed up, I'm sorry, I'll do better.* "That's tough for even the most cold-hearted to resist," says Goldsmith.

Facts. Provide objective information that introduces the bad news. For example, in a memo announcing cutbacks in the hours of the employees' cafeteria, you might say, *During the past five years, the number of employees eating breakfast in our cafeteria has dropped from 32 percent to 12 percent.*

Understanding. Show that you care about the reader. Notice how in this letter to customers announcing a product defect, the writer expresses concern: *We know that you expect superior performance from all the products you purchase from OfficeCity. That's why we're writing personally about the Omega printer cartridges you recently ordered.*

Apologizing

You learned about making apologies in adjustment messages discussed in Chapter 8. We expand that discussion here because apologies are often part of negative-news messages. The truth is that sincere apologies work. Peter Post, great-grandson of famed etiquette expert Emily Post and director of the Emily Post Institute, said that Americans love apologies. They will forgive almost anything if presented with a sincere apology.[11] An apology is defined as an "admission of blameworthiness and regret for an undesirable event."[12] Apologies to customers are especially important if you or your company erred. They cost nothing, and they go a long way in soothing hard feelings. Here are some tips on how to apologize effectively in business messages:

- **Apologize sincerely.** People dislike apologies that sound hollow (*We regret that you were inconvenienced* or *We regret that you are disturbed*). Focusing on your regret does not convey sincerity. Explaining what you will do to prevent recurrence of the problem projects sincerity in an apology.
- **Accept responsibility.** One CEO was criticized for the following weak apology: *I want our customers to know how much I personally regret any difficulties you may experience as a result of the unauthorized intrusion into our computer systems.* Apology experts faulted this apology because it did not acknowledge responsibility.[13]
- **Use good judgment.** Don't admit blame if it might prompt a lawsuit.

Ethics Check

Apology or Excuse?

District Attorney Mike Nifong apologized to three Duke University lacrosse players that he had indicted on charges of attacking an exotic dancer. How ethical and effective is his apology? "To the extent that I made judgments that ultimately proved to be incorrect, I apologize to the three students that were wrongly accused."

Consider these poor and improved apologies:

Poor apology: *We regret that you are unhappy with the price of ice cream purchased at one of our scoop shops.*
Improved apology: *We are genuinely sorry that you were disappointed in the price of ice cream recently purchased at one of our scoop shops. Your opinion is important to us, and we appreciate your giving us the opportunity to look into the problem you describe.*

Poor apology: *We apologize if anyone was affected.*
Improved apology: *I apologize for the frustration our delay caused you. As soon as I received your message, I began looking into the cause of the delay and realized that our delivery tracking system must be improved.*

Poor apology: *We are sorry that mistakes were made in filling your order.*
Improved apology: *You are right to be concerned. We sincerely apologize for the mistakes we made in filling your order. To prevent recurrence of this problem, we are . . . .*

Conveying Empathy

What is empathy, and how can it be conveyed?

One of the hardest things to do in negative messages is to conveying sympathy and empathy. As discussed in Chapter 3, *empathy* is the ability to understand and enter into the feelings of another. When ice storms trapped JetBlue Airways passengers on hot planes for hours, CEO Neeleman wrote a letter of apology that sounded as if it came from his heart. He said, "Dear JetBlue Customers: We are sorry and embarrassed. But most of all, we are deeply sorry." Later in his letter he said, "Words cannot express how truly sorry we are for the anxiety, frustration, and inconvenience that you, your family, friends, and colleagues experienced."[14] Neeleman put himself into the shoes of his customers and tried to experience their pain.

Here are other examples of ways to express empathy in written messages:

- In writing to an unhappy customer: *We did not intentionally delay the shipment, and we sincerely regret the disappointment and frustration you must have suffered.*
- In laying off employees: *It is with great regret that we must take this step. Rest assured that I will be more than happy to write letters of recommendation for anyone who asks.*
- In responding to a complaint: *I am deeply saddened that our service failure disrupted your sale, and we will do everything in our power to. . . .*
- In showing genuine feelings: *You have every right to be disappointed. I am truly sorry that. . . .*

Presenting the Reasons

What is the most important part of a bad-news message? Why?

The most important part of a negative message is the section devoted to reasons. Without sound reasons for denying a request, refusing a claim, or revealing other bad news, a message will fail, no matter how cleverly it is organized or written. For example, if you must deny a customer's request, as part of your planning before writing, you analyzed the request and decided to refuse it for specific reasons. Where do you place your reasons? In the indirect strategy, explain your reasons before disclosing the bad news. In the direct strategy, the reasons appear immediately after the disclosure of the bad news. Providing an explanation reduces feelings of ill will and improves the chances that readers will accept the bad news.

Explaining Clearly. If the reasons are not confidential and if they will not create legal liability, you can be specific: *Growers supplied us with a limited number of patio roses, and our demand this year was twice that of last year.* In responding to a billing error, explain what happened: *After you informed us of an error on your January bill, we investigated the matter and admit the mistake was ours. Until our new automated system is fully online, we are still subject to the frailties of human error. Rest assured that your account has been credited as you will see on your next bill.* In refusing a speaking engagement, tell why the date is impossible: *On January 17 we have a board of directors meeting that I must attend.* Don't, however, make unrealistic or dangerous statements in an effort to be the "good guy."

Spotlight on Communicators

© Yvonne Hemsey/Contributor /Getty Images

Millionaire publisher Malcolm Forbes recognized that being agreeable while disagreeing is truly an art. He advised being positive and "nice." Contrary to the cliché, genuinely nice people most often finish first or very near it. He suggested using the acid test, particularly for a bad-news message. After you finish, read it out loud. You will know whether it sounds natural, positive, and respectful.

Citing Reader or Other Benefits, if Plausible. Readers are more open to bad news if in some way, even indirectly, it may help them. In refusing a customer's request for free hemming of skirts and slacks, Lands' End wrote: "We tested our ability to hem skirts a few months ago. This process proved to be very time-consuming. We have decided not to offer this service because the additional cost would have increased the selling price of our skirts substantially, and we did not want to impose that cost on all our customers."[15] Readers also accept bad news more readily if they recognize that someone or something else benefits, such as other workers or the environment: *Although we would like to consider your application, we prefer to fill managerial positions from within.* Avoid trying to show reader benefits, though, if they appear insincere: *To improve our service to you, we are increasing our brokerage fees.*

How can you reduce the resentment that people feel when told that company policy prohibits what they want?

Explaining Company Policy. Readers resent blanket policy statements prohibiting something: *Company policy prevents us from making cash refunds* or *Contract bids may be accepted from local companies only* or *Company policy requires us to promote from within.* Instead of hiding behind company policy, gently explain why the policy makes sense: *We prefer to promote from within because it rewards the loyalty of our employees. In addition, we have found that people familiar with our organization make the quickest contribution to our team effort.* By offering explanations, you demonstrate that you care about readers and are treating them as important individuals.

Choosing Positive Words. Because the words you use can affect a reader's response, choose carefully. Remember that the objective of the indirect strategy is holding the reader's attention until you have had a chance to explain the reasons justifying the bad news. To keep the reader in a receptive mood, avoid expressions with punitive, demoralizing, or otherwise negative connotations. Stay away from such words as *cannot, claim, denied, error, failure, fault, impossible, mistaken, misunderstand, never, regret, rejected, unable, unwilling, unfortunately,* and *violate.*

Showing That the Matter Was Treated Seriously and Fairly. In explaining reasons, demonstrate to the reader that you take the matter seriously, have investigated carefully, and are making an unbiased decision. Receivers are more accepting of disappointing news when they feel that their requests have been heard and that they have been treated fairly. In canceling funding for a program, board members provided this explanation: *As you know, the publication of* Urban Artist *was funded by a renewable annual grant from the National Endowment for the Arts. Recent cutbacks in federally sponsored city arts programs have left us with few funds. Because our grant has been discontinued, we have no alternative but to cease publication of* Urban Artist. *You have my assurance that the board has searched long and hard for some other viable funding, but every avenue of recourse has been closed before us. Accordingly, June's issue will be our last.*

Cushioning the Bad News

What writing techniques can be used to cushion bad news?

Although you can't prevent the disappointment that bad news brings, you can reduce the pain somewhat by breaking the news sensitively. Be especially considerate when the reader will suffer personally from the bad news. A number of thoughtful techniques can cushion the blow.

Positioning the Bad News Strategically. Instead of spotlighting it, sandwich the bad news between other sentences, perhaps among your reasons. Don't let the refusal begin or end a paragraph; the reader's eye will linger on these high-visibility spots. Another technique that reduces shock is putting a painful idea in a subordinate clause: *Although another candidate was hired, we appreciate your interest in our organization and wish you every success in your job search.* Subordinate clauses often begin with words such as *although, as, because, if,* and *since.*

Using the Passive Voice. Passive-voice verbs enable you to depersonalize an action. Whereas the active voice focuses attention on a person *(We don't give cash refunds),* the passive voice highlights the action *(Cash refunds are not given because . . .).* Use the passive voice for the bad news. In some instances you can combine passive-voice verbs and a subordinate clause: *Although franchise scoop shop owners cannot be required to lower their ice cream prices, we are happy to pass along your comments for their consideration.*

Accentuating the Positive. As you learned earlier, messages are far more effective when you describe what you can do instead of what you can't do. Rather than *We will no longer allow credit card purchases,* try a more positive appeal: *We are now selling gasoline at discount cash prices.*

Implying the Refusal. It is sometimes possible to avoid a direct statement of refusal. Often, your reasons and explanations leave no doubt that a request has been denied. Explicit refusals may be unnecessary and at times cruel. In this refusal to contribute to a charity, for example, the writer never actually says *no*: *Because we will soon be moving into new offices in Glendale, all our funds are earmarked for relocation costs. We hope that next year we will be able to support your worthwhile charity.* The danger of an implied refusal, of course, is that it is so subtle that the reader misses it. Be certain that you make the bad news clear, thus preventing the need for further correspondence.

Suggesting a Compromise or an Alternative. A refusal is not so depressing—for the sender or the receiver—if a suitable compromise, substitute, or alternative is available. In denying permission to a group of students to visit a historical private residence, for instance, this writer softens the bad news by proposing an alternative: *Although private tours of the grounds are not given, we do open the house and its gardens for one charitable event in the fall.* You can further reduce the impact of the bad news by refusing to dwell on it. Present it briefly (or imply it), and move on to your closing.

Closing Pleasantly

How can you close a negative message pleasantly?

After explaining the bad news sensitively, close the message with a pleasant statement that promotes goodwill. The closing should be personalized and may include a forward look, an alternative, good wishes, freebies, an off-the-subject remark, or resale information. *Resale* refers to mentioning a product or service favorably to reinforce the customer's choice. For example, *you chose our best-selling model.*

Forward Look. Anticipate future relations or business. A letter that refuses a contract proposal might read: *Thanks for your bid. We look forward to working with your talented staff when future projects demand your special expertise.*

Alternative Follow-Up. If an alternative exists, end your letter with follow-through advice. For example, in a letter rejecting a customer's demand for replacement of landscaping plants, you might say: *I will be happy to give you a free inspection and consultation. Please call 746-8112 to arrange a date for my visit.* In a message to a prospective homebuyer: *Although the lot you saw last week is now sold, we do have two excellent view lots available at a slightly higher price.* In reacting to an Internet misprint: *Please note that our Web site contained an unfortunate misprint offering $850-per-night Bora Bora bungalows at $85. Although we cannot honor that rate, we are offering a special half-price rate of $425 to those who responded.*

Good Wishes. A letter rejecting a job candidate might read: *We appreciate your interest in our company, and we extend to you our best wishes in your search to find the perfect match between your skills and job requirements.*

Freebies. When customers complain—primarily about food products or small consumer items—companies often send coupons, samples, or gifts to restore confidence and to promote future business. In response to a customer's complaint about a frozen dinner, you could write: *Your loyalty and your concern about our frozen entrées are genuinely appreciated. Because we want you to continue enjoying our healthful and convenient dinners, we are enclosing a coupon that you can take to your local market to select your next Green Valley entrée.*

Resale or Sales Promotion. When the bad news is not devastating or personal, references to resale information or promotion may be appropriate: *The computer workstations*

FIGURE 9.3 **Delivering Bad News Sensitively**

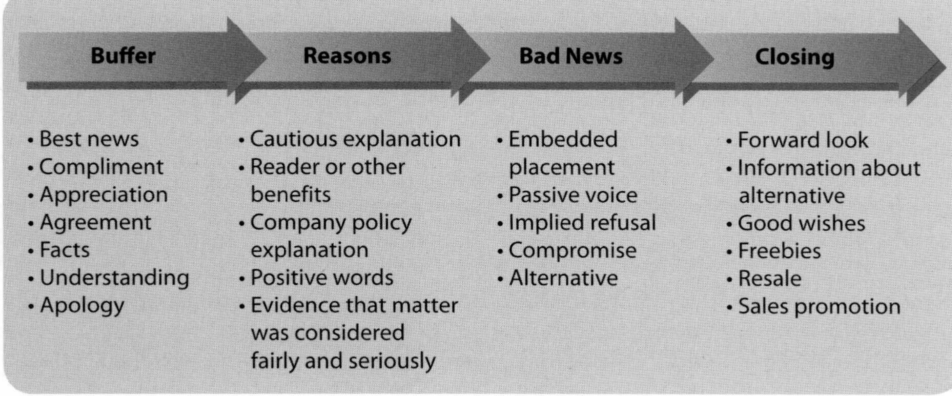

you ordered are unusually popular because of their stain-, heat-, and scratch-resistant finishes. To help you locate hard-to-find accessories for these workstations, we invite you to visit our Web site where our online catalog provides a huge selection of surge suppressors, multiple outlet strips, security devices, and PC tool kits.

Avoid endings that sound canned, insincere, inappropriate, or self-serving. Don't invite further correspondence *(If you have any questions, do not hesitate . . .)*, and don't refer to the bad news. Figure 9.3 reviews suggestions for delivering bad news sensitively.

Refusing Typical Requests

LEARNING OBJECTIVE 4
Describe and apply effective techniques for refusing typical requests.

As you move forward in your career and become a professional or a representative of an organization, you may receive requests for favors or contributions. You may also be invited to speak or give presentations. When you must refuse typical requests, you will first think about how the receiver will react to your refusal and decide whether to use the direct or the indirect strategy. If you have any doubt, use the indirect strategy.

Rejecting Requests for Favors, Money, Information, and Action

Why does the reasons-before-refusal plan work well when turning down requests for favors, money, information, and action?

Requests for favors, money, information, and action may come from charities, friends, or business partners. Many are from people representing commendable causes, and you may wish you could comply. However, resources are usually limited. In a letter from First Franklin Securities, shown in Figure 9.4, the company must refuse a request for a donation to a charity. Following the indirect strategy, the letter begins with a buffer acknowledging the request. It also praises the good works of the charity and uses those words as a transition to the second paragraph. In the second paragraph, the writer explains why the company cannot donate. Notice that the writer reveals the refusal without actually stating it (*Because of sales declines and organizational downsizing, we are forced to take a much harder look at funding requests that we receive this year*). This gentle refusal makes it unnecessary to be more blunt in stating the denial.

In some donation refusal letters, the reasons may not be fully explained: *Although we can't provide financial support at this time, we all unanimously agree that the Make-A-Wish Foundation contributes a valuable service to sick children.* The emphasis is on the foundation's good deeds rather than on an explanation for the refusal. In the letter shown in Figure 9.4, the writer felt a connection to the charity. Thus, he wanted to give a fuller explanation. If you were required to write frequent refusals, you might prepare a form letter, changing a few variables as needed.

Declining Invitations

What techniques can be used to decline an invitation?

When you must decline an invitation to speak or make a presentation, you generally try to provide a response that says more than *I can't* or *I don't want to*. Unless the reasons are confidential or business secrets, try to explain them. Because responses to invitations are often taken personally, make a special effort to soften the refusal. In the letter shown in Figure 9.5, an accountant must say no to the invitation from a friend's son to speak before the young man's college business club. This refusal starts with conviviality and compliments.

The writer then explains why she cannot accept. The refusal is embedded in a long paragraph and de-emphasized in a subordinate clause (*Although your invitation must be declined*). The reader naturally concentrates on the main clause that follows (*I would like to recommend . . .*). If no alternative is available, focus on something positive about the situation (*Although I'm not an expert, I commend your organization for selecting this topic*). Overall, the tone of this refusal is warm, upbeat, and positive.

Handling Bad News With Customers

LEARNING OBJECTIVE 5
Explain and apply effective techniques for handling bad news with customers.

Businesses must occasionally respond to disappointed customers. In some instances disappointed customers are turning to the Internet to air their grievances. Complaints about products and services now appear on sites such as Complaints.com and iRipoff.com, as well as on Facebook,

FIGURE 9.4 Refusing Donation Request

1 Prewriting

Analyze: The purpose of this letter is to reject the request for a monetary donation without causing bad will.

Anticipate: The reader is proud of her organization and the good work it pursues.

Adapt: The writer should strive to cushion the bad news and explain why it is necessary.

2 Writing

Research: Collect information about the receiver's organization as well as reasons for the refusal.

Organize: Use the indirect strategy. Begin with complimentary comments, present reasons, reveal the bad news gently, and close pleasantly.

Compose: Write message and consider keeping copy to serve as form letter.

3 Revising

Revise: Be sure that the tone of the message is positive and that it suggests that the matter was taken seriously.

Proofread: Check the receiver's name and address to be sure they are accurate. Check the letter's format.

Evaluate: Will this message retain the goodwill of the receiver despite its bad news?

First Franklin Securities

5820 Macon Cove Avenue
Memphis, TN 38135
800.640.2305
www.firstfranklinsecurities.com

May 18, 2012

Ms. Sierra Robinson
Executive Director
Outreach Children's Charity
3501 Beale Street
Memphis, TN 36110

Dear Ms. Robinson:

We appreciate your letter describing the care and support the Outreach Children's Charity gives to disadvantaged, physically challenged, sick, and needy children around the world. Your organization is to be commended for its significant achievements and outstanding projects such as the Sunshine Coach program, which provides passenger vans to worthy children's organizations around the globe.

Supporting the good work and worthwhile projects of your organization and others, although unrelated to our business, is a luxury we have enjoyed in past years. Because of sales declines and organizational downsizing, we are forced to take a much harder look at funding requests that we receive this year. We feel that we must focus our charitable contributions on areas that relate directly to our business.

We are hopeful that the worst days are behind us and that we will be able to renew our support for good work and worthwhile projects like yours next year.

Sincerely,

Andrew Hollingsworth

Andrew Hollingsworth
Vice President

Opens with praise and compliments

Transitions with repetition of key ideas (*good work and worthwhile projects*)

Closes graciously with forward look

Doesn't say *yes* or *no*

Explains sales decline and cutback in gifts, thus revealing refusal without actually stating it

FIGURE 9.5 **Declining an Invitation**

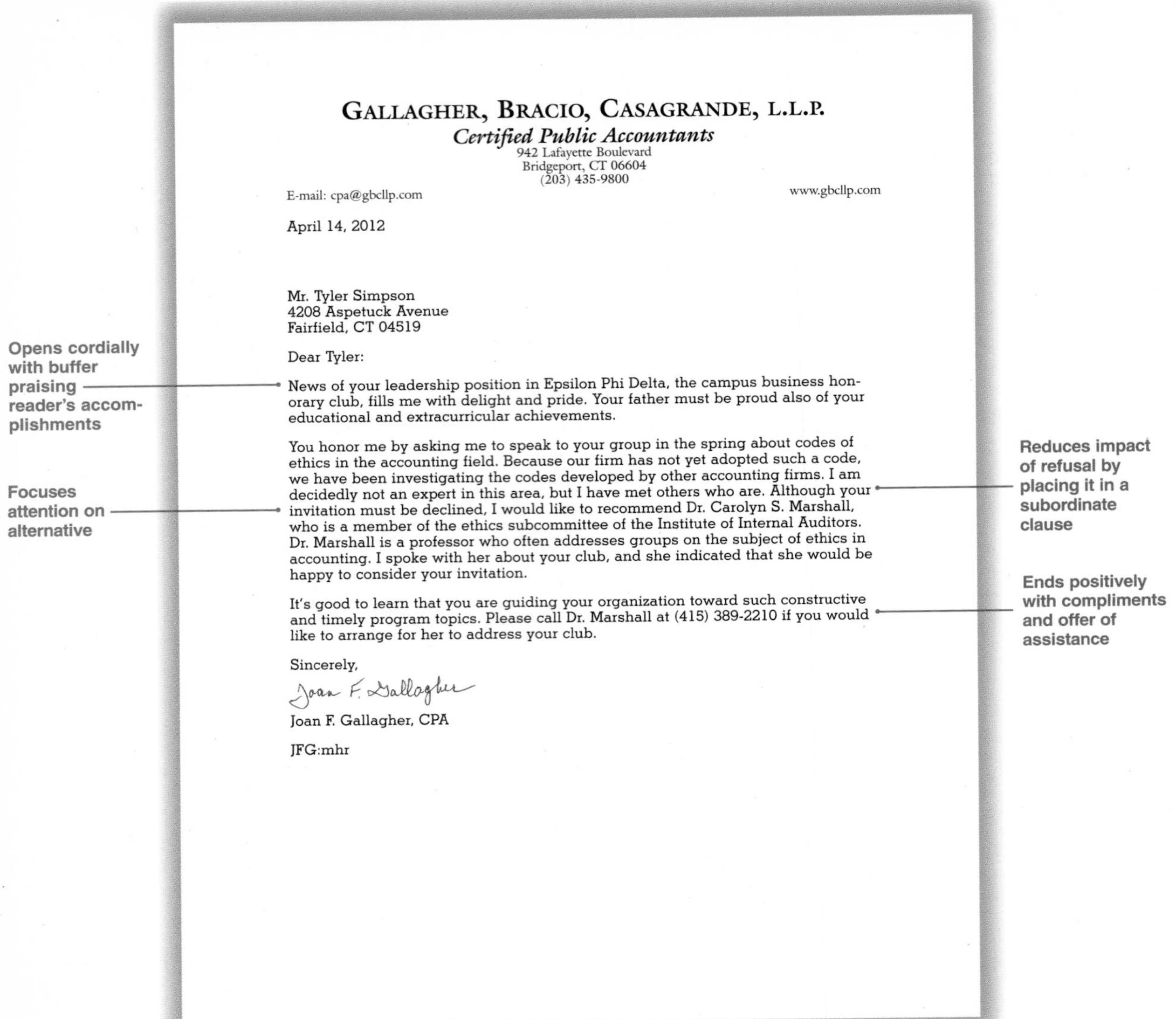

GALLAGHER, BRACIO, CASAGRANDE, L.L.P.
Certified Public Accountants
942 Lafayette Boulevard
Bridgeport, CT 06604
(203) 435-9800
E-mail: cpa@gbcllp.com www.gbcllp.com

April 14, 2012

Mr. Tyler Simpson
4208 Aspetuck Avenue
Fairfield, CT 04519

Dear Tyler:

News of your leadership position in Epsilon Phi Delta, the campus business honorary club, fills me with delight and pride. Your father must be proud also of your educational and extracurricular achievements.

You honor me by asking me to speak to your group in the spring about codes of ethics in the accounting field. Because our firm has not yet adopted such a code, we have been investigating the codes developed by other accounting firms. I am decidedly not an expert in this area, but I have met others who are. Although your invitation must be declined, I would like to recommend Dr. Carolyn S. Marshall, who is a member of the ethics subcommittee of the Institute of Internal Auditors. Dr. Marshall is a professor who often addresses groups on the subject of ethics in accounting. I spoke with her about your club, and she indicated that she would be happy to consider your invitation.

It's good to learn that you are guiding your organization toward such constructive and timely program topics. Please call Dr. Marshall at (415) 389-2210 if you would like to arrange for her to address your club.

Sincerely,

Joan F. Gallagher

Joan F. Gallagher, CPA

JFG:mhr

Opens cordially with buffer praising reader's accomplishments
Focuses attention on alternative
Reduces impact of refusal by placing it in a subordinate clause
Ends positively with compliments and offer of assistance

Twitter, and MySpace. See the accompanying Plugged In box for tips on how companies are responding to negative messages appearing in these emerging communication channels.

Whether companies deal with unhappy customers in cyberspace or up close and personal, they face the same challenges. Maintaining market share and preserving goodwill require sensitive and skillful communication. In Chapter 8 you learned to use the direct strategy in granting claims and making adjustments—because these were essentially good-news messages. But in some situations, you have little good news to share. Sometimes your company is at fault, in which case an apology is generally in order. Other times the problem is with orders you can't fill, claims you must refuse, or credit you must deny. Messages with bad news for customers generally follow the same pattern as other negative messages. Customer messages, though, differ in one major way: they usually include resale information or sales promotions.

Damage Control: Dealing With Disappointed Customers

When a customer problem arises and your company is at fault, how should you react?

All companies occasionally disappoint their customers. Merchandise is not delivered on time, a product fails to perform as expected, service is deficient, charges are erroneous, or customers are misunderstood. All businesses offering products or services must sometimes deal with troublesome situations that cause unhappiness to customers. Whenever possible, these problems should be dealt with immediately and personally. Most business professionals strive to control the damage and resolve such problems in the following manner:[16]

As the global recession deepens and budget shortfalls spread to all sectors of the economy, city managers are struggling to deliver negative news to workers. Faced with a $522 million annual deficit, San Francisco Mayor Gavin Newsom delivered pink slips to more than 15,000 city workers as part of a plan for "saving people's jobs and city services." In response to criticism over his characterization of the situation, Mayor Newsom replied that he was "lawyered up." *How can employers avoid legal liability in conveying bad news?*

- Call the individual involved.
- Describe the problem and apologize.
- Explain why the problem occurred, what you are doing to resolve it, and how you will prevent it from happening again.
- Follow up with a message that documents the phone call and promotes goodwill.

Dealing with problems immediately is very important in resolving conflict and retaining goodwill. Written correspondence is generally too slow for problems that demand immediate attention. But written messages are important (a) when personal contact is impossible, (b) to establish a record of the incident, (c) to formally confirm follow-up procedures, and (d) to promote good relations.

A bad-news follow-up letter is shown in Figure 9.6. Consultant Catherine Martinez found herself in the embarrassing position of explaining why she had given out the name of her client to a salesperson. The client, Alliance Resource International, had hired her firm, Cartus Consulting Associates, to help find an appropriate service for outsourcing its payroll functions. Without realizing it, Catherine had mentioned to a potential vendor (Payroll Services, Inc.) that her client was considering hiring an outside service to handle its payroll. An overeager salesperson from Payroll Services immediately called on Alliance, thus angering the client. The client had hired the consultant to avoid this very kind of intrusion. Alliance did not want to be hounded by vendors selling their payroll services.

Why are follow-up messages important in the damage-control process?

When she learned of the problem, the first thing consultant Catherine Martinez did was call her client to explain and apologize. She was careful to control her voice and rate of speaking. A low-pitched, deliberate pace gives the impression that you are thinking clearly, logically, and reasonably—not emotionally and certainly not irrationally. However, she also followed up with the letter shown in Figure 9.6. The letter not only confirms the telephone conversation but also adds the right touch of formality. It sends the nonverbal message that the writer takes the matter seriously and that it is important enough to warrant a written letter.

Many consumer problems are handled with letters, either written by consumers as complaints or by companies in response. However, the social networking sites on the Internet are an emerging channel for delivering complaints and negative messages.

Spotlight on Communicators

When Amazon discovered that it lacked permission to offer two classic books, *1984* and *Animal Farm*, on its Kindle e-reader, it removed them—without warning and without explanation. Zap—the titles just disappeared! The ensuing firestorm of protest forced founder and CEO Jeff Bezos to control the damage by admitting the company's error and promising not to repeat its mistake. He said, "Our 'solution' to the problem was stupid, self-inflicted, and we deserve the criticism we've received. We will use the scar tissue from this painful mistake to help make better decisions going forward, ones that match our mission."

FIGURE 9.6 Bad-News Follow-Up Message

CARTUS CONSULTING ASSOCIATES

4350 Camelback Blvd.
Scottsdale, AZ 85255

Voice: (480) 259-0971
Web: www.cartusassociates.com

May 7, 2012

Mr. Eric Nasserizad
Director, Administrative Operations
Alliance Resource International
538 Maricopa Plaza, Suite 1210
Phoenix, AZ 85001

Dear Mr. Nasserizad:

Opens with agreement and apology

You have every right to expect complete confidentiality in your transactions with an independent consultant. As I explained in yesterday's telephone call, I am very distressed that you were called by a salesperson from Payroll Services, Inc. This should not have happened, and I apologize to you again for inadvertently mentioning your company's name in a conversation with a potential vendor, Payroll Services, Inc.

Explains what caused the problem and how it was resolved

Takes responsibility and promises to prevent recurrence

All clients of Cartus Consulting are assured that their dealings with our firm are held in the strictest confidence. Because your company's payroll needs are so individual and because you have so many contract workers, I was forced to explain how your employees differed from those of other companies. Revealing your company name was my error, and I take full responsibility for the lapse. I can assure you that it will not happen again. I have informed Payroll Services that it had no authorization to call you directly and its actions have forced me to reconsider using its services for my future clients.

Closes with forward look

A number of other payroll services offer outstanding programs. I'm sure we can find the perfect partner to enable you to outsource your payroll responsibilities, thus allowing your company to focus its financial and human resources on its core business. I look forward to our next appointment when you may choose from a number of excellent payroll outsourcing firms.

Sincerely,

Catherine Martinez

Catherine Martinez
Partner

Tips for Resolving Problems and Following Up

- Whenever possible, call or see the individual linvolved.
- Describe the problem and apologize.
- Explain why the problem occurred.
- Take responsibility, if appropriate.
- Explain what you are doing to resolve it.
- Explain what you are doing to prevent recurrence.
- Follow up with a message that documents the personal contact.
- Look forward to positive future relations.

Handling Problems With Orders

What strategy should you follow when your company can't fill an order?

Not all customer orders can be filled as received. Suppliers may be able to send only part of an order or none at all. Substitutions may be necessary, or the delivery date may be delayed. Suppliers may suspect that all or part of the order is a mistake; the customer may actually want something else. In writing to customers about problem orders, it is generally wise to use the direct strategy if the message has some good-news elements. However, when the message is disappointing, the indirect strategy may be more appropriate.

Let's say you represent Live and Learn Toys, a large West Coast toy manufacturer, and you are scrambling for business in a slow year. A big customer, Child Land, calls in August and asks you to hold a block of your best-selling toy, the Space Station. Like most vendors, you require a deposit on large orders. September rolls around, and you still haven't received any money from Child Land. You must now write a tactful letter asking for the deposit—or else

PLUGGED IN

Managing Negative News on Facebook, Twitter, and Other Web Sites

Today's consumers eagerly embrace the idea of delivering their complaints to social networking sites rather than telling friends or calling customer service departments. Why rely on word of mouth or send a letter to a company about poor service or a defective product when you can shout your grievance to the entire world? Internet sites such as Complaints.com, Ripoff Report, and iRipoff .com encourage consumers to quickly share complaints about stores, products, and services that fall short of their standards. Twitter and Facebook are also favorite sites for consumers to make public their ire.

Why are online complaints so popular?
Complaint sites are gaining momentum for many reasons. Consumers may receive faster responses to tweets than to customer service calls. Airing gripes in public also helps other consumers avoid the same problems and may improve the complainer's leverage in solving a problem. In addition, sending a 140-word tweet is much easier and more satisfying than writing a complaint letter to a customer service department or navigating endless telephone menus to reach an agent.

How can business organizations manage negative news on social networking sites and blogs?

- **Recognize social networks as an emerging communication channel.** Instead of fearing social networks as a disruptive force, smart companies greet these channels as exciting opportunities to look into the true mind-set of customers.
- **Become proactive.** Company blogs and active Web sites with community forums help companies listen to their customers as well as to spread the word about their own good deeds. Home Depot's site describing its foundation, workshops, and careers now outranks Home DepotSucks.com, which used to rank No. 1 for searches on the keywords *home depot*.
- **Join the fun.** Wise companies have joined sites such as Twitter, Facebook, Flickr, YouTube, and LinkedIn so they can see how these sites function and benefit from site interaction.
- **Monitor comments.** Many companies employ tech-savvy staff members to monitor comments and respond immediately whenever possible. At Southwest Airlines, Paula Berg, manager of emerging media and affectionately called Blog Girl, manages a staff of seven who listen online to what people are saying about Southwest. Its policy is to engage the positive and address the negative.

Career Application
Visit Complaints.com, Ripoff Report, or another complaint site. Study ten or more complaints about products or companies (e.g., iPod, Starbucks, Delta Airline). Select one complaint and, as a company employee, respond to it employing some of the techniques presented in this chapter. Submit a copy of the complaint along with your response to your instructor.

you will release the toy to other buyers. The problem, of course, is delivering the bad news without losing the customer's order and goodwill. Another challenge is making sure the reader understands the bad news. An effective letter might begin with a positive statement that also reveals the facts:

> *You were smart to reserve a block of 500 Space Stations, which we have been holding for you since August. As the holidays approach, the demand for all our learning toys, including the Space Station, is rapidly increasing.*

Next, the letter should explain why the payment is needed and what will happen if it is not received:

> *Toy stores from Florida to California are asking us to ship these Space Stations. One reason the Space Station is moving out of our warehouses so quickly is its assortment of gizmos that children love, including a land rover vehicle, a shuttle craft, a hover craft, astronauts, and even a robotic arm. As soon as we receive your deposit of $4,000, we will have this popular item on its way to your stores. Without a deposit by September 20, though, we must release this block to other retailers.*

The closing makes it easy to respond and motivates action:

> *Use the enclosed envelope to send us your check immediately. You can begin showing this fascinating Live and Learn toy in your stores by November 1.*

Announcing Rate Increases and Price Hikes

How can you introduce the concept of audience benefits into messages announcing rate increases and price hikes?

Informing customers and clients of rate increases or price hikes can be like handling a live grenade. These messages necessarily cause consumers to recoil. With skill, however, you can help your customers understand why the rate or price increase is necessary.

The important steps in these negative messages are explaining the reasons and hooking the increase to benefits. For example, a price increase might be necessitated by higher material costs, rising taxes, escalating insurance, driver pay increase—all reasons you cannot control. You might cite changing industry trends or technology innovations as causes of increased costs.

In developing audience benefits and building goodwill, think about how the increase will add new value or better features, make use more efficient, or make customers' lives easier. Whenever possible, give advance warning of rate increases—for example: *Because you are an important customer to us, I wanted to inform you about this right away. Our energy costs have almost doubled over the last year, forcing us to put through a 10 percent price increase effective July 1. You order these items regularly, so I thought I'd better check with you to see if it would make sense to reorder now to save you money and prevent last-minute surprises.*

In today's digital environment, rate and price increases may be announced online, as shown in Figure 9.7. DVD City had to increase the charge for access to Blu-ray movies. In its blog it explained how Blu-ray discs are not only superior to DVDs but also more expensive. To provide its customers with a comprehensive library of Blu-ray movies, DVD City has to raise its rates. Notice that the rate increase is tied to benefits to customers.

FIGURE 9.7 Blog Announcing Price Increase

DVD CITY — DVD CITY Blog

Wednesday, June 16, 2010

Price Update for Access to Blu-ray Movies

Hi, Rocko Raider here, VP of Marketing, with a message for our valued members who have added Blu-ray access to their accounts.

Blu-ray represents a huge leap forward in the DVD viewing experience with greatly enhanced HD video and audio quality as well as advanced interactivity and networking features. The number of titles available for us to purchase on Blu-ray has increased significantly. Our Blu-ray selection has grown more than 70 percent in just 6 months to over 2,300 titles. Blu-ray adoption among our members has also grown–it's now close to 10 percent. As we buy more, you are able to choose from a rapidly expanding selection of Blu-ray titles. And, as you've probably heard, Blu-ray discs are substantially more expensive than standard definition DVDs–often as much as 30 percent more.

Because DVD CITY is committed to providing an extensive library of high quality Blu-ray films for our members who choose to add Blu-ray access, we need to adjust Blu-ray pricing. As a result, the monthly charge for Blu-ray access is increasing for most plans and will now vary by plan.

This change will take effect on your next billing date. You will receive an e-mail from us letting you know the monthly charge for your plan. For more information, call Betsy at 1-800-556-2002.

LINKS
DVD CITY Community Forums
Facebook DVD CITY Page
DVD CITY Home Page
-------> RSS Feed Page
-------> Top Releases This Week

ABOUT THE DVD CITY BLOG
Thanks for visiting the official DVD CITY Blog! We bloggers are members of the DVD CITY team and are all certifiably rabid movie fans. We want to make this an exciting forum for us to talk about what we are doing and for you to tell us what you think.

Explains expansion of Blu-ray DVD movie collection and describes how costly these films are, thus justifying a price increase

Connects increase in cost to bigger library and wider choice of best movies for customers

Provides name and number for more information

Courtesy of M.E. Guffey

Denying Claims

Customers occasionally want something they are not entitled to or that you can't grant. They may misunderstand warranties or make unreasonable demands. Because these customers are often unhappy with a product or service, they are emotionally involved. Letters that say no to emotionally involved receivers will probably be your most challenging communication task. As publisher Malcolm Forbes observed, "To be agreeable while disagreeing—that's an art."[17]

Should the direct or indirect strategy be used in denying customer claims?

Fortunately, the reasons-before-refusal plan helps you be empathic and artful in breaking bad news. Obviously, in denial letters you will need to adopt the proper tone. Don't blame customers, even if they are at fault. Avoid *you* statements that sound preachy *(You would have known that cash refunds are impossible if you had read your contract)*. Use neutral, objective language to explain why the claim must be refused. Consider offering resale information to rebuild the customer's confidence in your products or organization. In Figure 9.8 the writer denies a customer's claim for the difference between the price the customer paid for speakers and the price he saw advertised locally (which would have

FIGURE 9.8 Denying a Claim

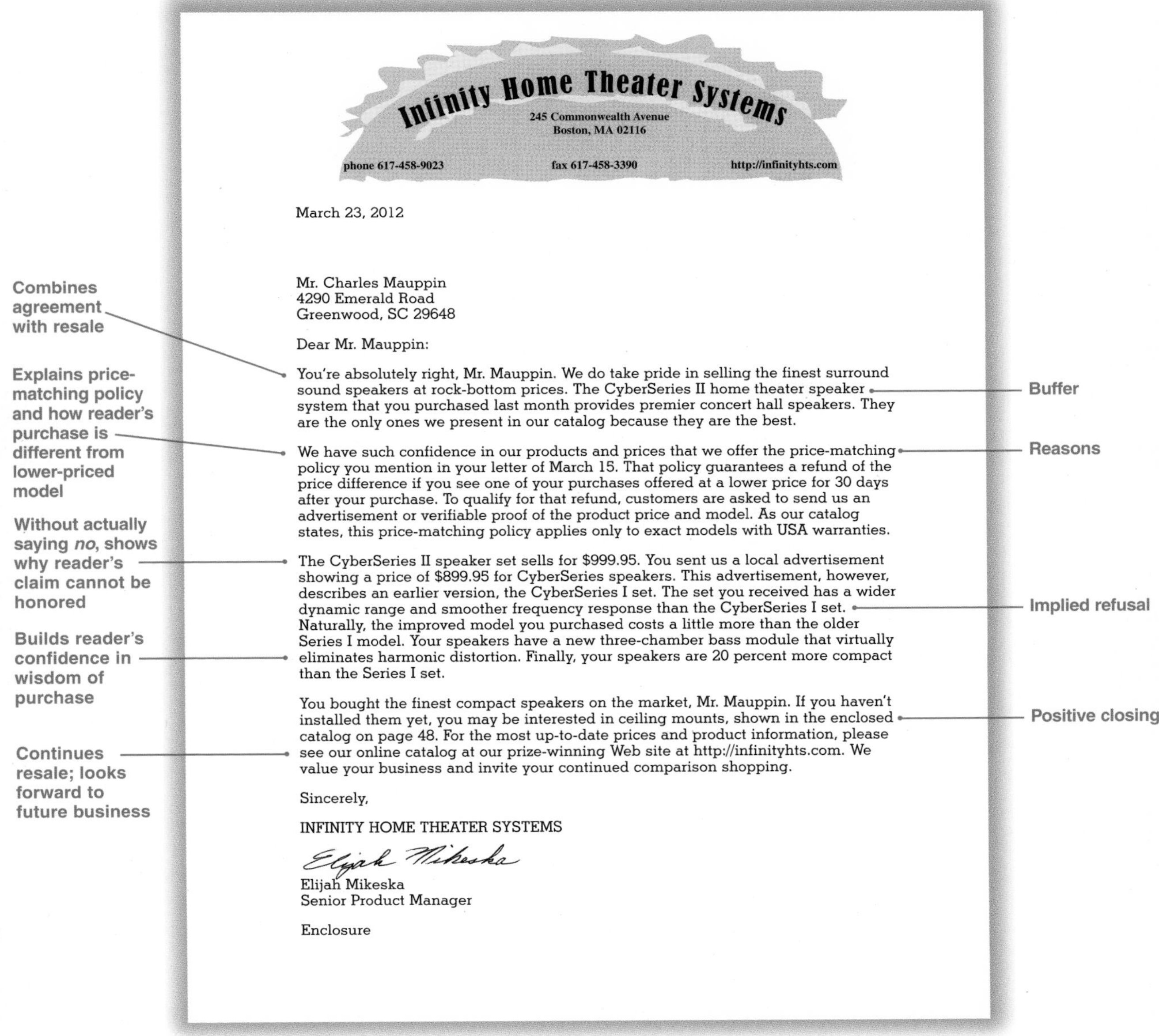

Infinity Home Theater Systems
245 Commonwealth Avenue
Boston, MA 02116
phone 617-458-9023 fax 617-458-3390 http://infinityhts.com

March 23, 2012

Mr. Charles Mauppin
4290 Emerald Road
Greenwood, SC 29648

Dear Mr. Mauppin:

You're absolutely right, Mr. Mauppin. We do take pride in selling the finest surround sound speakers at rock-bottom prices. The CyberSeries II home theater speaker system that you purchased last month provides premier concert hall speakers. They are the only ones we present in our catalog because they are the best.

We have such confidence in our products and prices that we offer the price-matching policy you mention in your letter of March 15. That policy guarantees a refund of the price difference if you see one of your purchases offered at a lower price for 30 days after your purchase. To qualify for that refund, customers are asked to send us an advertisement or verifiable proof of the product price and model. As our catalog states, this price-matching policy applies only to exact models with USA warranties.

The CyberSeries II speaker set sells for $999.95. You sent us a local advertisement showing a price of $899.95 for CyberSeries speakers. This advertisement, however, describes an earlier version, the CyberSeries I set. The set you received has a wider dynamic range and smoother frequency response than the CyberSeries I set. Naturally, the improved model you purchased costs a little more than the older Series I model. Your speakers have a new three-chamber bass module that virtually eliminates harmonic distortion. Finally, your speakers are 20 percent more compact than the Series I set.

You bought the finest compact speakers on the market, Mr. Mauppin. If you haven't installed them yet, you may be interested in ceiling mounts, shown in the enclosed catalog on page 48. For the most up-to-date prices and product information, please see our online catalog at our prize-winning Web site at http://infinityhts.com. We value your business and invite your continued comparison shopping.

Sincerely,

INFINITY HOME THEATER SYSTEMS

Elijah Mikeska

Elijah Mikeska
Senior Product Manager

Enclosure

resulted in a cash refund of $100). Although the catalog service does match any advertised lower price, the price-matching policy applies *only* to exact models. This claim must be rejected because the advertisement the customer submitted showed a different, older speaker model.

The letter to Charles Mauppin opens with a buffer that agrees with a statement in the customer's letter. It repeats the key idea of product confidence as a transition to the second paragraph. Next comes an explanation of the price-matching policy. The writer does not assume that the customer is trying to pull a fast one. Nor does he suggest that the customer is a dummy who didn't read or understand the price-matching policy. The safest path is a neutral explanation of the policy along with precise distinctions between the customer's speakers and the older ones. The writer also gets a chance to resell the customer's speakers and demonstrate what a quality product they are. By the end of the third paragraph, it is evident to the reader that his claim is unjustified.

Refusing Credit

What are the writer's goals when refusing credit to a customer?

When customers apply for credit, they must be notified if that application is rejected. The Fair Credit Reporting Act and Equal Credit Opportunity Act state that consumers who are denied loans must receive a notice of "adverse action" explaining the decision.[18] This notification may come directly from the credit reporting agency, such as Experian, Equifax, or TransUnion. More often, however, the credit agency reports its findings to the business. The business then makes a decision whether to grant credit based on the information supplied.

If you must write a letter to a customer denying credit, you have four goals in conveying the refusal:

- Avoiding language that causes hard feelings
- Retaining the customer on a cash basis
- Preparing for possible future credit without raising false expectations
- Avoiding disclosures that could cause a lawsuit

Because credit applicants are likely to continue to do business with an organization even if they are denied credit, you will want to do everything possible to encourage that patronage. Thus, keep the refusal respectful, sensitive, and upbeat. A letter to a customer denying her credit application might begin as follows:

> *We genuinely appreciate your application of January 12 for a Fashion Express credit account.*

To avoid possible litigation, many companies offer no explanation of the reasons for a credit refusal. Instead, they provide the name of the credit reporting agency and suggest that inquiries be directed to it. In the following example, notice the use of passive voice (*credit cannot be extended)* and a long sentence to de-emphasize the bad news:

> *After we received a report of your current credit record from Experian, it is apparent that credit cannot be extended at this time. To learn more about your record, you may call an Experian credit counselor at (212) 356-0922.*

The cordial closing looks forward to the possibility of a future reapplication:

> *Thanks, Ms. Love, for the confidence you have shown in Fashion Express. We invite you to continue shopping at our stores, and we look forward to your reapplication in the future.*

Some businesses do provide reasons explaining credit denials *(Credit cannot be granted because your firm's current and long-term credit obligations are nearly twice as great as your firm's total assets)*. They may also provide alternatives, such as deferred billing or cash discounts. When the letter denies a credit application that accompanies an order, the message may contain resale information. The writer tries to convert the order from credit to cash. For example, if a big order cannot be filled on a credit basis, perhaps part of the order could be filled on a cash basis.

Whatever form the bad-news message takes, it is a good idea to have the message reviewed by legal counsel because of the litigation land mines awaiting unwary communicators in this area.

Zooming In

PART 2

Southwest Airlines

For Fred Taylor, Southwest's senior manager of proactive customer communications, delivering bad news and apologizing to customers is all in a day's work. He is the point person when it comes to informing employees of problem situations and providing them with appropriate responses. When Southwest falls short of satisfying its customers, he prepares personal apology letters to passengers—about 20,000 in an average year, covering more than 180 flight disruptions. The letters have his direct phone number, and many include a free flight voucher. As he explained to customers on a recent flight from Phoenix to Albuquerque, the strange odor in the plane was from a defective valve but not dangerous. "Erring on the side of caution, our captain decided to return to Phoenix rather than second-guess the smell that was in the cabin," he wrote. Southwest's apologies even cover circumstances beyond Southwest's control, such as an ice storm that delayed a St. Louis flight. "It's not something we had to do," he says. "It's just something we feel our customers deserve."[19]

Critical Thinking

- What are the advantages to Southwest of its proactive approach to passenger problems?
- How might Fred Taylor use the writing plan suggested in this chapter to compose his apology letters to passengers?
- Contrast the strategies Taylor would develop to deliver bad news to Southwest's employees and to its passengers.

Delivering Bad News Within Organizations

LEARNING OBJECTIVE 6
Understand and apply effective techniques for delivering bad news within organizations.

A tactful tone and a reasons-first approach help preserve friendly relations with customers. These same techniques are useful when delivering bad news within organizations. Interpersonal bad news might involve telling the boss that something went wrong or confronting an employee about poor performance. Organizational bad news might involve declining profits, lost contracts, harmful lawsuits, public relations controversies, and changes in policy. Whether you use a direct or an indirect strategy in delivering that news depends primarily on the anticipated reaction of the audience. Generally, bad news is better received when reasons are given first. Within organizations, you may find yourself giving bad news in person or in writing.

Giving Bad News Personally

Whether you are an employee or a supervisor, you may have the unhappy responsibility of delivering bad news. First, decide whether the negative information is newsworthy. For example, trivial, noncriminal mistakes or one-time bad behaviors are best left alone. However, fraudulent travel claims, consistent hostile behavior, or failing projects must be reported.[20] For example, you might have to tell the boss that the team's computer crashed losing all its important files. As a team leader or supervisor, you might be required to confront an underperforming employee. If you know that the news will upset the receiver, the reasons-first strategy is most effective. When the bad news involves one person or a small group nearby, you should generally deliver that news in person. Here are pointers on how to do so tactfully, professionally, and safely:[21]

When delivering bad news in person, how can you do it tactfully, professionally, and safely?

- **Gather all the information.** Cool down and have all the facts before marching in on the boss or confronting someone. Remember that every story has two sides.
- **Prepare and rehearse.** Outline what you plan to say so that you are confident, coherent, and dispassionate.
- **Explain: past, present, future.** If you are telling the boss about a problem such as the computer crash, explain what caused the crash, the current situation, and how and when you plan to fix it.
- **Consider taking a partner.** If you fear a "shoot the messenger" reaction, especially from your boss, bring a colleague with you. Each person should have a consistent and credible

part in the presentation. If possible, take advantage of your organization's internal resources. To lend credibility to your view, call on auditors, inspectors, or human resources experts.

- **Think about timing.** Don't deliver bad news when someone is already stressed or grumpy. Experts also advise against giving bad news on Friday afternoon when people have the weekend to dwell on it.
- **Be patient with the reaction.** Give the receiver time to vent, think, recover, and act wisely.

Refusing Internal Requests

How can organizations retain employee morale when communicating bad news?

Occasionally, managers must refuse requests from employees. In Figure 9.9 you see the first draft and revision of a message responding to a request from a key specialist, Zachary Stapleton. He wants permission to attend a conference. However, he can't attend the conference because the timing is bad; he must be present at budget planning meetings scheduled for the same two weeks. Normally, this matter would be discussed in person. However, Zach has been traveling among branch offices, and he just hasn't been in the office recently.

The first inclination of Victoria Blaylock, vice president, was to send a quickie e-mail, as shown in Figure 9.9 draft, and "tell it like it is." However, she realized that this message was

FIGURE 9.9 Refusing an Internal Request

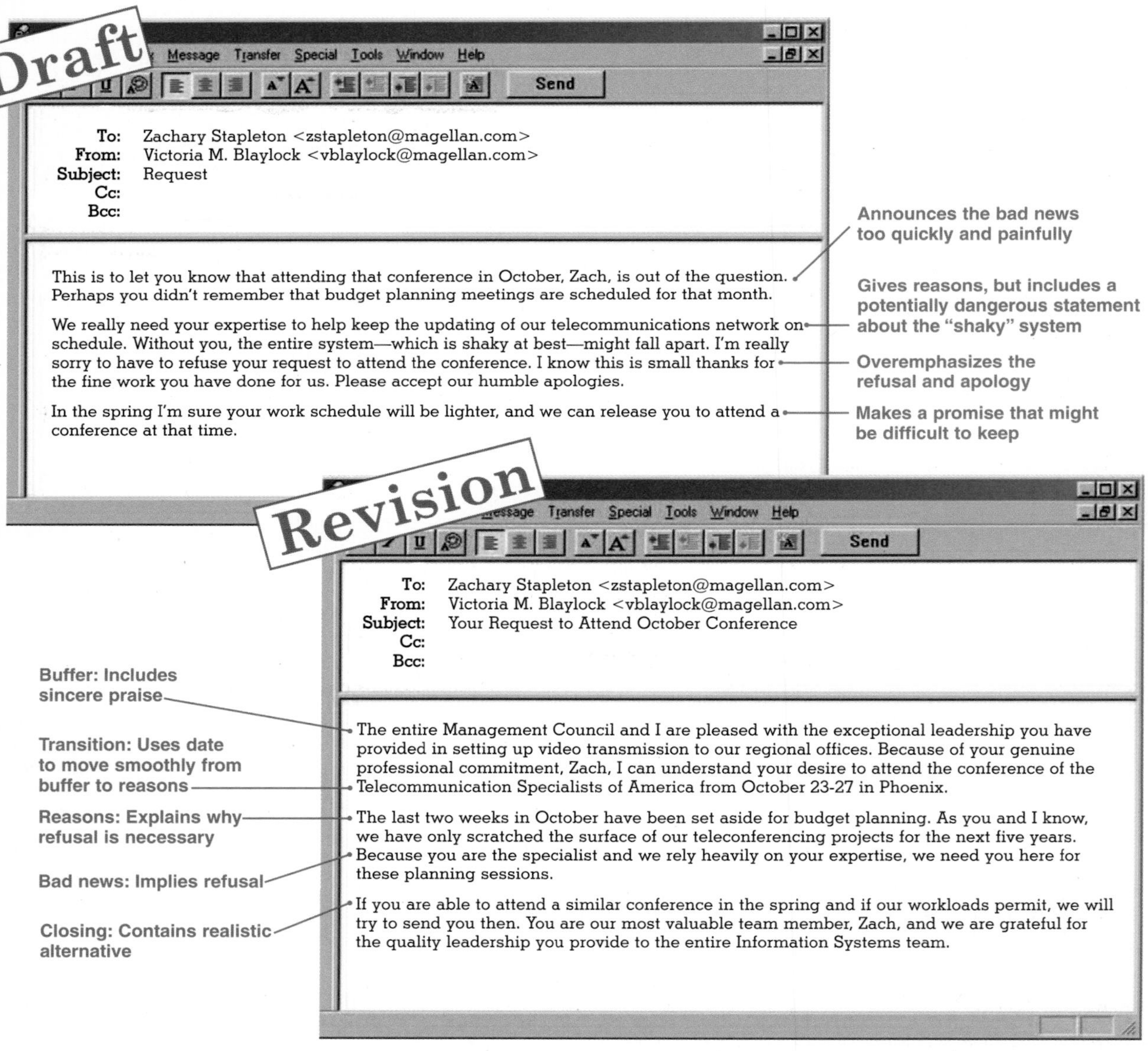
Draft
Message Transfer Special Tools Window Help
Send
To: Zachary Stapleton <zstapleton@magellan.com>
From: Victoria M. Blaylock <vblaylock@magellan.com>
Subject: Request
Cc:
Bcc:
This is to let you know that attending that conference in October, Zach, is out of the question. Perhaps you didn't remember that budget planning meetings are scheduled for that month.
We really need your expertise to help keep the updating of our telecommunications network on schedule. Without you, the entire system—which is shaky at best—might fall apart. I'm really sorry to have to refuse your request to attend the conference. I know this is small thanks for the fine work you have done for us. Please accept our humble apologies.
In the spring I'm sure your work schedule will be lighter, and we can release you to attend a conference at that time.
Announces the bad news too quickly and painfully
Gives reasons, but includes a potentially dangerous statement about the "shaky" system
Overemphasizes the refusal and apology
Makes a promise that might be difficult to keep
Revision
Message Transfer Special Tools Window Help
Send
To: Zachary Stapleton <zstapleton@magellan.com>
From: Victoria M. Blaylock <vblaylock@magellan.com>
Subject: Your Request to Attend October Conference
Cc:
Bcc:
The entire Management Council and I are pleased with the exceptional leadership you have provided in setting up video transmission to our regional offices. Because of your genuine professional commitment, Zach, I can understand your desire to attend the conference of the Telecommunication Specialists of America from October 23-27 in Phoenix.
The last two weeks in October have been set aside for budget planning. As you and I know, we have only scratched the surface of our teleconferencing projects for the next five years. Because you are the specialist and we rely heavily on your expertise, we need you here for these planning sessions.
If you are able to attend a similar conference in the spring and if our workloads permit, we will try to send you then. You are our most valuable team member, Zach, and we are grateful for the quality leadership you provide to the entire Information Systems team.
Buffer: Includes sincere praise
Transition: Uses date to move smoothly from buffer to reasons
Reasons: Explains why refusal is necessary
Bad news: Implies refusal
Closing: Contains realistic alternative

going to hurt and that it had possible danger areas. Moreover, the message misses a chance to give Zach positive feedback. An improved version of the e-mail starts with a buffer that delivers honest praise (*pleased with the exceptional leadership you have provided* and *your genuine professional commitment*). By the way, don't be stingy with compliments; they cost you nothing. As a philosopher once observed: "We don't live by bread alone. We need buttering up once in a while." The buffer also includes the date of the meeting, used strategically to connect the reasons that follow. You will recall from Chapter 5 that repetition of a key idea is an effective transitional device to provide smooth flow between components of a message.

The middle paragraph provides reasons for the refusal. Notice that they focus on positive elements: Zach is the specialist; the company relies on his expertise; and everyone will benefit if he passes up the conference. In this section it becomes obvious that the request will be refused. The writer is not forced to say, *No, you may not attend.* Although the refusal is implied, the reader gets the message.

The closing suggests a qualified alternative (*if our workloads permit, we will try to send you then*). It also ends positively with gratitude for Zach's contributions to the organization and with another compliment (*you're a valuable player*). The improved version focuses on explanations and praise rather than on refusals and apologies. The success of this message depends on attention to the entire writing process, not just on using a buffer or scattering a few compliments throughout.

Delivering Bad News to Groups

Should bad news to groups of employees be delivered personally or in writing?

Many of the same techniques used to deliver bad news personally are useful when organizations face a crisis or must deliver bad news to groups. Smart organizations involved in a crisis prefer to communicate the news openly to employees and stockholders. A crisis might involve serious performance problems, a major relocation, massive layoffs, a management shakeup, or public controversy. Instead of letting rumors distort the truth, managers explain the organization's side of the story honestly and early. Morale can be destroyed when employees learn of major events affecting their jobs through the grapevine or from news accounts—rather than from management.

When bad news must be delivered to employees, management may want to deliver the news personally. With large groups, however, this is generally impossible. Instead, organizations deliver bad news through hard-copy memos, which are formal and create a permanent record. Today's organizations are also experimenting with other delivery channels such as e-mail, videos, webcasts, and voice mail.

The draft of the memo shown in Figure 9.10 announces a substantial increase in the cost of employee health care benefits. However, the memo suffers from many problems. It announces jolting news bluntly in the first sentence. Worse, it offers little or no explanation for the steep increase in costs. It also sounds insincere (*We did everything possible* ...) and arbitrary. In a final miscue, the writer fails to give credit to the company for absorbing previous health cost increases.

Ethics Check

Canned by E-Mail

When downsizing, RadioShack used e-mail to fire about 400 employees at its Fort Worth headquarters. The messages said, "The work force reduction notification is currently in progress. Unfortunately, your position is one that has been eliminated." Is it ethical to send such bad news by e-mail, and how do you feel about the tone of the message?

The revision of this bad-news memo uses the indirect strategy and improves the tone considerably. Notice that it opens with a relevant, upbeat buffer regarding health care—but says nothing about increasing costs. For a smooth transition, the second paragraph begins with a key idea from the opening (*comprehensive package*). The reasons section discusses rising costs with explanations and figures. The bad news (*you will be paying $119 a month*) is clearly presented but embedded within the paragraph. Throughout, the writer strives to show the fairness of the company's position. The ending, which does not refer to the bad news, emphasizes how much the company is paying and what a wise investment it is.

Notice that the entire memo demonstrates a kinder, gentler approach than that shown in the first draft. Of prime importance in breaking bad news to employees is providing clear, convincing reasons that explain the decision. This message could have been sent by e-mail, but a memo is more formal, more permanent, and more appropriate for bad news. This channel choice, however, may change as e-mail increasingly gains acceptance.

Saying No to Job Applicants

Should you include specifics in messages that refuse job candidates?

Being refused a job is one of life's major rejections. Tactless letters intensify the blow (*Unfortunately, you were not among the candidates selected for* ...).

FIGURE 9.10 Announcing Bad News to Employees

1 Prewriting

Analyze: The purpose of this memo is to tell employees that they must share with the company the cost of increasing health care costs.

Anticipate: The audience will be employees who are unaware of specific health care costs and, most likely, reluctant to pay more.

Adapt: Because the readers will be unhappy, use the indirect strategy. Choose to send an interoffice memo, which is more permanent and more formal than e-mail.

2 Writing

Research: Collect facts and statistics that document health care costs.

Organize: Begin with a buffer describing the company's commitment to health benefits. Provide an explanation of health care costs. Announce the bad news. In the closing, focus on the company's major share of the cost.

Compose: Draft the first version with the expectation to revise.

3 Revising

Revise: Remove negativity (*unfortunately, we can't, the company was forced, inadvisable*). Explain the increase with specific figures.

Proofread: Use quotation marks around *defensive* to show its special sense. Spell out *percent* after *300*.

Evaluate: Is there any other way to help readers accept this bad news?

Draft

Beginning January 1 your monthly payment for health care benefits will be increased $119 a month for a total payment of $639 for each employee.

Every year health care costs go up. Although we considered dropping other benefits, Northern decided that the best plan was to keep the present comprehensive package. Unfortunately, we can't do that unless we pass along some of the extra cost to you. Last year the company was forced to absorb the total increase in health care premiums. However, such a plan this year is inadvisable.

We did everything possible to avoid the sharp increase in costs to you this year. A rate schedule describing the increases in payments for your family and dependents is enclosed.

Hits readers with bad news without any preparation

Offers no explanation for increase

Sounds defensive and arbitrary

Fails to take credit for absorbing previous increases

Revision

NORTHERN INDUSTRIES, INC.
MEMORANDUM

Date: October 2, 2012

To: Fellow Employees

From: Victor Q. Markelson, President VQM

Subject: Maintaining Quality Health Care

Begins with positive buffer

Health care programs have always been an important part of our commitment to employees at Northern Industries, Inc. We are proud that our total benefits package continues to rank among the best in the country.

Offers reason explaining why costs are rising

Such a comprehensive package does not come cheaply. In the last decade, health care costs alone have risen over 300 percent. We are told that several factors fuel the cost spiral: aging population, technology improvements, increased cost of patient services, and "defensive" medicine practiced by doctors to prevent lawsuits.

Reveals bad news clearly but embeds it in paragraph

Just two years ago our monthly health care cost for each employee was $515. It rose to $569 last year. We were able to absorb that jump without increasing your contribution. But this year's hike to $639 forces us to ask you to share the increase. To maintain your current health care benefits, you will be paying $119 a month. The enclosed rate schedule describes the costs for families and dependents.

Ends positively by stressing the company's major share of the costs

Northern continues to pay the major portion of your health care program ($520 each month). We think it's a wise investment.

Enclosure

FIGURE 9.11 Saying No to Job Candidate

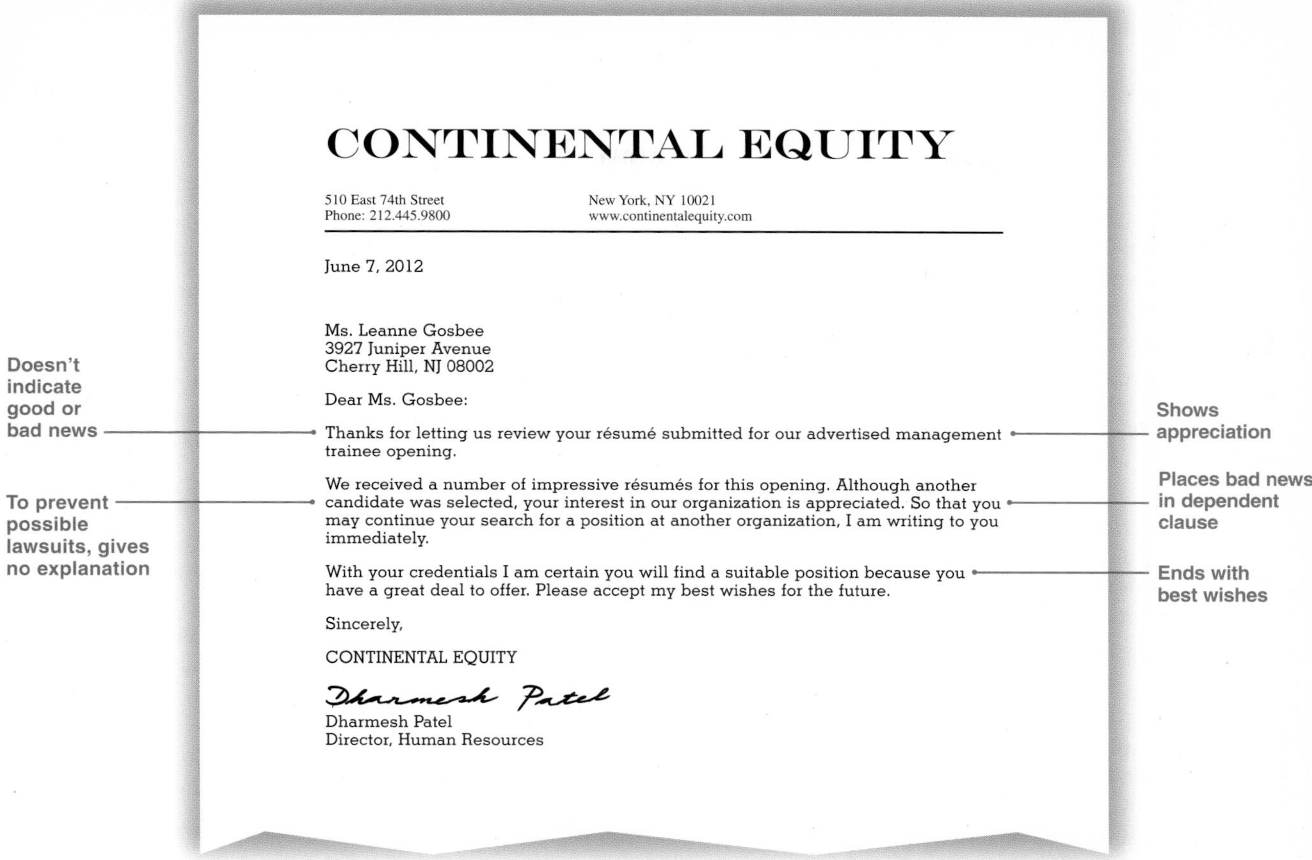

CONTINENTAL EQUITY

510 East 74th Street
Phone: 212.445.9800

New York, NY 10021
www.continentalequity.com

June 7, 2012

Ms. Leanne Gosbee
3927 Juniper Avenue
Cherry Hill, NJ 08002

Dear Ms. Gosbee:

Thanks for letting us review your résumé submitted for our advertised management trainee opening.

We received a number of impressive résumés for this opening. Although another candidate was selected, your interest in our organization is appreciated. So that you may continue your search for a position at another organization, I am writing to you immediately.

With your credentials I am certain you will find a suitable position because you have a great deal to offer. Please accept my best wishes for the future.

Sincerely,

CONTINENTAL EQUITY

Dharmesh Patel

Dharmesh Patel
Director, Human Resources

You can reduce the receiver's disappointment somewhat by using the indirect strategy—with one important variation. In the reasons section, it is wise to be vague in explaining why the candidate was not selected. First, giving concrete reasons may be painful to the receiver *(Your grade point average of 2.7 was low compared with the GPAs of other candidates)*. Second, and more important, providing extra information may prove fatal in a lawsuit. Hiring and firing decisions generate considerable litigation today. To avoid charges of discrimination or wrongful actions, legal advisors warn organizations to keep employment rejection letters general, simple, and short.

The job refusal letter shown in Figure 9.11 is tactful but intentionally vague. It implies that the applicant's qualifications don't match those needed for the position, but the letter doesn't reveal anything specific. The writer could have included this alternate closing: *We wish you every success in finding a position that exactly fits your qualifications.*

The checklist on page 282 summarizes tips on how to communicate negative news inside and outside your organization.

Presenting Bad News in Other Cultures

LEARNING OBJECTIVE 7

Compare strategies for revealing bad news in other cultures.

To minimize disappointment, Americans generally prefer to present negative messages indirectly. Communicators in other cultures may treat bad news differently.

In Germany, for example, business communicators occasionally use buffers but tend to present bad news directly. British writers also tend to be straightforward with bad news, seeing no reason to soften its announcement. In Latin countries the question is not how to organize negative messages but whether to present them at all. It is considered disrespectful and impolite to report bad news to superiors. Thus, reluctant employees may fail to report accurately any negative situations to their bosses.

Checklist

Conveying Negative News

Prewrite

- Decide whether to use the direct or indirect strategy. If the bad news is minor and will not upset the receiver, open directly. If the message is personally damaging and will upset the receiver, consider techniques to reduce its pain.
- Think through the reasons for the bad news.
- Remember that your primary goal is to make the receiver understand and accept the bad news as well as maintain a positive image of you and your organization.

Plan the Opening

- In the indirect strategy, start with a buffer. Pay a compliment to the reader, show appreciation for something done, or mention some mutual understanding. Avoid raising false hopes or thanking the reader for something you will refuse.
- In the direct strategy, begin with a straightforward statement of the bad news.

Provide Reasons in the Body

- Except in credit and job refusals, explain the reasons for the negative message.
- In customer mishaps, clarify what went wrong, what you are doing to resolve the problem, and how you will prevent it from happening again.
- Use objective, nonjudgmental, and nondiscriminatory language.
- Avoid negativity (e.g., words such as *unfortunately, unwilling,* and *impossible)* and potentially damaging statements.
- Show how your decision is fair and perhaps benefits the reader or others, if possible.

Soften the Bad News

- Reduce the impact of bad news by using (a) a subordinate clause, (b) the passive voice, (c) a long sentence, or (d) a long paragraph.
- Consider implying the refusal, but be certain it is clear.
- Suggest an alternative, such as a lower price, a different product, a longer payment period, or a substitute. Provide help in implementing an alternative.
- Offset disappointment by offering gifts, a reduced price, benefits, tokens of appreciation, or something appropriate.

Close Pleasantly

- Supply more information about an alternative, look forward to future relations, or offer good wishes and compliments.
- Maintain a bright, personal tone. Avoid referring to the refusal.

Why might it be necessary to use a different strategy when communicating bad news in other cultures?

In Asian cultures, harmony and peace are sought in all relationships. Disrupting the harmony with bad news is avoided. To prevent discord, Japanese communicators use a number of techniques to indicate *no*—without being forced to say it. In conversation they may respond with silence or with a counter question, such as *Why do you ask?* They may change the subject or tell a white lie to save face for themselves and for the questioner. Sometimes the answer sounds like a qualified yes: *I will do my best, but if I cannot, I hope you will understand.* If the response is *Yes, but ...*, or *Yes* followed by an apology, beware. All of these responses should be recognized as meaning *no.*

In China, Westerners often have difficulty understanding the hints given by communicators.

> *I agree* might mean *I agree with 15 percent of what you say.*
> *We might be able to* could mean *Not a chance.*
> *We will consider* could mean *WE will, but the real decision maker will not.*
> *That is a little too much* might equate to *That is outrageous.*[22]

Why might low-context, literal-minded communicators misunderstand subtle messages from some Asians?

In Thailand the negativism represented by a refusal is completely alien; the word *no* does not exist. In many cultures negative news is offered with such subtlety or in such a positive light that it may be overlooked or misunderstood by literal-minded Americans.

In many high-context cultures, saving face is important. A refusal is a potential loss of face for both parties. To save face, a person who must refuse an invitation to dine out with a business associate might say, *You must be very tired and want to have a quiet evening.*[23] This subtle refusal avoids putting it in words. To understand the meaning of what's really being communicated, we must look beyond an individual's actual words and consider the communication style, the culture, and especially the context.

Zooming In — YOUR TURN

Applying Your Skills at Southwest Airlines

Southwest Airlines, whose motto is "Share the Spirit," is actively involved in the communities it serves. Its high level of participation has earned the company a place on the 100 Best Corporate Citizens list. Employees volunteer in dozens of local events. On a national level, it partners with a wide range of charities, including the Hispanic Association of Colleges and Universities' national educational travel award program, the Ronald McDonald House, Junior Achievement, Read Across America, and Parkland Burn Camp. Through its award-winning Adopt-a-Pilot program, a fifth-grade classroom is paired with a pilot mentor for four weeks. Students correspond with their pilots and track their travels, engaging in aviation-themed science, math, research, writing, history, geography, and career-planning lessons and activities.

With such a high public profile, the airline receives many requests for donations, from monetary contributions and event sponsorships to numerous appeals for free flight tickets from charities holding fund-raising events. Its detailed guidelines for groups seeking donations, published on its Web site, state, "A standard donation is two round-trip passes good for transportation between any two cities Southwest Airlines serves within the continental U.S." Charities must mail their requests for free tickets to the Charitable Giving Department at Southwest's Dallas headquarters, which then determines the recipients.

Your Task

© Justin Sullivan/Getty Images

Assume that you are an intern in the Southwest Airlines Charitable Giving Department. Your manager hands you a letter from Elizabeth Dunbar, Director, Animal Rescue League of Iowa, 5452 Northeast 22nd Street, Des Moines, IA 50313. This organization never turns away an animal in need, but it has run out of space and desperately needs a new shelter. To build a $6.5 million state-of-the-art facility, it is sponsoring a local raffle. One prize would be ten round-trip tickets anywhere in the United States, and it asks Southwest to provide those tickets. The problem is that the request arrived 30 days before the event and is nonstandard. Deny the request, but offer an alternative. You like animals, too!

A recent study showed that business letters conveying bad news in Latin America were quite short and did not employ buffers. This may be a result of the desire to avoid negative news completely, feeling it is discourteous to bring bad news.[24]

Conveying bad news in any culture is tricky and requires sensitivity to and awareness of cultural practices.

Want to do well on tests and excel in your course?
Go to **www.meguffey.com** for helpful interactive resources.

- **Review the Chapter 9 PowerPoint slides to prepare for the first quiz.**

Summary of Learning Objectives

1 Describe the goals and strategies of business communicators in conveying negative news effectively, including applying the writing process and avoiding legal liability. All businesses occasionally deal with problems. Good communicators have many goals in delivering bad news: explaining clearly and completely, projecting a professional image, conveying empathy and sensitivity, being fair, and maintaining friendly relations. Applying the 3-x-3 writing process helps you prepare, compose, and revise your message so that it accomplishes your purpose. Careful communicators avoid careless and abusive language, which is actionable when it is false, damages a person's reputation, and is "published" (spoken within the presence of others or written). Messages written on company stationery represent that company and can be legally binding.

2 Decide whether to use the direct or indirect strategy in conveying negative news. The indirect strategy involves beginning with a buffer and delaying the bad news until reasons have been presented. The direct strategy reveals the main idea immediately. The direct strategy is preferable when the bad news is not damaging, when the receiver may overlook the bad news, when the organization policy suggests directness, when the receiver prefers directness, and when firmness is necessary. The indirect strategy works well when the bad news is personally upsetting, provokes a hostile reaction, threatens the customer relationship, and is unexpected.

3 Analyze the components of effective negative messages, including opening with a buffer, apologizing, conveying empathy, presenting the reasons, cushioning the bad news, and closing pleasantly. If you use the indirect strategy for a negative message, begin with a buffer, such as a compliment, appreciation, a point of agreement, objective information, understanding, or some part of the message that represents good news. Then explain the reasons that necessitate the bad news, trying to cite benefits to the reader or others. If you use the direct strategy, begin directly with the bad news followed by the reasons. When apologizing, do so sincerely, accept responsibility, and use good judgment. Throughout a negative message, strive to cushion the bad news by positioning it strategically, using the passive voice, accentuating the positive, choosing positive words, and suggesting a compromise or alternative. Close pleasantly with a forward-looking goodwill statement.

4 Describe and apply effective techniques for refusing typical requests. Typical requests ask for favors, money, information, action, and other items. When the answer will be disappointing, use the reasons-before-refusal pattern. Open with a buffer; provide reasons; announce the refusal sensitively; suggest possible alternatives; and end with a positive, forward-looking comment.

5 Explain and apply effective techniques for handling bad news with customers. When a company disappoints its customers, most organizations (a) call the individual involved, (b) describe the problem and apologize (when the company is to blame), (c) explain why the problem occurred and what is being done to prevent its recurrence, and (d) follow up with a message that documents the phone call and promotes goodwill. Some organizations also offer gifts or benefits to offset customers' disappointment and to reestablish the business relationship. In announcing rate increases and price hikes, tie the increase to customer benefits. In denying claims, begin indirectly, provide reasons for the refusal, and close pleasantly, looking forward to future business. When appropriate, resell a product or service. When refusing credit, avoid language that causes hard feelings, strive to retain the customer on a cash basis, prepare for possible future credit, and avoid disclosures that could cause a lawsuit.

6 Understand and apply effective techniques for delivering bad news within organizations. When delivering bad news personally to a superior, gather all the information, prepare and rehearse, explain what happened and how the problem will be repaired, consider taking a colleague with you, think about timing, and be patient with the reaction. In delivering bad news to groups of employees, use the indirect strategy but be sure to provide clear, convincing reasons that explain the decision. In refusing job applicants, however, keep letters short, general, and tactful.

7 Compare strategies for revealing bad news in other cultures. American communicators often prefer to break bad news slowly and indirectly. In other low-context cultures, such as Germany and Britain, however, bad news is revealed directly. In most high-context cultures, such as China and Japan, straightforwardness is avoided. In Latin cultures bad news may be totally suppressed. In Asian cultures negativism is avoided and hints may suggest bad news. Subtle meanings must be interpreted carefully.

Chapter Review

1. When delivering bad news, how can a communicator reduce the bad feelings of the receiver? (Obj. 1)
2. What is the most important part of Phase 1 of the writing process for negative messages? (Obj. 1)
3. When should you use the direct strategy in delivering bad news? (Obj. 2)
4. When should you use the indirect strategy in delivering bad news? (Obj. 2)
5. What are the major differences between the direct and indirect strategies in delivering bad news? (Obj. 2)
6. What is a buffer? Name five or more techniques to buffer the opening of a bad-news message. (Obj. 3)
7. What is an apology? When should an apology be offered to customers? (Obj. 3)
8. Name four or more techniques that cushion the delivery of bad news. (Obj. 3)
9. What are some typical requests that big and small businesses must refuse? (Obj. 4)
10. Identify a process used by a majority of business professionals in resolving problems with disappointed customers. (Obj. 5)
11. If you must deny the claim of a customer who is clearly at fault, should you respond by putting the blame squarely on the customer? (Obj. 5)
12. What is an effective technique in announcing rate increases and price hikes? (Obj. 5)
13. How can a subordinate tactfully, professionally, and safely deliver upsetting news personally to a superior? (Obj. 6)
14. What are some channels that large organizations may use when delivering bad news to employees? (Obj. 6)
15. In Latin countries why may employees sometimes fail to report accurately any negative situations to management? (Obj. 7)

Critical Thinking

1. Communication author Dana Bristol-Smith likens delivering bad news to removing a Band-Aid—you can do it slowly or quickly. She thinks that quickly is better, particularly when companies must give bad news to employees.[25] Do you agree or disagree? (Objs. 1–6)
2. Respected industry analyst Gartner Research issued a report naming social networking as one of the top ten disruptive influences shaping information technology in the next five years.[26] Should organizations fear Web sites where consumers post negative messages about products and services? What actions can companies take in response to this disruptive influence? (Objs. 1–5)
3. Consider times when you have been aware that others were using the indirect strategy in writing or speaking to you. How did you react? (Obj. 2)
4. When Boeing Aircraft reported that a laptop containing the names, salary information, and social security numbers of 382,000 employees had been stolen from an employee's car, CEO Jim McNerney wrote this e-mail to employees: "I've received many e-mails over the past 24 hours from employees expressing disappointment, frustration, and downright anger about yesterday's announcement of personal information belonging to thousands of employees and retirees being on a stolen computer. I'm just as disappointed as you are about it. I know that many of us feel that this data loss amounts to a betrayal of the trust we place in the company to safeguard our personal information. I certainly do." Critics have faulted this apology for its timing and content. Do you agree?
5. **Ethical Issue:** You work for a large corporation with headquarters in a small town. Recently you received shoddy repair work and a huge bill from a local garage. Your car's transmission has the same problems that it did before you took it in for repair. You know that a complaint letter written on your corporation's stationery would be much more authoritative than one written on plain stationery. Should you use corporation stationery? (Obj. 1)

Writing Improvement Exercises

9.1 Organizational Strategies (Objs. 1–5)

Your Task. Identify which organizational strategy you would use for the following messages: direct or indirect.

a. A letter from a credit card company announcing a small increase in rates.
b. A letter from a theme park refusing the request of a visitor who wants free tickets. The visitor was unhappy that he had to wait in line a very long time to ride a new thrill roller coaster.
c. An e-mail from a manager refusing an employee's request for funds and time off to attend a professional seminar.
d. A letter refusing a request by a charitable organization to use your office equipment on the weekend.
e. A memo from the manager denying an employee's request for special parking privileges. The employee works closely with the manager on many projects.
f. An announcement to employees that a financial specialist has canceled a scheduled lunchtime talk and cannot reschedule.
g. A letter to bank customers revealing that its central computer system had been hacked revealing customer addresses, dates of birth, account numbers, and the value of investments.
h. A form letter from an insurance company announcing new policy requirements that many policyholders may resent. If policyholders do not indicate the plan they prefer, they may lose their insurance coverage.

i. A memo from an executive refusing a manager's proposal to economize by purchasing reconditioned computers. The executive and the manager both appreciate efficient, straightforward messages.
j. A letter informing a company that the majority of the company's equipment order will not be available for six weeks.

9.2 Employing Passive-Voice Verbs (Obj. 3)

Your Task. Revise the following sentences to present the bad news with passive-voice verbs.

a. We cannot offer free shipping after January 1.
b. Our retail stores will no longer be accepting credit cards for purchases under $5.
c. Because management now requires more stringent security, we are postponing indefinitely requests for company tours.
d. We do not examine patients until we have verified their insurance coverage.
e. Your car rental insurance coverage does not cover large SUVs.
f. Company policy prevents us from offering health and dental benefits until employees have been on the job for 12 months.

9.3 Subordinating Bad News (Obj. 3)

Your Task. Revise the following sentences to position the bad news in a subordinate clause. (**Hint:** Consider beginning the clause with *Although*.) Use passive-voice verbs for the bad news.

a. We regret that we cannot replace the cabinet hinge you need. The manufacturer no longer offers it. A new hinge should work for you, and we are sending it to you.
b. State law does not allow smoking within 5 feet of a state building. But the college has set aside 16 outdoor smoking areas.
c. We now offer all of our catalog choices at our Web site, which is always current. Unfortunately, we no longer print or mail a complete catalog.
d. We are sorry to report that we are unable to ship your complete order at this point in time. However, we are able to send two corner workstations now, and you should receive them within five days.
e. We appreciate your interest in our organization, but we are unable to extend an employment offer to you at this time.

9.4 Implying Bad News (Obj. 3)

Your Task. Revise the following statements to *imply* the bad news. If possible, use passive-voice verbs and subordinate clauses to further de-emphasize the bad news.

a. Unfortunately, we find it impossible to contribute to your excellent and worthwhile fund-raising campaign this year. At present all the funds of my organization are needed to lease equipment and offices for our new branch in Hartford. We hope to be able to support this commendable endeavor in the future.
b. We cannot ship our fresh fruit baskets c.o.d. Your order was not accompanied by payment, so we are not shipping it. We have it ready, though, and will rush it to its destination as soon as you call us with your credit card number.
c. Because of the holiday period, all our billboard space was used this month. Therefore, we are sorry to say that we could not give your charitable group free display space. However, next month, after the holidays, we hope to display your message as we promised.

Activities

Note: All Documents for Analysis are provided at **www.meguffey.com** for you to download and revise.

9.5 Document for Analysis: Wedding Request Refusal (Objs. 1–4)

Your Task. Analyze the following poorly written request refusal. List its weaknesses. If your instructor directs, revise it using the suggestions you learned in this chapter.

Current date

Ms. Sonya Capretta
2459 Sierra Avenue
Fresno, CA 93710

Dear Ms. Capretta:

We regret to inform you that the wedding date you request in your letter of February 2 at the Napa Valley Inn is unavailable. Unfortunately, we are fully booked for all of the Saturdays in June, as you probably already suspected.

June is our busiest month, and smart brides make their reservations many months—even years—in advance. That's because the Napa Valley Inn is the ideal romantic getaway for weddings. With unparalleled cuisine and service, along with panoramic Napa Valley and vineyard views, our Inn offers unique, intimate ambiance in a breathtaking location for your special event.

We apologize if we have caused you any inconvenience. However, if you could change your wedding date to the middle of the week, we would try to accommodate your party. We do have a few midweek spots open in June, but even those dates are rapidly filling up. With 45 Mediterranean-style rooms and suites, each with its own sunny private terrace, the Napa Valley Inn is the perfect location for you and your partner to begin your married lives. Afternoon ceremonies typically begin at 11 a.m., while golden sunsets at the Napa Valley Inn offer a romantic prelude of the evening to come. Evening ceremonies usually begin at 6 p.m. I'm available if you want to arrange something.

Sincerely,

9.6 Document for Analysis: Copier Request Refusal (Objs. 1–4)

Your Task. Analyze the following letter. List its weaknesses. If your instructor directs, revise it using the suggestions you learned in this chapter. Add any needed information.

Current date

Mr. Tyler Venable
Great Atlantic Financial Services
105 Washington Avenue
Glassboro, NJ 08071

Dear Mr. Venable:

We find it impossible to convert the payments you have been making on your Sharp CopyCenter C20 to the purchase of a new copier. This request has been forwarded to me, and I see that you have been making regular payments for the past 11 months.

Some time ago we instituted a company policy prohibiting such conversion of leasing monies. Perhaps you have noticed that we offer extremely low leasing and purchase prices. Obviously, these low prices would never be possible if we agreed to many proposals such as yours. Because we are striving to stay in business, we must deny your request asking us to convert all 11 months of rental payments toward the purchase of our popular new equipment.

It is our understanding, Mr. Venable, that you have been using the Sharp CopyCenter C20 color copier for 11 months, and you claim that it has been reliable and versatile. We would like to tell you about another Sharp model—one that is perhaps closer to your limited budget.

Sincerely,

9.7 Document for Analysis: Refusing Internal Request for Time Off (Objs. 1–4, 6)

Your Task. Analyze the following poorly written e-mail, and list its weaknesses. If your instructor directs, revise it using the suggestions you learned in this and previous chapters.

To: Sylvia Greene (sgreene@financialsolutions.com)
From: Chester Goings (cgoings@financialsolutions.com)
Subject: No Go on Baby Charity Thing
Cc:
Bcc:

Hey, Syl, you're one in a million. But we can't give you time off to work on that charity fashion show/luncheon thingy you want to coordinate. And Financial Solutions can't make a big contribution as we've done in previous years. It's no, no, no, all the way around.

Look, we admire the work you have done for the Newborn Hope Foundation. It has raised millions of dollars to make differences in the lives of babies, particularly premature ones. But we need you here!

With the upcoming release of our Planning Guide 5.0, we need you to interview clients. We need you to make video testimonials, and you are the one to search for stories about customer successes. Plus a zillion other tasks! Our new Web site will launch in just six short weeks, and all that content stuff must be in final form. With the economy in the tank and our bare-bones staff, you certainly must realize that each and every team member must be here and making a difference. If our Planning Guide 5.0 doesn't make a big splash, we'll all have a lot of time off.

Due to the fact that we're the worldwide leader in on-demand financial planning and reporting software, and in view of the fact that we are about to launch our most important new product ever, you must understand our position. When things get better, we might be able to return back to our past practices. But not now!

Chet

9.8 Document for Analysis: Refusing a Job Applicant (Objs. 1, 2, and 6)

Your Task. Analyze the following letter. List its weaknesses. If your instructor directs, revise it.

Current date

Mr. Kent W. Bradshaw
2140 Azalea Avenue
Louisville, KY 40216

Dear Mr. Bradshaw:

Mrs. Lujan and I wish to thank you for the pleasure of allowing us to interview you last Thursday. We were totally delighted to learn about your superb academic record, and we also appreciated your attentiveness in listening to our description of the operations of Appalachian Technologies.

Unfortunately, we had many well-qualified applicants who were interested in the advertised position of human resources assistant. As you may have guessed, we were particularly eager to find a minority individual who could help us fill our diversity goals. Although you did not fit one of our goal areas, we enjoyed talking with you. We hired a female graduate from the University of Kentucky who had most of the qualities we sought.

We realize that the job market is difficult at this time, and you have our heartfelt wishes for good luck in finding precisely what you are looking for.

Sincerely,

9.9 Request Refusal: Helping Abused Children (Objs. 1–4)

As a vice president of a financial services company, you serve many clients and they sometimes ask your company to contribute to their favorite charities. You recently received a letter from Olivia Hernandez asking for a substantial contribution to the National Court Appointed Special Advocate (CASA) Association. On visits to your office, she has told you about its programs to recruit, train, and support volunteers in their work with abused children. She herself is active in your town as a CASA volunteer, helping neglected children find safe, permanent homes. She told you that children with CASA volunteers are more likely to be adopted and are less likely to reenter the child welfare system. You have a soft spot in your heart for children and especially for those who are mistreated. You sincerely want to support CASA and its good work. But times are tough, and you can't be as generous as you have been in the past. Ms. Hernandez wrote a special letter to you asking you to become a Key contributor, with a pledge of $1,000.

Your Task. Write a refusal letter that maintains good relations with your client. Address it to Ms. Olivia Hernandez, 3592 Marine Creek Parkway, Fort Worth, TX 76179.

9.10 Request Refusal: Jamba Asks for Juicy Favor (Objs. 1–4)

In an aggressive expansion effort, Jamba Juice became a good customer of your software company. You have enjoyed the business it brought, and you are also quite fond of its products—especially Banana Berry and Mega Mango smoothies. Jamba Inc. is in the midst of expanding its menu with the goal of becoming the Starbucks of the smoothie. "Just as Starbucks defined the category of coffee, Jamba has the opportunity to define the category of the healthy snack," said analyst Brian Moore. One goal of Jamba is to boost the frequency of customer visits by offering some products that are more filling. Then it could attract hungry customers as well as thirsty ones. It was experimenting with adding grains such as oatmeal or nuts such as almonds so that a smoothie packs more substance and could substitute for a meal.

You receive a letter from Joe Wong, your business friend and contact at Jamba Juice. He asks you to do him and Jamba Juice a favor. He wants to set up a juice tasting bar in your company cafeteria to test his new experimental drinks. All the drinks would be free, of course, but employees would have to fill out forms to evaluate each recipe. The details could be worked out later.

You definitely support healthy snacks, but you think this idea is terrible. First of all, your company doesn't even have a cafeteria. It has a small lunchroom, and employees bring their own food. Secondly, you would be embarrassed to ask your boss to do this favor for Jamba Juice, despite the business it has brought your company.

Your Task. Write a letter that retains good customer relations with Jamba Juice but refuses this request. What reasons can you give, and what alternatives are available? Address your message to Joe Wong, Vice President, Product Development, Jamba Inc., 450 Golden Gate Avenue, San Francisco, CA 94102.[27]

9.11 Request Refusal: Greening the Office (Objs. 1–4)

Hines, an international real estate firm, has developed a green office program designed to enhance the sustainable features and operation of its 230 offices on four continents. Its program, called HinesGO (short for Hines Green Office), helps identify and implement no-cost and low-cost green alternatives for standard indoor office environments. What's outstanding about the HinesGo program is its emphasis on improvements that can be achieved at minimal cost. For example, installation of occupancy light sensors can save enough money to offset the up-front investment.

Scored on a scale of 100, offices are evaluated in seven categories: energy efficiency; people and atmosphere; travel and commuting; reduce, reuse, and recycle; cleaning and pest control; remodeling and construction; and LEED and/or ENERGY STAR. (LEED is an internationally recognized green building certification system.) When a specific strategy has been implemented in the HinesGo program, participants earn Leaf Credits.[28]

Although its HinesGO program was initially intended for Hines offices only, the program generated so much attention that other businesses now want to duplicate its success. As a manager at Hines in charge of communication for HinesGo, you receive numerous invitations to speak to groups interested in creating greener workplace choices. However, you can't always accept. The most recent invitation came from Florida, where a group of realtors wants you to tell them about the HinesGO program. You were invited to speak October 12, but you are booked up. You don't see an opening until sometime in late January.

Your Task. Prepare a letter that refuses the invitation but suggests an alternative and promotes the HinesGO program. Send your letter to Donna Payne, Society of Commercial Realtors of Greater Fort Lauderdale, 1765 NE 26th Street, Fort Lauderdale, FL 33305.

9.12 Request Refusal: Rejecting Agent's Appeal for Wireless Device (Objs. 1–4)

Warren R. Sims, founder of Sims South Florida Realty, runs a successful real estate brokerage with 22 agents in three offices. Jon Tabaldo, an eager, new, tech-savvy agent, has discovered a handheld device that he thinks is the perfect tool to continuously access and monitor multiple listing service (MLS) data. This wireless device provides fast, complete Web access, enabling real estate professionals to increase productivity. They spend less time in the office and more time with their customers. The device also increases customer satisfaction because agents can respond quickly with data and full graphics for any-where-anytime service. Jon sent a persuasive e-mail to his boss asking that the realty company provide these handheld devices for all agents.

Mr. Sims uses e-mail, but he is not keen on employing technology to sell real estate. Regardless, he gave considerable thought to Jon's message recommending the devices. Mr. Sims did the math and figures it would cost him close to $8,000 for the initial investment plus $5,000 per year/per office for updates. He thinks this is a lot of money for technology he's not convinced is needed or that may not be used. He also worries about ownership responsibility.

He could pick up the phone and talk to Jon personally. But Mr. Sims wants to respond in an interoffice memo because he can control exactly what he says. He also thinks that a written response is more forceful and that it provides a permanent record of this decision in case agents make similar requests in the future. The more he ponders the request, the more Mr. Sims thinks that this kind of investment in software and hardware should be made by agents themselves—not by the agency. Don't they already purchase their own laptops?

Your Task. Put yourself in the place of Mr. Sims and prepare an interoffice memo that refuses the request but retains the goodwill of the agent. What reasons can you give for the refusal?

9.13 Request Refusal: Fun Ship Slams Door on Under-21 Crowd (Objs. 1–4)

The world's largest cruise line finds itself in a difficult position. Carnival climbed to the No. 1 spot by promoting fun at sea and pitching its appeal to younger customers who were drawn to on-board discos, swim-up bars, and hassle-free partying. But apparently the partying of high school and college students went too far. Roving bands of teens had virtually taken over some cruises in recent years. Travel agents complained of "drunken, loud behavior," as reported by Mike Driscoll, editor of *Cruise Week*.

To crack down, Carnival raised the drinking age from 18 to 21 and required more chaperoning of school groups. But young individual travelers were still unruly and disruptive. Therefore, Carnival instituted a new policy, effective immediately. No one under 21 may travel unless accompanied by an adult over 25. Vicki Freed, Carnival's vice president for marketing, said, "We will turn them back at the docks, and they will not get refunds." As Demetrice Hawkins, a Carnival marketing manager, you must respond to the inquiry of Elizabeth Neil, of Leisure World Travel, a Chicago travel agency that features special spring- and summer-break packages for college and high school students.

Leisure World Travel has been one of Carnival's best customers. However, Carnival no longer wants to encourage unaccompanied young people. You must refuse the request of Ms. Neil to help set up student tour packages. Carnival discourages even chaperoned tours. Its target market is now families. You must write to Leisure World Travel and break the bad news. Try to promote fun-filled, carefree cruises destined for sunny, exotic ports of call that remove guests from the stresses of everyday life. By the way, Carnival attracts more passengers than any other cruise line—over a million people a year from all over the world. Over 98 percent of Carnival's guests say that they were well satisfied.

Your Task. Write your letter to Elizabeth Neil, Leisure World Travel Agency, 636 South Michigan Avenue, Chicago, IL 60605. Send her a schedule for spring and summer Caribbean cruises. Tell her you will call during the week of January 15 to help her plan special family tour packages.[29]

9.14 Request Refusal: Can't Evict Noisy Tenant (Objs. 1-4)

Web

As the owner of Peachtree Business Plaza, you must respond to the request of Michael Vazquez, one of the tenants in your three-story office building. Mr. Vazquez, a CPA, demands that you immediately evict a neighboring tenant who plays loud music throughout the day, interfering with Mr. Vazquez' conversations with clients and with his concentration. The noisy tenant, Anthony Chomko, seems to operate an entertainment booking agency and spends long hours in his office. You know you can't evict Mr. Chomko because, as a legal commercial tenant, he is entitled to conduct his business. However, you might consider adding soundproofing, an expense that you would prefer to share with Mr. Chomko and Mr. Vazquez. You might also discuss limiting the time of day that Mr. Chomko could make noise.

Your Task. Before responding to Mr. Vazquez, you decide to find out more about commercial tenancy. Use the Web to search the keywords *commercial eviction*. Then develop a course of action. In a letter to Mr. Vazquez, deny his request but retain his goodwill. Tell him how you plan to resolve the problem. Write to Michael Vazquez, CPA, Suite 230, Peachtree Business Plaza, 116 Krog Street, Atlanta, GA 30307. Your instructor may also ask you to write an appropriate message to Mr. Anthony Chomko, Suite 225.

9.15 Claim Denial: Refusing Refund for Japandroids and Bugskull Concert (Objs. 1–4)

As manager of Promotions and Advertising at Adventureland Park, you must respond to a recent letter. Avianna Jones complained that she was "taken" by Adventureland when the park had to substitute performers for the Japandroids and Bugskull Summertime Slam performance Sunday, July 4. Explain to her that the concert was planned by an independent promoter. Your only obligation was to provide the venue and advertising. Three days before the event, the promoter left town, taking with him all advance payments from financial backers. As it turned out, many of the artists he had promised to deliver were not even planning to attend.

Left with a messy situation, you decided on Thursday to go ahead with a modified version of the event because you had been advertising it and many would come expecting some kind of talent. At that time you changed your radio advertising to say that for reasons beyond your control, the Japandroids and Bugskull bands would not be appearing. You described the new talent and posted signs at the entrance and in the parking lot announcing the change. Contrary to Ms. Jones's claim, no newspaper advertising featuring Japandroids or Bugskull appeared on the day of the concert (at least you did not pay for any to appear that day). Somehow she must have missed your corrective radio advertising and signs at the entrance. You feel you made a genuine effort to communicate the changed program. In your opinion, most people who attended the concert thought that Adventureland had done everything possible to salvage a rather unfortunate situation.

Ms. Jones wants a cash refund of $160 (two tickets at $80 each). Adventureland has a no-money-back policy on concerts after the event takes place. If Ms. Jones had come to the box office before the event started, you could have returned her money. But she stayed to see the concert. She claims that she didn't know anything about the talent change until after the event was well underway. This sounds unlikely, but you don't quarrel with customers. Nevertheless, you can't give her cash back. You already took a loss on this event. But you can give two complimentary passes to Adventureland Park.

Your Task. Write a refusal letter to Ms. Avianna Jones, 2045 Live Oak Drive, Sacramento, CA 95841. Invite her and a friend to return as guests under happier circumstances.

9.16 Claim Denial: She Wants Reimbursement for Her Eyeglasses (Objs. 1–4)

American Southern Airline (ASA) had an unhappy customer. Annette Boyer-Parker flew from New York to Los Angeles. The flight stopped briefly at Chicago O'Hare, where she got off the plane for half an hour. When she returned to her seat, her $400 prescription reading glasses were gone. She asked the flight attendant where the glasses were, and the attendant said they probably were thrown away since the cleaning crew had come in with big bags and tossed everything in them. Ms. Tomlinson tried to locate the glasses through the airline's lost-and-found service, but she failed.

Then she wrote a strong letter to the airline demanding reimbursement for the loss. She felt that it was obvious that she was returning to her seat. The airline, however, knows that an overwhelming number of passengers arriving at hubs switch planes for their connecting flights. The airline does not know who is returning. What's more, flight attendants usually announce that the plane is continuing to another city and that passengers who are returning should take their belongings. Cabin cleaning crews speed through planes removing newspapers, magazines, leftover foods, and trash. Airlines feel no responsibility for personal items left in cabins.[30]

Your Task. As a staff member of the customer relations department of American Southern Airline, deny the customer's claim but retain her goodwill using techniques learned in this chapter. The airline never refunds cash, but it might consider travel vouchers for the value of the glasses. Remember that apologies cost nothing. Write a claim denial to Mrs. Annette Boyer-Parker, 3560 Veteran Avenue, Santa Monica, CA 90401.

9.17 Claim Denial: Sorry—Smokers Must Pay (Objs. 1–4)

Recently the Century Park Hotel embarked on a two-year plan to provide enhanced value and improved product quality to its guests. It always strives to exceed guest expectations. As part of this effort, Century Park has been refurbishing many rooms with updated finishes. The new carpet, paint, upholstery, and draperies, however, absorb the heavy odor of cigarette smoke. In order to protect the hotel's investment, Century Park enforces a strict nonsmoking policy for its nonsmoking rooms.

Century Park makes sure that guests know about its policy regarding smoking in nonsmoking rooms. It posts a notice in each nonsmoking room, and it gives guests a handout from the manager detailing its policy and the consequences for smoking in nonsmoking rooms. The handout clearly says, "Should a guest opt to disregard our nonsmoking policy, we will process a fee of $150 to the guest's account." For those guests who prefer to smoke, a smoking accommodation can be provided.

On May 10 Wilson M. Weber was a guest in the hotel. He stayed in a room clearly marked "Nonsmoking." After he left, the room cleaners reported that the room smelled of smoke. According to hotel policy, a charge of $150 was processed to Mr. Weber's credit card. Mr. Weber has written to demand that the $150 charge be removed. He doesn't deny that he smoked in the room. He just thinks that he should not have to pay.

Your Task. As hotel manager, deny Mr. Weber's claim. You would certainly like to see Mr. Weber return as a Century Park guest, but you cannot budge on your smoking policy. Address your response to Mr. Wilson M. Weber, 634 Wetmore Avenue, Everett, WA 98201.

9.18 Bad News to Customers: The StairClimber or the LifeStep? (Objs. 1–3, 5)

You are delighted to receive a large order from Greg Waller at New Bodies Gym. This order includes two Lifecycle Trainers (at $1,295 each), four Pro Abdominal Boards (at $295 each), three Tunturi Muscle Trainers (at $749 each), and three Dual-Action StairClimbers (at $1,545 each).

You could ship immediately except for one problem. The Dual-Action StairClimber is intended for home use, not for gym or club use. Customers like it because they say it is more like scaling a mountain than climbing a flight of stairs. With each step, users exercise their arms to pull or push themselves up. Its special cylinders absorb shock so that no harmful running impact results. However, this model is not what you would recommend for gym use. You feel Mr. Waller should order your premier stair climber, the LifeStep (at $2,395 each) This unit has sturdier construction and is meant for heavy use. Its sophisticated electronics provide a selection of customer-pleasing programs that challenge muscles progressively with a choice of workouts. It also quickly multiplies workout gains with computer-controlled interval training. Electronic monitors inform users of step height, calories burned, elapsed time, upcoming levels, and adherence to fitness goals. For gym use the LifeStep is clearly better than the StairClimber. The bad news is that the LifeStep is considerably more expensive.

You get no response when you try to telephone Mr. Waller to discuss the problem. Should you ship what you can, or hold the entire order until you learn whether he wants the StairClimber or the LifeStep? Or perhaps you should substitute the LifeStep and send only two of them.

Your Task. Decide what to do and write a letter to Greg Waller, New Bodies Gym, 3402 Copeland Drive, Athens, OH 45701.

9.19 Bad News to Customers: University Admission Message Erroneously Welcomes All Who Applied (Objs. 1–3, 5)

E-mail

The University of California, San Diego, recently made a big mistake. It inadvertently invited all applicants to the LaJolla campus to an orientation—even those who had been rejected. The message said, "We're thrilled that you've been admitted to UC San Diego, and we're showcasing our beautiful campus on Admit Day." That message was intended to be sent to about 18,000 students who had been accepted. Instead, it went to all 47,000 students who applied. Admissions Director Mae Brown quickly realized the mistake. "The minute the e-mails were sent out, we noted that it was sent to a much larger pool than was admitted. We immediately recognized the error," she said.

What could the university do to correct this massive slip-up? One applicant, who had already received a rejection from UCSD, said she was confused. Her mother said, "It is adding insult to injury for kids who have already been through the wringer." When asked if anyone had been disciplined for the mistake, Brown said that the university was undertaking a complete review of the process.[31]

Your Task. For Admissions Director Mae Brown, write an appropriate bad-news message to the students who received the message in error. Many applicants will be wondering what their real admission status is.

9.20 Bad News to Customers: Rate Increase of Your Choice (Objs. 1–3, 5)

Select a product or service that you now use. It could be your newspaper, Internet service provider, local water or electricity company, propane or natural gas supplier, cell or landline provider, car insurance company, or some other product or service you regularly use. Assume that the provider must raise its rates, and you are the employee who must notify customers. Should you use a letter, e-mail, company Web site, or blog? Decide whether you should use the direct or indirect strategy. Gather as much information as you can about the product or service. What, if anything, justifies the increase? What benefits can be cited?

Your Task. Prepare a rate increase announcement. Submit it along with a memo explaining your rationale for the strategy you chose.

9.21 Bad News to Customers: Your Credit Card Is Refused (Objs. 1–3, 5)

Travel writer Arlene Getz was mystified when the sales clerk at a Paris department store refused her credit card. "Sorry," the clerk said, "your credit card is not being accepted. I don't know why." Getz found out soon enough. Her bank had frozen her account because of an "unusual" spending pattern. The problem? "We've never had a charge from you in France before," a bank official told her. The bank didn't seem to remember that Getz had repeatedly used that card in cities ranging from Boston to Tokyo to Cape Town over the past six years, each time without incident.

Getz was a victim of neural-network technology, a tool that is intended to protect credit cardholders from thieves who steal cards and immediately run up huge purchases. This technology tracks spending patterns. If it detects anything unusual—such as a sudden splurge on easy-to-fence items like jewelry—it sets off an alarm. Robert Boxberger, senior vice president of fraud management at Fleet Credit Card Services, says that the system is "geared toward not declining any travel and entertainment expenses, like hotels, restaurants, or car rentals." But somehow it goofed and did not recognize that Arlene Getz was traveling, although she had used her card earlier to rent a car in Paris, a sure sign that she was traveling.

Getz was what the credit card industry calls a false positive—a legitimate cardholder inconvenienced by the hunt for fraudsters. What particularly riled her was finding out that 75 percent of the transactions caught in the neural network turn out to be legitimate. Yet the technology has been immensely successful for credit card companies. Since Visa started using the program, its fraud rate dropped from 15 cents to 6 cents per $100. To avoid inconveniencing cardholders, the company doesn't automatically suspend a card when it suspects fraud. Instead, it telephones the cardholder to verify purchases. Of course, cardholders who are traveling are impossible to reach.

Angry at the inconvenience and embarrassment she experienced, Getz sent a letter to Visa demanding an explanation in writing.

Your Task. As an assistant to the vice president in charge of fraud detection at Visa, you have been asked to draft a letter that can be used to respond to Arlene Getz as well as to other unhappy customers whose cards were wrongly refused by your software. You know that the program has been an overwhelming success. It can, however, inconvenience people, especially when they are traveling. You have heard your boss tell travelers that it is a good idea to touch base with the bank before leaving and take along the card's customer service number (1-800-553-0321). Write a letter that explains what happened, retains the goodwill of the customer, and suggests reader benefits. Address your letter to Ms. Arlene Getz, 68 Riverside Drive, Apt. 35, New York, NY 10025.

9.22 Damage Control for Disappointed Customers: J. Crew Goofs on Cashmere Turtleneck (Objs. 1–3, 5)

E-mail

Who wouldn't want a cashmere zip turtleneck sweater for $18? At the J. Crew Web site, many delighted shoppers scrambled to order the bargain cashmere. Unfortunately, the price should have been $218! Before

J. Crew officials could correct the mistake, several hundred e-shoppers had bagged the bargain sweater for their digital shopping carts.

When the mistake was discovered, J. Crew immediately sent an e-mail to the soon-to-be disappointed shoppers. The subject line shouted "Big Mistake!" Emily Woods, chairwoman of J. Crew, began her message with this statement: "I wish we could sell such an amazing sweater for only $18. Our price mistake on your new cashmere zip turtleneck probably went right by you, but rather than charge you such a large difference, I'm writing to alert you that this item has been removed from your recent order."

As an assistant in the communication department at J. Crew, you saw the e-mail that was sent to customers and you tactfully suggested that the bad news might have been broken differently. Your boss says, "OK, hot stuff. Give it your best shot."

Your Task. Although you have only a portion of the message, analyze the customer bad-news message sent by J. Crew. Using the principles suggested in this chapter, write an improved e-mail. In the end, J. Crew decided to allow customers who ordered the sweater at $18 to reorder it for $118.80 to $130.80, depending on the size. Customers were given a special Web site to go to, to reorder (make up an address). Remember that J. Crew customers are youthful and hip. Keep your message upbeat.[32]

9.23 Damage Control for Disappointed Customers: No Payroll Checks (Objs. 1–3, 5)

Team

Trenton Hughes, a printing company sales manager, must tell one of his clients that the payroll checks his company ordered are not going to be ready by the date Hughes had promised. The printing company's job scheduler overlooked the job and didn't get the checks into production in time to meet the deadline. As a result, Hughes' client, a major insurance company, is going to miss its pay run.

Hughes meets with internal department heads. They decide on the following plan to remedy the situation: (a) move the check order to the front of the production line; (b) make up for the late production date by shipping some of the checks—enough to meet their client's immediate payroll needs—by air freight; (c) deliver the remaining checks by truck.[33]

Your Task. Form groups of three to four students. Discuss the following issues about how to present the bad news to Jessica Dyhala, Hughes' contact person at the insurance company.

a. Should Hughes call Dyhala directly or delegate the task to his assistant?
b. When should Dyhala be informed of the problem?
c. What is the best procedure for delivering the bad news?
d. What follow-up would you recommend to Hughes?

Be prepared to share your group's responses during a class discussion. Your instructor may ask two students to role-play the presentation of the bad news.

9.24 Damage Control for Disappointed Customers: Worms in Her PowerBars! (Objs. 1–3, 5)

Web

In a recent trip to her local grocery store, Kelly Keeler decided for the first time to stock up on PowerBars. These are low-fat, high-carbohydrate energy bars that are touted as a highly nutritious snack food specially formulated to deliver long-lasting energy. Since 1986, PowerBar (**http://www.powerbar.com**) has been dedicated to helping athletes and active people achieve peak performance. It claims to be "the fuel of choice" for top athletes around the world. Kelly is a serious runner and participates in many track meets every year.

On her way to a recent meet, Kelly grabbed a PowerBar and unwrapped it while driving. As she started to take her first bite, she noticed something white and shiny in the corner of the wrapping. An unexpected protein source wriggled out of her energy bar—a worm! Kelly's first inclination was to toss it out the window and never buy another PowerBar. On second thought, though, she decided to tell the company. When she called the toll-free number on the wrapper, Sophie, who answered the phone, was incredibly nice, extremely apologetic, and very informative about what happened. "I'm very sorry you experienced an infested product," said Sophie.

She explained that the infamous Indian meal moth is a pantry pest that causes millions of dollars in damage worldwide. It feeds on grains or grain-based products, such as cereal, flour, dry pasta, crackers, dried fruits, nuts, spices, and pet food. The tiny moth eggs lie dormant for some time or hatch quickly into tiny larvae (worms) that penetrate food wrappers and enter products.

At its manufacturing facilities, PowerBar takes stringent measures to protect against infestation. It inspects incoming grains, supplies proper ventilation, and shields all grain-storage areas with screens to prevent insects from entering. It also uses light traps and electrocuters; these devices eradicate moths with the least environmental impact.

PowerBar President Brian Maxwell makes sure every complaint is followed up immediately with a personal letter. His letters generally tell customers that it is rare for infestations like this to occur. Entomologists say that the worms are not toxic and will not harm humans. Nevertheless, as President Maxwell says, "it is extremely disgusting to find these worms in food."

Your Task. For the signature of Brian Maxwell, PowerBar president, write a bad-news follow-up letter to Kelly Keeler, 932 Opperman Drive, Eagan, MN 55123. Keep the letter informal and personal. Explain how pests get into grain-based products and what you are doing to prevent infestation. You can learn more about the Indian meal moth by searching the Web. In your letter include a brochure titled "Notes About the Indian Meal Moth," along with a kit for Kelly to mail the culprit PowerBar to the company for analysis in Boise, Idaho. Also send a check reimbursing Kelly $26.85 for her purchase.[34]

9.25 Damage Control for Disappointed Customers: Costly SUV Upgrade to a Ford Excursion (Obj. 4)

Steven Chan, a consultant from Oakland, California, was surprised when he picked up his rental car from Budget in Seattle over Easter weekend. He had reserved a full-size car, but the rental agent told him he could upgrade to a Ford Excursion for an additional $25 a day. "She told me it was easy to drive," Mr. Chan reported. "But when I saw it, I realized it was huge—like a tank. You could fit a full-size bed inside."

On his trip Mr. Chan managed to scratch the paint and damage the rear-door step. He didn't worry, though, because he thought the damage would be covered since he had charged the rental on his American Express card. He knew that the company offered backup car rental insurance coverage. To his dismay, he discovered that its car rental coverage excluded large SUVs. "I just assumed they'd cover it," he confessed. He wrote to Budget to complain about not being warned that certain credit cards may not cover damage to large SUVs or luxury cars.

Budget agents always encourage renters to sign up for Budget's own "risk product." But they don't feel that it is their responsibility to study the policies of customers' insurance carriers and explain what may or may not be covered. Moreover, they try to move customers into their rental cars as quickly as possible and avoid lengthy discussions of insurance coverage. Customers who do not purchase insurance are at risk. Mr. Chan does not make any claim against Budget, but he is upset about being "pitched" to upgrade to the larger SUV, which he didn't really want.[35]

Your Task. As a member of the communication staff at Budget, respond to Mr. Chan's complaint. Budget obviously is not going to pay for the SUV repairs, but it does want to salvage his goodwill and future business. Offer him a coupon worth two days' free rental of any full-size sedan. Write to Steven Chan, 5300 Park Ridge, Apt. 4A, Oakland, CA 93578.

9.26 Credit Refusal: Paying Cash at Atlanta Athletic Club (Objs. 1–4)

As manager of the Atlanta Athletic Club, you must refuse the application of Cherie Liotta for an Extended Membership. This is strictly a business decision. You liked Cherie very much when she applied, and she seems genuinely interested in fitness and a healthful lifestyle. However, your Extended Membership plan qualifies the member for all your testing, exercise, recreation, yoga, and aerobics programs. This multiservice program is expensive for the club to maintain because of the large staff required. Applicants must have a solid credit rating to join. To your disappointment, you learned that Cherie's credit rating is decidedly negative. Her credit report indicates that she is delinquent in payments to four businesses, including Total Body Fitness Center, your principal competitor.

You do have other programs, including your Drop In and Work Out plan, which offers use of available facilities on a cash basis. This plan enables a member to reserve space on the racquetball and handball courts. The member can also sign up for yoga and exercise classes, space permitting. Since Cherie is far in debt, you would feel guilty allowing her to plunge in any more deeply.

Your Task. Refuse Cherie Liotta's credit application, but encourage her cash business. Suggest that she make an inquiry to the credit reporting company Experian to learn about her credit report. She is eligible to receive a free credit report if she mentions this application. Write to Cherie Liotta, 2015 Springdale Hills, Apt. 15, Sandy Springs, GA 30328.

9.27 Credit Refusal: Camcorders for Rudy's Camera Shop (Objs. 1–3, 5)

As a Uniworld Electronics sales manager, you are delighted to land a sizable order for your new Canon Vixia camcorder. This hot new camcorder features sleek lightweight design, brilliant optical quality, vibrant images, and outstanding image capture in low light conditions.

The purchase order comes from Rudy's Camera Shop, a retail distributor in Beaumont, Texas. You send the order on to Pamela Kahn, your credit manager, for approval of the credit application attached. To your disappointment, Pam tells you that Rudy's Camera doesn't qualify for credit. Experian Credit Services reports that extending credit to Rudy's would be risky for Uniworld.

Because you think you can be more effective in writing than on the telephone, you decide to write to Rudy's Camera with the bad news and offer an alternative. Suggest that Rudy's order a smaller number of the Canon camcorders. If it pays cash, it can receive a 2 percent discount. After Rudy's has sold these fast-moving camcorders, it can place another cash order through your toll-free order number. With your fast delivery system, its inventory will never be depleted. Rudy's can get the camcorders it wants now and can replace its inventory almost overnight. Credit Manager Kahn tells you that your company generally reveals to credit applicants the name of the credit reporting service it used and encourages them to investigate their credit record.

Your Task. Write a credit refusal to Ron Kasbekar, Rudy's Camera Shop, 3016 East Lucas Drive, Beaumont, TX 77657. Add any information needed.

9.28 Bad News to Employees: Company Games Are Not Date Nights (Objs. 1–3, 6)

E-mail

As director of Human Resources at Weyerman Paper Company, you received an unusual request. Several employees asked that their spouses or friends be allowed to participate in Weyerman intramural sports teams. Although the teams play only once a week during the season, these employees claim that they can't afford more time away from friends and family. Over 100 employees currently participate in the eight coed volleyball, softball, and tennis teams, which are open to company employees only. The teams were designed to improve employee friendships and to give employees a regular occasion to have fun together.

If nonemployees were to participate, you fear that employee interaction would be limited. Although some team members might have fun if spouses or friends were included, you are not so sure all employees would enjoy it. You are not interested in turning intramural sports into "date night." Furthermore, the company would have to create additional teams if many nonemployees joined, and you don't want the administrative or equipment costs of more teams. Adding teams also would require changes to team rosters and game schedules. This could create a problem for some employees. You do understand the need for social time with friends and families, but guests are welcome as spectators at all intramural games. Also, the company already sponsors a family holiday party and an annual company picnic.

Your Task. Write an e-mail or hard-copy memo to the staff denying the request of several employees to include nonemployees on Weyerman's intramural sports teams.

9.29 Bad News to Employees: We Can't Pay Your Tuition (Objs. 1–3, 6)

Team

Yasmin Qajar, a hardworking bank teller, has sent a request asking that the company create a program to reimburse the tuition and book expenses for employees taking college courses. Although some companies have such a program, Middleton Bank has not felt that it could indulge in such an expensive employee perk. Moreover, the CEO is not convinced that companies see any direct benefit from such programs. Employees improve their educational credentials and skills, but what is to keep them from moving that education and those skill sets to other employers? Middleton Bank has over 200 employees. If even a fraction of them started classes, the company could see a huge bill for the cost of tuition and books. Because the bank is facing stiff competition and its profits are sinking, the expense of such a program is out of the question. In addition, it would involve administration—applications, monitoring, and record keeping. It is just too much of a hassle. When employees were hard to hire and retain, companies had to offer employment perks. But with a soft economy, such inducements are unnecessary.

Your Task. As director of Human Resources, send an individual response to Yasmin Qajar. The answer is a definite no, but you want to soften the blow and retain the loyalty of this conscientious employee.

9.30 Negative News in Other Cultures (Obj. 7)

Your Task. Interview fellow students or work colleagues who are from other cultures. How is negative news handled in their cultures? How would typical individuals refuse a request for a favor, for example? How would a business refuse credit to customers? How would an individual be turned down for a job? Is directness practiced? Report your findings to the class.

Video Resource

Video Library 2, Bad News: BuyCostumes

This video features BuyCostumes, the world's largest online costume and accessories retailer. After watching the video, play the part of a customer service representative.

BuyCostumes is proud of its extensive stock of costumes, its liberal return policy, and its many satisfied customers. But one day a letter arrived with a request that went beyond the company's ability to deliver. The customer said that he had ordered the Gorilla Blinky Eye With Chest costume. This popular gorilla costume comes with a unique gorilla mask, attractive suit with rubber chest, foot covers, and hands. The customer complained that the gorilla costume did not arrive until two days after his Halloween party. He planned an elaborate party with a gorilla theme, and he was extremely unhappy that he did not have his costume. He asks BuyCostumes to reimburse $300 that he spent on theme-related decorations, which he says were useless when he failed to receive his costume.

As a customer service representative, you checked his order and found that it was not received until five days before Halloween, the busiest time of the year for your company. The order was filled the next day, but standard shipping requires three to six business days for delivery. The customer did not order express or premium delivery; his shipping option was marked "Standard."

You showed the letter to the owner, Mr. Getz, who said that this request was ludicrous. However, he wanted to retain the customer's goodwill. Obviously, BuyCostumes was not going to shell out $300 for late delivery of a costume. But Mr. Getz suggested that the company would allow the customer to return the costume (in its original packaging). In addition, BuyCostumes would send a coupon for $20 off on the next costume purchase.

Your Task. Mr. Getz asks you to write a letter that retains the goodwill of this customer. Address your bad-news letter to Mr. Christopher King, 3579 Elm Street, Buffalo, NY 14202. Check the company Web site (**http://www.buycostumes.com**) for more information.

Chat About It

In each chapter you will find five discussion questions related to the chapter material. Your instructor may assign these topics for you to discuss in class, in an online chat room, or on an online discussion board. Some of the discussion topics may require outside research. You may also be asked to read and respond to postings made by your classmates.

Topic 1: Describe a time when a company delivered negative news to you effectively; that is, you understood and accepted the news. Explain why the company's strategy was effective.

Topic 2: Many people say they prefer the direct approach when receiving bad news. What situational factors might cause you to use the indirect approach with these people?

Topic 3: Create an effective buffer that you might use if you were a professor who had to tell a student expecting to earn an A that the student actually earned a C instead.

Topic 4: A flyer at a city bus stop announced a fare increase with the title *Rate Changes*. Was this title effective? If not, what title might have worked better?

Topic 5: You are an executive at a company that suddenly has to lay off 400 employees within three days or risk financial disaster. You have to make the cuts quickly, but you don't want to be impersonal by announcing the cuts by e-mail. How would you announce the bad news?

Grammar and Mechanics C.L.U.E. Review 9

Confusing Words and Frequently Misspelled Words

Review the lists of confusing words and frequently misspelled words in Appendix A, Grammar and Mechanics Guide, beginning on page A-1. On a separate sheet, revise the following sentences to correct word usage errors. Sentences may have more than one error. If a sentence is correct, write *C*. When you finish, check your answers on page Key-1.

Example: Have you allready sent the reccomendation?
Revision: Have you **already** sent the **recommendation?**

1. Included in her bad-news message was a complement and valuable advise.
2. His principle reason for declining the invitation was his busy calander.
3. In her damage-control message, the manager made a conscience effort to regain the customer's confidence.
4. In your every day business affairs, you must show patients even when irritated.
5. Before you procede with the report, please check those embarassing statistics.
6. Although we will look into this matter farther, I am not suprised at your report.
7. The judge declared that the comments of there attorneys were irrevelant to the case at hand.
8. Because the property was to difficult to apprise, its value was unrecorded.
9. Meredith hoped to illicit advice from her counselor, but she was disapointed.
10. The manager reccommended that we switch to an annual maintinance schedule.

Are you ready? Get more practice at **www.meguffey.com**

CHAPTER 10

Persuasive and Sales Messages

OBJECTIVES

After studying this chapter, you should be able to

1. Define the concept of persuasion, identify effective and ineffective persuasive techniques, and apply the 3-x-3 writing process to persuasive messages.
2. Explain the four major elements in successful persuasive messages and how to blend those elements into effective and ethical business messages.
3. Write persuasive messages that request favors and actions, make claims, and deliver complaints.
4. Write persuasive messages within organizations.
5. Write effective and ethical direct-mail and e-mail sales messages.
6. Compare effective persuasion techniques in high- and low-context cultures.
7. Understand basic patterns and techniques in developing persuasive press releases.

Want to do well on tests and excel in your course?
Go to **www.meguffey.com** for helpful interactive resources.

- **Review the Chapter 10 PowerPoint slides to prepare for the first quiz.**

Zooming In PART 1

Hands on Miami

"We make a living by what we get, but we make a life by what we give," said Winston Churchill. To the people at Hands on Miami, this is a creed to live by.

"For me, it is about trying to make a difference in my community," said Pat Morris, former CEO of Hands on Miami, a volunteer organization dedicated to making Miami a better place to live. "Giving to others," said Morris, "often comes back to you many, many times."[1]

Morris helped found Hands on Miami (HOM) to create a user-friendly approach to community service. HOM's new method involves making it easy for volunteers to participate regardless of their hectic schedules. Projects take place outside traditional work hours, and flexible time commitments permit volunteers to serve once a week, once a month, or whenever they can.

Hands on Miami partners with schools, social service organizations, and environmental organizations to offer more than 80 service opportunities each month. This gives thousands of Miamians the chance to make a difference in their community. Volunteers can spend a morning delivering care packages to AIDS patients in a local hospital, an afternoon planting native vegetation to restore natural beauty and ecosystems, or an evening reading bedtime stories to children at an emergency shelter. What's distinctive about HOM's program is that it makes community service accessible to anyone regardless of schedule. Because volunteerism is essential to enriching a community's well-being, most HOM projects are team based and take place in the evenings and on weekends, making it easy for busy people to give back to the community. HOM's hallmark flexible volunteering program has been a resounding success.

In addition to organizing volunteers, HOM acts as a consultant on a fee-for-service basis to design volunteer opportunities to meet a company's particular needs. Carnival Cruise Lines and other local companies often use the expertise of HOM in planning their own volunteer programs. Corporate donors provide further assistance by sponsoring big events such as Hands on Miami Day.

As CEO, Pat Morris used persuasion to keep his staff energized, motivated, and organized. He had to be persuasive in reaching out to corporate donors to persuade them to send volunteers to participate in Hands on Miami programs. He also had to sway corporations to sponsor events with cash contributions. Persuasion is a large part of the leadership role at Hands on Miami, as well as in every organization.[2] You will learn more about Hands on Miami on page 303.

© Jeff Greenberg/PhotoEdit

Critical Thinking

- Persuasion is vital to the CEO at Hands on Miami. Who must the CEO effectively persuade to ensure the success of the organization?
- In your own career, when might you find it necessary to be persuasive?
- From your experience, what techniques are effective or ineffective in persuading others to accept your views?

http://www.handsonmiami.org

Understanding Persuasion and How to Use It Effectively and Ethically

LEARNING OBJECTIVE 1

Define the concept of persuasion, identify effective and ineffective persuasive techniques, and apply the 3-x-3 writing process to persuasive messages.

Convincing others that your point of view is the right one is a critical business communication skill. At Hands on Miami, CEO Pat Morris had to be persuasive in all aspects of his job—in convincing his staff about the importance of their tasks, in winning over corporate sponsors, and in swaying volunteers to support community projects. For all businesspeople, persuasion is a critical skill. However, many of us do it poorly or unconsciously.[3] You have already studied techniques for writing routine request messages that required subtle forms of persuasion. This chapter focuses on messages that require deliberate and skilled persuasion. You will learn what persuasion is and how to apply it effectively when you write requests for favors and actions, make claims, and prepare sales messages. This is one of the most important chapters in the book because much of your success in business depends on how skilled you are at persuading people to believe, accept, and act on what you are saying.

What Is Persuasion?

Persuasion is defined as the ability to use argument or discussion to influence an individual's beliefs or actions. Parents use persuasion to cajole their kids into doing their homework. A team member uses persuasion to convince her technology-averse manager that instant messaging is an excellent tool to keep all team members informed about a project. You might want to persuade your boss to allow you to work at home part of the time. In Figure 10.1 Charmaine Williams, general manager of Oak Park Town Center, uses persuasion in a memo to the mall owner and president. She wants to convince him to restrict the access of unchaperoned teenagers on weekends and evenings.

Some people think that persuasion involves coercion or trickery. They think that you can achieve what you seek only if you twist an arm or deceive someone. Such negative tactics are ineffective and unethical. What's more, these tactics don't truly represent persuasion. To persuade is to present information enabling others to see the benefits of what you are offering, without browbeating or tricking them into agreement.

Successful persuasion depends largely on the reasonableness of your request, your credibility, and your ability to make the request attractive to the receiver. Many techniques can help you be effective in getting your ideas accepted by your fellow workers, superiors, and clients.

Effective Persuasion Techniques

What techniques can make your persuasive arguments more effective?

When you want your ideas to prevail, spend some time thinking about how to present them. Listeners and readers will be more inclined to accept what you are offering if you focus on the following important strategies, which are outlined here and further discussed with illustrations throughout the chapter.

- **Establish credibility.** To be persuasive, you must engender trust. People must believe that you are telling the truth, are experienced, and know what you are talking about. Most of us would not be swayed if a soccer or film star told us how to ease world tensions. If you lack credentials or experience, use testimonials, expert opinion, and research to support your position.

- **Make a reasonable, precise request.** Persuasion is most effective if your request is realistic, doable, and attainable. Don't ask for $100,000 worth of equipment when your department's budget is $5,000. Also, be clear about your objective. In one research study, students posed as beggars and asked for money. If they asked for an unspecified amount, they received money 44 percent of the time. If they asked for a precise sum (say, $1), they received money 64 percent of the time.[4] Precise requests are more effective than vague ones.

In one of the most unusual marketing campaigns of recent memory, Domino's Pizza sided with critics who said that its pies were little more than cardboard and ketchup. A pizza franchising wonder during the 1980s, Domino's has lost market share to rival chains and become the target of bad-food jokes, especially for ranking alongside Chuck E. Cheese in taste surveys. Instead of hiding the pizza's reputation for blandness, marketers endorsed the company's harshest consumer feedback and commissioned expert chefs to perform a complete makeover the product. *What makes the Domino's "pizza turnaround" campaign persuasive?*

- **Tie facts to benefits.** Line up solid information to support your view. Use statistics, printed resources, examples, and analogies to help people understand. Remember, however, that information alone rarely changes attitudes. Marketers have pumped huge sums into failed advertising and public relations campaigns that provided facts alone. More important is converting those facts into benefits for the audience, as Charmaine did in Figure 10.1.
- **Recognize the power of loss.** Describing the benefits of your proposal is a powerful motivator. Another powerful motivator is the thought of what the other person will lose if he or she doesn't agree. The threat of losing something one already possesses—such as time, money, competitive advantage, profits, reputation—seems to be more likely to motivate people than the idea of gaining that very same thing.[5]
- **Expect and overcome resistance.** When proposing ideas, be prepared for resistance. This may arise in the form of conflicting beliefs, negative attitudes, apathy, skepticism, and opposing loyalties. Recognize any weakness in your proposal and be prepared to counter with well-reasoned arguments and facts. In Figure 10.1 Charmaine realized that

FIGURE 10.1 Persuasive Action Request

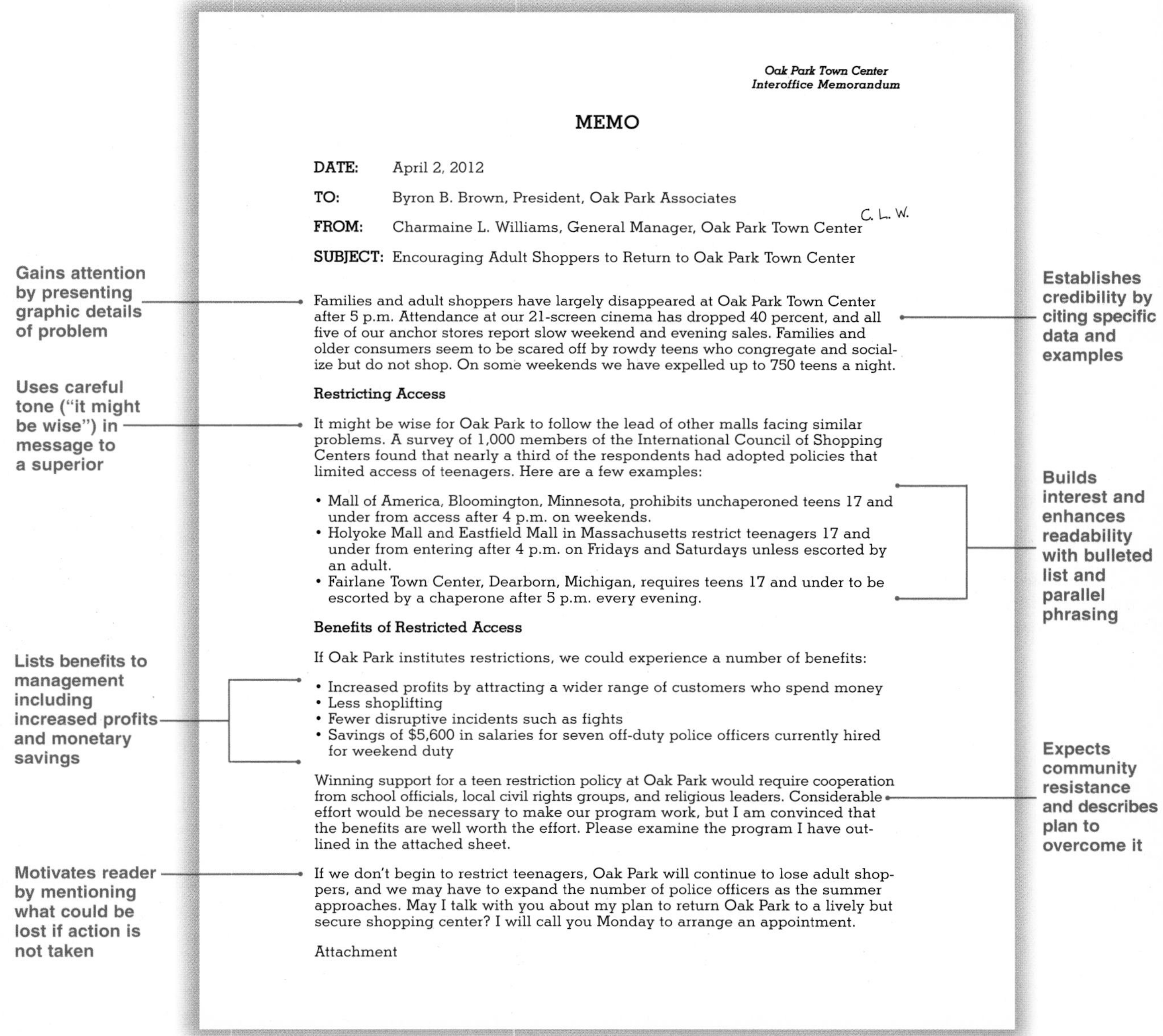

Oak Park Town Center
Interoffice Memorandum

MEMO

DATE: April 2, 2012

TO: Byron B. Brown, President, Oak Park Associates

FROM: Charmaine L. Williams, General Manager, Oak Park Town Center C. L. W.

SUBJECT: Encouraging Adult Shoppers to Return to Oak Park Town Center

Families and adult shoppers have largely disappeared at Oak Park Town Center after 5 p.m. Attendance at our 21-screen cinema has dropped 40 percent, and all five of our anchor stores report slow weekend and evening sales. Families and older consumers seem to be scared off by rowdy teens who congregate and socialize but do not shop. On some weekends we have expelled up to 750 teens a night.

Restricting Access

It might be wise for Oak Park to follow the lead of other malls facing similar problems. A survey of 1,000 members of the International Council of Shopping Centers found that nearly a third of the respondents had adopted policies that limited access of teenagers. Here are a few examples:

- Mall of America, Bloomington, Minnesota, prohibits unchaperoned teens 17 and under from access after 4 p.m. on weekends.
- Holyoke Mall and Eastfield Mall in Massachusetts restrict teenagers 17 and under from entering after 4 p.m. on Fridays and Saturdays unless escorted by an adult.
- Fairlane Town Center, Dearborn, Michigan, requires teens 17 and under to be escorted by a chaperone after 5 p.m. every evening.

Benefits of Restricted Access

If Oak Park institutes restrictions, we could experience a number of benefits:

- Increased profits by attracting a wider range of customers who spend money
- Less shoplifting
- Fewer disruptive incidents such as fights
- Savings of $5,600 in salaries for seven off-duty police officers currently hired for weekend duty

Winning support for a teen restriction policy at Oak Park would require cooperation from school officials, local civil rights groups, and religious leaders. Considerable effort would be necessary to make our program work, but I am convinced that the benefits are well worth the effort. Please examine the program I have outlined in the attached sheet.

If we don't begin to restrict teenagers, Oak Park will continue to lose adult shoppers, and we may have to expand the number of police officers as the summer approaches. May I talk with you about my plan to return Oak Park to a lively but secure shopping center? I will call you Monday to arrange an appointment.

Attachment

Gains attention by presenting graphic details of problem
Uses careful tone ("it might be wise") in message to a superior
Lists benefits to management including increased profits and monetary savings
Motivates reader by mentioning what could be lost if action is not taken
Establishes credibility by citing specific data and examples
Builds interest and enhances readability with bulleted list and parallel phrasing
Expects community resistance and describes plan to overcome it

her proposal to restrict the access of unchaperoned teenagers would require acceptance and cooperation from community groups.

- **Share solutions and compromise.** The process of persuasion may involve being flexible and working out a solution that is acceptable to all concerned. Sharing a solution requires listening to people and developing a new position that incorporates their input. When others' views become part of a solution, they gain a sense of ownership; they buy in and are more eager to implement the solution.

The Importance of Tone

How can the tone of a persuasive argument be improved?

Tone is particularly important in persuasion today because the workplace has changed. Gone are the days when managers could simply demand compliance. Today's managers and team leaders strive to generate cooperation and buy-in instead of using intimidation, threats, and punishment to gain compliance.[6] Team members no longer accept command-and-control, top-down, unquestioned authority.[7] How can persuaders improve the tone of their requests?

- **Avoid sounding preachy or parental.** People don't want to be lectured or instructed in a demeaning manner. No one likes to be treated like a child.
- **Don't pull rank.** Effective persuasion doesn't result from status or authority. People want to be recognized as individuals of worth. Pulling rank may secure compliance but not buy-in.
- **Avoid making threats.** People may comply when threatened, but their compliance may disappear over time. For example, many drivers follow the speed limit only when a patrol car is near. Threats also may result in retaliation, reduced productivity, and low morale.
- **Soften your words when persuading upward.** When you must persuade someone who has more clout than you, use words such as *suggest* and *recommend*. Craft sentences that begin with *It might be a good idea to.* . . . Make suggestions without threatening authority.
- **Be enthusiastic, positive, and likable.** Convey your passion for an idea through your body language, voice, and words. When you enthusiastically request something to be done, people feel more confident that they can do it. Use sincere compliments and praise. Describe what a positive impact others have had. Offer to reciprocate, if you are asking a favor.

Applying the 3-x-3 Writing Process to Persuasive Messages

Persuasion means changing people's views, and that's often a difficult task. Pulling it off demands planning and perception. The 3-x-3 writing process provides you with a helpful structure for laying a foundation for persuasion. Of particular importance here are (a) analyzing the purpose, (b) adapting to the audience, (c) collecting information, and (d) organizing the message.

Why is it important to analyze your purpose before preparing a persuasive message?

Analyzing the Purpose: Knowing What You Want to Achieve. The purpose of a persuasive message is to convert the receiver to your ideas or to motivate action. A message without a clear purpose is doomed. Not only must you know what your purpose is and what response you want, but you must know these things when you start writing your message or planning a presentation. Too often, inexperienced writers reach the end of the first draft of a message before discovering exactly what they want the receiver to do. Then they must start over, giving the request a different spin or emphasis. Because your purpose establishes the strategy of the message, determine it first.

Let's say you must convince Rachel, your department manager, that you could be more productive if you could work from home. Before approaching Rachel, know exactly what you want. How much time do you want to work at home? Full time? Part time? On special projects? Do you want Rachel to merely talk about it with you? Do you want her to set a time when you could start? Should you suggest a trial period? By identifying your purpose up front, you can shape the message to point toward it. This planning effort saves considerable rewriting time and produces the most successful persuasive messages.

Adapting to the Audience by Finding Ways to Make Your Message Heard. While you are considering the purpose of a persuasive message, you also need to concentrate on the receiver. How can you adapt your request to that individual so that your message is heard? Zorba the Greek wisely observed, "You can knock forever on a deaf man's door." A persuasive message is equally futile unless it meets the needs of its audience. In a broad sense, you will be seeking to show how your request helps the receiver achieve some of life's major goals or fulfills key needs: money, power, comfort, confidence, importance, friends, peace of mind, and recognition, to name a few.

On a more practical level, you want to show how your request solves a problem, achieves a personal or work objective, or just makes life easier for your audience. In your request for a flexible work schedule, you could appeal to Rachel's expressed concern for increasing productivity. Your goal is to make the boss look good by granting your request. To adapt your request to the receiver, consider these questions that receivers will very likely be asking themselves:

Why should I?
What's in it for me?
What's in it for you?
Who cares?

Spotlight on Communicators

Kraft Foods CEO Irene Rosenfeld can be very persuasive. Early in her career with Kraft, she convinced her bosses that Kool-Aid should be marketed at kids (not mothers) and that Jell-O could be modernized with new flavors. In Canada she was persuasive in turning around Kraft's troubled business. "When she is trying to persuade you of something, she will be relentless in coming back with facts and showing you she has the support of other people," said a former Kraft executive. With a PhD in marketing and statistics, Rosenfeld conducts meticulous research. In building interest and reducing resistance, "she will be totally emotionally and intellectually committed to her idea."

© MIKE CASSESE/Reuters/Landov

Adapting to your audience means being ready to answer these questions. It means learning about audience members and analyzing why they might resist your proposal. It means searching for ways to connect your purpose with their needs. If completed before you begin writing, such analysis goes a long way toward overcoming resistance and achieving your goal.

Researching and Organizing Persuasive Data. Once you have analyzed the audience and considered how to adapt your message to its needs, you are ready to collect data and organize it. You might brainstorm and prepare cluster diagrams to provide a rough outline of ideas. For your request for a flexible work schedule, you might gather information describing how other comparable companies have developed telecommuting programs and how effective they are. You could work out a possible schedule outlining when you would be working at home and when you would be in the office for meetings and face-to-face discussions. You are certain you could complete more work at home, but how can you prove it in your request? To overcome resistance, you might describe your work-at-home office, equipment, and procedures. You could also explain your plan for staying in touch with and being responsive to inquiries and requests.

The next step in a persuasive message is organizing your data into a logical sequence. If you are asking for something that you know will be approved, little persuasion is required. Thus, you would make a direct request, as you studied in Chapter 8. But when you expect resistance or when you need to educate the receiver, the indirect strategy often works better. The following four-part indirect strategy works well for many persuasive requests:

1. Gain attention
2. Build interest
3. Reduce resistance
4. Motivate action

Blending Four Major Elements in Successful Persuasive Messages

LEARNING OBJECTIVE 2
Explain the four major elements in successful persuasive messages and how to blend those elements into effective and ethical business messages.

Although the indirect strategy appears to contain separate steps, successful persuasive messages actually blend the four steps into a seamless whole. Also, the sequence of the elements may change depending on the situation and the emphasis. Regardless of where they are placed, the key elements in persuasive requests are (a) gaining your audience's attention, (b) building interest by convincing your audience that your proposal is worthy, (c) reducing resistance, and (d) motivating action.

How can you gain attention in a persuasive message?

Gaining Attention in Persuasive Messages

To grab attention, the opening statement in a persuasive request should be brief, relevant, and engaging. When only mild persuasion is necessary, the opener can be low-key and factual. If, however, your request is substantial and you anticipate strong resistance, provide a thoughtful, provocative opening. Following are some examples.

- **Problem description.** In a recommendation to hire temporary employees: *Last month legal division staff members were forced to work 120 overtime hours, costing us $6,000 and causing considerable employee unhappiness.* With this opener you have presented a capsule of the problem your proposal will help solve.
- **Unexpected statement.** In a memo to encourage employees to attend an optional sensitivity seminar: *Men and women draw the line at decidedly different places in identifying what behavior constitutes sexual harassment.* Note how this opener gets readers thinking immediately.
- **Reader benefit.** In a letter promoting Clear Card, a service that helps employees make credit card purchases without paying interest: *The average employee carries nearly $13,000 in revolving debt and pays $2,800 in interest and late fees. The Clear Card charges zero percent interest. You can't beat it!* Employers immediately see this offer as a benefit it can offer employees.
- **Compliment.** In a letter inviting a business executive to speak: *Because our members admire your success and value your managerial expertise, they want you to be our speaker.* In offering praise or compliments, however, be careful to avoid obvious flattery.
- **Related facts.** In a message to company executives who are considering restricting cell phone use by employee drivers: *A recent study revealed that employers pay an average of $16,500 each time an employee is in a traffic accident.* This relevant fact sets the scene for the interest-building section that follows.
- **Stimulating question.** In a plea for funds to support environmental causes: *What do golden tortoise beetles, bark spiders, flounders, and Arctic foxes have in common?* Readers will be curious to find the answer to this intriguing question. [They all change color depending on their surroundings.]

What techniques help you build interest in a persuasive message?

Building Interest in Persuasive Messages

After capturing attention, a persuasive request must retain that attention and convince the audience that the request is reasonable. To justify your request, be prepared to invest in a few paragraphs of explanation. Persuasive requests are likely to be longer than direct requests because the audience must be convinced rather than simply instructed. You can build interest and conviction through the use of the following:

- Facts, statistics
- Expert opinion
- Direct benefits
- Examples
- Specific details
- Indirect benefits

Showing how your request can benefit the audience directly or indirectly is a key factor in persuasion. If you were asking alumni to contribute money to a college foundation, for example, you might promote *direct benefits* such as listing the donor's name in the college magazine or sending a sweatshirt with the college logo. Another direct benefit is a tax write-off for the contribution. An *indirect benefit* might be feeling good about helping the college and knowing that students will benefit from the gift. Nearly all charities rely in large part on indirect benefits to promote their causes.

How can you reduce resistance in persuasive requests?

Reducing Resistance in Persuasive Requests

One of the biggest mistakes in persuasive requests is the failure to anticipate and offset audience resistance. How will the receiver object to your request? In brainstorming for clues, try *What if?* scenarios. Let's say you are trying to convince management that the employees' cafeteria should switch from paper and plastic plates and cups to ceramic. What if managers say the change is too expensive? What if they argue that they are careful recyclers of paper and plastic? What if they contend that ceramic dishes would increase cafeteria labor and energy costs tremendously? What if they protest that ceramic is less hygienic? For each of these *What if?* scenarios, you need a counterargument.

Unless you anticipate resistance, you give the receiver an easy opportunity to dismiss your request. Countering this resistance is important, but you must do it with finesse *(Although ceramic dishes cost more at first, they actually save money over time)*. You can minimize objections by presenting your counterarguments in sentences that emphasize benefits: *Ceramic dishes may require a little more effort in cleaning, but they bring warmth and graciousness to meals. Most important, they help save the environment by requiring fewer resources and eliminating waste.* However, don't spend too much time on counterarguments, thus making them overly important. Finally, avoid bringing up objections that may never have occurred to the receiver in the first place.

Another factor that reduces resistance is credibility. Receivers are less resistant if your request is reasonable and if you are believable. When the receiver does not know you, you may have to establish your expertise, refer to your credentials, or demonstrate your competence. Even when you are known, you may have to establish your knowledge in a given area. If you are asking your manager for a new laptop computer, you might have to establish your credibility by showing your manager articles about the latest laptops. You could point out that a laptop would enable you to work away from the office while staying in touch by e-mail. Some charities establish their credibility by displaying on their stationery the names of famous people who serve on their boards. The credibility of speakers making presentations is usually outlined by someone who introduces them.

Motivating Action in Persuasive Messages

How can you motivate action in the closing of a persuasive message?

After gaining attention, building interest, and reducing resistance, you will want to inspire the receiver to act. This is where your planning pays dividends. Knowing exactly what action you favor before you start to write enables you to point your arguments toward this important final paragraph. Here you will make your recommendation as specifically and confidently as possible—without seeming pushy. A proposal from one manager to another might conclude with, *So that we can begin using the employment assessment tests by May 1, please send a return e-mail immediately.* In making a request, don't sound apologetic *(I'm sorry to have to ask you this, but . . .)*, and don't supply excuses *(If you can spare the time, . . .)*. Compare the following closings for a persuasive memo recommending training seminars in communication skills.

Too General
We are certain we can develop a series of training sessions that will improve the communication skills of your employees.

Too Timid
If you agree that our training proposal has merit, perhaps we could begin the series in June.

Too Pushy
Because we are convinced that you will want to begin improving the skills of your employees immediately, we have scheduled your series to begin in June.

Effective
You will see decided improvement in the communication skills of your employees. Please call me at 439-2201 by May 1 to give your approval so that training sessions may start in June, as we discussed.

Note how the last opening suggests a specific and easy-to-follow action. It also provides a deadline and a reason for that date. Figure 10.2 summarizes a four-part plan for overcoming resistance and crafting successful persuasive messages.

Being Persuasive and Ethical

What techniques do unethical persuaders use?

Business communicators may be tempted to make their persuasion even more forceful by fudging on the facts, exaggerating a point, omitting something crucial, or providing deceptive emphasis. Consider the case of a manager who sought to persuade employees to accept a

FIGURE 10.2 Four-Part Plan for Persuasive Messages

Gaining Attention	Building Interest	Reducing Resistance	Motivating Action
Summary of problem	Facts, figures	Anticipate objections	Describe specific request
Unexpected statement	Expert opinion	Offer counterarguments	Sound confident
Reader benefit	Examples	Employ *What if?* scenarios	Make action easy to take
Compliment	Specific details	Establish credibility	Offer incentive
Related fact	Direct benefits	Demonstrate competence	Don't provide excuses
Stimulating question	Indirect benefits	Show value of proposal	Repeat main benefit

change in insurance benefits. His memo emphasized a small perk (easier handling of claims) but de-emphasized a major reduction in total coverage. Some readers missed the main point—as the manager intended. Others recognized the deception, however, and before long the manager's credibility was lost. A persuader is effective only when he or she is believable. If receivers suspect that they are being manipulated or misled or if they find any part of the argument untruthful, the total argument fails. Persuaders can also fall into traps of logic without even being aware of it. Take a look at the accompanying Ethical Insights box to learn about common logical fallacies that you will want to avoid.

Persuasion becomes unethical when facts are distorted, overlooked, or manipulated with an intent to deceive. Of course, persuaders naturally want to put forth their strongest case. But that argument must be based on truth, objectivity, and fairness.

In prompting ethical and truthful persuasion, two factors act as powerful motivators. The first is the desire to preserve your reputation and credibility. Once lost, a good name or reputation is difficult to regain. An equally important force prompting ethical behavior, though, is your opinion of yourself. Glen Senk, president of the retailer Anthropologie, tells a story of a supersaleswoman at his store. She vastly outsold her colleagues on virtually every shift she worked. Senk went to her store one day to watch and realized that the saleswoman would push anything on customers. It didn't matter whether items matched or the clothes looked good. She was fired. "Our customers are our friends," explained Senk. "It's never about the quick sale."[8] Senk was more concerned with preserving the store's reputation and his own self-image than making money.

ETHICAL INSIGHT

What's Fair in Persuasion? Avoiding Common Logical Fallacies

While being persuasive, we must be careful to remain ethical. In our eagerness to win others over to our views, we may inadvertently overstep the bounds of fair play. Philosophers through the years have pinpointed a number of logical fallacies. Here are three you will want to avoid in your persuasive messages.

- **Circular reasoning.** When the support given for a contention merely restates the contention, the reasoning is circular. For example, *Investing in the stock market is dangerous for short-term investors because it is unsafe.* The evidence (*because it is unsafe*) offers no proof. It merely circles back to the original contention. Revision: *Investing in the stock market is dangerous for short-term investors because stock prices fluctuate widely.*
- **Begging the question.** A statement such as *That dishonest CEO should be replaced* begs the question. Merely asserting that the CEO is dishonest is not enough. Be sure to supply solid evidence for such assertions. Revision: *That CEO is dishonest because he awards contracts only to his friends. A good manager would require open bidding.*
- **Post hoc (*after, thus, because*).** Although two events may have happened in immediate sequence, the first did not necessarily cause the second. For example, *The company switched to team-based management, and its stock price rose immediately afterward.* Switching to teams probably had no effect on the stock price. Revision: *At about the same time the company switched to team-based management, its stock price began to rise, although the two events are probably unrelated.*

Career Application

In teams or in a class discussion, cite examples of how these fallacies could be used in persuasive messages or sales letters. Provide a logical, ethical revision for each.

Zooming In PART 2

Hands on Miami

Being good corporate citizens ranks high with many businesses today, and Hands on Miami helps them do just that. Its Corporate Services Program assists businesses in developing community service projects. More and more business organizations today realize that their commitment to social responsibility provides many advantages. In a Points of Light Foundation poll, 90 percent of companies surveyed believed their employer-sponsored community service programs enhanced their public image, boosted employee morale and job satisfaction, helped recruit and retain quality employees, and built better work teams.

Volunteerism gives corporations an edge. Many corporations, however, do not have the staff resources or expertise to develop and manage corporate volunteer efforts. That's where Hands on Miami's Corporate Services program comes in. Its fee-based consulting services can survey employees about their volunteer interests, develop employee volunteer programs, and design and lead corporate volunteer days. It can also facilitate long-term employee volunteering, train and educate employee volunteers, and track employee volunteer hours.

Hands on Miami helped organize and now serves as advisor to Carnival Cruise Lines' employee volunteer program, the F.U.N. Team (Friends Uniting Neighbors). Their ongoing volunteer activities not only support the community but also improve company pride, teamwork, and leadership skills.

Hands on Miami knows that its Corporate Services program can help organizations develop successful employee volunteer initiatives that fit their business climate, employees' interests, and community goals. The problem is persuading more corporations to do it.

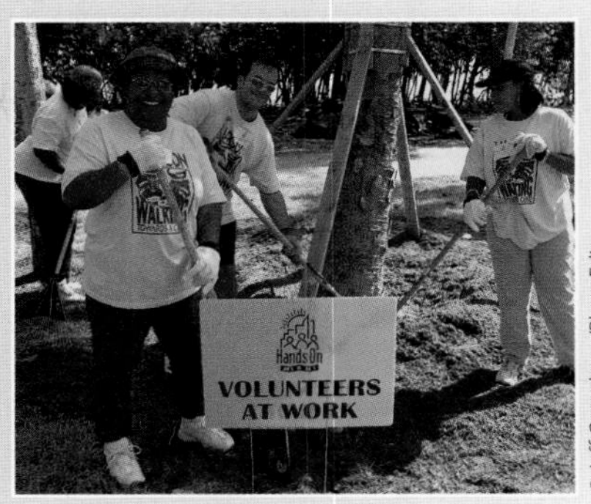

© Jeff Greenberg/PhotoEdit

Critical Thinking

- Do you agree that corporations derive benefits from sponsoring volunteer programs and encouraging employees to participate?
- The CEO of Hands on Miami must write a letter persuading Miami corporations to use its fee-based Corporate Services program. What direct benefits could be cited?
- What indirect benefits could the CEO cite in a persuasive letter?

Requesting Favors and Actions, Making Claims, and Delivering Complaints

LEARNING OBJECTIVE 3
Write persuasive messages that request favors and actions, make claims, and deliver complaints.

Many of your persuasive messages will be requests for favors or actions. For example, you may ask a businessperson to make a presentation to your club. You might ask a company to encourage its employees to participate in a charity drive. Another form of persuasion involves claims or complaints. All of these messages require skill in persuasion. Convincing someone to change a belief or to perform an action when that person is reluctant requires planning and skill—and sometimes a little luck. A written, rather than face-to-face, request may require more preparation but can be more effective. Persuasion is often more precise and controlled when you can think through your purpose and prepare a thoughtful message in writing. The indirect strategy gives you an effective structure.

Preparing Persuasive Requests for Favors and Actions

Why are individuals and companies willing to grant requests for time, money, information, cooperation, and special privileges?

Persuading someone to do something that largely benefits you may not be the easiest task. Fortunately, many individuals and companies are willing to grant requests for time, money, information, cooperation, and special privileges. They grant these favors for a variety of reasons. They may just happen to be interested in your project, or they may see goodwill potential for themselves. Professionals sometimes feel obligated to contribute their time or expertise to "pay their dues." Often, though, businesses and individuals comply because they see that others will benefit from the request.

Figure 10.3 shows a persuasive favor request from Michelle Moreno. Her research firm seeks to persuade other companies to complete a questionnaire revealing salary data. To most organizations, salary information is strictly confidential. What can she do to convince strangers to part with such private information?

FIGURE 10.3 Persuasive Favor Request

1 Prewriting

Analyze: The purpose of this letter is to persuade the reader to complete and return a questionnaire.

Anticipate: Although the reader is busy, he may respond to appeals to his professionalism and to his need for salary data in his own business.

Adapt: Because the reader may be uninterested at first and require persuasion, use the indirect strategy.

2 Writing

Research: Study the receiver's business and find ways to relate this request to company success.

Organize: Gain attention by opening with relevant questions. Build interest by showing how the reader's compliance will help his company and others. Reduce resistance by promising confidentiality and offering free data.

Compose: Prepare a first draft with the intention to revise.

3 Revising

Revise: Revise to show direct and indirect benefits more clearly. Make sure the message is as concise as possible.

Proofread: In the first sentence, spell out *percent* rather than using the symbol. Check the use of all question marks. Start all lines at the left for a block-style letter.

Evaluate: Will this letter convince the reader to complete and return the questionnaire?

ITHACA RESEARCH INSTITUTE
430 Seneca Street, Ithaca, NY 14850 www.ithacaresearch.com
PH 570.888.2300
FAX 570.888.4359

May 17, 2012

Mr. Trevor M. Mansker
All-Star Financial Advisors
240 Lomb Memorial Drive
Rochester, NY 14623

Dear Mr. Mansker:

Have you ever added a unique job title but had no idea what compensation the position demanded? Has your company ever lost a valued employee to another organization that offered 20 percent more in salary for the same position?

To remain competitive in hiring and to retain qualified workers, companies rely on survey data showing current salaries. Ithaca Research Institute has been collecting business data for a quarter century and has been honored by the American Management Association for its accurate data. We need your help in collecting salary data for today's workers. Information from the enclosed questionnaire will supply companies like yours with such data.

Your information, of course, will be treated confidentially. The questionnaire takes but a few moments to complete, and it can provide substantial dividends for professional organizations that need comparative salary data.

To show our gratitude for your participation, we will send you comprehensive salary surveys for your industry and your metropolitan area. Not only will you find basic salaries, but you will also learn about bonus and incentive plans, special pay differentials, expense reimbursements, and perquisites such as a company car and credit card.

Comparative salary data are impossible to provide without the support of professionals like you. Please complete the questionnaire and return it in the prepaid envelope before June 1, our spring deadline. Participating in this survey means that you will no longer be in the dark about how much your employees earn compared with others in your industry.

Sincerely yours,

ITHACA RESEARCH INSTITUTE

Michelle Moreno

Michelle Moreno
Director, Survey Research

Enclosures

Margin annotations (left):
- Poses two short questions related to the reader
- Presents reader benefit tied to request explanation; establishes credibility
- Anticipates and counters resistance to confidentiality and time/effort objections
- Offers free salary data as a direct benefit
- Provides deadline and a final benefit to prompt action

Margin annotations (right):
- Gains attention
- Builds interest
- Reduces resistance
- Appeals to professionalism, an indirect benefit
- Motivates action

To gain attention, she begins her persuasive favor request by posing two short questions that spotlight the need for salary information. To build interest and establish trust, she mentions that Ithaca Research Institute has been collecting business data for a quarter century and has received awards from the American Management Association. Developing credibility is especially important when persuading strangers to do something. Making a reasonable request tied to benefits is also important. Michelle does this by emphasizing the need for current salary information.

To reduce resistance, Michelle promises confidentiality and explains that the questionnaire takes but a few moments to complete. She offers free salary data as a direct benefit. This data may help the receiver learn how its salary scale compares with others in its industry. But Michelle doesn't count on this offer as the only motivator. As an indirect benefit, she appeals to the professionalism of the receiver. She's hoping that the receiver will recognize the value of providing salary data to the entire profession. To motivate action, Michelle closes with a deadline and reminds the reader that her company need not be in the dark about comparative salaries within its industry.

This favor request incorporates many of the techniques that are effective in persuasion: establishing credibility, making a reasonable and precise request, tying facts to benefits, and overcoming resistance.

Writing Persuasive Claims

Persuasive claims typically involve damaged products, mistaken billing, inaccurate shipments, warranty problems, limited return policies, insurance snafus, faulty merchandise, and so on. Generally, the direct strategy is best for requesting straightforward adjustments (see Chapter 8). When you feel your request is justified and will be granted, the direct strategy is most efficient. But if a past request has been refused or ignored or if you anticipate reluctance, then the indirect strategy is appropriate.

When making a claim or delivering a complaint, when is the direct strategy appropriate? When is the indirect strategy appropriate?

Developing a Logical Persuasive Argument. Strive for logical development in a claim letter. You might open with sincere praise, an objective statement of the problem, a point of agreement, or a quick review of what you have done to resolve the problem. Then you can explain precisely what happened or why your claim is legitimate. Don't provide a blow-by-blow chronology of details; just hit the highlights. Be sure to enclose copies of relevant invoices, shipping orders, warranties, and payments. Close with a clear statement of what you want done: a refund, replacement, credit to your account, or other action. Be sure to think through the possibilities and make your request reasonable.

Using a Moderate Tone. The tone of your message is important. Don't suggest that the receiver intentionally deceived you or intentionally created the problem. Rather, appeal to the receiver's sense of responsibility and pride in the company's good name. Calmly express your disappointment in view of your high expectations of the product and of the company. Communicating your feelings without rancor is often your strongest appeal.

ETHICS CHECK

Complaint Bullying

As any salesperson will tell you, some customers seem to believe that if they vent their anger and make a scene at the store, bullying and intimidating a fearful sales representative, they are more likely to get their way. Indeed, some sales staff may cave in, wishing to defuse the ruckus. Is it fair to resort to such tactics to get what one wants? Does the end justify the means?

Composing Effective Complaints

As their name suggests, complaints deliver bad news. Some complaint messages just vent anger. However, if the goal is to change something (and why bother to write except to motivate change?), then persuasion is necessary. Effective claim messages make a reasonable and valid request, present a logical case with clear facts, and adopt a moderate tone. Anger and emotion are not effective persuaders.

Martine Romaniack's letter, shown in Figure 10.4, follows the persuasive pattern as she seeks credit for two VoIP (voice over Internet protocol) systems. Actually, she was quite upset because her company was counting on these new Internet systems to reduce its phone bills. Instead, the handsets produced so much static that incoming and outgoing calls were all but impossible to hear. What's more, she was frustrated that the Return Merchandise Authorization form she filled out at the company's Web site seemed to sink into a dark hole in cyberspace. She had reason to be angry! But she resolved to use a moderate tone in writing her complaint letter.

Why are anger and emotion poor persuaders?

Notice that her tone is objective, rational, and unemotional. She begins with a compliment and explains why her company needs a VoIP system. She provides identifying data and justifies her claim by explaining that installation instructions were carefully followed. Claim messages are particularly effective when writers express their personal disappointment and feelings. Martine explains her strong disappointment in view of the promotional statement assuring a clear signal. She would like to have been more forceful, but she knew that a calm, unemotional tone would be more effective. She wondered whether she should say that she was really ticked off that she had spent hours researching the product. The new system took additional hours to install and troubleshoot. After all that work, she couldn't use it because of the static. Nevertheless, she stuck to the plan of using a positive opening, a well-documented claim, and a request for specific action in the closing.

FIGURE 10.4 Claim (Complaint) Letter

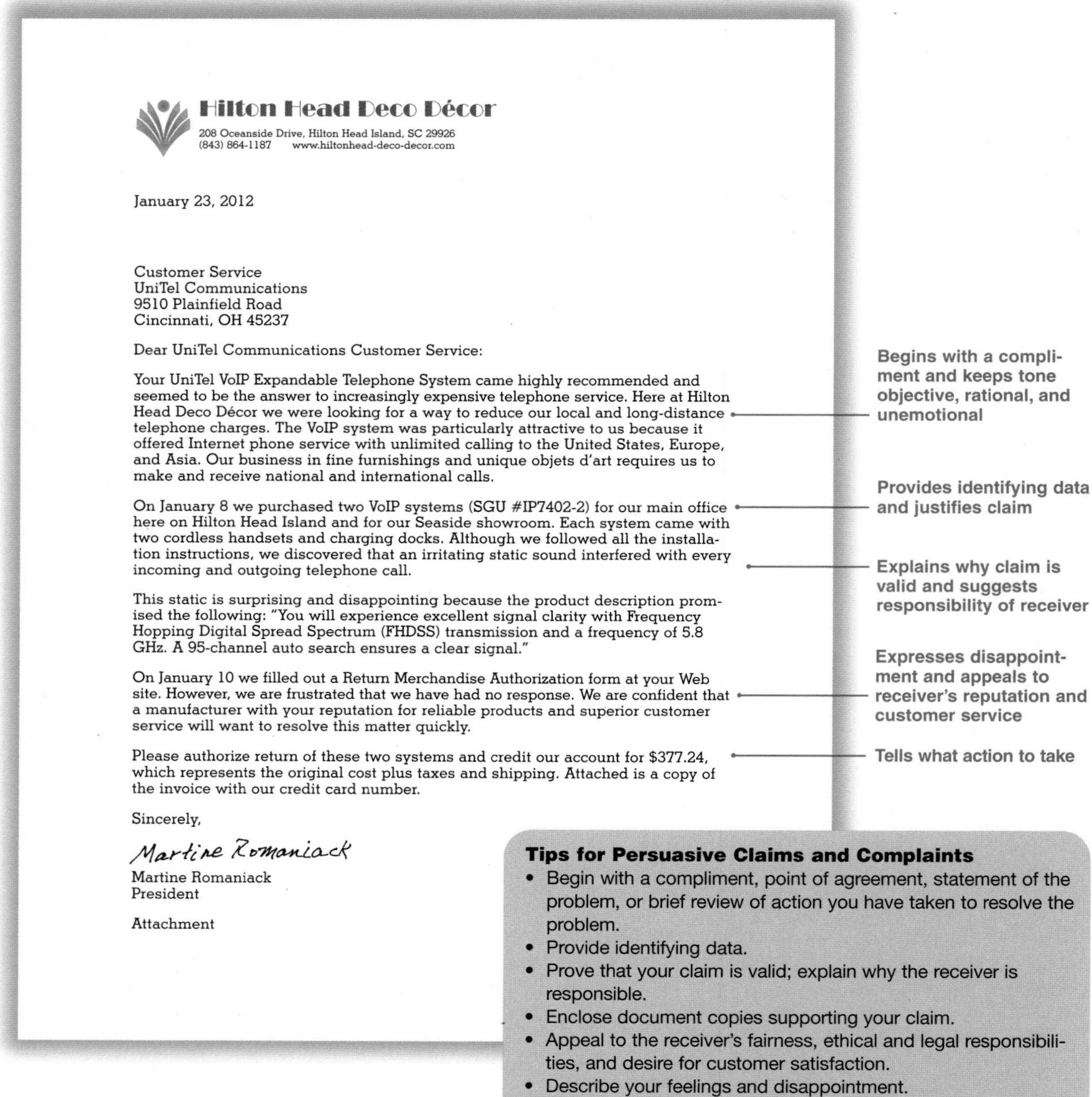

Hilton Head Deco Décor
208 Oceanside Drive, Hilton Head Island, SC 29926
(843) 864-1187 www.hiltonhead-deco-decor.com

January 23, 2012

Customer Service
UniTel Communications
9510 Plainfield Road
Cincinnati, OH 45237

Dear UniTel Communications Customer Service:

Your UniTel VoIP Expandable Telephone System came highly recommended and seemed to be the answer to increasingly expensive telephone service. Here at Hilton Head Deco Décor we were looking for a way to reduce our local and long-distance telephone charges. The VoIP system was particularly attractive to us because it offered Internet phone service with unlimited calling to the United States, Europe, and Asia. Our business in fine furnishings and unique objets d'art requires us to make and receive national and international calls.

On January 8 we purchased two VoIP systems (SGU #IP7402-2) for our main office here on Hilton Head Island and for our Seaside showroom. Each system came with two cordless handsets and charging docks. Although we followed all the installation instructions, we discovered that an irritating static sound interfered with every incoming and outgoing telephone call.

This static is surprising and disappointing because the product description promised the following: "You will experience excellent signal clarity with Frequency Hopping Digital Spread Spectrum (FHDSS) transmission and a frequency of 5.8 GHz. A 95-channel auto search ensures a clear signal."

On January 10 we filled out a Return Merchandise Authorization form at your Web site. However, we are frustrated that we have had no response. We are confident that a manufacturer with your reputation for reliable products and superior customer service will want to resolve this matter quickly.

Please authorize return of these two systems and credit our account for $377.24, which represents the original cost plus taxes and shipping. Attached is a copy of the invoice with our credit card number.

Sincerely,

Martine Romaniack

Martine Romaniack
President

Attachment

Begins with a compliment and keeps tone objective, rational, and unemotional
Provides identifying data and justifies claim
Explains why claim is valid and suggests responsibility of receiver
Expresses disappointment and appeals to receiver's reputation and customer service
Tells what action to take

Tips for Persuasive Claims and Complaints

- Begin with a compliment, point of agreement, statement of the problem, or brief review of action you have taken to resolve the problem.
- Provide identifying data.
- Prove that your claim is valid; explain why the receiver is responsible.
- Enclose document copies supporting your claim.
- Appeal to the receiver's fairness, ethical and legal responsibilities, and desire for customer satisfaction.
- Describe your feelings and disappointment.
- Avoid sounding angry, emotional, or irrational.
- Close by telling exactly what you want done.

Checklist

Requesting Favors and Actions, Making Claims, Delivering Complaints

Prewrite

- Determine your purpose. Know exactly what you are requesting.
- Anticipate the reaction of your audience. Remember that the receiver is thinking *Why should I? What's in it for me? What's in it for you? Who cares?*

Gain Attention

- Use the indirect strategy rather than blurting out the request immediately.
- Begin with a problem description, unexpected statement, compliment, praise, related facts, stimulating question, or reader benefit to grab attention.

Build Interest

- Develop interest by using facts, statistics, examples, testimonials, and specific details.
- Establish your credibility, if necessary, by explaining your background and expertise. Use testimonials, expert opinion, or research if necessary.
- Support your request by tying facts to direct benefits (increased profits, more efficient operations, better customer relations, saving money, a returned favor) or indirect benefits (improving the community, giving back to the profession, helping the environment).
- In claims and complaints, be objective but prove the validity of your request.

Reduce Resistance

- Anticipate objections to your request and provide counterarguments.
- Suggest what might be lost if the request is not granted, but don't make it sound like a threat.
- In claims and complaints, use a moderate, unemotional tone.

Motivate Action

- Make a precise request that spells out exactly what you want done. Add a deadline date if necessary.
- Repeat a benefit, provide additional details, or offer an incentive. Express appreciation.

Writing Persuasive Messages Within Organizations

LEARNING OBJECTIVE 4
Write persuasive messages within organizations.

As discussed in Chapter 1, messages within organizations move in one of three ways: downward, upward, or horizontally. The strategies and tone employed in these messages depend on the organizational position of the sender and that of the receiver. Let's say you want to persuade your boss to handle orders differently on the company's Web site. Your message would follow the indirect strategy. But the tone and content of your message would be different from that of the boss sending a similar persuasive message on the same topic. In this section we focus on messages flowing downward and upward within organizations. Horizontal messages traveling between coworkers are similar to those discussed earlier in requesting favors and actions.

Persuading Employees: Messages Flowing Downward

Why do messages flowing downward require attention to tone?

Instructions or directives moving downward from superiors to subordinates usually require little persuasion. Employees expect to be directed in how to perform their jobs. These messages (such as information about procedures, equipment, or customer service) use the direct strategy, with the purpose immediately stated. However, employees are sometimes asked to volunteer for projects. For example, some organizations ask employees to join programs to stop smoking, lose weight, or start exercising. Organizations may ask employees to participate in capacities outside their work roles—such as spending their free time volunteering for charity projects. In such cases, the four-part indirect strategy provides a helpful structure.

Messages flowing downward require attention to tone. Warm words and a conversational tone convey a caring attitude. Persuasive requests coming from a trusted superior are more likely to be accepted than requests from a dictatorial executive who relies on threats and punishments to secure compliance. As mentioned earlier, the proverbial carrot has always been more persuasive than the stick. Managers should avoid sounding preachy or parental.

Employees don't want to be treated as children. Because the words *should* and *must* sometimes convey a negative tone, be careful in using them.

Figure 10.5 shows a memo from Jessica Jeffers, director of Human Resources at a large bank. Her goal is to persuade employees to participate in Hands on Miami Day, a fund-raising and community service event that her bank sponsors. In addition to volunteering their services for a day, employees also have to pay $20 to register! You can see that this will be no small persuasion task for Jessica.

Jessica decides to follow the four-part indirect strategy beginning with gaining attention. Notice that she strives to capture attention by describing specific benefits of volunteering in Miami. She explains ways that volunteers make Miami a better place to live and work. Feeding the homeless, providing companionship to the elderly, building low-income housing, restoring the natural environment—all these examples of selfless giving not only gain attention but also suggest indirect benefits to the reader.

The second paragraph of this persuasive message builds interest by listing examples of what volunteers have accomplished during previous Hands on Miami events. Volunteers can

FIGURE 10.5 Persuasive Organizational Message Flowing Downward

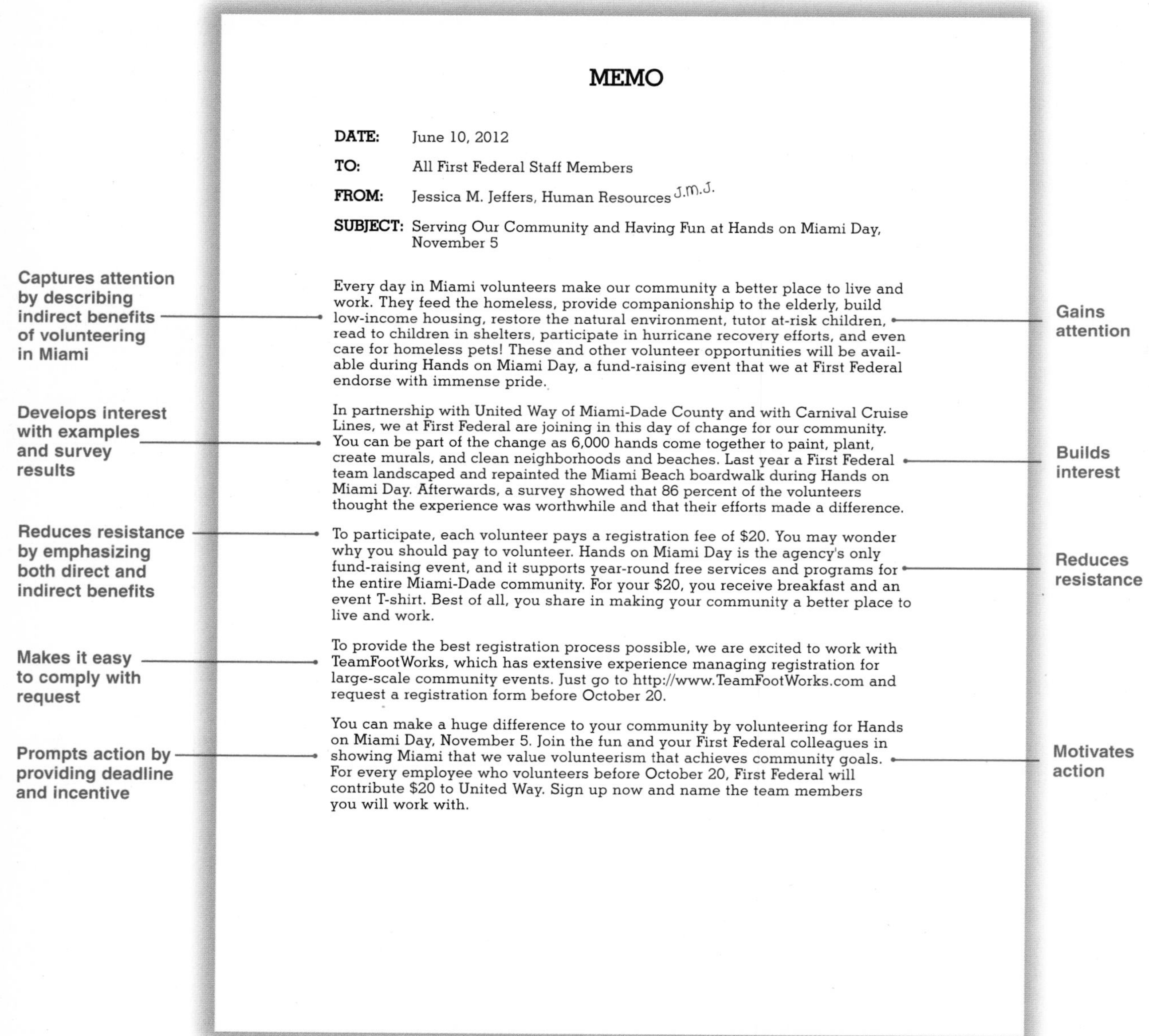

MEMO

DATE: June 10, 2012

TO: All First Federal Staff Members

FROM: Jessica M. Jeffers, Human Resources J.M.J.

SUBJECT: Serving Our Community and Having Fun at Hands on Miami Day, November 5

Captures attention by describing indirect benefits of volunteering in Miami / **Gains attention**

Every day in Miami volunteers make our community a better place to live and work. They feed the homeless, provide companionship to the elderly, build low-income housing, restore the natural environment, tutor at-risk children, read to children in shelters, participate in hurricane recovery efforts, and even care for homeless pets! These and other volunteer opportunities will be available during Hands on Miami Day, a fund-raising event that we at First Federal endorse with immense pride.

Develops interest with examples and survey results / **Builds interest**

In partnership with United Way of Miami-Dade County and with Carnival Cruise Lines, we at First Federal are joining in this day of change for our community. You can be part of the change as 6,000 hands come together to paint, plant, create murals, and clean neighborhoods and beaches. Last year a First Federal team landscaped and repainted the Miami Beach boardwalk during Hands on Miami Day. Afterwards, a survey showed that 86 percent of the volunteers thought the experience was worthwhile and that their efforts made a difference.

Reduces resistance by emphasizing both direct and indirect benefits / **Reduces resistance**

To participate, each volunteer pays a registration fee of $20. You may wonder why you should pay to volunteer. Hands on Miami Day is the agency's only fund-raising event, and it supports year-round free services and programs for the entire Miami-Dade community. For your $20, you receive breakfast and an event T-shirt. Best of all, you share in making your community a better place to live and work.

Makes it easy to comply with request

To provide the best registration process possible, we are excited to work with TeamFootWorks, which has extensive experience managing registration for large-scale community events. Just go to http://www.TeamFootWorks.com and request a registration form before October 20.

Prompts action by providing deadline and incentive / **Motivates action**

You can make a huge difference to your community by volunteering for Hands on Miami Day, November 5. Join the fun and your First Federal colleagues in showing Miami that we value volunteerism that achieves community goals. For every employee who volunteers before October 20, First Federal will contribute $20 to United Way. Sign up now and name the team members you will work with.

expect to join 6,000 other "hands" who paint, plant, create murals, and clean neighborhoods and beaches. To build further interest, the letter includes the results of a survey showing that a vast majority of volunteers thought the experience was worthwhile and that their efforts made a difference. People are more inclined to agree to do something if they know that others have done it in the past and found it beneficial.

Why are audience benefits important in persuasive messages?

To reduce resistance, the third paragraph explains why the $20 fee makes sense. Jessica skillfully combines both direct benefits (free breakfast and an event T-shirt) with indirect benefits (sharing in making the community a better place to live and work).

Good persuasive requests close by making it easy to comply and by finding some way to motivate action. In complying with the request in this message, all the reader has to do is go to a Web site and request a registration form. To motivate action in the closing, Jessica saved a strong indirect benefit. The bank will chip in $20 for every employee who volunteers before the deadline. Readers can see that their participation reaches beyond their individual contribution. Although readers don't benefit directly from the company's contribution to United Way, they can see that others will benefit. This significant indirect benefit along with the direct benefits of having fun and joining colleagues in a community activity combine for a strong persuasive message.

Persuading the Boss: Messages Flowing Upward

Why is saving money important in selling ideas to management?

Another form of persuasion within organizations centers on suggestions made by subordinates. Convincing management to adopt a procedure or invest in a product or new equipment requires skillful communication. Managers are just as resistant to change as others are. Providing evidence is critical when subordinates submit recommendations to their bosses. Be ready to back up your request with facts, figures, and evidence. When selling an idea to management, strive to make a strong dollars-and-cents case.[9] A request that emphasizes how the proposal saves money or benefits the business is more persuasive than one that simply announces a good deal or tells how a plan works.

In describing an idea to your boss, state it confidently and fairly. Don't undermine your suggestions with statements such as *This may sound crazy* or *I know we tried this once before but. . . .* Show that you have thought through the suggestion by describing the risks involved as well as the potential benefits. You may wonder whether you should even mention the downside of a suggestion. Most bosses will be relieved and impressed to know that you have considered the risks as well as the benefits to a proposal.[10] Two-sided arguments are generally more persuasive because they make you sound credible and fair. Presenting only one side of a proposal reduces its effectiveness because such a proposal seems biased, subjective, and flawed. You can make a stronger argument by acknowledging and neutralizing opposing points of view.

Persuasive messages traveling upward require a special sensitivity to tone. When asking superiors to change views or take action, use words such as *suggest* and *recommend* rather than *you must* and *we should*. Avoid sounding pushy or argumentative. Strive for a conversational, yet professional, tone that conveys warmth, competence, and confidence.

When Marketing Manager Monique Hartung wanted her boss to authorize the purchase of a multifunction color laser copier, she knew she had to be persuasive. Her memo, shown in Figure 10.6, illustrates an effective approach. First, she researched prices, features, and the maintenance of color laser copiers. These machines often serve as copiers, faxes, scanners, and printers and can cost several thousand dollars. Monique found an outstanding deal offered by a local office supplier. Because she knew that her boss, Samuel Neesen, favored "cold, hard facts," she listed current monthly costs for copying at Copy Quick to increase her chances of gaining approval. Finally, she calculated the amortization of the purchase price and monthly costs of running the new color copier.

Are persuasive messages that are developed indirectly longer or shorter than those developed directly? Why?

Notice that Monique's memo isn't short. A successful persuasive message will typically take more space than a direct message because proving a case requires evidence. In the end, Monique chose to send her memo as an e-mail attachment accompanied by a polite short e-mail because she wanted to keep the document format in MS Word intact. She also felt that the message was too long to paste into her e-mail program. Monique's persuasive memo and her e-mail include subject lines that announce the purpose of the message without disclosing the actual request. By delaying the request until she has had a chance to describe the problem and discuss a solution, Monique prevented the reader's premature rejection.

FIGURE 10.6 **Persuasive E-Mail and Memo Flowing Upward**

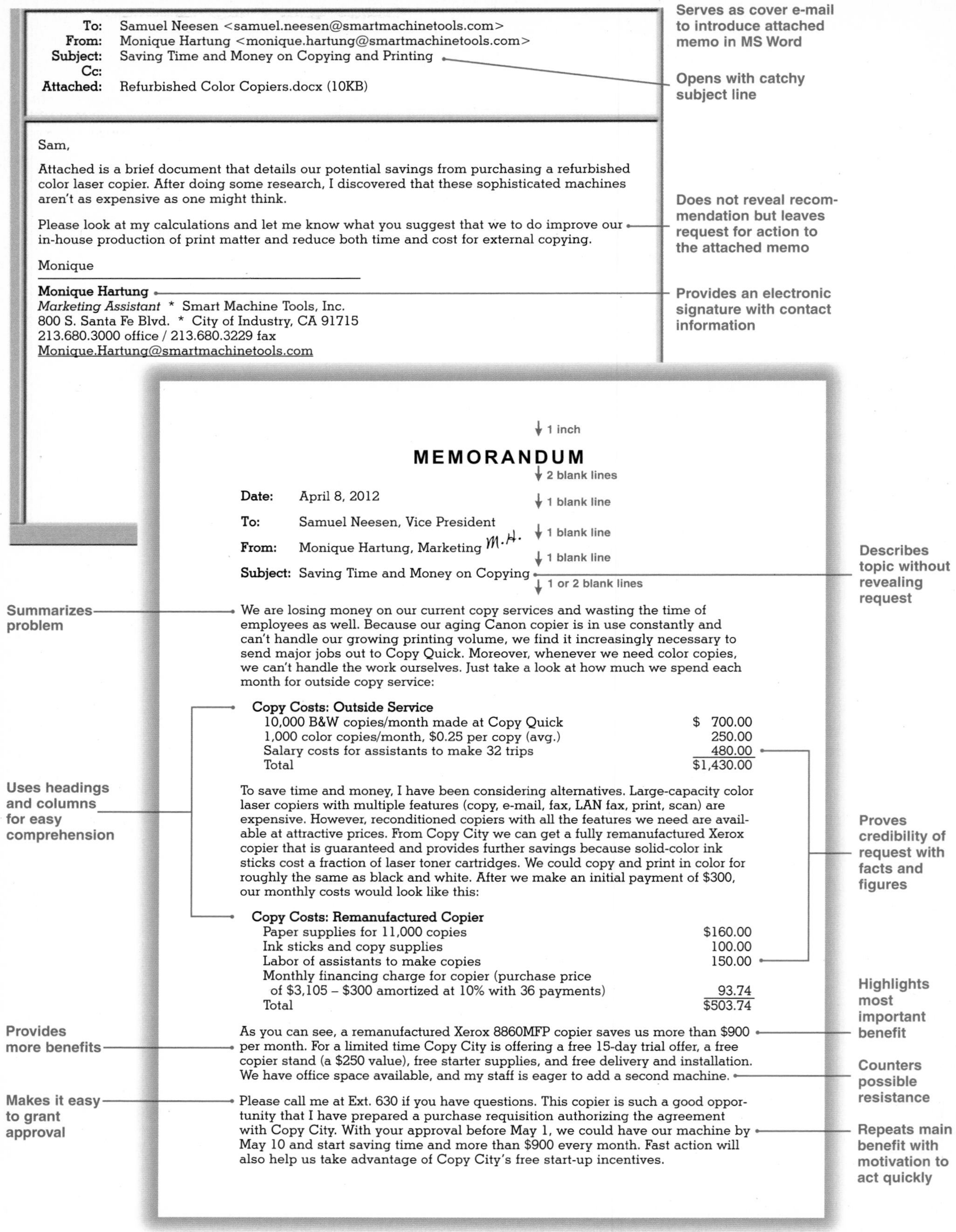
To: Samuel Neesen <samuel.neesen@smartmachinetools.com>
From: Monique Hartung <monique.hartung@smartmachinetools.com>
Subject: Saving Time and Money on Copying and Printing
Cc:
Attached: Refurbished Color Copiers.docx (10KB)

Sam,

Attached is a brief document that details our potential savings from purchasing a refurbished color laser copier. After doing some research, I discovered that these sophisticated machines aren't as expensive as one might think.

Please look at my calculations and let me know what you suggest that we to do improve our in-house production of print matter and reduce both time and cost for external copying.

Monique

Monique Hartung
Marketing Assistant * Smart Machine Tools, Inc.
800 S. Santa Fe Blvd. * City of Industry, CA 91715
213.680.3000 office / 213.680.3229 fax
Monique.Hartung@smartmachinetools.com

MEMORANDUM

Date: April 8, 2012

To: Samuel Neesen, Vice President

From: Monique Hartung, Marketing M.H.

Subject: Saving Time and Money on Copying

We are losing money on our current copy services and wasting the time of employees as well. Because our aging Canon copier is in use constantly and can't handle our growing printing volume, we find it increasingly necessary to send major jobs out to Copy Quick. Moreover, whenever we need color copies, we can't handle the work ourselves. Just take a look at how much we spend each month for outside copy service:

Copy Costs: Outside Service	
10,000 B&W copies/month made at Copy Quick	$ 700.00
1,000 color copies/month, $0.25 per copy (avg.)	250.00
Salary costs for assistants to make 32 trips	480.00
Total	$1,430.00

To save time and money, I have been considering alternatives. Large-capacity color laser copiers with multiple features (copy, e-mail, fax, LAN fax, print, scan) are expensive. However, reconditioned copiers with all the features we need are available at attractive prices. From Copy City we can get a fully remanufactured Xerox copier that is guaranteed and provides further savings because solid-color ink sticks cost a fraction of laser toner cartridges. We could copy and print in color for roughly the same as black and white. After we make an initial payment of $300, our monthly costs would look like this:

Copy Costs: Remanufactured Copier	
Paper supplies for 11,000 copies	$160.00
Ink sticks and copy supplies	100.00
Labor of assistants to make copies	150.00
Monthly financing charge for copier (purchase price of $3,105 – $300 amortized at 10% with 36 payments)	93.74
Total	$503.74

As you can see, a remanufactured Xerox 8860MFP copier saves us more than $900 per month. For a limited time Copy City is offering a free 15-day trial offer, a free copier stand (a $250 value), free starter supplies, and free delivery and installation. We have office space available, and my staff is eager to add a second machine.

Please call me at Ext. 630 if you have questions. This copier is such a good opportunity that I have prepared a purchase requisition authorizing the agreement with Copy City. With your approval before May 1, we could have our machine by May 10 and start saving time and more than $900 every month. Fast action will also help us take advantage of Copy City's free start-up incentives.

Serves as cover e-mail to introduce attached memo in MS Word
Opens with catchy subject line
Does not reveal recommendation but leaves request for action to the attached memo
Provides an electronic signature with contact information
1 inch
2 blank lines
1 blank line
1 blank line
1 blank line
1 or 2 blank lines
Describes topic without revealing request
Summarizes problem
Uses headings and columns for easy comprehension
Proves credibility of request with facts and figures
Highlights most important benefit
Provides more benefits
Counters possible resistance
Makes it easy to grant approval
Repeats main benefit with motivation to act quickly

Checklist

Writing Persuasive Messages Within Organizations

Prewrite

- Know your purpose and be able to state it precisely and concisely. What do you want the receiver to do? Make sure your request is doable and attainable.
- Profile the audience. Play *What if?* scenarios to anticipate how the receiver will react to your request. What direct or indirect benefits can you cite?

Gain Attention

- Make the reader aware of a problem, use a startling statement, provide a significant fact related to the request, describe possible benefits, ask a stimulating question, or offer compliments and praise.
- Establish your credibility, but don't pull rank.

Build Interest

- Use facts, statistics, examples, and specific details to build a solid foundation for your request.
- Strive for a personal but professional tone. Be enthusiastic and positive.
- Soften your words when persuading upward. Suggest benefits to the reader.

Reduce Resistance

- Recognize any weakness in your proposal and suggest well-reasoned counterarguments and facts.
- In requests flowing upward, consider making a strong dollars-and-cents appeal for requests involving budgets.
- In requests flowing downward, avoid sounding preachy, parental, or overly authoritarian.

Motivate Action

- State a specific request including a deadline if appropriate. Suggest ways to make it effortless and painless for the receiver to respond.
- Repeat a major benefit that appeals to the reader.
- Include an incentive or reason to act, and express appreciation if appropriate.

The strength of this persuasive document, though, is in the clear presentation of comparison figures showing how much money the company can save by purchasing a remanufactured copier. Buying a copier that uses low-cost solid ink instead of expensive laser cartridges is another argument in this machine's favor. Although the organization pattern is not obvious, the memo begins with an attention-getter (a frank description of the problem), builds interest (with easy-to-read facts and figures), provides benefits, and reduces resistance. Notice that the conclusion tells what action is to be taken, makes it easy to respond, and repeats the main benefit to motivate action.

Planning and Composing Effective Direct-Mail and E-Mail Sales Messages

LEARNING OBJECTIVE 5
Write effective and ethical direct-mail and e-mail sales messages.

Sales messages use persuasion to promote specific products and services. In our coverage we are most concerned with sales messages delivered by mail or by e-mail. Many of the concepts you will learn about sales persuasion, however, can be applied to online, wireless, TV, print, radio, and other media. The best sales messages, whether delivered by direct mail or by e-mail, have much in common. In this section we look at how to apply the 3-x-3 writing process to sales messages. We also present techniques developed by experts to draft effective sales messages, both in print and online.

Applying the 3-x-3 Writing Process to Sales Messages

Marketing professionals analyze and perfect every aspect of a sales message to encourage consumers to read and act on the message. Like the experts, you will want to pay close attention to the preparatory steps of analysis and adaptation before writing the actual message.

What aspects of a product should you study before writing a sales message promoting it?

Analyzing the Product and Purpose for Writing. Prior to sitting down to write a sales message promoting a product, you must study the item carefully. What can you learn about its design, construction, raw materials, and manufacturing process? What can you learn about its ease of use, efficiency, durability, and applications? Be sure to consider warranties, service, price, premiums, exclusivity, and special appeals. At the same time, evaluate the competition so that you can compare your product's strengths against the competitor's weaknesses.

Now you are ready to identify your central selling points. At Lands' End a central selling point for one marketing campaign was economical custom clothing. The company used a testimonial from a real customer who said that the $49 Lands' End custom dress shirts he bought were better than the $120 shirts he previously purchased from custom shops.[11] Analyzing your product and studying the competition help you determine what to emphasize in your sales letter.

Equally important is determining the specific purpose of your letter. Do you want the reader to call for a free video and brochure? Listen to a podcast at your Web site? Fill out an order form? Send a credit card authorization? Before you write the first word of your message, know what response you want and what central selling points you will emphasize to achieve that purpose.

How do the senders of direct-mail messages target audiences?

Adapting a Sales Message to Its Audience. Blanket mailings sent "cold" to occupants generally produce low responses—typically less than 2 percent. That means that 98 percent of the receivers usually toss direct-mail sales letters right into the trash. But the response rate can be increased dramatically by targeting the audience through selected database mailing lists. These lists can be purchased or compiled. By directing your message to a selected group, you can make certain assumptions about the receivers. Let's say you are selling fitness equipment. A good mailing list might come from subscribers to fitness or exercise magazines. You would expect similar interests, needs, and demographics (age, income, and other characteristics). With this knowledge you can adapt the sales letter to a specific audience.

Crafting Direct-Mail Sales Letters

What advantages do direct-mail messages enjoy?

Sales letters are usually part of direct-mail marketing campaigns. These letters are a powerful means to make sales, generate leads, boost retail traffic, solicit donations, and direct consumers to Web sites. Direct mail allows a personalized, tangible, three-dimensional message that is less invasive than telephone solicitations and less reviled than unsolicited e-mail.

Professionals who specialize in traditional direct-mail services have made it a science. They analyze a market, develop an effective mailing list, study the product, prepare a sophisticated campaign aimed at a target audience, and motivate the reader to act. You have probably received many direct-mail packages, often called junk mail. These packages typically contain a sales letter, a brochure, a price list, illustrations of the product, testimonials, and other persuasive appeals.

What is a primary goal of a sales message?

We are most concerned here with the sales letter: its strategy, organization, and evidence. Because sales letters are generally written by specialists, you may never write one on the job. Why, then, learn how to write a sales letter? In many ways, every letter we create is a form of sales letter. We sell our ideas, our organizations, and ourselves. Learning the techniques of sales writing will help you be more successful in any communication that requires persuasion and promotion. What's more, you will recognize sales strategies that enable you to become a more perceptive consumer of ideas, products, and services.

Your primary goal in writing a sales message is to get someone to devote a few moments of attention to it. You may be promoting a product, a service, an idea, or yourself. In each case the most effective messages will (a) gain attention, (b) build interest, (c) reduce resistance, and (d) motivate action. This is the same recipe we studied earlier, but the ingredients are different.

Spotlight on Communicators

© Jon Freilich/Bloomberg via Getty Images

In writing winning sales messages, beware of impossible promises, warns Herb Kelleher, cofounder of Southwest Airlines. He believes his company has the quickest baggage delivery in the industry—only eight minutes from Jetway to pickup. But when his marketing staff proposed making such a promise in the Southwest baggage promotions, Kelleher balked. On rare occasions Southwest wouldn't be able to deliver, he reasoned, and broken promises are not easily forgotten.

Gaining Attention in Sales Messages. One of the most critical elements of a sales message is its opening paragraph. This opener should be short (one to five lines), honest, relevant, and stimulating. Marketing pros have found that eye-catching typographical arrangements or provocative messages, such as the following, can hook a reader's attention:

What sales message openers are effective in gaining attention?

- **Offer:** *A free trip to Hawaii is just the beginning!*
- **Promise:** *Now you can raise your sales income by 50 percent or even more with the proven techniques found in . . . .*
- **Question:** *Do you yearn for an honest, fulfilling relationship?*
- **Quotation or proverb:** *Necessity is the mother of invention.*
- **Fact:** *The Greenland Eskimos ate more fat than anyone in the world. And yet . . . they had virtually no heart disease.*
- **Product feature:** *Volvo's snazzy new convertible ensures your safety with a roll bar that pops out when the car tips 40 degrees to the side.*
- **Testimonial:** *My name is Sheldon Schulman. I am a practicing medical doctor. I am also a multimillionaire. I didn't make my millions by practicing medicine, though. I made them by investing in my spare time.*
- **Startling statement:** *Let the poor and hungry feed themselves! For just $100 they can.*
- **Personalized action setting:** *It's 4:30 p.m. and you've got to make a decision. You need everybody's opinion, no matter where they are. Before you pick up your phone to call them one at a time, pick up this card: WebEx Teleconference Services.*

Other openings calculated to capture attention might include a solution to a problem, an anecdote, a personalized statement using the receiver's name, or a relevant current event.

Building Interest With Rational and Emotional Appeals. In this phase of your sales message, you should describe clearly the product or service. In simple language emphasize the central selling points that you identified during your prewriting analysis. Those selling points can be developed using rational or emotional appeals.

Rational appeals are associated with reason and intellect. They translate selling points into references to making or saving money, increasing efficiency, or making the best use of resources. In general, rational appeals are appropriate when a product is expensive, long-lasting, or important to health, security, and financial success. Emotional appeals relate to status, ego, and sensual feelings. Appealing to the emotions is sometimes effective when a product

With motorists at risk from texting while driving, highway safety groups are sending the message that texting kills. One police department in the United Kingdom sparked controversy by creating a Hollywood-styled PSA so disturbing that viewers complained it should not air on television. The graphic video, which follows three teenage girls as they text-and-drive their way into a head-on collision with another vehicle, left international viewers shocked and in tears. But one tracking firm found that 80 percent of viewers planned to quit texting while on the road. *Are safety messages delivered best using emotional appeals?*

How are rational appeals different from emotional appeals?

is inexpensive, short-lived, or nonessential. Many clever sales messages, however, combine emotional and rational strategies for a dual appeal. Consider these examples:

Rational Appeal
You can buy the things you need and want, pay household bills, and pay off higher-cost loans and credit cards—as soon as you are approved and your Credit-Line account is opened.

Emotional Appeal
Leave the urban bustle behind and escape to sun-soaked Bermuda! To recharge your batteries with an injection of sun and surf, all you need are your bathing suit, a little suntan lotion, and your Credit-Line card.

Dual Appeal
New Credit-Line cardholders are immediately eligible for a $200 travel certificate and additional discounts at fun-filled resorts. Save up to 40 percent while lying on a beach in picturesque, sun-soaked Bermuda, the year-round resort island.

ETHICS CHECK

Scare Tactics

Direct marketers sometimes resort to scare tactics—for example, to make us purchase alarm systems or subscribe to monitoring services. They may also appeal to our compassion and guilt before the holidays in soliciting money for the less fortunate. Are such emotional appeals ethical?

A physical description of your product is not enough, however. Zig Ziglar, thought by some to be America's greatest salesperson, pointed out that no matter how well you know your product, no one is persuaded by cold, hard facts alone. In the end, people buy because of product benefits.[12] Your job is to translate those cold facts into warm feelings and reader benefits. Let's say a sales message promotes a hand cream made with aloe and cocoa butter extracts, along with vitamin A. Those facts become, *Nature's hand helpers—including soothing aloe and cocoa extracts, along with firming vitamin A—form invisible gloves that protect your sensitive skin against the hardships of work, harsh detergents, and constant environmental assaults.*

Why is it important to turn facts into warm feelings and benefits?

Reducing Resistance and Building Desire. Marketing specialists use a number of techniques to overcome resistance and build desire. When price is an obstacle, consider these suggestions:

- Delay mentioning price until after you've created a desire for the product.
- Show the price in small units, such as the price per issue of a magazine.
- Demonstrate how the reader saves money—for instance, by subscribing for two or three years.
- Compare your prices with those of a competitor.

In addition, you need to anticipate other objections and questions the receiver may have. When possible, translate these objections into selling points *(If you are worried about training your staff members on the new software, remember that our offer includes $1,000 worth of on-site one-on-one instruction)*. Other techniques to overcome resistance and prove the credibility of the product include the following:

What techniques are effective in reducing resistance?

- **Testimonials:** *"I never stopped eating, yet I lost 107 pounds." — Tina Rivers, Greenwood, South Carolina*
- **Names of satisfied users** (with permission, of course): *Enclosed is a partial list of private pilots who enthusiastically subscribe to our service.*
- **Money-back guarantee or warranty:** *We offer the longest warranties in the business—all parts and service on-site for five years!*
- **Free trial or sample:** *We are so confident that you will like our new accounting program that we want you to try it absolutely free.*
- **Performance tests, polls, or awards:** *Our TP-3000 was named Best Web Phone, and* Etown.com *voted it Smartphone of the Year.*

How can you motivate action in a sales message?

Motivating Action at the Conclusion of a Sales Message. All the effort put into a sales message goes to waste if the reader fails to act. To make it easy for readers to act, you can provide a reply card, a stamped and preaddressed envelope, a toll-free telephone number, an easy-to-scan Web site, or a promise of a follow-up call. Because readers often need an extra push, consider including additional motivators, such as the following:

- **Offer a gift:** *You will receive a free cell phone with the purchase of any new car.*
- **Promise an incentive:** *With every new, paid subscription, we will plant a tree in one of America's Heritage Forests.*
- **Limit the offer:** *Only the first 100 customers receive free travel mugs.*
- **Set a deadline:** *You must act before June 1 to get these low prices.*
- **Guarantee satisfaction:** *We will return your full payment if you are not entirely satisfied—no questions asked.*

The final paragraph of the sales letter carries the punch line. This is where you tell readers what you want them to do and give them reasons for doing it. Most sales letters also include postscripts because they make irresistible reading. Even readers who might skim over or bypass paragraphs are drawn to a P.S. Therefore, use a postscript to reveal your strongest motivator, to add a special inducement for a quick response, or to reemphasize a central selling point.

Although you want to be persuasive in sales letters, you must guard against overstepping legal and ethical boundaries. Information contained in sales letters has landed some writers in hot water. See the accompanying Ethical Insights box to learn how to stay out of trouble.

ETHICAL INSIGHT

What's Legal and What's Not in Sales Messages

In promoting products and writing sales message, be careful about the words you use and the claims you make. How far can you go in praising and selling your product?

- **Puffery.** In a sales message, you can write, *Hey, we've got something fantastic! It's the very best product on the market!* Called "puffery," such promotional claims are not taken literally by reasonable consumers.
- **Proving your claims.** If you write that *three out of four dentists recommend* your toothpaste, you had better have competent and reliable scientific evidence to support the claim. Such a claim goes beyond puffery and requires proof. Vital Basics paid a $1 million settlement for claiming that its Focus Factor helped improve memory, a claim unsubstantiated by proof, said the Federal Trade Commission.[13] As part of a crackdown on deceptive drug advertising, the Food and Drug Administration forced Bayer to run new ads correcting its previous marketing overstating the ability of its birth control pill Yaz to improve women's moods and clear up acne.[14] Similarly, UPS had to stop running ads saying it was the "most reliable" shipping company after FedEx sued.[15]
- **Celebrities.** The unauthorized use of a celebrity's name, likeness, or nickname is not permitted in sales messages. For example, late-night talk show host Johnny Carson won a case against a portable toilet firm that promoted a "Here's Johnny" toilet. Similarly, film star Dustin Hoffman won millions of dollars for the unauthorized use of a digitally altered photo showing him in an evening gown and Ralph Lauren heels. Even a commercial showing the image of a celebrity such as Beyonce on a camera phone is risky.
- **Misleading statements.** You cannot tell people that they are winners or finalists in a sweepstake unless they actually are. American Family Publishers was found guilty of sending letters tricking people into buying magazine subscription in the belief that they had won $1.1 million. Similarly, the Damart clothing company was reprimanded for sending a mailing with *final reminder* printed in bold, red lettering on the envelope. Instead of referring to an overdue bill, it merely referred to a final reminder about a Damart offer, clearly a deceptive message.[16] Companies also may not misrepresent the nature, characteristics, qualities, or geographic origin of goods or services they are promoting.
- **Unwanted merchandise.** If you enclose unsolicited merchandise with a letter, don't expect the receiver to be required to pay for it or return it. Express Publishing, for example, sent a copy of its *Food & Wine Magazine's Cookbook with a letter* inviting recipients to preview the book. It read: "If you don't want to preview the book, simply return the advance notice card within 14 days." Courts, however, have ruled that recipients are allowed to retain, use, or discard any unsolicited merchandise without paying for it or returning it.

Career Application

Bring to class at least three sales letters or advertisements that may represent issues described here. What examples of puffery can you identify? Are claims substantiated by reliable evidence? What proof is offered? Do any of your examples include names, images, or nicknames of celebrities? How likely is it that the celebrity authorized this use? Have you ever received unwanted merchandise as part of a sales campaign? What were you to do with it?

Putting Together All the Parts of a Sales Message. Sales letters are a preferred marketing medium because they can be personalized, directed to target audiences, and filled with a more complete message than other advertising media. But direct mail is expensive. That's why crafting and assembling all the parts of a sales message are so critical.

Figure 10.7 shows a sales letter addressed to a target group of small business owners. To sell the new magazine *Small Business Monthly*, the letter incorporates all four components of an effective persuasive message. Notice that the personalized action-setting opener places the reader in a familiar situation (getting into an elevator) and draws an analogy between failing to reach the top floor and failing to achieve a business goal. The writer develops a rational central selling point (a magazine that provides valuable information for a growing small business) and repeats this selling point in all the components of the letter. Notice, too, how a testimonial from a small business executive lends support to the sales message and how the closing pushes for action. Because the price of the magazine is not a selling feature, price is mentioned only on the reply card. This sales letter saves its strongest motivator—a free booklet—for the high-impact P.S. line.

Writing Successful E-Mail Sales Messages

How are direct-mail and e-marketing similar, and how are they different?

To make the best use of limited advertising dollars while reaching a great number of potential customers, many businesses are turning to the Internet and to e-mail marketing campaigns in particular. E-mails cost about $7 per consumer response versus about $48 per response for traditional direct mail.[17] Much like traditional direct mail, e-mail marketing can attract new customers, keep existing ones, encourage future sales, cross-sell, and cut costs. However, e-marketers can create and send a promotion in half the time it takes to print and distribute a traditional message. As consumers feel more comfortable and secure with online purchases, e-marketing has become more popular.

Selling by E-Mail. If you will be writing online sales messages for your organization, try using the following techniques gleaned from the best-performing e-mails. Although much e-marketing dazzles receivers with colorful graphics, we focus on the words involved in persuasive sales messages.

What is the first rule of e-marketing?

The first rule of e-marketing is to communicate only with those who have given permission. By sending messages only to "opt-in" folks, you greatly increase your "open rate"—those e-mails that will be opened. E-mail users detest spam. However, receivers are surprisingly receptive to offers tailored specifically for them. Remember that today's customer is somebody—not just anybody. Here are a few guidelines that will help you create effective e-mail sales messages:

- **Craft a catchy subject line.** Offer discounts or premiums: *Spring Sale: Buy now and save 20 percent!* Promise solutions to everyday work-related problems. Highlight hot new industry topics. Invite readers to scan a top-ten list of items such as issues, trends, or people.
- **Keep the main information "above the fold."** E-mails should be top heavy. Primary points should appear early in the message so that they capture the reader's attention.
- **Make the message short, conversational, and focused.** Because on-screen text is taxing to read, be brief. Focus on one or two central selling points only.
- **Convey urgency.** Top-performing e-mails state an offer deadline or demonstrate why the state of the industry demands action on the reader's part. Good messages also tie the product to relevant current events.
- **Sprinkle testimonials throughout the copy.** Consumers' own words are the best sales copy. These comments can serve as callouts or be integrated into the copy.
- **Provide a means for opting out.** It's polite and a good business tactic to include a statement that tells receivers how to be removed from the sender's mailing database.

Whether you actually write sales message on the job or merely receive them, you will better understand their organization and appeals by reviewing this chapter and the tips in the checklist on page 318.

FIGURE 10.7 **Sales Letter**

Prewriting

Analyze: The purpose of this letter is to persuade the reader to return the reply card and subscribe to *Small Business Monthly*.

Anticipate: The targeted audience consists of small-business owners. The central selling point is providing practical business data that will help their business grow.

Adapt: Because readers will be reluctant, use the indirect pattern.

Writing

Research: Gather facts to promote your product, including testimonials.

Organize: Gain attention by opening with a personalized action picture. Build interest with an analogy and a description of magazine features. Use a testimonial to reduce resistance. Motivate action with a free booklet and an easy-reply card.

Compose: Prepare first draft for pilot study.

Revising

Revise: Use short paragraphs and short sentences. Replace *malfunction* with *glitch*.

Proofread: Indent long quotations on the left and right sides. Italicize or underscore titles of publications. Hyphenate *hard-headed* and *first-of-its-kind*.

Evaluate: Monitor the response rate to this letter to assess its effectiveness.

small business monthly
28 North Ferry Road • Waterford, CT 06386

April 15, 2012

Mr. James Wehrley
1608 Montlieu Avenue
High Point, NC 27262

Dear Mr. Wehrley:

You walk into the elevator and push the button for the top floor. The elevator glides upwards. You step back and relax.

But the elevator never reaches the top. A glitch in the electronics prevents it from processing the information it needs to take you to your destination.

Do you see a similarity between your growing company and this elevator? You're aiming for the top, but a lack of information halts your progress. Now you can put your company into gear and propel it toward success with a new publication—*Small Business Monthly*.

This first-of-its-kind magazine brings you marketing tips, hard-headed business pointers, opportunities, and inspiration. This is the kind of current information you need today to be where you want to be tomorrow. One executive wrote:

> As president of a small manufacturing company, I read several top business publications, but I get my "bread and butter" from *Small Business Monthly*. I'm not interested in a lot of "pie in the sky" and theory. I find practical problems and how to solve them in *SBM*.
> —Mitchell M. Perry, Bowling Green, Ohio

Mr. Perry's words are the best recommendation I can offer you to try *SBM*. In less time than you might spend on an average business lunch, you learn the latest in management, operations, finance, taxes, business law, compensation, and advertising.

To evaluate *Small Business Monthly* without cost or obligation, let me send you a free issue. Just initial and return the enclosed card to start receiving a wealth of practical information that could keep your company traveling upward to its goal.

Cordially,

Cheryl Owings

Cheryl Owings
Vice President, Circulation

P.S. Act before May 15 and I'll send you our valuable booklet, *Managing for Success*, revealing more than 100 secrets for helping small businesses grow.

Puts reader into action setting

Gains attention

Suggests analogy

Emphasizes central selling point

Builds interest

Uses testimonial for credibility

Reduces resistance

Repeats central sales pitch in last sentence

Motivates action

Spotlights free offer in P.S. to prompt immediate reply

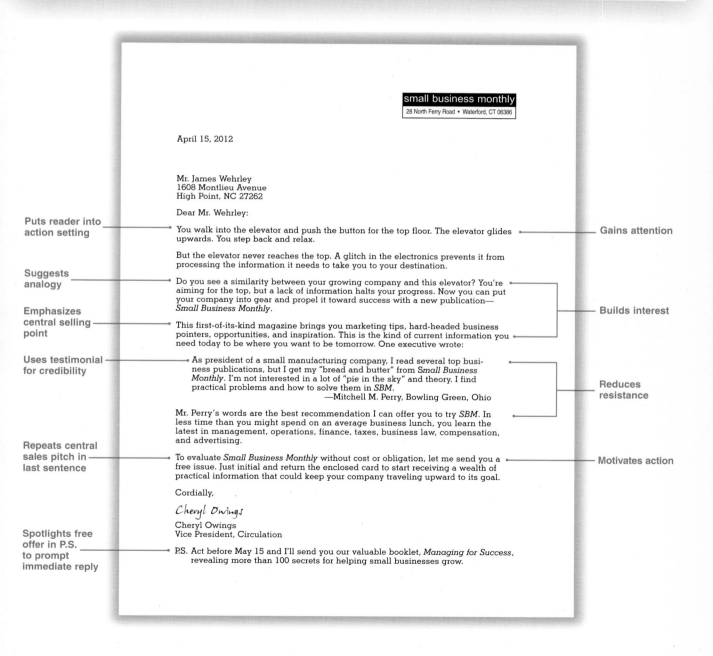

Checklist

Preparing Persuasive Direct-Mail and E-Mail Sales Messages

Prewrite

- Analyze your product or service. What makes it special? What central selling points should you emphasize? How does it compare with the competition?
- Profile your audience. How will this product or service benefit this audience?
- Decide what you want the audience to do at the end of your message.
- For e-mails, send only to those who have opted in.

Gain Attention

- Describe a product feature, present a testimonial, make a startling statement, or show the reader in an action setting.
- Offer something valuable, promise the reader a result, or pose a stimulating question.
- Suggest a solution to a problem, offer a relevant anecdote, use the receiver's name, or mention a meaningful current event.

Build Interest

- Describe the product or service in terms of what it does for the reader. Connect cold facts with warm feelings and needs.
- Use rational appeals if the product or service is expensive, long-lasting, or important to health, security, and financial success. Use emotional appeals to suggest status, ego, or sensual feelings.
- Explain how the product or service can save or make money, reduce effort, improve health, produce pleasure, or boost status.

Reduce Resistance

- Counter anticipated reluctance with testimonials, money-back guarantees, attractive warranties, trial offers, or free samples.
- Build credibility with results of performance tests, polls, or awards.
- If price is not a selling feature, describe it in small units *(only 99 cents an issue)*, show it as savings, or tell how it compares favorably with that of the competition.

Motivate Action

- Close by repeating a central selling point and describing an easy-to-take action.
- Prompt the reader to act immediately with a gift, incentive, limited offer, deadline, or guarantee of satisfaction.
- Put the strongest motivator in a postscript.
- In e-mails include an opportunity to opt out.

Comparing Persuasion in High- and Low-Context Cultures

LEARNING OBJECTIVE 6
Compare effective persuasion techniques in high- and low-context cultures.

The explosion of global communication, transportation, and marketing, along with the continuing migration of people, has moved all of us closer to a global society. As a business communicator, you can expect to interact with people from different cultures both at home and abroad. To be effective, as discussed in Chapter 3, you must be aware of your own culture. In addition, you should learn about other cultures to better understand how to be effective and to avoid confusion and miscommunication. What works in a low-context culture such as the United States may not be as effective in a high-context culture such as China.

Being Persuasive in High-Context Cultures

Countries in Asia, Africa, South America, and much of the Middle East are considered *high context.* As you learned in Chapter 3, high-context cultures generally value group sense rather than individualism. In such cultures, much information is not explicit; that is, it is not transmitted as words in a message. Meaning may be conveyed by clues in the situational context. Advertisements in high-context cultures are often indirect, polite, modest, and ambiguous. Even business messages can be so subtle that the meaning is unclear. Advertisements tend to emphasize harmony and beauty. For example, pictures of butterflies, flowers, nature scenes, and cultural artifacts are often seen on Japanese Web sites. Because of the respect for harmony and politeness, direct comparisons in persuasive messages are considered in bad taste. Nike advertisements in Japan would not mention its superior styling compared to Reebok or another named brand.

In high-context cultures, advertisements, Web sites, and sales letters such as that shown in Figure 10.8 may be characterized by the following:

How are persuasive efforts in high-context cultures characterized?

- **Indirectness.** Use of indirect expressions (such as *perhaps, probably, somewhat*). Preference for softened words (*would appreciate* rather than *must* or *expect*). Aversion to blunt hard-sell tactics and long, verbose messages.
- **Politeness.** Expressions of politeness, use of honorifics *(Esteemed* and *Revered Customer),* flowery language, wishful requests (*we hope)*, and overall humility.
- **Soft-sell approach.** Use of simple facts without embellishment or superlatives. Web sites may feature an entertainment theme to promote products. Emphasis on harmony.
- **Relationship appeal.** Attempts to establish a long-term relationship.
- **Collectivist view.** Emphasis on *we* and *our* rather than on *I* or the "you" view.

FIGURE 10.8 Sales Message From High-Context Culture (English translation)

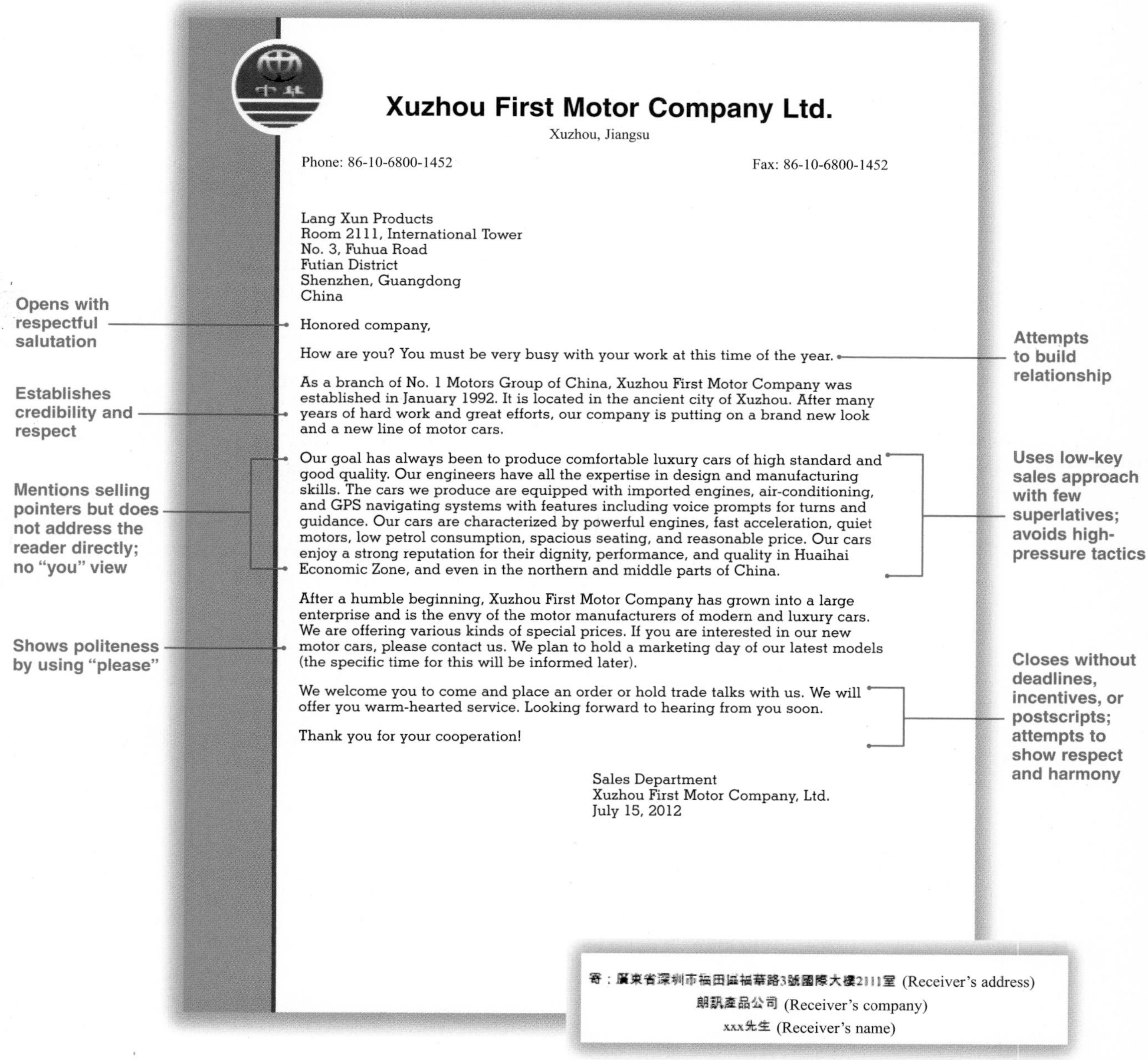

Xuzhou First Motor Company Ltd.
Xuzhou, Jiangsu

Phone: 86-10-6800-1452 Fax: 86-10-6800-1452

Lang Xun Products
Room 2111, International Tower
No. 3, Fuhua Road
Futian District
Shenzhen, Guangdong
China

Honored company,

How are you? You must be very busy with your work at this time of the year.

As a branch of No. 1 Motors Group of China, Xuzhou First Motor Company was established in January 1992. It is located in the ancient city of Xuzhou. After many years of hard work and great efforts, our company is putting on a brand new look and a new line of motor cars.

Our goal has always been to produce comfortable luxury cars of high standard and good quality. Our engineers have all the expertise in design and manufacturing skills. The cars we produce are equipped with imported engines, air-conditioning, and GPS navigating systems with features including voice prompts for turns and guidance. Our cars are characterized by powerful engines, fast acceleration, quiet motors, low petrol consumption, spacious seating, and reasonable price. Our cars enjoy a strong reputation for their dignity, performance, and quality in Huaihai Economic Zone, and even in the northern and middle parts of China.

After a humble beginning, Xuzhou First Motor Company has grown into a large enterprise and is the envy of the motor manufacturers of modern and luxury cars. We are offering various kinds of special prices. If you are interested in our new motor cars, please contact us. We plan to hold a marketing day of our latest models (the specific time for this will be informed later).

We welcome you to come and place an order or hold trade talks with us. We will offer you warm-hearted service. Looking forward to hearing from you soon.

Thank you for your cooperation!

Sales Department
Xuzhou First Motor Company, Ltd.
July 15, 2012

寄：廣東省深圳市福田區福華路3號國際大樓2111室 (Receiver's address)
朗訊產品公司 (Receiver's company)
xxx先生 (Receiver's name)

Analyzing a High-Context Sales Letter. Sales letters in high-context cultures definitely aim to be persuasive, but the tone and strategy are different from the techniques discussed thus far in this chapter. The letter from the Xuzhou First Motor Company in China, shown in Figure 10.8, promotes its renovated facilities and new line of motor cars. The formal salutation (*Honored company*) reflects respect for the addressee. The first sentences in the letter (*How are you? You must be very busy with your work at this time of the year*) are quite different from typical U.S. sales letters. These leisurely opening sentences attempt to build a relationship. They signal that the company is interested in more than a quick sale. Although such an opening might be considered naïve in this country, it is seen differently in China. The motor company wants to appear friendly and recognizes that all business dealings proceed more smoothly when the goal is a long-term relationship.

To establish its credibility, the company points out that it is part of a large national motor car manufacturer. This ensures that readers will respect the company because it is not a small-time facility, lacking the skills, expertise, and automobile models of a big company. To build interest, the letter uses facts and details about its cars (*imported engines, air-conditioning, GPS navigation systems*). The letter touts the cars' features (*powerful engines, fast acceleration, quiet motors, low petrol consumption, spacious seating, reasonable price*). Notice, however, that the letter neither uses superlatives (*the biggest and best GPS system in today's cars!*), nor attempts to focus on benefits to the reader. No effort is made to develop a "you" view; benefits are described in general terms. The entire approach is low-key, rather than focusing on appeals to the reader. Notice, too, that most references are to *our* and *we*, which are appropriate in a collectivist culture.

In reducing resistance, the letter again refers to the motor company's size (*a large enterprise*) and its reputation (*the envy of motor manufacturers*). However, the statements are all fairly formal, dignified, polite, and bland. One clear contrast with sales letters in this country and in other low-context cultures is the lack of high pressure. Notice that the closing is genteel and friendly (*we welcome you to come and place an order*). Again, it attempts to build a relationship, assuring *warm-hearted service*. This sales letter lacks high-pressure incentives, deadlines, and P.S. statements hammering home important reader benefits. The letter is also fairly short, contrasting with longer sales letters in this country. In low-context cultures, writers tend to use more words to ensure that they can be precise in explaining and persuading.

Being Persuasive in Low-Context Cultures

How are persuasive efforts in low-context cultures characterized?

Countries in Northern Europe, North America, Scandinavia, and Australia are classified as *low context*. As discussed in Chapter 3, low-context cultures tend to be logical, linear, and action oriented. Information is explicit and formalized in written documents. People in low-context cultures use words precisely and expect them to be understood literally. They rely less on the unspoken context and nonverbal clues to convey important messages. They are comfortable with direct, explicit, and confrontational appeals in advertising and persuasion. Sales letters, advertisements, Web sites, and other persuasive efforts within low-context cultures may be characterized by the following:

- **Directness.** Expression of requests may be made directly without attempts to use soft wording. Precision in expression is preferred.
- **Superlatives.** Use of superlatives such as *The lowest price, highest quality, and best customer service on the planet!* Little hesitation to "toot one's own horn." General acceptance of puffery. No expectation of humility or modesty in advertising or sales.
- **Hard-sell approach.** Aggressive promotions, incentives, testimonials, deadlines, and an emphasis on product advantages using explicit comparisons with competitors.
- **Short-term goal.** Little attempt to establish long-term relationships. Tendency to develop transitory personal relationships.
- **"You" view.** Emphasis on projecting benefits to an individual, instead of focusing on group perspectives.

As globalization expands and the huge markets of China and India open up, Western business practices may become more dominant even in high-context cultures. We may see more evidence of low-context strategies in sales messages in high-context cultures. Underlying cultural differences, however, will continue to exert considerable influence. Savvy business communicators who understand the powerful influence of high- and low-context cultures will always have a distinct advantage.

Developing Persuasive Press Releases

LEARNING OBJECTIVE 7
Understand basic patterns and techniques in developing persuasive press releases.

Press (news) releases announce information about your company to the media: new products, new managers, new location, sponsorships, participation in community projects, awards given or received, joint ventures, donations, or seminars and demonstrations. Naturally, you hope that this news will be published and provide good publicity for your company. But this kind of largely

FIGURE 10.9 Press Release Announces Chocolate Shop

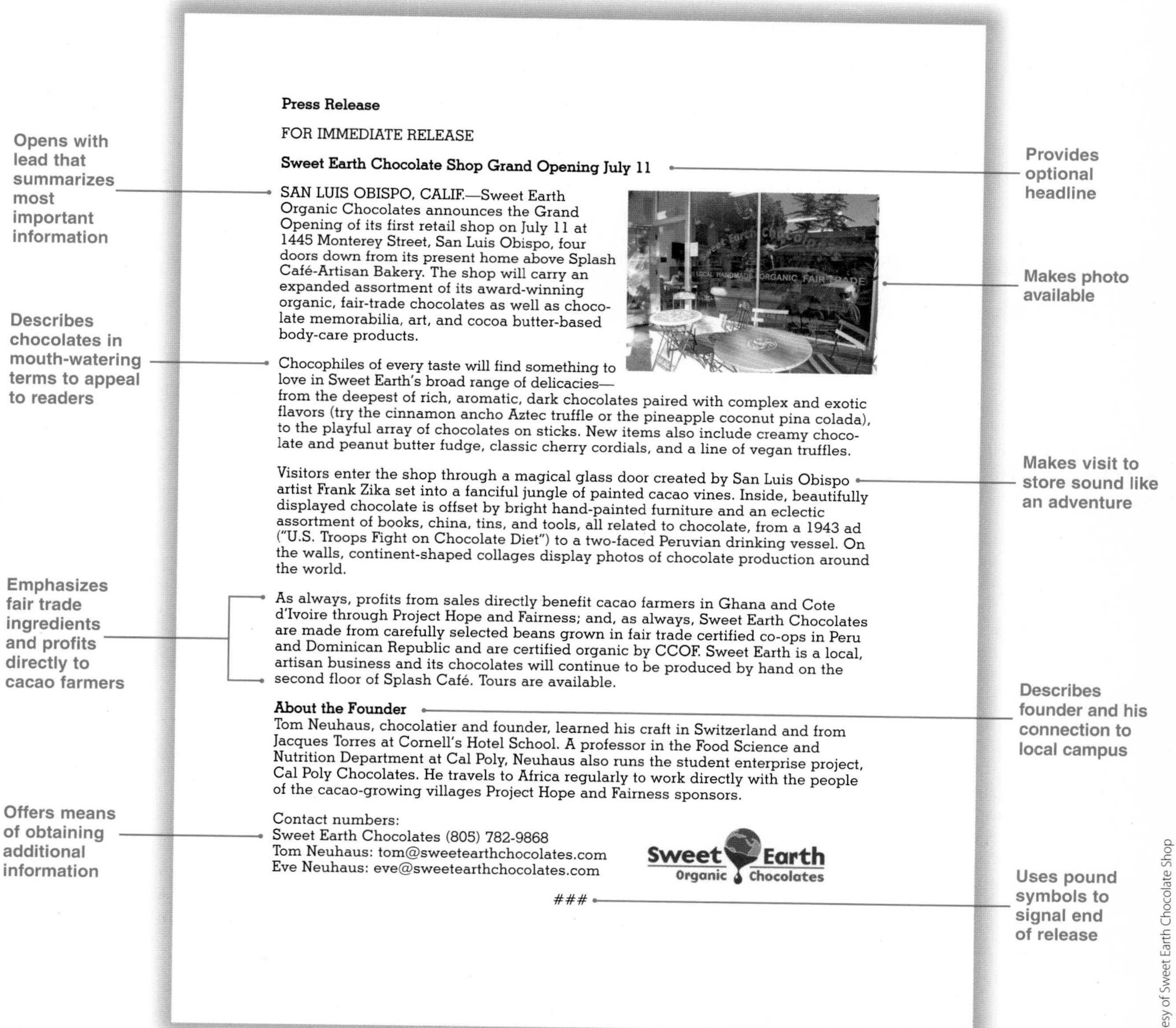
Press Release

FOR IMMEDIATE RELEASE

Sweet Earth Chocolate Shop Grand Opening July 11

SAN LUIS OBISPO, CALIF.—Sweet Earth Organic Chocolates announces the Grand Opening of its first retail shop on July 11 at 1445 Monterey Street, San Luis Obispo, four doors down from its present home above Splash Café-Artisan Bakery. The shop will carry an expanded assortment of its award-winning organic, fair-trade chocolates as well as chocolate memorabilia, art, and cocoa butter-based body-care products.

Chocophiles of every taste will find something to love in Sweet Earth's broad range of delicacies—from the deepest of rich, aromatic, dark chocolates paired with complex and exotic flavors (try the cinnamon ancho Aztec truffle or the pineapple coconut pina colada), to the playful array of chocolates on sticks. New items also include creamy chocolate and peanut butter fudge, classic cherry cordials, and a line of vegan truffles.

Visitors enter the shop through a magical glass door created by San Luis Obispo artist Frank Zika set into a fanciful jungle of painted cacao vines. Inside, beautifully displayed chocolate is offset by bright hand-painted furniture and an eclectic assortment of books, china, tins, and tools, all related to chocolate, from a 1943 ad ("U.S. Troops Fight on Chocolate Diet") to a two-faced Peruvian drinking vessel. On the walls, continent-shaped collages display photos of chocolate production around the world.

As always, profits from sales directly benefit cacao farmers in Ghana and Cote d'Ivoire through Project Hope and Fairness; and, as always, Sweet Earth Chocolates are made from carefully selected beans grown in fair trade certified co-ops in Peru and Dominican Republic and are certified organic by CCOF. Sweet Earth is a local, artisan business and its chocolates will continue to be produced by hand on the second floor of Splash Café. Tours are available.

About the Founder
Tom Neuhaus, chocolatier and founder, learned his craft in Switzerland and from Jacques Torres at Cornell's Hotel School. A professor in the Food Science and Nutrition Department at Cal Poly, Neuhaus also runs the student enterprise project, Cal Poly Chocolates. He travels to Africa regularly to work directly with the people of the cacao-growing villages Project Hope and Fairness sponsors.

Contact numbers:
Sweet Earth Chocolates (805) 782-9868
Tom Neuhaus: tom@sweetearthchocolates.com
Eve Neuhaus: eve@sweetearthchocolates.com

###

Opens with lead that summarizes most important information
Describes chocolates in mouth-watering terms to appeal to readers
Emphasizes fair trade ingredients and profits directly to cacao farmers
Offers means of obtaining additional information
Provides optional headline
Makes photo available
Makes visit to store sound like an adventure
Describes founder and his connection to local campus
Uses pound symbols to signal end of release
LOCAL HANDMADE ORGANIC FAIR TRADE
Sweet Earth
Organic Chocolates

Courtesy of Sweet Earth Chocolate Shop

What are press releases, and how are they usually organized?

self-serving information is not always appealing to magazine and newspaper editors or to TV producers. To get them to read beyond the first sentence, try these suggestions:

- Open with an attention-getting lead or a summary of the important facts.
- Include answers to the five *W*s and one *H* (*who, what, when, where, why*, and *how*) in the article—but not all in the first sentence!
- Appeal to the audience of the target media. Emphasize reader benefits written in the style of the focus publication or newscast.
- Present the most important information early, followed by supporting information. Don't put your best ideas last because they may be chopped off or ignored.
- Make the release visually appealing. Limit the text to one or two double-spaced pages with attractive formatting.
- Look and sound credible—no typos, no imaginative spelling or punctuation, no factual errors.

The most important ingredient of a press release, of course, is *news*. Articles that merely plug products end up in the circular file. The press release in Figure 10.9 announced the grand opening of Sweet Earth Chocolate Shop in the college town of San Luis Obispo, California. Sweet Earth features hand-made organic, fair-trade chocolates as well as chocolate memorabilia, art, and cocoa butter-based body care products.

Zooming In — YOUR TURN

Applying Your Skills at Hands on Miami

As a communication intern at Hands on Miami, you have been learning the ropes about publicizing and organizing programs. One day your boss sees a newspaper article and says to you, "Listen to this! Did you know that service organizations can earn up to $10 for used print cartridges and up to $20 for recycled cell phones? This sounds like a terrific idea for raising funds for our Community Bridges program. Why don't you do some research and find out more about this. Then I'd like you to draft a message that we could send to Miami businesses letting them know how they can help our programs. This is a good chance for you to try out your persuasion skills!"

In your research you discover that 300 million ink cartridges are discarded every year. You are horrified to learn that the industrial plastics in these cartridges take a thousand years to decompose. You find out that 40,000 tons of plastic could be diverted from landfills every year if ink cartridges were recycled. Your research also reveals that hundreds of thousands of cell phones are no longer being used as new models flood the market. Where do all of those unused cell phones go?

In doing your research, you discover that cartridges and cell phones may be dropped off at recycling centers. They can also be mailed in, or they can even be picked up. The best way for businesses to learn how to do this is to visit **http://www.miamidaderecycling.org** or call 1-800-534-9989 for details.

Your boss has asked you to focus on raising funds for Community Bridges, one of the flexible calendar programs at Hands on Miami. Volunteers like this program because it allows them to choose their hours and be personally involved. Some volunteers provide food service at the Miami Rescue Mission. Some are part of work crews to restore mangroves to wetlands, and those with carpentry skills enjoy working with Habitat for Humanity. Some volunteers help maintain the Miami Beach Botanical Gardens. One group of business professionals reads bedtime stories at the Salvation Army. Other volunteers care for animals at the humane society. These are just a few of the many volunteer services that make Miami a better place to live and work.

© Jeff Greenberg/PhotoEdit

Your Task

In teams or individually, draft a persuasive letter to be sent to 50 or more Miami area businesses. Ask the businesses to save used ink cartridges and old cell phones for Hands on Miami. As you compose your letter, follow the plan described in this chapter. You know the benefits that Hands on Miami will enjoy, but what benefits can you cite for the receiver? What incentive or final idea can you use to motivate action? Use your imagination, but stay within reason.

Figure 10.9 illustrates many good techniques for creating effective press releases. The announcement provides a headline, interesting photo, and descriptions of the shop's chocolate delicacies ranging from cinnamon Aztec truffles to pineapple-coconut pina coladas and vegan truffles. The best press releases focus on information that appeals to a targeted audience. To attract college students and educated townspeople, this press release describes the shop's use of fair trade ingredients with profits from sales directly benefitting cacao farmers in Ghana and Cote d'Ivorie. The press release also makes a visit to Sweet Earth Chocolates sound like an adventure by featuring a magical glass door, local art works, and chocolate memorabilia.

Newspapers and magazines are more likely to publish a press release that is informative, interesting, and helpful. The Web sites of many companies today provide readily available press information including releases and photos.

Want to do well on tests and excel in your course?
Go to **www.meguffey.com** for helpful interactive resources.

- **Review the Chapter 10 PowerPoint slides to prepare for the first quiz.**

Summary of Learning Objectives

1 Define the concept of persuasion, identify effective and ineffective persuasive techniques, and apply the 3-x-3 writing process to persuasive messages. Persuasion may be defined as the ability to use argument or discussion to influence an individual's beliefs or actions. Effective persuasive techniques include establishing credibility, making a reasonable and precise request, tying facts to benefits, recognizing the power of loss, expecting and overcoming resistance, sharing solutions, and compromising. Persuasion is more effective if one avoids sounding preachy or parental, doesn't pull rank, softens the tone when persuading upward, sounds enthusiastic, and presents a positive and likeable image. The first step in the writing process for a persuasive message is deciding what you want the receiver to do or think. The second step involves thinking of ways to adapt the message to the audience. The writer must collect information and organize it into an appropriate strategy. An indirect strategy is best if the audience might resist the request.

2 Explain the four major elements in successful persuasive messages and how to blend those elements into effective and ethical business messages. The most effective persuasive messages include four major elements: gaining attention, building interest, reducing resistance, and motivating action. Writers gain attention by opening with a problem, unexpected statement, reader benefit, compliment, related fact, stimulating question, or similar device. They build interest with facts, expert opinions, examples, details, and direct and indirect reader benefits. They reduce resistance by anticipating objections and presenting counterarguments. They conclude by motivating a specific action and making it easy for the reader to respond. Skilled communicators avoid distortion, exaggeration, and deception when making persuasive arguments.

3 Write persuasive messages that request favors and actions, make claims, and deliver complaints. In asking for favors and actions, writers must know exactly what they are requesting and anticipate the receiver's reaction. The opening may begin indirectly with a problem description, an unexpected statement, a compliment, praise, related facts, a stimulating question, or a reader benefit. Interest is built with facts, statistics, examples, testimonials, and details. Claims and complaints require an objective, unemotional tone and proof of the validity of the request. Resistance can be reduced by anticipating objections and providing counterarguments. Action is motivated by stating exactly what is to be done and by when. Add a deadline date if necessary and express appreciation.

4 Write persuasive messages within organizations. Before writing a persuasive business message, writers should profile the audience, know exactly what the receiver is to do or believe, and anticipate resistance. To gain attention, the writer might make the receiver aware of a problem, use a startling statement, provide a significant fact related to the request, describe possible benefits, ask a stimulating question, or offer compliments and praise. Facts, statistics, examples, and specific details build a foundation for the request. Receivers are interested in direct benefits such as how agreeing to the request will help them solve problems or improve

Are you ready? Get more practice at **www.meguffey.com**

their work and career. Recognizing weaknesses in the proposal and offering well-reasoned counterarguments are effective ways to reduce resistance. In messages flowing downward, avoid sounding preachy or overly authoritarian. In messages flowing upward, consider making a strong dollars-and-cents appeal for requests involving budgets. Persuasive messages should end with a specific request and a deadline if appropriate.

5 **Write effective and ethical print and e-mail sales messages.** Careful analysis of the product or service is necessary before one composes a sales message. Effective sales messages usually begin with an attention-getting statement that is short, honest, relevant, and stimulating. Simple language describing appropriate appeals builds interest. Testimonials, a money-back guarantee, a free trial, or some other device can reduce resistance. A gift, incentive, deadline, or other device can motivate action. E-marketing messages should be sent only to opt-in receivers. Writers of effective e-mails begin with a catchy subject line, keep the main information "above the fold," make the message short and focused, convey urgency, sprinkle testimonials throughout, and provide a means for opting out.

6 **Compare effective persuasion techniques in high- and low-context cultures.** Sales letters, advertisements, Web sites, and other persuasive efforts aimed at high-context cultures often exhibit politeness, indirectness, a soft-sell approach, and attempts to establish a long-term client relationship. Persuasive messages in low-context cultures, on the other hand, may be characterized by directness, superlatives, and a hard-sell approach.

7 **Understand basic patterns and techniques in developing persuasive press releases.** Press releases usually open with an attention-getting lead or summary of the important facts. They attempt to answer the questions *who, what, when, where, why*, and *how*. They are written carefully to appeal to the audience of the target media. The best press releases present the most important information early, are visually appealing, and look and sound credible.

Chapter Review

1. What is persuasion? (Obj. 1)
2. What four questions are receivers of persuasive messages likely to be asking themselves? (Obj. 2)
3. What are the four parts of successful persuasive messages? (Obj. 2)
4. List six ways to gain attention in a persuasive message. (Obj. 2)
5. Why is a written favor request or action request often more effective than a face-to-face request? (Obj.3)
6. Name five of more examples of typical situations requiring persuasive claim messages. (Obj. 3)
7. How can you reduce resistance in requesting favors, making claims, and delivering complaints? (Obj. 3)
8. When is persuasion necessary in business messages flowing downward in an organization? (Obj. 4)
9. When might persuasion be necessary in messages flowing upward? (Obj. 4)
10. Before composing a letter to sell a product, what should the writer do? (Obj. 5)
11. Name eight or more ways to attract attention in the opening of a sales message. (Obj. 5)
12. How can a writer motivate action in a sales letter? (Obj. 5)
13. Name four areas of the world where the culture is generally considered to be high context. Name four areas of the world where the culture is generally considered to be low context. (Obj. 6)
14. How do persuasive messages in high- and low-context cultures differ? (Obj. 6)
15. List five or more topics that an organization might feature in a press release. (Obj. 7)

Critical Thinking

1. The word *persuasion* turns some people off. What negative connotations can it have? (Obj. 1)
2. What are some of the underlying motivations that prompt individuals to agree to requests that do not directly benefit themselves or their organizations? (Obj. 2)
3. Why is it important to know your needs and have documentation when you make requests of superiors? (Obj. 4)
4. How are direct-mail sales messages and e-mail sales messages similar, and how are they different? (Obj. 5)
5. **Ethical Issue:** What is puffery, and how can it be justified in marketing messages? Consider the following: Dr. Phil calls himself "America's most trusted relationship counselor." Rush Limbaugh claims to be "America's anchorman." Sony's Cyber-Shot camera advertisement says "Make time stand still."

Are you ready? Get more practice at **www.meguffey.com**

Activities

Note: All Documents for Analysis are provided at **www.meguffey.com** for you to download and revise.

10.1 Document for Analysis: Going Bananas at 7-Eleven (Objs. 1–3)

Your Task. Analyze the following poorly written persuasive e-mail request. List its weaknesses. If your instructor directs, revise it using the suggestions you learned in this chapter.

To: Members of the 7-Eleven Franchise Owners Association of Chicagoland
From: Nicholas Barajas <nicholas.barajas@hotmail.com>
Subject: Can You Believe Plastic-Wrapped Bananas?
Cc:
Bcc:

Hey, have you heard about this new thing coming at us? As a 7-Eleven franchise owner and member of the 7-Eleven Franchise Owners Association of Chicagoland, I am seriously put off about this move to wrap our bananas in plastic. Sure, it would extend their shelf life to five days. And I know that our customers want yellow–not brown—bananas. But wrapping them in plastic?? I mentioned this at home, and my teenage daughter immediately turned up her nose and said, "A banana wrapped in plastic? Eeeyooo! Do we really need more plastic clogging up the environment?" She's been studying sustainability and said that more plastic packaging is not a sustainable solution to our problem.

I realize that we 7-Eleven franchisees are increasingly dependent on fresh food sales as cigarette sales tank. But plastic-wrapped bananas is going too far, even if the wrapping slows ripening. As members of the 7-Eleven Franchise Owners Association, we have to do something. I think we could insist that our supplier Fresh Del Monte come up with a wrapper that's biodegradable. On the other hand, extending the shelf life of bananas cuts the carbon footprint by cutting down all those deliveries to our stores.

We have a meeting of franchisees coming up on January 20. Let's resist this banana thing!

Nick

10.2 Document for Analysis: Weak Favor Request (Obj. 3)

Your Task. Analyze the following poorly written invitation. List its weaknesses. If your instructor directs, revise the letter. Add appropriate information if needed.

Current date

Ms. Danielle Watkins
The Beverly Hills Hotel
9641 Sunset Boulevard
Beverly Hills, CA 90210

Dear Ms. Watkins:

We know you are a very busy hospitality professional as chef at the Beverly Hills Hotel, but we would like you to make a presentation to the San Francisco chapter of the National Restaurant Association. I was asked to write you since I am program chair.

I heard that you made a good presentation at your local chapter in Los Angeles recently. I think you gave a talk called "Avoiding the Seven Cardinal Sins in Food Service" or something like that. Whatever it was, I'm sure we would like to hear the same or a similar presentation. All restaurant operators are interested in doing what we can to avoid potential problems involving discrimination, safety at work, how we hire people, etc. As you well know, operating a fast-paced restaurant is frustrating—even on a good day. We are all in a gigantic rush from opening the door early in the morning to shutting it again after the last customer has gone. It's a rat race and easy to fall into the trap with food service faults that push a big operation into trouble.

Enclosed please find a list of questions that our members listed. We would like you to talk in the neighborhood of 45 minutes. Our June 10 meeting will be in the Oak Room of the Westin St. Francis Hotel in San Francisco and dinner begins at 7 p.m.

How can we get you to come to San Francisco? We can only offer you an honorarium of $200, but we would pay for any travel expenses. You can expect a large crowd of restaurateurs who are known for hooting and hollering when they hear good stuff! As you can see, we are a rather informal group. Hope you can join us!

Sincerely,

10.3 Document for Analysis: Weak Persuasive Memo Flowing Upward (Obj. 4)

Your Task. Analyze the following memo, which suffers from many writing faults. List its weaknesses. If your instructor directs, revise the letter.

DATE: Current
TO: Bryanna Mazzetta, Vice President, Marketing
FROM: Luke Downey, Exhibit Manager
SUBJECT: Possible Change for Saving Money

We always try our best to meet customers and sell Worldclass Trainer equipment at numerous trade shows. But instead of expanding our visits to these trade shows, the company continues to cut back the number that we attend. And we have fewer staff members attending. I know that you have been asking us to find ways to reduce costs, but I don't think we are going about it right.

With increased airfares and hotel charges, my staff has tried to find ways to live within our very tight budget. Yet, we are being asked to find other ways to reduce our costs. I'm currently thinking ahead to the big Las Vegas trade show coming up in September.

One area where we could make a change is in the gift that we give away. In the past we have presented booth visitors with a nine-color T-shirt that is silk-screened and gorgeous. But it comes at a cost of $23 for each and every one of these beauties from a top-name designer. To save money, I suggest that we try a $6 T-shirt made in China, which is reasonably presentable. It's got our name on it, and, after all, folks just use these shirts for workouts. Who cares if it is a fancy silk-screened T-shirt or a functional Chinese one that has "Worldclass Trainer" plastered on the chest? Because we give away 2,000 T-shirts at our largest show, we could save big bucks by dumping the designer shirt. But we have to act quickly. I've enclosed a cheap one for you to see.

Let me know what you think.

10.4 Document for Analysis: Poor Claim Letter (Obj. 3)

Your Task. Analyze the following poorly written claim letter. List its weaknesses. If your instructor directs, revise it.

Current date

Mr. Jason M. Amato
TEK Copier Solutions
13429 North 59th Avenue
Glendale, AZ 85307

Dear Sir:

I hate to write to you with a complaint, but my company purchased four of your Multifunction SX500 photocopiers, and we've had nothing but trouble ever since.

Your salesperson, Gary Kazan, assured us that the Multifunction SX500 could easily handle our volume of 3,000 copies a day. This seemed strange since the sales brochure said that the Multifunction SX500 was meant for 500 copies a day. But we put our faith in Mr. Kazan. What a mistake! Our four SX copiers are down constantly, and we can't go on like this. Because they are still under warranty, they eventually get repaired. But we are losing considerable business in downtime.

Because your Mr. Kazan has been less than helpful, I telephoned the district manager, Victor Martineau. I suggested that we trade in our Multifunction SX500 copiers (which we got for $2,500 each) on two Multifunction XX800 models (at $13,500 each). However, Mr. Martineau said he would have to charge 50 percent depreciation on our SX500 copiers. What a rip-off! I think that 20 percent depreciation is more reasonable since we've had the machines only three months. Mr. Martineau said he would get back to me, and I haven't heard from him since.

Now I'm forced to write to your headquarters because I have no faith in either Ms. Kazan or Mr. Martineau, and I need to see some action on these machines. If you understood anything about business, you would see what a sweet deal I'm offering you. I'm willing to stick with your company and purchase your most expensive model—but I can't take such a steep loss on the SX500 copiers. These copiers are relatively new; you should be able to sell them with no trouble. And think of all the money you will save by not having your repair technicians making constant trips to service our underpowered Multifunction SX500 copiers! Please let me hear from you immediately.

Sincerely yours,

10.5 Persuasive Favor/Action Request: Inviting an Alumna to Speak (Obj. 3)

E-mail

As public relations director for the Business and Accounting Association on your campus, you have been asked to find a keynote speaker for the first meeting of the school year. The owner of a successful local firm, TempHelp4You, is an alumna of your university. You think not only that many students would enjoy learning about how she started her business, but also that some might like to sign up with her temporary help agency. She would need to prepare a 30-minute speech and take questions after the talk. The event will be held from noon until 1:30 p.m. on a date of your choosing in Branford Hall. You can offer her lunch at the event and provide her with a parking permit that she can pick up at the information kiosk at the main entrance to your campus. You need to have her response by a deadline you set.

Your Task. Write a direct approach e-mail to Marion Minter in which you ask her to speak at your club's meeting. Send it to *mminter@temphelp4you.com*.

10.6 Persuasive Favor/Action Request: Asking Beijing to Use Excel (Objs. 3, 6)

Intercultural

Mario Franchini, regional sales manager for a multinational manufacturer, is always in a hurry and doesn't take the time to write careful messages. As his assistant, you sometimes revise messages for him. Today he asks you to look over his message to Zhu Chen, regional sales manager for the company's prosperous branch in Beijing. On his way out the door, Mario says to you, "Please fix up the following memo. Make it sound better!"

> Hi there, Zhu! I know you haven't heard from me 4 a while, so don't hit the panic button! I need you to do me a big favor. I'm going to skip the bull and drive right to the point. I need your sales figures to be submitted in Excel spreadsheets. You could hit a home run by zeroing in on the sales for your region and zapping them to us in a better format. We just can't use the ledger account forms you usually send. They may work for your office in Beijing, but they won't fly here in Seattle. I'm counting on you to come through for me by using Excel in submitting your future sales figures. You already have the software available through our home office intranet. Just download it. You will see it's easy as pie to learn. When you send your next quarterly figures at the end of September, I expect to see them in Excel. Chow!

Your Task. You know that messages to your office from Beijing are usually more formal and often begin with a friendly greeting. You decide to try out your intercultural skills in writing a better favor request. For your boss's signature, revise this message using memo format. After approval, the memo will be faxed.

10.7 Persuasive Favor/Action Request: Borrowing Suits for Interviews (Obj. 3)

You saw an interesting article describing a Suitable Suits program at Barnard College. Its College of Career Development kept a closet filled with 21 crisp black suits that students could borrow for job interviews. Students made an appointment with the office and agreed to dry clean the suits before returning them. At Barnard the program was paid for with a grant from a prominent financial firm.[18] You think that a Suitable Suits program is worth exploring with your dean.

Your Task. Write a persuasive letter requesting an appointment with your dean to discuss a Suitable Suits program at your school. You don't have all the answers and you are not sure how such a program would operate, but you think the idea is worth discussing. Can you convince the dean to see you?

10.8 Persuasive Favor/Action Request: A Helping Hand for College Expenses (Obj. 3)

Team

After working a few years, you would like to extend your college education on a part-time basis. You know that your education can benefit your employer, but you can't really afford the fees for tuition and books. You have heard that many companies offer reimbursement for fees and books when employees complete approved courses with a grade of C or higher.

Your Task. In teams discuss the best way to approach an employer whom you wish to persuade to start a tuition/books reimbursement program. How could such a program help the employer? Remember that the most successful requests help receivers see what's in it for them. What objections might your employer raise? How can you counter them? After discussing strategies in teams, write a team memo or individual memos to your boss (for a company where you now work or one with which you are familiar). Persuade her or him to act on your action request.

10.9 Persuasive Favor/Action Request: Dear Senator or Representative (Obj. 3)

Web

Assume you are upset about an issue, and you want your representative or senator to know your position. Choose a national issue about which you feel strongly: student loans, social security depletion, human rights in other countries, the federal deficit, federal safety regulations for employees, environmental protection, gun control, taxation of married couples, finding a cure for obesity, or some other area regulated by Congress.

How does one write to a congressional representative? For the best results, consider these tips:

a. Use the proper form of address (*The Honorable John Smith, Dear Senator Smith* or *The Honorable Joan Doe, Dear Representative Doe*).
b. Identify yourself as a member of his or her state or district.
c. Immediately state your position (*I urge you to support/oppose . . . because . . .*).
d. Present facts and illustrations and explain how they affect you personally. If legislation were enacted, how would you or your organization be better or worse off? Avoid generalities.
e. Offer to provide further information.
f. Keep the message polite, constructive, and brief (one page, tops).

Your Task. Search the Web to obtain your congressional representative's address. Try the search term *contacting Congress*. You should be able to find e-mail and land addresses, along with fax and telephone numbers. Remember that although e-mail and fax messages are fast, they don't carry as much influence as personal letters. Moreover, congressional representatives are having trouble responding to the overload of e-mails they receive. Decide whether it would be better to send an e-mail or a letter.

10.10 Persuasive Favor/Action Request: School Vending Machines Become Weighty Problem (Obj. 3)

Team Web

© Glow Images/Photolibrary

"If I start to get huge, then, yeah, I'll cut out the chips and Coke," says 17-year-old Nicole O'Neill, as she munches sour-cream-and-onion potato chips and downs a cold can of soda fresh from the snack machine. Most days her lunch comes from a vending machine. The trim high school junior, however, isn't too concerned about how junk food affects her weight or overall health. Although she admits she would prefer a granola bar or fruit, few healthful selections are available from school vending machines.

Vending machines loaded with soft drinks and snacks are increasingly under attack in schools and lunchrooms. Some school boards, however, see them as cash cows. In Gresham, Oregon, the school district is considering a lucrative soft drink contract. If it signs an exclusive 12-year agreement with Coca-Cola to allow vending machines at Gresham High School, the school district will receive $75,000 up front. Then it will receive an additional $75,000 three years later. Commission sales on the 75-cent drinks will bring in an additional $322,000 over the 12-year contract, provided the school sells 67,000 cans and bottles every year. In the past the vending machine payments supported student body activities such as sending students to choir concerts and paying athletic participation fees. Vending machine funds also paid for an electronic reader board in front of the school and a sound system for the gym. The latest contract would bring in $150,000, which is already earmarked for new artificial turf on the school athletic field.

Coca-Cola's vending machines would dispense soft drinks, Fruitopia, Minute Maid juices, Powerade, and Dasani water. The hands-down student favorite, of course, is calorie-laden Coke. Because increasing childhood and adolescent obesity across the nation is a major health concern, the Gresham Parent Teacher Association (PTA) decided to oppose the contract. The PTA realizes that the school board is heavily influenced by the income generated from the Coca-Cola contract. It wonders what other school districts are doing about their vending machine contracts.

Your Task. As part of a PTA committee, you have been given the task of researching and composing a persuasive but concise (no more than one page) letter addressed to the school board. Use the Web or databases to locate articles that might help you develop arguments, alternatives, and counterarguments. Meet with your team to discuss your findings. Then, individually or as a group, write a letter to the Board of Directors, Gresham-Barlow School District, P.O. Box 310, Gresham, OR 97033.

10.11 Persuasive Claim: Overcharged and Unhappy (Obj. 3)

As regional manager for an electronics parts manufacturer, you and two other employees attended a conference in Nashville. You stayed at the Country Inn because your company recommends that employees use this hotel chain. Generally, your employees have liked their accommodations, and the rates have been within your company's budget.

Now, however, you are unhappy with the charges you see on your company's credit statement from Country Inn. When your department's administrative assistant made the reservations, she was assured that you would receive the weekend rates and that a hot breakfast—in the hotel restaurant, the Atrium—would be included in the rate. You hate those cold sweet rolls and instant coffee "continental" breakfasts, especially when you have to leave early and won't get another meal until afternoon. So you and the other two employees went to the restaurant and ordered a hot meal from the menu.

When you received the credit statement, though, you see a charge for $114 for three champagne buffet breakfasts in the Atrium. You hit the ceiling! For one thing, you didn't have a buffet breakfast and certainly no champagne. The three of you got there so early that no buffet had been set up. You ordered pancakes and sausage, and for this you were billed $35 each. You are outraged! What's worse, your company may charge you personally for exceeding the expected rates.

In looking back at this event, you remembered that other guests on your floor were having a "continental" breakfast in a lounge on your floor. Perhaps that's where the hotel expected all guests on the weekend rate to eat. However, your administrative assistant had specifically asked about this matter when she made the reservations, and she was told that you could order breakfast from the menu at the hotel's restaurant.

Your Task. You want to straighten out this matter, and you can't do it by telephone because you suspect that you will need a written record of this entire mess. Write a claim request to Customer Service, Country Inn, Inc., 428 Church Street, Nashville, TN 37219. Should you include a copy of the credit statement showing the charge?

10.12 Persuasive Claim: Legal Costs for Sharing a Slice of Heaven (Obj. 3)

Originally a shipbuilding village, the town of Mystic, Connecticut, captures the spirit of the nineteenth-century seafaring era. But it is best known for Mystic Pizza, a bustling local pizzeria featured in a movie that launched the film career of Julia Roberts. Today, customers line the sidewalk waiting to taste its pizza, called by some "a slice of Heaven."

Assume that you are the business manager for Mystic Pizza's owners. They were approached by an independent vendor who wants to use the Mystic Pizza name and secret recipes to distribute frozen pizza through grocery and convenience stores. As business manager, you worked with a law firm, Giordano, Murphy, and Associates. This firm was to draw up contracts regarding the use of Mystic Pizza's name and quality standards for the product. When you received the bill from Henry Giordano, you were flabbergasted. It itemized 38 hours of attorney preparation, at $400 per hour, and 55 hours of paralegal assistance, at $100 per hour. The bill also showed $415 for telephone calls, which might be accurate because Mr. Giordano had to talk with the owners, who were vacationing in Italy at the time. You seriously doubt, however, that an experienced attorney would require 38 hours to draw up the contracts in question. When you began checking, you discovered that excellent legal advice could be obtained for $200 an hour.

Your Task. Decide what you want to request, and then write a persuasive request to Henry Giordano, Attorney at Law, Giordano, Murphy, and Associates, 254 Sherborn Street, Boston, MA 02215. Include an end date and a reason for it.

10.13 Persuasive Claim: Botched Print Job (Obj. 3)

As president of Holiday Travel, you brought a very complex print job to the Jiffy Printers in Brighton, New York. It took almost 15 minutes to explain the particulars of this job to the printer. When you left, you wondered whether all of the instructions would be followed precisely. You even brought in your own special paper, which added to the cost of printing.

When you got the job back (a total of 1,500 sheets of paper) and returned to your office, you discovered a host of problems. One of the pages had 300 copies made on cheap 20-pound paper. This means that the printer must have run out of your special paper and substituted something else for one of the runs. The printer also made copies of your original photos and graphics, so that all the final prints were run from second-generation prints, which reduced the quality of the graphics enormously. What's more, many of the sheets were poorly or improperly cut. In short, the job was unacceptable.

Because you were desperate to complete the job, you allowed the print shop to repeat the job using its paper supply. When you inquired about the cost, the counter person Don was noncommittal. He said you would have to talk to the owner, who worked in the Rochester shop. The repeat print job turned out fairly well, and you paid the full price of $782. But you are unhappy, and Don sensed that Jiffy Printers would not see Holiday Travel again as a customer. He encouraged you to write to the owner and ask for an adjustment.

Your Task. Write a claim letter to Mr. Howard Moscatelli, Jiffy Printers, 3402 South Main Street, Rochester, NY 14634. What is a reasonable claim to make? Do you simply want to register your unhappiness, or do you want a refund? Supply any needed information.

10.14 Persuasive Claim: Honolulu Country Club Gets Scammed on Phony Toner Phoner (Obj. 3)

Heather W. was new to her job as administrative assistant at the Waialae Country Club in Honolulu. Alone in the office one morning, she answered a phone call from Rick, who said he was the country club's copier contractor. "Hey, look, Babydoll," Rick purred, "the price on the toner you use is about to go way up. I can offer you a great price on this toner if you order right now." Heather knew that the copy machine regularly needed toner, and she thought she should probably go ahead and place the order to save the country club some money. Ten days later two bottles of toner arrived, and Heather was pleased at the perfect timing. The copy machine needed it right away. Three weeks later Maureen, the bookkeeper, called to report a bill from Copy Machine Specialists for $960.43 for two bottles of toner. "What's going on here?" said Maureen. "We don't purchase supplies from this company, and this price is totally off the charts!"[19]

Heather spoke to the manager, Steven Tanaka, who immediately knew what had happened. He blamed himself for not training Heather. "Never, never order anything from a telephone solicitor, no matter how fast-talking or smooth he sounds," warned Steven. He outlined an office policy for future supplies purchases. Only certain people can authorize or finalize a purchase, and purchases require a confirmed price including shipping costs settled in advance. But what to do about this $960.43 bill? The country club had already begun to use the toner, although the current copies were looking faint and streaked.

Your Task. As Steven Tanaka, decide how to respond to this obvious scam. Should you pay the bill? Should you return the unused bottle? Write a persuasive claim to Copy Machine Specialists, 4320 Admiralty Way, Honolulu, HI 96643. Supply any details necessary.

10.15 Persuasive Organizational Message Flowing Upward: How About a Four-Day Week? (Obj. 4)

Team | Web

Gas prices are skyrocketing, and many companies and municipalities are switching to a four-day workweek to reduce gas consumption and air pollution. Compressing the workweek into four 10-hour days sounds pretty good to you. You would much prefer having Friday free to schedule medical appointments and take care of family business, in addition to leisurely three-day weekends.

As a manager at Skin Essentials, a mineral-based skin care products and natural cosmetics company, you are convinced that the company's 400 employees could switch to a four-day workweek with many resulting benefits. For one thing, they would save on gasoline and commute time. You know that many cities and companies have already implemented a four-day workweek with considerable success. You took a quick poll of immediate employees and managers and found that 80 percent thought that a four-day workweek was a good idea. One said, "This would be great! Think of what I could save on babysitting and lunches!"

Your Task. With a group of other managers, conduct research on the Web and discuss your findings. What are the advantages of a four-day workweek? What organizations have already tried it? What appeals could be used to persuade management to adopt a four-day workweek? What arguments could be expected, and how would you counter them? Individually or as a group, prepare a one-page persuasive memo addressed to Skin Essentials Management Council. Decide on a goal. Do you want to suggest a pilot study? Meet with management to present your ideas? Start a four-day workweek immediately?

10.16 Persuasive Organizational Message Flowing Upward: Providing Handheld GPS Devices to Hotel Guests (Obj. 4)

Always seeking to solve problems, you have a great idea for an amenity at the hotel where you work. Hotel guests often ask for directions to local restaurants or special local sights. But they sometimes get lost or exasperated when they can't find what they seek. Guests also go walking, jogging, or sightseeing and can't find their way back to the hotel.

As the assistant manager at an upscale hotel in your town or area, you saw a newspaper article about the five-star Rosewood hotel chain. It offers use of handheld GPS navigators free at select properties. You have a GPS device in your car, and you know how amazing it is when it can talk you right to your destination. Clearly, your hotel could distinguish itself competitively and be among the first to offer this new perk to guests. Rosewood hotels offering this service include The Carlyle (Manhattan), The Mansion on Turtle Creek (Dallas), and Hotel Crescent Court (Dallas).[20] La Jolla Shores, near San Diego, also offers this amenity.

You would like to convince your manager to offer this service. On the Web you discover that a Garmin nüvi 260 is just the right size. If a hotel guest is out jogging or sightseeing and loses the way, the guest can hit "home" and the GPS tells the direction back to the hotel from anywhere. The Garmin costs $250, which you think is not excessive. Although your manager is cost-conscious, he loves gadgets. You think that if the GPS device could attract just two guests per month, it would probably be worth it. You like the fact that when hotel guests at Rosewood hotels ask for directions, a concierge can plug in the desired location, hit "go," and the GPS will talk guests through the drive or walk until they arrive.

Your Task. Write a convincing message to Manager Martin Zatari. Before writing, decide what you want to ask. Should you ask for a meeting to discuss the proposal? Should you request a trial period in which you try out one or two GPS navigators? You haven't worked out all of the details of a GPS program, but you think the idea is worth talking about. You will need to gather information about a GPS device that might work for your purpose. Name specific restaurants or local attractions in your memo. What benefits can you suggest for your manager and for the hotel?

10.17 Persuasive Organizational Message Flowing Upward: An Apple a Day (Obj. 4)

During the recent economic downturn, Omni Hotels looked for ways to slice expenses. Omni operates 43 luxury hotels and resorts in leading business gateways and leisure destinations across North America. From exceptional golf and spa retreats to dynamic business settings, each Omni showcases the local flavor of the destination while featuring four-diamond services.

Omni Hotels ranks in the top three in "Highest in Guest Satisfaction Among Upscale Hotel Chains," according to J. D. Power. One signature amenity it has offered for years is a bowl of free apples in its lobbies. However, the practice of providing apples costs hundreds of thousands of dollars a year. They have to cut costs somewhere, and executives are debating whether to cut out apples as a way to save money with minimum impact on guests.

Omni Hotels prides itself on providing guests with superior service through The Power of One, a service program that provides associates the training and authority to make decisions that exceed the expectations of guests. The entire culture of the hotel provides a positive, supportive environment that rewards associates through the Omni Service Champions program. As an Omni associate, you are disturbed that the hotel is considering giving up its free apples. You hope that executives will find other ways to cut expenses, such as purchasing food in smaller amounts or reducing the hours of its lobby cafes.[21]

Your Task. In the true sense of The Power of One, you decide to express your views to management. Write a persuasive message to Richard Johnson, (*rjohnson@omni.com*), Vice President, Operations, Omni Hotels, 420 Decker Drive, Irving, TX 75062. Should you write a letter or an e-mail? In a separate note to your instructor, explain your rationale for your channel choice and your message strategy.

10.18 Persuasive Organizational Message Flowing Upward: Keeping Track of Office Projects (Obj. 4)

E-mail

© iStockphoto.com/Justin Horrocks

As the supervisor of administrative support at an architectural engineering firm, you serve five project managers. You find it difficult to keep track of what everybody is doing and where they are working. Mike is in New Orleans, Jason just left for Kansas City, Brian is working on a project in St. Louis, and Andrea is completing a job in Houston. With so many people working on projects in various places, it is hard to know where people are and what they are doing. Assigning administrative assistants and tracking their work is difficult. Although digital tools would be ideal, this office has shown no interest in wikis or similar collaborative tools. You decide that you and your managers need a dry erase board in the office to record projects and their status. Plain dry erase boards are not expensive at Wal-Mart. But can you persuade the managers to accept this new tool? They are largely independent engineers who are not attuned to following office procedures. Moreover, who will keep the board current?

Your Task. Write a convincing e-mail that persuades managers that your office needs a dry erase board to record weekly projects. Outline the benefits. How can you make it easy for them to buy in to using this new tool? Fill in any details from your imagination, but keep the message fairly simple. Address the first e-mail to *Mike.Kuryia@walters_inc.com*.

10.19 Persuasive Organizational Message Flowing Upward: Training Telecommuters (Obj. 4)

E-mail Team Web

James Lush arose from bed in his Connecticut home and looked outside to see a heavy snowstorm creating a fairyland of white. But he felt none of the giddiness that usually accompanies a potential snow day. Such days were a gift from heaven when schools closed, businesses shut down, and the world ground to a halt. As an on-and-off telecommuter for many years, he knew that snow days were a thing of the past. These days, work for James Lush and 23.5 million other American employees is no farther than their home office.[22]

More and more employees are becoming telecommuters. They want to work at home, where they feel they can be more productive and avoid the hassle of driving to work. Some need to telecommute only temporarily, while they take care of family obligations, births, illnesses, or personal problems. Others are highly skilled individuals who can do their work at home as easily as in the office. Businesses definitely see advantages to telecommuting. They don't have to supply office space for workers. What's more, as businesses continue to flatten management structures, bosses no longer have time to micromanage employees. Increasingly, they are leaving workers to their own devices.

But the results have not been totally satisfactory. For one thing, in-house workers resent those who work at home. More important are problems of structure and feedback. Telecommuters don't always have the best work habits, and lack of communication is a major issue. Unless the telecommuter is expert at coordinating projects and leaving instructions, productivity can fizzle. Appreciating the freedom but recognizing that they need guidance, employees are saying, "Push me, but don't leave me out there all alone!"

As human resources manager at your company, you already have 83 employees who are either full- or part-time telecommuters. With increasing numbers asking to work in remote locations, you decide that workers and their managers must receive training on how to do it effectively. You are considering hiring a consultant to train your prospective telecommuters and their managers. Another possibility is developing an in-house training program.

Your Task. As human resources manager, you must convince Victor Vasquez, vice president, that your company needs a training program for all workers who are currently telecommuting or who plan to do so. Their managers should also receive training. You decide to ask your staff of four to help you gather information. Using the Web, you and your team read several articles on what such training should include. Now you must decide what action you want the vice president to take. Meet with you to discuss a training program? Commit to a budget item for future training? Hire a consultant or agency to come in and conduct training programs? Individually or as a team, write a convincing e-mail to *victor.vasquet@beta.com* that describes the problem, suggests what the training should include, and asks for action by a specific date. Add any reasonable details necessary to build your case.

10.20 Persuasive Organizational Message Flowing Upward: Dear Boss (Obj. 4)

E-mail

In your own work or organization experience, identify a problem for which you have a solution. Should a procedure be altered to improve performance? Would a new or different piece of equipment help you perform your work better? Could some tasks be scheduled more efficiently? Are employees being used most effectively? Could customers be better served by changing something? Do you want to work other hours or perform other tasks? Do you deserve a promotion? Do you have a suggestion to improve profitability?

Your Task. Once you have identified a situation requiring persuasion, write a memo or an e-mail to your boss or organization head. Use actual names and facts. Employ the concepts and techniques in this chapter to help you convince your boss that your idea should prevail. Include concrete examples, anticipate objections, emphasize reader benefits, and end with a specific action to be taken.

10.21 Persuasive Organizational Message Flowing Upward: Demanding Mandatory Tipping (Obj. 4)

Team

Centered in the heart of a 2,400-acre Florida paradise, the Bayside Inn Golf and Beach Resort offers gracious hospitality and beautiful accommodations. Its restaurant, Dolphin Watch, overlooks the scenic Choctawhatchee Bay, a perfect place to spy dolphins. As a server in the Dolphin Watch, you enjoy working in this resort setting—except for one thing. You have occasionally been "stiffed" by a patron who left no tip. You know your service is excellent, but some customers just don't get it. They seem to think that tips are optional, a sign of appreciation. For servers, however, tips are 80 percent of their income.

In a recent *New York Times* article, you learned that some restaurants—such as the famous Coach House Restaurant in New York—automatically add a 15 percent tip to the bill. In Santa Monica the Lula restaurant prints "gratuity guidelines" on checks, showing customers what a 15 or 20 percent tip would be. You also know that American Express recently developed a gratuity calculation feature on its terminals. This means that diners don't even have to do the math!

Your Task. Because they know you are studying business communication, your fellow servers have asked you to write a serious letter to Nicholas Ruiz, General Manager, Bayside Inn Golf and Beach Resort, 9300 Emerald Coast Parkway West, Sandestin, FL 32550-7268. Persuade him to adopt mandatory tipping guidelines in the restaurant. Talk with fellow servers (your classmates) to develop logical persuasive arguments.

10.22 Persuasive Organizational Message Flowing Downward: Reducing Your Health Insurance Costs (Obj. 4)

As part of the management team at Bank of Westfield, you want to help your employees improve their health and reduce their health costs at the same time. Because the Bank of Westfield is a small company, its risk is greater than those of larger firms. Individuals with health problems have always paid more for health insurance. However, federal law requires that all employees who are covered by employer insurance programs must pay the same premium. That means that those with poor health cannot be charged more for insurance than those with good health. Recent legislation now allows some exceptions if employers offer wellness programs.

Working with its insurance carrier, the Bank of Westfield developed a plan that would enable employees to reduce their deductible $500 for each health benchmark the employee reached. For example, a nonsmoker receives a $500 deduction in the overall deductible of $2,500. Other benchmark categories are cholesterol, body mass index, and blood pressure. If the Bank of Westfield can persuade employees to meet benchmarks in these areas, employees can reduce their deductibles by $500 for each benchmark. This should help quiet the grumbling that resulted last year when the insurance deductible jumped from $500 to $2,500.

All of the benchmarks are explained in the "Road to Health" brochure provided by the insurance carrier. To get employees started, the Bank of Westfield wants them to fill out an application (before January 15) to see a fitness counselor who will develop a customized fitness plan for each employee who signs up. The company will provide literature, fitness programs, and counseling to help employees meet their benchmarks.

Your Task. As Melissa Mendoza, Human Resources, prepare a persuasive action request memo to send to Bank of Westfield staff members. Promote both direct and indirect benefits. Anticipate obstacles and address them. Close with an action request. Your message should tell exactly what you want the receiver to do and provide an extension number for anyone who has questions. Send a memo rather than an e-mail because you want to enclose the "Road to Health" brochure and application.

10.23 Persuasive Organizational Messages Flowing Downward: And Now We Want Your Blood! (Obj. 4)

Team

Companies are increasingly asking employees to take on-site blood tests. Because forcing employees to do so would invade their privacy, companies must persuade them to volunteer. Why should companies bother?

Blood tests are part of health risk assessment. Such assessments are considered the first step toward controlling chronic and expensive health problems such as diabetes, obesity, and tobacco addiction. According to American Healthways, employers using blood tests have seen between a $300 and $1,440 decrease in health care costs per participant, depending on what kind of incentive they offer to participants.

Snap-on, a well-known manufacturer of power and hand tools, began offering blood tests as part of a health assessment program a year ago. Although the first-year sign-up was slow, Snap-on saw a 50 percent increase in sign-ups the following year as employees became familiar with the plan. Employees filled out health risk questionnaires. Then they received the results of their questionnaires so that they could see how their blood work compared with their own assessments. Snap-on assured employees that the company would never see the results. The blood tests, conducted by American Healthways, screened for cholesterol, diabetes, hypertension, body fat, liver function, and nicotine. Employers receive only combined data about their employees.

Even though employees were the benefactors of these blood tests, Snap-on had to offer an incentive to urge them to participate. Employees received a $20 monthly discount on health care premiums for agreeing to the full assessment process, including the blood test.

However, another company found that the penalty approach was more effective in encouraging employee participation. Westell Technologies, which makes broadband communication equipment, charged employees 10 percent higher health care premiums if they refused to take the blood tests. This penalty program resulted in 80 percent participation. Regardless of the method used to encourage participation, any on-site blood testing must be voluntary.[23]

Assume you are part of a group of interns at manufacturer Colman International, which employs 900 people. The director of interns, Christine Davis, is also vice president of Human Resources. One day she calls your group together and says, "Listen up! Colman needs employees to take these blood tests and fill out health risk assessment forms. We know this is a hard sell, but we think it is the right thing to do—not only for employees but also for the company because it will lower our skyrocketing health care costs. So here's what I want you interns to do as a training exercise. Get together and decide what you think is the best way for us to persuade employees to participate. Should we offer incentives or threaten penalties?"

Seeing the blank expressions on your faces, she said, "Oh, you can assume that the company will back whatever decision you make—so long as it's not out of line with what other companies are doing. Once you decide what to do, I want you to prepare a message to employees. Medical staff from American Healthways will be in the human resources training room to conduct the blood tests on Monday, November 17, through Friday, November 21. Appointments are available between 7:30 a.m. and 5:30 p.m. Employees may sign up for appointments by e-mailing me before November 10 at *cdavis@colman.com* and requesting an appointment time. They will receive a confirmation e-mail stating the date and appointment time."

Your Task. Individually or as a group, prepare two messages. Address one to Christine Davis. Explain what your group decided and justify the rationale for your decisions. Address the second message to Colman employees for the signature of Ms. Davis. Persuade employees to participate in the program. Remember to anticipate objections to your request. How can these objections be overcome? Should you emphasize benefits to the reader or to the company? What direct and indirect benefits can you name? What is the best communication channel for this message? How can you make it easy for receivers to respond?

10.24 Persuasive Organizational Message Flowing Downward: Cutting Overnight Shipping Costs (Obj. 4)

As office manager of an East Coast software company, write a memo persuading your technicians, engineers, programmers, and other employees to reduce the number of overnight or second-day mail shipments. Your FedEx and other shipping bills have been sky high, and you feel that staff members are overusing these services.

You think employees should send messages by e-mail or fax. Sending a zipped file or PDF file as an e-mail attachment costs very little. What's more, a fax costs only about 35 cents a page to most long-distance areas and nothing to local areas. Compare this with $15 to $20 for FedEx service! Whenever possible, staff members should obtain the FedEx account number of the recipient and use it for charging the shipment. If staff members plan ahead and allow enough time, they can use UPS or FedEx ground service, which takes three to five days and is much cheaper. You wonder whether staff members consider whether the recipient is really going to use the message as soon as it arrives. Does it justify an overnight shipment? You would like to reduce overnight delivery services voluntarily by 50 percent over the next two months. Unless a sizable reduction occurs, the CEO threatens severe restrictions in the future.

Your Task. Address your memo to all staff members. What other ways could employees reduce shipping costs?

10.25 Persuasive Organizational Message Flowing Downward: Supporting Project H.E.L.P. (Obj. 4)

E-mail

As employee relations manager of The Prudential Insurance Company, one of your tasks is to promote Project H.E.L.P. (Higher Education Learning Program), an on-the-job learning opportunity. Project H.E.L.P. is a combined effort of major corporations and the Newark Unified School District. You must recruit 12 employees who will volunteer as instructors for 50 or more students. The students will spend four hours a week at the Prudential Newark facility earning an average of five units of credit a semester.

This semester the students will be serving in the Claims, Word Processing, Corporate Media Services, Marketing, Communications, Library, and Administrative Support departments. Your task is to convince employees in these departments to volunteer. They will be expected to supervise and instruct the students. In return, employees will receive two hours of release time per week to work with the students. The program has been very successful thus far. School officials, students, and employees alike express satisfaction with the experience and the outcomes.

Your Task. Write a persuasive memo or e-mail with convincing appeals that will bring you 12 volunteers to work with Project H.E.L.P.

10.26 Persuasive Organizational Message Flowing Downward: Revising Miserable Memo (Obj. 4)

The following memo (with names changed) was actually sent.

Your Task. Based on what you have learned in this chapter, improve the memo. Expect the staff to be somewhat resistant because they have never before had meeting restrictions.

TO: All Managers and Employees
FROM: Rita Nelson, CEO
SUBJECT: Scheduling Meetings

Please be reminded that travel in the greater Los Angeles area is time consuming. In the future we are asking that you set up meetings that

1. Are of critical importance
2. Consider travel time for the participants
3. Consider phone conferences (or video or e-mail) in lieu of face-to-face meetings
4. Meetings should be at the location where most of the participants work and at the most opportune travel times
5. Traveling together is another way to save time and resources.

We all have our traffic horror stories. A recent one is that a certain manager was asked to attend a one-hour meeting in Burbank. This required one hour travel in advance of the meeting, one hour for the meeting, and two and a half hours of travel through Los Angeles afterward. This meeting was scheduled for 4 p.m. Total time consumed by the manager for the one-hour meeting was four and a half hours.

Thank you for your consideration.

10.27 Persuasive Organizational Message Flowing Downward: Curbing Profanity on the Job (Obj. 4)

E-mail | Web

As sales manager for a large irrigation parts manufacturer, you are concerned about the use of profanity by your sales associates. Some defend profanity, claiming that it helps them fit in. Your female sales reps have said that it helps relax listeners, drives home a point, and makes them "one of the boys." You have done some research, however, and learned that courts have ruled that profanity can constitute sexual harassment—whether in person or in print. In addition to causing legal problems, profanity on the job projects a negative image of the individual and of the company. Although foul language is heard increasingly on TV and in the movies, you think it is a bad habit and you want to see it curbed on the job.

Your Task. Use the Web or databases to locate articles related to the use of profanity and strategies employed by organizations for dealing with it. One good resource is **http://www.cusscontrol.com**. In small groups or in class, discuss the place of formal and informal language in communication. Prepare a list of reasons people curse and reasons not to do so. Your instructor may ask you to interview employers to learn their reactions to the issue of workplace profanity. As sales manager at Rain City, compose a persuasive e-mail or memo to your sales staff that will encourage them to curb their use of profanity.[24]

10.28 Sales Letter Analysis (Obj. 5)

Your Task. Select a one- or two-page sales letter received by you or a friend. Study the letter and then answer these questions:

a. What techniques capture the reader's attention?
b. Is the opening effective? Explain.
c. What are the central selling points?
d. Does the letter use rational, emotional, or a combination of appeals? Explain.
e. What reader benefits are suggested?
f. How does the letter build interest in the product or service?
g. How is price handled?
h. How does the letter anticipate reader resistance and offer counter-arguments?
i. What action is the reader to take? How is the action made easy?
j. What motivators spur the reader to act quickly?

10.29 Sales Letter: Weighing In at Work (Obj. 5)

Web

Nearly 68 percent of adults in America are overweight, and 34 percent are obese.[25] In addition to the risks to individuals, obesity costs American companies billions in lost productivity caused by disability, illness, and death.[26] Companies from Wall Street to the Rust Belt are launching or improving programs to help employees lose weight. Union Pacific Railroad is considering giving out pedometers to track workers around the office, as well as dispensing weight loss drugs. Merrill Lynch sponsors Weight Watchers meetings. Caterpillar instituted the Healthy Balance program. It promotes long-term behavioral change and healthier lifestyles for Caterpillar workers. Estimates suggest that employers and employees could save a total of $1,200 a year for each person's medical costs if overweight employees shed their excess pounds.

As a sales representative for Fitness for Life, one of the country's leading fitness operators, you are convinced that your fitness equipment and programs are instrumental in helping people lose weight. With regular exercise at an on-site fitness center, employees lose weight and improve overall health. As employee health improves, absenteeism is reduced and overall productivity increases. What's more, employees love working out before or after work. They make the routine part of their workday, and they often have work buddies who share their fitness regimens.

Although many companies resist spending money to save money, fitness centers need not be large or expensive to be effective. Studies show that moderately sized centers coupled with motivational and training programs yield the greatest success. For just $30,000, Fitness for Life will provide exercise equipment including treadmills, elliptical trainers, exercise bikes, multigyms, and weight machines. Their fitness experts will design a fitness room, set up the equipment, and create appropriate programs. Best of all, the one-time cost is usually offset by cost savings within one year of center installation. For additional fees Fitness for Life can provide fitness consultants for employee fitness assessments. Fitness for Life specialists will also train employees on the proper use of the equipment and clean and manage the facility—for an extra charge, of course.

Your Task. Use the Web to update your obesity statistics. Then prepare a sales letter addressed to Carol Wong, Director, Human Resources, Prophecy Financial Services, 790 Lafayette Boulevard, Bridgeport, CT 06604. Ask for an appointment to meet with her. Send a brochure detailing the products and services that Fitness for Life provides. As an incentive, offer a free fitness assessment for all employees if Prophecy Financial Services installs a fitness facility by December 1.

10.30 Sales Message: Adapting From Low Context to High Context (Obj. 6)

Intercultural | Team

The following letter, adapted from an Australian sales message, is intended for a low-context culture.[27]

Your Task. In teams, study the following letter. List at least six factors and techniques used in this letter that typify low-context persuasive sales messages. Then discuss how the letter could be changed to appeal to high-context cultures. Your instructor may ask your team to compose a high-context version of the letter.

Dear Mr. Smith,

Since you are one of our important customers who appreciate convenience and value, I am writing to share an opportunity to enjoy both!

For example, would you like to choose $60 worth of Innovations merchandise—absolutely FREE? And could you benefit from a very convenient credit card—one that offers you a free Rewards program, unsurpassed card protection, free PhotoCard, free Purchase Cover, exceptional personal customer service—and is accepted at over 400,000 locations in Australia, more than 14 million establishments worldwide, and gives you cash access at over 341,000 ATMs?

Realistically, how could you pass up these attractive opportunities? They each represent the very practical (and innovative!) reasons for you to apply for a Citibank Visa or MasterCard. Because I feel so confident that you will truly appreciate a Citibank Credit Card, I would like you to have two $30 vouchers for anything in our Innovations catalogue. Use them separately or together. They are valid until 28 February on your choice of items. But you must reply to this very special offer before 28 November.

= = = = = = = = = [More incentives detailed here]

I hope you will take a moment to complete and mail (or fax) the enclosed application for your Citibank Credit Card today. I'm certain you will enjoy its many benefits—as well as $60 of vouchers for Innovations merchandise with our compliments. Happy shopping!

Yours sincerely,

Judy Powell, Managing Director

P.S. We can only reserve this exclusive offer until 28 November. So apply for your Citibank Visa or MasterCard today. Once you are approved, you will receive $60 of Innovations vouchers shortly after your new card. And for Double Rewards points, use your card on any Innovations purchase until 28 February of next year!

10.31 Sales Letter: Promoting Your Product or Service (Obj. 5)

Identify a situation in your current job or a previous one in which a sales letter is or was needed. Using suggestions from this chapter, write an appropriate sales letter that promotes a product or service. Use actual names, information, and examples. If you have no work experience, imagine a business you would like to start: word processing, pet grooming, car detailing, tutoring, specialty knitting, balloon decorating, delivery service, child care, gardening, lawn care, or something else. Write a letter selling your product or service to be distributed to your prospective customers. Be sure to tell them how to respond.

10.32 Press Release: Preparing News for Your Local Newspaper (Obj. 7)

Web

You have been interviewed for a terrific job in corporate communications at an exciting organization. To test your writing skills, the organization asks you to rewrite one of its press releases for possible submission to your local newspaper. This means revising the information you find into a new press release that your local newspaper would be interested in publishing.

Your Task. Select an organization and study its press releases. For example, search the Web for *FBI press release, Ben & Jerry's press release, Mars candy press release, World Honda news release, Screen Actors Guild press release*, or an organization of your choice. Study its current press releases. Select one event or product that you think would interest your local newspaper. Although you can use the information from current press releases, don't copy the exact wording because the interviewer wants to see how you would present that information. Use the organization's format and submit the press release to your instructor with a cover note identifying the newspaper or other publication where you would like to see your press release published.

10.33 Press Release: This Is New! (Obj. 7)

Your Task. For a company where you now work or an organization you belong to, identify a product or service that could be publicized. Consider writing a press release announcing a new course at your college, a new president, new equipment, or a campaign to raise funds. The press release is intended for your local newspaper.

Video Resources

Video Library 2, Hard Rock Café

This video takes you inside the Hard Rock Café where you learn about changes it has undergone in surviving over 30 years in the rough-and-tumble world of hospitality. One problem involves difficulty in maintaining its well-known logo around the world. As you watch the video, look for references to the changes taking place and the discussion of brand control.

Your Task. As an assistant in the Hard Rock Corporate Identity Division, you have been asked to draft a persuasive message to be sent to the Edinburgh Festival Fringe. In doing research, you learned that this festival is the largest arts festival in the world, bringing thousands of performances to Scotland's capital city. An annual event, the Edinburgh Festival takes over the city in August with stand-up comedy, cabaret, theater, street performance, film, television, radio, and visual arts programs. Some of the programs raise funds for charity.

The problem is that the festival is staging some of its events at the Hard Rock Café, and the festival is using outdated Hard Rock logos at its Web site and in print announcements. Your task is to persuade the Edinburgh Festival Fringe organizers to stop using the old logos. Explain why it is necessary to use the official Hard Rock logo. Make it easy for them to obtain the official logo at **http://hardrock.com/corporate/logos/logos.asp**. Organizers must also sign the logo usage agreement. Organizers may be resistant because they have invested in announcements and Web designs with the old logo. If they don't comply by June 1, Hard Rock attorneys may begin legal actions. However, you need to present this date without making it sound like a threat. Your boss wants this message to develop goodwill, not motivate antagonism.

Write a persuasive e-mail to Edinburgh Festival Fringe organizer Barry Cook at *bcook@edinburghfestival.com*. Add any reasonable details.

Video Library 2, Innovation, Learning, and Communication: A Study of Yahoo

This video familiarizes you with managers and inside operating strategies at the Internet company Yahoo. After watching the film, assume the role of assistant to John Briggs, senior producer, who appeared in the video. John has just received a letter asking for permission from another film company to use Yahoo offices and personnel in an educational video, similar to the one you just saw.

Briggs wants you to draft a message for him to send to the operations manager, Ceci Lang, asking for permission for VX Studios to film. VX says it needs about 15 hours of filming time and would like to interview four or five managers as well as founders David Filo and Jerry Yang. VX would need to set up its mobile studio van in the parking lot and would need permission to use advertising film clips. Although VX hopes to film in May, it is flexible about the date. John Briggs reminds you that Yahoo has participated in a number of films in the past two years, and some managers are complaining that they can't get their work done.

Your Task. After watching the video, write a persuasive memo or e-mail to Ceci Lang, operations manager, asking her to allow VX Studios to film at Yahoo. Your message should probably emphasize the value of these projects in enhancing Yahoo's image among future users. Provide any other details you think are necessary to create a convincing request message that will win authorization from Ceci Lang to schedule this filming.

Chat About It

In each chapter you will find five discussion questions related to the chapter material. Your instructor may assign these topics for you to discuss in class, in an online chat room, or on an online discussion board. Some of the discussion topics may require outside research. You may also be asked to read and respond to postings made by your classmates.

Topic 1: When you think about persuasion, does the term suggest deception or dishonesty? Compare negative and positive aspects of persuasion. Share descriptions of when you have experienced both kinds of persuasion.

Topic 2: In your own experience, when have you had to persuade someone (boss, parent, instructor, friend, colleague) to do something or to change a belief? What strategies did you use? Were they successful? How could you improve your technique?

Topic 3: When have you had to complain to a company, organization, or person about something that went wrong or that offended you? Share your experience. What channel did you use for your complaint? How effective was your channel choice and strategy? What would you change in your method for future complaints?

Topic 4: Think of a product you have used and like. If you were trying to sell that product, what rational appeals would you use? What emotional appeals would you use? Try to sell that product to your classmates.

Grammar and Mechanics C.L.U.E. Review 10

Number Use

Review Guides 47–50 about number usage in Appendix A, Grammar and Mechanics Guide, beginning on page xxx. On a separate sheet, revise the following sentences to correct number usage errors. For each error that you locate, write the guide number that reflects this usage. Sentences may have more than one error. If a sentence is correct, write *C*. When you finish, check your answers on page Key-1.

Example: 13 candidates submitted applications for the position.
Revision: Thirteen candidates submitted applications for the position. [Guide 47]

1. Susan showed me 5 different customer messages with the same 2 complaints.
2. 28 employees indicated they would change their health benefits.
3. Did Mike request three hundred dollars to attend the 1-day seminar?
4. Most deliveries arrive before 10:00 o'clock a.m.
5. Personal income tax returns must be mailed by April 15th.
6. We earned 2.5% dividends on our three thousand dollar investment.
7. Our company applied for a one hundred thousand dollar loan at six%.
8. Average attendance at Major League Baseball games totaled 80,000,000 in the United States and Canada.
9. I bought the item on eBay for one dollar and fifty cents and sold it for fifteen dollars.
10. That store offers a thirty-day customer satisfaction return policy.

Grammar and Mechanics Guide

APPENDIX A

Competent Language Usage Essentials (C.L.U.E.)

In the business world, people are often judged by the way they speak and write. Using the language competently can mean the difference between success and failure. Often a speaker sounds accomplished; but when that same individual puts ideas in print, errors in language usage destroy his or her credibility. One student observed, "When I talk, I get by on my personality; but when I write, the flaws in my communication show through. That's why I'm in this class."

How This Grammar and Mechanics Guide Can Help You

This grammar and mechanics guide contains 50 guidelines covering sentence structure, grammar, usage, punctuation, capitalization, and number style. These guidelines focus on the most frequently used—and abused—language elements. Frequent checkpoint exercises enable you to try your skills immediately. In addition to the 50 language guides in this appendix, you will find a list of 160 frequently misspelled words plus a quick review of selected confusing words.

The concentrated materials in this guide help novice business communicators focus on the major areas of language use. The guide is not meant to teach or review *all* the principles of English grammar and punctuation. It focuses on a limited number of language guidelines and troublesome words. Your objective should be mastery of these language principles and words, which represent a majority of the problems typically encountered by business writers.

How to Use This Grammar and Mechanics Guide

Your instructor may give you the short C.L.U.E. language diagnostic test (located in the Instructor's Manual) to help you assess your competency. A longer self-administered diagnostic test is available as part of Your Personal Language Trainer at **www.meguffey.com**. Either test will give you an idea of your language competence. After taking either diagnostic test, read and work your way through the 50 guidelines. You should also use the self-teaching Trainer exercises, all of which correlate with this Grammar and Mechanics Guide. Concentrate on areas in which you are weak. Memorize the spellings and definitions of the confusing words at the end of this appendix.

In this text you will find two kinds of exercises for your practice. (1) *Checkpoints,* located in this appendix, focus on a small group of language guidelines. Use them to test your comprehension as you complete each section. (2) *Review exercises,* located at the end of each chapter, help reinforce your language skills at the same time you are learning about the processes and products of business communication.

Many students want all the help they can get in improving their language skills. For additional assistance with grammar and language fundamentals, *Business Communication: Process and Product,* 7e, offers you unparalleled interactive and print resources:

- **Your Personal Language Trainer.** This self-paced learning tool is located at **www. meguffey.com.** Dr. Guffey acts as your personal trainer in helping you pump up your language muscles. Your Personal Language Trainer provides the rules plus hundreds of sentence applications so that you can test your knowledge and build your skills with immediate feedback and explanations.

- **Speak Right!,** found at **www.meguffey.com,** reviews frequently mispronounced words. You will hear correct pronunciations from Dr. Guffey so that you will never be embarrassed by mispronouncing these terms.
- **Spell Right!,** found at **www.meguffey.com**, presents frequently misspelled words along with exercises to help you improve your spelling.
- **Reference Books.** A more comprehensive treatment of grammar and punctuation guidelines can be found in Clark and Clark's *A Handbook for Office Workers* and Guffey's *Business English*.

Grammar and Mechanics Guidelines

Sentence Structure

GUIDE 1: Avoid sentence fragments. A fragment is an incomplete sentence. You can recognize a complete sentence because it (a) includes a subject (a noun or pronoun that interacts with a verb), (b) includes a verb (a word expressing action or describing a condition), and (c) makes sense (comes to a closure). A complete sentence is an independent clause. One of the most serious errors a writer can make is punctuating a fragment as if it were a complete sentence.

Fragment	**Improved**
Because 90 percent of all business transactions involve written messages. Good writing skills are critical.	Because 90 percent of all business transactions involve written messages, good writing skills are critical.
The recruiter requested a writing sample. Even though the candidate seemed to communicate well.	The recruiter requested a writing sample, even though the candidate seemed to communicate well.

Tip. Fragments often can be identified by the words that introduce them—words such as *although, as, because, even, except, for example, if, instead of, since, so, such as, that, which,* and *when.* These words introduce dependent clauses. Make sure such clauses are always connected to independent clauses.

DEPENDENT CLAUSE / INDEPENDENT CLAUSE

Since she became supervisor, she had to write more memos and reports.

GUIDE 2: Avoid run-on (fused) sentences. A sentence with two independent clauses must be joined by a coordinating conjunction *(and, or, nor, but)* or by a semicolon (;). Without a conjunction or a semicolon, a run-on sentence results.

Run-on	**Improved**
Ramon visited resorts of the rich and the famous he also dropped in on luxury spas.	Ramon visited resorts of the rich and famous, and he also dropped in on luxury spas.
	Ramon visited resorts of the rich and famous; he also dropped in on luxury spas.

GUIDE 3: Avoid comma-splice sentences. A comma splice results when a writer joins (splices together) two independent clauses—without using a coordinating conjunction *(and, or, nor, but).*

Comma Splice	**Improved**
Disney World operates in Orlando, EuroDisney serves Paris.	Disney World operates in Orlando; EuroDisney serves Paris.
	Disney World operates in Orlando, and EuroDisney serves Paris.
Visitors wanted a resort vacation, however they were disappointed.	Visitors wanted a resort vacation; however, they were disappointed.

Tip. In joining independent clauses, beware of using a comma and words such as *consequently, furthermore, however, therefore, then, thus,* and so on. These conjunctive adverbs require semicolons.

Note: Sentence structure is also covered in Chapter 5.

✓ *Checkpoint*

Revise the following to rectify sentence fragments, comma splices, and run-ons.

1. Although it began as a side business for Disney. Destination weddings now represent a major income source.
2. About 2,000 weddings are held yearly. Which is twice the number just ten years ago.
3. Weddings may take place in less than one hour, however the cost may be as much as $5,000.
4. Limousines line up outside Disney's wedding pavilion, they are scheduled in two-hour intervals.
5. Most couples prefer a traditional wedding, others request a fantasy experience.

For all the Checkpoint sentences, compare your responses with the answers at the end of Appendix A.

Grammar

Verb Tense

GUIDE 4: Use present tense, past tense, and past participle verb forms correctly.

Present Tense	Past Tense	Past Participle
Today I______)	(Yesterday I______)	(I have______)
am	was	been
begin	began	begun
break	broke	broken
bring	brought	brought
choose	chose	chosen
come	came	come
do	did	done
give	gave	given
go	went	gone
know	knew	known
pay	paid	paid
see	saw	seen
steal	stole	stolen
take	took	taken
write	wrote	written

The package *came* yesterday, and Kevin *knew* what it contained.

If I *had seen* the shipper's bill, I *would have paid* it immediately.

I *know* the answer now; I wish I *had known* it yesterday.

Tip. Probably the most frequent mistake in tenses results from substituting the past-participle form for the past tense. Notice that the past-participle tense requires auxiliary verbs such as *has, had, have, would have,* and *could have.*

Faulty	**Correct**
When he *come* over last night, he *brung* pizza.	When he *came* over last night, he *brought* pizza.
If he *had came* earlier, we *could have saw* the video.	If he *had come* earlier, we *could have seen* the video.

Verb Mood

GUIDE 5: Use the subjunctive mood to express hypothetical (untrue) ideas. The most frequent misuse of the subjunctive mood involves using *was* instead of *were* in clauses introduced by *if* and *as though* or containing *wish.*

If I *were* (not *was*) you, I would take a business writing course.

Sometimes I wish I *were* (not *was*) the manager of this department.

He acts as though he *were* (not *was*) in charge of this department.

Tip. If the statement could possibly be true, use *was.*

If I *was* to blame, I accept the consequences.

✓ *Checkpoint*

Correct faults in verb tenses and mood.

6. If I was you, I would have went to the ten o'clock meeting.

7. The manager could have wrote a better report if he had began earlier.

8. When the vice president seen the report, he immediately come to my office.

9. I wish the vice president was in your shoes for just one day.

10. If the manager had knew all that we do, I'm sure he would have gave us better reviews.

Verb Voice

For a discussion of active- and passive-voice verbs, see pages 151–152 in Chapter 5.

Verb Agreement

GUIDE 6: Make subjects agree with verbs despite intervening phrases and clauses. Become a detective in locating *true* subjects. Don't be deceived by prepositional phrases and parenthetic words that often disguise the true subject.

Our study of annual budgets, five-year plans, and sales proposals *is* (not *are*) progressing on schedule. (The true subject is *study.*)

The budgeted item, despite additions proposed yesterday, *remains* (not *remain*) as submitted. (The true subject is *item.*)

A vendor's evaluation of the prospects for a sale, together with plans for follow-up action, *is* (not *are*) what we need. (The true subject is *evaluation.*)

Tip. Subjects are nouns or pronouns that control verbs. To find subjects, cross out prepositional phrases beginning with words such as *about, at, by, for, from, of,* and *to.* Subjects of verbs are not found in prepositional phrases. Also, don't be tricked by expressions introduced by *together with, in addition to,* and *along with.*

GUIDE 7: Subjects joined by *and* require plural verbs. Watch for true subjects joined by the conjunction *and.* They require plural verbs.

The CEO and one of his assistants *have* (not *has*) ordered a limo.

Considerable time and money *were* (not *was*) spent on remodeling.

Exercising in the gym and jogging every day *are* (not *is*) how he keeps fit.

GUIDE 8: Subjects joined by *or* or *nor* may require singular or plural verbs. The verb should agree with the closer subject.

Either the software or the printer *is* (not *are*) causing the glitch. (The verb is controlled by the closer subject, *printer.*)

Neither St. Louis nor Chicago *has* (not *have*) a chance of winning. (The verb is controlled by *Chicago.*)

Tip. In joining singular and plural subjects with *or* or *nor,* place the plural subject closer to the verb. Then, the plural verb sounds natural. For example, *Either the manufacturer or the distributors are responsible.*

GUIDE 9: Use singular verbs for most indefinite pronouns. The following pronouns all take singular verbs: *anyone, anybody, anything, each, either, every, everyone, everybody, everything, neither, nobody, nothing, someone, somebody,* and *something.*

Everyone in both offices *was* (not *were*) given a bonus.

Each of the employees *is* (not *are*) being interviewed.

GUIDE 10: Use singular or plural verbs for collective nouns, depending on whether the members of the group are operating as a unit or individually. Words such as *faculty, administration, class, crowd,* and *committee* are considered *collective* nouns. If the members of the collective are acting as a unit, treat them as singular subjects. If they are acting individually, it is usually better to add the word *members* and use a plural verb.

Correct

The Finance Committee *is* working harmoniously. (*Committee* is singular because its action is unified.)

The Planning Committee *are* having difficulty agreeing. (*Committee* is plural because its members are acting individually.)

Improved

The Planning Committee members *are* having difficulty agreeing. (Add the word *members* if a plural meaning is intended.)

Tip. In the United States collective nouns are generally considered singular. In Britain these collective nouns are generally considered plural.

✓ *Checkpoint*

Correct the errors in subject–verb agreement.

11. The agency's time and talent was spent trying to develop a blockbuster ad campaign.

12. Your e-mail message, along with both of its attachments, were not delivered to my computer.

13. Each of the Fortune 500 companies are being sent a survey regarding women in management.

14. A full list of names and addresses are necessary before we can begin.

15. Either the judge or the attorney have asked for a recess.

Pronoun Case

GUIDE 11: Learn the three cases of pronouns and how each is used. Pronouns are substitutes for nouns. Every business writer must know the following pronoun cases.

Subjective (Nominative) Case	Objective Case	Possessive Case
Used for subjects of verbs and subject complements	Used for objects of prepositions and objects of verbs	Used to show possession
I	me	my, mine
we	us	our, ours
you	you	you, yours
he	him	his
she	her	her, hers

Subjective (Nominative) Case	Objective Case	Possessive Case
Used for subjects of verbs and subject complements	Used for objects of prepositions and objects of verbs	Used to show possession
it	it	its
they	them	their, theirs
who, whoever	whom, whomever	whose

GUIDE 12: Use subjective-case pronouns as subjects of verbs and as complements. Complements are words that follow linking verbs (such as *am, is, are, was, were, be, being,* and *been)* and rename the words to which they refer.

> *She* and *I* (not *her* and *me*) are looking for entry-level jobs. (Use subjective-case pronouns as the subjects of the verb phrase *are looking.*)
>
> We hope that Marci and *he* (not *him*) will be hired. (Use a subjective-case pronoun as the subject of the verb phrase *will be hired.*)
>
> It must have been *she* (not *her*) who called last night. (Use a subjective-case pronoun as a subject complement.)

Tip. If you feel awkward using subjective pronouns after linking verbs, rephrase the sentence to avoid the dilemma. Instead of *It is she who is the boss,* say, *She is the boss.*

GUIDE 13: Use objective-case pronouns as objects of prepositions and verbs.

> Send the e-mail to *her* and *me* (not *she* and *I*). (The pronouns *her* and *me* are objects of the preposition *to.*)
>
> The CEO appointed Rick and *him* (not *he*) to the committee. (The pronoun *him* is the object of the verb *appointed.*)

Tip. When a pronoun appears in combination with a noun or another pronoun, ignore the extra noun or pronoun and its conjunction. Then, the case of the pronoun becomes more obvious.

Jason asked Jennifer and *me* (not *I*) to lunch. (Ignore *Jennifer and*.)

The waiter brought hamburgers to Jason and *me* (not *I*). (Ignore *Jason and*.)

Tip. Be especially alert to the following prepositions: *except, between, but,* and *like.* Be sure to use objective pronouns as their objects.

Just between you and *me* (not *I*), that mineral water comes from the tap.

Everyone except Robert and *him* (not *he*) responded to the invitation.

GUIDE 14: Use possessive pronouns to show ownership.

Possessive pronouns (such as *hers, yours, whose, ours, theirs,* and *its)* require no apostrophes.

All reports except *yours* (not *your's*) have to be rewritten.

The apartment and *its* (not *it's*) contents are *hers* (not *her's*) until June.

Tip. Don't confuse possessive pronouns and contractions. Contractions are shortened forms of subject–verb phrases (such as *it's* for *it is, there's* for *there is, who's* for *who is,* and *they're* for *they are).*

✓ Checkpoint

Correct errors in pronoun case.

16. My partner and me have looked at many apartments, but your's has the best location.

17. We thought the car was her's, but it's license plate does not match.

18. Just between you and I, do you think there printer is working?

19. Theres not much the boss or me can do if its broken, but its condition should have been reported to him or I earlier.

20. We received several applications, but your's and her's were missing

GUIDE 15: Use pronouns ending in *self* only when they refer to previously mentioned nouns or pronouns.

The president *himself* ate all the M&Ms.

Send the package to Mike or *me* (not *myself*).

Tip. Trying to sound less egocentric, some radio and TV announcers incorrectly substitute *myself* when they should use *I*. For example, "Jerry and *myself* (should be *I*) are cohosting the telethon."

GUIDE 16: Use *who* or *whoever* for subjective-case constructions and *whom* or *whomever* for objective-case constructions.

In determining the correct choice, it is helpful to substitute *he* for *who* or *whoever* and *him* for *whom* or *whomever.*

For *whom* was this software ordered? (The software was ordered for *him*.)

Who did you say called? (You did say *he* called?)

Give the supplies to *whoever* asked for them. (In this sentence the clause *whoever asked for them* functions as the object of the preposition *to.* Within the clause *whoever* is the subject of the verb *asked.* Again, try substituting *he: he asked for them.*)

✓ Checkpoint

Correct any errors in the use of *self*-ending pronouns and *who/whom.*

21. The boss herself is willing to call whoever we decide to honor.

22. Who have you asked to develop ads for our new products?

23. I have a pizza for whomever placed the telephone order.

24. The meeting is set for Wednesday; however, Matt and myself cannot attend.

25. Incident reports must be submitted by whomever experiences a personnel problem.

Pronoun Reference

GUIDE 17: Make pronouns agree in number and gender with the words to which they refer (their antecedents). When the gender of the antecedent is obvious, pronoun references are simple.

> One of the boys lost *his* (not *their*) new tennis shoes. (The singular pronoun *his* refers to the singular *One*.)
>
> Each of the female nurses was escorted to *her car* (not *their cars*). (The singular pronoun *her* and singular noun *car* are necessary because they refer to the singular subject *Each*.)
>
> Somebody on the girls' team left *her* (not *their*) headlights on.

When the gender of the antecedent could be male or female, sensitive writers today have a number of options.

Faulty

Every employee should receive *their* check Friday. (The plural pronoun *their* does not agree with its singular antecedent *employee*.)

Improved

All employees should receive *their* checks Friday. (Make the subject plural so that the plural pronoun *their* is acceptable. This option is preferred by many writers today.)

All employees should receive checks Friday. (Omit the possessive pronoun entirely.)

Every employee should receive *a* check Friday. (Substitute *a* for a pronoun.)

Every employee should receive *his or her* check Friday. (Use the combination *his or her*. However, this option is wordy and should be avoided.)

GUIDE 18: Be sure that pronouns such as *it, which, this,* and *that* refer to clear antecedents. Vague pronouns confuse the reader because they have no clear single antecedent. The most troublesome are *it, which, this,* and *that*. Replace vague pronouns with concrete nouns, or provide these pronouns with clear antecedents.

Faulty	Improved
Our office recycles as much paper as possible because *it* helps the environment. (Does *it* refer to *paper, recycling,* or *office?*)	Our office recycles as much paper as possible because *such efforts* help the environment. (Replace *it* with *such efforts*.)
The disadvantages of local area networks can offset their advantages. That merits further evaluation. (What merits evaluation: advantages, disadvantages, or the offsetting of one by the other?)	The disadvantages of local area networks can offset their advantages. That fact merits further evaluation. (*Fact* supplies a concrete noun for the vague pronoun *that*.)
Negotiators announced an expanded health care plan, reductions in dental coverage, and a proposal of on-site child care facilities. *This* caused employee protests. (What exactly caused employee protests?)	Negotiators announced an expanded health care plan, reductions in dental coverage, and a proposal of on-site child care facilities. *This* reduction in child care facilities caused employee protests. (The pronoun *This* now has a clear reference.)

Tip. Whenever you use the words *this, that, these,* and *those* by themselves, a red flag should pop up. These words are dangerous when they stand alone. Inexperienced writers often use them to refer to an entire previous idea, rather than to a specific antecedent, as shown in the preceding examples. You can usually solve the problem by adding another idea to the pronoun (such as *this reduction).*

✓ *Checkpoint*

Correct the faulty and vague pronoun references in the following sentences. Numerous remedies exist.

26. Every employee must wear their picture identification badge.

27. Flexible working hours may mean slower career advancement, but it appeals to many workers.

28. Any renter must pay his rent by the first of the month.

29. Someone in this office reported that his computer had a virus.

30. Obtaining agreement on job standards, listening to coworkers, and encouraging employee suggestions all helped to open lines of communication. This is particularly important in team projects.

Adjectives and Adverbs

GUIDE 19: Use adverbs, not adjectives, to describe or limit the action of verbs. Use adjectives after linking verbs.

Andrew said he did *well* (not *good*) on the exam. (The adverb *well* describes how he did.)

After its tune-up, the engine is running *smoothly* (not *smooth*). (The adverb *smoothly* describes the verb *is running.*)

Don't take the manager's criticism *personally* (not *personal*). (The adverb *personally* tells how to take the criticism.)

She finished her homework *more quickly* (not *quicker*) than expected. (The adverb *more quickly*) explains how she finished her homework.)

Liam felt bad (not badly) after he heard the news. (The adjective *bad* follows the linking verb *felt.*)

GUIDE 20: Hyphenate two or more adjectives that are joined to create a compound modifier before a noun.

Follow the *step-by-step* instructions to construct the *low-cost* bookshelves.

A *well-designed* keyboard is part of this *state-of-the-art* equipment.

Tip. Don't confuse adverbs ending in *-ly* with compound adjectives: *newly enacted* law and *highly regarded* CEO would not be hyphenated.

✓ *Checkpoint*

Correct any problems in the use of pronouns, adjectives, and adverbs.

31. My manager and me could not resist the once in a lifetime opportunity.

32. Because John and him finished their task so quick, they made a fast trip to the recently opened snack bar.

33. If I do good on the exam, I qualify for many part time jobs and a few full time positions.

34. The vice president told him and I not to take the announcement personal.

35. In the not too distant future, we may enjoy more practical uses of robots.

Punctuation

GUIDE 21: Use commas to separate three or more items (words, phrases, or short clauses) in a series. (CmSer)

Downward communication delivers job instructions, procedures, and appraisals.

In preparing your résumé, try to keep it brief, make it easy to read, and include only job-related information.

The new ice cream flavors include cookie dough, chocolate raspberry truffle, cappuccino, and almond amaretto.

Tip. Some professional writers omit the comma before *and.* However, most business writers prefer to retain that comma because it prevents misreading the last two items as one item. Notice in the previous example how the final two ice cream flavors could have been misread if the comma had been omitted.

GUIDE 22: Use commas to separate introductory clauses and certain phrases from independent clauses. (CmIntro) This guideline describes the comma most often omitted by business writers. Sentences that open with dependent clauses (frequently introduced by words such as *since, when, if, as, although,* and *because)* require commas to separate them from the main idea. The comma helps readers recognize where the introduction ends and the big idea begins. Introductory phrases of four or more words or phrases containing verbal elements also require commas.

If you recognize introductory clauses, you will have no trouble placing the comma. (A comma separates the introductory dependent clause from the main clause.)

When you have mastered this rule, half the battle with commas will be won.

As expected, additional explanations are necessary. (Use a comma even if the introductory clause omits the understood subject: *As we expected.*)

In the spring of last year, we opened our franchise. (Use a comma after a phrase containing four or more words.)

Having considered several alternatives, we decided to invest. (Use a comma after an introductory verbal phrase.)

To invest, we needed $100,000. (Use a comma after an introductory verbal phrase, regardless of its length.)

Tip. Short introductory prepositional phrases (three or fewer words) require no commas. Don't clutter your writing with unnecessary commas after introductory phrases such as *by 2012, in the fall* or *at this time.*

GUIDE 23: Use a comma before the coordinating conjunction in a compound sentence. (CmConj) The most common coordinating conjunctions are *and, or, nor,* and *but.* Occasionally, *for, yet,* and *so* may also function as coordinating conjunctions. When coordinating conjunctions join two independent clauses, commas are needed.

The investment sounded too good to be true, *and* many investors were dubious about it. (Use a comma before the coordinating conjunction *and* in a compound sentence.)

Southern California is the financial fraud capital of the world, *but* some investors refuse to heed warning signs.

Tip. Before inserting a comma, test the two clauses. Can each of them stand alone as a complete sentence? If either is incomplete, skip the comma.

Promoters said the investment offer was for a limited time and could not be extended even one day. (Omit a comma before *and* because the second part of the sentence is not a complete independent clause.)

Lease payments are based largely on your down payment and on the value of the car at the end of the lease. (Omit a comma before *and* because the second half of the sentence is not a complete clause.)

✓ *Checkpoint*

Add appropriate commas.

36. Before she enrolled in this class Erin used to sprinkle her writing with commas semicolons and dashes.

37. After studying punctuation she learned to use commas more carefully and to reduce her reliance on dashes.

38. At this time Erin is engaged in a serious yoga program but she also finds time to enlighten her mind.

39. Next fall Erin may enroll in communication and merchandising or she may work for a semester to earn money.

40. When she completes her junior year she plans to apply for an internship in Los Angeles Burbank or Long Beach.

GUIDE 24: Use commas appropriately in dates, addresses, geographical names, degrees, and long numbers. (CmDate)

September 30, 1963, is his birthday. (For dates use commas before and after the year.)

Send the application to James Kirby, 20045 45th Avenue, Lynnwood, WA 98036, as soon as possible. (For addresses use commas to separate all units except the two-letter state abbreviation and the zip code.)

Lisa expects to move from Cupertino, California, to Sonoma, Arizona, next fall. (For geographical areas use commas to enclose the second element)

Karen Munson, CPA, and Richard B. Larsen, PhD, were the speakers. (For professional designations and academic degrees following names, use commas to enclose each item.)

The latest census figures show the city's population to be 342,000. (In figures use commas to separate every three digits, counting from the right.)

GUIDE 25: Use commas to set off internal sentence interrupters. (CmIn)

Sentence interrupters may be verbal phrases, dependent clauses, contrasting elements, or parenthetical expressions (also called transitional phrases). These interrupters often provide information that is not grammatically essential.

Harvard researchers, working steadily for 18 months, developed a new cancer therapy. (Use commas to set off an internal interrupting verbal phrase.)

The new therapy, which applies a genetically engineered virus, raises hopes among cancer specialists. (Use commas to set off nonessential dependent clauses.)

Dr. James C. Morrison, who is one of the researchers, made the announcement. (Use commas to set off nonessential dependent clauses.)

It was Dr. Morrison, not Dr. Arturo, who led the team effort. (Use commas to set off a contrasting element.)

This new therapy, by the way, was developed from a herpes virus. (Use commas to set off a parenthetical expression.)

Tip. Parenthetical (transitional) expressions are helpful words that guide the reader from one thought to the next. Here are typical parenthetical expressions that require commas:

As a matter of fact	in addition	of course
As a result	in the meantime	on the other hand
Consequently	nevertheless	therefore
for example		

Tip. Always use *two* commas to set off an interrupter, unless it begins or ends a sentence.

✓ *Checkpoint*

Insert necessary commas.

41. James listed 1805 Martin Luther King Street San Antonio Texas 78220 as his forwarding address.

42. This report is not however one that must be classified.

43. Employment of paralegals which is expected to increase 32 percent next year is growing rapidly because of the expanding legal services industry.

44. The contract was signed May 15 2009 and remains in effect until May 15 2015.

45. As a matter of fact the average American drinks enough coffee to require 12 pounds of coffee beans annually.

GUIDE 26: Avoid unnecessary commas. Do not use commas between sentence elements that belong together. Do not automatically insert commas before every *and* or at points where your voice might drop if you were saying the sentence out loud.

Faulty

Growth will be spurred by the increasing complexity of business operations, and by large employment gains in trade and services. (A comma unnecessarily precedes *and.*)

All students with high grades, are eligible for the honor society. (A comma unnecessarily separates the subject and verb.)

One of the reasons for the success of the business honor society is, that it is very active. (A comma unnecessarily separates the verb and its complement.)

Our honor society has, at this time, over 50 members. (Commas unnecessarily separate a prepositional phrase from the sentence.)

✓ *Checkpoint*

Remove unnecessary commas. Add necessary ones.

46. Car companies promote leasing because it brings customers back into their showrooms sooner, and gives dealers a steady supply of late-model used cars.

47. When shopping for a car you may be offered a fantastic leasing deal.

48. The trouble with many leases is, that the value of the car at the end of the lease may be less than expected.

49. We think on the other hand, that you should compare the costs of leasing and buying, and that you should talk to a tax adviser.

50. American and Japanese automakers are, at this time, offering intriguing lease deals.

Semicolons, Colons

GUIDE 27: Use a semicolon to join closely related independent clauses. Experienced writers use semicolons to show readers that two thoughts are closely associated. If the ideas are not related, they should be expressed in separate sentences. Often, but not always, the second independent clause contains a conjunctive adverb (such as *however, consequently, therefore,* or *furthermore)* to show the relation between the two clauses. Use a semicolon before a conjunctive adverb of two or more syllables (such as *however, consequently, therefore*, or *furthermore*) and a comma after it.

Learning history is easy; learning its lessons is almost impossible. (A semicolon joins two independent clauses.)

He was determined to complete his degree; consequently, he studied diligently. (A semicolon precedes the conjunctive adverb, and a comma follows it.)

Serena wanted a luxury apartment located near campus; however, she couldn't afford the rent. (A semicolon precedes the conjunctive adverb, and a comma follows it.)

Tip. Don't use a semicolon unless each clause is truly independent. Try the sentence test. Omit the semicolon if each clause could not stand alone as a complete sentence.

Faulty	**Improved**
There is no point in speaking; unless you can improve on silence. (The second half of the sentence is a dependent clause. It could not stand alone as a sentence.)	There is no point in speaking unless you can improve on silence.
Although I cannot change the direction of the wind; I can adjust my sails to reach my destination. (The first clause could not stand alone.)	Although I cannot change the direction of the wind, I can adjust my sails to reach my destination.

GUIDE 28: Use a semicolon to separate items in a series when one or more of the items contains internal commas.

Representatives from as far away as Blue Bell, Pennsylvania; Bowling Green, Ohio; and Phoenix, Arizona, attended the conference.

Stories circulated about Henry Ford, founder, Ford Motor Company; Lee Iacocca, former CEO, Chrysler Motor Company; and Shoichiro Toyoda, founder, Toyota Motor Company.

GUIDE 29: Use a colon after a complete thought that introduces a list of items.

Words such as *these, the following,* and *as follows* may introduce the list or they may be implied.

The following cities are on the tour: Louisville, Memphis, and New Orleans.

An alternate tour includes several West Coast cities: Seattle, San Francisco, and San Diego.

Tip. Be sure that the statement before a colon is grammatically complete. An introductory statement that ends with a preposition (such as *by, for, at,* and *to)* or a verb (such as *is, are,* or *were)* is incomplete. The list following a preposition or a verb actually functions as an object or as a complement to finish the sentence.

Faulty	**Improved**
Three Big Macs were ordered by: Pam, Jim, and Lee. (Do not use a colon after an incomplete statement.)	Three Big Macs were ordered by Pam, Jim, and Lee.
Other items that they ordered were: fries, Cokes, and salads. (Do not use a colon after an incomplete statement)	Other items that they ordered were fries, Cokes, and salads.

GUIDE 30: Use a colon after business letter salutations and to introduce long quotations.

Dear Mr. Duran: Dear Lisa:

The Asian consultant bluntly said: "Americans tend to be too blabby, too impatient, and too informal for Asian tastes. To succeed in trade with Pacific Rim countries, Americans must become more willing to adapt to native cultures."

Tip. Use a comma to introduce short quotations. Use a colon to introduce long one-sentence quotations and quotations of two or more sentences.

✓ *Checkpoint*

Add appropriate semicolons and colons.

51. Marco's short-term goal is an entry-level job his long-term goal however is a management position.

52. Speakers included the following professors Rebecca Hilbrink University of Alaska Lora Lindsey Ohio University and Michael Malone Central Florida College.

53. The recruiter was looking for three qualities loyalty initiative and enthusiasm.

54. Microsoft seeks experienced individuals however it will hire recent graduates who are skilled.

55. South Florida is an expanding region therefore many business opportunities are available.

Apostrophe

GUIDE 31: Add an apostrophe plus *s* to an ownership word that does not end in an *s* sound.

We hope to show a profit in one year's time. (Add *'s* because the ownership word *year* does not end in *s*.)

The company's assets rose in value. (Add *'s* because the ownership word *company* does not end in *s*.)

All the women's votes were counted. (Add *'s* because the ownership word *women* does not end in *s*.)

GUIDE 32: Add only an apostrophe to an ownership word that ends in an *s* sound—unless an extra syllable can be pronounced easily.

Some workers' benefits will cost more. (Add only an apostrophe because the ownership word *workers* ends in *s*.)

Several months' rent are now due. (Add only an apostrophe because the ownership word *months* ends in *s*.)

The boss's son got the job. (Add *'s* because an extra syllable can be pronounced easily.)

Tip. To determine whether an ownership word ends in *'s*, use it in an *of* phrase. For example, *one month's salary* becomes *the salary of one month*. By isolating the ownership word without its apostrophe, you can decide whether it ends in *s*.

GUIDE 33: Use a possessive pronoun or add *'s* to make a noun possessive when it precedes a gerund (a verb form used as a noun).

We all protested *Laura's* (not *Laura*) smoking. (Add *'s* to the noun preceding the gerund.)

His (not *Him*) talking on his cell phone angered moviegoers. (Use a possessive pronoun before the gerund.)

I appreciate *your* (not *you*) answering the telephone while I was gone. (Use a possessive pronoun before the gerund.)

✓ *Checkpoint*

Correct any problems with possessives.

56. Both companies executives received huge bonuses, even when employees salaries were falling.

57. In just one weeks time, we promise to verify all members names and addresses.

58. The manager and I certainly appreciate you bringing this matter to our CPAs attention.

59. All beneficiaries names must be revealed when insurance companies write policies.

60. Is your sister-in-laws job downtown?

Other Punctuation

GUIDE 34: Use one period to end a statement, command, indirect question, or polite request. Never use two periods.

Matt worked at BioTech, Inc. (Statement. Use only one period.)

Deliver it before 5 p.m. (Command. Use only one period.)

Stacy asked whether she could use the car next weekend. (Indirect question)

Will you please send me an employment application. (Polite request)

Tip. Polite requests often sound like questions. To determine the punctuation, apply the action test. If the request prompts an action, use a period. If it prompts a verbal response, use a question mark.

Faulty	**Improved**
Could you please correct the balance on my next statement? (This polite request prompts an action rather than a verbal response.)	Could you please correct the balance on my next statement.

Tip. To avoid the punctuation dilemma with polite requests, do not phrase the request as a question. Phrase it as a command: *Please correct the balance on my next statement.* It still sounds polite, and the punctuation problem disappears.

GUIDE 35: Use a question mark after a direct question and after statements with questions appended.

Are they hiring at BioTech, Inc.?

Most of their training is in-house, isn't it?

GUIDE 36: Use a dash to (a) set off parenthetical elements containing internal commas, (b) emphasize a sentence interruption, or (c) separate an introductory list from a summarizing statement. The dash has legitimate uses. However, some writers use it whenever they know that punctuation is necessary, but they are not sure exactly what. The dash can be very effective, if not misused.

Three top students—Gene Engle, Donna Hersh, and Mika Sato—won awards. (Use dashes to set off elements with internal commas.)

Executives at IBM—despite rampant rumors in the stock market—remained quiet regarding dividend earnings. (Use dashes to emphasize a sentence interruption.)

Japan, Taiwan, and Turkey—these were areas hit by recent earthquakes. (Use a dash to separate an introductory list from a summarizing statement.)

GUIDE 37: Use parentheses to set off nonessential sentence elements, such as explanations, directions, questions, or references.

Researchers find that the office grapevine (see Chapter 1 for more discussion) carries surprisingly accurate information.

Only two dates (February 15 and March 1) are suitable for the meeting.

Tip. Careful writers use parentheses to de-emphasize and the dash to emphasize parenthetical information. One expert said, "Dashes shout the news; parentheses whisper it."

GUIDE 38: Use quotation marks to (a) enclose the exact words of a speaker or writer; (b) distinguish words used in a special sense, such as slang; or (c) enclose titles of articles, chapters, or other short works.

"If you make your job important," said the consultant, "it's quite likely to return the favor."

The recruiter said that she was looking for candidates with good communication skills. (Omit quotation marks because the exact words of the speaker are not quoted.)

This office discourages "rad" hair styles and clothing. (Use quotes for slang.)

In *BusinessWeek* I saw an article titled "Communication for Global Markets." (Use quotation marks around the title of an article; use all caps, underlines, or italics for the name of the publication.)

Tip. Never use quotation marks arbitrarily, as in *Our "spring" sale starts April 1.*

✓ *Checkpoint*

Add appropriate punctuation.

61. Will you please send your print catalog as soon as possible

62. (Direct quotation) Our Super Bowl promotion said the CEO will cost nearly $500,000

63. (De-emphasize) Two kinds of batteries see page 16 of the instruction booklet may be used in this camera

64. Tim wondered whether sentences could end with two periods

65. All computers have virus protection don't they

Capitalization

GUIDE 39: Capitalize proper nouns and proper adjectives. Capitalize the *specific* names of persons, places, institutions, buildings, religions, holidays, months, organizations, laws, races, languages, and so forth. Do not capitalize seasons, and do not capitalize common nouns that make *general* references.

Proper Nouns	**Common Nouns**
Michelle Deluca	the manufacturer's rep
Everglades National Park	the wilderness park
College of the Redwoods	the community college
Empire State Building	the downtown building
Environmental Protection Agency	the federal agency
Persian, Armenian, Hindi	modern foreign languages
Annual Spring Festival	in the spring

Proper Adjectives

Hispanic markets	Italian dressing
Xerox copy	Japanese executives
Swiss chocolates	Reagan economics

GUIDE 40: Capitalize only specific academic courses and degrees.

Professor Donna Howard, PhD, will teach Accounting 121 next spring.

James Barker, who holds bachelor's and master's degrees, teaches marketing.

Jessica enrolled in classes in management, English, and business law.

GUIDE 41: Capitalize courtesy, professional, religious, government, family, and business titles when they precede names.

Mr. Jameson, Mrs. Alvarez, and Ms. Robinson (Courtesy titles)

Professor Andrews, Dr. Lee (Professional titles)

Rabbi Cohen, Pastor Williams, Pope Benedict (Religious titles)

Senator Tom Harrison, Mayor Jackson (Government titles)

Uncle Edward, Mother Teresa, Cousin Vinney (Family titles)

Vice President Morris, Budget Director Lopez (Business titles)

Do not capitalize a title when it is followed by an appositive (that is, when the title is followed by a noun that renames or explains it).

Only one professor, Jonathan Marcus, favored a tuition hike.

Local candidates counted on their governor, Lee Jones, to help raise funds.

Do not capitalize titles following names unless they are part of an address:

Mark Yoder, president of Yoder Enterprises, hired all employees.

Paula Beech, director of Human Resources, interviewed all candidates.

Send the package to Amanda Harr, Advertising Manager, Cambridge Publishers, 20 Park Plaza, Boston, MA 02116.

Generally, do not capitalize a title that replaces a person's name.

Only the president, his chief of staff, and one senator made the trip.

The director of marketing and the sales manager will meet at 1 p.m.

Do not capitalize family titles used with possessive pronouns.

my mother, his father, your cousin

GUIDE 42: Capitalize the main words in titles, subject lines, and headings.

Main words are all words except (a) the articles *a, an,* and *the;* (b) the conjunctions *and, but, or,* and *nor,* (c) prepositions containing two or three letters (e.g., *of, for, in, on, by*); (d) the word *to* in infinitives (such as *to work, to write,* and *to talk*); (e) the word *as*—unless any of these words are the first or last words in the title, subject line, or heading.

I enjoyed the book *A Customer Is More Than a Name.* (Book title)

Team Meeting to Discuss Deadlines Rescheduled for Friday (Subject line)

We liked the article titled "Advice From a Pro: How to Say It With Pictures." (Article)

Check the Advice and Resources link at the *CareerBuilder* Web site.

(Note that the titles of books are underlined or italicized but the titles of articles are enclosed in quotation marks.)

GUIDE 43: Capitalize names of geographic locations. Capitalize *north, south, east, west,* and their derivatives only when they represent specific geographical regions.

from the Pacific Northwest

living in the West

Midwesterners, Southerners

peace in the Middle East

heading northwest on the highway

west of the city

western Oregon, southern Ohio

a location east of the middle of the city

GUIDE 44: Capitalize the main words in the specific names of departments, divisions, or committees within business organizations. Do not capitalize general references.

All forms are available from our Department of Human Resources.

The Consumer Electronics Division launched an upbeat marketing campaign.

We volunteered for the Employee Social Responsibility Committee.

You might send an application to their personnel department.

GUIDE 45: Capitalize product names only when they refer to trademarked items. Do not capitalize the common names following manufacturers' names.

Dell laptop computer	Skippy peanut butter	NordicTrack treadmill
Eveready Energizer	Norelco razor	Kodak color copier
Coca-Cola	Panasonic plasma television	Big Mac sandwich

GUIDE 46: Capitalize most nouns followed by numbers or letters (except in page, paragraph, line, and verse references).

Room 14	Exhibit A	Flight 12, Gate 43
Figure 2.1	Plan No. 1	Model Z2010

✓ *Checkpoint*

Capitalize all appropriate words.

66. vice president moore bought a new nokia cell phone before leaving for the east coast.

67. when you come on tuesday, travel west on highway 5 and exit at mt. mckinley street.

68. The director of our human resources department called a meeting of the company's building security committee.

69. our manager and president are flying on american airlines flight 34 leaving from gate 69 at the las vegas international airport.

70. my father read a businessweek article titled can you build loyalty with bricks and mortar?

Number Usage

GUIDE 47: Use word form to express (a) numbers *ten* and under and (b) numbers beginning sentences. General references to numbers *ten* and under should be expressed in word form. Also use word form for numbers that begin sentences. If the resulting number involves more than two words, however, recast the sentence so that the number does not fall at the beginning.

We answered *six* telephone calls for the *four* sales reps.

Fifteen customers responded to the *three* advertisements today.

A total of 155 cameras were awarded as prizes. (Avoid beginning the sentence with a long number such as *one hundred fifty-five.*)

GUIDE 48: Use figures to express most references to numbers 11 and over.

Over *150* people from *53* companies attended the two-day workshop.

A four-ounce serving of Haagen-Dazs toffee crunch ice cream contains *300* calories and *19* grams of fat.

GUIDE 49: Use figures to express money, dates, clock time, decimals, and percents.

One item costs only *$1.95*; most, however, were priced between *$10* and *$35*. (Omit the decimals and zeros in even sums of money.)

We scheduled a meeting for May 12. (Notice that we do *not* write May 12th.)

We expect deliveries at 10:15 a.m. and again at 4 p.m. (Use lowercase *a.m.* and *p.m.*)

All packages must be ready by 4 o'clock. (Do *not* write 4:00 o'clock.)

When U.S. sales dropped *4.7* percent, net income fell *9.8* percent. (In contextual material use the word *percent* instead of the symbol %.)

GUIDE 50: Use a combination of words and figures to express sums of 1 million and over. Use words for small fractions.

Orion lost *$62.9 million* in the latest fiscal year on revenues of *$584 million*. (Use a combination of words and figures for sums of 1 million and over.)

Only one half of the registered voters turned out. (Use words for small fractions.)

Tip. To ease your memory load, concentrate on the numbers normally expressed in words: numbers *ten* and under, numbers at the beginning of a sentence, and small fractions. Nearly everything else in business is generally written with figures.

✓ *Checkpoint*

Correct any inappropriate expression of numbers.

71. Although he budgeted fifty dollars, Jake spent 94 dollars and 34 cents for supplies.

72. Is the meeting on November 7th or November 14th?

73. UPS deliveries arrive at nine AM and again at four fifteen PM.

74. The company applied for a fifty thousand dollar loan at six%.

75. The U.S. population is just over 300,000,000, and the world population is estimated to be nearly 6,500,000,000.

Key to Grammar and Mechanics Checkpoint Exercises in Appendix A

This key shows all corrections. If you marked anything else, double-check the appropriate guideline.

1. Disney, destination

2. yearly, which

3. hour; however,

4. pavilion;

5. wedding;

6. If I *were* you, I would have *gone* ....

7. could have *written* ... had *begun* earlier.

8. vice president *saw* ... immediately *came*

9. vice president *were*

10. manager had *known* ... would have *given*

11. time and talent *were* spent (Note that two subjects require a plural verb.)

12. attachments, *was* (Note that the subject is *message*.)

13. Each of ... companies *is* (Note that the subject is *Each*.)

14. list of names and addresses *is* (Note that the subject is *list*.)

15. attorney *has*

16. My partner and *I* .... but *yours*

17. was *hers*, but *its*

18. you and *me* ... *their* printer

19. *There's* not much the boss or *I* can do if *it's* broken, ... reported to him or *me* earlier.

20. but *yours* and *hers*

21. *whomever*

22. *Whom* have you asked ....

23. for *whoever*

24. Matt and *I*

25. by *whoever*

26. Every employee must wear *a* picture identification badge, *OR: All employees* must wear *picture identification badges*.

27. slower career advancement, but *flexible scheduling* appeals to many workers. (Revise to avoid the vague pronoun *it*.)

28. Any renter must pay *the* rent .... *OR: All renters* must pay *their* rent ....

29. reported that *a* computer ... *OR*: reported that *his or her* computer ....

30. communication. *These techniques are* particularly important (Revise to avoid the vague pronoun *This*.)

31. My manager and *I* could not resist the *once-in-a-lifetime* opportunity.

32. John and *he* finished their task so *quickly* (Do not hyphenate *recently opened*.)

33. do *well* ... *part-time* jobs and a few *full-time*

34. told him and *me* ... *personally*.

35. *not-too-distant* future

36. class, Erin ... with commas, semicolons,

37. studying punctuation,

38. program,

39. merchandising,

40. junior year, ... in Los Angeles, Burbank,

41. Street, San Antonio, Texas 78220,

42. not, however,

43. paralegals, ... next year,

44. May 15, 2009, ... May 15, 2015.

45. fact,

46. sooner [delete comma]

47. car,

48. is [delete comma]

49. think, on the other hand, ... buying [delete comma]

50. automakers are [delete comma] at this time [delete comma]

51. entry-level job; his long-term goal, however,

52. professors: Rebecca Hilbrink, University of Alaska; Lora Lindsey, Ohio University; and Michael Malone, Central Florida College.

53. qualities: loyalty, initiative,

54. individuals; however,

55. region; therefore,

56. companies' ... employees'

57. one week's time, ... members'

58. appreciate *your* ... CPA's

59. beneficiaries'

60. sister-in-law's

61. possible.

62. "Our Super Bowl promotion," said the CEO, "will cost nearly $500,000."

63. Two kinds of batteries (see page 16 of the instruction booklet)

64. two periods.

65. protection, don't they?

66. Vice President Moore ... Nokia ... East Coast

67. When ...Tuesday, ... Highway 5 ... Mt. McKinley Street.

68. Human Resources Department ... Building Security Committee

69. Our ... American Airlines Flight 34 ... Gate 69 at the Las Vegas International Airport

70. My ... *BusinessWeek* article titled "Can You Build Loyalty With Bricks and Mortar?"

71. $50 ... $94.34

72. November 7 or November 14 [delete *th*]

73. 9 a.m.... 4:15 p.m. (Note only one period at the end of the sentence.)

74. $50,000 ... 6 percent.

75. 300 million ... 6.5 billion

Confusing Words

accede:	to agree or consent
exceed:	over a limit
accept:	to receive
except:	to exclude; (prep) but
adverse:	opposing; antagonistic
averse:	unwilling; reluctant
advice:	suggestion, opinion
advise:	to counsel or recommend
affect:	to influence
effect:	(n) outcome, result; (v) to bring about, to create
all ready:	prepared
already:	by this time
all right:	satisfactory
alright:	unacceptable variant spelling
altar:	structure for worship
alter:	to change
appraise:	to estimate
apprise:	to inform
ascent:	(n) rising or going up
assent:	(v) to agree or consent
assure:	to promise
ensure:	to make certain
insure:	to protect from loss
capital:	(n) city that is seat of government; wealth of an individual; (adj) chief
capitol:	building that houses state or national lawmakers
cereal:	breakfast food
serial:	arranged in sequence
cite:	to quote; to summon
site:	location
sight:	a view; to see
coarse:	rough texture
course:	a route; part of a meal; a unit of learning
complement:	that which completes
compliment:	(n) praise or flattery; (v) to praise or flatter
conscience:	regard for fairness
conscious:	aware
council:	governing body
counsel:	(n) advice, attorney, consultant; (v) to give advice
credible:	believable
creditable:	good enough for praise or esteem; reliable
desert:	(n) arid land; (v) to abandon
dessert:	sweet food
device:	invention or mechanism
devise:	to design or arrange
disburse:	to pay out
disperse:	to scatter widely
elicit:	to draw out
illicit:	unlawful
envelop:	(v) to wrap, surround, or conceal
envelope:	(n) a container for a written message
every day:	each single day
everyday:	ordinary
farther:	a greater distance
further:	additional
formally:	in a formal manner
formerly:	in the past
grate:	(v) to reduce to small particles; to cause irritation; (n) a frame of crossed bars blocking a passage
great:	(adj) large in size; numerous; eminent or distinguished
hole:	an opening
whole:	complete
imply:	to suggest indirectly
infer:	to reach a conclusion
lean:	(v) to rest against; (adj) not fat
lien:	(n) legal right or claim to property
liable:	legally responsible
libel:	damaging written statement
loose:	not fastened
lose:	to misplace
miner:	person working in a mine
minor:	(adj) lesser; (n) person under age
patience:	calm perseverance
patients:	people receiving medical treatment
personal:	private, individual
personnel:	employees
plaintiff:	(n) one who initiates a lawsuit
plaintive:	(adj) expressive of suffering or woe
populace:	(n) the masses; population of a place
populous:	(adj) densely populated
precede:	to go before
proceed:	to continue
precedence:	priority
precedents:	events used as an example
principal:	(n) capital sum; school official; (adj) chief

principle:	rule of action
stationary:	immovable
stationery:	writing material
than:	conjunction showing comparison
then:	adverb meaning "at that time"
their:	possessive form of *they*
there:	at that place or point
they're:	contraction of *they are*
to:	a preposition; the sign of the infinitive
too:	an adverb meaning "also" or "to an excessive extent"
two:	a number
waiver:	abandonment of a claim
waver:	to shake or fluctuate

160 Frequently Misspelled Words

absence
accommodate
achieve
acknowledgment
across
adequate
advisable
analyze
annually
appointment
argument
automatically
bankruptcy
becoming
beneficial
budget
business
calendar
canceled
catalog
changeable
column
committee
congratulate
conscience
conscious
consecutive
consensus
consistent
control
convenient
correspondence
courteous
criticize
decision
deductible
defendant
definitely
dependent
describe
desirable
destroy
development
disappoint
dissatisfied
division
efficient
embarrass
emphasis
emphasize
employee
envelope
equipped
especially
evidently
exaggerate
excellent
exempt
existence
extraordinary
familiar
fascinate
feasible
February
fiscal
foreign
forty
fourth
friend
genuine
government
grammar
grateful
guarantee
harass
height
hoping
immediate
incidentally
incredible
independent
indispensable
interrupt
irrelevant
itinerary
judgment
knowledge
legitimate
library
license
maintenance
manageable
manufacturer
mileage
miscellaneous
mortgage
necessary
nevertheless
ninety
ninth
noticeable
occasionally
occurred
offered
omission
omitted
opportunity
opposite
ordinarily
paid
pamphlet
permanent
permitted
pleasant
practical
prevalent
privilege
probably
procedure
profited
prominent
quality
quantity
questionnaire
receipt
receive
recognize
recommendation
referred
regarding
remittance
representative
restaurant
schedule
secretary
separate
similar
sincerely
software
succeed
sufficient
supervisor
surprise
tenant
therefore
thorough
though
through
truly
undoubtedly
unnecessarily
usable
usage
using
usually
valuable
volume
weekday
writing
yield

Document Format Guide

APPENDIX B

Business communicators produce numerous documents that have standardized formats. Becoming familiar with these formats is important because business documents actually carry two kinds of messages. Verbal messages are conveyed by the words chosen to express the writer's ideas. Nonverbal messages are conveyed largely by the appearance of a document and its adherence to recognized formats. To ensure that your documents carry favorable nonverbal messages about you and your organization, you will want to give special attention to the appearance and formatting of your e-mails, letters, envelopes, and fax cover sheets.

E-Mail

E-mails are sent by computers through networks. After reading e-mails, receivers may print, store, or delete them. E-mail is an appropriate channel for *short* messages. E-mails should not replace business letters or memos that are lengthy, require permanent records, or transmit confidential or sensitive information. Chapter 7 presented guidelines for preparing e-mails. This section provides additional information on formats and usage. The following suggestions, illustrated in Figure B.1 and also in Figure 7.1 on page 194, may guide you in setting up the parts of any e-mail. Always check, however, with your organization so that you can follow its practices.

FIGURE B.1 E-Mail

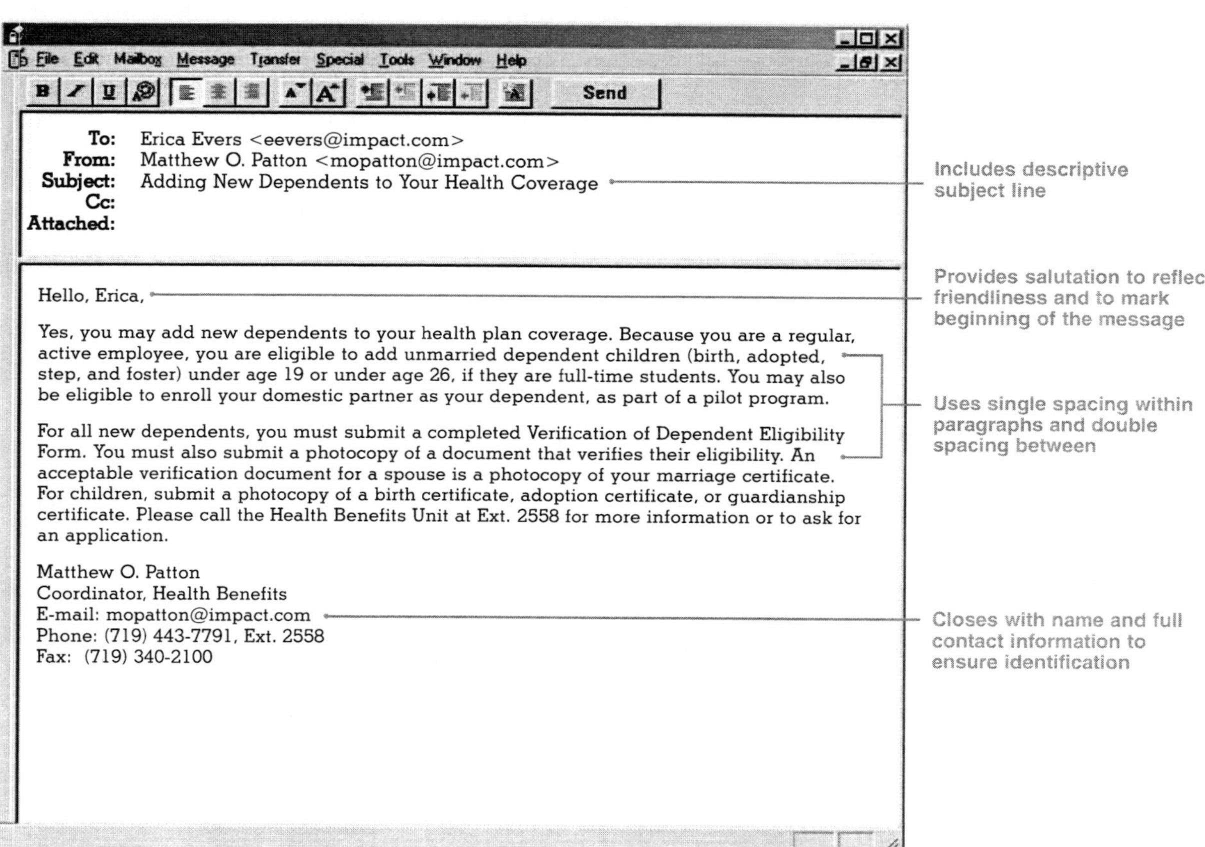

***To* Line.** Include the receiver's e-mail address after *To*. If the receiver's address is recorded in your address book, you just have to click on it. Be sure to enter all addresses very carefully since one mistyped letter prevents delivery.

***From* Line.** Most mail programs automatically include your name and e-mail address after *From*.

***Cc* and *Bcc*.** Insert the e-mail address of anyone who is to receive a copy of the message. *Cc* stands for carbon copy or courtesy copy. Don't be tempted, though, to send needless copies just because it is easy. *Bcc* stands for blind carbon copy. Some writers use *bcc* to send a copy of the message without the addressee's knowledge. Writers also use the *bcc* line for mailing lists. When a message is sent to a number of people and their e-mail addresses should not be revealed, the *bcc* line works well to conceal the names and addresses of all receivers.

Subject. Identify the subject of the e-mail with a brief but descriptive summary of the topic. Be sure to include enough information to be clear and compelling. Capitalize the initial letters of main words. Main words are all words except (a) the articles *a, an,* and *the*; (b) prepositions containing two or three letters (such as *at, to, on, by, for*); (c) the word *to* in an infinitive (*to work, to write*); and (d) the word *as*—unless any of these words are the first or last word in the subject line.

Salutation. Include a brief greeting, if you like. Some writers use a salutation such as *Dear Erica* followed by a comma or a colon. Others are more informal with *Hi, Erica; Hello, Erica; Good morning*; or *Greetings*. See Chapter 7 for additional discussion of e-mail greetings.

Message. Cover just one topic in your message, and try to keep your total message under three screens in length. Single-space and be sure to use both upper- and lowercase letters. Double-space between paragraphs.

Closing. Conclude an e-mail, if you like, with *Cheers, Best wishes,* or *Warm regards,* followed by your name and complete contact information. Some people omit their e-mail address because they think it is provided automatically. However, programs and routers do not always transmit the address. Therefore, always include it along with other identifying information in the closing.

Attachment. Use the attachment window or button to select the path and file name of any file you wish to send with your e-mail. You can also attach a Web page to your message.

Business Letters

Business communicators write business letters primarily to correspond with people outside the organization. Letters may go to customers, vendors, other businesses, and the government, as discussed in Chapters 8, 9, and 10. The following information will help you format your letters following conventional guidelines.

Spacing and Punctuation

For some time typists left two spaces after end punctuation (periods, question marks, and so forth). This practice was necessary, it was thought, because typewriters did not have proportional spacing and sentences were easier to read if two spaces separated them. Professional typesetters, however, never followed this practice because they used proportional spacing, and readability was not a problem. Influenced by the look of typeset publications, many writers now leave only one space after end punctuation. As a practical matter, however, it is not wrong to use two spaces.

Letter Placement and Line Endings

The easiest way to place letters on the page is to use the defaults of your word processing program. In Microsoft Word 2003, default side margins are set at 1¼ inch; in Word 2007 they are set at 1 inch. Many companies today find these margins acceptable. If you want to adjust your margins to better balance shorter letters, use the following chart:

Words in Body of Letter	Margin Settings	Blank Lines After Date
Under 200	1½ inches	4 to 10
Over 200	1 inch	2 to 3

Experts say that a ragged-right margin is easier to read than a justified (even) margin. You might want to turn off the justification feature of your word processing program if it automatically justifies the right margin.

Business Letter Parts

Professional-looking business letters are arranged in a conventional sequence with standard parts. Following is a discussion of how to use these letter parts properly. Figure B.2 illustrates the parts of a block style letter. See Chapter 8 for additional discussion of letters and their parts.

Letterhead. Most business organizations use 8½ × 11-inch paper printed with a letterhead displaying their official name, street address, Web address, e-mail address, and telephone and fax numbers. The letterhead may also include a logo and an advertising message.

Dateline. On letterhead paper you should place the date one blank line below the last line of the letterhead or 2 inches from the top edge of the paper (line 13). On plain paper place the date immediately below your return address. Because the date goes on line 13, start the return address an appropriate number of lines above it. The most common dateline format is as follows: *June 9, 2012*. Don't use *th* (or *rd, nd* or *st*) when the date is written this way. For European or military correspondence, use the following dateline format: *9 June 2012*. Notice that no commas are used.

Addressee and Delivery Notations. Delivery notations such as *FAX TRANSMISSION, FEDEX, MESSENGER DELIVERY, CONFIDENTIAL,* or *CERTIFIED MAIL* are typed in all capital letters two blank lines above the inside address.

Inside Address. Type the inside address—that is, the address of the organization or person receiving the letter—single-spaced, starting at the left margin. The number of lines between the dateline and the inside address depends on the size of the letter body, the type size (point or pitch size), and the length of the typing lines. Generally, one to nine blank lines are appropriate.

Be careful to duplicate the exact wording and spelling of the recipient's name and address on your documents. Usually, you can copy this information from the letterhead of the correspondence you are answering. If, for example, you are responding to *Jackson & Perkins Company*, do not address your letter to *Jackson and Perkins Corp.*

Always be sure to include a courtesy title such as *Mr., Ms., Mrs., Dr.,* or *Professor* before a person's name in the inside address—for both the letter and the envelope. Although many women in business today favor *Ms.*, you should use whatever title the addressee prefers.

In general, avoid abbreviations such as *Ave.* or *Co.* unless they appear in the printed letterhead of the document being answered.

Attention Line. An attention line allows you to send your message officially to an organization but to direct it to a specific individual, officer, or department. However, if you know an individual's complete name, it is always better to use it as the first line of the inside address and avoid an attention line. Two common formats for attention lines follow:

The MultiMedia Company
931 Calkins Avenue
Rochester, NY 14301

ATTENTION MARKETING DIRECTOR

The MultiMedia Company
Attention: Marketing Director
931 Calkins Avenue
Rochester, NY 14301

FIGURE B.2 Block and Modified Block Letter Styles

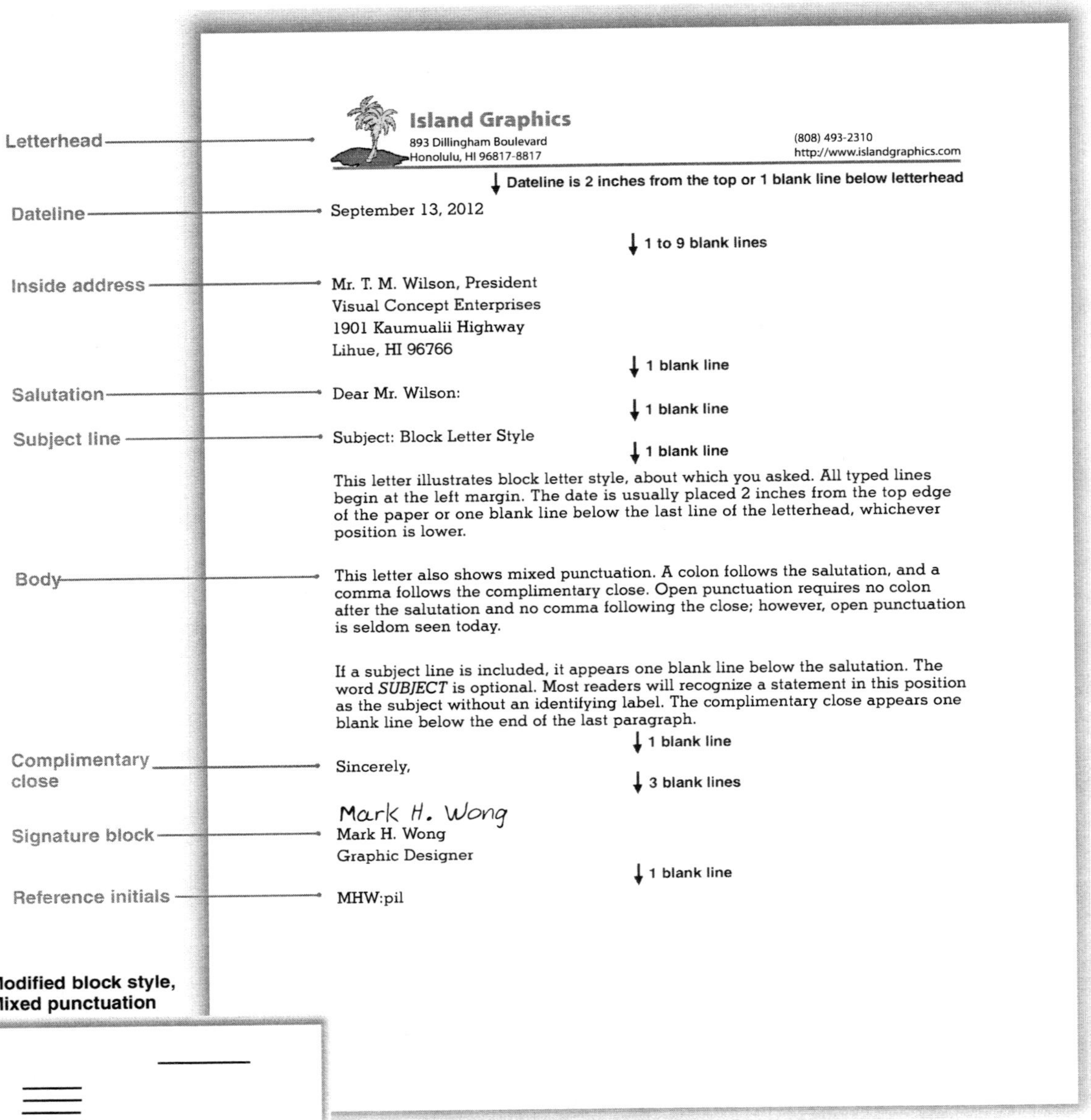

Letterhead — **Island Graphics**
893 Dillingham Boulevard
Honolulu, HI 96817-8817
(808) 493-2310
http://www.islandgraphics.com

↓ Dateline is 2 inches from the top or 1 blank line below letterhead

Dateline — September 13, 2012

↓ 1 to 9 blank lines

Inside address — Mr. T. M. Wilson, President
Visual Concept Enterprises
1901 Kaumualii Highway
Lihue, HI 96766

↓ 1 blank line

Salutation — Dear Mr. Wilson:

↓ 1 blank line

Subject line — Subject: Block Letter Style

↓ 1 blank line

Body — This letter illustrates block letter style, about which you asked. All typed lines begin at the left margin. The date is usually placed 2 inches from the top edge of the paper or one blank line below the last line of the letterhead, whichever position is lower.

This letter also shows mixed punctuation. A colon follows the salutation, and a comma follows the complimentary close. Open punctuation requires no colon after the salutation and no comma following the close; however, open punctuation is seldom seen today.

If a subject line is included, it appears one blank line below the salutation. The word *SUBJECT* is optional. Most readers will recognize a statement in this position as the subject without an identifying label. The complimentary close appears one blank line below the end of the last paragraph.

↓ 1 blank line

Complimentary close — Sincerely,

↓ 3 blank lines

Mark H. Wong

Signature block — Mark H. Wong
Graphic Designer

↓ 1 blank line

Reference initials — MHW:pil

Modified block style, Mixed punctuation

In the modified block style letter shown at the left, the date is centered or aligned with the complimentary close and signature block, which start at the center. Mixed punctuation includes a colon after the salutation and a comma after the complimentary close, as shown above and at the left.

Attention lines may be typed in all caps or with upper- and lowercase letters. The colon following *Attention* is optional. Notice that an attention line may be placed one blank line below the address block or printed as the second line of the inside address. Use the latter format so that you may copy the address block to the envelope and the attention line will not interfere with the last-line placement of the zip code. Mail can be sorted more easily if the zip code appears in the last line of a typed address. Whenever possible, use a person's name as the first line of an address instead of putting that name in an attention line.

Salutation. For most letter styles, place the letter greeting, or salutation, one blank line below the last line of the inside address or the attention line (if used). If the letter is addressed to an individual, use that person's courtesy title and last name (*Dear Mr. Lanham*). Even if you are on a first-name basis (*Dear Leslie*), be sure to add a colon (not a comma or a semicolon) after the salutation. Do not use an individual's full name in the salutation (not *Dear Mr. Leslie Lanham*) unless you are unsure of gender (*Dear Leslie Lanham*).

For letters with attention lines or those addressed to organizations, the selection of an appropriate salutation has become more difficult. Formerly, writers used *Gentlemen* generically for all organizations. With increasing numbers of women in business management today, however, *Gentlemen* is problematic. Because no universally acceptable salutation has emerged as yet, you could use *Ladies and Gentlemen* or *Gentlemen and Ladies*.

Subject and Reference Lines. Although experts suggest placing the subject line one blank line below the salutation, many businesses actually place it above the salutation. Use whatever style your organization prefers. Reference lines often show policy or file numbers; they generally appear one blank line above the salutation. Use initial capital letters for the main words or all capital letters.

Body. Most business letters and memorandums are single-spaced, with double-spacing between paragraphs. Very short messages may be double-spaced with indented paragraphs.

Complimentary Close. Typed one blank line below the last line of the letter, the complimentary close may be formal (*Very truly yours*) or informal (*Sincerely* or *Cordially*).

Signature Block. In most letter styles, the writer's typed name and optional identification appear three or four blank lines below the complimentary close. The combination of name, title, and organization information should be arranged to achieve a balanced look. The name and title may appear on the same line or on separate lines, depending on the length of each. Use commas to separate categories within the same line, but not to conclude a line.

Sincerely yours,

Jeremy M. Wood

Jeremy M. Wood, Manager
Technical Sales and Services

Cordially yours,

Casandra Baker-Murillo

Casandra Baker-Murillo
Executive Vice President

Some organizations include their names in the signature block. In such cases the organization name appears in all caps one blank line below the complimentary close, as shown here:

Cordially,

LIPTON COMPUTER SERVICES

Shelina A. Simpson

Shelina A. Simpson
Executive Assistant

FIGURE B.3 Second-Page Heading

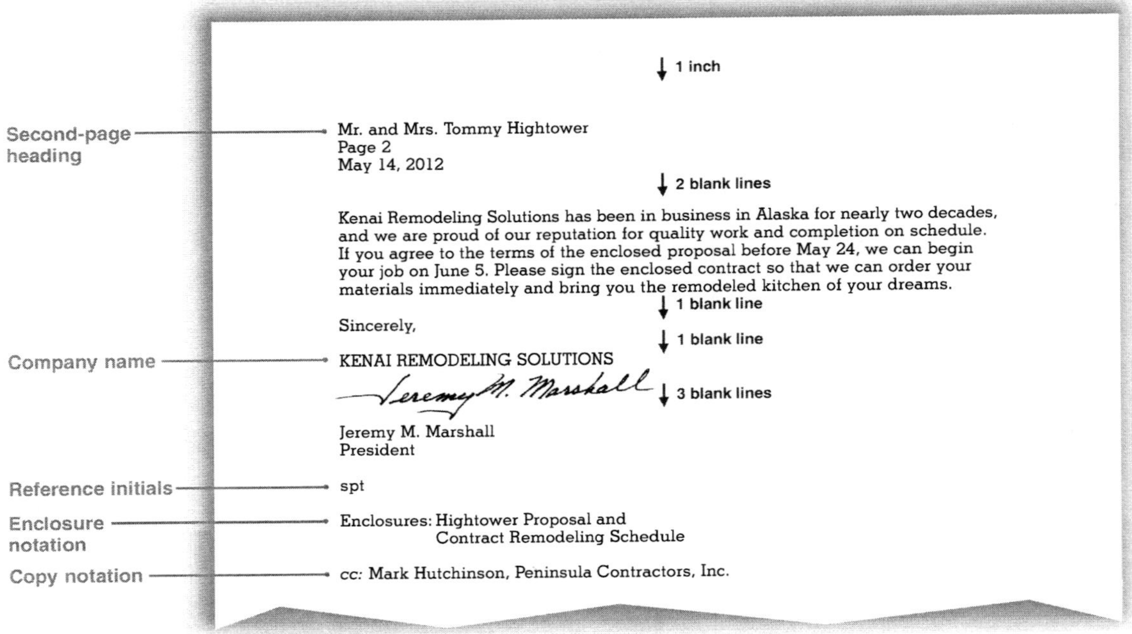

Reference Initials. If used, the initials of the typist and writer are typed one blank line below the writer's name and title. Generally, the writer's initials are capitalized and the typist's are lowercased, but this format varies.

Enclosure Notation. When an enclosure or attachment accompanies a document, a notation to that effect appears one blank line below the reference initials. This notation reminds the typist to insert the enclosure in the envelope, and it reminds the recipient to look for the enclosure or attachment. The notation may be spelled out (*Enclosure, Attachment*), or it may be abbreviated (*Enc., Att.*). It may indicate the number of enclosures or attachments, and it may also identify a specific enclosure (*Enclosure: Form 1099*).

Copy Notation. If you make copies of correspondence for other individuals, you may use *cc* to indicate courtesy copy, *pc* to indicate photocopy, or merely *c* for any kind of copy. A colon following the initial(s) is optional.

Second-Page Heading. When a letter extends beyond one page, use plain paper of the same quality and color as the first page. Identify the second and succeeding pages with a heading consisting of the name of the addressee, the page number, and the date. Use the following format or the one shown in Figure B.3:

Ms. Sara Hendricks   2   May 3, 2012

Both headings appear six blank lines (1 inch) from the top edge of the paper followed by two blank lines to separate them from the continuing text. Avoid using a second page if you have only one line or the complimentary close and signature block to fill that page.

Plain-Paper Return Address. If you prepare a personal or business letter on plain paper, place your address immediately above the date as shown at the top of the next page. Do not include your name; you will type (and sign) your name at the end of your letter. If your return address contains two lines, begin typing so that the date appears 2 inches from the top. Avoid abbreviations except for a two-letter state abbreviation.

580 East Leffels Street
Springfield, OH 45501
December 14, 2012

Ms. Ellen Siemens
Escrow Department
TransOhio First Federal
1220 Wooster Boulevard
Columbus, OH 43218-2900

Dear Ms. Siemens:

The above return address and inside address illustrate the personal business style. For letters in the block style, type the return address at the left margin. For modified block style letters, start the return address at the center to align with the complimentary close.

Letter and Punctuation Styles

Most business letters today are prepared in either block or modified block style, and they generally use mixed punctuation.

Block Style. In the block style, shown in Figure B.2 on page B-4, all lines begin at the left margin. This style is a favorite because it is easy to format.

Modified Block Style. The modified block style differs from block style in that the date and closing lines appear in the center, as shown at the bottom of Figure B.2. The date may be (a) centered, (b) begun at the center of the page (to align with the closing lines), or (c) backspaced from the right margin. The signature block—including the complimentary close, writer's name and title, or organization identification—begins at the center. The first line of each paragraph may begin at the left margin or may be indented five or ten spaces. All other lines begin at the left margin.

Mixed Punctuation Style. Most businesses today use mixed punctuation, shown in Figure B.2. It requires a colon after the salutation and a comma after the complimentary close. Even when the salutation is a first name, a colon is appropriate.

Envelopes

An envelope should be of the same quality and color of stationery as the letter it carries. Because the envelope introduces your message and makes the first impression, you need to be especially careful in addressing it. Moreover, how you fold the letter is important.

Return Address. The return address is usually printed in the upper left corner of an envelope, as shown in Figure B.4 on the next page. In large companies some form of identification (the writer's initials, name, or location) may be typed above the company name and address. This identification helps return the letter to the sender in case of nondelivery.

On an envelope without a printed return address, single-space the return address in the upper left corner. Beginning on line 3 on the fourth space (½ inch) from the left edge, type the writer's name, title, company, and mailing address. On a word processor, select the appropriate envelope size and make adjustments to approximate this return address location.

Mailing Address. On legal-sized No. 10 envelopes (4⅛ x 9½ inches), begin the address on line 13 about 4¼ inches from the left edge, as shown in Figure B.4. For small envelopes (3⅝ x 6½ inches), begin typing on line 12 about 2½ inches from the left edge. On a word processor, select the correct envelope size and check to be sure your address falls in the desired location.

The U.S. Postal Service recommends that addresses be typed in all caps without any punctuation. This Postal Service style, shown in the small envelope in Figure B.4, was originally developed to facilitate scanning by optical character readers. Today's OCRs, however, are so sophisticated that they scan upper- and lowercase letters easily. Many companies today do not follow the Postal Service format because they prefer to use the same format for the envelope as for the inside address. If the same format is used, writers can take advantage of word processing programs to copy the inside address to the envelope, thus saving keystrokes and reducing errors. Having the same format on both the inside address and the envelope also looks more professional and consistent. For those reasons you may choose to use the familiar upper- and lowercase combination format. But you will want to check with your organization to learn its preference.

In addressing your envelopes for delivery in this country or in Canada, use the two-letter state and province abbreviations shown in Figure B.5. Notice that these abbreviations are in capital letters without periods.

Folding. The way a letter is folded and inserted into an envelope sends additional nonverbal messages about a writer's professionalism and carefulness. Most businesspeople follow the procedures shown here, which produce the least number of creases to distract readers.

For large No. 10 envelopes, begin with the letter face up. Fold slightly less than one third of the sheet toward the top, as shown in the following diagram. Then fold down the top third to within ⅓ inch of the bottom fold. Insert the letter into the envelope with the last fold toward the bottom of the envelope.

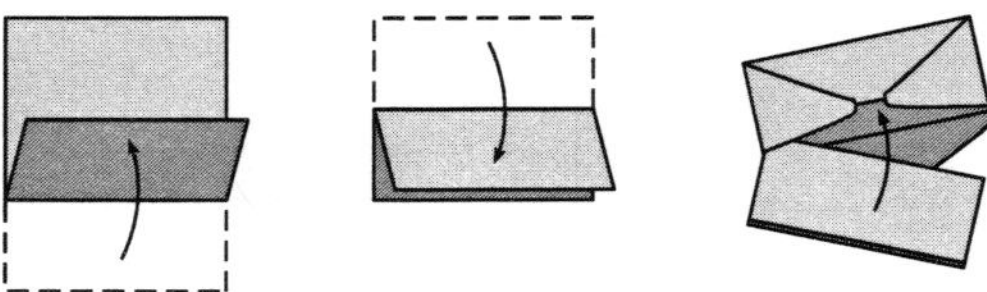

For small No. 6¾ envelopes, begin by folding the bottom up to within ⅓ inch of the top edge. Then fold the right third over to the left. Fold the left third to within ⅓ inch of the last fold. Insert the last fold into the envelope first.

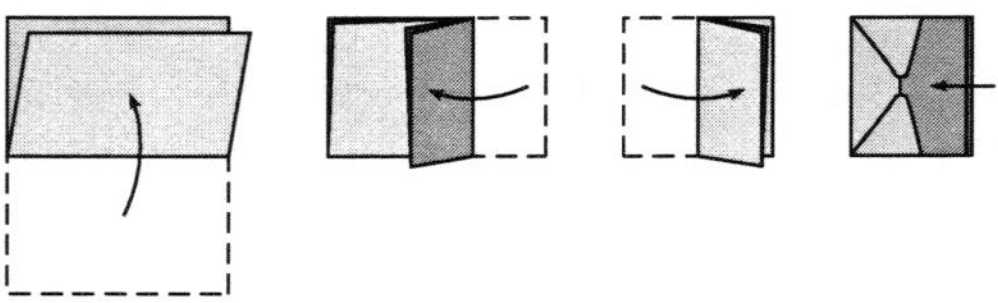

FIGURE B.4 **Envelope Formats**

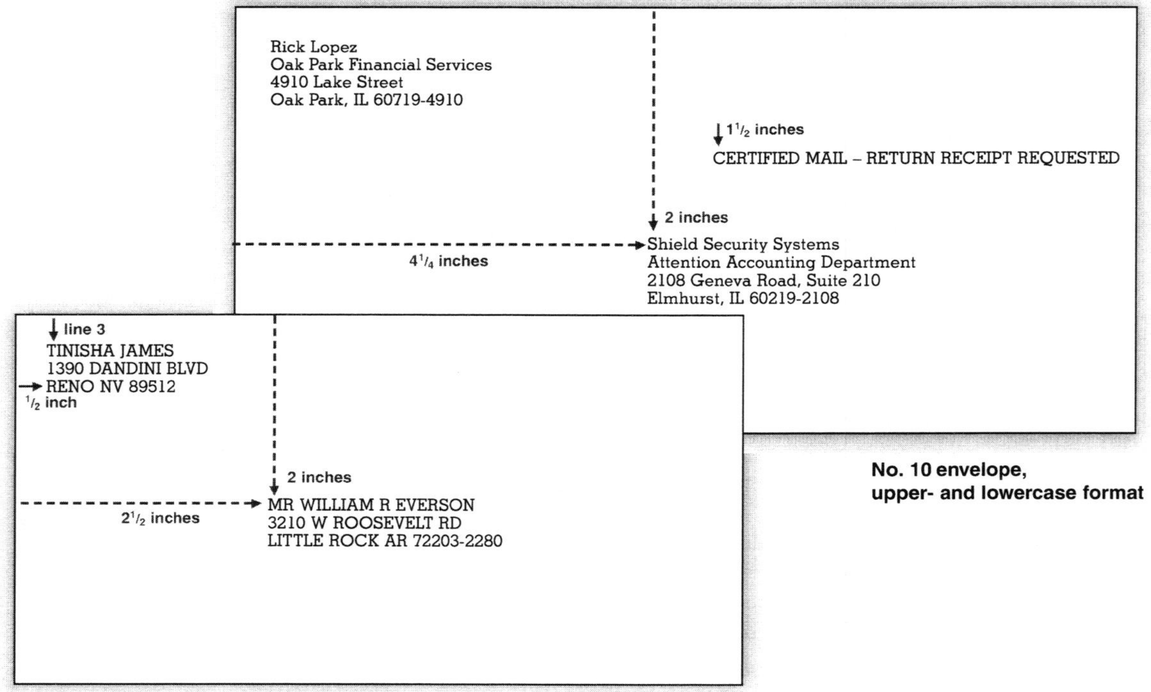

No. 10 envelope, upper- and lowercase format

No. 6¾ envelope, Postal Service uppercase format

FIGURE B.5 Abbreviations of States, Territories, and Provinces

State or Territory	Two-Letter Abbreviation	State or Territory	Two-Letter Abbreviation
Alabama	AL	North Carolina	NC
Alaska	AK	North Dakota	ND
Arizona	AZ	Ohio	OH
Arkansas	AR	Oklahoma	OK
California	CA	Oregon	OR
Canal Zone	CZ	Pennsylvania	PA
Colorado	CO	Puerto Rico	PR
Connecticut	CT	Rhode Island	RI
Delaware	DE	South Carolina	SC
District of Columbia	DC	South Dakota	SD
Florida	FL	Tennessee	TN
Georgia	GA	Texas	TX
Guam	GU	Utah	UT
Hawaii	HI	Vermont	VT
Idaho	ID	Virgin Islands	VI
Illinois	IL	Virginia	VA
Indiana	IN	Washington	WA
Iowa	IA	West Virginia	WV
Kansas	KS	Wisconsin	WI
Kentucky	KY	Wyoming	WY
Louisiana	LA	**Canadian Province**	
Maine	ME	Alberta	AB
Maryland	MD	British Columbia	BC
Massachusetts	MA	Labrador	LB
Michigan	MI	Manitoba	MB
Minnesota	MN	New Brunswick	NB
Mississippi	MS	Newfoundland	NF
Missouri	MO	Northwest Territories	NT
Montana	MT	Nova Scotia	NS
Nebraska	NE	Ontario	ON
Nevada	NV	Prince Edward Island	PE
New Hampshire	NH	Quebec	PQ
New Jersey	NJ	Saskatchewan	SK
New Mexico	NM	Yukon Territory	YT
New York	NY		

Fax Cover Sheet

Documents transmitted by fax are usually introduced by a cover sheet, such as that shown in Figure B.6. As with memos, the format varies considerably. Important items to include are (a) the name and fax number of the receiver, (b) the name and fax number of the sender, (c) the number of pages being sent, and (d) the name and telephone number of the person to notify in case of unsatisfactory transmission.

When the document being transmitted requires little explanation, you may prefer to attach an adhesive note (such as a Post-it fax transmittal form) instead of a full cover sheet. These notes carry essentially the same information as shown in our printed fax cover sheet. They are perfectly acceptable in most business organizations and can save considerable paper and transmission costs.

FIGURE B.6 Fax Cover Sheet

FAX TRANSMISSION

DATE: ______________________________

TO: ______________________________ FAX NUMBER: ____________________
____
____

FROM: ______________________________ FAX NUMBER: ____________________
____
____

NUMBER OF PAGES TRANSMITTED INCLUDING THIS COVER SHEET: ____________________

MESSAGE:

If any part of this fax transmission is missing or not clearly received, please call:

NAME: ______________________________

PHONE: ______________________________

Documentation Guide

APPENDIX C

For many reasons business writers are careful to properly document report data. Citing sources strengthens a writer's argument, as you learned in Chapter 11. Acknowledging sources also shields writers from charges of plagiarism. Moreover, good references help readers pursue further research.

Before we discuss specific documentation formats, you must understand the difference between *source* notes and *content* notes. Source notes identify quotations, paraphrased passages, and author references. They lead readers to the sources of cited information, and they must follow a consistent format. Content notes, on the other hand, enable writers to add comments, explain information not directly related to the text, or refer readers to other sections of a report. Because content notes are generally infrequent, most writers identify them in the text with a raised asterisk (*). At the bottom of the page, the asterisk is repeated with the content note following. If two content notes appear on one page, a double asterisk identifies the second reference.

Your real concern will be with source notes. These identify quotations or paraphrased ideas in the text, and they direct readers to a complete list of references (a bibliography) at the end of your report. Researchers have struggled for years to develop the perfect documentation system, one that is efficient for the writer and crystal clear to the reader. As a result, many systems exist, each with its advantages. The important thing for you is to adopt one system and use it consistently.

Students frequently ask, "But what documentation system is most used in business?" Actually, no one method dominates. Many businesses have developed their own hybrid systems. These companies generally supply guidelines illustrating their in-house style to employees. Before starting any research project on the job, you will want to inquire about your organization's preferred documentation style. You can also look in the files for examples of previous reports.

References are usually cited in two places: (a) a brief citation appears in the text, and (b) a complete citation appears in a bibliography at the end of the report. The two most common formats for citations and bibliographies in academic work are those of the Modern Language Association (MLA) and the American Psychological Association (APA). Each has its own style for textual references and bibliography lists. The citations in this textbook are based on the APA style, which is increasingly the standard in business communication.

Modern Language Association Format

Writers in the humanities and liberal arts frequently use the MLA format, which is illustrated in Figure C.1. In parentheses close to the textual reference appears the author's name and page cited. If no author is known, a shortened version of the source title is used. At the end of the report, the writer lists alphabetically all references in a bibliography called "Works Cited." The MLA no longer requires the use of URLs in Web citations because Web addresses change and most readers can find Web addresses by using a Web browser and searching for the publication title. In another recent change, MLA style now requires identification of the publication medium, such as *Print* or *Web.* For more information consult *MLA Handbook for Writers of Research Papers,* 7e (New York: The Modern Language Association of America, 2009) or Rossiter's *The MLA Pocket Handbook* (DW Publishing).

MLA In-Text Format. In-text citations generally appear close to the point where the reference is mentioned or at the end of the sentence inside the closing period. Follow these guidelines:

- Include the last name of the author(s) and the page number. Do not use a comma, as (Smith 310).

FIGURE C.1 Portions of MLA Text Page and Works Cited

Peanut butter was first delivered to the world by a St. Louis physician in 1890. As discussed at the Peanut Advisory Board's Web site, peanut butter was originally promoted as a protein substitute for elderly patients ("History"). However, it was the 1905 Universal Exposition in St. Louis that truly launched peanut butter. Since then, annual peanut butter consumption has zoomed to 3.3 pounds a person in the United States (Barrons).

America's farmers produce 1.6 million tons of peanuts annually, about half of which is used for oil, nuts, and candy. Lisa Gibbons, executive secretary of the Peanut Advisory Board, says that "peanuts in some form are in the top four candies: Snickers, Reese's Peanut Butter Cups, Peanut M & Ms, and Butterfingers" (Meadows 32).

Works Cited

Barrons, Elizabeth Ruth. "A Comparison of Domestic and International Consumption of Legumes." *Journal of Economic Agriculture* 23 (2010): 45–49. Print.

"History of Peanut Butter." *Peanut Advisory Board.* Alabama Peanut Producers Association. (n.d.) Web. Retrieved 19 Jan. 2011.

Meadows, Mark Allen. "Peanut Crop Is Anything but Peanuts at Home and Overseas." *Business Monthly* May 2011: 31–34. Print.

- If the author's name is mentioned in the text, cite only the page number in parentheses. Do not include either the word *page* or the abbreviations *p.* or *pp.*
- If no author is known, refer to the document title or a shortened version of it, as ("Facts at Fingertips" 102).

MLA Bibliographic Format. In the "Works Cited" bibliography, list all references cited in a report. Some writers include all works consulted. A portion of an MLA bibliography is shown in Figure C.1. A more complete list of model references appears in Figure C.2. Following are selected guidelines summarizing important points regarding MLA bibliographic format:

- Use italics for the titles of books, magazines, newspapers, journals, and Web sites. Capitalize all main words.
- Enclose the titles of magazine, newspaper, and journal articles in quotation marks. Include volume and issue numbers for journals only.
- Use the following sequence for electronic sources: author; article name in quotation marks; title of Web site, project, or book in italics; name of institution, organization, or publisher affiliated with the site; page numbers if available; URL (only if necessary for retrieval); and publication medium (such as *Web, Print,* or *PDF*); and access date.

American Psychological Association Format

Popular in the social and physical sciences, the American Psychological Association (APA) documentation style uses parenthetic citations. That is, each author reference is shown in parentheses when cited in the text, as shown in Figure C.3. At the end of the report, all references are listed alphabetically in a bibliography called "References." Because online materials can change, APA now recommends providing a digital object identifier (DOI) when available rather than the URL. In another departure from previous advice, APA style no longer requires the date of retrieval. For more information about APA formats, see the *Publication Manual of the American Psychological Association*, 6e (Washington, DC: American Psychological Association, 2009) or Rossiter's *The APA Pocket Handbook* (DW Publishing).

FIGURE C.2 MLA Sample Works Cited

Works Cited

American Airlines. *2011 Annual Report.* Fort Worth, TX: AMR Corporation. Print. — Annual report, print

Atamian, Richard A., and Ellen Ferranto. *Driving Market Forces.* New York: HarperCollins, 2010. Print. — Book, two authors, print

"Audio Conferencing." *Encyclopaedia Britannica*. 2010. *Britannica.com*. Web. 19 Oct. 2010. — Encyclopedia, Web

Austin, Anthony. Personal interview. 16 Jan. 2012. — Interview

Balcazar, Saul. "The Future of Investing," *Fortune* 1 Mar. 2010: 62–67. *ABI/Inform*. Web. 15 Mar. 2010. — Magazine article, Web database

Berss, Marcia. "Protein Man," *Forbes* 24 Oct. 2011: 65–66. Print. — Magazine article, print

Cantrell, Mark R., and Hilary Watson. "Violence in Today's Workplace." *Office Review* 10 Jan. 2010: 24–27. PDF file. 23 May 2011. — Magazine article, PDF file

"Globalization Often Means That the Fast Track Leads Overseas." *The Washington Post* 16 June 2011: A1, A4. Print. — Newspaper article, no author, print

Grover, Hal. "When Taking a Tip From a Job Network, Proceed With Caution." *The Wall Street Journal* 7 Feb. 2011: B1. Print. — Newspaper article, one author, print

Gutzman, Debra. "Corporate Ghostwriting," *Financial Times* 14 Apr. 2011: n.pag. *FT.com.* Web. 20 Apr. 2011. — Newspaper article, Web, no page

Lynch, Diane. "Wired Women: Gender in High-Tech Workplace." *abcnews.go.com Technology*. n.d. Web. 24 Apr. 2011. — Web document without print version

U.S. Dept. of Labor. *Child Care as a Workforce Issue*. Washington: Government Printing Office, 2010. Print. — Government publication

Vitalari, Nicholas P., James C. Patton, and Andrew Milner. "Key Trends in Systems Development in Europe and North America." *Journal of Global Information Management* 3.2 (2010): 5–20. Print. [*3.2* signifies volume 3, issue 2] — Journal article with volume and issue numbers, print

Walker, Robyn C., and Jolanta Aritz. "Cognitive Organization and Identity Maintenance in Multicultural Teams," *Journal of Business Communication* 47.1 (2010): 20–41. Business Source Complete database. Web. 15 Mar. 2011. — Journal, electronic database

"Writing With Inferential Statistics." *The OWL at Purdue*. Purdue University Online Writing Lab, n.d. Web. 20 Feb. 2011. — Web document, no author, no date

Yellin, Mike. "Re: Managing Managers and Cell Phones." 9 Sept. 2011. *Yahoo Groups*. E-commerce. Web. 15 Sept. 2011. — Listserv, discussion group, blog posting

Note 1: MLA style no longer recommends listing URLs for Web sites.

Note 2: To prevent confusion, you might add the words *Accessed* or *Retrieved* preceding the date you accessed the online source.

Note 3: Although MLA style prescribes double-spacing for the works sited, we show single spacing to conserve space and to represent preferred business usage.

APA In-Text Format. Within the text, document each specific textual source with a short description in parentheses. Following are selected guidelines summarizing important elements of APA style:

- For a direct quotation, include the last name of the author(s), date of publication, and page number, as (Jones, 2010, p. 36). Use *n.d.* if no date is available.
- If no author is known, refer to the first few words of the reference list entry and the year, as (Computer Privacy, 2011).
- Include page numbers only for direct quotations.

APA Reference Format. List all citations alphabetically in a section called "References." A portion of an APA reference page is shown in Figure C.3. A more complete list of model references appears in Figure C.4. APA style requires specific capitalization and sequencing guidelines, some of which are summarized here:

- Include an author's name with the last name first followed by initials, such as *Smith, M. A.* First and middle names are not used.
- Show the date of publication in parentheses immediately after the author's name, as *Smith, M. A. (2011, March 2).*
- Italicize the titles of books. Use "sentence-style" capitalization. This means capitalize only the first word of a title, proper nouns, and the first word after an internal colon.
- Do not italicize or underscore the titles of magazine and journal articles. Use sentence-style capitalization for article titles.
- Italicize the names of magazines, newspapers, and journals. Capitalize the initial letters of all main words.
- Include the document object identifier (DOI) when available for online periodicals. If no DOI is available, include the URL but no date of retrieval.
- For an online periodical that also appears in a printed version, include *Electronic version* in brackets after the article's title. Do not include a URL.
- For articles easily obtained from an online database (such as that in a school library), provide print information. The database need not be identified. You may include an accession number in parentheses at the end, but APA style does not require it.

FIGURE C.3 Portions of APA Text Page and References

Peanut butter was first delivered to the world by a St. Louis physician in 1890. As discussed at the Peanut Advisory Board's Web site, peanut butter was originally promoted as a protein substitute for elderly patients (History, n.d.). However, it was the 1905 Universal Exposition in St. Louis that truly launched peanut butter. Since then, annual peanut butter consumption has zoomed to 3.3 pounds a person in the United States (Barrons, 2010, p. 46).

America's farmers produce 1.6 million tons of peanuts annually, about half of which is used for oil, nuts, and candy. Lisa Gibbons, executive secretary of the Peanut Advisory Board, says that "peanuts in some form are in the top four candies: Snickers, Reese's Peanut Butter Cups, Peanut M & Ms, and Butterfingers" (Meadows, 2011, p. 32).

References

Barrons, E. R. (2010, November). A comparison of domestic and international consumption of legumes. *Journal of Economic Agriculture, 23*(3), 45–49.

History of peanut butter. (n.d.). Peanut Advisory Board. Alabama Peanut Producers Association. Retrieved from http://www.alpeanuts.com/consumer_interest/articles.phtml?articleID=102

Meadows, M. A. (2011, May). Peanut crop is anything but peanuts at home and overseas. *Business Monthly*, 31–34.

FIGURE C.4 **APA Sample References**

References

American Airlines. (2011). *2011 Annual Report.* Fort Worth, TX: AMR Corporation. — Annual report

Atamian, R. A., & Ferranto, E. (2010). *Driving market forces.* New York: HarperCollins. — Book, two authors

Audio conferencing. (2010). In *Encyclopaedia Britannica*. Retrieved October 19, 2011, from Encyclopaedia Britannica Online: http//www.britannica.com/eb/article-61669 — Encyclopedia, online

Balcazar, S. (2010, March 1). The future of investing. [Electronic version]. *Fortune*, 62–67. — Magazine article, online, without DOI, print version available

Beardsley, E. (2011, April 6). Building gone wild in China. [Electronic version]. Asia Today, 102, pp. 42–44. doi: 10.1090/14733300410001676403 — Magazine article, with DOI

Berss, M. (2008, October 24). Protein man. *Forbes*, 65–66. — Magazine article, print

Clay, R. (2008, June). Science vs. ideology: Psychologists fight back about the misuse of research. *Monitor on Psychology*, 39(6). Retrieved from http://www.apa.org.monitor/ — Magazine article, online

Globalization often means that the fast track leads overseas. (2011, June 16). *The Washington Post*, pp. A1, A4. — Newspaper article, no author, print

Guzman, D. (2011, April 20). Corporate ghostwriting. *Financial Times*. Retrieved from http://www.ft.com — Newspaper article, online

U.S. Department of Health and Human Services, National Institutes of Health, National Heart, Lung, and Blood Institute. (2003). *Managing asthma: A guide for schools* (NIH Publication No. 02-2650). Retrieved from http://www.nhlbi.nih.gov/health/prof/lung/asthma/asth_sch.pdf — Government report

Varma, P., Sivakumaran, B., and Marshall, R. (2010, March). Impulse buying and variety seeking: A trait-correlates perspective. *Journal of Business Research, 63*(3), 276–283. [*63*(3) signifies volume 63, series or issue 3] — Journal article from database (see Note 1 below)

Vitalari, N. P., Patton, J. C., & Milner, A. (2010, May). Key trends in systems development in Europe and North America. *Journal of Global Information Management, 3*(2), 5–20. — Journal article without DOI

Walker, R. D., & Aritz, J. (2010, January). Cognitive organization and identity maintenance in multicultural teams. [Electronic version]. *Journal of Business Communication*, 47(1): 20–41. doi: 10.1177/0021943609340669 — Journal article with DOI

Writing with inferential statistics. (n.d.). *The OWL at Purdue*. Retrieved from http://owl.english.purdue.edu/owl/resource/672/06/ — Web document, no author, no date

Yerkes, J. (2010, February 24). Re: Emerging business models [Online forum comment]. Retrieved from http://www1.wipo.int:8080/roller/trackback/ipisforum/Weblog/theme_nine_emerging_business_models — Web posting to newsgroup, online forum, or discussion group

Note 1: Database identification is unnecessary if the article is easily located through its primary publication.

Note 2: Do not include retrieval dates unless the source material may change over time (e.g., wikis).

Note 3: Although APA style prescribes double-spacing for the References page, we show single spacing to conserve space and to represent preferred business usage.

Correction Symbols

APPENDIX D

In marking your papers, your instructor may use the following symbols or abbreviations to indicate writing or formatting weaknesses. You will find that studying these symbols and suggestions will help you understand your instructor's remarks. Knowing this information can also help you evaluate and improve your own letters, memos, e-mail messages, reports, and other writing. To improve your command of grammar and mechanics, please review the guides in the Grammar and Mechanics Guide in Appendix A. You can also build your skills by completing the exercises in Your Personal Language Trainer at **www.meguffey.com**.

Grammar and Mechanics

Act	Use active-voice verbs.
Apos	Use apostrophe correctly.
Art	Use a correct article (*a, an,* or *the).*
Cap	Correct capitalization error.
Cm	Insert a comma.
CmConj	Use a comma before a coordinating conjunction (*and, or, nor, but*) that joins independent clauses.
CmIntr	Use a comma after an introductory clause or a long phrase.
CmSer	Insert commas to separate items in a series.
CS	Correct a comma splice by separating clauses with a period or a semicolon.
DM	Correct a misplaced or dangling modifier by moving the modifier closer to the word it describes or by supplying a clear subject.
Exp	Eliminate expletives (*there is, there are,* and *it is*)
Frag	Revise sentence fragment to express a complete thought.
Num	Express numbers in appropriate word or figure form.
ProAgr	Make pronoun agree in number with its antecedent.
ProCase	Use appropriate nominative, objective, or possessive case.
Ref	Correct vague pronoun reference. Avoid pronoun that refers to a phrase, clause, sentence, or paragraph.
RO	Revise run-on or fused sentence by adding a period or a semicolon to separate independent clauses.
Sp	Correct spelling error.
S/V	Make verbs agree with their subjects.
Vb	Use correct verb tense.
V/Shift	Avoid unnecessary shifts in verb tense.
UnCm	Eliminate unnecessary comma.

Content, Organization, and Style

Asgn	Follow assignment instructions.
Awk	Recast to avoid awkward expression.
Ch	Use longer sentences to avoid choppiness. Vary sentence patterns.
Cl	Improve clarity of ideas or expression.
Coh	Develop coherence between ideas. Repeat key ideas, use pronouns, or add transitional expression.
Cop	Avoid copying textbook examples or wording.
DirSt	Start directly with the main idea.
Exp	Expand or explain an incomplete idea.
IS	Use indirect strategy by explaining before introducing main idea.
Log	Reconsider faulty logic.
Neg	Revise negative expression with more positive view.
Ob	Avoid stating the obvious.
Org	Improve organization by grouping similar ideas.
Par	Express ideas in parallel form.
Redun	Avoid redundant expression.
Tone	Use conversational, positive tone that promotes goodwill.
You	Emphasize the "you" view.
WC	Improve word choice.

Format

DS	Insert a double space.
F	Choose an appropriate format for this document.
GH	Use graphic highlighting (bullets, lists, indentions, or headings) to enhance readability.
Mar	Improve margins to fit document attractively on the page.
SS	Insert a single space.
TS	Insert a triple space.

Key to Grammar and Mechanics C.L.U.E. Exercises

Chapter 1

1. Whether you are already working or about to enter today's **workplace, communication** skills are critical to your career success. [Guide 1, Fragment]
2. Surveys of employers consistently show that communication skills are important to job **success; job** advertisements often request excellent oral and written communication skills. [Use a semicolon or start a new sentence with "Job." Guide 3, Comma splice]
3. C.
4. We cannot predict future **jobs;** however, they will undoubtedly require brainpower and education. [Guide 3, Comma splice]
5. Face-to-face conversations have many **advantages even** though they produce no written record and sometimes waste time. [No punctuation required. Guide 1, Fragment]
6. A vital part of the communication process is **feedback. It** helps the sender know that the message was received and understood. [Start a new sentence or join clauses with a semicolon. Guide 3, Comma splice]
7. Knowledge workers must be critical **thinkers. They** must be able to make decisions and communicate those decisions. [Start a new sentence or join clauses with a semicolon. Guide 2, Run-on sentence]
8. Management uses many methods to distribute information **downward such** as newsletters, announcements, meetings, videos, and company intranets. [No additional punctuation is required. Guide 1, Fragment]
9. C.
10. You may be expected to agree to a company's code of **ethics. You** will also be expected to know the laws applying to your job. [Guide 3, Comma splice]

Chapter 2

1. Our recruiter must **choose** from among four strong candidates. [Guide 4]
2. The use of smartphones and laptops during meetings **is** prohibited. [Guide 6]
3. If I **were** you, I would finish my degree program. [Guide 5]
4. Considerable time and money **were** spent on communication training for employees. [Guide 7]
5. Neither the president nor the operations manager **has** read the complete report. [Guide 8]
6. Disagreement and dissension **are** normal and should be expected in team interactions. [Guide 7]
7. Everything in the meeting minutes and company reports **is** open to public view. [Guide 9]
8. A committee of three employees and two managers **is** working to establish office priorities.[Guide 10]
9. Greg said that he **saw** the report before it was distributed to management. [Guide 4]
10. Each of the office divisions **is** expected to work together to create common procedures. [Guide 9]

Chapter 3

1. Direct the visitors to my boss and **me**; she and I will give them a tour of our facility. [Guide 13]
2. Judging by you and **me** alone, this department will be the most productive one in the company. [Guide 13]
3. The team knew that **its** project was doomed once the funding was cut. [Guide 14]
4. You and **I** did the work of three; she only did hers and poorly so. [Guide 12]
5. The shift manager and I will work overtime tonight, so please direct all calls to him or **me**. [Guide 15]
6. Each new job candidate must be accompanied to **his or her** interview by a staff member.

   OR: All new job candidates must be accompanied to **their** interviews by a staff member. [Guide 17]
7. Please deliver the printer supplies to **whoever** ordered them. [Guide 16]
8. Most applications arrived on time, but **yours** and **hers** were not received. [Guide 14]
9. *C* [Guide 13]
10. **Who** did you say left messages for Connie and me? [Guide 16]

Chapter 4

1. Business writers strive to use **easy-to-understand** language and familiar words. [Guide 20]
2. Luis said he did **well** in his employment interview. [Guide 19]
3. Having prepared for months, we won the contract **easily**. [Guide 19]
4. Collaboration on **team-written** documents is necessary for big projects. [Guide 20]
5. Jenna felt **bad** when her team project was completed. [Guide 19]
6. The 3-x-3 writing plan provides **step-by-step** instructions for writing messages. [Guide 20]
7. Our **recently revised** office handbook outlined all recommended document formats. [Guide 20]
8. The project ran **smoothly** after Maria organized the team. [Guide 19]
9. **Locally installed** online collaboration tools are **easy to use** and work well. [Guide 20]
10. **Well-written** safety messages include short, familiar words. [Guide 20]

Chapter 5

1. The 3-x-3 writing process includes prewriting, **writing,** and revising. [Guide 21, CmSer]
2. Before asking others for **information,** see what you can find yourself. [Guide 22, CmIntr]
3. Formal research methods include accessing electronically, searching **manually,** and investigating primary sources. [Guide 21, CmSer]
4. If a project is **complex,** consider organizing it by outlining the major points. [Guide 22, CmIntr]
5. Careful writers define the main **topic,** and they divide it into three to five components. [Guide 23, CmConj]
6. We decided that Jill **Hawkins,** who is the best writer on the **team,** should prepare the final draft. [Guide 25, CmIn]
7. The company's executives expected new office construction to be finished by September 1, **2012,** in **Boulder,** Colorado. [Guide 24, CmDate]
8. Grammar **checkers,** by the **way,** often highlight passive voice as a grammar fault. [Guide 25, CmIn]
9. When you must be tactful and avoid naming the doer of an **action,** the passive voice can be helpful. [Guide 22, CmIntr]
10. *C* [Guide 26]

Chapter 6

1. Successful product names may appear to have been named by **magic; however,** the naming process is methodical and deliberate. [Guide 27]
2. Choosing the right name and tagline is **critical; consequently,** companies are eager to hire specialists. [Guide 27]
3. Naming is a costly **endeavor;** fees may range up to $70,000 for a global name. [Guide 27]
4. Expanding markets are in **Paris, France; Beijing, China;** and **Dubai City,** United Arab Emirates. [Guide 28]
5. As she was about to name a fashion product, Rachel Hermes **said:** "If I am launching a new fashion label, the task becomes very difficult. I have to find a name that communicates the creative style that the brand is to embody." [Guide 30]
6. For a new unisex perfume, Hermes considered the following **names:** Declaration, Serenity, and Earth. [Guide 29]
7. Naming is not a problem for small **companies; however,** it is a big problem for global brands. [Guide 27]
8. Hermes started with a thorough competitive **analysis;** it included quantifying the tone and strength of competing names. [Guide 27]
9. Attending the naming sessions were James Harper, marketing **director;** Reva Cruz, product **manager;** and Cheryl Chang, vice president. [Guide 28]
10. Distribution of goods has become **global; therefore,** names have to be registered in many countries. [Guide 27]

Chapter 7

1. Facebook **users'** accounts will be suspended if the members don't abide by the **site's** policies. [Guides 32, 31]
2. **James's** performance review was outstanding again. [Guide 32]
3. Would you please give me directions to your downtown headquarters. [Use period, not question mark. Guide 34]
4. The shipping supervisor resented **Barbara's** being late almost every morning. [Guide 33]
5. Is it true that the CEO decided to write a weekly blog. [Guide 34]
6. You must replace the ink cartridge **(see** page 8 in the **manual)** before printing. [Guide 37]
7. Justin wondered whether all the sales **managers'** databases needed to be updated. [Guide 32]
8. (Direct quotation) "**Health** care **costs,"** said the CEO, "**will** increase substantially this **year."** [Guide 38]
9. In just two **months'** time, we expect to interview five candidates for the opening. [Guide 32]
10. The meeting starts at 10 a.m. sharp, doesn't **it?** [Guide 35]

Chapter 8

1. Once the **management team** and the **union** members finally agreed, **Mayor Knox** signed the **agreement.** [Guides 39, 41]
2. All **Delta Airlines** passengers must exit the **plane** at **Gate** 14 when they reach **Los Angeles International Airport.** [Guides 39, 46]
3. The vice president of the **United States** urged members of the **European Union** to continue to seek peace in the **Middle East**. [Guides 39, 43]
4. My **uncle**, who lives in the **South**, has Skippy **peanut butter** and **Coca-Cola** for **breakfast**. [Guides 41, 43, 45]
5. Our **marketing manager** and **director** of **sales** thought that the **company** should purchase BlackBerry **smartphones** for all **sales reps**. [Guides 41, 45]
6. Personal **tax rates** for **Japanese** citizens are low by **international** standards, according to **Professor Yamaguchi** at **Osaka University**. [Guides 39, 41]
7. Jinhee Kim, who heads our **Customer Communication Division**, has a **master's degree** in social psychology from the **University** of **New Mexico**. [Guides 44, 40, 39]
8. Please consult **Figure** 4.5 in **Chapter** 4 to obtain **U.S. Census Bureau** population figures for the **Pacific Northwest.** [Guides 46, 39, 43]
9. Last **fall** did you see the article titled "The **Global Consequences** of **Using Crops** for **Fuel**"? [Guides 39, 42]
10. Toby plans to take courses in **marketing, business law,** and **English** in the **spring**. [Guides 40, 39]

Chapter 9

1. Included in her bad-news message were a **compliment** and valuable **advice**.
2. His **principal** reason for declining the invitation was his busy **calendar**.
3. In her damage-control message, the manager made a **conscious** effort to regain the customer's confidence.
4. In your **everyday** business affairs, you must show **patience** even when irritated.
5. Before you **proceed** with the report, please check those **embarrassing** statistics.
6. Although we will look into this matter **further**, I am not **surprised** at your report.
7. The judge declared that the comments of **their** attorneys were **irrelevant** to the case at hand.
8. Because the property was **too** difficult to **appraise**, its value was unrecorded.
9. Meredith hoped to **elicit** advice from her counselor, but she was **disappointed**.
10. The manager **recommended** that we switch to an annual **maintenance** schedule.

Chapter 10

1. Susan showed me **five** different customer messages with the same **two** complaints. [Guide 47]
2. **Twenty-eight** employees indicated they would change their health benefits. [Guide 47]

3. Did Mike request **$300** to attend the **one**-day seminar? [Guides 49, 47]
4. Most deliveries arrive before **10 a.m.** [Guide 49]
5. Personal income tax returns must be mailed by April **15**. [Guide 49]
6. We earned 2.5 **percent** dividends on our **$3,000** investment. [Guide 49]
7. Our company applied for a **$100,000** loan at **6 percent**. [Guide 49]
8. Average attendance at Major League Baseball games totaled **80 million** in the United States and Canada. [Guide 50]
9. I bought the item on eBay for **$1.50** and sold it for **$15.** [Guide 49]
10. That store offers a **30**-day customer satisfaction return policy. [Guide 48]

Chapter 11

1. The recruiter cited **studies** showing that **managers** leave [delete comma] when they lose their autonomy.
2. As they work more than **40 hours** a week without overtime pay, most **professionals** today are wondering **whether** their jobs can survive the recession.
3. One organization paid **$3,000** each for **12** employees to attend a **one-week** workshop in communication training.
4. My company **spends $500** on ink cartridges every month, but the cost doesn't worry my partner and **me** because our printed materials look sharp and professional.
5. If you find **an** open document on a colleague's computer **screen**, [add comma] **it's** inappropriate to peek.
6. **Today's** workers should brush up their marketable **skills; otherwise,** they may not find another job after being laid off.
7. On June **1** our company **president** revealed a **$4 million** drop in profits, which was bad news for everyone.
8. Most of us prefer to be let down **gently** [delete comma] when we are being refused **something;** that is why the **reasons-before-refusal** pattern is effective.
9. Between you and **me,** if we **were** to share a ride each **morning**, [insert comma] we would save a lot of money.
10. Despite the recent economic **downturn**, [insert comma] our **president** and CEO gave an optimistic assessment of the **company's** outlook.

Chapter 12

1. Toyota, the best-selling **Japanese** carmaker, has enjoyed a strong favorable perception of high **quality; therefore,** it long remained unharmed by a string of much-publicized recalls.
2. The **auditor's** report, which my boss and **I** read very closely, featured the following three main **flaws:** factual inaccuracies, omissions, and incomprehensible language.
3. **Eight** of the 20 workers in my department were **fired;** as a result, we had to work much harder to **achieve** our objectives.
4. As a matter of **principle**, we offer some form of financial support to more than **60** percent of our current MBA **candidates, which** proves our commitment to executive education.
5. To post easily to your blog on the **Web,** you could use Mozilla's **Web** browser **Firefox** and an add-on called ScribeFire.
6. **Peter's** presentation for a nonprofit group on advanced Internet marketing netted him only **$200**, a fifth of his usual **honorarium,** but he believes in pro bono work.
7. The old company manual covers the basics **of** [delete colon] searching, **selecting, interpreting,** and organizing data.
8. Our latest press **release,** which was written in our Corporate Communication **Department,** announces the opening of **three** Canadian offices.
9. Letter reports **usually have** side margins of **1¼** inches.
10. The CEO and **manager,** who had **gone** to a meeting in the West, delivered a report to Jeff and **me** when they returned.

Chapter 13

1. Lack of job security and high unemployment **are** here to **stay** [delete period] even if we do our work **well**.
2. Managers in **three departments** complained that **their** departments were over budget for supplies.
3. After sending many e-mails to Frank and **me**, the client felt **bad** about barraging us with messages to solicit a response from our two **teams**.
4. The new vice president and **she** decided to move up the launch to **May 3;** as a result, the software was buggy.
5. Managers of big **corporations** sometimes do not know how to **motivate;** consequently, the executives miss an opportunity to develop their **workers**.
6. The **director** of marketing wanted to speak to you and **me** about the poor **morale** in our division.
7. Laura and **he** decided to **accept** assistance with their **proposal;** therefore, they completed the project by the deadline.
8. We invited **75** employees to hear **two** experts **disperse** information about wellness.
9. **Memos** usually contain four necessary **parts:** subject line, opening, **body,** and action closing.
10. Darrin **Jizmejian,** who was recently evaluated, wondered whether his formal report would be presented at the **March 13 meeting.**

Chapter 14

1. If you are planning a short **presentation,** you should focus on about **three** main points and limit yourself to **20** minutes.
2. Because he was **president** of the **company,** Mr. Yost made at least **six** major presentations every year.
3. The **company's** CPA asked me to explain the **principal** ways we planned to finance the **30**-year mortgage.
4. My accountant and **I** are **grateful** to be able to give a short **presentation;** however, we may not be able to cover the entire budget.
5. The introduction to a presentation should accomplish three **goals:** (a) **capture** attention, (b) establish credibility, and (**c**) preview main points.
6. Steven wondered whether focusing on what the audience is to **remember** [delete comma] and summarizing main points **were** equally **important.** [delete question mark]
7. A list of suggestions for a **speaker's** ideas **is** found in the article titled "How **to** Improve Your Listening Skills."
8. The appearance and mannerisms of a speaker **definitely affect** a **listener's** evaluation of the message.
9. Melody Hobson, who is an expert **speaker,** said that reading from slides is the **kiss** of **death** in a presentation.
10. In a poll of **3,000 workers,** only one third felt that **their** companies valued their opinions.

Chapter 15

1. Many employers use **sites** like Facebook to learn about potential employees**, which means** job seekers must maintain a professional online presence.
2. To conduct a safe online job search, you **must** [delete colon] (a) **use** only reputable job boards, **(b)** keep careful records, and (c) limit the number of sites on which you post your résumé.
3. When **Melissa's** job search was **complete,** she had received **four** job offers.
4. If you **lose** your **job, don't** be discouraged by the thought of having to find another.
5. Joseph wondered whether it was **all right** to ask his professor for employment **advice.** [change question mark to period]

6. At last **month's** staff **meeting,** team members examined several **candidates'** résumés.
7. Rather **than** schedule **face-to-face interviews,** the team investigated videoconferencing.
8. **Twelve** applicants will be interviewed on **April 10;** consequently, we may need to work late to accommodate them.
9. Professional e-mail manners **reflect** on you and your **company;** however, **too** few employees are trained properly.
10. In the last issue of ***Newsweek,*** did you see the article titled "Should a **Résumé Include** a Career Objective?"

Chapter 16

1. Before going to a job **interview,** you should do the **following:** [delete hyphen] research the company, practice answering questions, rehearse success **stories,** and choose appropriate clothing.
2. I wonder how many **companies** go online to find out more about **candidates' backgrounds.** [delete question mark]
3. Even with the popularity of **e-mail,** most **employers** [delete apostrophe] contact job applicants by telephone to set up **their** interviews.
4. Initial contacts by employers are **usually** made by **telephone;** therefore, **ensure** that you keep important information nearby.
5. If you have gaps in your employment **history,** explain what you did during this **time** [delete comma] and how you stayed **up-to-date** in your field.
6. Interviewees should not **criticize** anyone or **anything,** and they should not focus on **their** imperfections.
7. Evan was asked whether he had a **bachelor's degree** [delete comma] and whether he had five **years'** experience.
8. If you are **hoping** to create a good **impression,** be sure to write a **thank-you** message after a job interview.
9. When **Robin's** interview was **over,** she told friends that she had done **well**.
10. Robin was **all ready** to send a thank-you **message** [delete comma] when she realized she could not spell the **interviewer's** name.

Notes

Chapter 1

[1] PepsiCo's Indian icon. (2001, January 8). *Business India*. Retrieved March 23, 2009, from http://www.answers.com/topic/indra-nooyi. See also Brady, D. (2007, June 11). Keeping cool in hot water. *BusinessWeek*. Retrieved March 20, 2009, from http://www.businessweek.com; and Useem, M. (2008, December 1–8). New ideas for this Pepsi generation. *U.S. News & World Report*, p. 49.

[2] Kinsman, M. (2004, February 1). Are poor writing skills holding back your career? *California Job Journal*. Retrieved April 24, 2009, from http://www.jobjournal.com; Tucker, M. L., & McCarthy, A. M. (2001, Summer). Presentation self-efficacy: Increasing communication skills through service-learning. *Journal of Managerial Issues*, 227–244; Cohen, A. (1999). The right stuff. *Sales and Marketing Management*, p. 151; and Messmer, M. (1999, August). Skills for a new millennium. *Strategic Finance*, pp. 10–12.

[3] Koncz, A. (2009, January 29). Employers cite qualities, attributes of "perfect" job candidate. National Association of Colleges and Employers. Press release retrieved April 24, 2009, from http://www.naceweb.org

[4] Moody, J., Stewart, B., & Bolt-Lee, C. (2002, March). Showcasing the skilled business graduate: Expanding the tool kit. *Business Communication Quarterly, 65*(1), 23.

[5] Vance, E. (2007, February 2). College graduates lack key skills, report says. *The Chronicle of Higher Education*, p. A30.

[6] Communication skills—Start here! (n.d.). *MindTools*. Retrieved April 24, 2009, from http://www.mindtools.com

[7] Schwartz, E. (2006, June 29). Brushing up on your soft skills. *InfoWorld*. Retrieved April 24, 2009, from http://www.infoworld.com

[8] The National Commission on Writing. [press release] (2004, September 14). Writing skills necessary for employment, says big business. Retrieved April 24, 2009, from http://www.writingcommission.org/pr/writing_for_employ.html

[9] Ibid.

[10] Daniels, C. (2004, June 28). 50 best companies for minorities. *Fortune*, p. 136.

[11] Anderson, R. (2009, April 26). He wants subjects, verbs and objects. *The New York Times*, p. 2 BU Y.

[12] Drucker, P. (1989, May). New realities, new ways of managing. *Business Month*, pp. 50–51.

[13] Schadler, T. (2009). A day in the life of a U.S. information worker. Forrester Research. Retrieved October 31, 2009, from http://www.forrester.com. See also Grimes, A. (2002, June 27). Techno talk. *The Wall Street Journal*, p. B4.

[14] Haag, S., Cummings, M., & Phillips, A. (2003). *Management information systems for the information age* (3rd ed.). New York: McGraw-Hill Higher Education.

[15] Thinking for a living. (2006, January 21). *The Economist* (U.S.). Retrieved May 14, 2009, from InfoTrac College Edition database.

[16] O'Toole, J. & Lawler, E. E., III. (2006, July). *The new American workplace*. New York: Palgrave Macmillan, p. 17.

[17] Koncz, A. (2009, January 29). Employers cite qualities, attributes of "perfect" job candidate. NACE Web Press Release. Retrieved April 26, 2009, from http://www.naceweb.org

[18] Jargon, J. (2008, May 1) Kraft reformulates Oreo, scores in China. *The Wall Street Journal*, p. B1.

[19] Welcome to McDonald's Russia. (n.d.). Retrieved April 26, 2009, from http://www.mcdonalds.com/countries/russia.html; see also Arvedlund, E. E. (2005, March 17). McDonald's commands a real estate empire in Russia. *The New York Times*, p. C5.

[20] Heller, L. (2006, August 7). Customer experience evolves in China. *Retailing Today, 45*(14), 42. Retrieved May 29, 2009, from InfoTrac database.

[21] Balfour, F., & Kiley, D. (2005, April 25). Ad agencies unchained. *BusinessWeek*, p. 51.

[22] Friedman, T. L. (2005). *The world is flat*. New York: Farrar, Straus and Giroux, pp. 178–179.

[23] Malone, T. W. (2004). *The future of work*. Cambridge: Harvard Business School Press, p. 32.

[24] Weintraub, A. (2007, June 18). J & J's new baby. *BusinessWeek*, p. 48.

[25] Miller, C. C. (2008, June 2). Higher office. *Forbes*, p. 62. See also Shinkle, K. (2008, March 10). Running an office by wiki and e-mail. *U.S. News & World Report*, p. 50.

[26] Holland, K. (2008, September 28). The anywhere, anytime office. *The New York Times*, p. 14 BU Y.

[27] Telework trendlines (2009, February). Retrieved April 16, 2009, from Worldatwork, http://www.workingfromanywhere.org/news/Trendlines_2009.pdf

[28] Holland, K. (2008, September 28). The anywhere, anytime office. *The New York Times*, p. 14 BU Y.

[29] About Google Wave. Google Web site. Retrieved January 2, 2010, from http://wave.google.com/help/wave/about.html

[30] Karoly, L. A., & Panis, C. W. A. (2004). *The 21st century at work*. Santa Monica, CA: Rand Corporation, pp. 36–39.

[31] Shifting workplace demographics and delayed retirement. (2002, May). *Monthly Labor Review*. Retrieved October 11, 2006, from http://www.microsoft.com/enable/aging/references.aspx

[32] DeMars, N. (2008, April). Office ethics: News from the front lines. *OfficePro*, p. 28.

[33] Hamilton, C., & Parker, C. (1996). *Communicating for results* (6th ed.). Belmont, CA: Wadsworth, p. 7.

[34] Sullivan, J., Karmeda, N., & Nobu, T. (1992, January/February). Bypassing in managerial communication. *Business Horizons, 34*(1), 72.

[35] Brewer, E., & Holmes, T. (2009, October). Obfuscating the obvious: Miscommunication issues in the interpretation of common terms. *Journal of Business Communication, 46*(4), 480–496.

[36] McGirt, E. (2006, March 20). Getting out from under: Beset by interruptions, information overload, and irksome technology, knowledge workers need help: A survival guide. *Fortune*, p. 88.

[37] Drucker, P. (1990). *Managing the non-profit organization: Practices and principles*. New York: HarperCollins, p. 46.

[38] E-mail becoming crime's new smoking gun. (2005). *USA Today*. Retrieved May 14, 2009, from http://www.usatoday.com/tech/news/2002-08-15-email-evidence_x.htm

[39] Sims, R. R., Veres, J. G., III, Jackson, K. A., & Facteau, C. L. (2001). *The challenge of front-line management*. Westport, CT: Quorum, p. 10.

[40] Steelcase Inc. (2007, August 9). Steelcase Workplace Index Survey examines 'water cooler' conversations at work. Retrieved May 4, 2009, from http://www.prnewswire.com

[41] Ibid.

[42] Useem, M. (2008, December 8). New ideas for this Pepsi generation. *U.S. News & World Report*, p. 49.

[43] PepsiCo releases sustainable development report. (2009, January 6). PepsiCo press release. Retrieved March 21, 2009, from http://ca.csrwire.com

[44] Steelcase Inc., ibid. See also Karathanos, P., & Auriemmo, A. (1999, March-April). Care and feeding of the organizational grapevine. *Industrial Management, 41*(2), 26. Retrieved May 4, 2009, from InfoTrac College Edition database.

[45] Goman, C. K. (2006, June). I heard it through the grapevine. Paper presented at the International Association of Business Communicators, Vancouver, Canada. Retrieved October 22, 2006, from http://common.iabc.com/employee/2006/06

[46] Zimmermann, S., Davenport, B., & Haas, J. W. (1996, April). A communication metamyth in the workplace: The assumption that more is better. *Journal of Business Communication, 33*(2), 185–204.

[47] DeMars, N. (2008). What you can do when you're the latest topic on the rumor mill. Retrieved May 4, 2009, from http://www.office-ethics.com/columns/gossip.html

[48] Gentile, M. C. (2009, February 5). Business schools: A failing grade on ethics. *BusinessWeek*. Retrieved March 29, 2009, from http://www.businessweek.com

[49] Gardiner, B. (2009, March 26). B-schools rethink curricula amid crisis. Wall Street Journal Online. Retrieved April 1, 2009, from http://online.wsj.com

[50] DeMars, N. (2008, April). Office ethics: News from the front lines. *OfficePro*, p. 28.

[51] Pfanner, E. (2009, April 18). Four convicted in Internet piracy case. *The New York Times*, p. B1.

[52] Campbell, A. (2003, November 25). More women starting businesses. Small business trends. Retrieved April 15, 2009, from http://smallbiztrends.com

[53] Trudel, R., & Cotte, J. (2008, May 12). Does being ethical pay? *The Wall Street Journal*, p. R4.

[54] O'Connell, V. (2009, January 7). Test for dwindling retail jobs spawns a culture of cheating. *The Wall Street Journal*, p. A1.

[55] Henriques, D. (2009, June 29). Madoff Is Sentenced to 150 Years for Ponzi Scheme. *New York Times*. Retrieved December 19, 2009, from http://www.nytimes.com/2009/06/30/business/30madoff.html

[56] Nooyi, I. (n.d.). Meritocracy. Cornell University eClips. Video transcript. Retrieved March 24, 2009, from http://eclips.cornell.edu/clip.do?id=12279&tab=TabClipPage

[57] Do your reps' writing skills need a refresher? (2002, February). *Customer Contact Management Report*, p. 7.

[58] Sandberg, J. (2008, January 19). Global-market woes are more personality than nationality. *The Wall Street Journal*, p. B1.

[59] Sandberg, J. (2006, September 18). What exactly was it that the boss said? You can only imagine. *The Wall Street Journal*, p. B1.

[60] Ahmad, A. (2006, May). To the manner born at the workplace. *The Economic Times*. Retrieved January 7, 2007, from InfoTrac College Edition database.

[61] Armour, S. (2007, September 7). Did you hear the real story about office gossip? *USA Today*, p. 1B.

[62] The Wall Street Journal ethics quiz. (1999, October 21). *The Wall Street Journal*, p. B1.

[63] El Pollo Loco. (n.d.) Healthier dining. Retrieved May 15, 2009, from http://www.elpolloloco.com/menu/healthydinning.html

[64] Jargon, J. (2008, May 9). Rival chicken chain calls out KFC. *USA Today*, p. B5.

Chapter 2

[1] Thomas, D., senior manager, Sales Development and Education, FedEx Office (personal communication with Mary Ellen Guffey, November 11, 2009).

[2] Brent, P. (2006, November). Soft skills speak volumes. *CA Magazine, 139*, 112. Retrieved June 3, 2009, from InfoTrac College Edition database.

[3] O'Toole, J., & Lawler, E. E., III. (2005). *The new American workplace*. New York: Palgrave Macmillan, p. 20.

[4] Mueller, F., Procter, S., & Buchanan, D. (2000, November). Teamworking in its context(s): Antecedents, nature and dimensions. *Human Relations, 53*, 1387. Retrieved June 3, 2009, from Business Source Complete database.

[5] DiSanza, J. R., & Legge, N. J. (2000). *Business and professional communication*. Boston: Allyn and Bacon, p. 98.

[6] Coutu, D., & Beschloss, M. (2009, May). Why teams don't work. *Harvard Business Review, (87)*, 5, 98-105. Retrieved June 1, 2009, from Business Source Complete database.

[7] Hymowitz, C. (2006, February 13). Rewarding competitors over collaborators no longer makes sense. *The Wall Street Journal*, p. B1.

[8] Ennen, S. (2003, April). Red baron soars with teamwork. *Food Processing, 64*, 40. Retrieved June 3, 2009, from http://www.foodprocessing.com/articles/2003/141.html

[9] Edmondson, G. (2006, October 16). BMW's dream factory. *BusinessWeek*, p. 80.

[10] Katzenbach, J. R., & Smith, K. (1994). *The wisdom of teams*. New York: HarperBusiness, pp. 68–69.

[11] Crash course in managing a virtual team. (2007, September 3). *Management Today*. Retrieved June 3, 2009, from InfoTrac College Edition database.

[12] Lipnack, J., & Stamps, J. (2000). *Virtual teams: People working across boundaries with technology* (2nd ed.). New York: Wiley, p. 18.

[13] Kiger, P. J. (2006, September 25). Flexibility to the fullest: Throwing out the rules of work—Part 1 of 2. *Workforce Management, 85*(18), 1. See also Holland, K. (2006, December 3).When work time isn't face time. *The New York Times*, p. BU 3.

[14] Cutler, G. (2007, January-February). Mike leads his first virtual team. *Research-Technology Management, 50*(1), 66. Retrieved June 3, 2009, from InfoTrac College Edition database.

[15] Miculka, J. H. (2007). *Speaking for success* (2nd ed.). Cincinnati, OH: South-Western, pp. 96–97.

[16] Janis, I. L. (1982). *Groupthink: Psychological studies on policy decisions and fiascoes*. Boston: Houghton Mifflin. See also Miranda, S. M., & Saunders, C. (1995, Summer). Group support systems: An organization development intervention to combat groupthink. *Public Administration Quarterly, 19*, 193–216. Retrieved June 1, 2009, from Business Source Complete database.

[17] Amason, A. C., Hochwarter, W. A., Thompson, K. R., & Harrison, A. W. (1995, Autumn). Conflict: An important dimension in successful management teams. *Organizational Dynamics, 24*, 1. Retrieved June 2, 2009, from InfoTrac College Edition database.

[18] Parnell, C. (1996, November 1). Teamwork: Not a new idea, but it's transforming the workplace. *Executive Speeches, 63*, 46. Retrieved December 11, 2006, from InfoTrac College Edition database.

[19] Katzenbach & Smith. (1994). *Wisdom of teams*. New York: HarperBusiness, p. 45.

[20] Makower, J. (1995, Winter). Managing diversity in the workplace. *Business & Society Review*, 48. Retrieved June 2, 2009, from Business Source Complete database.

[21] Bayot, J. (2000, November 8). Developers bet on theaters in glutted L.A. *The Wall Street Journal*, Eastern edition, p. C1.

[22] Callahan, D. (2009, April 21). Breaking the ice; success through teamwork and partnerships. Retrieved June 1, 2009, from Your Great Lakes Coast Guard blog at http://uscgd9.blogspot.com

[23] Survey finds workers average only three productive days per week. (2005, March 15). Microsoft survey retrieved June 8, 2009, from http://www.microsoft.com. See also Herring, H. B. (2006, June 18). Endless meetings: The black holes of the workday. *The New York Times*. Retrieved June 4, 2009, from http://www.nytimes.com

[24] Loechner, J. (2009, May 12). Meeting optimization too. Retrieved June 4, 2009, from http://www.mediapost.com

[25] Herring, H. B. (2006, June 18). Endless meetings: The black holes of the workday. *The New York Times*. Retrieved June 4, 2009, from http://www.nytimes.com

[26] Lancaster, H. (1998, May 26). Learning some ways to make meetings less awful. *The Wall Street Journal*, p. B1.

[27] Maher, K. (2004, January 13). The jungle. *The Wall Street Journal*, p. B6.

[28] Bruening, J. C. (1996, July). There's good news about meetings. *Managing Office Technology, 41*, 24–25. Retrieved December 4, 2006, from InfoTrac College Edition database.

[29] Marquis, C. (2003, July). Doing well and doing good. *The New York Times*, p. BU2.

[30] Schabacker, K. (1991, June). A short, snappy guide to meaningful meetings. *Working Women*, 73.

[31] Based on the following: Master the meeting madness. (2008). *Briefings Bonus*, Communication Briefings; and Egan, M. (2006, March 13). Meetings can make or break your career. *Insurance Advocate, 117*, 24.

[32] Lohr, S. (2008, July 22). As travel costs rise, more meetings go virtual. *The New York Times*. Retrieved June 4, 2009, from http://www.nytimes.com

[33] Bulkeley, W. M. (2006, September 28). Better virtual meetings. *The Wall Street Journal*, p. B1.

[34] Lohr, S. (2008, July 22). As travel costs rise, more meetings go virtual. *The New York Times*. Retrieved June 5, 2009, from http://www.nytimes.com

[35] Yu, R. (2009, June 23). Videoconferencing eyes growth spurt. *USA Today*, p. 3B.

[36] Lohr, S. (2008, July 22). As travel costs rise, more meetings go virtual. *The New York Times*. Retrieved June 5, 2009, from http://www.nytimes.com

[37] Schindler, E. (2008, February 15). Running an effective teleconference or virtual meeting. *CIO*. Retrieved June 5, 2009, from www.cio.com. See also Brenowitz, Randi S. (2004, May). Virtual meeting etiquette. Article 601, *Innovative Leader*. Retrieved June 5, 2009, from http://www.winstonbrill.com

[38] Ibid.

[39] Robbins, H., & Finley, M. (1995). *Why teams don't work*. Princeton, NJ: Peterson's/Pacesetter Books, p. 123.

[40] Pellet, J. (2003, April). Anatomy of a turnaround guru. *Chief Executive*, 41; Mounter, P. (2003). Global internal communication: A model. *Journal of Communication Management, 3*, 265; Feiertag, H. (2002, July 15). Listening skills, enthusiasm top list of salespeople's best traits. *Hotel and Motel Management*, 20; Goby, V. P., & Lewis, J. H. (2000, June). The key role of listening in business: A study of the Singapore insurance industry. *Business Communication Quarterly, 63*, 41–51; Cooper, L. O. (1997, December). Listening competency in the workplace: A model for training. *Business Communication Quarterly, 60*, 75–84; and Penley, L. E., Alexander, E. R., Jerigan, I. E., & Henwood, C. I. (1997). Communication abilities of managers: The relationship to performance. *Journal of Management, 17*, 57–76.

[41] Awang, F., Anderson, M. A., & Baker, C. J. (2003, Winter). Entry-level information services and support personnel: Needed workplace and technology skills. *The Delta Pi Epsilon Journal*, 48; and American Management Association. (1999, August). The challenges facing workers in the future. *HR Focus*, 6.

[42] Harris, T. W. (1989, June). Listen carefully. *Nation's Business*, 78.

[43] Steil, L. K., Barker, L. I., & Watson, K. W. (1983). *Effective listening: Key to your success* Reading, MA: Addison-Wesley; and Harris, J. A. (1998, August). Hear what's really being said. *New Zealand Management, 45*, 18.

[44] Nelson, E., & Gypen, J. (1979, September/October). The subordinate's predicament. *Harvard Business Review*, 133.

[45] International Listening Association. (2009). Listening and speech rates. Retrieved June 20, 2009, from http://www.listen.org

[46] Wolvin, A., & Coakley, C. G. (1996). *Listening* (5th ed.). New York: McGraw-Hill, pp. 136–137.

[47] Effective communication. (1994, November). *Training Tomorrow*, 32–33.

[48] Wood, J. T. (2003). *Gendered lives: Communication, gender, and culture* (5th ed.). Belmont, CA: Wadsworth, pp. 119–120; Anderson, K. J., & Leaper, C. (1998, August). Meta-analyses of gender effects on conversational interruption: Who, what, when, where, and how. *Sex Roles: A Journal of Research*, 225; and Booth-Butterfield, M. (1984). She hears: What they hear and why. *Personnel Journal, 44*, 39.

[49] Tear. J. (1995, November 20). They just don't understand gender dynamics. *The Wall Street Journal*, p. A12; and Wolfe, A. (1994, December 12). She just doesn't understand. *New Republic*, 26–34.

[50] Burgoon, J., Coker, D., & Coker, R. (1986). Communication explanations. *Human Communication Research*, 463–494.

[51] Tarsala, M. (1997, November 7). Remec's Ronald Ragland: Drawing rivals to his team by making their concerns his. *Investor's Business Daily*, A1.

[52] Birdwhistel, R. (1970). *Kinesics and context*. Philadelphia: University of Pennsylvania Press.

[53] What's A-O.K. in the U.S.A. is lewd and worthless beyond. (1996, August 18). *The New York Times*, p. E7.

[54] Zielinski, D. (2001, April). Body language. *Presentations*, 15, 36–42. Retrieved July 1, 2009, from InfoTrac College Edition database.

[55] Body speak: What are you saying? (2000, October). *Successful Meetings*, 49–51.

[56] Finney, P. (2007, October 23). Redefining business casual. *The New York Times*. Retrieved June 10, 2009, from InfoTrac College Edition database. See also Osterman, R. (2006, March 20). Casual loses its cool in business: More employers are trying to tighten up workplace clothing standards. *Sacramento Bee*. Retrieved June 10, 2009, from InfoTrac College Edition database; and Business casual: Out of style? (2005, May). *HR Focus*, 9. Retrieved June 10, 2009, from InfoTrac College Edition database.

[57] Wilkie, H. (2003, Fall). Professional presence. *The Canadian Manager*, 14; and Kaplan-Leiserson, L. (2000, November). Casual dress/back to business attire. *Training & Development*, 38–39.

[58] Kennedy, M. M. (1997, September–October). Is business casual here to stay? *Executive Female*, 31.

[59] Wood, N., & Benitez, T. (2003, April). Does the suit fit? *Incentive*, 31.

[60] Business casual out of style. (2005, May). *HR Focus, 82*, 16. Retrieved December 16, 2006, from InfoTrac database; Egodigwe, L. (2003, March). Here come the suits. *Black Enterprise, 33*, 59. Retrieved June 4, 2009, from InfoTrac College Edition database; and Summerson, C. (2002, November 18). The suit is back in business. *BusinessWeek*, 130.

[61] Chao, L. (2006, January 17). Not-so-nice costs. *The Wall Street Journal*, p. B1.

[62] Workplace rudeness is common and costly. (2002, May). *USA Today Magazine*, 9.

[63] Coutu, D., & Beschloss, M. (2009, May). Why teams don't work. *Harvard Business Review, (87)*, 5, 98–105.

Retrieved June 1, 2009, from Business Source Complete database.

64 Maturo, D. (2007, Winter). Being a technician is not enough: Develop leadership and communication skills. *The Pennsylvania CPA Journal*. Retrieved June 4, 2009, from http://www.picpa.org/asp/Journal/journal_article_details.asp?action=Normal&ID=1294

65 Horovitz, B. (2008, May 23). Denny's wants to rock 'n' roll all night long. *USA Today*, p. 3B.

66 Arrien, A. (2003, March–April). Geese teach lessons on teamwork. *Motion Systems Distributor*, *17*, 32. Retrieved June 15, 2009, from InfoTrac College Edition database; and Flying like the geese. (2001, December). *Design Engineering*, 9. Retrieved June 15, 2009, from InfoTrac College Edition database.

67 Office Team poll. (2008, June 23). Meetings and productivity. Graphic appearing in *USA Today*, p. 1.

68 What's the universal hand sign for "I goofed"? (1996, December 16). *Santa Barbara News-Press*, p. D2.

69 Bell, A. H. (1999, September). Using nonverbal cues. *Incentive*, *173*, 162. Retrieved June 5, 2009, from Business Source Complete database.

70 McCarty, M. (2007, January/February). Tattoos: Not just for sailors anymore. *OfficePro*, 26.

71 Williams, A. (2008, June 24). At meetings, it's mind your BlackBerry or mind your manners. *The New York Times*, pp. A1, A3.

Chapter 3

1 Landler, M., & Barbaro, M. (2006, August 2). No, not always. *New York Times*, p. 1. Retrieved July 23, 2009, from http://www.nytimes.com

2 Metro's chief executive, Hans-Joachim Koerber, in Hall, A., & Bawden, T. (2006, July 29). Wal-Mart pulls out of Germany at cost of $1bn. *The Times Online*. Retrieved July 7, 2009, from http://business.timesonline.co.uk/tol/business/industry_sectors/retailing/article694345.ece

3 Landler, M., & Barbaro, M. (2006, August 2). No, not always. *New York Times*, p. 1. Retrieved July 23, 2009, from http://www.nytimes.com

4 Ibid.

5 David Rogers, president of DSR Marketing Systems, Deerfield, Illinois, quoted in Davis, G. (2008, May 26). World vision (Walmart). *Supermarket News*, *56*(21). Retrieved July 7, 2009, from Factiva database.

6 Holstein, W. (2007). Why Wal-Mart can't find happiness in Japan. *Fortune*, *156*(3), pp. 73-78. Retrieved July 23, 2009, from ProQuest database.

7 Smith, J. (2007). The perils of prediction. *World Trade*, *20*(1), 39-44. Retrieved July 20, 2009, from Business Source Premier database.

8 Flannery, R. (2004, May 10). China is a big prize. *Forbes*, *173*(10), p. 163. Retrieved July 25, 2009, from ProQuest database.

9 Sewell, D. (2009, June 10). Report: P&G's McDonald to succeed Lafley. *USAToday.com*. Retrieved July 25, 2009, from http://www.usatoday.com/money/industries/manufacturing/2009-06-09-pg-ceo_N.htm

10 Seven-Eleven Japan (2007). Retrieved July 25, 2009, from http://www.sej.co.jp/english/company/g_stores.html

11 Flannery, R. (2004, May 10). China is a big prize. *Forbes*, *173*(10), p. 163. Retrieved July 25, 2009, from ProQuest database.

12 Holmes, S. (2003, July 21). The real Nike news is happening abroad. *BusinessWeek*, p. 30; Ronaldo decisivo. (2009, March 26). Nike Futebol. Retrieved July 25, 2009, from http://inside.nike.com/blogs/nikefootball-pt_BR/tags/v%C3%ADdeo?view=all

13 Browning, E. S. (1992, April 23). In pursuit of the elusive Euroconsumer. *The Wall Street Journal*, p. B1. Retrieved July 25, 2009, from ProQuest database; and Wheatley, M. (1995). The branding of Europe. *Management Today*, 66. Retrieved July 25, 2009, from ProQuest database.

14 Stern, G. (1992, November 21). Heinz aims to export taste for ketchup. *The Wall Street Journal*, p. B1. Retrieved July 25, 2009, from ProQuest database.

15 International Specialty Regional Toppings. (2008). Inside Domino's. Retrieved July 25, 2009, from http://www.dominos.com/

16 Brooks, S. (2006, December). Tomorrow, the world. *Restaurant Business*, *105*(12), pp. 26–32. Retrieved July 25, 2009, from Wilson Web database.

17 Adamy, J. (2007, January 17). Dunkin' begins new push into China. *The Wall Street Journal*, p. A4. Retrieved July 25, 2009, from ProQuest database.

18 Creative jobs destruction. (2004, January 6). *The Wall Street Journal*, p. A18. Retrieved July 25, 2009, from ProQuest database.

19 Glater, J. D. (2004, January 3). Offshore services grow in lean times. *The New York Times*, p. B1. Retrieved July 25, 2009, from Business Full Text (Wilson) database.

20 Kalin, S. (1997, June 9). Global net knits East to West at Liz Claiborne. *Computerworld*, G4-G6. Retrieved July 25, 2009, from ProQuest database.

21 U.S. Department of Labor. (2007). Futurework: Trends and challenges for work in the 21st century. Retrieved July 25, 2009, from http://www.dol.gov/oasam/programs/history/herman/reports/futurework/report/chapter1/main.htm#1b

22 Gleckman, H. (1998, August). A rich stew in the melting pot. *BusinessWeek*, p. 76.

23 Pollack, A. (1996, December 22). Barbie's journey in Japan. *The New York Times*, p. E3. Retrieved July 25, 2009, from http://www.nytimes.com/1996/12/22/weekinreview/barbie-s-journey-in-japan.html

24 Hall, E. T., & Hall, M. R. (1990). *Understanding cultural differences*. Yarmouth, ME: Intercultural Press, pp. 183–184.

25 Chaney, L. H., & Martin, J. S. (2000). *Intercultural business communication* (2nd ed.). Upper Saddle River, NJ: Prentice Hall, p. 83.

26 Zunker, V. (2008). Career, work, and mental health. Thousand Oaks, CA: Sage Publications, p. 140; see also Reardon, K. K. (1987). *Where minds meet*. Belmont, CA: Wadsworth, p. 199.

27 Sheer, V. C., & Chen, L. (2003, January). Successful Sino-Western business negotiation: Participants' accounts of national and professional cultures. *The Journal of Business Communication*, *40*(1), 62; see also Luk, L., Patel, M., & White, K. (1990, December). Personal attributes of American and Chinese business associates. *The Bulletin of the Association for Business Communication*, 67.

28 Gallois, C., & Callan, V. (1997). *Communication and culture*. New York: Wiley, p. 24.

29 Jarvis, S. S. (1990, June). Preparing employees to work south of the border. *Personnel*, p. 763. Retrieved July 25, 2009, from Business Full Text (Wilson) database; Murtagh, B. (2008, August 22). Working south of the border. Pittsburgh Business Times. Retrieved July 25, 2009, from http://pittsburgh.bizjournals.com/pittsburgh/stories/2008/08/25/focus1.html?page=2

30 Gallois, C., & Callan, V. (1997). *Communication and culture*. New York: Wiley, p. 29.

31 Copeland, L., & Griggs, L. (1985). *Going international*. New York: Penguin, p. 94.

32 Ibid., p. 108.

33 Ibid., p. 12.

34 Copeland, J. (1990, December 15). Stare less, listen more. American Airlines: *American Way*, p. 32.

35 Chen, G. M., & Starosta, W. J. (1998). *Foundations of intercultural communication*. Boston: Allyn and Bacon, p. 40.

36 Varner, I., & Beamer, L. (2001). *Intercultural communication in the global workplace*. Boston: McGraw-Hill Irwin, p. 18.

37 Browning, E. S. (1994, May 3). Computer chip project brings rivals together, but the cultures clash. *The Wall Street Journal*, pp. A1, A11. Retrieved July 25, 2009, from ProQuest database.

38 Holstein, W. (2007). Why Wal-Mart can't find happiness in Japan. *Fortune*, *156*(3), pp. 73–78. Retrieved July 23, 2009, from ProQuest database.

39 Based on McGee, S. (2007, June 29). What's on the shelves in China's Wal-Marts? *MSN Money*. Retrieved July 8, 2009, from http://moneycentral.msn.com/home.asp

40 Martin, J. S., & Chaney, L. H. (2006). *Global business etiquette*. Westport, CT: Praeger, p. 69.

41 Hammer, M. R. (1993). Quoted in Chen and Starosta's *Foundations of intercultural communication*, p. 247.

42 Chaney, L. H., & Martin, J. S. (1995). *Intercultural business communication*. Englewood Cliffs, NJ: Prentice Hall Career and Technology, p. 67.

43 Weber, G. (2004, May). English rules. *Workforce Management*, 47–50; Desai, D. (2008). Globalization and the English skills gap. *Chief Learning Officer*, *7*(6), 62–63. Retrieved July 25, 2009, from Business Source Premier (EBSCO) database; and Dvorak, P. (2007, November 5). Plain English gets harder in global era. *Wall Street Journal*. Retrieved July 25, 2009, from ProQuest database.

44 Axtell, R. E. (Ed.). (1990). *Do's and taboos around the world* (2nd ed.) New York: Wiley, p. 7l.

45 Martin, J. S., & Chaney, L. H. (2006). *Global business etiquette*. Westport, CT: Praeger, p. 36.

46 Ibid., p. 191.

47 Finney, P. B. (2005, May 17). Shaking hands, greasing palms. *The New York Times*, p. C1.

48 Berenbeim, R. (2000, May). Global ethics. *Executive Excellence*, p. 7.

49 Kimes, M. (2009, February 16). Fluor's corporate crime fighter. *Fortune*, p. 26. Retrieved July 7, 2009, from Academic Search Premier database.

50 Dorroh, J. (2003, June). Stay out of the shadows: Mexican companies, government move to improve business ethics and values. *Business Mexico*, *13*(6), p. 42. Retrieved July 25, 2009, from ProQuest database.

51 Schubert, S., & Miller, T. C. (2008, December 21). Where bribery was just a line item. *New York Times*, p. BU1. Retrieved July 23, 2009, from ProQuest Newspapers database.

52 Going after Chiquita. (2008, March 24). *BusinessWeek*, p. 10.

53 Finney, P. B. (2005, May 17). Shaking hands, greasing palms. *The New York Times*, p. C1.

54 Wei, S-J. (2003, March 12). Corruption in developing countries. *Global Economics*. Retrieved July 23, 2009, from http://brookings.org/views/speeches/wei/20030312.htm

55 Bush, J. (2009, July 2). Why IKEA is fed up with Russia. *BusinessWeek.com*. Retrieved August 4, 2009, from http://www.businessweek.com/magazine/content/09_28/b4139033326721.htm

56 Alvarez, S. (2006, December). Global integrity: Transparency International's David Nussbaum is fighting for a world that is free of bribery and corruption. *Internal Auditor*, *63*(6), 53. Retrieved July 23, 2009, from Factiva database.

57 Hodgson, K. (1992, May). Adapting ethical decisions to a global marketplace. *Management Review*, 56. Retrieved July 23, 2009, from Factiva database. See also Digh, P. (1997, April). Shades of gray in the global marketplace. *HR Magazine*, p. 42. Retrieved July 23, 2009, from Business Full Text (Wilson) database.

58 Solomon, C. M. (1996, January). Put your ethics to a global test. *Personnel Journal*, 66–74. See also Smeltzer, L. R., & Jennings, M. M. (1998, January). Why an international code of business ethics would be good for business. *Journal of Business Ethics*, 57–66. See also Barker, T. S., & Cobb, S. L. (2000). A survey of ethics and cultural dimensions of MNCs [Multinational companies]. *Competitiveness Review*, *10*(2), 123. Retrieved July 23, 2009, from Academic Search Premier database.

59 Hodgson, K. (1992, May). Adapting ethical decisions to a global marketplace. *Management Review*, 54. Retrieved July 23, 2009, from Factiva database. See also Franke, G. R. (2008, March). Culture, economic development, and national ethical attitudes. *Journal of Business Research*, *61*(3). Retrieved July 23, 2009, from Business Source Premier database.

60 Based on 2000 U.S. Census figures, as reported by Little, J. S., & Triest, R. K. (2001). Proceedings from the Federal Reserve Bank of Boston Conference

Series. The impact of demographic change on U.S. labor markets. *Seismic shifts: The economic impact of demographic change*. Retrieved July 23, 2009, from http://www.bos.frb.org/economic/conf/conf46/conf46a.pdf

[61] Hansen, F. (2003, April). Tracing the value of diversity programs. *Workforce*, p. 31.

[62] Carbone, J. (2005, August 11). IBM says diverse suppliers are good for business. *Purchasing*, p. 27. Retrieved July 25, 2009, from Business Full Text (Wilson) database.

[63] Neff, J. (1998, February 16). Diversity. *Advertising Age*, p. S1.

[64] Terhune, C. (2005, April 19). Pepsi, vowing diversity isn't just image polish, seeks inclusive culture. *The Wall Street Journal*, p. B4.

[65] Andre, R. (1995, June). Diversity stress as morality stress. *Journal of Business Ethics*, 489–496.

[66] Ibid.

[67] Schwartz, J., & Wald, M. L. (2003, March 9). Smart people working collectively can be dumber than the sum of their brains. Appeared originally in *The New York Times*. Retrieved July 25, 2009, from http://www.mindfully.org/Reform/2003/Smart-People-Dumber9mar03.htm

[68] Capowski, G. (1996, June). Managing diversity. *Management Review*, p. 16.

[69] Makower, J. (1995, Winter). Managing diversity in the workplace. *Business and Society Review*, pp. 48–54.

[70] White, M. D. (2002). *A short course in international marketing blunders*. Novato, CA: World Trade Press, p. 46.

[71] Based on Walmart Brazil mobilizes suppliers and announces sustainability pact. (2009, June 23). *Facts & News/Walmart.com*. Retrieved July 23, 2009, from http://walmartstores.com/FactsNews/NewsRoom/9223.aspx; Winston, A. (2009, July 14). Wal-Mart Brazil thinks green. *BusinessWeek/Harvard Business Online*. Retrieved July 23, 2009, from http://www.businessweek.com; and Aston, A. (2009, May 14). Wal-Mart: Making its suppliers go green. *BusinessWeek Online*. Retrieved July 23, 2009, from http://www.businessweek.com/magazine/content/09_21/b4132044814736.htm

[72] Winston, A. (2009, July 14). Wal-Mart Brazil thinks green. *BusinessWeek/Harvard Business Online*. Retrieved July 23, 2009, from http://www.businessweek.com

[73] Rothrock, V. (2004, July 16). Culture clash. Retrieved July 23, 2009, from Business Source Premier database.

[74] Špaček, L. (2008). *Nová velká kniha etikety*. Prague: Mladá Fronta, p. 260.

[75] Cottrill, K. (2000, November 6). The world according to Hollywood. *Traffic World*, p. 15.

[76] Conlin, M. (2007, April 23). Go-go-going to pieces in China. *BusinessWeek*, p. 88.

[77] Nasr, O. (2009, June 15). Tear gas and Twitter: Iranians take their protests online. *CNN.com*. Retrieved July 20, 2009, from http://edition.cnn.com/2009/WORLD/meast/06/14/iran.protests.twitter/; Grossman, L. (2009, June 17). Iran protests: Twitter, the medium of the movement. *Time.com*. Retrieved July 18, 2009, from http://www.time.com/time/world/article/0,8599,1905125,00.html; and Sarno, D. (2009, March 6). Twittergates: Twitter's @billgates isn't really Bill Gates. *Los Angeles Times.com*. Retrieved July 20, 2009, from http://latimesblogs.latimes.com/technology/2009/03/latest-twitter.html

[78] Thapanachai, S. (2003, October 6). Awareness narrows cross-cultural gap in Thai management training courses. *Bangkok Post*. Retrieved July 21, 2009, from Factiva database.

[79] Dawson, D. (2005, March 1). At the top and still climbing. *High performance composites*. Retrieved January 22, 2007, from http://www.compositesworld.com/articles/at-the-top-and-still-climbing.aspx; and Wucker, M. (1998, December/January). Keep on trekking. *Working Woman*, pp. 32–36.

[80] Smith, J. (2008, July 29). Tracking Facebook's 2008 international growth by country. Inside Facebook. Retrieved July 22, 2009, from http://www.insidefacebook.com/2008/07/29/tracking-facebooks-2008-international-growth-by-country/

[81] Based on Knotts, R., & Thibodeaux, M. S. (1992). Verbal skills in cross-culture managerial communication. *European Business Review, 92*(2), pp. v–vii.

[82] Martin, K., & Walsh, S. M. (1996, October). Beware the Foreign Corrupt Practices Act. *International Commercial Litigation*, 25–27; and Lay-person's guide to Foreign Corrupt Practices Act (FCPA). (n.d.). United States Department of Justice. Retrieved July 21, 2009, from http://www.usdoj.gov/criminal/fraud/fcpa/

[83] Kellner, T. (2002, March 18). Insert foot. *Forbes*. Retrieved July 21, 2009, from Business Sources Premier database.

[84] Daniels, C. (2004, June 28). 50 best companies for minorities. *Fortune*, p. 138.

Chapter 4

[1] Welch, S. (2009, May 11). Suze Orman. *Time*, p. 67; and Fabrikant, G. (2006, March 5). Cleaning up messages, friend to friend [Suze Orman]. *The New York Times*, p. BU5. Retrieved July 13, 2009, from InfoTrac College Edition database.

[2] Grainger, D. (2003, June 16). The Suze Orman show. *Fortune*, pp. 82-88. Retrieved July 12, 2009, from Business Source Complete database.

[3] Erler, S. (2005, March 31). Suze Orman spills, signs books. *Times* (Munster, Indiana). Retrieved March 7, 2007, from InfoTrac College Edition database.

[4] Gallo, C. (2001, June). Best presentations. Suze Orman. *BusinessWeek Online*. Retrieved July 1, 2009, from http://images.businessweek.com/ss/06/01/best_communicators/index_01.htm

[5] Arnold, V. (1986, August). Benjamin Franklin on writing well. *Personnel Journal*, p. 17.

[6] Bacon, M. (1988, April). Quoted in Business writing: One-on-one speaks best to the masses. *Training*, p. 95. See also Effective communication: Remember to pack your writing with reader focus. (2009, March 22). *Sales Insider*. p. 4. Retrieved July 1, 2009, from Business Source Premier database; and Danziger, E. (1998, February). Communicate up. *Journal of Accountancy*, p. 67.

[7] Wallis, C., & Steptoe, S. (2006, January 26). The case for doing one thing at a time. *Time South Pacific* (Australia/New Zealand edition), issue 2, p. 50. Retrieved July 16, 2009, from Business Source Complete database.

[8] Ibid.

[9] Be positive. (2009, March). *Communication Briefings*, p. 5. Adapted from Brandi, J. *Winning at customer retention* at http://www.customercarecoach.com

[10] Based on Fichter, D. (2005, July/August). The many forms of e-collaboration: Blogs, wikis, portals, groupware, discussion boards, and instant messaging. *Online*, pp. 48-50. Retrieved July 15, 2009, from Business Source Complete database.

[11] Dahl, D. (2009, June). Connecting the dots: How to choose the right collaboration software for your company. *Inc.*, p. 103. Retrieved July 19, 2009, from InfoTrac College Edition database.

[12] Iwata, E. (2007, January 5). Diet pill sellers fined $25M. *USA Today*, p. B1.

[13] Woolever, K. (1990, June 2). Corporate language and the law: Avoiding liability in corporate communications. *IEE Transactions on Professional Communication*, pp. 95-98.

[14] Ibid.

[15] Newark, N. A. (2005). Avoiding an "implied" employment contract or drafting a favorable one: A primer. *FindLaw*. Retrieved July 14, 2009, from http://library.findlaw.com/2005/Mar/2/157726.html; see also Jenner, L. (1994, March). Employment-at-will liability: How protected are you? *HR Focus*, p. 11.

[16] Walter, R., & Sleeper, B. (2002, Spring). Employee recruitment and retention: When company inducements trigger liability. *Review of Business*, pp. 17–23.

[17] Pickens, J. (1985, August). Communication: Terms of equality: A guide to bias-free language. *Personnel Journal*, p. 5.

[18] Armour, S. (2005, June 14). Warning: Your clever little blog could get you fired. *USA Today*. Retrieved July 16, 2009, from http://www.usatoday.com/money/workplace/2005-06-14-worker-blogs-usat_x.htm

[19] Ziobro, P. (2009, July 14). Burger King scraps plans for $1 burger. *The Wall Street Journal*, p. B6.

[20] Templeton, B. (2004, October). 10 big myths about copyright explained. Retrieved February 24, 2007, from http://www.templetons.com/brad/copymyths.html

Chapter 5

[1] O'Donnell, J., & Fetterman, M. (2007, January 24). Can Gap be saved? *USA Today*, p. B1.

[2] Ibid.

[3] The misnomer of specialty apparel. (2009, February). *Chain Store Age*, p. 2. Retrieved January 5, 2010, from Business Source Complete database.

[4] Sutton, R. I. (2006, September 5). The truth about brainstorming. *BusinessWeek*, p. 17. Retrieved January 2, 2010, from InfoTrac College Edition database.

[5] Heslin, P. (2009, March). Better than brainstorming? *Journal of Occupational & Organizational Psychology, 82*(2), 129–145. Retrieved January 4, 2010, from Business Source Complete database.

[6] Harris, A., Finkelstein, D., et al. (2009, July 9). BRW Twitter Homepage. *BRW Magazine*, p. 7. Retrieved January 2, 2010, from Business Source Complete database.

[7] Based on information retrieved February 7, 2007, from http://www.gapinc.com

[8] Rindegard, J. (1999, November 22). Use clear writing to show you mean business. *InfoWorld*, p. 78.

[9] Working with factories. (2007). Gap Inc. Retrieved February 6, 2007, from http://www.gapinc.com/public/SocialResponsibility/sr_fac_wwf.shtml

[10] Factory approval process. (2007). Gap Inc. Retrieved February 6, 2007, from http://www.gapinc.com/public/SocialResponsibility/sr_fac_wwf_fap.shtml. See also Merrick, A. (2004, May 12). Gap offers unusual look at factory conditions. *The Wall Street Journal*, p. A1.

[11] Goddard, R. W. (1989, April). Communication: Use language effectively. *Personnel Journal*, 32.

[12] Toffler, B. L. quoted in Schmitt, R. B. (2002, November 5). Companies add ethics training; will it work? *The Wall Street Journal*, p. Bl.

[13] Mannes, G. (2006, September). Earning a degree in debt. *Money*, pp. 98–105. Retrieved August 3, 2009, from http://www.mutualofamerica.com/articles/Money/2006September/money2.asp. See also Kristof, K. M. (2003, September 14). More grads struggling to repay loans. *Los Angeles Times*, p. C3.

[14] United Press International. (2009, July 20). Programs seek to ease student loan debt. Retrieved January 4, 2010, from InfoTrac College Edition database.

Chapter 6

[1] Yum! brands recognized in corporate responsibility officer magazine's "100 best corporate citizens" list. (2009, March 25). *Biotech Week*, p. 4400. Retrieved January 2, 2010, from Business Source Complete database.

[2] Lockyer, S. E. (2006, December 18). Yum to expand Taco Bell breakfast test. *Nation's Restaurant News, 40*(51), 3. Retrieved January 3, 2010, from InfoTrac College Edition database.

[3] Yum Brands: Taco Bell to expand. (2009, January). *MarketWatch: Food*, p. 16. Retrieved January 3, 2010, from Business Source Complete database.

[4] Brumback, N. (1998, September 1). Yo quiero Mexican food. *Restaurant Business*, pp. 43–44.

[5] Elbow, P. (1998). *Writing with power: Techniques for mastering the writing process.* Oxford, UK: Oxford University Press, p. 30.

[6] Cook, C. K. (1985). *Line by line.* Boston: Houghton Mifflin, p. 17.

[7] van Roon, Ilja. (2006, May 23). Quoted in Sorry, no more excuses for bad business writing. *PR Newswire.* Retrieved January 4, 2010, from InfoTrac College Edition database.

Chapter 7

[1] Colker, D. (2009, August 13). CEO's wife tweets during childbirth. *Los Angeles Times*, p. B3.

[2] Hof, R. (2009, August 17). Betting on the real-time Web. *BusinessWeek*, p. 46.

[3] Ibid., p. 47.

[4] Ladaga, L. (2009, July 23). TMT: Too much Twitter? *Yahoo News.* Retrieved January 18, 2010, from http://news.yahoo.com

[5] Sandberg, J. (2006, September 26). Employees forsake dreaded email for the beloved phone. *The Wall Street Journal*, p. B1.

[6] Wikipedia. (2009, October 24). *Wikipedia, the free encyclopedia.* Retrieved February 24, 2010, from http://en.wikipedia.org/wiki/Wikipedia

[7] Tschabitscher, H. (2009). How many emails are sent every day? *About.com: Email.* Retrieved January 29, 2010, from http://email.about.com/od/emailtrivia/f/emails_per_day.htm

[8] Maney, K. (2003, July 24). How the big names tame e-mail. *USA Today*, p. 2A.

[9] American Management Association & The ePolicy Institute. (2004). Workplace e-mail and IM survey. *ePolicy Institute.com.* Retrieved January 28, 2010, from http://www.epolicyinstitute.com/

[10] E-mail becoming crime's new smoking gun. (2002, August 15). *USA Today.com.* Retrieved January 28, 2010, from http://www.usatoday.com/tech/news/2002-08-15-email-evidence_x.htm

[11] Revkin, A. C. (2009, November 20). Hacked e-mail is new fodder for climate dispute. *New York Times.* Retrieved January 28, 2010, from http://www.nytimes.com/2009/11/21/science/earth/21climate.html

[12] Goldsmith, M. (2007, May 16). Understanding the perils of e-mail. *BusinessWeek.* Retrieved January 20, 2010, from http://www.businessweek.com/careers/content/may2007/ca20070516_392697.htm?chan=rss_topEmailedStories_ssi_5

[13] Sanati, C. (2008, June 20). Dealbook extra: E-crimination. *The New York Times*, p. C6. Retrieved January 29, 2010, from LexisNexis Academic database; and Goldsmith, M. (2007, May 17). Understanding the perils of e-mail. *BusinessWeek Online*, p. 31. Retrieved January 19, 2010, from Academic Search Premier database.

[14] Living the fast, young life in Asia. (2008, April). *Change Agent.* Retrieved January 24, 2010, from http://www.synovate.com/changeagent/index.php/site/full_story/living_the_fast_living_young_in_asia/

[15] 5 ways Twitter can get you fired. (2009, October 8). *Applicant.com.* Retrieved January 28, 2010, from http://applicant.com/5-ways-twitter-can-get-you-fired/

[16] Baker, S., & Green, H. (2009, June 2). Beyond blogs. *BusinessWeek*, p. 49.

[17] Fortune 500 business blogging wiki. (2009, October 1). *Socialtext.net.* Retrieved January 14, 2010, from http://www.socialtext.net/bizblogs/index.cgi

[18] Beutler, W. (2007, April 10). Yes, but how many blogs are there really? Blog, P. I. Retrieved January 6, 2010, from http://www.blogpi.net/yes-but-how-many-blogs-are-there-really

[19] Baker, S., & Green, H. (2008, May 22). Beyond blogs: What business needs to know. *BusinessWeek Online.* Retrieved January 6, 2010, from http://www.businessweek.com/magazine/ content/08_22/b4086044617865.htm?chan=search

[20] Ibid.

[21] Reality check: State of the media democracy survey. (2008). Retrieved January 3, 2010, from www.deloitte.com/us/realitycheck

[22] Baker, S., & Green, H. (2008, June 2). Beyond blogs: What business needs to know. *BusinessWeek Online.* Retrieved January 6, 2010, from http://www.businessweek.com/magazine/ content/08_22/b4086044617865.htm?chan=search

[23] Taking cues from Facebook. (n.d.). *About McDonald's.* Retrieved January 14, 2010, from http://www.aboutmcdonalds.com/mcd/students/did_you_know/taking_cues_from_facebook.html?DCSext.destination=http://www.aboutmcdonalds.com/mcd/students/did_you_know/taking_cues_from_facebook.html

[24] Conlin, M., & MacMillan, D. (2009, June 1). Managing the tweets. *BusinessWeek*, p. 21.

[25] Baker, S., & Green, H. (2008, June 2). Beyond blogs. *BusinessWeek*, pp. 46, 48.

[26] Conlin, M., & MacMillan, D. (2009, June 1). Managing the tweets. *BusinessWeek*, p. 20.

[27] Ibid., pp. 20–21.

[28] Irvine, M. (2009, July 12). Young workers push employers for wider Web access. *USA Today.* Retrieved January 14, 2010, from http://www.usatoday.com/tech/webguide/internetlife/2009-07-13-blocked-internet_N.htm

[29] Ibid.

[30] Villano, M. (2009, April 26). The online divide between work and play. *The New York Times.* Retrieved February 14, 2010, from http://www.nytimes.com

[31] Ibid.

[32] Ibid.

[33] Ibid.

[34] Dougherty, C. cited in Hiring pros share insights about social networking. (2009). *Yahoo! Hotjobs.* Retrieved January 3, 2010, from http://hotjobs.yahoo.com/career-articles-hiring_pros_share_insights_about_social_networking_sites-1030

[35] Searcey, D. (2009, November 24). Some courts raise bar on reading employee email. *The Wall Street Journal*, p. A31. Retrieved January 28, 2010, from http://online.wsj.com/article/SB125859862658454923.html; and Na, G. (2006, October 17). Employee e-mail use: Big brother may be watching. *Mondaq Business Briefing.* Retrieved January 28, 2010, from Factiva database.

[36] Klein, K. E. (2009, December 1). Putting a fair Internet use policy in place. *BusinessWeek.com.* Retrieved January 28, 2010, from http://www.businessweek.com/smallbiz/content/dec2009/sb2009121_245449.htm

[37] Zetter, K. (2006, October). Employers crack down on personal net use: Misusing e-mail or browsing the wrong sites can cost you your job. *PC World*, p. 26. Retrieved January 28, 2010, from Factiva database.

[38] Breaton, S. (2007, January/February). Blogging: Priceless? *CA Magazine*, p. 13. Retrieved January 28, 2010, from Business Source Premier (EBSCO) database.

[39] Gardner, T. (2009, September 13). It may pay to Twitter. *Los Angeles Times*, p. L8.

[40] Needleman, S. E. (2009, August 4). For companies, a Tweet in time can avert PR mess. *The Wall Street Journal.* Retrieved February 4, 2010, from http://online.wsj.com

[41] Garvey, M. (2009, October 31). Fifth years of simplicity as style. *The Wall Street Journal*, p. A19.

[42] Greene, D. (Host). (2009, July 2). Twitter music reviews: Criticism as haiku. *Morning Edition.* Washington, DC: National Public Radio. Retrieved January 31, 2010, from http://www.npr.org/templates/story/story.php?storyId=106178234

[43] Ibid.

Chapter 8

[1] Based on Clark, N. (2009, August 12). The cold wars. *Marketing.* Retrieved January 20, 2010, from InfoTrac College Edition database; Ethical Companies. (2009, April 9), *Marketing Week*, p. 18. Retrieved January 19, 2010, from InfoTrac College Edition database; Ben & Jerry's Mission. (n.d.). Retrieved January 15, 2010, from http://www.benjerry.com/activism/mission-statement; Brown, K. (2004, April 15). Chilling at Ben & Jerry's: Cleaner, greener. *The Wall Street Journal*, p. B1; Arnold, M. (2001, May 3). Is Ben & Jerry's losing its Bohemian appeal? *Marketing*, p. 17; and Ben & Jerry's goes cage-free and expands fair trade. (2006, October 20). *Ice Cream Reporter*, p. 4. Retrieved January 20, 2010, from InfoTrac College Edition database.

[2] Messmer, M. (2001, January). Enhancing your writing skills. *Strategic Finance*, pp. 8–10. Retrieved January 15, 2010, from Business Source Complete database.

[3] Blachly, A., Ben & Jerry's (personal communication with Mary Ellen Guffey, January 12, 1993).

[4] Zhu, Y., and White, C. (2009, September). Practitioners' views about the use of business email within organizational settings: Implications for developing student generic competence. *Business Communication Quarterly, 72*(3), 292.

[5] Fallows, J. (2005, June 12). Enough keyword searches. Just answer my question. *The New York Times*, p. BU3.

[6] Quinley, K. (2008, May). Apology programs. *Claims*, pp. 14-16. Retrieved January 22, 2010, from Business Source Premier database. See also Runnels, M. (2009, Winter). Apologies all around: Advocating federal protection for the full apology in civil cases. *San Diego Law Review,46*(1), 137–160. Retrieved February 1, 2010, from Business Source Premier database.

[7] Davidow, M. (2003, February). Organizational responses to customer complaints: What works and what doesn't. *Journal of Service Research, 5*(3), 225. Retrieved February 2, 2010, from Business Source Premier database; Blackburn-Brockman, E., & Belanger, K. (1993, June). You-attitude and positive emphasis: Testing received wisdom in business communication. *The Bulletin of the Association for Business Communication*, 1–5; Mascolini, M. (1994, June). Another look at teaching the external negative message. *The Bulletin of the Association for Business Communication*, 46.

[8] Liao, H. (2007, March). Do it right this time: The role of employee service recovery performance in customer-perceived justice and customer loyalty after service failures. *Journal of Applied Psychology, 92*(2), 475. Retrieved January 25, 2010, from Business Source Premier database; Gilbert, P. (1996, December). Two words that can help a business thrive. *The Wall Street Journal*, p. A12.

[9] Martin, J. S., & Chaney, L. H. (2006). *Global business etiquette.* Westport, CT: Praeger, p. 150.

[10] Haneda, S., & Hirosuke, S. (1982). Japanese communication behavior as reflected in letter writing. *The Journal of Business Communication (1)*, 29. See also Varner, I., & Beamer, L. (2001). *Intercultural Communication*. Chicago: McGraw-Hill Irwin, pp. 131–132.

[11] Martin, J. S., & Chaney, L. H. (2006). *Global business etiquette.* Praeger: Westport, CT, p. 159.

[12] Loewy, D., German interpreter (personal communication with Mary Ellen Guffey, July 2007).

[13] Luciani-Samec, A., French instructor, & Samec, P. French businessman (personal communication with Mary Ellen Guffey, May 1995).

[14] Fallows, J. (2005, June 12). Enough keyword searches. Just answer my question. *The New York Times*, p. BU3.

[15] Based on Scarp, M. J. (1995, October 28). Hotel to cease pigeon poisoning. *Scottsdale Tribune.*

Chapter 9

[1] Southwest Airlines confirms passengers are not superstitious. (2009, November 13). *PR Newswire.* Retrieved January 4, 2010, from http://www.southwest.com

[2] Less baggage. (2008, June 12). *The Tampa Tribune* (Tampa, FL), p. 1.

[3] Edwards, J. (2008, September 22). Sour tweets get sweet results. *Brandweek*. Retrieved January 4, 2010, from InfoTrac College Edition database.

[4] Bailey, J. (2007, March 18). Airlines learn to fly on a wing and an apology. *The New York Times*, p. 1.1. Retrieved January 3, 2010, from http://www.nytimes.com; and Taylor, F. (2008, January 23, March 5). Being proactive—The next generation of customer service. Message posted to Nuts About Southwest blog. Retrieved January 3, 2010, from http://www.blogsouthwest.com/

[5] Mintz, J. (2009, February 23). Microsoft: Laid-off can keep extra pay after all. *USA Today*. Retrieved January 3, 2010, from http://www.usatoday.com/tech/news/2009-02-23-microsoft-layoffs_N.htm

[6] Greenwald, J. (2009, June 1). Layoffs may spark defamation suits. *Business Insurance*. Retrieved January 13, 2009, from Business Source Complete database.

[7] American Management Association. 2004 Survey on workplace e-mail and IM reveals unmanaged risks. (2004). Retrieved June 10, 2007, from http://www.amanet.org/press/amanews/im_survey.htm

[8] McCord, E. A. (1991, April). The business writer, the law, and routine business communication: A legal and rhetorical analysis. *Journal of Business and Technical Communication*, 183.

[9] Ibid.

[10] Shuit, D. P. (2003, September). Do it right or risk getting burned. *Workforce Management*, p. 80.

[11] Brodkin, J. (2007, March 19). Corporate apologies don't mean much. *Networkworld, 24*(11), p. 8. Retrieved January 4, 2010, from Business Source Complete database.

[12] Schweitzer, M. (2006, December). Wise negotiators know when to say "I'm sorry." *Negotiation*, 4. Retrieved January 4, 2010, from Business Source Complete database.

[13] Brodkin, J. (2007, March 19). Rating apologies. *Networkworld, 24*(11), p. 14. Retrieved January 3, 2010, from Business Source Complete database.

[14] Neeleman, D. (2007). An apology from David Neeleman. Retrieved January 4, 2010, from http://www.jetblue.com/about/ourcompany/apology/index.html

[15] Letters to Lands' End. (1991, February). 1991 Lands' End Catalog. Dodgeville, WI: Lands' End, p. 100.

[16] Mowatt, J. (2002, February). Breaking bad news to customers. *Agency Sales*, 30; and Dorn, E. M. (1999, March). Case method instruction in the business writing classroom. *Business Communication Quarterly, 62*(1), 51–52.

[17] Forbes, M. (1999). How to write a business letter. In K. Harty (Ed.), *Strategies for business and technical writing*. Boston: Allyn and Bacon, p. 108.

[18] Harris, D. (2004, July 5). Court: Dealerships need not repeat a lender's credit rejection notice. *Automotive News*, , p. 18. Retrieved January 5, 2010, from InfoTrac College Edition database.

[19] Mainz, C. (2005, June). Southwest Star of the Month: Fred Taylor. *Spirit*. Retrieved January 6, 2010, from http://www.fredtaylorjr.com/1894/10001.html; McGregor, J., Jespersen, F., Tucker, M., & Foust, D. (2007, March 5). Customer service champs. Retrieved January 6, 2010, from http://www.businessweek.com/magazine/content/07_10/b4024001.htm

[20] Browning, M. (2003, November 24). Work dilemma: Delivering bad news a good way. *Government Computer News*, p. 41; and Mowatt, J. (2002, February). Breaking bad news to customers. *Agency Sales*, p. 30.

[21] Ensall, S. (2007, January 30). Delivering bad news. *Personnel Today*, p. 31. Retrieved January 5, 2010, from Business Source Premier database; and Lewis, B. (1999, September 13). To be an effective leader, you need to perfect the art of delivering bad news. *InfoWorld*, p. 124.

[22] Gilsdorf, J. W. (1997, June). Metacommunication effects on international business negotiating in China. *Business Communication Quarterly, 60*(2), 27.

[23] Beamer, L., & Varner, I. (2001). *Intercultural communication in the global workplace*. New York: McGraw-Hill/Irwin, p. 141.

[24] Conaway, R. N., & Wardrope, W. J. (2004, December). Communication in Latin America. *Business Communication Quarterly, 67*(4), 472.

[25] Bristol-Smith, D. (2003, November). Quoted in Need to deliver bad news? How & why to tell it like it is. *HR Focus*, p. 3. Retrieved January 5, 2010, from InfoTrac College Edition database.

[26] Gartner identifies top ten disruptive technologies for 2008-2012. (n.d.) Press release. Retrieved January 5, 2010, from http://www.gartner.com/it/page.jsp?id=68117

[27] Based on Lee, L. (2007, June 11). A smoothie you can chew on. *BusinessWeek*, p. 64.

[28] Hines announces HinesGO sustainability tool to green office space. (2009, November 2). Retrieved January 5, 2010, from http://www.immo-news.net/Hines-announces-HinesGO-sustainability-tool-to-green-office-space_a5733.html

[29] Based on Sloan, G. (1996, November 29). Under 21? Carnival says cruise is off. *USA Today*; Sieder, J. (1995, October 16). Full steam ahead: Carnival Cruise Line makes boatloads of money by selling fun. *U.S. News & World Report*, p. 72; and About Carnival Cruise Line. Retrieved July 27, 2004, from http://www.cruisecritic./reviews/cruiseline.cfm?CruiseLineID=9

[30] Based on Burbank, L. (2007, June 8). Personal items can be swept away between flights. *USA Today*, p. 3D.

[31] Kucher, K. (2009, March 31). UCSD email erroneously welcomes all who applied. Retrieved January 10, 2010, from http://www3signonsandiego.com/stories/2009/mar31/bn31letter114447/

[32] Sorkin, A. R. (1999, November). J. Crew web goof results in discount. *The New York Times*, p. D3.

[33] Mishory, J. (2008, June). Don't shoot the messenger: How to deliver bad news and still keep customers satisfied. *Sales and Marketing Management*, 18.

[34] Based on Harari, O. (1999, July–August). The power of complaints. *Management Review*, p. 31.

[35] Based on SUV surprise. (2004, June 15). *The Wall Street Journal*, p. W7.

Chapter 10

[1] Betancourt, C. M. (1999, November 28). Head of Make-A-Wish chapter is a man with many missions. *The Miami Herald*, p. B1.

[2] Morris, P., president and CEO, Hands on Miami (personal communication with Mary Ellen Guffey, August 2, 2006).

[3] Hamilton, C. (2005). *Communicating for results* (7th ed.). Mason, OH: Wadsworth/Thomson, p. 334.

[4] Hoar, R. (2005, March 1). Be more persuasive. *Management Today*, 56.

[5] Cialdini, R. B. (1993). *Influence: The power of persuasion*. New York: Quill, William Morrow, p. 238.

[6] Fracaro, K. E. (2004, August). Managing by persuasion. *Contract Management, 44*(8), 4. Retrieved January 29, 2010, from InfoTrac College Edition database.

[7] Conde, C. (2010, January 17). Structure? The flatter the better. *The New York Times*, p. BU2.

[8] Newman, R. (2006, September 25). Lessons from the rule breakers. *U.S. News & World Report*, Executive Edition, p. 4. Retrieved January 30, 2010, from InfoTrac College Edition database.

[9] Pollock, T. (2003, June). How to sell an idea. *Supervision*, p. 15. Retrieved January 29, 2010, from InfoTrac College Edition database.

[10] Communicating with the boss. (2006, May). *Communication Briefings*, p. 8.

[11] Friesen, P. (2003, October). Customer testimonials. *Target Marketing*, p. 137.

[12] McLaughlin, K. (1990, October). Words of wisdom. *Entrepreneur*, 101. See also Wastphal, L. (2001, October). Empathy in sales letters. *Direct Marketing*, 55.

[13] Consumer complaints about Vital Basics—Focus Factor. Retrieved September 17, 2006, from http://www.consumeraffairs.com/nutrition/vital.html; see also Clifford, S. (2009, November 22). Are ads true? New lawsuits ask for proof. *The New York Times*, p. 1.

[14] Singer, N. (2009, February 11). A pill that promised too much. *The New York Times*, B1.

[15] Clifford, S. (2009, November 22). Are ads true? New lawsuits ask for proof. *The New York Times*, p. 1.

[16] Loathing of mail and Web activity on rise. (2006, April 28). *Precision Marketing*, p. 2.

[17] Howard, T. (2008, November 28). E-mail grows as direct-marketing tool. *USA Today*, p. 5B.

[18] Suited for employment. (2005, July 15). *The Chronicle of Higher Education*, p. A8.

[19] Based on Fritscher-Porter, K. (2003, June/July). Don't be duped by office supply scam artists. *OfficePro*, 9–10.

[20] Yancey, K. B. (2006, September 2). Hotels give guests a hand with GPS. *USA Today*, p. 1D.

[21] Based on Yu, R. (2009, 13 March). Hotels take action to pare down food, restaurant expenses. *USA Today*, p. 3D.

[22] Zbar, J. D. (2001, March). Training to telework. *Home Office Computing*, p. 72.

[23] Based on Marquez, J. (2006, January 16). On-site blood testing raises privacy issues. *Workplace Management*, p. 10.

[24] Based on DuFrene, D. D., & Lehman, C. M. (2002, March). Persuasive appeal for clean language. *Business Communication Quarterly, 65*(1), 48–55.

[25] Belluck, P. (2010, January 14). After a longtime rise, obesity rates in U.S. level off, data suggest. *The New York Times*, p. A20(L). Retrieved January 28, 2010, from InfoTrac College Edition database.

[26] Know the true cost of obesity: Related lost productivity. (2008, April 1). *Occupational Health Management*. Retrieved January 27, 2010, from InfoTrac College Edition database.

[27] Based on Yunxia, Z. (2000, December). Building knowledge structures in teaching cross-cultural sales genres. *Business Communication Quarterly, 63*(4), 66–67.

Chapter 11

[1] Flying with companion animals: Protect your precious "cargo." (n.d.). *HelpingAnimals.com*. Retrieved January 15, 2010, from http://www.helpinganimals.com/Travel_cargo.asp

[2] 2009/2010 National Pet Owners Survey cited by American Pet Products Association. (2010). *APPA.com*. Retrieved January 15, 2010, from http://www.americanpetproducts.org/press_industrytrends.asp

[3] Questions for David McCullough. (2006, July 7). *Workforce Management*, p. 9.

[4] Cohen, J. S. (2009, December 28). Top 10 favorite foods preferred by college students. *Chicago Tribune*. Retrieved January 22, 2010, from http://www.inyork.com/ci_14080691?source=most_viewed

[5] Giorgetti, D., & Sebastiani, F. (2003, December). Automating survey coding by multiclass text categories. *Journal of the American Society for Information Science and Technology, 54*(14), 1269. Retrieved January 22, 2010, from ABI/INFORM Global database; and Brennan, M., & Holdershaw, J. (1999). The effect of question tone and form on responses to open-ended questions: Further data. *Marketing Bulletin*, 57-64.

[6] Goldsmith, B. (2002, June). The awesome power of asking the right questions. *OfficeSolutions*, 52; and Bracey, G. W. (2001, November). Research-question authority. *Phi Delta Kappan*, 191.

[7] Berfield, S. (2009, August 17). Howard Schultz versus Howard Schultz. *BusinessWeek*, p. 31.

[8] Lenhart, A. (2009, October 8). The democratization of online social networks. *Pew Internet & American Life Project*, slide 4. Retrieved January 22, 2010, from http://www.pewinternet.org/Presentations/2009/41--The-Democratization-of-Online-Social-Networks.aspx

[9] Netcraft, Ltd. (n.d.) *January 2010 Web Server Survey*. Retrieved January 22, 2010, from http://news.netcraft.com/archives/web_server_survey.html

[10] Alpert, J., & Hajaj, N. (2008, July 25). We knew the Web was big . . . *The Official Google Blog*. Retrieved January 22, 2010, from http://googleblog.blogspot.com/2008/07/we-knew-web-was-big.html

[11] Little, L. (2006, March 7). Using a multiple search. *The Wall Street Journal*, p. D1. Retrieved January 23, 2010, from Factiva database.

[12] Vincent, J. (n.d.). Write or wrong: Thoughts on plagiarism. *Helium.com*. Retrieved January 22, 2010, from http://www.helium.com/items/982257-thoughts-on-plagiarism

[13] Arenson, K. W., & Gootman, E. (2008, February 21). Columbia cites plagiarism by a professor. *The New York Times*. Retrieved January 22, 2010, from http://www.nytimes.com/2008/02/21/education/21prof.html; and Bartlett, T. (2006, September 8). Professor faces firing for plagiarism. *Chronicle of Higher Education*, p. 11. Retrieved January 22, 2010, from Academic Search Elite database.

[14] Writing Tutorial Services, Indiana University. *Plagiarism: What it is and how to recognize and avoid it*. Retrieved January 22, 2010, from http://www.indiana.edu/~wts/pamphlets/plagiarism.shtml

[15] Brady, D. (2006, December 4). *!#?@ the e-mail. Can we talk? *BusinessWeek*, p. 109.

[16] Berfield, S. (2009, August 17). Howard Schultz versus Howard Schultz. *BusinessWeek*, p. 33.

[17] Spake, A. (2003, November 17). Hey kids! We've got sugar and toys. *U.S. News & World Report*, p. 62.

[18] Reena, J. (2006, October 16). Enough with the shoot-'em-ups. *BusinessWeek*, p. 92.

[19] Hibbard, J. (2006, October 9). How Yahoo! gave itself a face-lift. *BusinessWeek*, p. 77.

[20] Goldman, A. (2006, December 1). Wal-Mart limps into the holidays. *Los Angeles Times*, p. C4.

[21] 2010 College food trends: Students crave global, national and regional comfort food with a twist. (2009, December 14). *SodexoUSA.com*. Retrieved February 5, 2010, from http://www.sodexousa.com/usen/newsroom/press/press09/2010collegefoodtrends.asp

[22] Teens more "normal" than you think regarding media usage. (2009, June 25). *Nielsenwire*. Retrieved February 5, 2010, from http://blog.nielsen.com/nielsenwire/consumer/teens-more-normal-than-you-think-regarding-media-usage/

[23] Edwards, C., & Ihlwan, M. (2006, December 4). Upward mobility. *BusinessWeek*, pp. 68–82.

[24] World Internet usage and population statistics. (2009, September 30). *Internet World Stats*. Retrieved February 5, 2010, from http://www.internetworldstats.com/stats.htm

[25] Naughton, K. (2006, July 3). Corporate giant. *Newsweek*, p. 74. Retrieved February 4, 2010, from Business Source Premier (EBSCO) database.

[26] How undergraduate students use credit cards. (2009). *Sallie Mae*. Retrieved February 5, 2010, from http://www.salliemae.com/NR/rdonlyres/0BD600F1-9377-46EA-AB1F-6061FC763246/10744/SLMCreditCardUsageStudy41309FINAL2.pdf

Chapter 12

[1] Case based on Berfield, S. (2009, August 17). Howard Schultz versus Howard Schultz. *BusinessWeek*, pp. 28-33; Temkin, B. (2010, January 25). Starbucks brews a comeback with purpose. *BusinessExchange*. Retrieved February 15, 2010, from http://bx.businessweek.com/starbucks; Starbucks brews up instant coffee line. (2009, February 18). *The Boston Globe*. Retrieved February 15, 2010, from http://www.boston.com/business/articles/2009/02/18/starbucks_brews_up_instant_coffee_line; and Bramhall, J. (2007, January 1). Starbucks. *Hoover's Company Records*, 15745. Retrieved January 9, 2010, from ProQuest database.

[2] Ewing, J. (2007, May 4). First mover in mobile: How Nokia is selling cell phones to the developing world. *BusinessWeek Online*. Retrieved February 20, 2010, from http://www.businessweek.com

[3] Temkin, B. (2010, January 25). Starbucks brews a comeback with purpose. *Business Exchange*. Retrieved February 20, 2010, from http://bx.businessweek.com/starbucks/

[4] Groom, N., & Baertlein, L. (2008, April 24). Starbucks steps back from music business. *Business Exchange*. Retrieved February 15, 2010, from http://bx.businessweek.com/starbucks; and Van Riper, T. (2007, February 27). Dunkin' Donuts edges Starbucks. *Forbes.com*. Retrieved February 15, 2010, from http://www.forbes.com/2007/02/26/starbucks-dunkin-donuts-biz-cx_tvr_0227starbucks.html

[5] Toyo sets tire recall. (2010, February 23). *Tire Review*. Retrieved February 23, 2010, from http://www.tirereview.com/Article/71180/toyo_sets_tire_recall.aspx; and Aeppel, T. (2000, November 20). Firestone recall fuels interest in "smart" tires. *The Wall Street Journal*, p. B1.

[6] Cornish, A. (Writer). (2006, July 18). Nissan workers make Tennessee move. [Radio Broadcast episode]. In M. Block (Host). *All Things Considered*. Washington, DC: National Public Radio; Halcomb, R. (2005, October 20). Nissan may move its U.S. headquarters. *Autoblog*. Retrieved February 20, 2010, from http://www.autoblog.com/2005/10/20/nissan-may-move-its-u-s-headquarters; and Halcomb, R. (2005, November 3). Nissan to move headquarters to Tennessee. *Autoblog*. Retrieved February 20, 2010, from http://www.autoblog.com/2005/11/03/nissan-to-move-headquaters-to-tennessee/

[7] Berfield, S. (2009, August 17). Howard Schultz versus Howard Schultz. *BusinessWeek*, p. 33.

[8] Red light camera reform. (2003, May/June). *WestWays*, 19.

[9] Roberts, D., Engardio, P., Bernstein, A., Holmes, S., & Ji, X. (2006, November 27). Secrets, lies, and sweatshops. *BusinessWeek Online*. Retrieved February 20, 2010, from http://www.businessweek.com

Chapter 13

[1] Based on Grinyer, M., Raytheon proposal consultant (personal communication with Mary Ellen Guffey, July 23, 2007).

[2] City of Las Vegas. (2010, January 4). RFP for public private partnership parking initiative. *Onvia DemandStar*. Retrieved March 4, 2010, from http://www.lasvegasnevada.gov/Business/5990.htm?ID

[3] Buck Institute for Age Research. (n.d.). Architecture. Retrieved February 5, 2010, from http://www.buckinstitute.org/TheInstitute/architecture.asp

[4] Sant, T. (2004). Persuasive business proposals. New York: AMACOM, pp. 99–100.

[5] MasterPlans: Professional Business Plan Writers. (n.d.). Rapid development cycle. Retrieved March 5, 2010, from MasterPlans Web site: http://www.masterplans.com

[6] Turner, M. L. (2007). Guide to business plan consultants: Hiring help is the next best thing to writing your plan yourself. *Work.com*. Retrieved March 5, 2010, from http://www.work.com/business-plan-consultants-880/

[7] Nelson, F. (2004, September 5). Device from UCSB trio ready to take its first breath. *Santa Barbara News-Press*, p. F1.

Chapter 14

[1] Johnson, B. (2010, January 27). Apple iPad: The first review. *Guardian.co.uk*. Retrieved March 28, 2010, from http://www.guardian.co.uk/technology/2010/jan/27/apple-ipad-tablet-first-review

[2] Steve Jobs' obsession with secrecy and the "big-bang." (2009, December 8). *Edible Apple Blog*. Retrieved March 28, 2010, from http://www.edibleapple.com/steve-jobs-obsession-with-secrecy-and-the-big-bang/

[3] Ibid.

[4] Joy, D. (2007, April 26). Blog post: Do public speaking skills affect your technology career success? *Jobing.com*. Retrieved March 30, 2010, from http://glendale.jobing.com/blog_post.asp?post=4221

[5] Dr. John J. Medina as quoted by Reynolds, G. (2010). *Presentation zen design*. Berkeley, CA: New Riders, p. 97.

[6] Gallo, C. (2009, October 6). Uncovering Steve Jobs' presentation secrets. *BusinessWeek*. Retrieved March 28, 2010, from http://www.businessweek.com/smallbiz/content/oct2009/sb2009106_706829.htm

[7] Lewis, A. (2005, July 5). So many meetings, so little point, *The Denver Post*, p. C1. Retrieved March 20, 2010, from LexisNexis database; and Paradi, D. (2003). Are we wasting $250 million per day due to bad PowerPoint? *Think Outside The Slide*. Retrieved March 28, 2010, from http://www.thinkoutsidetheslide.com/articles/wasting_250M_bad_ppt.htm

[8] Stanford communication professor Clifford Nass quoted in Simons, T. (2001, July). When was the last time PowerPoint made you sing? *Presentations*, p. 6. See also Geoffrey Nunberg, G. (1999, December 20). The trouble with PowerPoint. *Fortune*, pp. 330–334.

[9] ThinkFree Office 3 and PodPresenter now available online. (2006, March 27). *ThinkFree Corporation*. Retrieved March 26, 2010, from http://company.thinkfree.com/views/jsp/user/company/articleList.jsp?currentPage=91&seq=33&type=&lang_type=en

[10] Bajaj, G. (2009, February 28). Impatica ShowMate. Retrieved March 28, 2010, from http://www.indezine.com/products/powerpoint/hardware/impaticashowmate.html

[11] Booher, D. (2003). *Speak with confidence: Powerful presentations that inform, inspire, and persuade*. New York: McGraw-Hill Professional, p. 126; Paradi, D. (2009, March 3). Choosing colors for your presentation slides. Retrieved March 26, 2010, from http://www.indezine.com/ideas/prescolors.html

[12] Bates, S. (2005). *Speak like a CEO: Secrets for commanding attention and getting results*. New York: McGraw-Hill Professional, p. 113.

[13] Bergells, L. (2007, May 2). Top nine visual clichés. Maniactive.com Blog. Retrieved March 15, 2010, from http://www.maniactive.com/states/2007/05/top-nine-visual-cliches.html; See also: How to avoid the 7 deadly sins of PowerPoint. (2004, July 30). *Yearbook of Experts News Release Wire*, Retrieved March 15, 2010, from LexisNexis Academic database.

[14] Burrows, P., Grover, R., & Green, H. (2006, February 6). Steve Jobs' magic kingdom. *BusinessWeek*, p. 62. Retrieved March 26, 2010, from http://www.businessweek.com; Gallo, C. (2006, April 6). How to wow 'em like Steve Jobs. *BusinessWeek*. Retrieved March 26, 2010, from http://www.businessweek.com

[15] See the PowerPoint preshow checklist at http://www.tlccreative.com/images/tutorials/PreShowChecklist.pdf

[16] Ellwood, J. (2004, August 4). Less PowerPoint, more powerful points, *The Times* (London), p. 6.

[17] Ozer, J. (2006, January 11). Ovation for PowerPoint. *PC Magazine*. Retrieved March 26, 2010, from http://www.pcmag.com/article2/0,1759,1921436,00.asp; See more information at http://www.adobe.com/products/ovation/

[18] For more information, go to http://www.turningtechnologies.com, http://www.audienceresponse.com, or http://www.optiontechnologies.com

[19] Boeri, R. J. (2002, March). Fear of flying? Or the mail? Try the Web conferencing cure. *Emedia Magazine*, p. 49.

[20] Booher, D. (2003). *Speak with confidence*. New York: McGraw-Hill Professional, p. 14; and Booher, D. (1991). *Executive's portfolio of model speeches for all occasions*. Englewood Cliffs, NJ: Prentice Hall, p. 259.

[21] Gallo, C. (2006, July 6). Steve Jobs' greatest presentation. *BusinessWeek Online*. Retrieved March 26, 2010, from http://www.businessweek.com; and

Evangelist, M. (2006, January 5). Behind the magic curtain. *The Guardian*. Retrieved March 26, 2010, from http://technology.guardian.co.uk

[22] Edmondson, G. (2006, October 16). The secret of BMW's success. *BusinessWeek Online*. Retrieved March 26, 2010, from http://www.businessweek.com/magazine/content/06_42/b4005078.htm

[23] Peterson, R. (n.d.). Presentations: Are you getting paid for overtime? *Presentation Coaching Institute*. Retrieved March 20, 2010, from http://www.passociates.com/getting_paid_for_overtime.shtml; The sales presentation: The bottom line is selling. (2001, March 14). *Marken Communications*. Retrieved March 20, 2010, from http://www.markencom.com/docs/01mar14.htm

[24] Schneider, P. (2001, August 12). Scenes from a marriage: Observations on the Daimler-Chrysler merger from a German living in America. *The New York Times Magazine*, p. 47.

[25] Wunderle, W. (2007, March/April). How to negotiate in the Middle East. *The U.S. Army Professional Writing Collection, 5*(7). Retrieved March 20, 2010, from http://www.army.mil/professionalwriting/volumes/volume5/july_2007/7_07_4.html; see also Marks, S. J. (2001, September). Nurturing global workplace connections. *Workforce*, p. 76.

[26] Brandel, M. (2006, February 20). Sidebar: Don't be the ugly American. *Computerworld*. Retrieved March 20, 2010, from http://www.computerworld.com/s/article/108772/Sidebar_Don_t_Be_the_Ugly_American

[27] Dulek, R. E., Fielden, J. S., & Hill, J. S. (1991, January/February). International communication: An executive primer. *Business Horizons*, p. 22.

[28] Davidson, R., & Rosen, M. Cited in Brandel, M. (2006, February 20). Sidebar: Don't be the ugly American. *Computerworld*. Retrieved March 20, 2010, from http://www.computerworld.com/s/article/108772/Sidebar_Don_t_Be_the_Ugly_American

[29] Burge, J. (2002, June). Telephone safety protocol for today. *The National Public Accountant*, p. 35.

[30] Vergano, D. (2004, August 31). Computers: Scientific friend or foe? *USA Today*, p. D6.

[31] Reynolds, G. (2008). *Presentation zen*. Berkeley, CA: New Riders, pp. 64ff.

[32] Jackson, M., quoted in Garbage In, Garbage Out. (1992, December). *Consumer Reports*, p. 755.

Chapter 15

[1] Ryan, L. (2007). Online job searching. *BusinessWeek Online*. Video interview retrieved February 12, 2010, from http://feedroom.businessweek.com/?fr_story=5e1ec1bacf73ae689d381f30e80dfea30cd52108&rf=sitemap

[2] Ryan, L. (2009). Five ways to grow your job-search army. *Yahoo HotJobs Articles*. Retrieved February 12, 2010, from http://ca.hotjobs.yahoo.com/career-experts-5_ways_to_grow_your_job_search_army-95

[3] Ryan, L. (2009). Ten boilerplate phrases that kill résumés. Retrieved February 12, 2010, from LizRyan.com at http://www.asklizryan.com/lizarticles/tenboilerplatephrasesthatkillsresumes.html

[4] Ryan, L. (2010). Job Seeker, Are you memorable? *Yahoo HotJobs Articles*. Retrieved February 12, 2010, from http://hotjobs.yahoo.com/career-experts-job_seeker_are_you_memorable-74

[5] U.S. Small Business Administration. FAQs: Frequently Asked Questions. Retrieved February 12, 2010, from http://web.sba.gov/faqs/

[6] Middleton, D. (2009, December 28). Landing a job of the future takes a two-track mind. *CareerJournal*. Retrieved February 12, 2010, from http://online.wsj.com/article/SB10001424052748703278604574624392641425278.html?mod=WSJ_WSJ_Careers_NewsTrends_4

[7] Kimmitt, R. M. (2007, January 23). Why job churn is good. *The Washington Post*, p. A17. Retrieved February 12, 2010, from http://www.washingtonpost.com/wp-dyn/content/article/2007/01/22/AR2007012201089.html

[8] Levy, R (2010). How to use social media in your job search. *About.com*. Retrieved February 12, 2010, from http://jobsearch.about.com/od/networking/a/socialmedia.htm

[9] Korkki, P. (2007, July 1). So easy to apply, so hard to be noticed. *The New York Times*. Retrieved July 8, 2008, from LexisNexis database.

[10] Marquardt, K. (2008, February 21). 5 tips on finding a new job. *U.S. News & World Report*. Retrieved February 16, 2010, from http://www.usnews.com/articles/business/careers/2008/02/21/5-tips-on-finding-a-new-job.html

[11] Crispin, G., & Mehler, M. (2009, February). CareerXroads 8th Annual Source of Hire Study. *CareerXroads.com*. Retrieved February 12, 2010, from http://www.careerxroads.com/news/SourcesOfHire09.pdf

[12] The top ten other job web sites for job-seekers. (2010). *QuintCareers.com*. Retrieved February 12, 2010, from http://www.quintcareers.com/top_10_sites.html

[13] Boyle, M. (2009, June 25). Recruiting: Enough to make a monster tremble. *BusinessWeek*. Retrieved February 17, 2010, from http://www.businessweek.com/magazine/content/09_27/b4138043180664.htm; and Shawbel, D. (2009, February 24). Top ten social sites for finding a job. *Mashable: The Social Media Guide*. Retrieved February 12, 2010, from http://mashable.com/2009/02/24/top-10-social-sites-for- finding-a-job/

[14] McConnon, A. (2007, August 30). Social networking graduates and hits the job market. *BusinessWeek*. Retrieved February 15, 2010, from http://www.businessweek.com/innovate/content/aug2007/id20070830_886412.htm?chan=search

[15] Cheeseman, J., quoted by Wolgemuth, L. (2008, February 25). Using the Web to search for a job. *U.S. News & World Report*. Retrieved February 15, 2010, from http://www.usnews.com/articles/business/careers/2008/02/25/using-the-web-to-search-for-a-job.html

[16] Brown, J., Cober, R. T., Kane, K., Levy, P. E., & Shalhoop, J. (2006). Proactive personality and the successful job search: A field investigation with college graduates. *Journal of Applied Psychology, 91*(3), 717–726. Retrieved July 15, 2007, from Business Source Premier (EBSCO) database.

[17] Koeppel, D. (2006, December 31). Those low grades in college may haunt your job search. *The New York Times*, p. 1. Retrieved February 15, 2010, from http://www.nytimes.com/2006/12/31/jobs/31gpa.html

[18] Black, D., quoted by Brandon, E. (2007, January 31). Tips for getting that first job. *U.S. News & World Report*. Retrieved February 15, 2010, from http://www.usnews.com/usnews/biztech/articles/070131/31firstjob.htm

[19] Gabbard, D. (2009, June 12). Unlocking the hidden job market. *Examiner.com Washington DC*. Retrieved February 15, 2010, from http://www.examiner.com/x-/x-11194-Cleveland-Unemployment-Examiner~y2009m6d12-Unlocking-the-hidden-job-market

[20] Borney, N. (2010, February 16). 10 ways to crack Michigan's hidden job market. *AnnArbor.com*. Retrieved February 17, 2010, from http://www.annarbor.com/business-review/ann-arbor-human-resources-experts-offer-tips-how-to-get-hired-in-2010/

[21] Salpeter, M. (2010). Leverage Twitter for your job search. *Twitip.com*. Retrieved February 15, 2010, from http://www.twitip.com/leverage-twitter-for-your-job-search/

[22] Résumés inching up. (2009, March 20). *Accountemps*. Retrieved February 15, 2010, from http://accountemps.rhi.mediaroom.com/index.php?s=189&item=210

[23] Isaacs, K. (2007). How to decide on résumé length. Retrieved February 15, 2010, from http://www.resumepower.com/resume-length.html

[24] Hansen, K. (2007). Should you use a career objective on your résumé? Retrieved February 15, 2010, from http://www.quintcareers.com/resume_objectives.html

[25] Coombes, A. (2010, February 7). First aid for your résumé. *The Wall Street Journal*. Retrieved February 15, 2010, from http://online.wsj.com/article/SB126550131743542087.html

[26] Korkki, P. (2007, July 1). So easy to apply, so hard to be noticed. *The New York Times*. Retrieved February 15, 2010, from http://www.nytimes.com/2007/07/01/business/yourmoney/01career.html

[27] Koeppel, D. (2006, December 31). Those low grades in college may haunt your job search. *The New York Times*, p. 1. Retrieved February 15, 2010, from http://www.nytimes.com/2006/12/31/jobs/31gpa.html

[28] Ibid.

[29] Build the résumé employers want. (n.d.). Retrieved July 21, 2007, from http://www.jobweb.com/resources/library/Interviews

[30] Locke, A. (2008, June 18). Is your resume telling the wrong story? *The Ladders.com*. Retrieved February 15, 2010, from http://www.theladders.com/career-advice/Is-Your-Resume-Telling-the-Wrong-Story

[31] Washington, T. (2007). Effective résumés bring results to life. Retrieved July 21, 2007, from http://www.careerjournal.com/jobhunting/resumes/20000913-washington.html

[32] Ryan, L. (2007). Online job searching. *BusinessWeek Online*. Video interview retrieved February 15, 2010, from http://feedroom.businessweek.com/?fr_story=5e1ec1bacf73ae689d381f30e80dfea30cd52108&rf=rss

[33] Ibid.

[34] Hansen, K. (2010). Tapping the power of keywords to enhance your résumé's effectiveness. *QuintCareers.com*. Retrieved February 16, 2010, from http://www.quintcareers.com/resume_keywords.html

[35] The video resume technique. (2007). Retrieved February 16, 2010, from http://www.collegegrad.com/jobsearch/guerrilla-insider-techniques/the-video-resume-technique/

[36] McGrath, B. (2006, October 23). Aleksey the Great. *New Yorker*. Retrieved February 16, 2010, from http://www.newyorker.com/archive/2006/10/23/061023ta_talk_mcgrath

[37] Zupek, R. (2008). Honesty is the best policy in résumés and interviews. Retrieved February 16, 2010, from http://www.careerbuilder.com/Article/CB-1180-Cover-Letters-and-Resumes-Honesty-is-the-Best-Policy-in-R%c3%a9sum%c3%a9s-and-Interviews/

[38] Needleman, S. E. (2007, March 6). Why sneaky tactics may not help résumé. *The Wall Street Journal*, p. B8.

[39] Korkki, P. (2009, July 18). Where, oh where, has my application gone? *The New York Times*. Retrieved February 16, 2010, from http://www.nytimes.com/2009/07/19/jobs/19career.html?_r=1&scp=1&sq=Where,%20oh%20where,%20has%20my%20application%20gone&st=cse

[40] Korkki, P. (2007, July 1). So easy to apply, so hard to be noticed. *The New York Times*. Retrieved February 16, 2010, from http://www.nytimes.com/2007/07/01/business/yourmoney/01career.html

Chapter 16

[1] Jones, E. (January 25, 2010). They're hiring! *CNNMoney.com*. Retrieved March 8, 2010, from http://money.cnn.com/galleries/2010/fortune/1001/gallery.bestcompanies_mosthiring.fortune/index.html

[2] Bock, L. (2007, June 6). Testimony of Google's Laszlo Bock, House Judiciary Subcommittee on Immigration, Citizenship, Refugees, Border Security, and International Law. *BusinessWeek Online*. Retrieved February 22, 2010, from http://www.businessweek.com/bwdaily/dnflash/content/jun2007/db20070606_682422.htm

[3] Hansell, S. (2007, January 3). Google answer to filling jobs is an algorithm. *The New York Times*. Retrieved February 22, 2010, from http://www.nytimes.com/2007/01/03/technology/03google.html

[4] Delaney, K. (2006, October 23). Google adjusts hiring process as needs grow. *The Wall Street Journal*, p. B1.

[5] Wilmott, N. (n.d.). Interviewing styles: Tips for interview approaches. *About.com: Human Resources*. Retrieved February 22, 2010, from http://humanresources.about.com/cs/selectionstaffing/a/interviews.htm

[6] Athavaley, A. (2007, June 20). A job interview you don't have to show up for. *The Wall Street Journal*. Retrieved February 22, 2010, from http://online.wsj.com/article/SB118229876637841321.html#articleTabs%3Darticle

[7] Ziebarth, B. (2009, December 10). Tips to ace your panel job interview. *Associated Content, Inc.* Retrieved February 22, 2010, from http://www.associatedcontent.com/article/2470148/tips_to_ace_your_panel_job_interview.html?cat=31

[8] Cristante, D. (2009, June 15). How to succeed in a group interview. *CareerFAQs*. Retrieved February 22, 2010, from http://www.careerfaqs.com.au/job-interview-tips/1116/How-to-succeed-in-a-group-interview

[9] Weiss, T. (2009, May 12). Going on the second interview. *Forbes*. Retrieved February 22, 2010, from http://www.forbes.com/2009/05/12/second-interview-advice-leadership-careers-basics.html

[10] Hansen, R. (2010). Situational interviews and stress interviews: What to make of them and how to succeed in them. *QuintCareers*. Retrieved February 22, 2010, from http://www.quintcareers.com/situational_stress_interviews.html

[11] Bergey, B. (2009, December 10). Online job interviews becoming more popular. *WKOWTV*. Retrieved February 22, 2010, from http://www.wkowtv.com/Global/story.asp?S=11655389

[12] Domeyer, D. (2007, January/February). *OfficePro*, p. 5.

[13] Maher, K. (2004, October 5). Job seekers and recruiters pay more attention to blogs. Retrieved August 12, 2007, from http://www.careerjournal.com/jobhunting/usingnet/20041005-maher.html

[14] Ryan, L. (2007, May 6). Job seekers: Prepare your stories. Retrieved February 22, 2010, from http://ezinearticles.com/?Job-Seekers:-Prepare-Your-Stories&id=142327

[15] Haefner, R. (2009, June 10). More employer screen candidates via social networking sites. *CareerBuilder*. Retrieved February 22, 2010, from http://www.careerbuilder.com/Article/CB-1337-Getting-Hired-More-Employers-Screening-Candidates-via-Social-Networking-Sites/

[16] Finder, A. (2006, June 11). For some, online persona undermines a résumé. *The New York Times*. Retrieved February 22, 2010, from http://www.nytimes.com/2006/06/11/us/11recruit.html?ex=1307678400&en=ddfbe1e3b386090b&ei=5090

[17] Haefner, R. (2009, June 10). More employer screen candidates via social networking sites. *CareerBuilder*. Retrieved February 22, 2010, from http://www.careerbuilder.com/Article/CB-1337-Getting-Hired-More-Employers-Screening-Candidates-via-Social-Networking-Sites/

[18] Mahoney, S. (2006, September 4). Finding postmodern marketers. *Advertising Age*. Retrieved March 2, 2010, from http://findarticles.com/p/articles/mi_hb6398/is_200609/ai_n25579339/

[19] Hiring process. (2010). *Google.com*. Retrieved March 13, 2010, from http://www.google.com/intl/en/jobs/joininggoogle/hiringprocess/

[20] Wright, D. (2004, August/September). Tell stories, get hired. *OfficePro*, pp. 32–33.

[21] FAQs about interview questions. (2009). Retrieved February 25, 2010, from University of Wisconsin-Eau Claire Career Center at http://www.uwec.edu/career/Online_Library/illegal_ques.htm

[22] Doyle, A. (n.d.). Illegal interview questions. *About.com*. Retrieved February 25, 2010, from http://jobsearchtech.about.com/od/interview/l/aa022403.htm

[23] Anten, T. (2008, October 15). How to handle illegal interview questions. Retrieved February 25, 2010, from http://www.careerservices.calpoly.edu/students/interviewing/illegal.htm; Illegal interview questions. (2010). Retrieved February 25, 2010, from http://www.jobinterviewquestions.org/questions/illegal-questions.asp; and Illegal interview questions. (2007). *FindLaw.com*. Retrieved February 25, 2010, from http://employment.findlaw.com/employment/employment-employee-hiring/employment-employee-hiring-interview-questions.html

[24] Lublin, J. S. (2008, February 5). Notes to interviewers should go beyond a simple thank you. *The Wall Street Journal*, p. B1. Retrieved February 25, 2010, from http://online.wsj.com/public/article_print/SB120215930971242053.html

[25] Ibid.

[26] Needleman, S. E. (2006, February 7). Be prepared when opportunity calls. *The Wall Street Journal*. Retrieved March 2, 2010, from http://online.wsj.com/article/SB113927577768966742.html

Acknowledgments

Chapter 1

p. 3 Opening case study based on Useem, M. (2008, December 8). New ideas for this Pepsi generation. *U.S. News & World Report*, p. 49; Indra K. Nooyi biography. (n.d.). Retrieved March 21, 2009, from http://www.notablebiographies.com; Brady, D. (2007, June 11). Keeping cool in hot water. Retrieved July 10, 2007, from Business Source Premier database; PepsiCo touts water, energy savings from 2007 (n.d.). Retrieved March 21, 2009, from http://www.greenbiz.com; and Nooyi, I. (n.d.). The best advice I ever got. Retrieved March 27, 2009, from www.cnnmoney.com.

p. 4 Spotlight (Aylwin Lewis) based on Berner, R. (2005, October 31). At Sears, a great communicator. *BusinessWeek*, p. 50.

p. 6 Spotlight (Oren Harari) based on Harari, O. (1997, November). Flood your organization with knowledge. *Management Review*, p. 33; and Harari, O (2006). *Break from the pack: How to compete in a copycat economy*. Upper Saddle River, NJ: FT Press.

p. 9 Photo essay about Google Wave. Google Web site. Retrieved January 2, 2010, from http://wave.google.com/help/wave/about.html

p. 12 Figure 1.3 based on U.S. 2001 Bureau of the Census figures appearing in Karoly, L. A., & Paris, C. W. A. *The 21st century at work*. Santa Monica, CA: Rand Corporation, pp. 36–39.

p. 14 Ethics Check (Bypassing or False Advertising?) based on Burnsed, B. BTW. (2009, June 29). *BusinessWeek*, p. 019.

p. 28 Photo essay based on Henriques, D. (2009, June 29). Madoff Is Sentenced to 150 Years for Ponzi Scheme. *New York Times*. Retrieved December 19, 2009, from http://www.nytimes.com/2009/06/30/business/30madoff.html

Chapter 2

p. 40 Photo essay based on Wilson, M., & Baker, A. (2009, January 15). A Quick Rescue Kept Death Toll at Zero. *The New York Times*. Retrieved December 21, 2009, from http://www.nytimes.com/2009/01/16/nyregion/16rescue.html

p. 42 Plugged In based on Schindler, E. (2008, February 15). Running an effective teleconference or virtual meeting. *CIO*. Retrieved June 28, 2009, from http://www.cio.com; Gordon, J. (2005, June). Do your virtual teams deliver only virtual performance? *Training*, 20; Brown-Johnston, N. (2005, January–February). Virtual teamwork: Smart business leaders are building high-performance virtual teams. *Detroiter*, 55; Managing virtual teams. (2004, March 16). *Info-Tech Advisor Newsletter*; Snyder, B. (2003, May). Teams that span time zones face new work rules. *Stanford Business Magazine*. Retrieved April 15, 2007, from http://www.gsb.stanford.edu/news/bmag/sbsm0305/feature_virtual_teams.shtml; Loudin, K. H. (2003, June). Building bridges: Virtual teamwork in the 21st century. *Contract Management*; and Armstrong, D. (2000, March). Building teams across borders. *Executive Excellence*, 10.

p. 43 Figure 2.1 adapted from Robbins, H. A., and Finley, M. (1995). *Why Teams Don't Work*. Princeton, NJ: Peterson's/Pacesetter Books, Chapters 5 to 16.

p. 43 Discussion of Tuckman's model based on Robbins, H. A., & Finley, M. (1995). *Why teams don't work*. Princeton, NJ: Peterson's/Pacesetter Books, Chapter 22.

pp. 44–45 Discussion of conflict and groupthink based on Toledo, R. (2008, June). Conflict is everywhere. *PM Network*. Retrieved June 28, 2009, from Business Source Complete database; McNamara, P. (2003, August/September). Conflict resolution strategies. *OfficePro*, p. 25; Weiss, W. (2002, November). Building and managing teams. *SuperVision*, p. 19; Eisenhardt, K. (1997, July/August). How management teams can have a good fight. *Harvard Business Review*, pp. 77–85; Brockmann, E. (1996, May). Removing the paradox of conflict from group decisions. *Academy of Management Executives*, pp. 61–62; and Beebe, S., & Masterson, J. (1999). *Communicating in small groups*. New York: Longman, pp. 198–200.

p. 45 Spotlight (Steve Ballmer) based on the following: CEO job was surprisingly different. (2007, April 30). *USA Today*, p. B2.

p. 46 Ethical Insights based on Wilson, G. (1996). *Groups in context*. New York: McGraw-Hill, pp. 24–27; and Robbins, H., & Finley, M. (1995). *Why teams don't work*. Princeton, NJ: Peterson's/Pacesetter Books, pp. 88–89.

p. 49 Spotlight (Reid Hastie) based on Hastie, R. (2009, January 18). Meetings are a matter of precious time. *The New York Times*, p. BU2.

p. 53 Figure 2.6 Courtesy of MeetingSense Software Corporation, http://www.meetingsense.com.

p. 61 Career Coach box (Listening to Nonnative Speakers) based on Marshall, T., & Vincent, J. Improving listening skills: Methods, activities, and resources; Instructor's Manual, *Business communication: Process and product*, 6e; Varner, I., & Beamer, L. (1995). *Intercultural communication in the global workplace*. (Boston: Irwin, McGraw-Hill), p. 37; and Lee, C. (1993, January). How to deal with the foreign accent. *Training*, pp. 72, 75.

p. 62 Spotlight (Oprah Winfrey) based on Marshall, L. (1998, November). The intentional Oprah. *InStyle*, p. 341.

Chapter 3

p. 81 Figure 3.1 based on Bellman, E. (2009, June 30). McDonald's to expand in India. *The Wall Street Journal*. Retrieved July 7, 2009, from http://online.wsj.com; Adams, B. (2007, July 19). McDonald's strange menu around the world. Retrieved July 7, 2009, from www.trifter.com; Adamy, J. (2007, October 16). As burgers boom in Russia, McDonald's touts discipline. *The Wall Street Journal*. Retrieved July 14, 2009, from http://online.wsj.com; and Steinberger, M. (2009, June 25). How McDonald's conquered France. *Slate*. Retrieved July 14, 2009, from http://www.slate.com/id/2221246/pagenum/all/

p. 82 Plugged In (Greenland and Iceland: The Most Connected Countries in the World?) based on the following: Internet usage statistics: The Internet big picture. (2009). *Internet World Stats*. Retrieved July 16, 2009, from http://www.internetworldstats.com/stats.htm

p. 85 Figure 3.2 based on Chaney, L. H., & Martin, J. S. (2000). *Intercultural business communication*, 2e. Upper Saddle River, NJ: Prentice Hall, Chapter 5; J. Chung's analysis appearing in Chen, G. M., & Starosta, W. J. *Foundations of intercultural communication*. Boston: Allyn and Bacon, 1998, p. 51; and O'Hara-Devereaux, M. & Johansen, R. (1994). *Globalwork: Bridging distance, culture, and time*. San Francisco: Jossey-Bass, p. 55.

p. 88 Ethical Insights based on Saslow, E. (2009, June 3). As the myths abound, so does Islamic outreach. *The Washington Post*, p. C1. Retrieved July 8, 2009, from Factiva database.

p. 89 Ethics Check (The World's Worst Tourists) based on Tandy, J., & Mackenzie, J. (2009, July 9). French tourists seen as world's worst: Survey. *Reuters.com*. Retrieved July 9, 2009, from http://www.reuters.com/

p. 91 Figure 3.3 based on Ostheimer, S. (1995, February). Internationalize yourself. *Business Education Forum*, p. 45. Reprinted with permission of Sondra Ostheimer, Southwest Wisconsin Technical College.

p. 93 Figure 3.4 based on Horwitz, S. (2002). Why the crazy dates? *PSA Journal*, 68(7), 11. Retrieved July 20, 2009, from Academic Search Premier database; and Horton, W. (1993, Fourth Quarter). The almost universal language: Graphics for international documents. *Technical Communication*, p. 690.

p. 96 Spotlight (International Perp Walk: Siemens Busted for Bribery) based on Schubert, S., & Miller, T. C. (2008, December 21). Where bribery was just a line item. *New York Times*, p. BU1. Retrieved July 23, 2009, from ProQuest Newspapers database.

p. 97 Figure 3.7 based on The 2008 Corruption Perceptions Index, Transparency International. Retrieved July 9, 2009, from http://www.transparency.org/policy_research/surveys_indices/cpi

p. 99 Spotlight (Ursula Burns) based on Byrnes, N., & Crockett, R. O. (2009, May 28). Ursula Burns: An historic succession at Xerox. *BusinessWeek.com*. Retrieved August 4, 2009, from http://www.businessweek.com/magazine/content/09_23/b4134018712853_page_3.htm

p. 100 Photo essay based on UPS Corporate Responsibility Web site. (2009). UPS Supplier Diversity Guidelines. Retrieved December 26, 2009, from http://www.community.ups.com/docs/UPS_Supplier_Diversity_Guidelines.pdf

p. 101 Spotlight (Andrea Jung) based on Adler, S. J. (2006, February 6). Avon, the Net, and glass ceilings: A conversation with Andrea Jung. *BusinessWeek.com*. Retrieved August 4, 2009, from http://www.businessweek.com/magazine/content/06_06/b3970143.htm; On the call: Avon Products CEO Andrea Jung. (2009, July 30). *Associated Press/BusinessWeek.com*. Retrieved August 4, 2009, from http://www.businessweek.com/ap/financialnews/D99OSFVO1.htm; and Jones, D. (2009, June 14). Avon's Andrea Jung: CEOs need to reinvent themselves. *USAToday*. Retrieved July 15, 2009, from http://www.usatoday.com/money/companies/management/advice/2009-06-14-jung-ceo-avon_N.htm

p. 101 Career Coach (He Said, She Said) based on Basow, S. A., & Rubenfeld, K. (2003, February). Troubles talk: Effects of gender and gender-typing. *Sex Roles: A Journal of Research*, 183. Retrieved July 23, 2009, from http://www.springerlink.com/content/rm75xx843786037q/fulltext.pdf; Wood, J. T. (2002).

Gendered lives. Belmont, CA: Wadsworth, p. 119; Tear, J. (1995, November 20). They just don't understand gender dynamics. *The Wall Street Journal*, p. A12. Retrieved July 23, 2009, from Factiva database; Roiphe, A. (1994, October). Talking trouble. *Working Woman*, pp. 28–31; Stuart, C. (1994, February). Why can't a woman be more like a man? *Training Tomorrow*, pp. 22–24; and Wolfe, A. (1994, December 12). She just doesn't understand. *New Republic*, *211*(24), pp. 26–34.

Chapter 4

p. 114 Ethics Check (Cramster) based on Foderaro, L. S. (2009, May 18). Psst! Need the answer to No. 7? Just click here. *The New York Times*, p. A17.

p. 117 Spotlight (Warren Buffett) based on the following: *A Plain English Handbook*, Preface. (1997). Retrieved August 12, 2009, from http://www.sec.gov/pdf/handbook.pdf

p. 120 Spotlight (John H. Johnson) based on the following: How he went from a tin-roof shack to the Forbes 400. (1998, March 26). *Investor's Business Daily*, p. 1.

p. 127 Photo essay based on Dahl, D. (2009, June 1). How to Choose the Right Collaboration Software. *Inc.* magazine. Retrieved December 28, 2009, from http://www.inc.com/magazine/20090601/how-to-choose-theright-collaboration-software.html

p. 128 Discussion of online collaboration tools based on the following: Beyond Google Docs: 7 Web-based collaboration tools. (2009, July 6). *Information Week*. Retrieved July 19, 2009, from InfoTrac College Edition database; Dahl, D. (2009, June). Connecting the dots: How to choose the right collaboration software for your company. *Inc.*, p. 103. Retrieved July 19, 2009, from InfoTrac College Edition database; and Fichter, D. (2005, July/August). The many forms of e-collaboration: Blogs, wikis, portals, groupware, discussion boards, and instant messaging. *Online*, pp. 48–50. Retrieved July 18, 2009, from Business Source Complete database.

p. 130 Ethics Check (Shepard Fairey) based on Crovitz, L. G. (2009, March 16). The fine art of copyright. *The Wall Street Journal*, p. A17.

Chapter 5

p. 141 Spotlight (Chris Heatherly and Len Mazzocco) based on Damian, J. (2009, July 2). Inside Disney's toy factory. *BusinessWeek Online*. Retrieved August 7, 2009, from Business Source Complete database.

p. 146 Ethics Check (How Sweet It Is) based on Lerner, I. (2009, May 25). Sweet nothings. *ICIS Chemical Business*. Retrieved August 18, 2009, from Business Source Complete database.

p. 152 Spotlight (Bob Knight) based on Knight, B. (2007, February). Guard against five common mistakes. *Writing That Works*, p. 2.

p. 154 Ethics Check (Blogging for Pay) Based on Frazier, M. (2006, October 30). Want to build up blog buzz? *Advertising Age*. Retrieved August 7, 2009, from InfoTrac College Edition.

Chapter 6

p. 163 Opening case study based on Lockyer, S. E. (2009, August 12). Yum lays out plans for Taco Bell. *Nation's Restaurant News*. Retrieved August 17, 2009, from Business Source Complete database; Lockyer, S. E. (2008, February 18). Yum readies menu tweaks aimed at boosting soft U.S. sales. *Nation's Restaurant News*. Retrieved August 19, 2009, from Business Source Complete database; Lockyer, S. E. (2006, December 18). Yum to expand Taco Bell breakfast test: Potential rollout anchors company's plan to boost core chains' flagging U.S. sales. *Nation's Restaurant News*. Retrieved August 18, 2009, from InfoTrac College Edition database; Analysis of Yum! Brands Inc. (2007, February 13). *M2 Presswire*. Retrieved April 17, 2007, from InfoTrac College Edition database; Wheaton, K. (2007, March 5). Yum Brands has a rat problem, but it will have customers, too. *Advertising Age*, p. 4. Retrieved April 7, 2007, from Business Source Premier database; and Sharma, S. (2007, January 10). Brand should not get trapped in low-price bracket. *The Economic Times*. Retrieved April 7, 2007, from InfoTrac College Edition database.

p. 169 Spotlight (Colin Powell) based on Powell, C. (1996, December). Quotations from Chairman Powell: A leadership primer. *Management Review*, p. 36.

p. 172 Spotlight (Arthur Levitt) based on Nielan, C. (2000, November). Arthur Levitt and the SEC: Promoting plain English. *Intercom*, p. 17. Retrieved August 19, 2009, from Business Source Complete database.

p. 173 Ethics Check (Costly Writing) based on Duffy, S. P. (2007, April 23). Attorney hit with $6.6 million malpractice verdict. *The Legal Intelligencer*. Retrieved August 16, 2009, from http://www.law.com.

p. 173 Spotlight (William Raspberry) based on Raspberry, W. (1998, April). Words to the wise on students' speech. *Writing Concepts*, p. 3.

p. 184 Activity 6.18 based on Pomerenke, P. J. (1998, December). Teaching ethics with apartment leases. *Business Communication Quarterly*, *61*(4), 119.

Chapter 7

p. 193 Spotlight (James E. Gaskin) based on Gaskin, J. E. (2009, August 19). Three tips for more effective e-mailing. *Network World*. Retrieved January 29, 2010, from http://www.networkworld.com/columnists/2009/090819-gaskin.html

p. 199 Spotlight (Nancy Flynn) based on Irvine, M. (2009, July 12). Young workers push employers for wider Web access. *Associated Press*. Retrieved January 13, 2010, from http://hosted.ap.org/dynamic/stories/U/US_TEC_BLOCKED_OFFICE_INTERNET?SITE=VTBEN&SECTION=HOME&TEMPLATE=DEFAULT

p. 200 Zooming In Part 2 (Got Something to Tweet About at Work? Think Again) based on 5 ways Twitter can get you fired. (2009, October 8). *Applicant.com*. Retrieved January 28, 2010, from http://applicant.com/5-ways-twitter-can-get-you-fired/

p. 201 Spotlight (Donagh Herlihy) based on Hamm, S. (2009, June 15). Cloud computing's big bang for business. *BusinessWeek*, pp. 42–44.

p. 201 Plugged In box (Cloud Computing) based on Hamm, S. (2009, June 15). Cloud computing's big bang for business. *BusinessWeek*, pp. 43–44; Wildstrom, S. H. (2009, April 6). What to entrust to the cloud. *BusinessWeek*, pp. 89–90; Burrows, P. (2009, August 17). Apple and Google: Another step apart. *BusinessWeek*, pp. 24–25; and Hamm, S. (2009, April 6). IBM reaches for the clouds. *BusinessWeek*, p. 34.

p. 204 Tips for Creating a Professional Blog based on Wuorio, J. (n.d.). Blogging for business: 7 tips for getting started. Microsoft Small Business Center. Retrieved January 14, 2010, from http://www.microsoft.com/smallbusiness/resources/marketing/online-marketing/small-business-blog.aspx#Smallbusinessblog

p. 204 Ethics Check (Fired for Blogging) based on Palan, E. (2008, May 29). Seven people fired for blogging. *Mental Floss*. Retrieved January 31, 2010, from http://www.mentalfloss.com/blogs/archives/15329

p. 205 The five main uses of wikis based on Nations, D. (2009). The business wiki. About.com: Web Trends. Retrieved February 13, 2010, from http://webtrends.about.com/od/wiki/a/business-wiki.htm

p. 208 Ethics Check (Social Media Help Spread Errors Like Wildfire) based on Anderson, M. (2009, August 12). Best Buy $9.99 TV offer was too good to be true. *Yahoo News*. Retrieved December 16, 2009, from http://news.yahoo.com; and Pricing blunder: Ecommerce. (2003, November 11.) *Webmaster World*. Retrieved December 16, 2009, from http://www.webmasterworld.com/forum22/1310.htm

p. 211 Spotlight (Scott Townsend) based on Karpinski, R. (2009, April 6). B-to-b followers flock to Twitter. *B to B*. Retrieved December 17, 2009, from ProQuest database.

Chapter 8

p. 223 Spotlight (Peggy Foran) based on Levitt, A. (2002). *Take on the street*. New York: Pantheon Books, p. 226.

p. 234 Ethics Check (Renting or Buying?) based on the following: An eagle eye on retail scams. (2005, August 8). *BusinessWeek*. Retrieved September 21, 2009, from http://www.businessweek.com

p. 234 Photo essay based on Zimmermann, S. (2007, June 24). The fixer: Honeymoon glitch—cruising to a solution. *The Chicago Sun-Times*. Retrieved June 29, 2007, from http://www.suntimes.com/news/zimmermann/440955,CST-NWS-fixer24.article

p. 240 Spotlight (Andrew S. Grove) based on the following: The fine art of feedback. (1992, February). *Working Woman*, p. 26.

p. 236–240 Discussion of claim and adjustment letters based on A new take on complaints. (2009, October). *Communication Briefings*, p. 4; McCartney, S. (2007, March 20). What airlines do when you complain. *The Wall Street Journal*, p. D5; Liao, H. (2007, March). Do it right this time: The role of employee service recovery performance in customer-perceived justice and customer loyalty after service failures. *Journal of Applied Psychology*, *92*(2), 475. Retrieved January 22, 2010, from Business Source Premier database; Davidow, M. (2003, February). Organizational responses to customer complaints: What works and what doesn't. *Journal of Service Research*, *5*(3) 31. Retrieved January 20, 2010, from Business Source Premier database; Michelson, M. W., Jr. (2003, December). Turning complaints into cash. *The American Salesman*, p. 22; Torp, J. R. (2003, March/April). In person, by phone, by mail, or online: Managing customer complaints. *ABA Bank Compliance*, p. 10; Kim, C., Kim, S., Im, S., & Shin, S. (2003). The effect of attitude and perception on consumer complaint intentions. *The Journal of Consumer Marketing*, *20*, 352; and David, D., & Baker, M. A. (1994). Rereading bad news: Compliance-gaining features in management memos. *The Journal of Business Communications*, 267–290.

Chapter 9

p. 264 Ethics Check based on Nifong issues apology to ex-lacrosse players. (2007, April 12). Retrieved January 19, 2010, from http://www.wral.com/news/local/story/1270348/?d_full_comments=1&d_comments_page=2

p. 264 Spotlight (Marshall Goldsmith) based on Goldsmith, M., & Reiter, M. (2007). *What got you here won't get you there*. New York: Hyperion Books. Excerpt retrieved January 20, 2010, from http://www.businessweek.com

p. 265 Spotlight (Malcolm Forbes) based on Forbes, M. (1999). How to write a business letter. In K. Harty (Ed.), *Strategies for business and technical writing*. Boston: Allyn and Bacon, p. 108.

p. 271 Spotlight (Jeff Bezos) based on Milliot, J. (2009, July 27). Cracks in Amazon's e-book empire. Retrieved January 11, 2010, from www.publishersweekly.com/article/CA6673024.html

p. 273 Plugged In box based on Weber, H. R. (2009, October 13). Social sites new conduits for customer service. Retrieved January 21, 2010, from, http://www.crmbuyer.com; Social networking and customer service. (n.d.) Retrieved January 21, 2010, from http://www.allthingscrm.com; Baker, L. (2008, July 24). How to combat complaints sites in Google. Retrieved January 21, 2010, from http://www.searchenginejournal.com; Whitehead, J. (2009, December 9). Are customer complaints on Twitter good for brands? Retrieved January 22, 2010, from http://www.brandrepublic.com; and Miles, S. (2009, October 26). Complain, complain, complain. Retrieved January 22, 2010, from http://www.recessionwire.com

p. 279 Ethics Check based on RadioShack uses e-mail to fire employees. (2006, August 30). Associated Press. Retrieved January 21, 2009, from http://www.sfgate.com/cgi-bin/article.cgi?f=/n/a/2006/08/30/financial/f131351D00.DTL

Chapter 10

p. 299 Spotlight (Irene Rosenfeld) based on Berfield, S., & Arndt, M. (2010, January 25). Kraft's sugar rush. *Bloomberg BusinessWeek*, p. 37.

p. 302 Ethical Insights box based on Troyka, L. Q. (2005). *Simon & Schuster handbook for writers* (7th ed.). Upper Saddle River, NJ: Prentice Hall, pp. 142–145; Crews, F. (1987). *The Random House Handbook*. New York: Random House, pp. 76–78; and Downes, S. (n.d.). Stephen's guide to the logical fallacies. Retrieved January 28, 2010, from http://onegoodmove.org/fallacy/

p. 312 Spotlight (Herb Kelleher) based on Krames, J. A. (2003, November). Performance culture. *Executive Excellence*, 16; and Kelleher, K. (1992). Beware the impossible guarantee. *Inc.*, p. 30.

p. 319 Figure 10.8. Letter adapted from Yunxia, Z. (2000, December). Building knowledge structures in teaching cross-cultural sales genres, Appendix B. *Business Communication Quarterly, 63*(4), 67–68. Permission to reprint granted by Association for Business Communication. Chinese characters provided by Dr. Bertha Du-Babcock.

p. 326 Activity 10.6. Sales letter adapted from Yunxia, Z. (2000, December). Building knowledge structures in teaching cross-cultural sales genres, Appendix A. *Business Communication Quarterly, 63*(4), 66–67. Permission to reprint granted by Association for Business Communication.

Chapter 11

p. 347 Zooming In, Part 2, based on Shah, D. (2006, October 16). Six interesting stats about startup success. *OnStartups.com*. Retrieved January 28, 2010, from http://onstartups.com/tabid/3339/bid/79/Six-Interesting-Stats-About-Startup-Success.aspx; and Kehrer, D. (2006). Upping the odds of startup success. *Business.com*. Retrieved January 28, 2010, from http://www.business.com/directory/advice/startup/getting-started-basics/upping-the-odds-of-startup-success/

p. 351 Figure 11.7's image published with permission of ProQuest. Further reproduction is prohibited without permission. Image produced by ProQuest. Inquires may be made to: ProQuest, P.O. Box 1346, 789 E. Eisenhower Parkway, Ann Arbor, MI 48106-1346 USA. Telephone (734) 761-7400; E-mail: info@proquest.com; Web-page: www.proquest.com

p. 354 Spotlight (Tom Peters) based on Peters, T. (1991). *Thriving on chaos*. New York: Knopf, pp. 230–231.

p. 356 Spotlight (Eric Dezenhall) based on Conlin, M. (2007, April 16). Web attack. *BusinessWeek*, p. 54.

p. 357 Figure 11.9 based on Search Engine Watch (2009, September 15). Top search providers for August 2009. SearchEngineWatch.com. Retrieved January 29, 2010, from http://searchenginewatch.com/3634991; Sullivan, D. (2006, August 21). ComScore media metrix search engine ratings. Retrieved January 28, 2010, from http://searchenginewatch.com/reports/article.php/2156431

p. 361 Spotlight (Jim Berkowitz) based on Jones, D. (2006, August 1). Authorship gets lost on Web: Some bloggers don't give credit where it's due. *USA Today*, p. B3. Retrieved January 22, 2010, from ProQuest database.

Chapter 12

p. 395 Spotlight (Relmond Van Daniker) based on Mosquera, M. (2008, February 20). Government accountants: Taxpayers distrust federal financial reporting. *Federal Computer Week*. Retrieved February 23, 2010, from http://fcw.com/Articles/2008/02/20/Government-accountants-Taxpayers-distrust-federal-financial-reporting.aspx?Page=1

p. 396 Career Coach box based on Booher, D. (2001, April). E-writing. *Executive Excellence*, p. 16; Bernstel, J. B., & Thomases, H. (2001, March). Writing words for the Web. *Bank Marketing*, pp. 16–21; and Graves, P. R., & Murry, J. E. (1990, Summer). Enhancing communication with effective page design and typography. *Delta Pi Epsilon* Instructional Strategies Series.

p. 402 Ethics Check based on Neuman, W. (2010, February 25). Hidden ingredient: The sweetener. *The New York Times*, pp. B1, B5.

p. 421 Activity 12.28 Feasibility Report: Can Rainbow Precision Instruments Afford a Children's Center? is based on a case study, "Excel Industries, Inc." by James S. O'Rourke, IV, and is used by permission. Copyright: 1995. Revised: 2005. University of Notre Dame. All rights reserved.

Chapter 13

p. 430 Spotlight (Michael Asner) based on Bellett, G. (2009, July 24). Expert on government contracts sees a winning bid as a work of art. *ProposalWorks.com*. Retrieved March 5, 2010, from http://www.proposalworks.com/articles/work-of-art.asp

p. 432 Spotlight (Tim Berry) based on Berry, T. (2009, November 1). Common business plan mistakes. *Bplans.com*. Retrieved March 9, 2010, from http://articles.bplans.com/writing-a-business-plan/common-business-plan-mistakes/31

p. 454 Figure 13.5 based on Sokuvitz, S., & George, A. M. (2003, June). Teaching culture: The challenges and opportunities of international public relations. *Business Communication Quarterly*, 97; Koh, A. C. (2003). Teaching understanding cultural differences for business in an Internet-based economy. *Journal of Teaching in International Business, 15*(2), 27; and Sterkel, K. S. (1988, September). Integrating intercultural communication and report writing in the communication class. *The Bulletin of the Association for Business Communication*, 13–16.

Chapter 14

p. 457 Zooming In Part 1 based on Johnson, B., & Arthur, C. (2010, January 27). Apple iPad launch: Live coverage. *Guardian.co.uk*. Retrieved March 28, 2010, from http://www.guardian.co.uk/technology/blog/2010/jan/27/apple-tablet-launch-live-coverage; Steve Jobs' obsession with secrecy and the "big-bang." (2009, December 8). *Edible Apple Blog*. Retrieved March 28, 2010, from http://www.edibleapple.com/steve-jobs-obsession-with-secrecy-and-the-big-bang/

p. 458 Spotlight (Guy Kawasaki) based on Bryant, A. (2010, March 21). Just give him 5 sentences, not "War and Peace." *The New York Times*, p. BU 2. Retrieved March 29, 2010, from http://www.nytimes.com/2010/03/21/business/21corner.html

p. 459 Figure 14.1 based on Elsea, J. G. (1985, September). Strategies for effective presentations. *Personnel Journal*, pp. 31–33 in Hamilton, C. (2001). *Communicating for results*. Belmont, CA: Wadsworth/Thomson Learning, p. 340.

p. 460 Career Coach (Guy Kawasaki) based on Kawasaki, G. (2005, December 30). The 10/20/30 rule of PowerPoint. *How to Change the World*. Retrieved March 20, 2010, from http://blog.guykawasaki.com/2005/12/the_102030_rule.html and on personal communication by e-mail on April 8, 2010.

p. 463 Spotlight (Dianna Booher) based on Booher, D. (2003). *Speak with confidence*. New York: McGraw-Hill Professional, p. 13.

p. 464 Spotlight (John Chambers) based on Gallo, C. (2007, January 4). The camera doesn't lie. *BusinessWeek Online*. Retrieved August 3, 2007, from http://www.businessweek.com/smallbiz/content/jan2007/sb20070103_877305.htm?chan=search

p. 466 Figure 14.3 based on Booher, D. (2003). *Speak with confidence*. New York: McGraw-Hill Professional, pp. 131–143; U.S. Department of Labor. (1996, May). Presenting effective presentations with visual aids. Retrieved March 26, 2010, from http://www.osha.gov/doc/outreachtraining/htmlfiles/traintec.html; and McConnon, S. (2002). *Presenting with power*. Oxford: How To Books, pp. 38–43.

p. 467 Zooming In Part 2 based on Gallo, C. (2009, October 6). Uncovering Steve Jobs' presentation secrets. *BusinessWeek*. Retrieved March 28, 2010, from http://www.businessweek.com/smallbiz/content/oct2009/sb2009106_706829.htm

p. 475 Photo essay based on Fisher, A. (2009, August 24). 50 Best Websites 2009: Kiva. *Time*. Retrieved April 10, 2010, from http://www.time.com; Schonfeld, E. (2009, November 1). Four years after founding, Kiva hits $100 million in microloans. *TechCrunch*. Retrieved April 10, 2010, from http://techcrunch.com

p. 483 Spotlight (Patrick Forsyth) based on Forsyth, P. (2000). *Telephone skills*. London: Management Shapers, pp. 21–23.

p. 489 Activity 14.11 based on Booher, D. (2003). *Speak with confidence*. New York: McGraw-Hill Professional, pp. 167–172.

Chapter 15

p. 497 Spotlight (Michael Dell) based on Dell Press Release (2010, January 25). Michael Dell shares vision for role of IT, entrepreneurialism in driving sustainable competitiveness. Retrieved February 25, 2010, from http://content.dell.com/us/en/corp/d/press-releases/2010-1-25-Michael-Dell-Speaks-at-GCF.aspx; Batelle, J., & Dell, M. (2004, May). Still giving 'em Dell twenty years in, Michael Dell's hair is a little grayer—but his taste for beating the competition remains as strong as ever. *Business2.0*, 99; and Turner, N. (1999, March 1). Entrepreneur Michael Dell. *Investor's Business Daily*, p. A8.

p. 502 Career Coach (networking) partially based on Gabbard, D. (2009, June 12). Unlocking the hidden job market. *Examiner.com Washington DC*. Retrieved February 15, 2010, from http://www.examiner.com/x-/x-11194-Cleveland-Unemployment-Examiner~y2009m6d12-Unlocking-the-hidden-job-market; Salpeter, M. (2010). Leverage Twitter for your job search. *Twitip.com*. Retrieved February 15, 2010, from http://www.twitip.com/leverage-twitter-for-your-job-search/; Dickler, J. (2009, June 10) The hidden job market. *CNNMoney.com*. Retrieved February 17, 2010, from http://money.cnn.com/2009/06/09/news/economy/hidden_jobs/; and Borney, N. (2010, February 16). 10 ways to crack Michigan's hidden job market. *AnnArbor.com*. Retrieved February 17, 2010, from http://www.annarbor.com/business-review/ann-arbor-human-resources-experts-offer-tips-how-to-get-hired-in-2010/

p. 506 Photo essay (George O'Leary) based on Di Meglio, F. (2009, June 8). The temptation to lie on your résumé. *BusinessWeek*. Retrieved February 19, 2010, from http://www.businessweek.com/bschools/blogs/mba_admissions/archives/2009/06/the_temptation.html; Zupek, R. (2007, September 24). Infamous résumé lies. *MSN.Careers*. Retrieved February 19, 2010, from http://msn.careerbuilder.com/Article/MSN-1154-Cover-Letters-Resumes-Infamous-R%c3%a9sum%c3%a9-Lies/?ArticleID=1154&cbRecursionCnt=1&cbsid=89a54a8c9fa14c02a47d88d64c184c64-319896364-R1-4

p. 516 Photo essay (video résumés) based on Athavaley, A. (2006, December 7). Posting your résumé on YouTube to stand out from the competition. *CareerJournal.com*. Retrieved July 31, 2007, from http://www.careerjournal.com/jobhunting/usingnet/20061207-athavaley.html

p. 524 Spotlight (Liz Ryan) based on Ryan, L. (2007). For job-hunters: How to find a contact name inside a target company. Retrieved July 2, 2007, from http://ezinearticles.com/?For-Job-Hunters:-How-to-Find-a-Contact-Name-Inside-a-Target-Company&id=101910

Chapter 16

p. 539 Photo essay (meal interview) based on Doyle, A. (2010). Interview etiquette: Manners, meals, and interviews. *About.com Guide*. Retrieved February 22, 2010, from http://jobsearch.about.com/cs/interviews/a/interviewdining.htm

p. 543 Photo essay (tattoos and piercings) based on Borlik, J. (2009, December 2). Tattoos still not overlooked in job search. *Central Michigan Life*. Retrieved March 8, 2010, from http://www.cm-life.com/2009/12/02/tattoos-still-not-overlooked-in-job-search/

p. 550 Career Coach (Let's Talk Money) based on Hansen, R. S. (2007). Salary negotiation do's and don'ts. Reprinted with permission of Quintessential Careers. Retrieved March 2, 2010, from http://www.quintcareers.com/salary-dos-donts.html

p. 551 Spotlight (Daisy Wright) based on Wright, D. (2004, August/September). Tell stories, get hired. *OfficePro*, pp. 32–33.

Index

A

B

C

F

G

H

I

J

K

L

M

N

O

Q

R

S

T

U

V

W

X

Y

Z